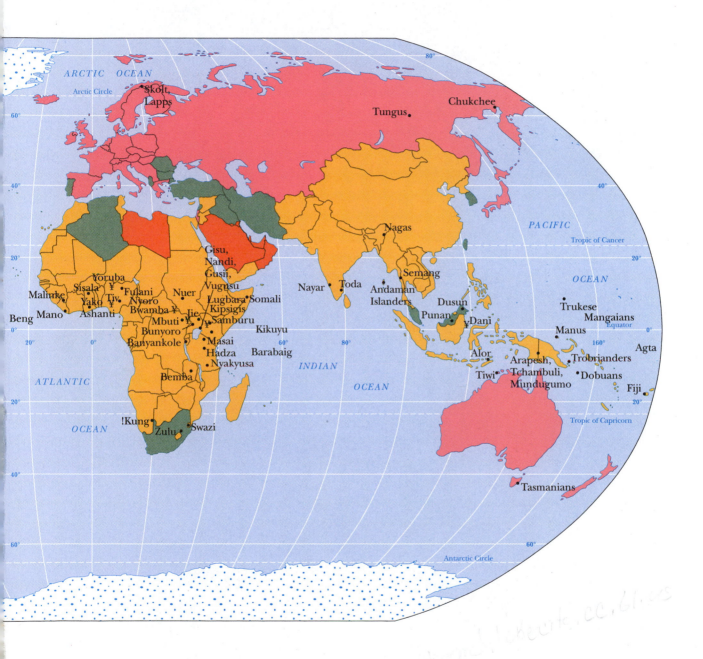

CULTURAL ANTHROPOLOGY

An Applied Perspective

FOURTH EDITION

Gary Ferraro

The University of North Carolina at Charlotte

Wadsworth
Thomson Learning™

Australia • Canada • Mexico • Singapore • Spain
United Kingdom • United States

For the Donati Nine

Anthropology Editor: Lin Marshall
Development Editor: Robert Jucha
Assistant Editor: Dee Dee Zobian
Editorial Assistant: Analie Barnett
Marketing Manager: Matthew Wright
Project Editor: Jerilyn Emori
Print Buyer: Karen Hunt
Permissions Editor: Robert Kauser
Production Service: Joan Keyes, Dovetail Publishing Services

Text and Cover Designer: Marilyn Perry
Photo Researcher: Linda L Rill
Copy Editor: Jennifer Gordon
Illustrators: Byron Gin, Electronic Publishing Services, Inc.,
    Dovetail Publishing Services
Cover Image: Peter Essick / AURORA
Cover Printer: Phoenix Color Corp.
Compositor: G & S Typesetters, Inc.
Printer: Quebecor World Book Services, Taunton

Wadsworth/Thomson Learning
10 Davis Drive
Belmont, CA 94002-3098
USA

For more information about our products, contact us:
Thomson Learning Academic Resource Center
1-800-423-0563
http://www.wadsworth.com

International Headquarters
Thomson Learning
International Division
290 Harbor Drive, 2nd Floor
Stamford, CT 06902-7477
USA

UK/Europe/Middle East/South Africa
Thomson Learning
Berkshire House
168-173 High Holborn
London WC1V 7AA
United Kingdom

Asia
Thomson Learning
60 Albert Street, #15-01
Albert Complex
Singapore 189969

Canada
Nelson Thomson Learning
1120 Birchmount Road
Toronto, Ontario M1K 5G4
Canada

ISBN: 0-534-55621-3

Contents in Brief

DETAILED CONTENTS

PREFACE

FROM THE BEGINNING, this text has had two major purposes. First, the book is designed to introduce university undergraduates to the field of cultural anthropology by drawing upon the rich ethnographic examples found within the discipline. With its comparative approach to the study of cultural diversity, the text provides a comprehensive overview of the discipline. Second, the text goes beyond the basic outline of introductory materials by applying the theory, insights, and methods of cultural anthropology to those contemporary situations that students, both majors and nonmajors, are likely to encounter in their professional and personal lives. Most students enrolled in introductory anthropology courses will never take another course in anthropology during their undergraduate careers. It is, therefore, important that they be exposed to the relevance of the discipline at the introductory level, rather than expecting them to take additional courses in more applied areas of anthropology.

FEATURES THAT INTEGRATE THE APPLIED PERSPECTIVE

The text's applied orientation is integrated into each of the chapters by the features called Applied Perspectives and Cross-Cultural Miscues. The Applied Perspectives, which appear in boxed format in Chapters 2 through 16, demonstrate how cultural anthropology has been used to solve specific societal problems in the areas of medicine, education, government, architecture, business, and economic development, among others. For example, in Chapter 3 of this Fourth Edition, students are shown how the study of Gypsie culture in San Francisco can lead to the delivery of better health care for this distinct cultural minority in the United States. And the Applied Perspective in Chapter 12 shows how the work of an ethnohistorian was used to secure official recognition of the Poarch Creek Indians by the federal government, a measure that had far reaching implications for the group's economic revitalization.

In recent years a number of leading introductory textbooks in the field have, to one degree or another, included some applied case studies in boxed format. I consider this imitation to be the sincerest form of flattery. Nevertheless, the Applied Perspective case studies in this text differ in some important respects. For example, each applied case study is selected to illustrate how certain understandings from each chapter have been applied to the solution of significant societal problems; there are a greater number of in-depth applied case studies in this text than in the others; and each of the case studies is followed by Questions for Further Thought, designed to encourage students to think critically about the broader implications of the applied case.

Two Cross-Cultural Miscues also appear in boxed format in Chapters 2 through 16. These short scenarios illustrate the potential negative results of failing to understand cultural differences. To illustrate, one miscue from Chapter 10 tells how a well-intentioned, but culturally insensitive, physician from the United States contributed to the death of an unmarried pregnant woman in Saudi Arabia.

Over the past decade an increasing number of cultural anthropologists have agreed with our basic premise: that an introductory text with an applied focus was long overdue. Anthropology instructors at a number of different types of institutions, public and private, large and small, two-year and four-year, have adopted the first three editions of this book. However, as well received as the previous editions have been, there is always room for improvement. Responding to many helpful suggestions of reviewers, the following changes have been made in the fourth edition.

CHANGES TO THE FOURTH EDITION
General

▶ The major format change in the new edition is that the Applied Perspectives—the signature feature of this book from the beginning—have been moved from the end of each chapter to boxes within the text itself. Because of this change, the feature of the third edition called Looking Ahead has been eliminated. The Cross-Cultural Miscues, which for the first three editions have been boxed throughout the chapters, will continue to be boxed. Thus, each of Chapters 2 through 16 will contain two Cross-Cultural Miscues and most chapters will contain two Applied Perspectives.

Moreover, most of the Applied Perspectives have been paired down slightly to make them easily readable and less obtrusive on the body of the text.

▶ Five new Applied Perspectives have been added to the fourth edition and two others have been substantially updated and supplemented.

▶ Nine of the Cross-Cultural Miscues are new to the fourth edition.

▶ All the Suggested Readings sections have been updated with current works.

▶ Most of the Internet exercises have been revised and many new ones added. In general, the exercises contain fewer specific URLs because they change frequently. In this new edition students are asked to conduct more generic searches which do not depend on the existence of a specific web site. Moreover, as part of the section entitled On the Net, some of the exercises bring students to Wadsworth's InfoTrac link, which should provide introductory students with at least a cursory exposure to this valuable research database.

▶ A deliberate effort has been made in this edition to make connections between the basic anthropological theories and insights *and* what is going on in the world around us as we enter the new millenium. The theme of *globalization* is discussed in a number of chapters including Chapter 8 (Economics), Chapter 12 (Political Organization and Social Control), Chapter 14 (Supernatural Beliefs), Chapter 15 (Art), and Chapter 16 (Cultural Change). Other contemporary events (from 1999) have also been integrated into the new edition. These include the creation of Nunavut, the Inuit's self-governing homeland in Canada; the controversy revolving around whale hunting by Native Americans in the State of Washington; the dispute between the Brooklyn Museum and Mayor Rudolph Giuliani of New York City over the Saatchi exhibition; and the way that Mia Hamm and her teammates on the U.S. World Cup Soccer Team have helped reshape our definition of femininity.

Chapter Changes

As with previous editions, all chapters have been revised with an eye toward streamlining, making materials more current, and reflecting recent trends in the discipline. For those familiar with previous editions of this book, a closer look at the specific changes made in each chapter will be helpful.

Chapter 1 (What is Anthropology) contains a new section entitled "Some Guiding Principles" which discusses the concepts of holism and cultural relativism. Another major addition is a section on "carry over skills" developed through the study of cultural anthropology. This discussion makes explicit to students (and their parents) the types of skills and capacities gained by studying cultural anthropology that are useful in whatever profession a student may ultimately pursue.

Chapter 2 (The Concept of Culture) provides a conceptual framework for understanding the central concept of the discipline of anthropology. The sections on ethnocentrism and cultural relativism, which appeared in Chapter 2 in the third edition have been moved to Chapter 1. The major addition to this chapter involves a new discussion on the related concepts of subcultures and pluralistic societies.

Chapter 3 (Applied Anthropology) no longer contains as much history of applied anthropology because a number of reviewers thought that it was not relevant to beginning students of anthropology. In place of the deleted history, three in-depth examples of how anthropology is applied have been added (ethnographic studies of teenage crack cocaine sellers, a medical project among the Zulu of South Africa, and a population study of the Shipibo in South America).

Chapter 4 (The Growth of Anthropological Theory) has been trimmed down. Some reviewers wanted to eliminate this chapter altogether, or put it in an appendix, while others wanted to keep it. As a reasonable compromise, we decided to make it less weighty. A new section on postmodernism has been added to the fourth edition.

Chapter 5 (Methods in Cultural Anthropology) includes a lengthy quote from an undergraduate who conducted fieldwork in a homeless shelter, a new section on the physical dangers of doing fieldwork, a contemporary example of doing fieldwork in Silicon Valley, California, and the inclusion of a student research project on sociometric tracking at a university cafeteria.

Chapter 6 (Language) has undergone considerable change. New topics include the threat of language extinction in small-scale societies; language acquisition among children; a major new section on historical linguistics, which discusses both language families and how languages change; and a discussion of dialect change in New York City. The chart on major languages of the world has also been updated.

Chapter 7 (Getting Food) includes new materials on changes in Inuit society, creation of the new Inuit homeland (Nunavut) by the Canadian Government, a discussion on why the Neolithic Revolution (domestication of plants and animals) was not such a great boon to humankind, and the contemporary problem of wild fires (and resulting air pollution) from slash and burn agriculture. Also new to this chapter is a discussion of the problems resulting from a "villagization" scheme among the pastoral Somali, how the use of the Internet has increased agricultural productivity, and some of the more deleterious effects of industrialized agriculture on the population and the environment.

Chapter 8 (Economics) has been streamlined, but also includes new discussions of land alienation among the Kikuyu of Kenya, how roles are allocated among the Abkhasians, and a discussion of "Big Women" and "Big Men" in the Pacific. Also new in this edition is a discussion of present day (1999) potlatching among Native Americans, a comparison between free-market economies and controlled markets, and a discussion of the globalization of world markets.

Chapter 9 (Marriage and the Family) has traded places with Chapter 10 (Kinship and Descent) since the last edition. New to this chapter is a discussion on the young age of marriage among girls in contemporary India, polygyny practiced in present-day Utah, and comparative data on bridewealth studies conducted in Africa during the 1970s, 1980s, and 1990s. Also, in the section on arranged marriages, there is a new discussion of a woman who is a professional matchmaker for top financial executives on Wall Street.

Chapter 10 (Kinship and Descent) has been revised to make the material less abstract, and thus, more understandable. The kinship diagrams are easier to read, and there is a new discussion of the meaning of legal parenthood by examining data from the Zambagua culture of highlands Ecuador.

Chapter 11 (Sex and Gender) has been expanded to include discussions of how the Women's U.S. World Cup Soccer Team has helped change our definition of femininity in the United States, gender discrimination in the classroom, and current information on gender discrimination in the area of finances. Lest we think that all gender discrimination occurs outside of the academic discipline of anthropology, this chapter includes a discussion of male bias in traditional ethnographic writing. Moreover, in the Exploitation section, new data are included on "honor killings" and "genital mutilation."

Chapter 12 (Political Organization and Social Control) now includes discussions of how the information revolution is affecting global politics in general, and dictatorships specifically. Closer to home, the effects of the Internet on the United States electoral process are examined. And, there is a major new discussion of warfare in the section on Social Control.

Chapter 13 (Social Stratification) includes a new section on the rising prominence of Hispanics in North America, new information on the growing gap in wealth in the United States, and a contemporary update on the untouchables of India. Also new to this chapter is a discussion of some inroads made by United States women in the area of occupational segregation, as well as the temporary "cease fire" in the gender wars. The fourth edition also includes an update on Bill Gates' wealth, which (given the mercurial ups and downs in the life of Microsoft) may need to be revised again before long.

Chapter 14 (Supernatural Beliefs), while retaining much of its content on different forms of supernatural belief systems, contains a good deal of contemporary information that is new to this edition. Specifically, there is information on the Wicca (witchcraft) movement in North America, the use of Buddhist priests by the city government of Portland to pray over the new transit system, the revival of shamanism in Siberia as a result of economic hard times in Russia, and revitalization movements in present-day Indonesia. In addition, this chapter includes a new section on the globalization of world religions.

Chapter 15 (Art) contains a number of new topics including how the political system is reflected in the type of body art found in certain Pacific societies, and the connections between art and the status quo in Bali (Indonesia). In an attempt to make the text as up-to-date as possible, this chapter includes a discussion of the on-going controversy raging between the mayor of New York and the Brooklyn Museum of Art. In addition, there is a new section on art and globalization, with a discussion of the resilience of various traditional art forms in Bali.

Chapter 16 (Cultural Change) in this edition recognizes the enormous changes that are taking place in the world today. Thus a major section discussing the nature of globalization of information, technology, and markets has been added. To better illustrate the selective nature of cultural diffusion, this chapter now contains a discussion of how certain western religious denominations have selectively adopted various elements from Buddhism. And finally, a new discussion of gers (tents) in Mongolian cities provides a physical example of how difficult it is to distinguish between rural and urban populations.

In addition to the many changes—both additions and deletions—to the various chapters, the bibliography and glossary have been revised to reflect the new content. The two appendices (Anthropology and Jobs and The Anthropology Student's Guide to the Internet) appearing in the third edition have been revised, and can now be found on the vastly enriched web site which supports the text.

CHAPTER FEATURES

As with all previous editions, the fourth edition contains a number of pedagogical features designed to enhance student learning. These include introductory questions alerting the student to what will be learned in the chapter; concise chapter summaries; key terms identified at the end of each chapter; Applied Perspectives, case studies illustrating how cultural anthropology is being applied to the solution of societal problems; Questions for Further Thought, designed to stimulate further thinking about the applied cases; Suggested Readings, which provide relevant references for students who want to learn more about a particular topic discussed in the chapter; and On the Net, exercises designed to help students both familiarize themselves with the Internet and use the vast resources of the Web to discover more anthropological content.

SUPPLEMENTS

Supplements for Instructors

INSTRUCTOR'S MANUAL WITH TEST BANK Written by Marlena Yvette Baber, the manual includes concept outlines, chapter overviews, learning objectives, and a Video/Film/Internet Resource Guide. The *Test Bank* provides 40 to 70 questions per chapter.

EXAMVIEW COMPUTERIZED AND ONLINE TESTING FROM WADSWORTH/THOMSON LEARNING Create, deliver, and customize tests and study guides (both print and online) in minutes with this easy-to-use assessment and tutorial system.

POWERPOINT Available free to adopters, this book-specific PowerPoint presentation can be viewed and downloaded from our website at *http://anthropology.wadsworth.com/ instructor/*. A username and password are available from your Wadsworth/Thomson Learning sales representative.

ANTHROLINK AnthroLink CD-ROM is an easy-to-use presentation tool that permits instructors to integrate media from this CD-ROM digital library into their lecture presentations. AnthroLink contains hundreds of pieces of graphic art from Wadsworth anthropology textbooks, photographs, and short video segments as well as the software to edit, sequence, and present customized lectures which can be saved and even posted to the Web.

VISUAL ANTHROPOLOGY VIDEO This video consists of sixteen clips, each three to four minutes in length, from some of the best-known ethnographic films. The shortness of the clips makes for maximum flexibility. Documentary Educational Resources produced the video exclusively for Wadsworth Publishing. Also available: *A Guide to Visual Anthropology*, which provides descriptions, discussion questions, and suggested classroom use for over 50 classical and contemporary anthropological films.

WADSWORTH ANTHROPOLOGY VIDEO LIBRARY Qualified adopters may select full-length videos from an extensive library of offerings drawn from such excellent educational video sources such as *NOVA, Films for the Humanities and Sciences,* and *The Disappearing World Video Series.*

CNN CULTURAL ANTHROPOLOGY TODAY VIDEO SERIES, VOLUMES I, II AND III The *CNN Cultural Anthropology Today Videos* is an exclusive series jointly created by Wadsworth and CNN for the cultural anthropology course. Each video in the series consists of approximately 45 minutes of footage originally broadcast on CNN within the last several years. The videos are broken into short two to seven minute segments, which are perfect for classroom use as lecture launchers, or to illustrate key anthropological concepts. An annotated table of contents accompanies each video with descriptions of the segments and suggestions for their possible use within the course.

Supplements for Students

APPLYING CULTURAL ANTHROPOLOGY: READINGS This reader prepared by Gary Ferraro contains 35 readings in applied anthropology. The readings focus on areas in which anthropology has been applied, such as business, medicine, education, government and law, criminal justice, and housing.

STUDY GUIDE A student study guide prepared by Marlena Yvette Baber is available. The study guide contains learning objectives, chapter outline reviews, and practice tests.

WEB-BASED RESOURCES

Anthropology Online: Wadsworth's Anthropology Resource Center

http://anthropology.wadsworth.com
At **Wadsworth's Anthropology Resource Center,** you will find surfing lessons (tips to find information on the Web), a career center, anthropology web-surfing links, InfoTrac College Edition, Anthropology in the News, and an online forum.

Visit the Ferraro, *Cultural Anthropology: An Applied Perspective, Fourth Edition* online resources at *http://anthropology.wadsworth.com/ferraro_4e/*. Features of the Ferraro online resources include:

- ▶ Hypercontents: Chapter-by-chapter resources available on the Internet
- ▶ Chapter Quizzes: Online self-quizzes for each chapter in the text
- ▶ InfoTrac College Edition
- ▶ Join the Forum: An online threaded discussion forum
- ▶ PowerPoint presentation: Available to the Instructor, it is easily viewable and downloadable. Please contact your local Wadsworth/Thomson Learning sales representative for a password to the Instructor Resources.

A special feature of the web site is **A Virtual Tour of Applying Anthropology** at *http://anthropology. wadsworth.com/applied/*. Visit this special section of the text's web site for a virtual tour of the various activities of applied anthropologists. Written by the text author, the tour uses photographs, video, hot links, and text to illustrate anthropologists at work in private business, as well as the environmental, medical, government, and political communities.

InfoTrac College Edition

Ignite discussions or augment your lectures with the latest developments in sociology and societal change. InfoTrac College Edition (available as a free option with newly purchased texts) gives you and your students four-month's free access to an easy-to-use online database of reliable, full-length articles (not abstracts) from hundreds of top academic journals and popular sources. Among the journals which are available 24 hours a day, 7 days a week are

American Anthropologist, Current Anthropology, and *Canadian Review of Sociology and Anthropology.* Contact your Wadsworth/Thomas Learning representative for more information.

WebTutor

WebTutor is a content-rich, Web-based teaching and learning tool which helps students succeed by taking the course beyond classroom boundaries to an anywhere–anytime environment. *WebTutor* is rich with study and mastery tools, communication tools, and course content. Professors can use *WebTutor* to provide virtual office hours, post syllabi, set up threaded discussions, track student progress with quizzing material, and more.

ACKNOWLEDGMENTS

Since its first appearance in 1992, this textbook has benefited enormously from excellent editorial guidance and the comments of many reviewers. I want to thank my original editor from West, Pete Marshall, for encouraging me to write an introductory textbook with an applied perspective in the first place, and for his support and advice for the first two editions. I also want to thank Bob Jucha, Senior Developmental Editor at Wadsworth, for his vision, counsel, and many excellent suggestions for improving the Fourth Edition. Thanks are also extended to Eve Howard, Publisher, and Jerilyn Emori, Project Editor at Wadsworth. Many thanks also to Jennifer Gordon for her meticulous copy editing, and to Joan Keyes of Dovetail Publishing Services for shepherding the book through the production process. Also, I am grateful to Kristin Labrie, a post-baccalaureate student at UNC Charlotte, for her invaluable help as a research assistant.

As with the previous editions, many reviewers have made valuable and insightful suggestions for strengthening the text. For this fourth edition, I would like to thank in particular the following colleagues:

Saul Arbess
Camosun College (Victoria, B.C.)

M. Yvette Baber
University of Memphis

William H. Breece
Orange Coast College

Richard Cerreto
Victor Valley College

Brian Donohue-Lynch
Quinebaug Valley Community-Technical College

Michael R. Fong
Chaffey College

Bonnie Glass-Coffin
Utah State University

Carol Hayman
Austin Community College

David Paul Lumsden
York University

Brian Leigh Molyneaux
University of South Dakota

Corey Pressman
Mt. Hood Community College

Martin Ottenheimer
Kansas State University

Orit Tamir
New Mexico Highlands University

Susan R. Trencher
George Mason University

John A. Young
Oregon State University

Cheryl L. Wright
University of Houston

I also want to thank the many unsolicited reviewers—both adopters and non-adopters—who have commented on various aspects of the text over the years. I trust that these reviewers will see that many of their helpful suggestions have been incorporated into the fourth edition. I encourage any readers, professors, or students to send me comments, corrections, and suggestions for improvements via e-mail at the following address:

gpferrar@email.uncc.edu.

And finally, I want to thank my many students who, over the last thirty years, have helped me define and refine the concepts and interpretations in this book.

ABOUT THE AUTHOR

Gary Ferraro, Professor of Anthropology, has taught at the University of North Carolina at Charlotte since 1971. Ferraro received his B.A. in history from Hamilton College and his M.A. and Ph.D. degrees from Syracuse University. He has been a Fulbright Scholar at the University of Swaziland in Southern Africa and has served as a visiting professor of anthropology in the University of Pittsburgh's Semester at Sea Program, a floating university that travels around the world.

With primary research interests in kinship and marriage systems in Eastern and Southern Africa, he has conducted research for extended periods of time in Kenya and Swaziland and has traveled widely throughout many other parts of the world. He has served as a consultant for such organizations as USAID, the Peace Corps, and the World Bank. In recent years he has taken a more applied focus in his work by conducting cross-cultural training seminars for international business people, educators, government officials, and medical practitioners. In 1996 he became Director of the Intercultural Training Institute at UNC–Charlotte, a consortium of cross-cultural trainers/educators from academia and business, designed to help regional organizations cope with cultural differences at home and abroad. In addition to publishing in a number of professional journals, he is the author of *The Two Worlds of Kamau* (1978), *The Cultural Dimension of International Business* (1998), *Cultural Anthropology: An Applied Perspective* (2001), and *Anthropology; an Applied Perspective* (1994).

Chapter One

WHAT IS ANTHROPOLOGY?

A young Morrocan woman peers from her window to see what is going on in the world around her, an activity in which students of cultural anthropology also engage.

WHAT WE WILL LEARN:

▼

How does anthropology differ from other social and behavioral sciences?

▼

What is the four-field approach to the discipline of anthropology?

▼

How can anthropology help solve social problems?

▼

What is meant by "cultural relativism," and why is it important?

▼

What skills will students develop from the study of anthropology?

▼

When most North Americans hear the word *anthropologist,* a number of images come to mind. They picture, for example,

- Dian Fossey devoting years of her life to making systematic observations of mountain gorillas in their natural environment in Rwanda
- A field anthropologist interviewing an exotic tribesman about the nature of his kinship system
- The excavation of a jawbone that will be used to demonstrate the evolutionary link between early and modern humans
- A linguist meticulously recording the words and sounds of a native informant speaking a language that has never been written down
- A cultural anthropologist living with a group of hard-core unemployed men in Washington, DC, while studying their culture
- A team of archaeologists in pith helmets unearthing an ancient temple from a rain forest in Guatemala

Each of these impressions—to one degree or another—accurately represents the concerns of scientists who call themselves anthropologists. Anthropologists do in fact travel to different parts of the world to study little-known cultures (cultural anthropologists) and languages (anthropological linguists), but they also study culturally distinct groups within their own cultures. There are also anthropologists who unearth fossil remains (physical anthropologists) and various artifacts (archaeologists) of people who lived thousands and, in some cases, millions of years ago. Even though these anthropological subspecialties engage in substantially different types of activities and generate different types of data, they are all directed toward a single purpose: the scientific study of humans, both biologically and culturally, in whatever form, time period, or region of the world they might be found.

Anthropology—derived from the Greek words *anthropos* for "human" and *logos* for "study"—is, if we take it literally, the study of humans. In one sense this is an accurate description to the extent that it raises a wide variety of questions about the human condition. And yet this literal definition is not particularly illuminating because a number of other academic disciplines—including sociology, biology, psychology, political science, economics, philosophy, and history—also study human beings. What is it that distinguishes anthropology from all of these other disciplines?

Anthropology is the study of people—their origins, their development, and contemporary variations, wherever and whenever they have been found on the face of the earth. Of all the disciplines that study humans, anthropology is by far the broadest in scope. The subject matter of anthropology includes fossilized skeletal remains of early humans, artifacts and other material remains from prehistoric and historic archaeological sites, and all of the contemporary and historical cultures of the world. The task that anthropology has set for itself is an enormous one. Anthropologists strive for an understanding of the biological and cultural origins and evolutionary development of the species. They are concerned with all humans, both past and present, as well as humans' behavior patterns, thought systems, and material possessions. In short, anthropology aims to describe, in the broadest sense, what it means to be human (see Peacock 1986).

In their search to understand the human condition, anthropologists—drawing on a wide variety of data and methods—have created a diverse field of study. Many specialists in the field of anthropology often engage in research that is directly relevant to other fields. It has been suggested (Wolf 1964) that anthropology spans the gap between the humanities, the social sciences, and the natural sciences. To illustrate, anthropological investigations of native art, folklore, values, and supernatural belief systems are primarily humanistic in nature; studies of social stratification, comparative political systems, and means of distribution have a good deal in common with the social science investigations of sociology, political science, and economics, respectively; and studies of comparative anatomy and radiocarbon dating are central to the natural sciences of biology and chemistry.

The breadth of anthropology becomes apparent when looking at the considerable range of topics discussed in papers published in the *American Anthropologist* (one of the primary professional journals in the field). For example, the following are just a few of the topics discussed in the *American Anthropologist* in the 1990s:

- ▶ The health and nutrition of a medieval Nubian population in the Sudan
- ▶ The origins of agriculture in the Near East
- ▶ The migration, education, and status of women in southern Nigeria
- ▶ An explanation of differences in overseas experiences among employees of the General Motors Corporation
- ▶ The sexual behavior of bonobos (pygmy chimpanzees)
- ▶ An analysis of tension between African Americans and Korean immigrants in Los Angeles
- ▶ Status and power in classical Mayan society
- ▶ Men's and women's speech patterns among the Creek Indians of Oklahoma
- ▶ The role of maize in bringing about political changes in Peru many centuries ago
- ▶ The distribution and consumption of Islamic religious paraphernalia in Egypt and how it has transformed urban religious consciousness
- ▶ The question of whether infants have religion
- ▶ The biocultural factors in school achievement for Mopan children in Belize

The global scope of anthropological studies has actually increased in recent years. In the early 1900s, anthropologists concentrated on the non-Western, preliterate, and technologically simple societies of the world and were content to leave the study of industrial societies to other disciplines. But for much of the twentieth century anthropologists have been studying, with increased frequency, cultural and subcultural groups in industrialized areas while continuing their studies of more exotic peoples of the world. It is not uncommon today for anthropologists to apply their field methods to the study of the Hutterites of Montana, rural communes in California, or urban street gangs in Chicago. Only when the whole range of human cultural variation is examined will we be in a position to test the accuracy of theories about human behavior.

Traditionally, anthropology as practiced in the United States during the twentieth century is divided into four distinct branches or subfields: physical anthropology, which deals with humans as biological organisms; archaeology, which attempts to reconstruct the cultures of the past, most of which have left no written records; anthropological linguistics, which focuses on the study of language in historical, structural, and social contexts; and cultural anthropology, which examines similarities and differences between contemporary cultures of the world (Table 1-1). Despite this four-field division, the discipline of anthropology has a long-standing tradition of emphasizing the interrelations among these four subfields. Moreover, in recent years there has been considerable blurring of the boundaries among the four branches. For example, the specialized area known as medical anthropology draws heavily from both physical and cultural anthropology; educational anthropology addresses issues that bridge the gap between cultural anthropology and linguistics; and sociobiology looks at the interaction between culture and biology. Although cultural anthropology is the central focus

TABLE 1-1
Branches of Anthropology

PHYSICAL ANTHROPOLOGY	ARCHAEOLOGY	ANTHROPOLOGICAL LINGUISTICS	CULTURAL ANTHROPOLOGY
Paleontology	Historical archaeology	Historical linguistics	Economic anthropology
Primatology	Prehistoric archaeology	Descriptive linguistics	Psychological anthropology
Human variation	Contract archaeology	Ethnolinguistics	Educational anthropology
Forensic anthropology		Sociolinguistics	Medical anthropology
			Urban anthropology
			Political anthropology

of this textbook, it is important to discuss the other three branches and to provide an adequate description of the whole discipline.

PHYSICAL ANTHROPOLOGY

THE STUDY OF HUMANS from a biological perspective is called **physical anthropology.** Essentially, physical anthropologists are concerned with two broad areas of investigation. First, they are interested in reconstructing the evolutionary record of the human species; that is, they ask questions about the emergence of humans and how humans have evolved up to the present time. This area of physical anthropology is known as **human paleontology** or **paleoanthropology.** The second area of concern to physical anthropologists deals with how and why the physical traits of contemporary human populations vary across the world. This area of investigation is called human variation. Physical anthropologists differ from comparative biologists in that they study how culture and environment have influenced these two areas of biological evolution and contemporary variations.

EVOLUTIONARY RECORD OF HUMANS

In their attempts to reconstruct human evolution, paleoanthropologists have drawn heavily on fossil remains (hardened organic matter such as bones and teeth) of humans, protohumans, and other primates. Once these fossil remains have been unearthed, the difficult job of compar-

= *Paleontologist Richard Leakey unearths some prehistoric fossil remains at Koobi Fora in Kenya.*

ison, analysis, and interpretation begins. To which species do the remains belong? Are the remains human or those of our prehuman ancestors? If not human, how do the remains relate to our own species? When did these primates live? How did they adapt to their environment? To answer these questions, paleoanthropologists use the techniques of comparative anatomy. They compare such physical features as cranial capacity, teeth, hands, position of the pelvis, and the shape of the head of the fossil remains with those of humans or other nonhuman primates. In addition to comparing physical features, paleoanthropologists look for signs of culture (such as tools) to help determine the humanity of the fossil remains. For example, if fossil remains are found in association with tools, and if it can be determined that the tools were made by these creatures, it is likely that the remains will be considered human.

The work of paleoanthropologists is often tedious and must be conducted with meticulous attention to detail. Even though the quantity of fossilized materials is growing each year, the paleoanthropologist has few data to analyze. Much of the evolutionary record remains underground. Of the fossils that have been found, many are partial or fragmentary, and more often than not, they are not found in association with cultural artifacts. Consequently, to fill in the human evolutionary record, physical anthropologists need to draw on the work of a number of other specialists: paleontologists (who specialize in prehistoric plant and animal life), archaeologists (who study prehistoric material culture), and geologists (who provide data on local physical and climatic conditions).

Since the 1950s, physical anthropologists have developed an area of specialization of their own that helps shed light on human evolution and adaptation over time and space. This field of study is known as **primatology**—the study of our nearest living relatives (apes, monkeys, and prosimians) in their natural habitat. Primatologists study the anatomy and social behavior of such nonhuman primate species as gorillas, baboons, and chimpanzees in an effort to gain clues about our own evolution as a species. Because physical anthropologists do not have the luxury of observing the behavior of our human ancestors several million years ago, we can learn how early humans responded to certain environmental conditions and changes in their developmental past by studying contemporary nonhuman primates in similar environments. For example, the simple yet very real division of labor among baboon troops can shed light on role specialization and social stratification in early human societies.

Primatologists study such nonhuman primates as this mountain gorilla of Rwanda.

PHYSICAL VARIATIONS AMONG HUMANS

Although all humans are members of the same species and therefore are capable of interbreeding, considerable *physical variation* exists among human populations. Some of these differences are based on visible physical traits, such as the shape of the nose, body stature, and color of the skin. Other variations are based on less visible biochemical factors, such as blood type or susceptibility to diseases.

For decades, physical anthropologists attempted to document human physical variations throughout the world by dividing the world's populations into various racial categories. (A **race** is a group of people who share a greater statistical frequency of genes and physical traits with one another than they do with people outside the group.) Today the physical anthropologist's attention is focused more on

trying to explain *why* the variations exist by asking such questions as, Are peoples of the Arctic better endowed physically to survive in colder climates? Why do some populations have darker skin than others? Why are most Chinese adults unable to digest milk? Why is the blood type B nonexistent among Australian aborigines? How have certain **human populations adapted** biologically to their local environments? To help answer these and other questions involving human biological variation, physical anthropologists draw on the work of three allied disciplines: **genetics** (the study of inherited physical traits), **population biology** (the study of the relationship between population characteristics and environment), and **epidemiology** (the study of differential clusterings of disease in populations over time).

Sometimes the study of physical anthropology leads to startling findings. While studying chimps in their natural habitat in Tanzania, primatologist Richard Wrangham noticed that young chimps occasionally ate the leaves of plants that were not in their normal diet. Because the chimps swallowed the leaves whole, Wrangham concluded that they perhaps were not ingesting these leaves primarily for nutritional purposes. Chemical analysis of the leaves by pharmacologist Eloy Rodriquez indicated that the plant contains substantial amounts of the chemical compound thiarubrine-A, which has strong antibiotic properties. Wrangham concluded that the chimps were medicating themselves, perhaps to help them control internal parasites. Seeing the potential for treating human illnesses, Rodriquez and Wrangham have applied for a patent. Interestingly, they plan to use part of the proceeds from their new drug to help preserve the chimpanzee habitat in Tanzania. According to Wrangham, "I like the idea of chimps showing us the medicine and then helping them to pay for their own conservation" (Howard 1991).

▪◾ ARCHAEOLOGY ◾▪

THE STUDY OF the lifeways of people from the past through excavating and analyzing the material culture they leave behind is called **archaeology**. The purpose of archaeology is not to fill up museums by collecting exotic relics from prehistoric societies. Rather, it is to understand cultural adaptations of ancient peoples by at least partially reconstructing their cultures. Because they concentrate on societies of the past, archaeologists are limited to working with material culture including, in some cases, written records. However, from these material remains archaeologists are able to infer many nonmaterial cultural aspects (ideas and behavior patterns) held by people thousands and, in some cases, millions of years ago.

Archaeologists work with three types of material remains: artifacts, features, and ecofacts. **Artifacts** are objects that have been made or modified by humans and that can be removed from the site and taken to the laboratory for further analysis. Tools, arrowheads, and fragments of pottery are examples of artifacts. **Features,** like artifacts, are made or modified by people, but they differ in that they cannot be readily carried away. Archaeological features include such things as house foundations, fireplaces, and post holes. **Ecofacts** are the third type of physical remains used by archaeologists. These include objects found in the natural environment (such as bones, seeds, and wood) that were not made or altered by humans but were used by them. Ecofacts provide archaeologists with important data concerning the environment and how the people used natural resources.

The data that archaeologists have at their disposal are very selective. Not only are archaeologists limited to material remains, but also the overwhelming majority of material possessions that may have been part of a culture do not survive thousands of years under the ground. As a result, archaeologists search for fragments of material evidence that will enable them to piece together as much of the culture as possible—such items as projectile points, hearths,

beads, and post holes. A prehistoric garbage dump is particularly revealing, for the archaeologist can learn a great deal about how people lived from what they threw away. These material remains are then used to make inferences about the nonmaterial aspects of the culture being studied. For example, the finding that all women and children are buried with their heads pointing in one direction, whereas the heads of adult males point in a different direction, could lead to the possible explanation that the society practiced matrilineal kinship (that is, children followed their mother's line of descent rather than their father's).

Once the archaeologist has collected the physical evidence, the difficult work of analysis and interpretation begins. By studying the bits and pieces of material culture left behind (within the context of both environmental data and anatomical remains), the archaeologist seeks to determine how the people supported themselves, whether they had a notion of an afterlife, how roles were allocated between men and women, whether some people were more prominent than others, whether the people engaged in trade with neighboring peoples, and how lifestyles have changed through time.

Present-day archaeologists work with both historic and prehistoric cultures. Historic archaeologists help to reconstruct the cultures of people who used writing and about whom historical documents have been written. For example, historical archaeologists have contributed significantly to our understanding of colonial American cultures by analyzing material remains that can supplement such historical documents as books, letters, graffiti, and government reports.

Prehistoric archaeology, on the other hand, deals with the vast segment of the human record before writing. In the several million years of human existence, writing is a very recent development. Writing first appeared about 5,500 years ago, and in many parts of the world is much more recent than that. Prehistoric archaeologists, then, study cultures that existed before the development of writing. Archaeology thus remains the one scientific enterprise that systematically focuses on prehistoric cultures, and, consequently, it has provided us with a much fuller time frame for understanding the record of human development.

The relevance of studying ancient artifacts often goes beyond helping us better understand our prehistoric past. In some cases, the study of stone tools can lead to improvements in our own modern technology. To illustrate, while experimentally replicating the manufacture of stone

= *Archaeologists excavate decorated vases on the Greek island of Santorini.*

tools, archaeologist Don Crabtree found that obsidian from the western part of the United States can be chipped to a very sharp edge. When examined under an electron microscope, the cutting edge of obsidian was found to be 200 times sharper than modern surgical scalpels. Some surgeons now use these obsidian scalpels because the healing is faster and the scarring is reduced (Sheets 1993).

•■ ANTHROPOLOGICAL ■• LINGUISTICS

THE BRANCH OF the discipline that studies human speech and language is called **anthropological linguistics.** Although humans are not the only species that has systems of symbolic communication, ours is by far the most complex form. In fact, some would argue that language is the most distinctive feature of being human, for without language we could not acquire and transmit our culture from one generation to the next.

Linguistic anthropology, which studies contemporary human languages as well as those of the past, is divided into four distinct branches: historical linguistics, descriptive linguistics, ethnolinguistics, and sociolinguistics.

Historical linguistics deals with the emergence of language in general and how specific languages have diverged over time. Some of the earliest anthropological interest in language focused on the historical connections between languages. For example, nineteenth-century linguists working with European languages demonstrated similarities in the sound systems between a particular language and an earlier parent language from which the language was derived. In other words, by comparing contemporary languages, linguists have been able to identify certain language families. More recently, through such techniques as **glottochronology**, linguists can now approximate when two related languages began to diverge from each other.

Descriptive linguistics is the study of sound systems, grammatical systems, and the meanings attached to words in specific languages. Every culture has a distinctive language with its own logical structure and set of rules for putting words and sounds together for the purpose of communicating. In its simplest form, the task of the descriptive linguist is to compile dictionaries and grammars for previously unwritten languages.

Ethnolinguistics is the branch of anthropological linguistics that examines the relationship between language and culture. In any culture, aspects that are emphasized (such as types of snow among the Inuit, cows among the pastoral Masai, or automobiles in U.S. culture) are reflected in the vocabulary of that culture's language. Moreover, ethnolinguists explore how different linguistic categories can affect how people categorize their experiences, how they think, and how they perceive the world around them.

The fourth branch of anthropological linguistics, known as **sociolinguistics,** examines the relationship between language and social relations. For example, sociolinguists are interested in investigating how social class influences the particular dialect a person speaks. They also study the situational use of language—that is, how people use different forms of a language depending on the social situation they find themselves in at any given time. To illustrate, the words, and even grammatical structures, a U.S. college student would choose when conversing with a roommate would be significantly different from the linguistic style used when talking to a grandparent, a priest, or a personnel director during a job interview.

For much of the twentieth century, anthropological linguists have performed the invaluable task of documenting the vocabularies, grammars, and phonetic systems of the many unwritten languages of the world. As we enter the twenty-first century, however, most of the hitherto unwritten languages have been recorded or have died out (that is, lost all of their native speakers). This has led some anthropologists to suggest that the field of anthropological linguistics has essentially completed its work and should no longer be regarded as one of the major branches of anthropology. Such a view, however, is shortsighted. Because languages are constantly changing, anthropological linguists will be needed to document these changes and to show how they relate to the culture at large. Moreover, in recent years anthropological linguists have expanded their research interests to include such areas as television advertising, linguistic aspects of popular culture, and even computer jargon.

•■ CULTURAL ANTHROPOLOGY ■•

THE BRANCH OF the discipline that deals with the study of specific contemporary cultures (**ethnography**) and the more general underlying patterns of human culture derived through cultural comparisons (**ethnology**) is called **cultural anthropology.** Before cultural anthropologists can examine cultural differences and similarities throughout the world, they must first describe the features of specific cultures in as much detail as possible. These detailed descriptions (ethnographies) are the result of extensive field studies (usually a year or two in duration) in which the anthropologist observes, talks to, and lives with the people he or she is studying. The writing of large numbers of ethnographies over the course of the twentieth century has provided an empirical basis for the comparative study of cultures. In the process of developing these descriptive accounts, cultural anthropologists may provide insights into such questions as, How are the marriage customs of a group of people related to the group's economy? What effect does urban migration have on the kinship system? In what ways have supernatural beliefs helped a group of people adapt more effectively to their environment? Thus, while describing the essential features of a culture, the cultural anthropologist may also explain why certain cultural patterns exist and how they may be related to one another.

Ethnology is the comparative study of contemporary cultures, wherever they may be found. Ethnologists seek to understand both why people today and in the recent past differ in terms of ideas and behavior patterns and what all cultures in the world have in common with one another. The primary objective of ethnology is to uncover general cultural principles, the "rules" that govern human behavior. Because all humans have culture and live in groups called societies, there are no populations in the world today that are not viable subjects for the ethnologist. The lifeways of Inuit living in the Arctic tundra, Greek peasants, !Kung hunters of the Kalahari Desert, and the residents of a retirement home in southern California have all been studied by cultural anthropologists.

Ethnographers and ethnologists face a task of great magnitude as they attempt to describe and compare the many peoples of the world during the twentieth century. A small number of cultural anthropologists must deal with enormous cultural diversity (thousands of distinct cultures where people speak mutually unintelligible languages), numerous features of culture that could be compared, and a wide range of theoretical frameworks for comparing them. To describe even the least complex cultures requires many months of interviewing people and observing their behavior. Even with this large expenditure of time, rarely do contemporary ethnographers describe total cultures. Instead, they usually describe only the more outstanding features of a culture and then investigate a particular aspect or problem in greater depth.

AREAS OF SPECIALIZATION

Because the description of a total culture is usually beyond the scope of a single ethnographer, in recent decades cultural anthropologists have tended to specialize, often identifying themselves with one or more of the following areas of specialization:

1. *Urban anthropology*. Cultural anthropologists during the first half of the twentieth century tended to concentrate their research on rural societies in non-Western areas. In the immediate post–World War II era, however, anthropologists in greater numbers turned their attention to the study of urban social systems. With increases in rural to urban migration in many parts of the world, it was becoming increasingly more difficult to think of rural populations as isolated, insulated entities. Because traditional rural populations were interacting with urban areas with increasing frequency during the 1950s and 1960s, cultural anthropologists began to assess the impacts that cities were having on these traditional rural societies. From that point it was a natural development to follow rural people into the cities to see how the two systems interacted. Thus was born the subdiscipline of urban anthropology.

By focusing on how such factors as size, density, and heterogeneity affect customary ways of behaving, urban anthropologists in recent decades have examined a number of important topics, including descriptive accounts of urban ethnic neighborhoods, rural urban linkages, labor migration, urban family and kinship patterns, social network analysis, emerging systems of urban stratification, squatter settlements, and informal economies. Urban anthropology has also focused on such social problems as homelessness, race relations, poverty, unemployment, crime, and health. Some recent studies have described the modern urban subcultures of truck drivers, cocktail waitresses, street gangs, drug addicts, skid row alcoholics, and prostitutes. Interestingly, few studies have been conducted in the suburbs, where various forms of social problems are also found.

2. *Medical anthropology*. Another recent area of specialization is medical anthropology, which studies the biological and sociocultural factors that affect health, disease, and illness now and in the past. Medical anthropology includes a variety of perspectives and concerns, ranging from a biological pole at one end of the spectrum to a sociocultural pole at the other. Medical anthropologists with a more biological focus tend to concentrate on such interests as the role of disease in human evolution, nutrition, growth and development, and **paleopathology** (the analysis of

disease in ancient populations). Medical anthropologists with more social or cultural interests focus their studies on ethnomedicine (belief systems that affect sickness and health), medical practitioners, and the relationship between traditional and Western medical systems. Contemporary medical anthropology represents both the biological and the sociocultural approaches, but we should not think of them as separate and autonomous. In actual practice, theory and data from one approach are often used by the other.

Medical anthropology, like many other specialty areas, deals with both theoretical and applied questions of research. To be certain, because beliefs and practices about medicine and healing are part of any culture, they deserve study in much the same way as would other features of culture such as economics, family patterns, or supernatural belief systems. But for many practitioners, medical anthropology has a strong applied or practical focus as well. Many medical anthropologists are motivated by the desire to apply the theories, methods, and insights to programs designed to improve health services at home and abroad.

3. *Educational anthropology.* In a general sense, educational anthropology involves the use of anthropological theory, data, and methods to study educational practices, institutions, and problems both at home and abroad. Just as cultural anthropologists study other cultural areas such as economic, political, or kinship systems, educational anthropologists examine the processes of learning (that is, acquiring one's culture) in its proper cultural context. The range of educational institutions studied varies from highly formal school systems in industrialized societies to very informal systems in which important cultural knowledge is passed down from generation to generation by kinspeople through such means as storytelling, experiential learning, and peer interaction.

The 1960s and 1970s witnessed a number of case studies in education and culture. For example, Thomas Williams (1969) wrote *A Borneo Childhood,* a study of how Dusun children learned what they needed to know at different stages of development; Margaret Read (1960) wrote *Children of Their Fathers,* an ethnography of growing up among the Ngoni of Malawi; and Bruce Grindal (1972), in his work *Growing Up in Two Worlds,* ethnographically examined how the Sisala children of northern Ghana were caught between traditional and more modern forms of education. At the same time, while educational anthropology was establishing itself as a viable subdiscipline of anthropology, some educational anthropologists were working closer to home. By using ethnographic methods in our own society, Gerry Rosenfeld (1971) studied school failure among Black children in Harlem schools, John Hostetler and Gertrude Huntington (1971) studied the process of education among the Amish in Ohio, and Martha Ward (1971) examined

Some applied anthropologists conduct research in multiracial classrooms such as this one in Fontana, California. Their findings enable teachers to better understand the cultural backgrounds of their students.

speech acquisition among Black children near New Orleans. Today some of the most interesting research is being done in ordinary classrooms where ethnographic methods are being used to observe interaction among students, teachers, administrators, staff, parents, and visitors. And many contemporary studies are not confined to the classroom, but rather follow students into their homes and neighborhoods, because learning must be viewed within the wider cultural context of family and peers.

4. *Economic anthropology.* Economic anthropology studies how goods and services are produced, distributed, and consumed within the total cultural contexts of which they are a part. The variety of topics studied by economic anthropologists is wide, including patterns of work, division of labor, patterns of exchange, and control of property. To illustrate, a collection of essays on economic anthropology might include a piece on traditional hunting patterns among the Hadza of Tanzania, a description of the decision-making process of a grandmother in rural Bolivia to join an economic cooperative, and an article on how the international price of cocoa beans affects the consumption patterns of a peasant farmer in Ghana. Early studies in economic anthropology during the late 1940s and early 1950s were largely descriptive in nature, but they have become more analytical in subsequent decades.

Like most cultural anthropologists, economic anthropologists have traditionally studied small-scale, non-Western societies that are not based on the profit motive. Economists, on the other hand, have examined institutions of production, distribution, and consumption primarily in Western, capitalistic societies. Although over the years economic anthropologists have borrowed some concepts from the discipline of economics, most economic anthropologists feel that classical economic theories derived from modern Western economies are inappropriate for understanding small-scale, non-Western economies.

5. *Psychological anthropology.* Psychological anthropology, one of the largest subspecialty areas of cultural anthropology, looks at the relationship between culture and the psychological makeup of individuals and groups. Concerned with understanding how psychological processes relate to cultural factors, psychological anthropology examines how culture may affect personality, cognition, attitudes, and emotions.

The early practitioners of psychological anthropology between the 1920s and 1950s—namely Benedict, Boas, and Sapir—were interested in the relationship between culture and personality. Many of these early theorists studied the effects of cultural features (such as feeding, weaning, and toilet training) on personality, but some, led by Abraham Kardiner, were interested in how group personality traits could be reflected in a culture. Stimulated by the need to know more about America's allies and enemies during World War II, some of the culture and personality anthropologists turned their analysis on large, complex societies in what came to be known as national character studies. Geoffrey Gorer and John Rickman (1949), for example, studied Russia while Ruth Benedict wrote her classic study of the Japanese national character in 1946. Today these studies are not taken very seriously because of the methodological difficulties involved in generalizing about large, complex societies with considerable class and ethnic diversity.

Since the 1960s, psychological anthropology has moved away from these broad national character studies and has focused on a more narrowly drawn set of problems. The early interest in large global assessments of personality or character has been largely replaced by investigations of more particular psycho-cultural phenomena such as symbolism, cognition, and consciousness in specific societies. Methodologies have become more varied, statistics have been more widely used, and psychological anthropologists have been engaged in more collaborative research with those from other disciplines such as psychology and linguistics.

These five areas are only a partial list of the specializations within cultural anthropology. Other specialties include agricultural anthropology, legal anthropology, ecological anthropology, political anthropology, the anthropology of work, and nutritional anthropology.

·■ GUIDING PRINCIPLES ■·

FOR THE PAST CENTURY, cultural anthropology has distinguished itself from other disciplines in the humanities and social sciences by several guiding principles. Although other disciplines have incorporated some of these major themes over the decades, they remain central to the discipline of cultural anthropology.

HOLISM

A distinguishing feature of the discipline of anthropology is its holistic approach to the study of human groups. The holism of anthropology is evident in a number of important respects. First, the anthropological approach involves both biological and sociocultural aspects of humanity. That is, anthropologists are interested in people's genetic endowment as well as what people acquire from their sociocultural environment after birth. Second, anthropology has the deepest possible time frame, starting with the earliest beginnings of humans several million years ago right up to the present. Anthropology is holistic to the extent that it studies all varieties of people wherever they may be found. That is, anthropology's global perspective considers the lifeways of East African pastoralists, Polynesian farmers, and Japanese businesspeople all to be equally legitimate subjects of study. And, finally, anthropology studies many different aspects of human experience. To illustrate, a cultural anthropologist who is conducting direct, participant-observation fieldwork may be collecting data on a wide variety of topics, including family structure, marital regulations, house construction, methods of conflict resolution, means of livelihood, religious beliefs, language, space usage, and art.

In the past, cultural anthropologists have made every effort to be holistic by covering as many aspects of a culture as possible in the total cultural context. More recently, however, the accumulated information from all over the world has become so vast that most anthropologists have needed to become more specialized or focused. This is called a problem-oriented research approach. To illustrate, one anthropologist may concentrate on marital patterns whereas another may focus on farming and land-use patterns. Despite the recent trend toward specialization, anthropologists continue to analyze their findings within their wider cultural context. Moreover, when all of the various specialties within the discipline are viewed together, they represent a very comprehensive or holistic view of the human condition.

ETHNOCENTRISM

While waiting to cross the street in Bombay, India, an American tourist stood next to a local resident, who proceeded to blow his nose, without handkerchief or Kleenex, into the street. The tourist's reaction was instantaneous and unequivocal: "How disgusting!" he thought to himself. He responded to this cross-cultural encounter by evaluating the Indian's behavior on the basis of standards of etiquette established by his own culture. According to those standards, it would be considered proper to use a handkerchief in such a situation. But if the man from Bombay were to see the American tourist blowing his nose into a handkerchief, he would be equally repulsed, thinking it strange indeed for the man to blow his nose into a handkerchief and then put the handkerchief back into his pocket and carry it around for the rest of the day.

Both the American and the Indian are evaluating each other's behavior based on the standards of their own cultural assumptions and practices. This way of responding to culturally different behavior is known as ethnocentrism: the belief that one's own culture is most desirable and superior to all others. In other words, it means viewing the rest of the world through the narrow lens of one's own culture.

Incidents of ethnocentrism are extensive. For example, we can see ethnocentrism operating in the historical accounts of the American Revolutionary War by both British and American historians. According to U.S. historians, George Washington was a folk hero of epic proportions. He led his underdog Continental Army successfully against the larger, better equipped redcoats, he threw a coin across the Potomac River, and he was so incredibly honest that he turned himself in for chopping down a cherry tree. What a guy! But according to many British historians, George Washington was a thug and a hooligan. Many of Washington's troops were the descendants of debtors and prisoners who couldn't make it in England. Moreover, Washington didn't fight fairly. Whereas the British were most gentlemanly about warfare (for example, standing out in open fields in their bright red coats, shooting at the enemy), Washington went sneaking around ambushing the British. Some British military historians have described Washington in much the same way that recent American historians have described the leaders of the Vietcong during the Vietnam conflict. Even though the U.S. and British historians were describing the same set of historical events, their own biased cultural perspectives lead to two very different interpretations.

No society has a monopoly on ethnocentrism. Marshall Hodgson (1974:19–20) reminds us that people view their own culture as superior and that they often see themselves as occupying the most prominent place on earth:

> In the sixteenth century the Italian missionary, Matteo Ricci, brought to China a European map of the world showing the new discoveries in America. The Chinese were glad to learn about America, but one aspect of the map offended them. Since the map split the earth's

surface down the Pacific, China appeared off at the right hand edge; whereas the Chinese thought of themselves as literally the "Middle Kingdom," which should be in the center of the map. . . . [The Chinese thought] . . . that the Temple of Heaven at the Emperor's capitol, Peking, marked the exact center of the earth's surface.

It should be quite obvious why ethnocentrism is so pervasive throughout the world. Because most people are raised in a single culture and never learn another culture during their lifetime, it is only logical that their own way of life—their values, attitudes, ideas, and ways of behaving—would seem to be the most natural. Even though ethnocentrism is present to some degree in all peoples and all cultures, it nevertheless serves as a major obstacle to the understanding of other cultures, which is, after all, the major objective of cultural anthropology. Even people who think of themselves as open-minded have difficulty controlling the impulse to evaluate the ideas or actions of culturally different people. And when individuals do make a value judgment, it is in all likelihood based on their own cultural standards. Because it is so difficult to suppress our ethnocentrism, we often find ourselves expressing surprise, horror, outrage, disgust, disapproval, or amusement when encountering a lifestyle different from our own. Although we cannot eliminate ethnocentrism totally, we can reduce it. By becoming aware of our own ethnocentrism, we can temporarily set aside our own value judgments long enough to learn how other cultures operate.

CULTURAL RELATIVISM

Since the beginning of the twentieth century, the discipline of anthropology has led a vigorous campaign against the perils of ethnocentrism. As cultural anthropologists began to conduct empirical fieldwork among the different cultures of the world, they recognized a need for dispassionate and objective descriptions of the people they were studying. Following the lead of Franz Boas in the United States and Bronislaw Malinowski in Britain, twentieth-century anthropologists have participated in a tradition that calls on the fieldworker to strive to prevent his or her own cultural values from coloring the descriptive accounts of the people under study.

According to Boas, the father of modern anthropology in the United States, the way anthropologists are to strive for that level of detachment is through the practice of cultural relativism. This is the notion that any part of a culture (such as an idea, a thing, or a behavior pattern) must be viewed in its proper cultural context rather than from

the viewpoint of the observer's culture. The cultural relativist asks, How does a cultural item fit into the rest of the cultural system of which it is a part? rather than, How does it fit into my own culture? First formulated by Boas and later developed by one of his students, Melville Herskovits (1972), cultural relativism rejects the notion that any culture, including our own, possesses a set of absolute standards by which all other cultures can be judged. Cultural relativity is a cognitive tool that helps us understand why people think and act the way they do.

Perhaps a specific example of cultural relativity will help to clarify the concept. Anthropologists over the years have described a number of cultural practices from around the world that appear to be morally reprehensible to most Westerners. For example, the Dani of western New Guinea customarily cut off a finger from the hand of any close female relative of a man who dies, the Kikuyu of Kenya routinely remove part of the genitalia of teenage girls for the sake of suppressing their maleness, and the Dodoth of Uganda extract the lower front teeth of young girls in an attempt to make them more attractive. Some Inuit groups practice a custom that would strike the typical Westerner as inhumane at best: When aging parents become too old to contribute their share of the workload, they are left out in the cold to die. If we view such a practice by the standards of our own Western culture (that is, ethnocentrically), we would have to conclude that it is cruel and heartless, hardly a way to treat those who brought you into the world. But the cultural relativist would look at this form of homicide in the context of the total culture of which it is a part. John Friedl and John Pfeiffer (1977:331) provide a culturally relativistic explanation of this custom:

> It is important to know . . . that this . . . [custom is not practiced] against the will of the old person. It is also necessary to recognize that this is an accepted practice for which people are adequately prepared throughout their lives, and not some kind of treachery sprung upon an individual as a result of a criminal conspiracy. Finally, it should be considered in light of the ecological situation in which the Eskimos live. Making a living in the Arctic is difficult at best, and the necessity of feeding an extra mouth, especially when there is little hope that the individual will again become productive in the food-procurement process, would mean that the whole group would suffer. It is not a question of Eskimos not liking old people, but rather a question of what is best for the entire group. We would not expect—and indeed we do not find—this practice to exist where there was adequate food to support those who were not able to contribute to the hunting effort.

For Boas, cultural relativism was an ethical mandate as well as a strategic methodology for understanding other cultures. In his attempt to counter the methodological abuses of his time and set anthropology on a more scientific footing, Boas perhaps overemphasized the importance of cultural relativism. If cultural relativism is taken to its logical extreme, we arrive at two indefensible positions. First, from a methodological perspective, if every society is a unique entity that can be evaluated only in terms of its own standards, then any type of cross-cultural comparison would be virtually impossible. Clearly, however, if cultural anthropology is to accomplish its major objective—that is, to scientifically describe and compare the world's cultures—it needs some basis for comparison.

A second difficulty with taking the notion of cultural relativism too literally is that, from an ethical standpoint, we would have to conclude that absolutely no behavior found in the world would be immoral provided that the people who practice it concur that it is morally acceptable or that it performs a function for the well-being of the society. Practicing cultural relativism, however, does not require that we view all cultural practices as morally equivalent. That is, not all cultural practices are equally worthy of tolerance and respect. To be certain, some cultural practices (such as the genocide perpetrated by Hitler or the Serbs in Bosnia and Kosovo) are morally indefensible within any cultural context. And, as Henry Bagash (1981) reminds us, if we refuse to acknowledge our own values and compare, evaluate, and judge other cultures, we may be paralyzed in coping with the everyday world. Yet, if our goal is to *understand* human behavior in its myriad forms, then cultural relativism can help us identify the inherent logic behind certain ideas and customs. Sometimes cultural anthropologists have been criticized for being overly nonjudgmental about the customs they study, but as Richard Barrett (1991:8) have suggested,

> The occasional tendency for anthropologists to treat other cultures with excessive approbation to the extent that they sometimes idealize them, is less cause for concern than the possibility that they will misrepresent other societies by viewing them through the prism of their own culture.

·■ CONTRIBUTIONS ■· OF ANTHROPOLOGY

ONE OF THE MAJOR contributions of anthropology to the understanding of the human condition stems from the very broad task it has set for itself. Whereas such disci-

plines as economics, political science, and psychology are considerably more narrow in scope, anthropology has carved out for itself the task of examining all aspects of humanity for all periods of time and for all parts of the globe. Because of the magnitude of the task, anthropologists must draw on theories and data from a number of other disciplines in the humanities, the social sciences, and the physical sciences. As a result, anthropology is in a good position to integrate the various disciplines dealing with human physiology and culture.

ENHANCING UNDERSTANDING

Because of its holistic approach, the data and theories of anthropology have served as a powerful corrective to deterministic thinking. That is, this broad, comparative perspective serves as a check against oversimplified explanations concerning all of humanity based on evidence obtained from the Western world. A case in point is the revision of the notion of what a city is. Based largely on the study of American and European cities in the first several decades of the twentieth century, Western social scientists defined a city as a social system in which kinship ties were less elaborate than in rural communities. Although this was an accurate picture of cities in the industrialized areas of Europe and the United States, it was not accurate as a universal definition of urbanism. Since the 1950s, urban anthropologists studying cities in the non-Western world have called into question this "universal" characteristic of the city. For example, Horace Miner (1953) found substantial kinship interaction—which took the form of joint activities, mutual assistance, and friendship ties—in the West African city of Timbuktu; Oscar Lewis (1952), in an article aptly titled "Urbanization Without Breakdown," found that extended kinship networks were every bit as real in Mexico City as they were in rural Tepoztlán; and more recent studies (Moock 1978–1979; Keefe 1988) have found equally significant kinship ties in urban areas. Thus, urban anthropology, with its broad cross-cultural approach, has revised our thinking about the theory of urbanism.

Cultural anthropology examines cultural differences and similarities among the contemporary peoples of the world. Although some people view cultural anthropology as devoted to documenting the exotic customs of people in far-off places, it is only by learning about cultural variations and similarities that we can avoid generalizing about human nature solely on the basis of observations from U.S. culture. It is not unusual for people to think that their

= *A cultural anthropologist working in Kitari, Kenya, operates her portable computer from a car battery.*

beliefs and behaviors are natural, reasonable, and therefore human while thinking that those who believe and act differently are somewhat less than human.

This strong comparative tradition in cultural anthropology helps to reduce the possibility that our theories about human nature will be culture bound. For example, studies in cultural anthropology have revealed that great works of art are found in all parts of the world; that social order can be maintained without having centralized, bureaucratic governments; that reason, logic, and rationality did not originate solely in ancient Greece; and that all morality does not stem from Judeo-Christian ethics. Cultural anthropology, in other words, prevents us from taking our own cultural perspective too seriously. As Clifford Geertz (1984:275) reminds us, one of the tasks of cultural anthropology is to "keep the world off balance; pulling out rugs, upsetting tea tables, setting off fire crackers. It has been the office of others to reassure; ours to unsettle."

Still another contribution of anthropology is that it helps us better understand ourselves. The early Greeks claimed that the educated person was the person with self-knowledge ("know thyself"). One of the best ways to gain self-knowledge is to know as much as possible about one's own culture, that is, to understand the forces that shape our own thinking, values, and behaviors (see, for example, De Vita and Armstrong 1993). And the best way of learning about our culture is to learn something about other cultures. The anthropological perspective, with its emphasis on the comparative study of cultures, should lead us to the conclusion that our culture is just one way of life among many found in the world and that it represents one way (from among many) to adapt to a particular set of environmental conditions. Through the process of contrasting and comparing, we gain a fuller understanding of both other cultures and our own.

APPLICATIONS

Anthropology, with its holistic, cross-cultural perspective, has contributed in a number of important ways to the scientific understanding of humanity. Moreover, the study of anthropology is important because it enables the individual to better comprehend and appreciate his or her own culture. But, it may be asked, does anthropology have any practical relevance to our everyday lives? Students of biochemistry can apply their skills to the discovery of new drugs, creative arts students can produce lasting works of art, and students of architecture can design buildings that are both beautiful and functional. As we hope to demonstrate in this book, anthropology has relevance for all of us, both personally and professionally. Because anthropology is concerned primarily with the scientific study of culture, and because our lives and our jobs are conducted within a cultural context, anthropologists do indeed have some practical things to say.

Anthropology, like other social science disciplines, engages in both basic and applied research. Basic research in anthropology is directed at gaining scientific understanding for its own sake rather than for any practical ends. Applied research in anthropology, on the other hand, seeks to gain scientific knowledge for the sake of solving particular social problems. For much of the twentieth century, anthropologists have devoted most of their energy to basic research—that is, testing hypotheses concerning such theoretical issues as the rise of civilization, the functions of religious institutions, and the variations in systems of social stratification.

Anthropologists from all four subdisciplines have applied many of the methods, theories, and insights gained from basic research to the solution of societal problems. For example, specialists in forensic anthropology, an applied branch of physical anthropology, use their expertise with bones to help medical examiners and coroners identify human skeletal remains for legal purposes (Stewart 1979). Archaeologists in recent decades have applied their unique skills to the area of cultural resource management, which evaluates and helps preserve a nation's cultural heritage (Hill and Dickens 1978). Anthropological linguistics has been applied in a wide range of settings, including the improvement of language instruction (Cowan 1979), the development of intercultural training programs (Samovar and Porter 1994), and public decision making for language use in specific language communities (Eastman 1983). Cultural anthropologists have applied their trade to the evaluation of various social programs both here and abroad, to market research, to classroom learning, and to the improvement of health delivery systems, to mention but a few.

Even though all four subfields of anthropology have well-developed applied components, this book focuses on applied *cultural* anthropology. As discussed in greater depth in Chapter 3, interest in applying cultural anthropology has increased over the past decade. Graduate and undergraduate courses in applied anthropology, as well as doctoral dissertations on applied topics, have been on the rise in recent years. Moreover, there has been a noticeable increase in the number of anthropologists working outside universities and museums in such capacities as administrators, evaluators, planners, and research analysts. In fact, in the last several years, there has been a movement in the American Anthropological Association to recognize applied anthropology as the fifth major subdivision of anthropology. In response to the increasing interest in making anthropology practical, this textbook focuses on *applying* cultural anthropology. To demonstrate how widely cultural anthropology has been applied to the solution of practical societal problems, each chapter in the remainder of the book includes applied case studies. Each case study has been selected to show how the information from the chapter has been applied to the solution of practical problems.

The study of anthropology looks at the human condition from both an evolutionary and a contemporary perspective. It examines how humans have changed physically and culturally over the course of the past several million years, and it studies the various similarities and differences among the thousands of linguistic and cultural groups that inhabit today's world. And although this

This gathering of retired and semiretired Airstream trailer owners in the United States would be a possible subject of study for present-day cultural anthropologists.

remains the core of anthropology, it is important to bear in mind that the study of anthropology does affect our personal and professional lives in some very significant ways.

BUILDING SKILLS FOR THE TWENTY-FIRST CENTURY

As discussed in the previous section, the study of cultural anthropology has relevance to our everyday lives. The *products* (that is, data, concepts, and insights) derived from the study of other cultures can help us better meet our professional goals and lead more satisfying lives in a multicultural society. But, the *process* of studying cultural anthropology is also valuable because of the skills and competencies that it develops. Activities such as taking courses about different cultures, participating in local internships with international organizations, living in the university's international dormitory, and participating in study abroad programs all combine to provide the student with valuable carry-over skills that go beyond the mere mastery of subject content.

As we begin the new millennium, educators and organizational specialists have written volumes on the subject of what behavioral traits, skills, and competencies will be needed for success in the twenty-first century. Although many of these writers have put a unique spin on their own list of competencies, there remains a basic core on which most can agree. These skills involve developing a broad perspective, appreciating other points of view, operating comfortably in ambiguous situations, working effectively in cross-cultural teams, and becoming emotionally resilient, open-minded, and perceptually aware. These traits have been identified as essential for coping with a world that is becoming increasingly more global and interdependent. And, most people fail to appreciate that the study of cultural anthropology (involving, as it does, immersing oneself in other cultures) is perhaps the very best way to develop those competencies. Let's examine briefly how the study of cultural anthropology helps us develop those skills and competencies needed for the twenty-first century.

Develop a Broad Perspective

This skill involves seeing the big picture and the interrelatedness of the parts. A basic anthropological strategy for understanding other cultures is to look at a cultural feature from within its original cultural context rather than looking at it from the perspective of one's own culture. In other words, the student of anthropology is continually be-

ing asked to analyze a part of a culture in relationship to the whole. What better way to develop this type of systems thinking?

Appreciate Other Perspectives

Most lists of competencies for the new millennium include the need to be curious, nonjudgmental, and open to new ways of thinking and explanation. This skill involves being sufficiently open and receptive to learning new ideas so as to be able to *adapt* to ever-changing environments. This means, essentially, that the individual is willing to learn and postpone making evaluations until more facts are known. Such a capacity also involves suppressing one's ego and letting go of old paradigms. This certainly *doesn't* mean giving up one's own cultural values in favor of others. But it does entail (at least temporarily) letting go of cultural certainty, learning how other cultures view us, and being willing to see the internal logic of another culture. This is exactly what students of cultural anthropology are encouraged to do in order to learn about other cultures.

Balance Contradictions

A major requirement for working and living effectively in a global society is to be able to balance contradictory needs and demands rather than trying to eliminate them. Contradictions and conflicts should be seen as opportunities, not as liabilities. Conflicting values, behaviors, and ideas are a fact of life in today's world. The study of cultural anthropology provides insights into the nature of the world's diversity and how each culture is a logical and coherent entity. When anthropology students are exposed to logical alternatives to their own way of thinking and behaving, they learn to cope with differences and contradictions and actually use these differences for the sake of achieving synergy.

Emphasize Global Teamwork

Success in the next century requires an emphasis on cultural awareness and cross-cultural teamwork, not just personal awareness and individual mastery. Both private and public institutions hiring students today are becoming increasingly more global in focus. For example, foreign subsidiaries, joint ventures with foreign firms, and overseas facilities are becoming ever-more commonplace in the world of business. If young people are to be successful at working within and leading these culturally complex organizations, they will need to know the underlying cultural assumptions of the diverse people on those multicultural teams. There is no academic discipline in higher education today that addresses this competency better than cultural anthropology.

Develop Cognitive Complexity

Citizens of the new millennium need what is referred to as cognitive complexity, which is made up of the twin abilities of differentiating and integrating. Differentiation involves being able to see how a single entity is composed of a number of different parts; integration, on the other hand, involves the capacity to identify how the various parts are interconnected. The cognitively complex person is able to engage in both types of thinking and can move comfortably between the two. One must be able to focus on the unique needs of the local situation while at the same time understanding how it fits into the operations of the total organization. The study of cultural anthropology encourages the examination of another culture, one's own culture, how both compare with each other, and how both relate to the generalized concept of culture. Thus, the student of anthropology gets practice at becoming cognitively complex by moving from the specific parts to the whole and back again.

Build Emotional Resilience

Being part of the global village in the twenty-first century will require the ability to bounce back rapidly after disappointment and frustrations. Although unanticipated problems always occur, they happen with greater regularity when operating in an environment in which the rules are imperfectly understood. Things rarely go as planned when living and working in a culturally different environment. Frustrations are frequent and stress is high. Thus, cultural anthropology—the study of another culture by living in it—prepares anthropology students to learn how to deal with unanticipated problems, frustrations, and stress.

Develop Perceptual Acuity

Living and working in the twenty-first century requires people to be perceptually acute in a number of ways. They need to accurately derive meaning from interactions with others from a wide variety of cultures and subcultures. This involves being attentive to both verbal and nonverbal communication by being an active listener, deriving meaning from social context, and being sensitive to the feelings of others and to one's effect on others. Studying other cultures—and particularly living in other cultures—forces the anthropology student to derive meaning not only from the words exchanged in cross-cultural encounters but also from the nonverbal cues, the social context, and the assumptions embedded in the other culture.

Thus, a number of skills and capacities that are considered to be essential for effective living and working in the twenty-first century can be mastered *while studying cultural anthropology.* Although a mere exposure to cultural anthropology does not guarantee that these skills will be developed, the comparative study of the world's cultural diversity and shared heritage is the single best classroom for acquiring these competencies.

SUMMARY

1. The academic discipline of anthropology involves the study of the biological and cultural origins of humans. The subject matter of anthropology is wide-ranging, including fossil remains, nonhuman primate anatomy and behavior, artifacts from past cultures, past and present languages, and all of the prehistoric, historic, and contemporary cultures of the world.

2. As practiced in the United States, the discipline of anthropology follows an integrated four-field approach comprising physical anthropology, archaeology, anthropological linguistics, and cultural anthropology.

3. The subdiscipline of physical anthropology focuses on three primary concerns: paleoanthropology (constructing the biological record of human evolution through the study of fossil remains), primatology (the study of nonhuman primate anatomy and behavior for the purpose of gaining insights into human adaptation to the environment), and studies in human physical variation (race) among the contemporary peoples of the world.

4. The subfield of archaeology has as its primary objective the reconstruction of past cultures, both his-

toric and prehistoric, from the material objects the cultures leave behind.

5. Anthropological linguistics, which studies both present and past languages, is divided into four major subdivisions: historical linguistics (the study of the emergence and divergence of languages over time), descriptive linguistics (the structural analysis of phonetic and grammar systems in contemporary languages), ethnolinguistics (the explanation of the relationship between language and culture), and sociolinguistics (how social relations affect language).

6. Cultural anthropology has as its aim the study of contemporary cultures wherever they may be found in the world. One part of the task of cultural anthropology involves describing particular cultures (ethnography); the other part involves comparing two or more cultures (ethnology). Cultural anthropologists tend to specialize in such areas as urban anthropology, medical anthropology, educational anthropology, economic anthropology, and psychological anthropology, among others.

7. A long-standing tradition in anthropology is the holistic approach. The discipline is holistic (or comprehensive) in four important respects: It looks at both the biological and the cultural aspects of human behavior; it has the broadest possible time frame by looking at contemporary, historic, and prehistoric societies; it is global in that it examines human cultures in every part of the world; and it studies many different aspects of human cultures.

8. There are essentially two ways of responding to unfamiliar cultures. One way is ethnocentrically—that is, from one's own cultural perspective. The other way is from the perspective of a cultural relativist—that is, from within the context of the other culture. Cultural anthropologists strongly recommend the second mode, yet they are aware of certain limitations.

9. The study of anthropology is valuable from a number of different viewpoints. From the perspective of the social and behavioral sciences, cultural anthropology is particularly valuable for testing theories about human behavior within the widest possible cross-cultural context. For the individual, the study of different cultures provides a much better understanding of one's own culture and develops valuable

leadership skills. From a societal point of view, the understanding of different cultures can contribute to the solution of pressing societal problems.

KEY TERMS

anthropological linguistics	genetics
archaeology	glottochronology
artifacts	historical linguistics
cultural anthropology	holism
cultural relativism	human paleontology
descriptive linguistics	paleoanthropology
ecofacts	paleopathology
epidemiology	physical anthropology
ethnocentrism	population biology
ethnography	primatology
ethnolinguistics	race
ethnology	sociolinguistics
features	

SUGGESTED READINGS

Barfield, Thomas, ed. *The Dictionary of Anthropology.* Malden, MA: Blackwell, 1997. A standard reference guide for students of anthropology containing substantial analytical articles dealing with key anthropological concepts.

Barrett, Richard. *Culture and Conduct: An Excursion in Anthropology.* 2d ed. Belmont, CA: Wadsworth, 1991. By examining some of the questions, ideas, and issues facing modern anthropology, Barrett provides an interesting introduction to how cultural anthropologists investigate unfamiliar cultures.

Chamberlain, Andrew. *Human Remains.* Berkeley: University of California Press, 1994. In this very brief account, Chamberlain shows how recent advances in medicine and science have been applied to the analysis of human remains, thereby shedding light on both the lives of the people and the nature of their communities.

Deutsch, Richard. *Perspectives: Anthropology.* St. Paul, MN: Coursewise, 1999. This selection of readings covering the field of cultural anthropology is a useful supplement to the broad-brush approach taken by most textbooks.

Fromkin, Victoria, and Robert Rodman. *An Introduction to Language.* 6th ed. Fort Worth: Dryden Press, 1997. A sprightly written introduction to the field of anthropological linguistics.

Kluckhohn, Clyde. *Mirror for Man: Anthropology and Modern Life.* New York: McGraw-Hill, 1949. Although written in 1949, this classic study remains one of the best introductions to the discipline because it demonstrates in a number of concrete ways how the study of different cultures—both past and present—can contribute to the solution of contemporary world problems.

Nash, Dennison. *A Little Anthropology.* 3d ed. Upper Saddle River, NJ: Prentice-Hall, 1999. A brief and easy-to-read introduction to cultural anthropology designed to give students an overview of the discipline.

Peacock, James L. *The Anthropological Lens.* Cambridge: Cambridge University Press, 1986. A very readable book that discusses the philosophical underpinnings of the discipline of anthropology, with special emphasis on cultural anthropology. The work is divided into three sections that deal with anthropology's substance, methods, and significance.

Tattersall, Ian. *The Fossil Trail.* New York: Oxford University Press, 1995. A current and clearly written analysis of what we know about human evolution from the fossil record. The interpretations are based on the latest paleontological findings set within the historical context of research that dates back to pre-Darwinian times.

Thomas, David Hurst. *Archaeology: Down to Earth.* Fort Worth: Harcourt, Brace, Jovanovich, 1998. An excellent introduction to the field of archaeology, written in a personal and witty style.

Vivelo, Frank R. *Cultural Anthropology: A Basic Introduction.* Lanham, MD: University Press of America, 1994. This concise introduction to the field of cultural anthropology conveys a number of key issues in the field without becoming bogged down in laborious theoretical debates or excessive ethnographic data.

On the Net

Each chapter in this textbook is followed by an Internet exercise. These exercises are designed to accomplish two separate objectives. First, they provide students with a chance to practice their computer and Internet skills, which will become increasingly more valuable in the years to come. Second, the exercises are designed to reinforce some of the substantive concepts and insights found in each chapter. In other words, they enable the student to learn the chapter content more effectively because of the experiential nature of the exercises.

Within the last several years, the Internet has become an extraordinarily important learning tool for scholars. We now have at our fingertips vast amounts of information obtainable (almost instantaneously) from all parts of the world. To illustrate, it is now possible for most students on their college campuses to send electronic messages to anyone in the world; from our own desktops, we can download enormous amounts of information that can be useful in our research. We can even receive full-screen color photographs and video clips via the Internet.

Because some students are intimidated and mystified by the Internet, they may have put off getting to know it. Others may have thrown themselves onto the Internet and feel quite comfortable there. Still others are such Internet experts that they are much more at home with the Internet than are some of their professors. Whether you are a novice or an expert, one thing is certain: The Internet is an extremely powerful learning tool, and its importance to our educational and professional success will continue to increase into the future.

But what is the Internet? Very simply put, the Internet is a vast network of computers that permits the exchange of information. Some of those computers are very small, perhaps like your own desktop computer; others are supercomputers. What the Internet does is to enable all of those computers (whether next door or on the other side of the earth) to talk with one another and share information. To be certain, there are many acronyms surrounding the use of the Internet. For example, you will encounter such terms as *URL, WAIS, FTP,* and *WWW.* Even though the Internet may seem daunting, the good news is that you don't need to know how it works technically in order to use it, just as you don't need to understand all of the technical features of the internal combustion engine in order to drive a car. (If you would like to read about the workings of the Internet in greater detail, you might want to consult any of a number of books such as the latest edition of *The Internet for Dummies* (Levine et al. 1999). For those of you who are just beginning, the best advice is not to become overwhelmed. Instead, just log on; you will learn as you go along. As you become more familiar with browsing the net, you will discover many exciting opportunities to learn applied cultural anthropology. So welcome to the Information Superhighway—but don't forget to buckle up!

A word of caution is in order before beginning. Internet addresses have the bad habit of changing every so often. All of the web links listed in the Internet exercises at the end of each chapter were correct at the time of publication. If an address has changed, often, but not always, there will be a new address to direct you to the new location. The addresses that appear in this book were selected because they are relevant to the content of the chapter. However, if the site no longer exists, a suitable substitute can often be found by conducting a subject search on one of the search engines.

The American Anthropological Association (AAA) is the major professional organization for anthropologists in the Americas and in fact is the largest such organization for anthropologists in the world. If you want information on what anthropology is and what anthropologists do, go to the web site of the AAA:

http://www.aaanet.org

1. Click on the section "About AAA." Next click on "What is anthropology?" Then, in several sentences for each, answer the following questions: (a) What are the four major subfields of anthropology? (b) What is meant by the term *comparative method?* (c) What is meant by the statement "Language is the hallmark of our species"? (d) What types of evidence do archaeologists rely on when reconstructing prehistoric cultures?

2. While you are in the section of the AAA home page titled "About AAA," click on the latest annual "Survey of Anthropology PhDs." According to the latest data, what percentage of anthropologists represent the four traditional fields (and the fifth field of applied anthropology)? Have there been any noticeable changes in the ethnic/racial composition of American anthropologists over the decades? Have there been any significant changes in gender composition over the decades? Roughly what percentage of anthropologists are employed in academic institutions (colleges and universities), and what percentage are employed in nonacademic jobs?

3. Now go back to "About AAA" and click on the section titled "Sections and Interest Groups." Browse the more than 30 specialized sections and interest groups that are officially recognized by the AAA. Select one such interest group and write a paragraph summary of what you think this group is all about.

Chapter Two

THE CONCEPT OF CULTURE

WHAT WE WILL LEARN:

▼

What do anthropologists mean by the term *culture*?

▼

How do we acquire our culture?

▼

Despite the enormous variation in different cultures, are some common features found in all cultures of the world?

▼

Tiwi dancers from northern Australia.

Although the term *culture* is used today by most of the social sciences, over the years it has received its most precise and thorough definition from the discipline

of anthropology. Whereas sociology has concentrated on the notion of society, economics on the concepts of production, distribution, and consumption, and political science on the concept of power, anthropology has focused on the culture concept. From anthropology's nineteenth-century beginnings, culture has been central to both ethnology and archaeology and has been an important, if not major, concern of physical anthropology. Anthropology, through its constant examining of different lifeways throughout space and time, has done more than any other scientific discipline to refine our understanding of the concept of culture.

·■ CULTURE DEFINED ■·

IN ITS ORDINARY, nonscientific usage, the term *culture* refers to such personal refinements as classical music, the fine arts, world philosophy, and gourmet cuisine. For example, according to this popular use of the term, the cultured person listens to Bach rather than Ricky Martin, orders escargot rather than barbecued ribs when dining out, can distinguish between the artistic styles of Monet and Toulouse-Lautrec, prefers Grand Marnier to Kool-Aid, and attends the ballet instead of professional wrestling. The anthropologist, however, uses the term in a much broader sense to include far more than just "the finer things in life." The anthropologist does not distinguish between cultured people and uncultured people. All people have culture, according to the anthropological definition. The Australian aborigines, living as they do with a bare minimum of technology, are as much cultural animals as Pavarotti and Baryshnikov. Thus, for the anthropologist, projectile points, creation myths, and grass huts are as legitimate

items of culture as a Beethoven symphony, a Warhol painting, and a Sondheim musical.

Over the past century, anthropologists have formulated a number of definitions of the concept of culture. In fact, in the often-cited work by Alfred Kroeber and Clyde Kluckhohn (1952), over 160 different definitions of culture were identified. This proliferation of definitions should not lead to the impression that anthropology is a chaotic battleground where no consensus exists among practicing anthropologists. In actual fact, many of these definitions say essentially the same thing. One early definition, which has been widely quoted up to the present time, was suggested by nineteenth-century British anthropologist Edward Tylor. According to Tylor, culture is "that complex whole which includes knowledge, belief, art, morals, law, custom, and any other capabilities and habits acquired by man as a member of society" (1871:1). More recently, culture has been defined as "a mental map which guides us in our relations to our surroundings and to other people" (Downs 1971:35), and perhaps most succinctly as "the way of life of a people" (Hatch 1985:178).

Adding to the already sizable number of definitions, for our purposes we will define the concept of culture as *everything that people have, think, and do as members of a society*. This definition can be instructive because the three verbs correspond to the three major components of culture. That is, everything that people *have* refers to material possessions; everything that people *think* refers to the things they carry around in their heads, such as ideas, values, and attitudes; and everything that people *do* refers to behavior patterns. Thus, all cultures comprise material objects; ideas, values, and attitudes; and patterned ways of behaving (Figure 2-1).

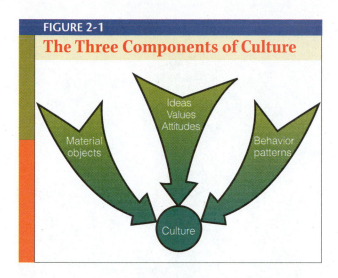

FIGURE 2-1

The Three Components of Culture

Ideas
Values
Attitudes

Material
objects

Behavior
patterns

Culture

•■ CULTURE IS SHARED ■•

THE LAST PHRASE in our working definition—*as members of a society*—should remind us that culture is a shared phenomenon. For a thing, idea, or behavior pattern to qualify as being cultural, it must have a meaning shared by most people in a society. It is this shared nature of culture that makes our lives less complicated. Because people share a common culture, they are able to predict, within limits, how others will think and behave. For example, when meeting someone for the first time in the United States, it is customary to shake the person's hand. If both people are from the United States, neither party will have to wonder what is meant by an outstretched hand. They will know, with nearly absolute certainty, that the extended hand is a nonverbal gesture signifying friendship rather than a sexual advance, a hostile attack, or an attempt to go for one's wallet. It is when we step outside our familiar cultural setting—where meanings are not shared with other people—that misunderstandings and breakdowns in communication occur. In fact, the ambiguity and uncertainty one experiences when trying to operate in an unfamiliar culture often lead to **culture shock,** a form of psychological distress that can result in depression, overeating, or irritability (see Chapter 5).

People from the same culture are able to predict one another's behavior because they have been exposed to similar cultural conditioning. Yet a word of caution is necessary. To say that culture *conditions* our thoughts, values, and behaviors is hardly to imply that culture *determines* them. People are influenced by their cultures, but we should not think of them as unthinking robots who live out their lives

exactly according to cultural dictates. If this were the case, we would expect total conformity to the cultural norms in all societies. But the study of anthropology informs us that although most of the people conform to most of the cultural norms most of the time, there will always be some segment of the culture's population that, for a number of reasons, deviates from those norms. For example, some people may deviate from expected norms for purely biological reasons such as hormonal imbalances, hyperactivity, or physiologically based mental disorders. Or an individual's personal history can lead to a culturally unorthodox way of thinking or acting (such as the person who was traumatized by a hurricane as a child and still expresses unreasonable reactions to inclement weather). Another explanation is that even in the most small-scale, homogeneous societies one can expect to find a certain amount of differentiation based on gender, class, age, religion, or ethnicity. For example, the daughter of a wealthy physician in Athens is likely to have a somewhat different set of values and behavioral expectations from the daughter of a rural Greek peasant farmer. Finally, societal rules are never adhered to strictly. Although culture exerts a powerful influence, people continue to exercise their free will either by reinterpreting the rules, downplaying their consequences, or disregarding them altogether (such as the Catholic who practices birth control or the conscientious objector who flees to another country rather than serve in a war).

The extent to which people within a society share their culture varies from culture to culture. However, in larger, more highly complex societies, such as the United States or Canada, one is likely to find a number of subcultural groups in addition to the mainstream culture. The use of the terms *subculture* and *mainstream culture* should in no way imply that subcultures are inferior or any less worthy of study. Rather, **subcultures** are subsets of the wider culture. They share a number of cultural features with the mainstream, but they retain a certain level of cultural uniqueness that sets them apart. Often, however, subcultural groups within a society are not afforded all of the benefits enjoyed by the mainstream. The mainstream both outnumber the various subcultural groups and also control the society's major institutional structures (government, economics, and education, for example).

An example of a long-standing subcultural group in the United States is the old order Amish of Pennsylvania, Indiana, and Ohio. Originating in Switzerland and coming to the United States as early as 1727, the Amish people today

= *According to the anthropological perspective, this Dani man from New Guinea has as much culture as this opera singer.*

number approximately 60,000. They have gone to considerable length to maintain the integrity of the traditional culture, no small feat in a country like the United States that places such a high premium on progress and change. The Amish value their religious beliefs, hard work, an agrarian way of life, pacifism, simplicity, and neighborly cooperation. They are a clearly visible subcultural group in that they wear simple black clothing, transport themselves by horse and buggy, and rarely send their children to public schools. According to John Hostetler and Gertrude Huntington (1971:4–9), Amish society is governed by the following five cultural themes:

1. *Separation from the World* Amish are expected to shun worldly material possessions, avoid marrying or taking as a business partner any non-Amish, and steer clear of violence and war. Although the Amish view themselves as special or chosen people, they do not behave toward non-Amish in an arrogant or exclusionary manner.

2. *Voluntary Acceptance of High Social Obligations* When Amish (as adults) agree to baptism, they also agree to walk the straight and narrow, live a good life, acknowledge that Christ is the Son of God, and live according the rules of the community.

3. *Maintenance of a Disciplined Church Community* Once baptized, Amish are expected, in fact morally committed, to adhere to the rules of the church community. Although not specified in writing, these rules are known only to the congregates and must be assented to unanimously in the church service before they can receive communion.

4. *Excommunication and Shunning* In order to keep the church community pure, those that fail to keep their social and spiritual commitments are to be shunned or excommunicated. Because the Amish want to keep their communities pure, there is no attempt to evangelize or seek converts.

5. *Harmony with Nature and the Soil* The Amish are strongly agrarian. As one Amish man put it, "The Lord told Adam to replenish the earth and to rule over the animals and the land—you can't do that in cities."

In their attempt to remain separate from the world, the Amish have sometimes been at odds with the wider society. There is no more volatile issue for the Amish than the schooling of their children; they have taken their case all the way to the U.S. Supreme Court. The Amish have insisted that their children attend school near their homes and that their teachers be committed to basic Amish values. Although the Amish have been able to preserve their culture by maintaining control over the education of their children, they have had to work hard to do so. In the process they have, no doubt, become even more distrustful of the society at large.

Although the Amish have been a long-standing subculture within the United States, there are others that are more recent and are likely to have less staying power. Some excellent examples of such subcultural groups are found in American high schools. "Metalheads," "jocks," and "ravers" are teen subcultures found in a number of secondary schools in North America that have their own distinct cultural traits setting them apart from the larger culture. To illustrate, ravers are fans of a specific music style (Reynolds 1998). They engage in late-night or all-night parties held in large warehouses or open fields where laser light shows, music, and sometimes such drugs as ecstasy combine to create a feeling of euphoria. Alchohol and aggressive behavior are generally nonexistent at these parties, and, by and large, devotees of this lifestyle are not likely to be aggressive in their personal lives. Clothing and personal adornment also serve to visually differentiate ravers from the larger culture. Bright colors, flower rings, baby doll clothing, oversized pants, and other whimsical items set ravers apart from their peers. Ravers tend to be more liberal about drug use as well as about both platonic and romantic relationships. Moreover, ravers maintain their group identity and cohesion through the use of specialized vocabulary, which further distinguishes them from those outside of this subculture.

Many societies, such as the United States, Canada, and the United Kingdom, are called **pluralistic societies** because they are composed of a number of subcultural groups. With the beginning of centralized state systems of government about 5,000 years ago, formerly independent cultures began to subsumed into a single pluralistic, or multicultural society. The centralized, hierarchical, and bureaucratic authority of the state mediated among the various cultural interest groups, permitting their coexistence within a single society. Such an arrangement, however, is not without its difficulties. With different cultural groups operating with different sets of values and behaviors, misunderstandings (or outright hostilities) are always possible. To illustrate the type of culture clash that can occur, Norine Dresser (1996) recounts an incident that took place in a sixth-grade classroom in the United States. The teacher noticed that one of his students, a Vietnamese girl, had strange red marks on her neck and forehead. Without giving the girl a chance to explain, the teacher notified lo-

cal authorities, who accused the girl's parents of child abuse. What the teacher did not understand was that in many Asian countries, and in Vietnam in particular, rubbing a coin rigorously on the back, neck, and forehead is a common folk remedy for headaches, colds, and respiratory problems. Unfortunately, the resulting red marks from this remedy were misinterpreted by school officials as signs of child abuse.

•■ CULTURE IS LEARNED ■•

CULTURE IS NOT TRANSMITTED genetically. Rather, it is acquired through the process of learning or interacting with one's cultural environment. This process of acquiring culture after we are born is called **enculturation.** We acquire our culture (ideas, values, and behavior patterns) by growing up in it. When an infant is born, he or she enters a cultural environment in which many solutions already exist to the universal problems facing all human populations. The child merely needs to learn or internalize those solutions in order to make a reasonable adjustment to his or her surroundings. A male child who is born in Kansas will probably watch a good deal of TV, attend schools with books, desks, and teachers, eventually learn to drive a car, and marry one wife at a time. On the other hand, a male child who is born among the Jie of Uganda is likely to grow up playing with cows, learn most of what he knows from peers and elders rather than teachers, undergo an initiation ceremony into adulthood that involves being anointed with the undigested stomach contents of an ox slaughtered for the occasion, and look forward to having at least three or four wives at one time. Even though these children were born into radically different cultures, they have in common one important thing: Both children were born into an already existing culture, and they have only to *learn* the ways of thinking and acting set down by their culture.

If we stop to think about it, a great deal of what we do during our waking hours is learned. Brushing our teeth, eating three meals a day, sweeping the floor, attending school, wearing a wristwatch, knowing to stop at a red light, sleeping on a mattress, and waving good-bye are all learned responses to our cultural environment. To be certain, some aspects of our behavior are not learned but are genetically based or instinctive. For example, a newborn infant does not need to attend a workshop on the "Art of Sucking." Or, if someone throws a brick at your head, you do not have to be taught to duck or throw your hands up in front of your face. Nevertheless, the

Anthropology and Architecture

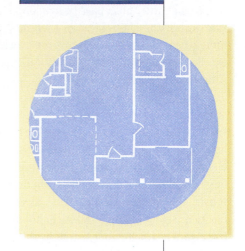

When designing buildings, architects need a thorough understanding of both the laws of physics and the nature of building materials if the structure is not to fall down. However, architecture involves more than bricks and mortar. Because buildings are used by people to serve certain functions, the architect must also pay particular attention to the culture or subculture of the people who will eventually use the building. Because people have different values, attitudes, and behavior patterns, it is likely that they will use their physical space differently. In other words, low-income housing in Djakarta, Indonesia, will look substantially different from low-income housing in Philadelphia.

In recent years, architects have increasingly collaborated with cultural anthropologists to ensure that buildings are designed in culturally appropriate ways. One such effort was the Payson Project, a U.S. government project aimed at building a community of homes for a group of Apaches in central Arizona during the late 1970s. Much to the credit of the project, anthropologist George Esber was invited to be part of the planning team by serving as a cultural advisor. His role involved conducting anthropological research on the space needs of the local Apache people and translating these needs into appropriate design features for the architects.

Esber's research (1977, 1987) was an interesting mixture of traditional methods and a creative technique designed specifically to elicit data relevant for this housing project. The initial data gathering involved ethnographic mapping of the location of houses in the existing community and the interior use of space in these houses. Interviewing was also used to determine the social networks of relationships that existed in the community. Esber gave each family a model house kit with movable wall segments and pieces of furniture so

overwhelming majority of our behavioral responses are the result of complex learning processes.

LEARNING VERSUS INSTINCTS

During the first half of the twentieth century, psychologists and other social scientists tended to explain human behavior in terms of various instincts or genetically based propensities. Gypsies traveled about because they were thought to have wanderlust in their blood; Black people were musical because they were believed to have natural rhythm; and some people, owing to their genetic makeup, were supposedly born criminals. Today most people have rejected this instinctual interpretation of human behavior. Instead, although acknowledging the role of biology, most social scientists would come closer to agreeing with the notion that humans are born with little predetermined behavior. If humans are to survive, they must learn most of their coping skills from others in their culture. This usually takes a number of years. As early as 1917, anthropologist Alfred Kroeber recognized the importance of learning for human adaptation to the environment:

that they could design their own housing preference. He then photographed and analyzed the families' model plans before sharing the information with the architects.

Esber's research revealed some important features of contemporary Apache life that had important design implications for the housing project. In terms of the internal house design, most Apaches preferred a layout that divided the space into sleeping areas and a large living area. Esber found that his informants preferred an open design very similar to that of traditional Apache houses, with a minimum of partitions in the general living space. Such a floor plan (combining cooking, eating, and general living in a single room) is very much in keeping with the Apaches' patterns of social interaction. Through systematic observations, Esber learned that Apaches enter social situations in a slow, gradual manner. This step-by-step approach permits the Apaches to determine whether they want to continue the interaction after having assessed the social situation.

This is just one example of how anthropological insights about the cultural needs of the Apaches were accommodated through architectural design. The anthropological contribution involved an understanding of patterns of social interaction and space usage among the Apaches. Unlike houses built for other Apache communities without anthropological input, the houses designed for the Payson Project met with a high degree of satisfaction. Many Apaches on other reservations were unwilling to move into new homes built on an Anglo (non-Apache) model that were not designed in collaboration with anthropologists. When they did, they found the new houses unsatisfying, and many moved back into their old homes.

QUESTIONS FOR FURTHER THOUGHT

1. How can the patterns of social interaction among members of a culture influence how they use space?
2. How would ideal housing interiors be different for contemporary Apaches and low-income families in Atlanta, Georgia?
3. If an anthropologist were to make recommendations for building the dream house for your family, what cultural and social factors would you want the anthropologist to consider?

Take a couple of ant eggs of the right sex—unhatched eggs, freshly laid. Blot out every individual and every other egg of the species. Give the pair a little attention as regards warmth, moisture, protection and food. The whole of ant "society," every one of the abilities, powers, accomplishments, and activities of the species . . . will be reproduced, and reproduced without diminution, in one generation. But place on a desert island . . . two or three hundred human infants of the best stock from the highest class of the most civilized nation; furnish them the necessary incubation and nourishment; leave them in total isolation from their kind; and what shall we have? . . . only a pair or a troop of mutes, without arts, knowledge, fire, without order or religion. Civilization would be blotted out within these confines—not disintegrated, not cut to the quick, but obliterated in one sweep. (1917:177–178)

LEARNING DIFFERENT CONTENT

Even though there is an enormous range of variation in cultural behavior throughout the world, all people acquire their culture by the same process. People often assume erroneously that if a Hadza adult of Tanzania does not know how to solve an algebraic equation, then she or he must be less intelligent than we are. Yet there is no evidence to suggest that people from some cultures are fast learners and people from others are slow learners. The study of comparative cultures has taught us that people in different cultures learn different cultural content (attitudes, values, ideas, and behavioral patterns) and that they accomplish this with similar efficiency. The Hadza has not learned algebra because such knowledge would not particularly enhance his adaptation to life in the East African grasslands. However, he would know how to track a wounded bush buck that he has not seen for three days, where to find groundwater, and how to build a house out of locally available materials. In short, people learn (with relatively equal efficiency) what they need to know to best adapt to their environment.

Some degree of learning is nearly universal among all animals. Yet, no other animal has a greater capacity for learning than do humans; and no other animal relies as heavily on learning for its very survival. This is an extraordinarily important notion, particularly for people who are directly involved in the solution of human problems. If human behavior were largely instinctive (genetic), there would be little reason for efforts aimed at changing people's behavior, such as programs in agricultural development, family planning, or community health.

■ CULTURE'S INFLUENCE ■ ON BIOLOGICAL PROCESSES

ALL ANIMALS, including humans, have certain biologically determined needs that must be met if they are to stay alive and well. We all need to ingest a minimal number of calories of food each day, protect ourselves from the elements, sleep, and eliminate wastes from our body, to mention a few. It is vital for us to distinguish between these needs and the ways in which we satisfy them. To illustrate, even though all people need to eliminate wastes from the body through defecation, how often, where, in what physical position, and under what social circumstances we defecate are all questions that are answered by our individual culture.

A dramatic example of how culture can influence or channel our biological processes was provided by anthropologist Clyde Kluckhohn (1949), who spent much of his career in the American Southwest studying the Navajo culture. Kluckhohn tells of a non-Navajo woman he knew in Arizona who took a somewhat perverse pleasure in causing a cultural response to food. At luncheon parties she often served sandwiches filled with a light meat that resembled tuna or chicken but had a distinctive taste. Only after everyone had finished lunch would the hostess in-

form her guests that what they had just eaten was neither tuna salad nor chicken salad but rather rattlesnake salad. Invariably, someone would vomit upon learning what they had eaten. Here, then, is an excellent example of how the biological process of digestion was influenced by a cultural idea. Not only was the process influenced, it was reversed! That is, the culturally based idea that rattlesnake meat is a despicable thing to eat triggered a violent reversal of the normal digestive process.

OUR BODIES AND CULTURE

The nonmaterial aspects of our culture, such as ideas, values, and attitudes, can have an appreciable effect on the human body. Culturally defined attitudes concerning male and female attractiveness, for example, have resulted in some dramatic effects on the body. Burmese women give the appearance of elongating their necks by depressing their clavicles and scapulas with heavy brass rings, Chinese women traditionally had their feet bound, men in New

= *People in all cultures alter their bodies because they believe it makes them more attractive.*

Guinea put bones through their noses, and scarification and tattooing are practiced in various parts of the world for the very same reasons that women and men in the United States pierce their ear lobes (that is, because their cultures tell them that it looks good). People intolerant of such different cultural practices often fail to realize that had they been raised in one of those other cultures, they would be practicing those allegedly disgusting or irrational customs.

Even our body stature is related to a large extent to our cultural ideas. In the Western world, people go to considerable lengths to become as slender as possible. They spend millions of dollars each year on running shoes, diet plans, appetite suppressants, and health spa memberships to help them take off those "ugly pounds." However, our Western notion of equating slimness with physical beauty is hardly universally accepted. In large parts of Africa, for example, Western women are perceived as emaciated and considered to be singularly unattractive. This point was made painfully obvious to me when I was conducting fieldwork in Kenya during the 1970s. After months of living in Kenya, I learned that many of my male Kikuyu friends pitied me for having such an unattractive wife (5 feet 5 inches tall and 114 pounds). Kikuyu friends often came by my house with a bowl of food or a chicken and discreetly whispered, "This is for your wife." Even though I considered my wife to be beautifully proportioned, my African friends thought she needed to be fattened up in order to be beautiful.

·■ CULTURE CHANGES ■·

THUS FAR, culture has been presented as a complex of things, ideas, and behavior patterns transmitted from generation to generation through the process of learning. Such a view of culture, focusing as it does on continuity between the generations, tends to emphasize its static rather than dynamic aspects. And yet a fundamental principle underlying all cultures is that there is nothing as constant as change. Some cultures—those that remain relatively insulated from the global economy—change quite slowly, whereas for others, change occurs more rapidly. Despite the wide variation in the speed by which cultures change, one thing is certain: No cultures remain completely static year after year.

THE PROCESSES OF CHANGE

Cultures change according to two basic processes: internal changes (innovations) and external changes (cultural diffusion). **Innovations**—the ultimate source of all culture change—can be spread to other cultures. Those same innovations can also occur at different times and in different cultures independently. But not all innovations lead to culture change. An individual can come up with a wonderfully novel thing or idea, but unless it is accepted and used by the wider society, it will not lead to a change in the culture.

The Western ideal of equating physical attractiveness with thinness is not shared by all cultures of the world.

CROSS-CULTURAL MISCUE

IN AN ATTEMPT to locate an outlet for its products in Europe, a large U.S. manufacturer sent one of its promising young executives to Frankfurt to make a presentation to a reputable German distributor. The U.S. company had considerable confidence in the choice of this particular junior executive because the man not only spoke fluent German but also knew a good deal about German culture. When the American entered the conference room where he would be making his presentation, he did all the right things. He shook hands firmly, greeted everyone with a friendly "Guten tag," and bowed his head slightly as is customary in Germany. Drawing on his experience as a past president of the Toastmasters Club in his hometown, the U.S. executive prefaced his presentation with a few humorous anecdotes to set a relaxed mood. At the end of his presentation, however, he sensed that his talk had not gone well. In actual fact, the presentation was not well received, and the German company chose not to distribute the U.S. company's product line.

What went wrong? Despite careful preparation, the U.S. firm made two tactical miscues that conflicted with German business culture. First, despite the American executive's knowledge of his product line and his fluency in German, his age was one important factor working against him. Because executives in German corporations tend to be older than their U.S. counterparts, any young U.S. executive, no matter how competent, is not likely to be taken seriously because of his or her inexperience. The second miscue was that the American attempted to set a relaxed tone by starting off with several jokes. Although this may have been an effective public-speaking technique for a luncheon talk at the Kiwanis Club, it was considered too frivolous and informal for a German business meeting.

Some internal changes involve only slight variations in already existing cultural patterns. In other cases, the changes involve fairly complex combinations of a number of existing cultural features to form a totally new cultural feature. To be certain, internal culture changes involve creativity, ingenuity, and in some cases genius. To a large extent, however, the internal changes possible in any given culture are usually limited to what already exists in a culture. The automobile was invented in Europe because it was part of a cultural tradition that included many previous innovations, such as the internal combustion engine and the locomotive. Because innovations depend on the recombination of already existing elements in a culture, innovations are most likely to occur in societies with the greatest number of cultural elements. This is another way of saying that internal culture change occurs more often in technologically complex societies than it does in less developed ones.

The other source of culture change, which comes from outside the culture, is known as **cultural diffusion**: the spreading of a cultural element from one culture to another. As important as innovations are to the process of culture change, cultural diffusion is actually responsible for the greatest amount of change that occurs in any society. In fact, it has been estimated that the majority of cultural elements found in any society at any time got there through the process of cultural diffusion rather than innovation. The reason for this is that it is easier to borrow a thing, an idea, or a behavior pattern than it is to invent it. This is not to suggest that people are essentially uninventive, but only that cultural items can be acquired with much less effort by borrowing than by inventing them.

CAUSES OF CULTURAL CHANGE

Most anthropologists acknowledge that cultures change by means of both internal and external mechanisms, but there is no such agreement on the primary causes of culture change. Do cultures change in response to changing technologies and economies, or do these changes originate in values and ideologies? Some people argue that the prime mover of change is technology. They cite, for example, the introduction of the automobile and its many effects on all aspects of the American way of life. Others assert that ideas and values lead to culture change to the extent that they can motivate people to explore new ways of interacting with the environment, thereby inventing new items of technology. Still others suggest that cultures change in response to changes in the physical and social environment. For example, U.S. attitudes concerning mothers working outside the home have changed because of changing economic conditions and the need for two salaries; or the traditional Fulani pastoral culture has been drastically altered during the twentieth century by the encroachment of the Sahara desert.

The discipline of anthropology has not been able to make definitive statements about the actual causes of culture change. No doubt the truth resides with a combination of these factors. The forces of culture change are so complex, particularly in more technologically advanced societies, that it is difficult, if not impossible, to identify any single factor as most important. The most reasonable way of viewing culture change, then, is as a phenomenon brought about by the interaction of a number of different factors, such as ecology, technology, ideology, and social relationships. The topic of culture change is discussed in greater depth in Chapter 16.

•■ CULTURAL UNIVERSALS ■•

SINCE THE EARLY twentieth century, hundreds of cultural anthropologists have described the wide variety of cultures found in the contemporary world. As a result, the discipline of anthropology has been far more effective at documenting cultural differences than at showing similarities among cultures. This preoccupation with different forms of behavior and different ways of meeting human needs was the result, at least in part, of wanting to move away from the premature generalizing about "human nature" that was so prevalent around the turn of the century.

This vast documentation of culturally different ways of behaving has been essential for our understanding of the human condition. The significant number of cultural differences illustrates how flexible and adaptable humans are compared to other animals because each culture has developed its own set of solutions to the universal human problems facing all societies. For example, every society, if it is to survive as an entity, needs a system of communication enabling its members to send and receive messages. That there are thousands of mutually unintelligible languages in the world today certainly attests to human flexibility. Yet, when viewed from a somewhat higher level of abstraction, all of these different linguistic communities have an important common denominator—that is, they all have developed some form of language. Thus, it is important to bear in mind that despite the many differences, all cultures of the world share a number of common features

Cultural diffusion, not independent invention, is responsible for the greatest amount of culture change in all societies.

= *Although the marriage practices in Africa and the United States differ in many respects, both sets of practices are responses to the universal need to have an orderly system of mating and child rearing.*

(**cultural universals**) because they have all worked out solutions to a whole series of problems facing all human societies. We can perhaps gain a clearer picture of cultural universals by looking in greater detail at the universal societal problems or needs that give rise to them.

Basic Needs

One of the most fundamental requirements of all societies is to see that the basic physiological needs of its people are met. Clearly, people cannot live unless they receive a minimum amount of food, water, and protection from the elements. Because a society will not last without living people, every society needs to work out systematic ways of producing (or procuring from the environment) absolutely essential commodities and then distributing what it regards as necessary to its members. In the United States, goods and services are distributed according to the capitalistic principle of "each according to his or her capacity to pay." In such socialist countries as Cuba and China, distribution takes place according to the principle of "each according to his or her need." The Hadza of Tanzania distribute meat according to how an individual is related to the person who killed the animal. The Mbuti of Central Africa engage in a system of distribution called silent barter, whereby they avoid having face-to-face interaction with their trading partners. Many societies distribute valu-

able commodities as part of the marriage system, sending considerable quantities of livestock from the family of the groom to the family of the bride. Even though the details of each of these systems of distribution vary greatly, every society has worked out a patterned way of ensuring that people get what they need for survival. As a result, we can say that every society has an *economic system*.

All societies face other universal needs besides the need to produce and distribute vital commodities to their members. For example, all societies need to make provisions for orderly mating and child rearing that give rise to patterned *systems of marriage and family*. If a society is to endure, it will need to develop a systematic way of passing on its culture from one generation to the next. This universal societal need for cultural transmission leads to some form of *educational system* in all societies. A prerequisite for the longevity of any society is the maintenance of social order. That is, most of the people must obey most of the rules most of the time. This universal societal need to avoid destruction through anarchy leads to a set of mechanisms that coerce people to obey the social norms that we call a *social control system*. Because people in all societies are faced with life occurrences that defy explanation or prediction, all societies have developed systems for explaining the unexplainable, most of which rely on some form of supernatural beliefs such as religion, witchcraft, magic, or sorcery. Thus, all societies have developed a *system of supernatural beliefs* that serve to explain otherwise inexplicable phenomena. And because all societies, if they are to function, need their members to be able to send and receive messages efficiently, they all have developed *systems of communication,* both verbal and nonverbal.

Despite what may appear to be an overwhelming amount of cultural variety found in the world today, all cultures, because they must meet certain universal needs, have a number of traits in common. Those just mentioned are some of the more obvious cultural universals, but many more could be cited. More than a half century ago, anthropologist George Peter Murdock (1945:124) compiled a list of cultural universals that can provide us with a look at what our species has in common (Table 2-1).

Sometimes the similarities (or universal aspects) of different cultural features are not always obvious. To illustrate, in middle-class America it is customary to spend a certain proportion of one's income on various types of insurance policies, including life insurance, medical insurance, and fire insurance. In many parts of the world today,

such as rural Swaziland, these forms of insurance are virtually unknown. This is not to suggest, however, that rural Swazis do not experience misfortune such as death, illness, or accidents. Nor do they suffer misfortunes without any support or safety net. Whereas most North Americans view the insurance company as their first line of security against such calamities as serious illness or death, Swazis have the extended family for support. If a husband dies prematurely, the widow and her children are provided for (financially, socially, and emotionally) by the relatives of the deceased. In Swaziland the extended family *is* the insurance company. Thus, the function of providing security and support in the face of misfortune is performed in both Swazi and North American cultures. Indeed, such security systems are found in all cultures, and consequently are universal. What differs, of course, are the agencies that provide the systems of support—in this case, either insurance companies or extended families.

For much of the twentieth century, cultural anthropologists have been focusing their efforts on explaining cultural differences. In an attempt to reestablish the discipline's focus that petered out with Murdock's list of

TABLE 2-1

Murdock's Cultural Universals

Are there any additional universals you would add to the following list?

Age grading	Etiquette	Joking	Postnatal care
Athletics	Faith healing	Kin groups	Pregnancy usages
Bodily adornment	Family	Kin terminology	Property rights
Calendar	Feasting	Language	Propitiation of
Cleanliness training	Fire making	Law	supernatural beings
Community organization	Folklore	Luck superstitions	Puberty customs
Cooking	Food taboos	Magic	Religious ritual
Cooperative labor	Funeral rites	Marriage	Residence rules
Cosmology	Games	Mealtimes	Sexual restrictions
Courtship	Gestures	Medicine	Soul concepts
Dancing	Gift giving	Modesty	Status differentiation
Decorative art	Government	Mourning	Surgery
Divination	Greetings	Music	Tool making
Division of labor	Hair styles	Mythology	Trade
Dream interpretation	Hospitality	Numerals	Visiting
Education	Housing	Obstetrics	Weaning
Eschatology	Hygiene	Penal sanctions	Weather control
Ethics	Incest taboos	Personal names	
Ethnobotany	Inheritance rules	Population policy	

SOURCE: George Peter Murdock, "The Common Denominator of Cultures," in Ralph Linton, ed., *The Science of Man in the World Crisis.* New York: Columbia University Press, 1945, p. 124.

cultural universals in the 1940s, Donald Brown (1991) has explored in considerable detail what is common to all cultures and societies. Of particular interest is Brown's description of "The Universal People," a composite culture of all peoples known to anthropologists. Drawing heavily from Murdock's 1945 list, as well as from Lionel Tiger and Robin Fox (1971) and Charles Hockett (1973), Brown makes a convincing case that cultural universals exist, are numerous, and are theoretically significant for carrying out the work of anthropology.

•■ CULTURE: ADAPTIVE ■•
AND MALADAPTIVE

CULTURE REPRESENTS the major way by which human populations adapt or relate to their environments so that they can continue to reproduce and survive. Most living organisms other than humans adapt to their environments by developing physiological features that equip them to maximize their chances for survival. For example, certain species of predators such as wolves, lions, and leopards have developed powerful jaws and canine teeth used for killing animals and ripping the flesh of the animal. Humans, on the other hand, have relied more on cultural than on biological features for adapting to their environments. Through the invention and use of such cultural tools as spears, arrows, guns, and knives, humans are able to kill and butcher animals even more efficiently than an animal could with its massive jaws and teeth. The discovery of such chemical substances as penicillin, quinine, and the polio vaccine has provided the human species a measure of protection against disease and death. The proliferation of agricultural technology over the past century has dramatically increased humans' capacity to feed themselves. Because humans rely much more heavily on cultural adaptation than on biological adaptation, we are enormously flexible in our ability to survive and thrive in a wide variety of natural environments. Because of the **adaptive nature of culture,** people are now able to live in many previously uninhabitable places, such as deserts, the polar region, under the sea, and even in outer space.

The notion that culture is adaptive should not lead us to the conclusion that every aspect of a culture is adaptive. It is possible for some features to be adaptively neutral, neither enhancing nor diminishing the capacity of a people to survive. Moreover, it is even possible for some features of a culture to be maladaptive or dysfunctional. To illustrate, the large-scale use of automobiles coupled with industrial pollutants is currently destroying the quality of the air in our environment. If this set of cultural behaviors continues unchecked, it will destroy our environment to such an extent that it will be unfit for human habitation. Thus, it is not likely that such a maladaptive practice will persist indefinitely. Either the practice will disappear when the people become extinct, or the culture will change so that the people will survive. Whichever occurs, the maladaptive cultural feature will eventually disappear.

An understanding of the adaptive nature of culture is further complicated by its relativity. What is adaptive in one culture may be maladaptive or adaptively neutral in another culture. For example, the mastery of such skills as algebra, word analogies, and reading comprehension is necessary for a successful adaptation to life in the United States, for these skills all contribute to academic success, landing a good job, and living in material comfort. However, such skills are of little value in helping the Nuer herdsman adapt to his environment in the Sudan. Furthermore, the adaptability of a cultural item varies over time within any particular culture. To illustrate, the survival capacity of traditional Inuit hunters living on the Alaskan tundra would no doubt be enhanced appreciably by the introduction of guns and snowmobiles. Initially, such innovations would be adaptive because they would enable the Inuit hunters to obtain caribou more easily, thereby enabling people to eat better, be more resistant to disease, and generally live longer. After several generations, however, the use of guns and snowmobiles would, in all likelihood, become maladaptive, for the newly acquired capacity to kill caribou more efficiently would eventually lead to the destruction of a primary food supply.

•■ CULTURES ARE GENERALLY ■•
INTEGRATED

TO SUGGEST THAT all cultures share a certain number of universal characteristics is not to imply that cultures comprise a laundry list of norms, values, and material objects. Instead, cultures should be thought of as integrated wholes, the parts of which, to some degree, are interconnected with one another. When we view cultures as integrated systems, we can begin to see how particular culture traits fit into the whole system and, consequently, how they tend to make sense within that context. Equipped with such a perspective, we can begin to better understand the "strange" customs found throughout the world.

One way of describing this integrated nature of cultures is by using the **organic analogy** made popular by some of the early functionalist anthropologists. This approach makes the analogy between a culture and a living organism such as the human body. The physical human body comprises a number of systems, all functioning to maintain the overall health of the organism; these systems include the respiratory, digestive, skeletal, excretory, reproductive, muscular, circulatory, endocrine, and lymphatic systems. Any anatomist or surgeon worth her or his salt knows where these systems are located in the body, what function each plays, and how the various parts of the body are interconnected. Surely no sane person would choose a surgeon to remove a malignant lung unless that surgeon knew how that organ was related to the rest of the body.

Cultural Interconnections

In the same way that human organisms comprise various parts that are both functional and interrelated, so too do cultures. When conducting empirical field research, the task of the cultural anthropologist is to describe the various parts of the culture, show how they function, and show how they are interconnected. When describing cultures, anthropologists often identify such parts or systems as the economic, kinship, social control, marriage, military, religious, aesthetic, technological, and linguistic systems, among others. These various parts of a culture are more than a random assortment of customs. Even though more often than not anthropologists fail to spell out clearly the nature and dimensions of these relationships, it is believed that many parts of a culture are to some degree interconnected. Thus, we can speak of cultures as being logical and coherent systems.

The notion of the interconnectedness of the parts of a culture can be illustrated with any culture. The Samburu of East Africa are seminomadic pastoralists who keep relatively large numbers of cows. An anthropologist studying the Samburu and their herds would no doubt describe the cow as part of the economic system. The cow's blood and milk are routinely consumed as a source of food; skins are used to make clothing, shoes, and jewelry; the cow's urine is used as an antiseptic; and cow dung is both a principal material for house construction and a fuel for cooking. Even though cows are an integral part of the economic system of the Samburu, they play an important role in (or are related to) other systems as well. To illustrate, because an exchange of cattle is necessary for a legal marriage to take place, cows are part of the marriage system; because cows are exchanged by men to establish obligations and bonds of friendship, cattle play an important role in social relationships; and because cows are often the subject of such artistic expressions as songs, poems, epics, and folktales, they are an integral part of the aesthetic system. Thus, to the extent that cattle function as part of a number of distinct components in the Samburu culture, we can see how the culture tends to be integrated.

▪■ "Primitive" Cultures ■▪

A **FUNDAMENTAL FEATURE** of the discipline of cultural anthropology is that it is comparative in approach. Whether studying religions, economic systems, ways of resolving conflicts, or art forms, cultural anthropologists look at these aspects of human behavior in the widest possible context, ranging from the most technologically simple foraging societies at one end of the continuum to the most highly industrialized societies at the other. Societies with simple technologies, once called primitive, are

For these Samburu pastoralists of East Africa, cattle are more than just an economic commodity. Because cattle also play roles in legitimizing marriages, allocating social status, and making religious sacrifices, we say that the various parts of a culture tend to be interconnected.

APPLIED PERSPECTIVE
Evaluating Educational Programs

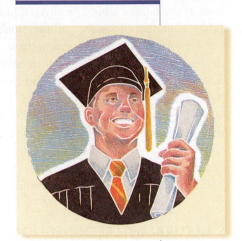

David Fetterman (1987, 1988) provides us with an excellent example of how cultural anthropology can be applied to the evaluation of a national educational program. Working for a private research corporation specializing in evaluation research, Fetterman was the anthropologist on a multidisciplinary team responsible for evaluating the Career Intern Program, an alternative high school program designed to enable dropouts and potential dropouts to earn a high school degree while working at their own pace. This federally funded program, allowing most students to complete their high school education on an accelerated basis, represents one of the few exemplary educational programs for economically disadvantaged minority youth.

Being in charge of the ethnographic portion of the evaluation, Fetterman was responsible for producing case studies of each of the four sites located in Bushwick, NY, Poughkeepsie, NY, East Detroit, MI, and Seattle. More specifically, his task involved analyzing all of the components in the program—the students, teachers, counselors, directors, disseminators, monitors, funders, and even the evaluators themselves—in order to identify the relationship between student outcomes and various program components. Fetterman used traditional data-gathering techniques such as participant observation and both structured and unstructured interviews. Fetterman's ethnographic research differed from more traditional types of anthropological research in that there was less fieldwork time available for this evaluation project. Rather than spending six or eight months in each site, he made intensive two-week visits to each site every three months for a total period of three years.

Fetterman's findings, some of which were couched in anthropological terminology, can be summarized as follows:

1. In his description of the culture of each site, Fetterman showed that while maintaining high expectations, teachers, counselors, and administrators created a supportive environment for students; the long list of rules and regulations gave students both behavioral guidelines and a feeling that people cared about them.

2. Fetterman described the role that certain rituals played in developing group loyalty and identity. These included basketball games, bake sales, student

described by contemporary cultural anthropologists by other terms such as *preliterate, small-scale, egalitarian,* or *technologically simple.* Because of the misleading implication that something primitive is both inferior and

earlier in a chronological sense, the term *primitive* will not be used in this book. Instead we will use the term **small-scale society,** which refers to societies that have small populations, are technologically simple, are usually

council elections, and periodic appreciation days where various students were recognized for their achievements in a number of areas. These rituals had the effect of bonding students and staff and bringing a sense of social solidarity to the entire school.

3. The ethnographic evaluation also identified the importance of certain rites of passage (ceremonies acknowledging one's change of status) for students' self-esteem. In addition to the final graduation ceremony itself, the programs were divided into "new groups" and "old groups." Fetterman found that the passing from the new group to the old group served as an important milestone for students, letting them know that they could in fact finish the program.

4. And finally, the ethnographic evaluation was able to document some significant outcomes such as positive attitudinal changes, increased attention spans, improved communication skills, enhanced cognitive skills, and greater ability to cope with authority.

The use of anthropology in evaluating a nationwide educational program provided the multidisciplinary team with a perspective it was not likely to get from other disciplines. One such ethnographic contribution was a picture of the sociocultural context in which the program was operating. Ethnographic descriptions of inner-city neighborhoods—where theft, drug abuse, prostitution, and murder are common occurrences—provided insights into the types of influences bearing on the students in the programs.

Fetterman's study represents one more instance of how anthropology can be applied to the solution of human problems. It differs from most other applied educational research projects in some important respects. For example, whereas most anthropological research applied to education is frequently conducted in a single location, Fetterman was looking at a large national educational program with multiple sites throughout the country. It does represent, however, an illustration of how cultural anthropology is carving out a role for itself in the area of the evaluation of educational programs.

QUESTIONS FOR FURTHER THOUGHT

1. In what ways was Fetterman's research different from traditional forms of anthropological research?
2. What rites of passage have you experienced in your life? Be specific.
3. In addition to the type of evaluation research conducted by Fetterman, in what other ways can ethnography be applied to formal educational systems?

preliterate (that is, without a written form of language), have little labor specialization, and are not stratified. Making such a distinction between small-scale and more complex societies should not be taken to imply that all societies can be pigeonholed into one or the other category. Rather, it would be more fruitful to view all of the societies of the world along a continuum from most small-scale to most complex.

CROSS-CULTURAL MISCUE

DURING THE 1960s, a group of recent Cuban American immigrants in New York City were planning a peaceful demonstration, for which they had a permit, in front of the United Nations building. On the day of the demonstration, one of the leaders approached a New York City policeman to ask where the demonstrators could gather. As the two men were talking, the police officer became increasingly uncomfortable as the demonstrator moved closer to him. The officer told the demonstrator to "get out of my face," but owing to language differences, the demonstrator didn't understand what the policeman wanted. The Cuban American continued talking while standing closer to the officer than the officer felt was appropriate. Within minutes the Cuban American was arrested for threatening the safety of a law enforcement officer.

This incident illustrates a cross-cultural misunderstanding involving a subtle aspect of culture. According to Edward T. Hall (1969), people in different parts of the world adhere to predictable spatial distances when communicating; in other words, our culture dictates how much space we need from another when we talk. To illustrate, Hall has found that most middle-class North Americans choose a normal conversational distance of no closer than 22 inches from one mouth to the other. However, for certain South American and Caribbean cultures (such as Cubans), the distance is approximately 15 inches, whereas Middle Eastern cultures maintain a distance of 9 to 10 inches. These culturally produced spatial patterns are extremely important when communicating, or trying to communicate, with culturally different people because they are so subtle, and thus, so frequently overlooked.

The problem that occurred between the Cuban American and the New York City policeman is that their two cultures had different ideas about spatial distancing. The Cuban American was attempting to establish what for him was a comfortable conversational distance of approximately 15 inches. Unfortunately, the policeman felt that his personal space, as defined by his culture, was being violated. Had either the policeman or the Cuban American demonstrator understood this aspect of cultural behavior, the breakdown in communication, and the arrest, could have been avoided.

CULTURE AND THE INDIVIDUAL

THROUGHOUT THIS CHAPTER we have used the term *culture* to refer to everything that people have, think, and do as members of a society. Whether we are talking about the Chinese, Yanamamo, or Samoans, all peoples have a shared set of meanings that serve as a collective guide to their behavior. Because people from the same culture learn essentially the same set of values, rules, and expected behaviors, their lives are made somewhat less complicated because they know, within broad limits, what to expect from one another. To illustrate, when walking down a crowded hallway in the United States, there is a general understanding that people will keep to their right. Because most people share that common cultural understanding, the traffic in a crowded hallway usually flows without serious interruption. If someone walks down the left-hand side of the hallway, it is likely that traffic will slow down because many people will be unsure of how to cope with the oncoming person. Such an incident is disruptive and anxiety-producing for the simple reason that normal, expected, and predictable behavior has not occurred.

This chapter has shown in a number of different ways how individuals are constrained, or at least influenced, by their cultures—the sets of material objects, ideas, and behavior patterns that they internalize from birth. And, in fact, how effectively people fit into their own group depends largely on the extent to which they adhere to those cultural expectations. To be certain, our cultures exert a powerful influence on our conduct, often without our even being aware of it. However, to assert that culture influences our behavior is hardly the same as asserting that it determines our behavior.

Deviance from the cultural norms is found in all societies. Because individual members of any society maintain, to varying degrees, a free will, they have the freedom to say no to cultural expectations. Unlike the honeybee, which behaves according to its genetic programming, humans can make a range of behavioral choices. Of course, choosing an alternative may result in unpleasant consequences, but all people have the option of doing things differently from what is culturally expected. People sometimes choose to go against cultural conventions for a number of reasons. In some cases where adherence to a social norm involves a hardship, people may justify their noncompliance by stretching the meaning of the norm. Or sometimes people flout a social norm or custom in order to make a social statement. Whatever the reason one has for deviating from the norms, the fact remains that social norms rarely, if ever, receive total compliance. For this reason, cultural anthropologists distinguish between ideal behavior (what people are expected to do) and real behavior (what people actually do).

SUMMARY

1. For purposes of this book, we have defined the term *culture* as everything that people have, think, and do as members of a society.

2. Culture is something that is shared by members of the same society. This shared nature of culture enables people to predict—within broad limits—the behavior of others in the society. Conversely, people become disoriented when attempting to interact in a culturally different society because they don't share that culture with members of that society.

3. Culture is acquired not genetically but through a process of learning, which anthropologists call enculturation. People in different cultures learn different things, but there is no evidence to suggest that people in some cultures learn more efficiently than people in other cultures.

4. Certain aspects of culture—such as ideas, beliefs, and values—can affect our physical bodies and our biological processes. More specifically, certain culturally produced ideas concerning physical beauty can influence the ways in which people alter their bodies.

5. Cultures—and their three basic components of things, ideas, and behavior patterns—are constantly experiencing change. Although the pace of culture change varies from society to society, no cultures are totally static. Cultures change internally (innovation) and by borrowing from other cultures (diffusion).

6. Although cultures found throughout the world vary considerably, certain common features (cultural universals) are found in all cultures. Cultural anthropology—the scientific study of cultures—looks at both similarities and differences in human cultures wherever they may be found.

7. Cultures function to help people adapt to their environments and consequently increase their chances for survival. It is also possible for cultures to negatively alter or even destroy their environments.

8. A culture is more than the sum of its parts. Rather, a culture should be seen as an integrated system with its parts interrelated to some degree. This cultural integration has important implications for the process of culture change because a change in one part of the system is likely to bring about changes in other parts.

9. Although culture exerts considerable influence on a person's thoughts and behaviors, it does not determine them.

KEY TERMS

adaptive nature of culture	innovations
cultural diffusion	organic analogy
cultural universals	pluralistic society
culture shock	small-scale society
enculturation	subcultures

SUGGESTED READINGS

Brown, Donald E. *Human Universals.* New York: McGraw-Hill, 1991. Drawing on the works of earlier theorists, this work argues convincingly that cultural universals (the aspects of culture shared by all cultures) are numerous and theoretically significant.

DeVita, Philip R., and James D. Armstrong. *Distant Mirrors: America as a Foreign Culture.* Belmont, CA: Wadsworth, 1993. A readable collection of 14 articles on American culture as seen through the eyes of foreign scholars who conducted field research in the United States. This slim volume, written from the critical perspective of foreign observers, should give American readers a different view of their own culture.

Freilich, Morris, Douglas Raybeck, and Joel Savishinsky, eds. *Deviance: Anthropological Perspectives.* South Hadley, MA: Bergin and Garvey, 1990. This collection of essays looks at the relationship between culture and deviance (or noncompliance with cultural prescriptions) in a wide range of societies throughout the world.

Gamst, Frederick C., and Edward Norbeck, eds. *Ideas of Culture: Sources and Uses.* New York: Holt, Rinehart & Winston, 1976. This is a collection of writings over the past hundred years on the notion of culture, the concept that is central to the discipline of anthropology.

Hall, Edward T. *The Hidden Dimension.* Garden City, NY: Doubleday, 1969. Hall introduces the science of proxemics to show how a very subtle aspect of culture—how people use space—can have a powerful impact on international business relations, cross-cultural encounters, and the fields of architecture and urban planning.

Kottak, Conrad. *Prime-Time Society: An Anthropological Analysis of Television and Culture.* Belmont, CA: Wadsworth, 1990. An interesting comparative study analyzing the effects of television on Brazilian and American societies.

Kuper, Adam. *Culture: The Anthropologists' Account.* Cambridge, MA: Harvard University Press, 1999. By drawing on the works of Parsons, Geertz, Schneider, and Sahlins, among others, Kuper thoughtfully traces the history of the concept of culture in American anthropology by showing its uses and limitations.

On the Net

As we have seen in this chapter, the concept of culture has been defined in a number of different ways over the years. Washington State University has a web site devoted to exploring some of the ways by which scholars have defined the concept. Using one of the major search engines, search the web for a site called "What is culture?" You may do a subject search using the name of the site or you can use the URL:

http://www.wsu.edu:8001/vcwsu/commons/topics/culture/culture-index.html

1. Once there, click on "a baseline definition of culture." According to the authors what is the "essential feature" of culture?
2. Read over the brief definitions of culture presented by Matthew Arnold, Raymond Williams, and Clifford Geertz. In a single paragraph, how do these three different definitions differ from one another?

Chapter Three

APPLIED ANTHROPOLOGY

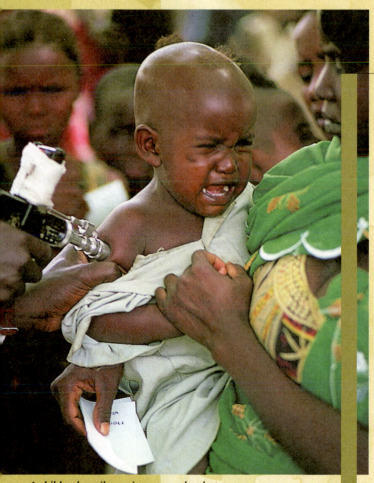

A child unhappily receives a measles shot in Chad, West Africa.

WHAT WE WILL LEARN:

▼

How have cultural anthropologists applied their theories, methods, and insights to the solution of practical problems during the course of this century?

▼

What special contributions can cultural anthropology make as an applied science?

▼

What ethical dilemmas do applied anthropologists face when conducting fieldwork?

▼

A distinguishing feature of cultural anthropology is its direct, experiential approach to research through the technique known as

participant-observation. By and large, cultural anthropologists conduct field research among populations experiencing serious societal problems, such as poor health, inadequate food production, high infant mortality, high crime rates, and rampant population growth, to mention but a few. The very nature of anthropological research—which involves living with people, sharing their lives, and often befriending them—makes it difficult for cultural anthropologists to ignore the enormity of the problems these societies face on an everyday basis. It should therefore come as no surprise that many cultural anthropologists feel a sense of responsibility for helping to solve—or at least alleviate—some of these pressing social problems.

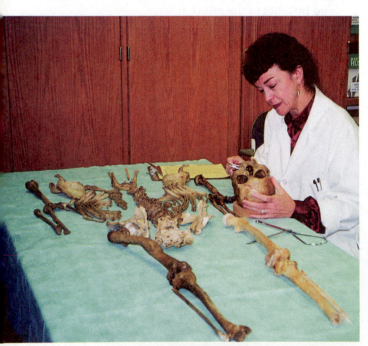

Forensic anthropology, as practiced here by Dr. Karen Ramey Burns, is a form of applied physical anthropology.

Although anthropologists have always applied their findings to the solution of human problems, an increasing number of anthropologists during the past half century have conducted research aimed very explicitly at practical applications. These practitioners represent a new and growing subdiscipline known as **applied anthropology,** which is characterized by **problem-oriented research** among the world's contemporary populations. Pragmatic anthropologists attempt to apply anthropological data, concepts, and strategies to the solution of social, economic, and technological problems, both at home and abroad. Over the past decades a number of terms have been given to these many attempts to use anthropological research for the improvement of human conditions. They include *action anthropology, development anthropology, practical anthropology,* and *advocacy anthropology.* For purposes of this chapter, however, we will use the more widely accepted and generic term, *applied anthropology.*

Our use of this term requires some delineation because applied anthropology cuts across all of the traditional four fields. Most anthropologists who would identify with an applied perspective are cultural anthropologists, but the other three traditional subdisciplines are certainly involved in their share of applied activities. For example, researchers in **forensic anthropology** for years have used traditional methods and theories to help identify the remains of crime and disaster victims; archaeologists, applying their traditional methods and insights to the study of contemporary landfills, have been responsible for helping develop policies on solid waste disposal; and applied anthropological linguists have contributed widely to problem solving and policy formation in the area of teaching English as a second language to nonmainstream students in the United States.

Much of the applied anthropology carried out in recent decades has been supported by large public and private organizations seeking to better understand the cultural dimension of their sponsored programs. These organizations include such international agencies as the U.S. Agency for International Development (USAID), the World Bank, the World Health Organization (WHO), the Ford Foundation, and the Population Council; certain national organizations such as the National Institutes of Health (NIH), the Bureau of Indian Affairs, and the U.S. Department of Agriculture; and on a more local level, various hospitals, private corporations, school systems, urban planning departments, substance abuse programs, facilities for the aged, and family planning clinics.

•■ APPLIED VERSUS PURE ■• ANTHROPOLOGY

FOR MUCH OF THE PAST CENTURY, many anthropologists have distinguished applied anthropology from pure or academic anthropology. So-called pure anthropology was seen as being concerned only with the advancement of the discipline in terms of refining its methods and theories and providing increasingly more valid and reliable anthropological data. Applied anthropology, on the other hand, was characterized as being primarily aimed at changing human behavior in order to ameliorate contemporary problems. The two types of anthropology are not mutually exclusive enterprises, however.

In fact, unlike the traditional four subfields of anthropology, applied anthropology, which has become for all practical purposes the fifth subfield, is considerably more difficult to define. Part of the difficulty in conceptualizing the applied subfield precisely is that it has always been a part of the discipline; in fact, both applied and theoretical anthropology have developed alongside each other. Throughout its history, anthropologists, to one degree or another, have been concerned with the utility of their findings for solving social problems. For example, in the early 1930s the Applied Anthropology Unit of Indian Affairs was created by President Roosevelt's Commissioner of Indian Affairs, John Collier (himself an anthropologist). The aim of this unit was to study the progress of self-governing organizations among some Indian groups as called for in the 1934 Indian Reorganization Act. As part of the Interdisciplinary Committee on Human Relations at the University of Chicago, anthropologist W. Lloyd Warner, Burleigh Gardner, and others conducted applied research in the areas of industrial management, productivity, and working conditions. Moreover, World War II provided vast opportunities for anthropologists to apply their skills and insights to the war effort, including strategies on improving national morale, studies of food preferences and rationing programs, and cultural information supplied to the Office of War Information on both our allies and our adversaries. In the decades following World War II, cultural anthropologists have conducted applied research in a wide variety of areas including agriculture, medicine, criminal

= *Applied cultural anthropologists study a wide variety of social settings including such Chinese neighborhoods as this one in New York City.*

justice, alcohol and drug use, housing, geriatric services, education, and business, among many others. Thus, as we can see, many cultural anthropologists have very purposefully engaged in applied research throughout the twentieth century, others have applied secondary anthropological data to help solve certain social problems, and still others, engaging in the investigation of a theoretical problem, have taken the additional step to explicate the practical implications of their findings for policymakers.

If we take the pure/applied distinction too literally, we might conclude that applied anthropologists are devoid of any theoretical concerns and that academic purists have no concern for the practical implications of their work. In actual practice, neither of these things are true. Applied anthropology, when it is done effectively, takes into account the theories, methods, and data that have been developed by the discipline as a whole. At the other polarity, the more theoretically oriented anthropologists are indebted to applied anthropologists for stimulating their interests in new areas of research and, in some cases, for contributing to the development of new theory. The beneficial consequences that can accrue from the interaction of theoretical and applied anthropologists are well stated by Walter Goldschmidt (1979:5):

> The more a field is engaged in practical affairs, the greater the intellectual ferment; for programmatic activities raise issues and often new approaches which would otherwise escape the attention of the discipline.

That the line between pure and applied anthropology is so murky is not surprising because both groups, by and large, receive the same form of training, usually in traditional anthropology doctoral programs. Moreover, both pure and applied forms of research—drawing as they do on such methods as participant-observation and ethnographic interviewing—are often indistinguishable from each other. The line is blurred still further by the fact that the two have experienced parallel development, have been mutually supportive, and often have claimed the same personnel. Thus, because pure and applied anthropologists share a wide variety of both theoretical and practical concerns, the task of defining the behavioral dimensions of applied anthropologists can become as elusive as trying to nail a custard pie to the wall.

•■ APPLIED ANTHROPOLOGY ■• IN THE TWENTIETH CENTURY

EVEN THOUGH ANTHROPOLOGISTS have been applying their insights since the beginning of the twentieth century, the real stimulus came in the 1940s when many of the leading cultural anthropologists of the time were asked to participate in efforts related to World War II. Anthropologists were recruited by the National Research Council to examine national morale during wartime, to learn about food preferences and wartime rationing, and to perform national character studies on our adversaries—the Germans,

Sometimes applied anthropologists serve as expert witnesses in court cases involving cultural issues.

= *Ruth Benedict's study of the Japanese national character was used by the U.S. Office of War Information during World War II.*

Italians, and Japanese. After the war, many anthropologists left government service and returned to positions in colleges and universities. This trend, with a return to more theoretical concerns, continued through the 1950s and 1960s. Whatever applied anthropology was conducted during the decades of the 1950s and 1960s was carried out by academic anthropologists engaged in short-term projects outside the university setting.

However, from the 1970s to the present, a new brand of applied anthropologist emerged. Whereas many of the applied anthropologists of the 1950s and 1960s were essentially academics engaged in short-term applied projects, the new applied anthropologists are not academics but rather full-time employees of the hiring agencies. Data from a recent survey conducted by the American Anthropological Association indicate that approximately 30 percent of all anthropology Ph.D.s work outside an academic setting for government organizations, nonprofits, or private-sector firms. This developmental stage is largely the result of two important trends essentially external to the discipline of anthropology. First, over the past two and

a half decades, the market for academic jobs has declined dramatically. The abundance of jobs that marked the 1950s and 1960s turned into a shortage of jobs during the 1970s, 1980s, and 1990s. A second factor contributing to the new applied anthropology has been the increase in federal legislation mandating policy research that can be accomplished effectively by cultural anthropologists. For example, the National Historic Preservation Act (1966), the National Environmental Policy Act (1969), the Foreign Assistance Act (1973), and the Community Development Act (1974) all provide for policy research of a cultural nature. As a consequence of these two factors (fewer academic jobs coupled with greater research opportunities), more anthropology Ph.D.s are finding permanent employment outside academia. This trend has been paralleled by increases in the number of M.A. programs in applied anthropology and the membership of such applied anthropology organizations as the Society for Applied Anthropology (SFAA) and the National Association of Practicing Anthropologists (NAPA).

EXAMPLES OF APPLIED ANTHROPOLOGY

An Ethnographic Study of Adolescent Drug Dealers

Because of cocaine's high cost, cocaine addiction historically has been viewed as a rich person's problem. In the last several decades, however, the introduction of a cheaper variety of cocaine—crack cocaine—has made this drug accessible to all segments of the population. By and large, the appearance of crack cocaine has been a destructive force for both individuals and society as a whole. Increased trafficking in crack cocaine has been responsible, at least in part, for increases in crime, in the incidence of AIDS (sex-for-crack exchanges), and in the number of children born with drug addictions. One of the more disturbing aspects of the crack cocaine epidemic is the high rate of cocaine dealing among adolescents.

In an attempt to learn more about adolescent drug dealing, Richard Dembo and his colleagues (1993) conducted an ethnographic study of adolescent drug dealers in west central Florida. Dembo interviewed 34 drug-dealing youth and 16 nondealer youth for about an hour each on such topics as the extent to which income from drugs was used to help meet family expenses, reasons for selling crack cocaine, the perceived risks of dealing in cocaine, and the negative effects of drug trafficking on the neighborhood. The adolescents who were dealing sold on average 21

APPLIED PERSPECTIVE

Mediating Between the Government and Trukese Villagers

Whenever central governments initiate programs of planned change—be it in the field of agriculture, medicine, family planning, or education—more likely than not problems will emerge with the local target population. This is because, generally, governments and local populations often have different cultural values and interests and start from a different set of cultural assumptions. In some cases, the plans and policies of the central government are so much at odds with the needs of the local population that an impasse develops. Demonstrations, petitions, and other forms of popular protest may arise in opposition to the government's plans; hostilities and mistrust may be generated in both camps; and, in some serious cases, the proposed project may come to a standstill. In such situations, cultural anthropologists have been recruited to serve as intercultural mediators between the government and the local people whose lives are being affected by the projects. In the words of Richard Salisbury (1976:255), anthropologists serve in the role of "societal ombudsmen."

In the late 1970s, the government of the Trust Territories for the Island of Truk (administered by the United States) made plans to expand the airport. The plans were drawn up, and the environmental impact study (required by U.S. law) was completed without any consultation with the local villagers. As proposed, the airport expansion would have created a number of problems for the local people. For example, proposed dredging operations would destroy certain local fishing areas, the expanded runway would prevent the villagers from mooring their boats near their homes, construction would destroy several cultural/historical landmarks, and during construction, the project would generate high levels of noise and dust. The people naturally objected. Protest demonstrations and the threat of a legal injunction to stop construction convinced the government that it had a serious problem.

In an attempt to address some of the complaints of the local people, the government appointed Thomas King, an archaeological consultant in historic preservation, to mediate officially between the government and the local villagers on matters pertaining to the construction's impact. Although she had no

weeks out of the year for an average weekly income of $672. The estimated mean financial worth of the adolescent dealers was $2,500. Most of the dealers said that they were not currently using cocaine. Two out of every three adolescent dealers said they had killed or hurt someone through their association with cocaine. The great majority of the dealers reported that they spent most of their income on personal luxury items (such as clothes and jewelry) or business expenses such as guns or protection. It is estimated that they contributed less than 10 percent of their income to their families. Most adolescent dealers said that they sold cocaine to earn a lot of money (because legiti-

official status in the mediation process, King's wife, Patricia Parker, a cultural anthropologist who was conducting ethnographic research on Trukese land law, played an important role by translating the villagers' concerns into language the government officials could understand (see Parker and King 1987).

The first order of business facing this wife–husband negotiating team was to work with the villagers to develop a list of specific grievances that could serve as the basis for negotiations. Meetings were held in the various villages to allow the local people themselves to reach some consensus on the nature of their complaints against the proposed airport expansion. Parker, the cultural anthropologist fluent in the local language, attended these meetings and provided detailed outlines of the villagers' concerns to King, who in turn brought the concerns up with the responsible government officials.

Parker and King were thus able to serve as cultural mediators or cultural brokers between the government and the local Trukese villagers. Because they came to understand the constraints and interests of both sides of the controversy, they were able to mediate from a fairly strong knowledge base, thereby avoiding a hardening of positions on either side. As a result of their mediating efforts, the following modifications were made. First, dredging operations were changed so that local fishing areas were only minimally affected; where they were affected, the villagers received block grant compensation for the potential loss of food. Second, the government agreed to construct a new anchorage for local fishing boats. Third, construction plans were altered so that the cultural/historic landmarks were not destroyed.

In the final analysis, the use of two anthropologists to mediate between the interests of the government and those of the local Trukese villagers worked out satisfactorily for all parties concerned. The villagers were pleased with most of the modifications made in the original plans and the compensation they received. The government now has an expanded airport. Although the cost of the airport was increased, its building was not delayed by litigation.

QUESTIONS FOR FURTHER THOUGHT

1. While mediating between the government and the villagers, are anthropologists responsible to the government, the Trukese villagers, or both?
2. What specialized role or roles (discussed in the chapter) did these applied anthropologists play?
3. What ethical concerns do you think the applied anthropologists faced in their work in Truk?

mate jobs pay too little), which would give them higher status among their peers.

This ethnographic study of the culture of adolescent cocaine dealers has important policy implications because it suggests certain strategies for dealing with this problem. For example, because wanting to make money is the major reason for selling cocaine, intervention strategies must include ways of improving the vocational and educational skills of adolescents so that they will have more access to legitimate work. Because most of the adolescent dealers were not using cocaine, there is little reason to treat the problem as one of drug dependency. Adolescent dealing is

CROSS-CULTURAL MISCUE

motivated by economics, not drug addiction. Knowing this about the culture of adolescent dealers suggests that the following would be a rational strategy for addressing the problem: Former dealers who have been successful in legitimate careers could serve as positive role models for adolescent dealers by encouraging and supporting those willing to enter legitimate career alternatives.

Understanding Food Consumption Patterns Contributes to a Successful Health Program

For at least the last half century, cultural anthropologists have been interested in the sociocultural aspects of medical problems. In fact, today medical anthropology is one of the largest branches of applied anthropology. But as early as the 1940s anthropologists were providing insights into the area of medical delivery systems. During the 1940s the Polela Health Center served the medical needs of approximately 16,000 Zulu living in South Africa's Natal Provence. Health conditions among these people were extremely poor. In addition to widespread occurrences of such infectious diseases as typhoid, typhus, smallpox, and tuberculosis, the Zulu suffered from kwashiorkor, a form of protein malnutrition. There were particularly high rates of kwashiorkor among married women. Health officials found this particularly puzzling because the Zulu keep cattle and thus should be able to use their milk supplies (which are rich in protein) to offset the often deadly effects of kwashiorkor.

The key to understanding why kwashiorkor was so prevalent among married women rested with the understanding of a deep-seated cultural belief that people are permitted to drink only the milk produced by the cows of their father's lineage. Although this dietary restriction applied to all Zulu, the situation was particularly problematic for married women. Zulu society is patrilocal—that is, having a residence pattern in which a married couple lives with or near the husband's parents. When a woman married, she moved away from her father's extended family and consequently lost access to the milk from her own father's cows. The only way that a married woman could have access to milk is if her father gave her a cow of her own when she married, an unlikely occurrence. Thus, milk as a source of protein, was, for all practical purposes, unavailable to Zulu women.

Even though the reasons for the dietary prohibition had long since been forgotten, the Zulu people had powerful feelings about maintaining it. Given such strong convictions, it would have served little purpose for the health professionals to try to argue the Zulu out of their belief. Much to their credit, the Polela health team overcame the cultural obstacle to improving the dietary intake of Zulu women by circumventing it. According to John Cassel,

Fortunately, it was possible to overcome this difficulty to a considerable extent by introducing powdered milk into the area. Even though people knew that this powder was in fact milk, it was not called milk in Zulu but was referred to as "powder" or "meal" and accepted by all families without protest. Even the most orthodox of husbands and mothers-in-law had no objection to their wives or daughters-in-law using the powder. (1972:308)

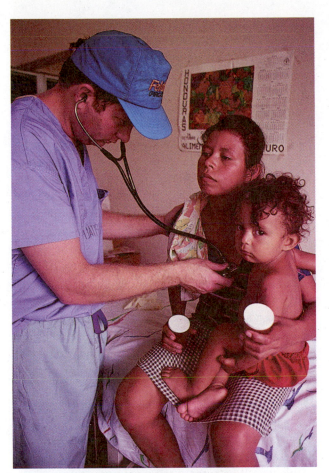

= *Applied anthropological research helps medical personnel provide more efficient services to peoples in developing countries. Here a Western doctor provides medical assistance in rural Honduras.*

Because the Polela health staff understood the essential features of Zulu culture, they were able to engage in some creative problem solving. All parties concerned were winners. The medical team was happy because it had improved the health of Zulu women. The Zulu themselves were happy because they were healthier. And it was all accomplished without having to do battle with a part of Zulu traditional culture. To be certain, not all obstacles to initiating health programs are always resolved so painlessly. Nevertheless, this preventive health program would not have succeeded without a thorough understanding and appreciation of traditional Zulu patterns of consumption and resource allocation. Although this example of applying anthropological knowledge had a happy ending, it is important to point out that the health-care system for the Zulu (and other Black South African groups) during apartheid was woefully inadequate.

An Understanding of Marital Patterns Sheds Light on Population Growth

As we will discuss in detail in Chapter 10, the majority of societies in the world, particularly in the non-Western world, practice a form of marriage known as polygyny, in which a man has more than one wife at a time. Over the course of the past century, Western missionaries have put considerable pressure on these small-scale societies to give up the practice of polygyny in favor of monogamy (the practice of having one wife at a time). The Christian missionaries argue that polygyny is immoral, even though most would be hard pressed to explain the widespread practice of polygyny in the Old Testament. In their well-intentioned yet short-sighted attempt to convert non-Western peoples to monogamy, missionaries have contributed to the serious worldwide problem of out-of-control population growth.

Warren Hern (1992), a medical anthropologist who has worked for decades with the Shipibo Indians in the Peruvian Amazon, has studied the relationship between polygyny and population growth. At first glance one might think that the practice of polygyny would contribute more to overall population growth than would the practice of monogamy. In actual fact, just the opposite is true. Although polygyny does permit some men to have more children than others, it permits women to have fewer children with longer intervals between births. Often associated with polygyny is postpartum sexual abstinence, in which a woman does not have sex with her husband for a certain period of time after giving birth. This sexual abstinence, which may last from several months to several years, functions to allow the child to breastfeed without competition, thereby improving its chances for survival. The overall effect of this abstinence is to lengthen the interval between pregnancies, thereby reducing the number of children born to wives in polygynous marriages.

Hern's research among the Shipibo Indians demonstrates that the practice of polygyny tends to keep overall birthrates down. In 1983 and 1984, Hern studied six Shipibo villages in various stages of modernization. In the most traditional Shipibo village, as many as 45 percent of the women were in polygynous marriages; this figure dropped to 5 percent in the least traditional village. Hern found that among all women in polygynous marriages, the average interval between births was 34 months, four months longer than for women in monogamous unions. Moreover, women in polygynous marriages on average had 1.3 fewer children during their lifetime than monogamous women.

Thus, for the Shipibo—and for many other traditionally polygynous peoples—the practices of polygyny and postpartum sexual abstinence tend to depress the overall birthrate. Consequently, when people convert from polygyny to monogamy (and are provided no alternative forms of birth control), the usual result is an increase in the overall number of births. Thus, Hern's findings are important for policymakers concerned with issues of population control.

THE ANTHROPOLOGIST'S INVOLVEMENT IN APPLIED PROJECTS

The extent to which an applied anthropologist becomes involved in any given project can vary considerably. At one extreme, the least interventionist end, are applied anthropologists who simply provide information for planners and decision makers. This information can range from very concrete observational data, through low- and intermediate-level concepts and propositions, to the most abstract level of general theory. Moving along the continuum, there are applied anthropologists, either working alone or as members of an interdisciplinary team, who use the collected data to construct a plan for bringing about a desired change in a particular population. And finally, at the most interventionist extreme, applied anthropologists become involved in actual implementation and evaluation of particular projects. Although rare, these "action anthropologists" feel a professional responsibility not only to make their research findings available but also to propose, advocate, and carry out policy positions.

•■ SPECIAL FEATURES ■• OF ANTHROPOLOGY

WHAT DOES THE DISCIPLINE of anthropology have to offer as an applied science? What unique contributions can anthropology make to social programs and agencies? The answer to these questions rests largely in the unique approach to the study of humans that anthropology has taken from its earliest beginnings. Among some of the special features of anthropology that contribute to its potential as a policy science are the following: participant-observation, the holistic perspective, the development of a regional expertise, the emic view, and the basic value orientation of cultural relativism.

Participant-Observation: Direct field observation, a hallmark of twentieth-century anthropology, can lead to a fuller understanding of the sociocultural realities than might be possible by relying on secondary sources of information. Also, the rapport developed while conducting participant-observation research can be drawn on in the implementation stage of the applied project.

The Holistic Perspective: This distinctive feature of anthropology forces us to look at multiple variables and see human problems in their historical, economic, and cultural contexts. This conceptual orientation reminds us that the various parts of a sociocultural system are interconnected so that a change in one part of the system is likely to cause changes in other parts. The holistic approach also encourages us to look at the problems in terms of both the short run and the long run.

Regional Expertise: Many anthropologists, despite recent trends toward specialization, continue to function as culture area specialists (such as Africanists and Micronesianists). The cultural anthropologist who has conducted doctoral research in Zambia, for example, often returns to that country for subsequent field studies. Thus, long-term association with a cultural region provides a depth of geographic coverage that most policymakers lack.

The Emic View: A major insight of anthropology in general—and applied anthropology specifically—is that linguistic and cultural differences invariably exist between project bureaucrats and the local client populations. Whatever the setting of a particular project—be it an agricultural development scheme in Zimbabwe, an inner-city hospital in Detroit, or a classroom in rural Peru—the applied anthropologist brings to the project the perspective of the local people, what anthropologists call the **emic view.** By describing the emic view (using the mental categories and assumptions of the local people) rather than their own technical/professional view (the **etic view**), anthropologists can provide program planners/administrators with strategic information that can seriously affect the outcome of programs of planned change.

Cultural Relativism: The basic principle of cultural relativism (refer to Chapter 2)—a vital part of every cultural anthropologist's training—tends to foster tolerance, which can be particularly relevant for applied anthropologists working in complex organizations. For example, tolerance stemming from the perspective of cultural relativism can help anthropologists cross class lines and relate to a wide range of people in the complex organization (such as a hospital or school system) in which they are working.

These five features of anthropology can very definitely enhance the discipline's effectiveness as a policy science. Nevertheless, when compared to other disciplines, anthropology has some drawbacks that limit its effectiveness in solving societal problems. First, anthropologists have not, by and large, developed many time-effective research methods; the premier anthropological data-gathering technique of participant-observation, which usually requires up to a year or more, is not particularly well suited to the accelerated time schedules of applied programs of change. Moreover, with their strong tradition of qualitative research methods, anthropologists have been unsophisticated in their use of quantitative data, although recently a number of anthropologists have begun to use more quantitative approaches.

SPECIALIZED ROLES OF APPLIED ANTHROPOLOGISTS

Applied anthropologists also play a number of specialized roles, which are more thoroughly described by Van Willigen (1993:3–6):

Policy Researcher: This role, perhaps the most common role for applied anthropologists, involves providing cultural data to policymakers so that they can make the most informed policy decisions.

Evaluator: This role is also quite common; evaluators use their research skills to determine how well a program or policy has succeeded in its objectives.

Impact Assessor: This role entails measuring or assessing the effect of a particular project, program, or policy on local peoples. For example, the anthropologist serving in the role of impact assessor may determine the consequences, both intended and unintended, that a federal highway construction project might have on the community through which the highway runs.

Planner: In this fairly common role, applied anthropologists actively participate in the design of various programs, policies, and projects.

Research Analyst: In this role, the applied anthropologist interprets research findings so that policymakers, planners, and administrators can make more culturally sensitive decisions.

Needs Assessor: This role involves the conduct of a fairly specialized type of research designed to determine ahead of time the need for a proposed program or project.

Trainer: This is essentially a teaching role, whereby the applied anthropologist imparts cultural knowledge about certain populations to different groups that are expected to work in cross-cultural situations (such as training a group of U.S. engineers to be better aware of the cultural environment of Saudi Arabia, where they will work for two years building a hotel complex).

Advocate: This rare role involves becoming an active supporter of a particular group of people. Usually involving at least some political action, this role is most often combined with other roles.

Expert Witness: This role, usually played on a short-term basis, involves the presentation of culturally

Industrial anthropologist Dr. Elizabeth Briody is a full-time employee of General Motors.

APPLIED PERSPECTIVE

Providing Medical Services to Gypsies in San Francisco

For years medical anthropologists have investigated disease from a cross-cultural perspective. They have studied folk remedies and curing practices in different cultures and, in recent years, have advised medical personnel about dealing with patients from different cultural backgrounds.

One such study, conducted by Anne Sutherland (1994), looked at the culture of the Rom Gypsies of San Francisco. Usually residing in the poorer sections of town, Gypsies often pass themselves off as members of other ethnic groups such as Mexican, Native Americans, or Rumanians. Men often earn money by engaging in auto body repair jobs while many women work as fortune tellers. They prefer living by themselves and usually avoid contact with non-Gypsies. Gypsies have a reputation for being difficult hospital patients, but Sutherland shows how an understanding of their culture can greatly facilitate the delivery of health-care services to this U.S. minority, which numbers over several hundred thousand people.

One feature of Gypsy culture is that illness is not just an individual concern but rather has broad social importance. Whenever a Gypsy becomes ill, a wide range of friends and relatives rush to his or her bedside. This customary gathering to the vicinity of the ill person is based on a sincere desire to be supportive during difficult times.

Rom Gypsies have a very strong notion of purity and impurity in both a physical and a moral sense. Cleanliness involves making sure that the upper part of the body from the waist up (which is considered clean) is kept separate from the lower half of the body, considered unclean because of its association with the secretions and emissions of the genitoanal area. These two parts of the body are kept separate to the extent that separate soap and towels are used to clean them. Menstruating women need to take particular care to keep clean because menstruation is considered a potentially polluting bodily function.

Sutherland's research found that there is also a strong belief that because non-Gypsies do not practice this body separation, they are a source of impurity and disease. So too are the places where non-Gypsies predominate, such as schools, offices, hospitals, public restrooms, and non-Gypsy houses, which

relevant research findings as part of judicial proceedings through legal briefs, depositions, or direct testimony.

Administrator/Manager: An applied anthropologist who assumes direct administrative responsibility for a particular project is working in this specialized role.

Cultural Broker: This role involves serving as a liaison between the program planner and administrators on one hand and local ethnic communities on the other,

Gypsies make every effort to avoid. When in these non-Gypsy places, Rom Gypsies avoid touching or having any physical contact with as many surfaces as possible.

As Gypsies become old, they take on higher status, are vested with political authority, and are almost venerated. Moreover, elders tend to enjoy a "cleaner" status, because it is thought that menstruation and sexual activity cease in old age. Given these and other features of Gypsy culture, Sutherland makes a number of important suggestions to hospital personnel when working with Gypsy patients:

1. In light of the dichotomy of the top (clean)/bottom (unclean) parts of the body, Gypsy patients should be provided separate soap and towels during their stay in the hospital. Moreover, when nurses and doctors touch the lower (unclean) part of their Gypsy patients' bodies, they should wash their hands before touching the upper (clean) parts of their bodies.

2. Because older relatives play an important role in making decisions about health care for younger family members, their thoughts and opinions must be taken into consideration and respected. These older relatives can be influential in gaining the cooperation of younger family members.

3. Given the strong belief that hospitals (frequented mostly by non-Gypsies) are unclean, fears of becoming polluted can be lessened by providing Gypsy patients with disposable paper cups, plates, eating utensils, and towels— that is, things that have not been used previously by non-Gypsies.

4. Because English is a second language for Gypsies, it is important that medical procedures be explained carefully and patiently. If certain remedies involve a violation of their religious beliefs, every effort should be made to use a medically sound alternative procedure.

5. Gypsy patients fear being left alone, separated from their wide network of families and friends. Allowing some relatives to rotate through the patient's room will reduce the anxiety and, in all likelihood, accelerate the recuperation time.

QUESTIONS FOR FURTHER THOUGHT

1. How would you characterize the distinction Gypsies make between "clean" and "unclean"?
2. Are there other minority groups living in North American cities to which Sutherland's recommendations would apply?
3. From the brief description of Gypsy culture above, what other recommendations might you make to hospital personnel in San Francisco?

or between mainstream hospital personnel and their ethnically distinct patients.

These specialized roles are not mutually exclusive. In many cases, applied anthropologists play two or more of these roles as part of the same job. For example, an applied anthropologist who is working as a policy researcher may also conduct research as a needs assessor before a program is initiated and as an impact assessor and evaluator after the program has concluded.

•■ THE ETHICS OF APPLIED ■• ANTHROPOLOGY

ALL FIELD ANTHROPOLOGISTS—both applied and theoretical—find themselves in social situations that are varied and complex because they work with people in a number of different role relationships. They are involved with and have responsibilities to their subjects, their discipline, their colleagues both in and outside anthropology, their host governments, their own governments, and their sponsoring agencies.

Applied anthropologists must operate in an even more complex situation, for their work often is aimed at facilitating some type of change in the culture of the local population. Under such socially complex conditions, it is likely that the anthropologist, having to choose between conflicting values, will be faced with a number of ethical dilemmas. For example, how do you make your findings public without jeopardizing the anonymity of your informants? Can you ever be certain that the data your informants gave you will not eventually be used to harm them? How can you be certain that the project you are working on will be beneficial for the target population? To what extent should you become personally involved in the lives of the people you are studying? Should you intervene to stop illegal activity? These are just a few of the ethical questions that arise in anthropological research. (For case materials on a wider range of ethical issues, see Appell 1978.) Although recognizing that anthropologists continually face such ethical decisions, the profession has made it clear that each member of the profession ultimately is respon-

sible for anticipating these ethical dilemmas and for resolving them in such a way as to do damage neither to their subjects nor to other scholars.

Today, federal law (in the United States) and policies at most research-oriented universities require that any faculty research (where human being are subjects) must comply with accepted ethical and professional standards. Generally, anthropologists are required to submit a description of their research to their university's Committee on Human Subjects and obtain approval for conducting the research. Many granting agencies will refuse to fund anthropological research unless the proposed research has been reviewed for potential ethical pitfalls.

A concern for professional ethics is hardly a recent phenomenon among anthropologists. As early as 1919, Franz Boas, the guru of the first generation of anthropologists in the United States, spoke out adamantly against the practice of anthropologists engaging in spying activities while allegedly conducting scientific research. Writing in the *Nation,* Boas (1919:797) commented, "A person who uses science as a cover for political spying . . . prostitutes science in an unpardonable way and forfeits the right to be classed as a scientist." Anthropologists have been aware of the ethical dilemmas they face since the beginning, but the profession did not adopt a comprehensive code of behavioral standards until the 1970s. In 1971 the AAA (American Anthropological Association) adopted its "Principles of Professional Responsibility" and established its Committee on Ethics, and the SFAA (Society for Applied Anthropology) published its "Statement on Professional and Ethical Responsibilities" in 1975.

= *Because programs designed to reduce rapid population growth must be sensitive to local cultural patterns, applied anthropology is playing an increasingly important role in family planning efforts throughout the world.*

CROSS-CULTURAL MISCUE

BRAD HUTCHISON, an applied anthropologist from California, was spending a semester as a visiting professor at Waseda University in Tokyo, Japan. Several days after arriving Hutchison made an appointment to meet with one of his colleagues in the anthropology department, Todashi Kobayashi. In response to Hutchison's general question about his colleague's latest research project, Kobayashi-san proceeded to describe his research in considerable detail. Although Hutchison was interested in the topic, he was becoming increasingly annoyed with Kobayashi-san, who kept pausing to ask whether Hutchison was understanding. Hutchison began to think that his Japanese colleague thought he was either inattentive or stupid.

This cross-cultural misunderstanding occurred because the role of the listener in Japan is substantially different from that in the United States. It is customary in Japan for listeners to use replies (*aizuchi*) such as "hai" ("yes"), which indicates that one is listening and understanding what is being said. Americans also do this (by saying "yes" or grunting "umhum"), but the Japanese use these to a much greater extent. Because Hutchison was not giving off any *aizuchi*, Kobayashi-san kept seeking reassurance that his message was getting through.

PROJECT CAMELOT

The publication of these professional codes of ethics in the 1970s was, to a large degree, precipitated by a controversial event that occurred in the preceding decade: **Project Camelot,** a $6 million research project funded by the U.S. Army to study the causes of civil violence in a number of countries in Asia, Latin America, Africa, and Europe. More specifically, Project Camelot was designed to gather data on counterinsurgency that would enable the U.S. Army to cope more effectively with internal revolutions in foreign countries.

The research project, which had hired the services of a number of prominent anthropologists and social scientists, was scheduled to begin its work in Latin America and later in other parts of the world. Six months after the project director was hired, however, Project Camelot was canceled by the secretary of defense. Word about this clandestine operation in Chile was brought to the attention of the Chilean senate, which reacted with outrage over the apparent U.S. interference in its internal affairs.

Although the project never really got under way, it had enormous repercussions on the social sciences in general and the discipline of anthropology in particular. The heated debate among anthropologists that followed revolved around two important questions. First, was Project Camelot a legitimately objective attempt to gather social science data, or was it a cover for the U.S. Army to intervene in the internal political affairs of a sovereign nation?

And second, were the participating anthropologists misled into thinking that scientific research was the project's sole objective, while they were really (and perhaps unwittingly) serving as undercover spies?

One of the very practical and immediate consequences of the Project Camelot controversy was the cloud of suspicion that fell over all legitimate anthropological research. For years afterward, many U.S. anthropologists experienced difficulties trying to prove that they were not engaged in secret research sponsored by the CIA or the Department of Defense. On a personal note, five years after the demise of Project Camelot in Chile, this author was questioned on several occasions by his Kikuyu informants in Kenya (who were aware of Project Camelot) about his possible links with the U.S. government.

The discipline of anthropology learned an important but costly lesson from the Project Camelot affair. That is, anthropologists have a responsibility to their subjects, their profession, their colleagues, and themselves to become much more aware of the motives, objectives, and assumptions of the organizations sponsoring their research. In other words, all anthropologists have an ethical responsibility to avoid employment or the receipt of funds from any organization that would use their research findings to support policies that are inhumane, potentially harmful to the research subjects, or in any way morally questionable. Given the nature of applied anthropology, such ethical questions are particularly relevant for the simple reason that they are more likely to present themselves.

ANTHROPOLOGISTS' MAJOR AREAS OF RESPONSIBILITY

The codes of professional ethics adopted by the AAA (revised 1998) and by the SFAA are not appreciably different. Both codes cover the major areas of responsibility for practicing anthropologists, including the following:

Responsibility to the People Studied: According to the AAA, the anthropologist's paramount responsibility is to the people he or she studies. Every effort must be made to protect the physical, psychological, and social well-being of the people under study. The aims and anticipated consequences of the research must be clearly communicated to the research subjects so that they can be in the best position to decide for themselves whether they wish to participate in the research. Participation is to be voluntary and should be based on the principle of informed consent. Informants should in no way be exploited, and their rights to remain anonymous must be protected.

Responsibility to the Public: Anthropologists have a fundamental responsibility to respect the dignity, integrity, and worth of the communities that will be directly affected by the research findings. In a more general sense, anthropologists have a responsibility to the general public to disseminate their findings truthfully and openly. They are also expected to make their findings available to the public for use in policy formation.

Responsibility to the Discipline: Anthropologists bear responsibility for maintaining the reputation of the discipline and their colleagues. They must avoid engaging in any research of which the results or sponsorship cannot be freely and openly reported. Anthropologists must refrain from any behavior that will jeopardize future research for other members of the profession.

Responsibility to Students: Anthropologists should be fair, candid, and nonexploitive when dealing with their students. They should alert students to the ethical problems of research and should acknowledge in print the contributions that students make to anthropologists' professional activities, including both research and publications.

Responsibility to Sponsors: Anthropologists have a professional responsibility to be honest about their qualifications, capabilities, and purposes. Before accepting employment or research funding, an anthropologist is obligated to reflect sincerely on the purposes of the

= *Federal legislation in the United States now requires environmental impact studies to be conducted before the building of interstate highways such as this one in Virginia. Applied anthropologists often conduct such studies to determine how certain populations will be disrupted by federally funded construction.*

sponsoring organizations and the potential uses to which the findings will be put. Anthropologists must retain the right to make all ethical decisions in their research while at the same time reporting the research findings accurately, openly, and completely.

Responsibility to One's Own and the Host Governments: Anthropologists should be honest and candid in their relationships with both their own and the host governments. They should demand assurances that they will not be asked to compromise their professional standards or ethics as a precondition for research clearance. They should not conduct clandestine research or write secret reports.

Sometimes, particularly when conducting potentially risky research, a fieldworker can be faced with conflicting ethical responsibilities. One such recent case involved Rik Scarce, an ethnographer from Washington State University who conducted a study of the radical environmental movement. Among the groups Scarce examined were Greenpeace, Earth First!, and the Animal Liberation Front (ALF). A year after the publication of his findings, one of the groups studied, the ALF, raided a federally funded animal research laboratory at Washington State University. Because some of the defendants in the case had been the ethnographer's informants, Scarce was subpoenaed before the grand jury to testify against the ALF defendants. Even though the above ethical guidelines call for dealing honestly with governmental officials, to do so in this case would have violated another ethical principle—that is, protecting the confidentiality of one's sources of information. Scarce argued before the court that if coerced to testify against his research subjects, he would be violating his own promise and obligation to maintain their anonymity. He further argued that to testify would jeopardize his own career as a social scientist because future research subjects would refuse to talk to him, and academic/research institutions would be reluctant to hire him as he would be considered an unethical researcher. Clearly, Scarce found himself at the horns of an ethical dilemma. Scarce's eventual choice not to violate the confidence of his research subjects resulted in his being jailed for 159 days for contempt of court. This case dramatically illustrates that field ethnographers in the United States have little legal protection in maintaining the confidentiality of their sources.

SUMMARY

1. Traditionally, many anthropologists have distinguished between pure anthropology (aimed at refining the discipline's theory, methods, and data) and applied anthropology (focusing on using anthropological insights toward the solution of practical social problems).

2. World War II provided vast opportunities for anthropologists to turn their efforts to applied projects relating to the war. The postwar boom in higher education lured many anthropologists back into academic positions during the 1950s and 1960s. But the subsequent decline in academic positions for anthropologists since the 1970s has resulted in an increase in applied types of employment outside academia and museums.

3. Cultural anthropology can make a number of unique contributions as a policy science. For example, anthropologists bring to a research setting their skills as participant-observers, the capacity to view sociocultural phenomena from a holistic perspective, their regional expertise, a willingness to see the world from the perspective of the local people (emic view), and the value orientation of cultural relativism.

4. Applied anthropologists work in a wide range of settings, both at home and abroad. Moreover, they play a number of specialized roles including policy researcher, impact assessor, expert witness, trainer, planner, and cultural broker.

5. Cultural anthropologists in general—but particularly applied anthropologists—face a number of ethical problems when conducting their research. One very important ethical issue to which applied anthropologists must be sensitive is whether the people being studied will benefit from the proposed changes. Both the American Anthropological Association and the Society for Applied Anthropology have identified areas of ethical responsibility for practicing anthropologists, including responsibilities to the people under study, the local communities, the host governments and their own government, other members of the scholarly community, organizations that sponsor research, and their own students.

KEY TERMS

applied anthropology	participant-observation
emic view	problem-oriented research
etic view	Project Camelot
forensic anthropology	

SUGGESTED READINGS

Ahmed, Akbar, and Cris Shore. *The Future of Anthropology: Its Relevance to the Contemporary World.* London: Athione, 1995. This collection of 12 articles explores the relevance of anthropology to the modern world by focusing on such key issues as HIV/AIDS research, tourism, aging, overseas development, and ethnic cleansing in the former Yugoslavia.

Bodley, John H. *Anthropology and Contemporary Human Problems.* Palo Alto, CA: Mayfield, 1984. Bodley argues that many of the problems facing the world today—overconsumption, resource depletion, hunger and starvation, overpopulation, violence, and war—are inherent in the basic cultural patterns of modern industrial civilization.

Crewe, Emma, and Elizabeth Harrison. *Whose Development?: An Ethnography of Aid.* London: Zed Books, 1999. A thoughtful ethnography of foreign aid programs showing the flawed assumptions in the minds of developers concerning progress, technology, race, and gender.

Eddy, Elizabeth, and W. Partridge, eds. *Applied Anthropology in America.* 2d ed. New York: Columbia University Press, 1987. A collection of essays by noted applied anthropologists on various aspects of applying anthropology to American society. The introductory essay by the editors is a particularly good discussion of the development of applied anthropology in the United States.

Ferraro, Gary. *Applying Cultural Anthropology: Readings.* Belmont, CA: Wadsworth, 1998. A collection of 39 articles illustrating how anthropological insights have been applied to the solution of problems in the areas of medicine, business, education, government and law, and economic development.

Van Willigen, John. *Applied Anthropology: An Introduction.* 2d ed. South Hadley, MA: Bergin & Garvey, 1993. An excellent introduction to the growing field of applied anthropology for students contemplating a nonacademic career in anthropology. Topics covered include the history of applied anthropology, various intervention strategies, ethical issues, and the role of applied anthropologists in evaluation research.

Wulff, Robert, and Shirley Fiske, eds. *Anthropological Praxis: Translating Knowledge into Action.* Boulder, CO: Westview Press, 1987. A collection of writings by applied anthropologists especially for this volume on how they applied their trade to the solution of specific societal problems. Dealing with cases from both home and abroad, all of the case studies are written in the same format and discuss how anthropologists make a difference.

On the Net

More and more anthropologists are conducting research that is applied in nature. This book tries to expose students to some of the more important applied research, but it touches on only a small percentage of the total. A leading journal in the field of applied anthropology is called *Human Organization* and is published by the Society for Applied Anthropology.

1. Go to the web site of the Society for Applied Anthropology by doing a subject search on any major search engine or by using the URL for the society:

http://www.sfaa.net/

Once there, click on "Publications" and then "Human Organization," which is the society's major professional journal containing scholarly articles on applied anthropology. This file contains summaries (abstracts) of recent and forthcoming research in applied anthropology. Browse the sections on forthcoming issues and recent and back issues. Read over the first 20 research summaries. Make a list of the range of social problems that have been addressed in these applied studies.

2. If you are interested in reading the original statement on ethics drafted by the American Anthropological Association and the Society for Applied Anthropology, you can find them on the Internet at:

http://www.aaanet.org/ethcode.htm

http://www.sfaa.net/sfaaethic.html

 LOG ON TO INFOTRAC COLLEGE EDITION to learn about business anthropologists, those applied anthropologists who serve as consultants to or who work for various business firms. Use the PowerTrac search with "business anthropology" as the key word index. Then write a one-page paper on ways that applied anthropologists are contributing to the world of business—through marketing, managing, human resources, and so on.

Chapter Four

THE GROWTH OF ANTHROPOLOGICAL THEORY

Masai Moran (warriors) from Central Kenya.

WHAT WE WILL LEARN:

▼

Who have been the important theorists in cultural anthropology since the mid-nineteenth century?

▼

What theories have anthropologists used to explain cultural differences and similarities among the people of the world?

▼

How can anthropological data be used to make large-scale comparisons among cultures?

▼

As anthropologists started to accumulate data on different cultures beginning in the mid-nineteenth century, they needed to be able to explain the

cultural differences and similarities they found. This desire to account for the vast cultural variations gave rise to anthropological theories. A **theory** is a statement that suggests a relationship among phenomena. Theories enable us to reduce reality into an abstract set of principles. These principles then allow us to make sense out of a variety of ethnographic information from different parts of the world. A good theory is one that can both explain and predict. In other words, theories as models of reality enable us to bring some measure of order to a complex world.

Even when theories remain unproven, they are useful for research, for they can generate **hypotheses** (unproven propositions that can provide a basis for further investigation) to be tested in an empirical research investigation. In testing a hypothesis, it is possible to determine how close the actual findings are to the expected findings. If what is found is consistent with what was expected, the theory will be strengthened; if not, the theory will probably be revised or abandoned. Anthropological theory changes constantly as new data come forth.

Anthropological theories attempt to answer such questions as, Why do people behave as they do? and, How do we account for human diversity? These questions guided the early nineteenth-century attempts to theorize and continue to be relevant today. We will explore—in roughly chronological order—the major theoretical schools of cultural anthropology that have developed since the mid-nineteenth century. Some of the earlier theoretical orientations (such as diffusionism) no longer attract much attention; others (such as evolutionism) have been refined and reworked into something new; and still others (such as functionalism) continue to command some popularity. It is easy, in hindsight, to demonstrate the inherent flaws in some of the early theoretical orientations. We should keep in mind, however, that contemporary anthropologi-

cal theories that may appear plausible today were built on what we learned from those older theories.

•■ EVOLUTIONISM ■•

TRYING TO ACCOUNT for the vast diversity in human cultures, the first group of early anthropologists, writing during the mid-nineteenth century, suggested the theory of cultural **evolutionism.** The basic premise of these early anthropological theorists was that all societies pass through a series of distinct evolutionary stages. We find differences in contemporary cultures because they are at different evolutionary stages of development. According to this theory, developed by Edward Tylor in England and Lewis Henry Morgan in the United States, Euro-American cultures were at the top of the evolutionary ladder and "less developed" cultures occupied the lower stages. The evolutionary process was thought to progress from simpler (lower) forms to increasingly more complex (higher) forms of culture. Thus, the "primitive" societies occupying the lower echelons of the evolutionary ladder need only wait an indeterminable length of time before eventually (and inevitably) rising to the top. It was assumed that all cultures pass through the same set of preordained evolutionary stages.

Even though this threefold evolutionary scheme appears terribly ethnocentric by today's standards, we must remember that it replaced the prevailing theory that explained the existence of small-scale, preliterate societies by claiming that they were people whose ancestors had fallen from grace. Hunters and gatherers, it had been argued previously, possessed simple levels of technology because their degeneration had made them intellectually inferior to peoples with more technological sophistication.

While Tylor (1832–1917) was writing in England, Morgan (1818–1881) was founding the evolutionary school in

= *Lewis Henry Morgan, a nineteenth-century evolutionist, held that all societies pass through certain distinctive evolutionary stages.*

the United States. A lawyer in Rochester, New York, Morgan was hired to represent the neighboring Iroquois Indians in a land grant dispute. After the lawsuit was resolved, Morgan conducted an ethnographic study of the Seneca Indians (one of the Iroquois group). Fascinated by the Senecas' matrilineal kinship system, Morgan circulated questionnaires and traveled fairly extensively around the United States gathering information about kinship systems among North American Indians and elsewhere in the world. This kinship research—which some have suggested may be Morgan's most enduring contribution to the comparative study of culture—was published in *Systems of Consanguinity and Affinity* in 1871.

Representing the American branch of the evolutionist school, Morgan wrote his famous book, *Ancient Society,* published in 1877. In keeping with the general tenor of the times, he developed a system of classifying cultures to determine their evolutionary niche. Morgan, like Tylor, used the categories of **savagery, barbarism,** and **civilization** but was more specific in defining them according to the presence or absence of certain technological features. Moreover, Morgan subdivided the stages of savagery and barbarism into three distinct subcategories: lower, middle,

and upper. Morgan defined these seven evolutionary stages—through which all societies allegedly passed—in the following way:

1. *Lower savagery:* From the earliest forms of humanity subsisting on fruits and nuts.
2. *Middle savagery:* Began with the discovery of fishing technology and the use of fire.
3. *Upper savagery:* Began with the invention of the bow and arrow.
4. *Lower barbarism:* Began with the art of pottery making.
5. *Middle barbarism:* Began with the domestication of plants and animals in the Old World and irrigation cultivation in the New World.
6. *Upper barbarism:* Began with the smelting of iron and use of iron tools.
7. *Civilization:* Began with the invention of the phonetic alphabet and writing. (1877:12)

The theories of early evolutionists Tylor and Morgan have been criticized by succeeding generations of anthropologists. Nineteenth-century evolutionists have been charged with being ethnocentric, for they concluded that Western societies represented the highest levels of human achievement. They have also been criticized for being armchair speculators, putting forth grand schemes to explain cultural diversity based on fragmentary data at best. Although there is considerable substance to these criticisms, we must evaluate the nineteenth-century evolutionists with an eye toward the times in which they were writing. As David Kaplan and Robert Manners (1986:39–43) remind us, Tylor and Morgan may have overstated their case somewhat because they were trying to establish what Tylor called "the science of culture," whereby human behavior was explained in terms of secular evolutionary processes rather than supernatural causes. In defense of Tylor and Morgan, we should acknowledge that they firmly established the notion, on which modern cultural anthropology now rests, that differences in human lifestyles are the result of certain identifiable cultural processes rather than biological processes or divine intervention. Moreover, Morgan's use of techno-economic factors to distinguish between fundamentally different types of cultures remains a viable concept.

EVOLUTIONISM IN BRIEF

▶ All cultures pass through the same developmental stages in the same order.

APPLIED PERSPECTIVE
Trees for Haiti

The Agroforestry Outreach Project (AOP), a reforestation program in Haiti, is an excellent example of how cultural anthropology can contribute to a multimillion-dollar development project (see Murray 1984, 1986, 1987). Rapid population growth, coupled with rapid urbanization, had created high market demands in Haiti for construction wood and charcoal. The cash-poor Haitian farmers have willingly met this demand by cutting down large numbers of trees (estimated at approximately 50 million trees per year). The effect of this deforestation on the long-term health of the nation's economy has been devastating, for it not only denuded the country of trees but also significantly lowered agricultural productivity through soil erosion.

Faced with this rapid deforestation, the U.S. Agency for International Development (USAID) hired Gerald Murray, an anthropologist who had conducted research on land tenure and population growth in Haiti, to direct a reforestation program. Previous reforestation projects in Haiti (and in other parts of the world) took a conservationist approach, whereby peasants were rewarded for planting trees and penalized in certain ways for cutting them down. Moreover, whatever trees were planted were defined as belonging to the general public. The peasants, in other words, had no particular ownership of the trees. Murray, however, took a very unorthodox approach by suggesting that farmers be given seedlings to plant on a cash-crop basis. Wood trees, in other words, were meant to be harvested and sold in much the same way as corn or beans. Murray based this radical (some might say heretical) assumption on previous ethnographic research that Haitian farmers are aggressive cash-croppers. Murray wanted to capitalize on this strong tradition of crop marketing by making wood trees just one more crop to be sold or traded.

Anthropologist Murray had three formidable barriers to overcome: He had to convince local farmers that the seedlings could mature in four years' time, that it was feasible to plant trees along with their food crops, and that whatever trees they grew on their land did, in fact, belong to them. Once he had convinced an initial group to participate in the tree planting program, Murray's project met with unprecedented success. The project, which lasted from

- ▶ Evolution is unidirectional and leads to higher (better) levels of culture.
- ▶ A deductive approach is used to apply general theories to specific cases.
- ▶ Evolutionism was ethnocentric because evolutionists put their own societies at the top.

▪▶ DIFFUSIONISM ▪▶

DURING THE LATE NINETEENTH and early twentieth centuries, the diffusionists, like the evolutionists, addressed the question of cultural differences in the world. They came up with a radically different answer to that

1981 to 1985, had set for itself the goal of having 6,000 farmers plant 3 million trees. When the project ended, some 20 million trees had been planted by 75,000 farmers! This reforestation project in Haiti was significant in that it not only drew heavily on anthropological insights but also was implemented and directed by an anthropologist. Anthropological data played an important role in the success of the project. That is, an understanding of the highly individualistic land tenure system of Haitian farmers, as well as their entrepreneurial nature, led to the decision to design a program based on a more free enterprise (cash-cropping) basis.

The project design was also directly affected by anthropological *theory*. Murray admits that his ideas about tree planting were heavily influenced by cultural evolutionary theories. Cultural evolutionists remind us that for the overwhelming majority of prehistory, humans, who were hunters and gatherers, faced food shortages. If hunters and gatherers became too efficient in exploiting their environments, they would eventually destroy their sources of food (wild plants and animals). The cultural evolutionists also remind us that this age-old problem of food shortages was not solved eventually by a conservationist's approach to the problem but rather by domesticating plants and animals. In other words, a quantum leap in the world's food supplies occurred when people began to produce food (around 10,000 years ago) rather than rely on what nature had to offer.

Murray saw the connections between tree planting in Haiti and the evolutionary theory of the origins of agriculture. He rejected the conservationist approach, which would have called for raising the consciousness of peasant farmers about the ecological need for conserving trees. Instead, he reasoned that trees will reemerge in Haiti when people start planting them as a harvestable crop, in much the same way that food supplies were dramatically increased when people started planting and harvesting food crops. Thus, the theory of plant domestication—arising from the anthropological study of the beginnings of agriculture—held the key to the solution of Haiti's tree problem.

QUESTIONS FOR FURTHER THOUGHT

1. How did an anthropologist contribute to the huge success of the reforestation project in Haiti?
2. What difficulties would the project have encountered if it had used a conservationist approach?
3. What applied anthropology role (discussed in the previous chapter) did Murray play?

question. Evolutionism may have overestimated human inventiveness by claiming that cultural features have arisen in different parts of the world independently of one another, due in large measure to the **psychic unity** of humankind. At the other extreme, **diffusionism** held that humans were essentially uninventive. According to the diffusionists, certain cultural features were invented originally in one or several parts of the world and then spread, through the process of diffusion, to other cultures.

Represented by Grafton Elliot Smith and W. J. Perry in England and Fritz Graebner and Wilhelm Schmidt in Germany and Austria, the diffusionists eventually ran their course by the early part of the twentieth century. To be certain, they started with a particularly sound anthropological concept—that is, cultural diffusion—and either took it to its illogical extreme or left too many questions unanswered. Few cultural anthropologists today would deny the central role that diffusion plays in the process of culture change, but some of the early diffusionists, particularly Smith and Perry, took this essentially valid concept ad absurdum by suggesting that everything found in the world could ultimately be traced back to the early Egyptians. Moreover, even though they collected considerable historical data, the diffusionists were not able to prove primary centers of invention. Nor were the diffusionists able to answer a number of important questions concerning the process of cultural diffusion. For example, when cultures come into contact with one another, what accounts for the diffusion of some cultural items but not others? What are the conditions required to bring about diffusion of a cultural item? What determines the rate at which a cultural item spreads throughout a geographic region? Furthermore, diffusionists failed to even raise some questions, such as why certain traits arise in the first place. Despite these limitations, however, the diffusionists made a major contribution to the study of comparative cultures: They were the first to point out the need to develop theories dealing with contact and interaction among cultures.

As we have seen, the nineteenth-century evolutionists and diffusionists tried to explain why the world was inhabited by large numbers of highly diverse cultures. The evolutionists invoked the principle of evolution as the major explanatory variable. Thus, according to Tylor and Morgan, the world's cultural diversity resulted from different cultures being at different stages of evolutionary development. The diffusionists proposed a different causal variable to explain the diversity, namely differential levels of cultural borrowing among societies. Even though these nineteenth-century schools offered different explanations for the diversity, they both took a **deductive** approach to the discipline (reasoning from the general to the specific). They started off with a general principle (either evolution or diffusion) and then used that principle to explain specific cases. The evolutionists and diffusionists based their theories on inadequate data at best. They seemed to be more interested in universal history than in discovering how different people of the world actually lived their lives. This type of genteel armchair speculation was poignantly illustrated by evolutionist Sir James Frazer, who, when asked if he had ever seen any of the people about whom he had written, replied, "God forbid!" (Beattie 1964:7).

DIFFUSIONISM IN BRIEF

▶ All societies change as a result of cultural borrowing from one another.
▶ A deductive approach is used by applying general theories to explain specific cases.
▶ The theory overemphasized the essentially valid idea of diffusion.

•◼ AMERICAN HISTORICISM ◼•

AROUND THE TURN of the century, **American historicism,** which was a reaction to this deductive approach, began, led primarily by Franz Boas (1858–1942). Coming from an academic background in physics and geography, Boas was appalled by what he saw as speculative theorizing masquerading as science. To Boas's way of thinking, anthropology was on the wrong path. Rather than dreaming up large, all-encompassing theories to explain why particular societies are the way they are, Boas wanted to turn the discipline 180 degrees by putting it on a sound **inductive** footing. That is, Boas wanted to start by collecting specific data and then move on to develop general theories. Boas felt that the enormous complexity of factors influencing the development of specific cultures rendered any type of sweeping generalization, such as those proposed by the evolutionists and diffusionists, totally inappropriate. Thus, Boas and his followers insisted on the collection of detailed ethnographic information and at the same time called for a moratorium on theorizing.

Some of Boas's more severe critics claimed that this antitheoretical stance was responsible for retarding the discipline of anthropology as a science. Yet, in retrospect, most commentators would agree that his experience in the areas of physics and mathematics enabled Boas to bring to the young discipline of anthropology both methodological rigor and a sense of how to define problems in scientific terms. Even though Boas himself did little theorizing, he did leave the discipline on a sound empirical footing.

The impact Boas had on anthropology is perhaps most eloquently demonstrated by the long list of anthropologists he trained. As the first anthropological guru in the United States, Boas trained virtually the entire first generation of American anthropologists. The list of Boas's students reads like a *Who's Who in Twentieth-Century U.S. Anthropology*: Margaret Mead, Robert Lowie, Alfred Kroeber, Edward Sapir, Melville J. Herskovits, Ruth Benedict, Paul Radin, Jules Henry, E. Adamson Hoebel, and Ruth Bunzel.

■ *Franz Boaz, the teacher of the first generation of cultural anthropologists in the United States, put the discipline on a firm empirical basis.*

In recruiting graduate students to study anthropology with him at Columbia University, Boas from the beginning was very purposeful about attracting women into the discipline. Recognizing that male fieldworkers would be excluded from observing certain aspects of a culture by virtue of their gender, Boas felt that the discipline needed both male and female ethnographers if all of a culture was to be described. Today, compared to other academic disciplines, the discipline of anthropology has a high number of women professionals, a legacy that can be traced back to Boas's methodological concerns when the discipline was in its formative period. Moreover, among other contributions to the fledgling discipline of anthropology, Boas took a strong stance against racism, and in fact, many of his antiracist ideas are still relevant today.

AMERICAN HISTORICISM IN BRIEF

- ▶ Collection of ethnographic facts must precede development of cultural theories (induction).
- ▶ Any culture is partially composed of traits diffused from other cultures.

- ▶ Direct fieldwork is absolutely essential.
- ▶ Each culture is, to some degree, unique.
- ▶ Ethnographers should try to get the view of those being studied, not their own view.

▪ FUNCTIONALISM ▪

WHILE FRANZ BOAS was putting anthropology on a more empirical footing in the United States, Bronislav Malinowski (1884–1942) was proceeding inductively by establishing a tradition of firsthand data collection in the United Kingdom. Like Boas, Malinowski was a strong advocate of fieldwork. Both men insisted on learning the local language and trying to understand a culture from the perspective of the native. They differed, however, in that Malinowski had no interest in asking how a cultural item got to be the way it is. Believing that little could be learned about the origins of small-scale societies, Malinowski concentrated on how contemporary cultures operated or functioned. This theoretical orientation, known as **functionalism,** assumed that cultures provided various means for satisfying both societal and individual needs. According to Malinowski, no matter how bizarre a cultural item might at first appear, it had a meaning and performed some useful function for the well-being of the individual or the society. The job of the fieldworker is to become sufficiently immersed in the culture and language to be able to identify these functions.

Not only do all aspects of a culture have a function, but, according to Malinowski, they are also related to one another. This functionalist tenet is no better illustrated than in Malinowski's own description of the kula ring, a system of trade found among the Trobriand Islanders (see Chapter 8). The kula not only performs the function of distributing goods within the society but is related to many other areas of Trobriand culture, including political structure, magic, technology, kinship, social status, myth, and social control. To illustrate, the kula involves the exchange of both ceremonial necklaces and bracelets and everyday commodities between trading partners on a large number of islands. Even though the exchanges are based on the principle of reciprocity, usually long periods of time elapse between repayments between trading partners. Alvin Gouldner (1960:174) has suggested that during these periods debtors are morally obligated to maintain peaceful relationships with their benefactors. If this is the case, we can see how the kula ring maintains peace and thereby functions as a mechanism of social control as well as a mechanism of material exchange. Thus, by examining a cultural

CROSS-CULTURAL MISCUE

THE EVOLUTIONISTS of the nineteenth century have been criticized for their assumption that all human societies go through the same set of evolutionary stages because of their basic "psychic unity." Ethnographic research during the twentieth century, however, has demonstrated that people from different cultures have very different ways of conceptualizing and making sense of the world around them. And, these different ways of ordering the world can sometimes lead to cross-cultural misunderstandings.

Dena Lassiter, a purchaser of ladies' apparel for a major U.S. department store, had just taken over the overseas accounts. Anxious to make a good impression on her European counterparts, Lassiter worked long, hard hours to provide information needed to close purchasing contracts in a timely manner. On May 1, Stefan, one of her Dutch associates in Amsterdam, sent an urgent message requiring information before the close of day on 6/5/97.

Although she thought it odd for the message to be marked "urgent" for information needed over a month away, Lassiter squeezed the request into her already busy schedule. She was pleased when she had pulled together the information and was able to fax it by May 10, three full weeks before the deadline. Pleased with herself, she placed a telephone call to Stefan to make sure that he had received the fax and was met with a hostile response. The department store not only lost the order at the agreed-upon cost, but the Dutch office asked that Lassiter be removed from their account.

Where did Lassiter go wrong? In most of Europe, when people write the date as 6/5/97, they are placing the day first, month second, and year last. So Stefan's request for information on 6/5 was not for June 5 but for May 6. Therefore, Lassiter was not three weeks early but five days late!

---

feature (such as the kula ring) in greater depth, the ethnographer, according to this functionalist perspective, will begin to see how it is related to many other aspects of the culture and what it contributes to both individuals and society as a whole.

Another form of functionalism was developed by the British anthropologist Alfred Reginald Radcliffe-Brown (1881–1955). Like Malinowski, Radcliffe-Brown held that the various aspects of a society should be studied in terms of the functions they perform. Whereas Malinowski viewed functions mostly as meeting the needs of the *individual,* Radcliffe-Brown saw them in terms of how they contributed to the well-being of the *society.* Because of this emphasis on social functions rather than individual functions, Radcliffe-Brown's theory has taken the name **structural functionalism.**

The functionalist approach, most closely associated with Malinowski and Radcliffe-Brown, is based on two fundamental principles. First, the notion of **universal functions** holds that every part of a culture has a function.

For example, the function of a hammer is to drive nails into wood, the function of a belief in an omnipotent god is to control people's behavior, and the function of shaking hands in the United States is to communicate nonverbally one's intentions to be friendly. The second principle, known as **functional unity,** states that a culture is an integrated whole composed of a number of interrelated parts. As a corollary to this second principle, it follows that if the parts of a culture are interconnected, then a change in one part of the culture is likely to result in changes in other parts.

Once functionalism was accepted into the discipline of anthropology, it appears that the functionalist anthropologists were distracted from reevaluating and revising their theory by the overwhelming demands of ethnographic field research. Even though anthropologists such as Malinowski and Radcliffe-Brown fought vigorously for the acceptance of the functionalist approach, the most effective revisions of functionalist theory have come from sociologists, most notably Robert Merton. For example, in his

The automobile is dysfunctional for society in some respects because it contributes to traffic congestion, air pollution, and respiratory diseases.

influential book *Social Theory and Social Structure* (1957), Merton suggests that although every cultural item *may* have a function, it is premature to assume that every item *must* have a function. As a result, Merton proposed the notion of **dysfunction,** which tends to cause stress or imbalance in a cultural system. According to Merton, whether a cultural trait is functional or dysfunctional can be resolved only by empirical research.

In addition, Merton took issue with Malinowski and Radcliffe-Brown's notion of functional unity. Though fully recognizing that all societies have some degree of functional integration, he could not accept the very high degree of interconnectedness suggested by the early British functionalists. Merton's more moderate views on the issue of functional unity are, at least in part, the result of his being a sociologist. Merton warns against applying these extreme functionalist assumptions (which may be more valid for small-scale, undifferentiated societies that anthropologists tend to study) to the large, complex societies that are most often studied by sociologists.

Functionalism in brief

- ▶ Through direct fieldwork, anthropologists seek to understand how the parts of contemporary cultures work for the well-being of the individual and the society.
- ▶ Society is like a biological organism with all of the parts interconnected.

- ▶ With this high level of integration, societies tend to be in a state of equilibrium; a change in one part of the system brings change in other parts.
- ▶ Empirical fieldwork is absolutely essential.
- ▶ The existing institutional structure of any society contains indispensable functions without which the society could not continue.

▪ PSYCHOLOGICAL ANTHROPOLOGY ▪

AS EARLY AS the 1920s and 1930s, some American anthropologists became interested in the relationship between culture and the individual. Radcliffe-Brown, warning against what he called psychological reductionism, looked almost exclusively to social structure for his explanations of human behavior. A number of Boas's students, however, were asking some theoretically powerful questions: What part do personality variables play in human behavior? Should personality be viewed as a part of the cultural system? If personality variables are part of culture, how are they causally related to the rest of the system? Wanting to relate some of the insights of Gestalt and Freudian psychology to the study of culture, the early psychological anthropologists looked at child-rearing practices and personality from a cross-cultural perspective. They held that child-rearing practices (which are an integral part of a culture) help shape the personality structure of the individual, which in turn influences the culture. Thus, they saw an interactive relationship between child-rearing practices, personality structure, and culture.

Although best known for his linguistic research, Edward Sapir (1884–1934) was very interested in the area of culture and personality. Individuals learn their cultural patterns unconsciously, Sapir suggested, in much the same way that they learn their language. Rejecting the notion that culture exists above the individual, Sapir believed that the true locus of culture was in the interaction of individuals. Even though Sapir did no direct fieldwork himself in this area of culture and personality, his writings and lectures stimulated interest in others, most notably Ruth Benedict and Margaret Mead. **Psychological anthropology,** which studies the relationship between culture and personality, would be interested in the question, How do the TV-watching habits of U.S. children affect children's personality structures, and how do these personality structures, in turn, affect other parts of the culture?

Margaret Mead (1901–1978), a student of both Benedict and Boas, was one of the earliest and most prolific writers in the field of culture and personality. After completing her graduate training under Boas at Columbia University, Mead became fascinated with the general topic of the emotional disruption that seemed to accompany adolescence in the United States. Psychologists at the time maintained that the stress and emotional problems found among American adolescents were a biological fact of life and occurred at puberty in all societies. But Mead wanted to know whether this emotional turbulence was the result of being an adolescent or of being an adolescent in the United States. In 1925 she left for Samoa to try to determine whether the strains of adolescence were universal (that is, biologically based) or varied from one culture to another. In her first book, *Coming of Age in Samoa* (1928), Mead reported that the permissive family structure and relaxed sexual patterns among Samoans were responsible for a calm adolescence. Thus, she concluded that the emotional turbulence found among adolescents in the United States was culturally rather than biologically based.

From the turbulence of adolescence, Mead next turned to the question of gender roles. Based on her research among the Arapesh, Tchambuli, and Mundugumor of New Guinea, she attempted to demonstrate that there were no universal temperaments that were exclusively masculine or feminine. More specifically, Mead reported that among the Arapesh, both men and women had what Westerners would consider feminine temperaments (that is, nurturing, cooperative, nonaggressive, maternal); both Mundugumor men and women displayed exactly the opposite traits (that is, ruthless, aggressive, violent demeanors), whereas among the Tchambuli there was a complete reversal of the male–female temperaments found in North American culture. Based on these findings, Mead concluded in her *Sex and Temperament in Three Primitive Societies* (1935) that our own Western conception of masculine and feminine are not sex-linked but rather is culturally determined.

Mead's formulations have been criticized on the basis of both accuracy and methodology. Being more qualitative than quantitative, Mead's research has been questioned in terms of such issues as sampling, controls, and experimental design. Despite these criticisms, however, Mead's major contribution to anthropological theory was her demonstration of the importance of cultural rather than biological

= *Psychological anthropologists would be interested in such questions as how the television-watching habits of U.S. children affect the children's personality structures and how these personality structures, in turn, affect other parts of the culture.*

= *Margaret Mead devoted much of her long and distinguished career in anthropology to the study of how culture affects the process of growing up.*

conditioning. Moreover, she popularized the discipline of cultural anthropology and served as a pioneer for many women who subsequently became anthropologists.

Psychological Anthropology in Brief

▶ Anthropologists need to explore the relationships between psychological and cultural variables.

▶ Personality is largely the result of cultural learning.

▶ Universal temperaments associated with males and females do not exist.

•■ Neoevolutionism ■•

AS WE HAVE SEEN, Franz Boas and others were extremely critical of the nineteenth-century evolutionists, in part because they were accustomed to making sweeping generalizations based on inadequate data. Despite the criticisms, however, no one, including Boas himself, was able to demonstrate that cultures do not develop or evolve in certain ways over time.

As early as the 1930s, Leslie White (1900–1975), a cultural anthropologist trained in the Boasian tradition, resurrected the theories of the nineteenth-century evolutionists. It was White's position that Tylor and Morgan had developed a useful theory. Their major shortcoming was that they lacked the data to demonstrate it. Like Tylor and Morgan, White believed that cultures evolve from simple to increasingly more complex forms and that cultural evolution is as real as biological evolution. White's unique contribution was to suggest the cause (or driving force) of evolution, which he called his "basic law of evolution." According to White (1959:368–369), "Culture evolves as the amount of energy harnessed per capita per year increases or as the efficiency of the means of putting energy to work is increased."

According to White's **neoevolutionism,** culture evolves when people are able to increase the amount of energy under their control. For most of human prehistory, while people were hunters and gatherers, the major source of energy was human power. But with the invention of agriculture, animal domestication, the steam engine, the internal combustion engine, and nuclear power, humans have been able to dramatically increase the levels of energy at their disposal. To illustrate, the daily average energy output for a healthy man is a small fraction of a horsepower per day; the amount of energy produced from a kilo of uranium in a nuclear reactor is approximately 33 billion horsepower! For White, the significant equation was $C = E \times T$, where C is culture, E is energy, and T is technology. Cultural evolution, in other words, is caused by advancing levels of technology and a culture's increasing capacity to "capture energy."

Another anthropologist who rejected the particularist orientation of Franz Boas in the mid-twentieth century was Julian Steward. Like White, Steward was interested in the relationship between cultural evolution and adaptation to the environment. But White's approach—which focused on the whole of human culture—was far too general for Steward. Even though Steward rejected Boasian particularism, he was equally unaccepting of approaches that were overly abstract. The main problem with White's theory is that it cannot explain why some cultures evolve by "capturing energy" whereas others do not. One way of characterizing the difference between these two prominent neoevolutionists is that White was interested in the broad concept of culture and Steward was more interested in developing propositions about specific cultures or groups of cultures.

Steward distinguished among three different types of evolutionary thought. First, there was **unilinear evolution** (Tylor and Morgan), which attempted to place particular cultures into certain evolutionary stages. Second, Steward called White's approach **universal evolution** because it is concerned with developing laws that apply to culture as a whole. In contrast to these two earlier forms of evolutionism, Steward called his own form **multilinear evolution**, which focuses on the evolution of specific cultures without assuming that all cultures follow the same evolutionary process.

Steward held that by examining sequences of change in different parts of the world, it would be possible to identify paths of development and some limited causal principles that would hold true for a number of societies. To test out his formulation, Steward selected areas of the world that had produced complex societies (civilizations), such as Egypt and the Middle East in the Old World and Mexico and Peru in the New World. In all of these cases, Steward tried to show certain recurring developmental sequences from earliest agriculture up through large, complex urbanized social systems. For example, in all of these instances, people were faced with dry environments that required them to develop some methods of irrigation to obtain water for their fields.

Steward's approach was based on analysis of the interaction between culture and environment. He argued that people who face similar environmental challenges (such as arid or semiarid conditions) are likely to develop similar technological solutions, which, in turn, lead to the parallel development of social and political institutions. Even though environment is a key variable in Steward's theory, he was not an environmental determinist, for he recognized the variety of human responses to similar environmental conditions. By focusing on the relationship among people, environment, and culture, Steward was the first and leading proponent of the study of **cultural ecology.**

Neoevolutionism in Brief

▶ Cultures evolve in direct proportion to their capacity to harness energy.

▶ Culture is shaped by environmental conditions.

▶ Through culture, human populations continuously adapt to techno-environmental conditions.

▶ Because technological and environmental factors shape culture, individual (personality) factors are de-emphasized.

= *According to the neoevolutionist theory of Leslie White, a society that produces nuclear power has reached an advanced stage of cultural evolution.*

▪ FRENCH STRUCTURALISM ▪

NO SINGLE THEORETICAL ORIENTATION is as closely associated with a single person as **French structuralism** is associated with Claude Lévi-Strauss (1908–). Although both Radcliffe-Brown and Lévi-Strauss are called structuralists, their approaches to cultural analysis are vastly different. Whereas Radcliffe-Brown focused on identifying how the parts of a society function as a systematic whole, Lévi-Strauss concentrates on identifying the mental structures that undergird social behavior. For Lévi-Strauss, ethnology tends to be more psychological or cognitive than sociological.

The approach taken by Lévi-Strauss draws heavily on the science of linguistics. After assuming for decades that language is purely a learned response, many linguists in recent years have hypothesized that basic grammatical structures are preprogrammed in the human mind. Likewise, Lévi-Strauss argues that certain codes programmed into the human mind are responsible for shaping cultures. Cultural differences occur, according to Lévi-Strauss, because these inherent mental codes are altered by environment and history. Although recognizing these surface differences, Lévi-Strauss suggests that in the final analysis the mental structure of all humans is essentially the same. Although the content of a cultural element may vary from one society to another, the structure of these elements is limited by the very nature of the human mind. In essence,

Lévi-Strauss has reintroduced his own version of the psychic unity of humankind.

One of the basic tenets of the human mind for Lévi-Strauss is that it is programmed to think in **binary oppositions,** or opposites. All people have a tendency to think in terms of such opposites as male–female, hot–cold, old–young, night–day, right–left, and us–them. It is these dichotomies that give shape to culture. Consider, for example, Lévi-Strauss's interpretation of totemism, a belief system found in many parts of the world that states a relationship between social groupings (such as clans or lineages) and aspects of the natural world (such as plants or animals). Lévi-Strauss suggests that totemic beliefs are complex mental devices that enable people to classify the units of their culture and relate them to the natural world.

Lévi-Strauss's structuralism has been criticized for being overly abstract. Because his theories, often brilliantly creative, are not susceptible to empirical testing, many anthropologists have rejected them. Even though French structuralism does not appeal to the more empirically oriented anthropologists, Lévi-Strauss has made a major contribution by directing our attention to the relationship between culture and cognition. Moreover, he has focused on the grand questions that anthropologists, in their twentieth-century quest for specialization, have largely abandoned: How does the human mind work? Even with the world's vast cultural variations, is there a psychic unity for all of humankind? In all likelihood, Lévi-Strauss will be remembered not for developing theories that will help explain the real world but rather for prodding other researchers to generate more imaginative hypotheses, which can then be tested through empirical research.

FRENCH STRUCTURALISM IN BRIEF

▶ Human cultures are shaped by certain preprogrammed codes of the human mind.
▶ Theory focuses on the underlying principles that generate behavior rather than the observable empirical behavior itself.
▶ Theory emphasizes repetitive structures rather than sociocultural change.
▶ Rather than examining attitudes, values, and beliefs, structural anthropologists concentrate on the unconscious level.
▶ It is assumed that the human mind categorizes phenomena in terms of binary oppositions.

▪ ETHNOSCIENCE ▪

THE THEORETICAL APPROACH of Lévi-Strauss is similar in several significant respects to that of the ethnoscientists, a small but vocal group of American cultural anthropologists who gained fleeting recognition during the 1950s and 1960s. For example, both approaches draw on a linguistic model, seek explanations in the human mind, and view human behavior from a logical or rational perspective. However, the methods are radically different. Whereas the French structuralists would infer mental structures or codes from cultural traits, ethnoscientists attempt to understand a culture from the point of view of the people themselves. Proponents of **ethnoscience** include Ward Goodenough (1956) and William Sturtevant (1964).

Aimed at making ethnographic description more accurate and replicable than in the past, ethnoscientists try to describe a culture in terms of how it is perceived, ordered, and categorized by the members of that culture rather than by imposing the categories of the ethnographer. To illustrate, traditionally Western ethnographers used categories from their own cultures for describing another culture. Whereas most middle-class North Americans would divide all of the items in the fresh produce department of a supermarket into either fruits or vegetables, people from some other cultures would not. Whereas English speakers have different words for turquoise, aqua, and green, other cultures might include them all under a single color term, and still others would have 30 or more different words for various shades of blues and greens. Whereas some cultures have different linguistic categories for mother's brother's daughter and mother's sister's daughter, in the United States these two family members are lumped together under the single kinship category of cousin. Thus, the primary aim of ethnoscience is to identify the implicit rules, principles, and codes that people use to classify the things and events in their world.

Ethnoscientists have distinguished between the emic and the etic approaches to methodology. The *emic approach*—which they strongly advocate—attempts to understand a culture from the native's point of view. The *etic approach*, on the other hand, describes a culture in terms of the categories of the ethnographer, from the outsider's point of view. The ethnoscientific approach assumes that if we can describe another culture by using native categories rather than our own, we can both minimize investigator bias and get a more accurate picture of reality.

Anthropologists as Cross-Cultural Trainers for Business

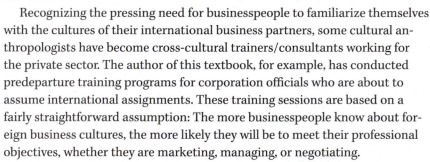

*I*t has become commonplace to say that the world is shrinking. To be certain, rapid technological developments in communications and transportation have brought the peoples of the world closer together in a physical sense. Yet, as we have greater contact with one another, there is an increasing need for better understandings of cultural differences. Nowhere is this more true than in international business. Unlike in the past, when U.S. businesses could stay at home and wait for their international customers to come to them, today's highly competitive world markets require Western businesspeople to conduct their business abroad, often in different cultures where the rules of conduct are unfamiliar.

Recognizing the pressing need for businesspeople to familiarize themselves with the cultures of their international business partners, some cultural anthropologists have become cross-cultural trainers/consultants working for the private sector. The author of this textbook, for example, has conducted predeparture training programs for corporation officials who are about to assume international assignments. These training sessions are based on a fairly straightforward assumption: The more businesspeople know about foreign business cultures, the more likely they will be to meet their professional objectives, whether they are marketing, managing, or negotiating.

Although anthropologists follow a variety of formats in conducting this type of predeparture training, this author (Ferraro 1998) used a fourfold approach: mastering information about a particular culture; developing an understanding of the communication system (both linguistic and nonverbal) of the culture being studied; gaining an awareness of one's own culture, a prerequisite for learning about other cultures; and understanding certain anthropological concepts (theories) that can be applied to any cross-cultural situation.

The fourth component—the application of basic concepts to a foreign business setting—can serve as an example. This part of the training program assumes that it is impossible for anyone to master all of the facts about all of the

Ethnoscientists have been criticized on several fronts. First, though admitting that it may be desirable to get the natives' viewpoint, some anthropologists feel that one's own conditioning and preconceptions make it impossible to get into the mind of someone from another culture. Second, even if it is possible to understand another culture from the natives' point of view, how does one communicate one's findings to others in one's own linguistic/cultural group? Third, if every ethnographer described specific cultures using native categories, there would be little or no basis for comparing different societies. And fourth, ethnoscience is extremely time-consuming. To date, ethnoscientific studies have been completed on very limited domains of culture, such as kinship terms or color categories.

thousands of different cultures in the world. Instead, a more conceptual approach is used, whereby the program presents useful concepts or generalizations that can be applied to any cross-cultural situation. In Chapter 2 we discussed a number of generalizations about the concept of culture that hold true for all cultures of the world. One such generalization—that culture is acquired through learning rather than through the genes—has some important implications for the conduct of international business. First, it reminds the international businessperson that no cultures are "dumber" than others. To be certain, different cultures learn different things, but no cultural groups are inherently slow learners. Thus, the general understanding that people from one culture learn every bit as effectively as people from other cultures can lead to greater tolerance for cultural differences, a prerequisite for effective intercultural communication in the business arena. Second, the concept of the learned nature of culture can lead to the understanding that because we have mastered (learned) our own culture, it is possible for us to learn to function in other cultures as well. Finally, the notion that culture is learned leads to the inescapable conclusion that foreign workforces, although perhaps lacking certain job-related skills today, are perfectly capable of learning those skills in the future, provided they are exposed to culturally relevant training programs.

This, then, is the type of general concept that cultural anthropologists can apply to the world of international business. When such general concepts are combined with other specific cultural information—such as language, customs, beliefs, values, and nonverbal forms of communication—cultural anthropologists are able to develop very effective cross-cultural training programs for international businesspeople.

QUESTIONS FOR FURTHER THOUGHT

1. Why is it so important for international businesspeople to be familiar with the cultural features of those with whom they are conducting business?
2. In addition to the notion that culture is learned, what other general concepts about culture can be helpful to those engaged in international business?
3. What other professions besides international business could benefit from cross-cultural training programs?
4. What are the business implications of the anthropological principle that culture is learned, not passed through the genes?

The completion of an ethnoscientific study of a total culture would, no doubt, be beyond the time capabilities of a single ethnographer. Despite its impracticality, the ethnoscientific approach has served as a useful reminder of a fundamentally sound anthropological principle: People from different cultural and linguistic backgrounds organize and categorize their world in essentially different ways.

ETHNOSCIENCE IN BRIEF

▶ This theory attempts to make ethnographic description more accurate and replicable.
▶ Ethnoscience describes a culture by using the categories of the people under study rather than by imposing categories from the ethnographer's culture (emic approach).

CROSS-CULTURAL MISCUE

A MAJOR LEGACY of the ethnoscientists is that they remind us to use the native categories (emic view) when trying to understand people from another culture. We can get ourselves into trouble if we assume that people from different cultures categorize the world around them exactly as we do. This point is well illustrated in the following cross-cultural misunderstanding.

Harold Josephson, an electronics engineer, had spent weeks negotiating with a Japanese parts distributor in Yokohama. The Japanese executive, Mr. Kushiro, was tough in the negotiations so progress had been slow. Eventually, Josephson felt they had found common ground and an equitable deal could be worked out to the advantage of both companies. On the final day of negotiations, Josephson was pleased to announce to Kushiro that their thinking was parallel and that he was ready to draw up the contract. Kushiro pleasantly thanked Josephson for his time and left the meeting without further discussion.

What Josephson failed to realize is that the word *parallel* has a different meaning to Japanese than it does to Americans. We think of the word *parallel* as meaning compatible, being on the same track, going in the same direction, or agreement. However, to the Japanese, it represents a lack of agreement, positions that will always remain apart, never to meet, as with two train tracks. When Josephson stated that their thinking was "parallel," Kushiro took that as an indication the negotiations were over because they would remain apart in their contract goals.

▶ Because of the time-consuming nature of their methodology, ethnoscientists have been confined to describing very small segments of a culture.

▶ It is difficult to compare data collected by ethnoscientists.

•■ CULTURAL MATERIALISM ■•

MOST CLOSELY ASSOCIATED with Marvin Harris (1968, 1979), **cultural materialism** is the theoretical position based on the concept that material conditions or modes of production determine human thoughts and behavior. According to this approach, the primary task of anthropology is to provide causal explanations for the similarities and differences in thought and behavior found among human groups. Cultural materialists do this by studying material constraints that arise from the universal needs of producing food, technology, tools, and shelter. These material constraints are distinguished from mental constraints, which include such human factors as values, ideas, religion, and aesthetics. Harris and the cultural materialists see the material constraints as the primary causal factors accounting for cultural variations.

Harris has been criticized for devaluing the importance of ideas and political activities as sources of cultural change. But rather than ignoring these nonmaterial factors, Harris suggests that they have a secondary, or less important, role in causing cultural changes and variations. Ideas and political ideologies can either accelerate or retard the process of change but are not themselves causes of the change.

Cultural materialists rely heavily on an etic research methodology—that is, one that assumes the viewpoint of the anthropologist rather than the native informant. This research strategy utilizes the scientific method, logical analysis, the testing of hypotheses, measurement, and quantification. Using these scientific methods, cultural materialists attempt to explain the similarities and differences among the sociocultural structures by focusing on the material and economic factors.

Although cultural materialism has much in common with the ideas of Karl Marx (in particular, a materialist interpretation), the two schools should not be equated. Cultural materialists reject the Marxist notion of dialectic materialism, which calls for destroying capitalism and empowering the working class. Cultural materialism, which doesn't have a particular political agenda, is committed to the scientific study of culture. At the same time, Harris is equally critical of cultural idealists, anthropologists who rely on an emic approach (native's point of view) and use ideas, values, and ideologies as the major explanatory factors. As Harris (1979) has argued, codes and rules (à la ethnoscientists) are not at all helpful in explaining such phenomena as poverty, underdevelopment, imperialism, population explosions, minorities, ethnic and class conflict, exploitation, taxation, private property, pollution, the military-industrial complex, political repression, crime, urban blight, unemployment, and war.

CULTURAL MATERIALISM IN BRIEF

- ▶ Material conditions determine human thoughts and behavior.
- ▶ Theorists assume the viewpoint of the anthropologist, not the native informant.
- ▶ Anthropology is seen as scientific, empirical, and capable of generating causal explanations.
- ▶ Cultural materialism de-emphasizes the role of ideas and values in determining the conditions of social life.

·■ POSTMODERNISM ■·

FOR MUCH of the twentieth century, anthropology saw itself as essentially a scientific enterprise. The nineteenth- and early twentieth-century founders of the discipline attempted to put anthropology on a solid scientific footing by offering an alternative to a theological explanation of human culture and behavior. Although many of the schools of anthropology discussed so far varied between hard and soft scientific approaches, they never abandoned such scientific canons as gathering empirical data, testing of hypotheses, looking for cause-and-effect relationships, and adhering to the scientific method. However, in the 1970s and 1980s a number of anthropologists, collectively referred to as postmodernists, questioned the very scientific nature of anthropology.

Although **postmodernism** means different things to different people, it grew out of the traditions of the structuralists, interpretative anthropology, and feminist anthropology. Essentially, postmodernists dispute the possibility that anthropology can construct a grand theory of human behavior. A basic tenet of postmodernism is that the "modernists" (scientific anthropologists) are extraordinarily arrogant to think that they can describe, inter-

pret, and give meaning to the lives of people from other cultures. The modernists' enterprise for much of the twentieth century, they claim, was based on the privileged status of science (held by most developed countries) and reflected the basic power imbalances between the wealthy, colonial countries and those developing countries where much anthropological research was conducted. It is impossible, they contend, for predominantly White, male, Euro-American anthropologists to step outside of their own culture so as to produce an objective view of another culture.

Rather than attempting to discover the "truth" about how the world works through empirical investigations, the postmodernists hold that all ethnographic accounts are subjective because they are conditioned by the experiences and personal histories of the ethnographer. Instead of the ethnographer being the sole authority, postmodernists call for a more collaborative approach to the study of culture. Written ethnography should consist of multiple authors, creating a dialogue between the anthropologist and the people being studied. This call for dialogue rather than monologue goes further than the attempts of the ethnoscientists to describe the culture using native categories (emic approach). Rather, it involves relinquishing sole authorship to include the voice of the research subjects themselves. Postmodernists contend that only through this dialogical process will meaning and interpretation emerge.

Another tenet of the postmodernist philosophy involves the rejection of generalizing and developing predictable theories. By emphasizing the uniqueness of every culture, postmodernists view culture as a changing set of individual meanings that require continual reinterpretation. For anthropologists to think that they can single-handedly develop generalizable theories of culture that have any level of predictability is both misguided and unethical. It is misguided because it cannot be done. It is unethical because grand theories tend to support the dominant ideology (usually that of the anthropologist) by promoting order and consistency at the expense of individual autonomy and variation. Whereas many of the twentieth-century schools of anthropology assume a scientific posture in which they are searching for generalizations, the postmodernists are more interested in *describing* and *interpreting* particular cultures. The postmodernists see cultural anthropology as a humanistic enterprise more than as a scientific one, having more in common with art and literature than with biology or psychology.

= *The collaboration between anthropologist Ruth Behar (left) and her Mexican informant, Esperanza, is a good example of interpretive anthropology.*

Interpretive anthropology, led by Clifford Geertz, is a major force in postmodernism. Rather than searching for general propositions about human behavior, Geertz (1973, 1983) and the interpretive anthropologists take a more descriptive approach by examining how the people themselves interpret their own values and behaviors. Cultures can best be understood by listening and recording the ways in which the natives explain their own customary behavior. Thus, like ethnoscientists, interpretive anthropologists are strongly wedded to the emic, rather than the etic, approach to the discipline. According to Geertz, the job of the anthropologist is not to generate laws or models that will predict human behavior, for they tend to ignore the complexity and living qualities of human cultures. Rather, Geertz would have anthropology concentrate on cultural description, literature, folklore, myths, and symbols.

The interpretive orientation is admittedly relativistic and is designed to sensitize anthropologists to their own views and values as well as those of the informant. Geertz advocates combining self-knowledge with knowledge of the people under study so that anthropologists learn something about themselves as they are learning about the culture of the informant. In fact, a reading of a postmodernist ethnography usually reveals as much about the anthropologist as it does about the people being studied. The recent writings of Cuban American anthropologist Ruth

Behar of the University of Michigan are an excellent example of what Geertz had in mind for interpretive anthropology. In her book *Translated Woman: Crossing the Border with Esperanza's Story* (1993), Behar tells how she started her research by listening to the life story of Esperanza, a Mexican woman she had befriended. Before long Behar found that Esperanza's life history was causing her to reflect on her own life. Anthropologist Behar began to question aspects of her own life and work, including the role of the ethnographer, the validity of comparing her life with Esperanza's, and her achievements as an affluent and successful academic. The book, written from an interpretive perspective, turned out to be two life stories rather than one.

Behar captured the interpretive or humanistic approach that Geertz advocates, for by telling Esperanza's story (and her own), she was able to retain the complexity and individuality of human behavior. The ascendancy of the interpretive approach to anthropology has been marked by a growing number of such studies, including Janice Boddy's (1989) study of the Zar possession cult in the northern Sudan, a study by Karen McCarthy Brown (1991) of a voodoo priestess in Brooklyn, and the study of a spirit possession troupe in Songhay, Niger, by Paul Stoller (1989).

POSTMODERNISM IN BRIEF

▶ Postmodernism called on anthropologists to switch from cultural generalization and laws to description, interpretation, and the search for meaning.
▶ Ethnographies should be written from several voices—that of the anthropologist along with those of the people under analysis.
▶ Postmodernism involves a distinct return to cultural relativism.

▪• CONCLUDING THOUGHTS ON ▪• ANTHROPOLOGICAL THEORY

THIS CHAPTER HAS BEEN WRITTEN with distinct subheadings dividing the field of anthropological theory into discrete schools. Table 4-1 summarizes the primary anthropological theories and their proponents. These divisions can serve as a useful device to help track, in general terms, the various emphases that anthropologists have taken since the mid-nineteenth century. However, these schools of anthropology are not particularly relevant categories for distinguishing among the different approaches

TABLE 4-1		
Anthropological Theories and Their Proponents		
SCHOOL	**MAJOR ASSUMPTION**	**ADVOCATES**
Evolutionism	All societies pass through a series of stages.	Tylor, Morgan
Diffusionism	All societies change as a result of cultural borrowing from one another.	Graebner, Smith
American historicism	Fieldwork must precede cultural theories.	Boas, Kroeber
Functionalism	Task of anthropology is to understand how parts of contemporary cultures work for well-being of the individual.	Malinowski
Structural functionalism	Anthropology's task is to determine how cultural elements function for the well-being of the society.	Radcliffe-Brown
Psychological anthropology	Anthropology's task is to show relationship among psychological and cultural variables.	Benedict, Mead
Neoevolutionism	Cultures evolve in direct proportion to their capacity to harness energy.	White, Steward
French structuralism	Human cultures are shaped by certain preprogrammed codes of the human mind.	Lévi-Strauss
Ethnoscience	Cultures must be described in terms of native categories.	Sturtevant, Goodenough
Cultural materialism	Material conditions determine human consciousness and behavior.	Harris
Postmodernism	Human behavior stems from the way people perceive and classify the world around them.	Geertz

used by contemporary anthropologists. Few anthropologists today would tie themselves to a single school or theoretical orientation such as neoevolutionist, structuralist, or functionalist. Contemporary anthropologists tend to be more eclectic and problem oriented, focusing on explaining cultural phenomena while drawing on a wide variety of research methods and sources of data. Today it is generally recognized that many of these theoretical schools are not mutually exclusive. That anthropology as a discipline is maturing is evident when its practitioners reject hard-drawn lines among themselves and thereby enrich one another's thinking.

SUMMARY

1. Anthropological theory, which arose from the desire to explain the great cultural diversity in the world, enables us to reduce reality to an abstract yet manageable set of principles.

2. The first group of anthropologists used the notion of evolution to account for the vast diversity in human cultures. Such nineteenth-century evolutionists as Tylor and Morgan suggested that all societies pass through a series of distinct evolutionary stages. Though criticized by their successors for being overly speculative and ethnocentric in their formulations, these early evolutionists fought and won the battle to establish that human behavior was the result of certain cultural processes rather than biological or supernatural processes.

3. The diffusionists explained cultural differences and similarities in terms of the extent of contact cultures had with one another. The British diffusionists, represented by Smith and Perry, held that all cultural features, wherever they may be found, had their origins in Egypt. The German/Austrian diffusionists, most notably Graebner and Schmidt, took a more methodologically sound approach by examining the diffusion of entire complexes of culture.

4. In contrast to the evolutionists and diffusionists, Boas took a more inductive approach to cultural anthropology, insisting on the collection of firsthand empirical data on a wide range of cultures before

developing anthropological theories. Though criticized for not engaging in much theorizing himself, the meticulous attention Boas gave to the methodology put the young discipline of cultural anthropology on a solid scientific footing.

5. The British functionalists Malinowski and Radcliffe-Brown, who, like Boas, were strong advocates of fieldwork, concentrated on how contemporary cultures functioned to meet the needs of the individual and perpetuate the society. Not only do all parts of a culture serve a function (universal functions), but they are interconnected (functional unity) so that a change in one part of the culture is likely to bring about changes in other parts.

6. The early psychological anthropologists, most notably Benedict and Mead, were interested in exploring the relationships between culture and the individual. By examining the configuration of traits, Benedict described whole cultures in terms of individual personality characteristics. Mead's early research efforts brought her to Samoa to study the emotional problems associated with adolescence and later to New Guinea to study male and female gender roles.

7. The theory of evolution was brought back into fashion during the twentieth century by White and Steward. White, like Tylor and Morgan before him, held that cultures evolve from simple to complex forms, but for White, the process of evolution was driven by his "basic law of evolution" ($C = E \times T$). Steward's major contribution was to introduce the concept of multilinear evolution, a form of evolution of specific cultures that did not assume that all cultures passed through the same stages.

8. Drawing heavily on the models of linguistics and cognitive psychology, Lévi-Strauss maintains that certain codes or mental structures preprogrammed in the human mind are responsible for culture and social behavior. A fundamental tenet of Lévi-Strauss's theory is that the human mind thinks in binary oppositions—opposites that enable people to classify the units of their culture and relate them to the world around them.

9. Like the French structuralism of Lévi-Strauss, the theoretical approach known as ethnoscience is cog-

nitive in that it seeks explanations in the human mind. By distinguishing between the emic and the etic approaches to research, ethnoscientists attempt to describe a culture in terms of how it is perceived, ordered, and categorized by members of that culture rather than by the codes or categories of the ethnographer's culture.

10. Led by Harris, cultural materialists believe that tools, technology, and material well-being are the most critical aspects of cultural systems.

11. Diametrically apposed to the cultural materialists are the postmodernists who advocate cultural description and interpretation rather than a search for generalizations and explanatory theories. A major debate in anthropological theory today is between the cultural materialists and the postmodernists.

KEY TERMS

American historicism	hypotheses
barbarism	inductive
binary oppositions	interpretive anthropology
civilization	multilinear evolution
cultural ecology	neoevolutionism
cultural materialism	postmodernism
deductive	psychic unity
diffusionism	psychological anthropology
dysfunction	savagery
ethnoscience	structural functionalism
evolutionism	theory
French structuralism	unilinear evolution
functionalism	universal evolution
functional unity	universal functions

SUGGESTED READINGS

Barrett, Stanley, R. *Anthropology: A Student's Guide to Theory and Method.* Toronto: University of Toronto Press, 1996. Starting with the foundations of anthropology during the nineteenth century, Barrett brings the reader up-to-date with the current trends of postmodernism and feminist criticism. This is one of the few books that attempts to integrate both anthropological theory and methods.

Bohannan, Paul, and Mark Glazer, eds. *High Points in Anthropology.* 2d ed. New York: Knopf, 1988. A collection of writings dating back to Spencer, Morgan, and Tylor, tracing the history and development of cultural anthropological thought up to the present time. Each selection is prefaced by editorial background notes on the theorists and their works.

Erickson, Paul A., and Liam Murphy. *A History of Anthropological Theory.* Peterborough, Ontario, Canada: Broadview Press, 1998. A readable introduction to the history of anthropological thought from ancient times to the postmodernists.

Garbarino, Merwyn S. *Sociocultural Theory in Anthropology: A Short History.* New York: Holt, Rinehart & Winston, 1977. An overview of anthropological theory in historical perspective, written for beginning undergraduates.

Harris, Marvin. *The Rise of Anthropological Theory: A History of Theories of Culture.* New York: Crowell, 1968. A comprehensive and critical review of the history of anthropological theory over the course of the past 200 years. Writing from his own cultural materialist perspective, Harris is quite willing to point out the theoretical and methodological shortcomings of all theoretical orientations other than his own. Despite its very opinionated stance, or perhaps because of it, this sprightly written book remains the best single history of anthropological theory.

Kaplan, David, and Robert A. Manners. *Culture Theory.* Prospect Heights, IL: Waveland Press, 1986. Discusses the major theoretical orientations of cultural anthropology and some of the major theoretical/ methodological issues facing contemporary ethnologists. In terms of depth of coverage, this volume is a nice compromise between the very brief overview of Garbarino and the more encyclopedic work of Harris.

Layton, Robert. *An Introduction to Theory in Anthropology.* Cambridge: Cambridge University Press, 1997. A concise and readable analysis of the ideas and theories that have inspired anthropologists during the nineteenth and twentieth centuries.

McGee, Jon, and Richard Warms. *Anthropological Theory: An Introductory History.* Mountain View, CA: Mayfield, 2000. A comprehensive collection of nineteenth- and twentieth-century anthropological theorists containing excellent introductions and annotations that will be helpful to students.

On the Net

1. By using any major search engine, conduct a subject search for some of the founders of anthropological theory, such as Franz Boas, Marvin Harris, Margaret Mead, Clifford Geertz, and Bronislav Malinowski. What additional information (not mentioned in the chapter) can you find about these giants of anthropology?

2. The University of Indiana has a web site dealing specifically with anthropological theory:

http://www.indiana.edu/~wanthro/theory.htm#sub

   Once there, select "psychological anthropology" from the section on subdisciplines. Write a one-page paper on what you consider to be the most distinctive feature of psychological anthropology.

3. Minnesota State University at Mankato has a web site devoted to biographies of famous cultural anthropologists. This site can be found at the following URL:

http://www.anthro.mankato.msus.edu/information/biography/index.shtml

   What information can you find on the professional careers of Franz Boas, Clifford Geertz, Marvin Harris, Margaret Mead, and Bronislav Malinowski that was not mentioned in the chapter?

Chapter Five

Methods
in cultural
anthropology

WHAT WE WILL LEARN:

▼

How do cultural anthropologists
conduct fieldwork?

▼

What types of data-gathering techniques
do cultural anthropologists use?

▼

What are some of the problems faced by
cultural anthropologists that make
fieldwork somewhat less than romantic?

▼

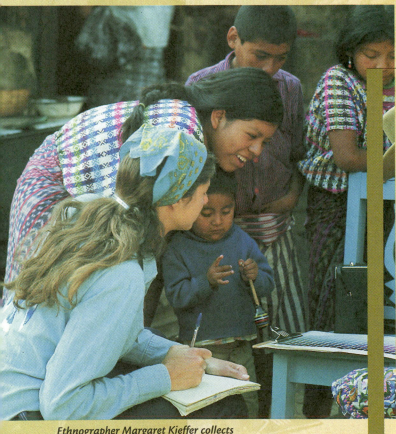

*Ethnographer Margaret Kieffer collects
information from a Mayan Indian of
Santiago Atitlan in Guatemala.*

A distinctive feature of twentieth-century cultural anthropology is the reliance on fieldwork as the primary way of conducting research. To be certain,

cultural anthropologists carry out their research in other contexts as well—such as libraries and museums—but they rely most heavily on experiential fieldwork. Like professionals from any other discipline, cultural anthropologists want to describe the basic subject matter of their discipline. They are interested in documenting the enormous variety of lifeways found among the peoples of the world today. How do people feed themselves? What do they believe? How do they legitimize marriages? In addition to learning the what and the how of different cultures, cultural anthropologists are interested in explaining *why* people in different parts of the world behave and think the way they do. To answer these questions of both description and explanation, cultural anthropologists collect their data and test their hypotheses by means of **fieldwork.**

As a research strategy, fieldwork is eminently experiential. That is, cultural anthropologists collect their primary data by throwing themselves into the cultures they are studying. This involves living with the people they study, asking them questions, surveying their environments and material possessions, and spending long periods of time observing their everyday behaviors and interactions in their natural setting. Doing firsthand fieldwork has become a necessary rite of passage for becoming a professional anthropologist. In fact, it is unusual to receive a Ph.D. in cultural anthropology in the United States without first having conducted fieldwork in a culture other than one's own.

The strong insistence on direct fieldwork has not always been an integral part of the discipline. Much of the theorizing of nineteenth-century anthropology was based on secondhand data at best and, often, on superficial and impressionistic writings of untrained observers. For example, Morgan's classic work *Ancient Society* (1877), discussed in Chapter 4, was based largely on data collected by ships'

captains, missionaries, explorers, and others who inadvertently came across cultures in some of the more exotic parts of the world. It wasn't until the early twentieth century that fieldwork became the normative mode of collecting cultural data.

Even though anthropologists have routinely conducted fieldwork for most of the twentieth century, they have not explicitly discussed their field techniques until quite recently. Before the 1960s, it was usual for an anthropologist to produce a book on "his" or "her" people several years after returning from a fieldwork experience. Nowhere in these books was there an explanation of field methods or of the fieldwork experience itself. The reader had no way of knowing, for instance, how long the investigator stayed in the field, how many people were interviewed and observed, how samples were selected, what data-gathering techniques were used, what problems were encountered, or how the data were analyzed. Because the credibility of any ethnographic study depends on its methodology, cultural anthropologists since the 1960s have been producing some excellent accounts of their own fieldwork experiences. Perhaps even more significantly, a number of books and articles have appeared in recent decades that explore the methodological issues involved in designing a fieldwork study, collecting the data, and analyzing the results.

Whereas the early twentieth-century cultural anthropologists did, in fact, concentrate their fieldwork studies on exotic, non–Euro-American cultures, more recently anthropologists have studied cultures or subcultures closer to home. In recent decades cultural anthropologists have conducted fieldwork in urban ethnic neighborhoods, retirement homes, industrial plants, hospitals, elementary schools, prisons, administrative bureaucracies, and among recreational vehicle owners, to mention but a few. One large-scale (and fairly long term) ethnographic field

▬ *No two anthropological field studies are the same. The study of everyday life in Warsaw, Poland presents different problems and challenges to the field anthropologist than does the study of village life in Zaire.*

project is the Silicon Valley Cultures Project headed by anthropologists June English-Lueck and Charles Darrah of San Jose State University. Silicon Valley, by anyone's definition, is the cutting edge of the global cyberculture. It is the leading region in the United States for technology exports; it received 3,500 patents in a single year; the average wage in the valley is 60 percent higher than in the rest of the country; and four of every 10 workers earn a living in the technology sector. The purpose of this ethnographic project in California is to learn as much as possible about the culture of the people at the center of the nation's—indeed, the world's—digital revolution. Companies and countries around the globe would like to understand what makes that culture tick—and possibly emulate it.

Any general discussion of how to do fieldwork is difficult because no two fieldwork situations are the same. The problems encountered while studying the reindeer-herding Chukchee of Siberia would be quite different from those faced when studying hard-core unemployed street people in Philadelphia or rural peasant farmers in Greece. Even studies of the same village by the same anthropologist at two different times involve different experiences because in the period between the two studies, both the anthropologist and the people under analysis have changed. Despite these differences, all fieldworkers have a number of concerns, problems, and issues in common. For example, everyone entering fieldwork must make many preparations before leaving home, gain acceptance into the community, select the most appropriate data-gathering techniques, understand how to operate within the local political structure, take precautions against investigator bias, choose knowledgeable **informants,** cope with culture

shock, learn a new language, and be willing to reevaluate his or her findings in the light of new evidence. This chapter explores these and other common concerns of the fieldworker, fully recognizing that every fieldwork situation has its own unique set of concerns, problems, and issues.

•▪ PREPARING FOR FIELDWORK ▪•

THE POPULAR IMAGE of the field anthropologist tends to be overly romanticized. Field anthropologists are often envisioned going about their data collection in an idyllic setting, reclining in their hammocks while being served noncarcinogenic foods by beautiful native people. In reality, conducting anthropological fieldwork is not a carefree vacation. Like any scientific enterprise, it makes serious demands on one's time, patience, and sense of humor and requires a lot of hard work and thoughtful preparation. Although luck is a factor, the success of a fieldwork experience is usually directly proportional to the thoroughness of one's preparations.

Any fieldwork project lasting more than a few months may well require a minimum of a year's lead time. If a fieldwork project of a year or two is to be a realistic possibility, the anthropologist must attend to a number of essential matters during this preparatory period. First, because doing fieldwork is expensive, it is necessary, unless the would-be fieldworker is independently wealthy, to obtain funding from a source that supports anthropological research, such as the Social Science Research Council, the National Science Foundation, or the Wenner-Gren Foundation. Financial support (covering living expenses, transportation to and from the field, and various research-related costs) is awarded on a highly competitive basis to the proposals that have the greatest scientific merit. Even though a proposal may require months of preparation, there is no guarantee that it will result in funding.

Second, prefieldwork preparation involves taking the proper health precautions. Before leaving home, it is imperative to obtain all relevant immunizations. A fieldworker traveling to a malaria-infested area must take malarial suppressants before leaving home. It is also prudent to obtain information about available health facilities ahead of time in case the anthropologist or a dependent becomes ill while in the field.

Third, if the field research is to be conducted in a foreign country (as most is), permission or clearance must be obtained from the host government. Because field projects usually last a year or longer, no foreign government will allow an anthropologist to conduct research without prior approval. Some parts of the world are simply off-limits to U.S. citizens because of travel restrictions established by either U.S. officials or the governments of the particular countries. Even countries that are hospitable to Westerners require that the researcher spell out the nature of his or her research in considerable detail. The host government officials often want to make sure that the research will not be embarrassing or politically sensitive, that the findings will be useful, and that the researcher's presence in the host country will not jeopardize the safety, privacy, or jobs of any local citizens. Moreover, host governments often require cultural anthropologists to affiliate with local academic institutions to share their research experiences with local scholars and students. Sometimes, particularly in developing countries, the approval process can be very slow.

A fourth concern that must be addressed before leaving for the field is proficiency in the local language. An important part of the tradition of anthropological fieldwork is that it must be conducted using the native language. If the fieldworker is not fluent in the language of the culture to be studied, she or he should learn the language before leaving home. That may not always be possible, however, depending on the language. Dictionaries and grammar books may not even exist for some of the more esoteric languages, and finding a native speaker to serve as a tutor while still at home may not be possible. In such cases, the ethnographer will have to learn the language after arriving in the field.

Finally, the soon-to-be fieldworker must take care of a host of personal details before leaving home. Arrangements must be made for personal possessions such as houses, cars, and pets while out of the country; decisions

have to be made about what to ship and what to purchase abroad; if families are involved, arrangements must be made for children's education; equipment such as cameras and tape recorders must be purchased, insured, and protected against adverse environmental conditions; up-to-date passports must be obtained; and a schedule for transferring money must be worked out between one's bank at home and a convenient bank in the host country. These and other predeparture details should put an end to the illusion that fieldwork is a romantic holiday.

•■ STAGES OF FIELD RESEARCH ■•

EVEN THOUGH NO TWO fieldwork experiences are ever the same, every study should progress through the same basic stages:

1. Selecting a research problem
2. Formulating a research design
3. Collecting the data
4. Analyzing the data
5. Interpreting the data

Rather than describing these five stages in abstract terms, it will perhaps be more meaningful to discuss them within the framework of an actual fieldwork project (the Kenya Kinship Study, a comparative analysis of rural and urban kinship interaction in Kenya) conducted by the author during the 1970s.

STAGE 1: SELECTING A RESEARCH PROBLEM

In the early twentieth century, the major aim of fieldwork was to describe a culture in as much ethnographic detail as possible. In recent decades, however, fieldworkers have moved away from general ethnographies to research that is focused, specific, and problem oriented. That is, rather than study all of the parts of a culture equally, contemporary cultural anthropologists are more likely to examine specific theoretical issues dealing with the relationships among various phenomena, such as the relationship between matrilineal kinship and high levels of divorce or the relationship between nutrition and food-getting strategies. This shift to a problem-oriented approach has resulted in the formulation of hypotheses (stating the predicted relationship between two or more variables) that are then tested in a fieldwork setting.

The theoretical issue that gave rise to the Kenya Kinship Study (KKS) was the relationship between family interaction and urbanization. What happens to family patterns in the face of rapid urbanization? Throughout most of

Western social thought, there has been general agreement concerning the effects of urbanization on the family. The general proposition—which has been stated in one form or another since the mid-nineteenth century—sees a "nuclearization" of the family when confronted with urbanization. This relationship is perhaps best stated by William Goode, who holds that urbanization brings with it "fewer kinship ties with distant relatives and a greater emphasis on the 'nuclear' family unit of couple and children" (1963:1). The purpose of the KKS was to see whether this alleged relationship between family interaction and urbanization held up in Kenya, a country that has been experiencing rapid urbanization since independence in the early 1960s. The general research problem thus generated the following hypothesis: As Kenya becomes more urbanized, extended family interaction will be replaced by more nuclear family interaction.

STAGE 2: FORMULATING A RESEARCH DESIGN

In the **research design** stage, the would-be fieldworker must decide how to measure the two major variables in the hypothesis: urbanization and family interaction. In this hypothesis, urbanization is the **independent variable** (that is, the variable that is capable of affecting change in the other variable), and family interaction is the **dependent variable** (that is, the variable whose value is dependent on the other variable). In our research design, the dependent variable (family interaction) is the variable we wish to explain, whereas the independent variable (urbanization) is the hypothesized explanation.

Both the dependent and the independent variable in our hypothesis must be made less abstract and more concrete and measurable so as to test the validity of the relationship. One way to do this with regard to the concept of urbanization is to design the study in a comparative fashion. This involves selecting two different populations in Kenya —one rural and one urban. The urban sample selected was from Nairobi, by far the largest city in Kenya and indeed in all of East Africa; the rural sample was selected from a small village very isolated from Nairobi and having none of the major features of a city, such as large populations, industrialization, or labor specialization. If we find that rural people interact with extended family members to a greater extent than urban people, the hypothesis is supported. If we find no appreciable differences in patterns of family interaction between rural and urban populations, the hypothesis will be rejected.

The dependent variable in our hypothesis (family interaction) must be defined more specifically so that it can be measured quantitatively. The task, in other words, is to identify certain concrete measures of family interaction. The KKS identified several such measures:

1. *Residence patterns:* Who lives with whom in the same house or compound? How close do people live to various types of family members?
2. *Visitation patterns:* How often do people have face-to-face interaction with various types of family members?
3. *Mutual assistance:* How often and to what extent do people exchange gifts or money with various types of family members?
4. *Formal family gatherings:* How often and to what extent do people get together for formal family meetings or ceremonies?

When designing a research project, it is important to control for any extraneous factors that might interfere with the testing of the hypothesis. If we are examining differences in kinship interaction between rural and urban residents, it is important that we eliminate any variable (other than degree of urbanism) that might explain the differences. For example, if we select the rural sample from among the Kikuyu and the urban sample from a neighborhood comprising Luo and Nandi, the differences in family interaction may be the result of tribal affiliation (ethnicity) rather than degree of urbanization. Consequently, to control for this ethnic variable, only one ethnic group (the Kikuyu) was used for both rural and urban samples.

STAGE 3: COLLECTING THE DATA

Once the hypothesis has been made concrete, the next step, **collecting data,** involves selecting the appropriate data-gathering techniques for measuring the variables. The KKS used three principal data-gathering techniques: participant-observation, structured interviews, and day histories, a type of biographical interview that focuses on what a person did and with whom he or she interacted during a 24-hour period.

Participant-observation and interviewing—two primary field techniques used by cultural anthropologists— are discussed in the next section of this chapter. Because the day history technique was developed (or at least modified) especially for this study, it is described here in some detail. Day histories were designed to answer such questions as, Whom were you with? What relationship is this person to you? How much time did you spend with this person? How long have you known this person? How often do you see this person? What did you do while you were together?

Day histories were collected from 53 informants from the rural sample and 86 from the urban sample. Although there are obvious limitations to the usefulness of this technique, in the KKS day histories generated specific quantitative data on family interaction. Moreover, the day histories proved beneficial as an initial device for gathering general sociocultural data that were later helpful in the construction of the questionnaire used in the structured interviews.

STAGE 4: ANALYZING THE DATA

Once the day histories have been collected, **analyzing data** begins. The content of the day histories was analyzed, and the various time segments were categorized into one of nine types of social interaction (such as interaction with nonrelatives, interaction with nuclear family members, and interaction with extended family members). Because every hour of the 24-hour period was accounted for, it was a straightforward matter to code the various time segments according to one of the nine categories. The next step in the analysis involved simply counting the number of minutes per 24-hour period that each interviewee spent in nuclear family interaction and the number of minutes spent in extended family interaction. From there, it was a routine mathematical exercise to determine the mean number of minutes spent in each type of family interaction for both rural and urban samples.

When all of the data were coded and analyzed, no significant differences in family interaction emerged between urban and rural samples. In fact, part of the urban sample (those having resided in Nairobi for five years or longer) showed greater involvement with extended family members than did those in the rural sample. These data generated from the day histories were supported by data collected from 298 structured interviews and 13 months of participant-observation. The KKS concluded that living and working within the highly differentiated, industrial urban complex of Nairobi does not in itself lead to the truncation of extended kinship ties.

STAGE 5: INTERPRETING THE DATA

Like any science, the discipline of anthropology does more than simply describe specific cultures. **Interpreting data** —perhaps the most difficult step—involves explaining or interpreting the findings. Has the original hypothesis been confirmed or rejected? What factors can be identified that will help explain the findings? How do these findings compare with the findings of other similar studies? How generalizable are the findings to wider populations? Have these findings raised methodological or theoretical issues that have bearing on the discipline? These are the types of questions with which the anthropologist must wrestle, usually after returning home from the fieldwork experience.

The significant lack of fit between the data and the socalled nuclearization hypothesis in the KKS requires an explanation. The key to understanding these data lies in the general socioeconomic status of the people under study.

= *Cultural anthropologists gather information by having direct contact with the people being studied.*

CROSS-CULTURAL MISCUE

WHILE CONDUCTING URBAN FIELDWORK in Kuala Lumpur, Malaysia, medical anthropologist Jennifer Roberts was devoting the first several weeks of her research time to establishing her credibility, building social networks, and getting to know the local people. Her research assistant introduced Roberts to a woman who was accompanied by her 5-year-old daughter. Roberts was so taken by the girl's beauty that she patted the girl on the head while commenting to the mother what a gorgeous child she had. Much to Robert's surprise, the mother responded by saying that the girl was not very pretty at all and then abruptly left. What had Roberts done? She was simply trying to pay the woman and her daughter a compliment.

In fact, Roberts had inadvertently committed two cross-cultural gaffes. First, in this part of the world, the head is considered to be the most sacred part of the body, where one's spiritual power resides. Although patting a child on the head in North America is a gesture of endearment, in Malaysia it is viewed as a violation of the most sacred part of the body. Second, complimenting a child on her beauty or health is regarded in Malaysia as inviting bad fortune for the child. If evil people or evil spirits believe that a child is particularly healthy or beautiful, they might become jealous and want to harm the child. So, unlike parents in North America who often boast of their children's beauty, health, and intelligence, parents in Malaysia will downplay those traits to protect their children from harm.

Kenya, like most other African nations in the 1970s, was a nation with a dual economy comprising two quite distinct categories of people. On one hand was a small elite with secure, well-paying jobs and potential for further upward mobility; on the other hand was everyone else, with either poor-paying jobs or no jobs at all and little or no economic mobility. The critical dimension, then, is between the haves and the have-nots, and with few exceptions, all of the people in both rural and urban samples clearly qualify for have-not status.

The wide range of family interaction found among both rural and urban populations in Kenya can be understood largely in terms of a lack of money and economic security. For example, in the absence of a public welfare program protecting workers against accidents, illness, old age, and unemployment, it is reasonable to expect that welfare will continue to take place along already established lines of kinship. Moreover, family ties between rural and urban areas remain high in Kenya because of two important economic facts of life: the instability of employment in Kenya and the Kikuyu land tenure system, whereby most land remains in the hands of the lineage (extended family). Urban migrants who neglect their rural kinship obligations are, in effect, relinquishing their rights to a portion of their lineage land, which for most impoverished migrants remains their sole retreat from the insecurities of urban employment. Thus, given the national economy within which all Kikuyu are operating, the maintenance of strong kinship ties for both rural and urban residents is the most rational choice they can make.

DATA-GATHERING TECHNIQUES

A CENTRAL PROBLEM FACING any anthropological fieldworker is determining the most appropriate methods for collecting data. Data collection methods that might work in one culture may be totally inappropriate for a neighboring culture. Given the wide variety of cultures in the world, it is important that anthropologists have a number of options so that they can match the appropriate set of data-gathering techniques to each fieldwork situation. There is a need to be flexible, however, for the techniques originally planned in the **research proposal** may prove to be inappropriate when actually used in the field. Whatever techniques are finally chosen, a variety of methods is needed so that the findings from one technique can be used to check the findings from others.

PARTICIPANT-OBSERVATION

It seems only fitting to start a discussion of data-gathering techniques with participant-observation because anthropologists use this technique more than any other single technique and more extensively than any other social science discipline (see Jorgensen 1989). Participant-observation, as the name implies, means becoming involved in the culture under study while making systematic observations of what is going on. When fieldworkers participate, they become as immersed in the culture as the local people permit. They share activities, attend ceremonies, eat together, and generally become part of the rhythm of everyday life. H. Russell Bernard captured the complexity of participant-observation:

> It involves establishing rapport in a new community; learning to act so that people go about their business as usual when you show up; and removing yourself every day from cultural immersion so you can intellectualize what you've learned, put it into perspective, and write about it convincingly. If you are a successful participant observer you will know when to laugh at what your informant thinks is funny; and when informants laugh at what you say, it will be because you meant it to be a joke. (1988:148)

From the very first day of fieldwork, gaining entry into the community presents a major problem for the participant-observer. Cultural anthropologists in the field can hardly expect to be accepted as soon as they walk into the local community. Under the best of circumstances, the fieldworker, as an outsider, will be an object of curiosity. More often, however, the beginning fieldworker encounters a wide variety of fears, suspicions, and hostilities on the part of the local people that must be overcome. There is no reason whatsoever for traditional Samoan fishermen or Pygmy hunters to understand who the fieldworker is or what he or she is doing in their midst. In his classic study of the Nuer of the Sudan, E. E. Evans-Pritchard stated that the Nuer were so suspicious and reluctant to cooperate with him that after just several weeks of fieldwork "one displays, if the pun be allowed, the most evident symptoms of Nuerosis" (1940:13).

Guidelines for Participant-Observation Fieldwork

By and large, the anthropologist conducting participant-observation fieldwork for the first time has probably received little instruction in how to cope with these initial problems of resistance. For most of the twentieth century, cultural anthropology has been notorious for its sink-or-swim approach to preparing doctoral candidates for fieldwork. In a sense, it is not really possible to prepare the first-time fieldworker for every eventuality for the obvious reason that no two fieldwork situations, cultures, or ethnographers are ever the same. Nevertheless, it is possible to identify some general guidelines applicable to most fieldwork situations (see, for example, Fetterman [1989] and Jorgensen [1989]).

= *One disadvantage of participant-observation research is that the presence of the cultural anthropologist affects the very thing that is under study: people's normal way of life. Here the arrival of the anthropologist at a small village causes a stir.*

APPLIED PERSPECTIVE
Anthropological Research and AIDS

*I*n the early 1980s, very few Americans had ever heard of acquired immune deficiency syndrome (AIDS). By 1998, however, AIDS had assumed the title of the leading infectious cause of death in the world. Virtually unknown in the late 1970s, AIDS has spread so dramatically that by 1999 over 33 million people worldwide were living with HIV/AIDS. In 1998 alone 5.8 million new HIV infections occurred worldwide, nearly 16,000 cases each day. Tragically, 95 percent of all new AIDS cases are occurring in the poorest countries that are least equipped to handle the epidemic. The situation is most grim on the continent of Africa, where approximately 2 million people have already died. The World Health Organization (WHO) estimates that 19 percent of all deaths in Africa in 1998 were due to AIDS. In the United States, NIH reports that 688,200 cases of AIDS had been reported by the beginning of 1999. AIDS is now the fifth leading cause of death in the United States among people ages 25–44.

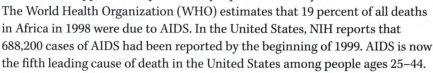

The AIDS epidemic is particularly difficult to get under control for several reasons. First, the disease attacks the human immune system, one of the most complex and inadequately understood systems of the body. Second, the group of viruses thought to cause the disease are so poorly understood that a chemical cure is not likely to be found in the immediate future. Thus, the biological factors in solving the AIDS threat are highly complex. Efforts to stem the epidemic are further complicated by cultural factors. That is, the high-risk populations (gay males, intravenous drug users, and prostitutes) are not visible subcultures. This creates additional problems for programs of AIDS prevention.

Until a vaccine for AIDS is developed, education remains the best strategy for reducing the spread of the disease. Because AIDS is sexually transmitted, the world's populations must learn as much as possible about how to avoid contracting the disease. Yet before public health officials can design effective educational programs, they need a good deal of cultural and behavioral information on high-risk populations. Cultural anthropologists have made significant contributions to programs of preventive education by conducting ethnographic research on the cultural patterns of sexual behavior among these high-risk groups.

First, because the participant-observer is interested in studying people at the grassroots level, it is always advisable to work one's way down the political hierarchy. Before entering a country on a long-term visa, the fieldworker must obtain **research clearance** from a high level of the national government. In the case of the KKS, research clearance came in the form of a brief letter from the office of the president of the country. Starting with this letter from the top of the political pyramid, courtesy calls were made on each descending rung of the administrative ladder (from the provincial commissioner, through the district commissioner, location chief, sublocation chief, and finally to the local headman in the area where the study was to be conducted). Because the study had the approval

One such study was conducted by anthropologist Michelle Renaud (1993, 1997) who worked with registered (legal) prostitutes in Kaolack, Senegal. Because Kaolack is a crossroads town with a steady flow of truck drivers and rural migrants, this particular town has a thriving sexual trade and a correspondingly high rate of sexually transmitted diseases. It was estimated that approximately four of every 10 of Kaolack's registered prostitutes were HIV positive as compared to 10 percent nationally. Renaud worked out of a local health clinic where registered prostitutes came for their bimonthly examinations as well as for treatment of sexually transmitted diseases.

Drawing on structured and unstructured interviews, as well as participant-observation, Renaud gathered valuable data on the lifestyles, worldviews, and decision making of these legal prostitutes. A primary finding of the study was that almost all prostitutes enforced condom use among their clients. However, in their roles as girlfriends, these same prostitutes required their partners to use condoms only 71 percent of the time. Similarly, nonprostitutes in Renaud's sample were reluctant to insist that their sexual partners use condoms. Renaud concluded that both prostitutes and nonprostitutes did "not want to risk losing their partners by implying that one of them might be HIV positive" (1993:28). Armed with this empirical finding, she could then recommend to the Senegalese health officials that future AIDS education programs target groups other than just the prostitutes, including the clients of the prostitutes and particularly their boyfriends.

Applied anthropological studies such as Renaud's have their limitations. The collection of behavioral data on sexual practices among any group of people will always be difficult because of its highly personal nature. When seeking such sensitive information from a subgroup often stigmatized by the wider society, problems of data validity are greatly magnified. Nevertheless, cultural anthropology has an important role to play in the monumental effort it will take to eradicate this disease. Anthropologists such as Renaud, who are interested in both anthropology and epidemiology, can contribute to the design of successful prevention programs by providing both attitudinal and behavioral data from the ethnographic study of at-risk communities at home and abroad.

QUESTIONS FOR FURTHER THOUGHT

1. Why is the AIDS epidemic so difficult to control?
2. How could culture be a factor in the distribution of a disease such as AIDS?
3. What other areas concerning the AIDS epidemic must be investigated by anthropologists?

of the president, it was not likely that any of the administrators down the line would oppose it.

Second, when introducing oneself, it is important to select one role and use it consistently. There are a number of ways that a field anthropologist could answer the question, Who are you? (a question, incidentally, that will be asked frequently and requires an honest and straightforward an-

swer). In my own case when conducting the KKS, I could have said, with total honesty, that I was a student (I was finishing my Ph.D.), an anthropologist (my research was funded by NIMH), Pam's husband, a visiting research associate at the University of Nairobi, Kathryn's father, a teacher, a former basketball player, Charles's son, a Catholic, and a member of the Democratic party. Yet many of these roles, though accurate, were not particularly understandable to the people asking the question. Even though the reason for my being there was that I was an anthropologist, that particular role has little meaning to people with little or no education. So I selected a role that was comprehensible: the role of teacher, a role that was both well known and, much to my advantage, well respected. Even though I wasn't teaching at the time, I had taught professionally before doing fieldwork, and I had planned on a career in college teaching upon returning to the States. So, when asked who I was and what was I doing there, I always said that I was a teacher collecting information about Kikuyu culture so that I could teach my students about it. Had I not standardized my introductions, but instead told one person that I was an anthropologist, another that I was a student, and still another that I was a teacher, the local people would have thought that either I was lying or, perhaps equally bad, that I didn't know who I was.

A third general piece of advice for most fieldworkers is to proceed slowly. Coming from a society that places a high value on time, most U.S. anthropologists do not take kindly to the suggestion to slow down. After all, because they will be in the field for a limited amount of time, most Western anthropologists feel that they must make the best use of that time by collecting as much data as possible. The natural tendency for most Westerners is to want to hit the ground running. There seems to be so much to learn and so little time.

There are compelling reasons for not rushing into asking highly specific questions from day one. First, because most fieldworkers have such an imperfect understanding of the culture during the initial weeks and months, they often do not know enough to even ask the right types of questions. And, second, the very quality of one's data will vary directly with the amount of social groundwork the fieldworker has been able to lay. In other words, ethnographers must invest a considerable amount of time and energy establishing their credibility by allowing the local people to get to know them. For example, in the KKS, I spent the first three months engaging in a number of activities that didn't seem particularly scientific, including helping people with their tax forms, showing teenage boys how to shoot a 15-foot jump shot, taking people for rides in my car, sharing large quantities of food, and talking about life in the United States. None of these activities involved the deliberate gathering of cultural data about the Kikuyu, but they did help to demonstrate that I was interested in them as people rather than merely as sources of information. Once the local people got to know and trust me, they were far more willing to give me the type of cultural information I was looking for.

Fourth, the fieldworker must communicate to the local people, in a genuine way, that she or he is a *student,* wanting to learn more about a subject on which they are the experts. For example, fieldworkers are not interested in sim-

= *Ethnographers in the field are interested in studying all segments of a population. They would include these Salvadorian children as well as their parents.*

ply studying the physical environment (rivers, grasslands, livestock, homes, and so on) of a pastoral people; instead they try to discover how the people define and value these aspects of their physical surroundings. They don't attempt to study marriage and kinship by superimposing already existing notions of how relatives deal with one another; rather, they are interested in the insider's view of how different categories of kin are expected to relate to one another in that society. To assume a student's role, while putting the local informant in the role of the teacher, is more than just a cynical way of enticing people to give you information. The reason the fieldworker is there is to gather information on the local culture, a subject on which he or she has a very imperfect understanding at best. The local people, on the other hand, certainly know their own culture better than anyone else. When people are put in their well-deserved position of teacher–expert, they are likely to be most willing to share the knowledge that is near and dear to their hearts.

Advantages of Participant-Observation

Using participant-observation has certain methodological advantages for enhancing the quality of the data obtained. For example, people in most cultures appreciate any attempt on the part of the anthropologist to live according to the rules of their culture. No matter how ridiculous one might appear at first, the very fact that the fieldworker takes an interest in the local culture is likely to enhance rapport. And as trust levels increase, so do the quantity and quality of the data.

Another major advantage of participant-observation is that it enables the fieldworker to distinguish between normative and real behavior—that is, between what people *should do* and what people *actually do*. When conducting an interview, there is no way to know for certain whether people behave as they say they do. The participant-observer, however, has the advantage of seeing actual behavior rather than relying on hearsay. To illustrate, as part of the KKS, urban informants were asked how often they traveled to their rural homelands to visit family. A number of male informants who lived up to 95 miles away said that they went home every weekend to visit family. Through participant-observation, however, it became apparent that many of the men remained in the city for a number of consecutive weekends. When confronted with this discrepancy between what they said they did and what they actually did, the men claimed that their families wanted them to come home every weekend, but

THE FAR SIDE By GARY LARSON

"Anthropologists! Anthropologists!"
Reprinted by permission of United Press Syndicate.

it was usually too costly and time-consuming. In actual fact, they traveled home on an average of once a month. The difference between once a week and once a month is a 400-percent error in the data. Thus, the participant-observer gains a more accurate picture of the culture by seeing what people actually do rather than merely relying on what they say they do.

Disadvantages of Participant-Observation

On the other hand, participant-observation poses certain methodological problems that can diminish the quality of the data. For example, the very nature of participant-observation precludes a large sample size. Because participant-observation studies are both in-depth and time-consuming, fewer people are actually studied than would be using questionnaires or surveys. A second problem with participant-observation is that the data are often hard to code or categorize, which makes synthesizing and comparing the data difficult. Third, participant-observers face special problems when recording their observations because it may be difficult, if not impossible, to record

TABLE 5-1
Methodological Advantages and Disadvantages of Participant-Observation

METHODOLOGICAL ADVANTAGES	METHODOLOGICAL DISADVANTAGES
Generally enhances rapport	Small sample size
Enables fieldworkers to distinguish actual from expected behavior	Difficult to obtain standardized comparable data
Permits observation of nonverbal behavior	Problems of recording
	Obtrusive effect on subject matter

notes while attending a circumcision ceremony, participating in a feast, or chasing through the forest after a wild pig. The more time that passes between the event and its recording, the more details are forgotten. And, finally, a major methodological shortcoming of participant-observation is that it has an obtrusive effect on the very thing that is being studied. Inhibited by the anthropologist's presence, many people are likely to behave in a way they would not behave if the anthropologist was not there. Table 5-1 lists the methodological advantages and disadvantages of participant-observation.

INTERVIEWING

In addition to using participant-observation, cultural anthropologists in the field rely heavily on ethnographic interviewing. This technique is used for obtaining information on what people think or feel (**attitudinal data**) as well as on what they do (**behavioral data**). Even though interviewing is used widely by a number of different disciplines (including sociology, economics, political science, and psychology), the ethnographic interview is unique in several important respects. First, in the ethnographic interview, the interviewer and the subject almost always speak different first languages. Second, the ethnographic interview is often much broader in scope because it elicits information on the entire culture. Third, the ethnographic interview cannot be used alone but must be used in conjunction with other data-gathering techniques.

Structured and Unstructured Interviews

Ethnographic interviews can be unstructured or structured, depending on the level of control retained by the interviewer. In **unstructured interviews,** which involve a minimum of control, the interviewer asks open-ended questions on a general topic and allows interviewees to respond at their own pace using their own words. At the other extreme, in **structured interviews,** the interviewer asks all informants exactly the same set of questions, in the same sequence, and preferably under the same set of conditions. If we can draw an analogy between interviews and school examinations, structured interviews would be comparable to short-answer tests whereas unstructured interviews would be more like open-ended essay tests.

Structured and unstructured interviews have advantages that tend to complement each other. Unstructured interviews, which are usually used early in the data-gathering process, have the advantage of allowing informants to decide what is important to include in their information. In an unstructured interview, for example, an informant might be asked to describe all of the steps necessary for getting married in her or his culture. Structured interviews, on the other hand, have the advantage of producing large quantities of data that are comparable and thus lend themselves well to statistical descriptions. Because structured interviews ask questions based on highly specific cultural information, they are used most commonly late in the fieldwork, only after the anthropologist knows enough about the culture to ask highly specific questions.

Guidelines for Conducting Interviews

In the past, some field anthropologists to one degree or another have used certain field guides that identify various aspects of culture about which questions can be asked. The two most widely used field guides are *Notes and Queries on Anthropology,* published approximately a century ago by the Royal Anthropological Institute of Great Britain and Ireland, and the more recent *Outline of Cultural Materials,* published by George Peter Murdock as part of the Human Relations Area Files. The use of such field guides can be helpful in eliciting certain aspects of culture expected but not yet observed or aspects of culture that are not particularly obvious in people's behavior (such as values, attitudes, and beliefs). The danger in relying too heavily on such field guides for structuring ethnographic interviews is that they can force one's thinking into Western categories that have little relevance for the culture being studied.

When using interviewing as a data-gathering technique, the fieldworker must take certain precautions to minimize distortions in the data. For example, it has been found that respondents are more likely to answer a question negatively when it is worded negatively. The fieldworker is less likely to bias the response by phrasing a question positively (for example, Do you smoke cigarettes?) rather than negatively (You don't smoke, do you?). Moreover, questions asked as part of a structured interview should be pretested—that is, given to a small number of people so as to eliminate ambiguous or misleading questions.

It is also important to be aware of the social situation in which the interview takes place. In other words, what effect does the presence of other people have on the validity of the data? In his field study of the Dusun, Thomas Williams explains how sex, age, or status influenced the way his informants answered questions in front of others:

> Women would not talk about childbirth before nonrelated males, adolescent boys did not want to talk about their games before young men for fear of being held childish, and most informants did not wish to appear to be questioning the status of a senior man or woman among the onlookers. (1967:27)

Validity of the Data Collected

The cultural anthropologist in the field must devise ways of checking the validity of interview data. One way of accomplishing this is to ask a number of different people the same question; if all people independent of one another answer the question in essentially the same way, it is safe to assume that the data are valid. Another method of checking the validity of interview data is to ask a person the same question over a certain period of time. If the person answers the question differently, there is reason to believe that one of the responses might not be truthful. A third way of determining validity is to compare the responses with people's actual behavior. As we saw in the discussion on participant-observation, what people do is not always the same as what they say they do.

ADDITIONAL DATA-GATHERING TECHNIQUES

Even though participant-observation and interviewing are the mainstays of anthropological fieldwork, cultural anthropologists use other techniques for the collection of cultural data at various stages of the field study. These techniques include census taking, mapping, document analysis, genealogizing, and photography, although this list is hardly exhaustive.

Census Taking

Early on in the fieldwork, anthropologists usually conduct a **census** of the area under investigation. Because this involves the collection of basic demographic data—such as

CROSS-CULTURAL MISCUE

WITHIN THE FIRST SEVERAL WEEKS of conducting fieldwork in rural Kenya, anthropologist Peter Sutton decided to photograph the physical surroundings of the village he was studying. He wanted to visually document the location of houses and fields so as to better understand how the people used space. But within minutes of his photographing the environment (which unavoidably also included some people), several men in the village began shaking their fists and shouting angrily at him. Sutton retreated and rarely used his camera again during his 18 months of fieldwork.

Sutton learned an important lesson from this incident: Photography has different meanings in different cultures. Even though cameras can be useful for documenting cultural features, they must be used with caution. In addition to being an invasion of privacy—as it may be in our own society—there are additional reasons why East Africans are reluctant to have their pictures taken. For example, because some East Africans (particularly in the coastal region) are Islamic, they feel strongly about not violating the Koranic prohibition against making images of the human form. Moreover, people who do not understand the nature of photography may believe that having one's picture taken involves the entrapment of their souls in the camera. In those societies where witchcraft is practiced, the prospect of having one's soul captured, particularly by a witch, can be terrifying.

age, occupation, marital status, and household composition—it is generally nonthreatening to the local people. It is important for the fieldworker to update the census data continuously as he or she learns more about the people and their culture.

Mapping

Another data-gathering tool used in the early stages of fieldwork is **ethnographic mapping**: the attempt to locate people, material culture, and environmental features in space. To illustrate, anthropologists are interested in mapping where people live, where they pasture their livestock, where various public and private buildings are located, how people divide up their land, and how the people position themselves in relation to such environmental features as rivers, mountains, or oceans. We can learn a good deal about a culture by examining how people interact with their physical environment. Aerial and panoramic photography are particularly useful techniques for mapping a community's ecology.

Document Analysis

Cultural anthropologists may do **documentary analysis** to supplement the information collected through interviewing and observation. Some examples of the types of documents used by anthropologists in certain circumstances are personal diaries, colonial administrative records, newspapers, marriage registration data, census information, and various aspects of popular culture, such as song lyrics, television programs, and children's nursery rhymes. As an illustration of how anthropologists can use

already existing documents, consider how tax records in Swaziland from the 1920s and 1930s can shed light on the changing practice of polygyny (a man having more than one wife at a time). For example, an anthropologist might be interested in determining how the incidence of polygyny has changed over time. The present practice of polygyny can be assessed by using such direct methods as interviewing and participant-observation. To compare the present practice of polygyny with the practice in the 1930s, one needs only to consult the tax rolls because during the decade of colonial rule (the 1930s), men were taxed according to the number of wives they had. A man with three wives paid three times as much tax as a man with one wife. The advantages of using this type of historical tax data are obvious: It provides large quantities of data, it is inexpensive, and it is totally unobtrusive.

Collecting Genealogies

Another technique used to collect cultural data is **genealogizing**, which involves writing down all of the relatives of a particular informant. Collecting this type of information is especially important in the small-scale, preliterate societies that anthropologists often study because kinship relationships tend to be the primary ones in those societies. Whereas in Western societies much of our lives are played out with people who are not family members, such as teachers, employers, coworkers, and friends, in small-scale societies people tend to interact primarily with their family. When using the genealogical method, each informant is asked to state the name and relationship of all

Cultural anthropologist David Maybury-Lewis collects cultural information while working among the Xavante of Brazil.

family members and how they are referred to, addressed, and treated. From this information the anthropologist can deduce how family members interact with one another and what behavioral expectations exist between different categories of kin.

Photography

A particularly important aid to the fieldworker's collection of data is **photography,** both motion pictures and still photography. Recent decades have witnessed a proliferation of ethnographic films portraying a wide variety of cultures from all parts of the globe. Ethnographic films are valuable for introducing anthropology students to different cultures, but filmmaking can also have more specific uses for anthropological research. To illustrate, motion pictures can be extremely helpful in **proxemic analysis** (that is, how people in different cultures distance themselves from one another in normal interaction) or **event analysis** (that is, documenting such events as circumcision ceremonies, marriages, or funerals). Because of technological advances in recent years, videocameras (which are less expensive, more versatile, and easier to use) have largely replaced motion picture photography.

Still photography has become such an important part of anthropological research that it is hard to imagine an anthropologist in the field without a 35mm camera. As a research tool, the camera can be put to many uses. First, as mentioned above, the camera can produce a lasting record of land-use patterns and the general ecological arrangements in the community under study. Second, as the adage suggests, a picture is worth a thousand words. Still photography can document the technology of the culture (tools, weapons, machines, utensils), how these items are used (by whom, where, when, in what combinations, and so on), the sequences in a crafts process, and the sex roles associated with different items of technology. Third, photographs can be used as probes in the interview process. Because the photograph becomes the object of discussion, the informant feels less like a subject and more like an expert commentator. And finally, still photography can be used for **sociometric tracking.** If enough photos are taken of people interacting over a period of time, it is possible to quantify which members spend time with whom.

As an example of the use of still photography for sociometric tracking, a study of voluntary interaction was conducted in the cafeteria of the author's university by anthropology students. They were interested in determining the extent to which people from different segments of the university actually *chose* to interact with one another dur-

= *Photographs taken in the field can serve as probes during an interview as well as useful sources of information.*

ing lunchtime. The students took a series of still photographs of the same set of tables at the university cafeteria over a two-week period. Then, by identifying the people who chose to sit together for lunch (commuter students, international students, jocks, Greeks, minority students, and so forth), they were able to determine the extent to which university social life was either segregated or integrated. Their findings—that the various groups of students stayed very much to themselves—made a dramatic statement about the nature of the university which, by definition, should be a place where diverse people from different backgrounds can share their ideas with one another.

Still photography has certain methodological advantages. Among its special assets, the camera allows us to see without fatigue; the last exposure is as clear as the first. Unlike the human eye, the camera is not selective; it captures everything in any particular frame. Photographs are

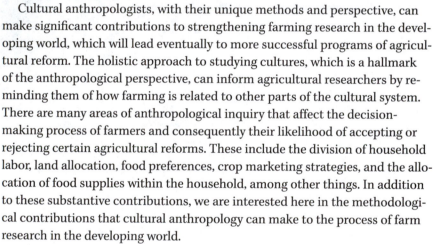

APPLIED PERSPECTIVE
Agricultural Anthropology in Ecuador

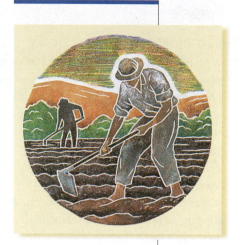

The use of participant-observation to study human behavior has relevance for a vast number of domains of human society. One such area is planned agricultural reform in developing countries. International foreign aid organizations spend millions of dollars each year on programs designed to improve agricultural productivity among the developing nations of the world. Before more productive techniques can be introduced, research needs to be conducted on (a) the nature of the traditional farming practices, (b) technical issues of farming such as soil composition and climatic conditions, and (c) the psychological, political, and social obstacles to change. In recent years, however, the effectiveness of farming research in developing countries has been called into question.

Cultural anthropologists, with their unique methods and perspective, can make significant contributions to strengthening farming research in the developing world, which will lead eventually to more successful programs of agricultural reform. The holistic approach to studying cultures, which is a hallmark of the anthropological perspective, can inform agricultural researchers by reminding them of how farming is related to other parts of the cultural system. There are many areas of anthropological inquiry that affect the decision-making process of farmers and consequently their likelihood of accepting or rejecting certain agricultural reforms. These include the division of household labor, land allocation, food preferences, crop marketing strategies, and the allocation of food supplies within the household, among other things. In addition to these substantive contributions, we are interested here in the methodological contributions that cultural anthropology can make to the process of farm research in the developing world.

Robert Tripp (1985) has shown how a type of agricultural research called on-farm research (OFR) draws heavily upon the use of anthropological field

a lasting record that can be used long after returning from the field. Photography also is often an easier and less time-consuming mode of data collection than written description.

However, the camera is not without its drawbacks. For example, some people object to being photographed, such as certain African peoples who believe that to be photographed is to have one's soul entrapped in the camera, or the Amish, whose religion forbids graven images. Moreover, photography can cause certain headaches for the fieldworker; for example, in some societies the person whose picture is taken may ask for multiple copies of the photo to give to friends and relatives.

Choosing a Technique

Which of the variety of data-gathering techniques will be used depends largely on the nature of the problem being investigated. Kinship studies are likely to draw heavily on the genealogical method, studies of child-rearing practices rely on observation of parent–child relationships, and studies of values will probably use the interview (a technique particularly well suited to generating attitudinal data).

methods. In past decades agricultural research was based largely on lengthy surveys and questionnaires. This approach, however, is neither cost-effective nor convenient for planners to translate into practical terms. A new research strategy, the *sondeo,* was designed to correct these two shortcomings (Hildebrand, 1981). The *sondeo* involves the use of informal interviews and participant-observation by teams of agricultural and social scientists. Over the course of several weeks the research team is able to develop a composite picture of the local farming system. This relatively rapid and effective approach to diagnostic research is a direct application of the experiential and interactive methodology of the cultural anthropologist.

Tripp illustrates how a program of farm research in northern Ecuador utilized a modified form of the *sondeo* for collecting diagnostic information. Because of a scarcity of resources, the biological scientists (agronomists) were required to conduct all of the research themselves. These agronomists, however, were schooled in anthropological field methods, including participant-observation, informal interviewing, and systematic note taking. As part of the research process, the agricultural researchers learned how to visit with local farmers in their fields and homes and participate in local community events. They also developed skills of recording the data they observed, which, in the final analysis, improved the quality of the research. And, finally, by using these personal, interactive research methods, the agronomists learned to assume an attitude central to anthropological fieldwork—that is, an attitude of honest curiosity rather than one of scientific or intellectual superiority. Thus, by using these anthropological methods these agricultural researchers were able to collect information that was timely, relevant, and cost-effective.

QUESTIONS FOR FURTHER THOUGHT

1. Why do foreign aid organizations spend millions of dollars each year on agricultural development programs?
2. How does on-farm research (OFR) draw on traditional anthropological field methods?
3. What are the advantages of the *sondeo* over the use of surveys and questionnaires?

Another significant factor influencing the choice of techniques is the receptivity of the people being studied. It is important that the fieldworker carefully plan which techniques will be appropriate to use and determine the types of data to collect, as well as the segments of the population to study. If, after entering the field, the anthropologist finds that a technique is not working, he or she must be flexible enough to revise the research design and creative enough to come up with a workable alternative. Whatever technique is selected, it should be used in conjunction with other techniques. By using multiple techniques, the investigator can collect different types of data around the same set of issues, which can be used to cross-check one another.

THE PAINS AND GAINS OF FIELDWORK

IT SHOULD BE CLEAR by now that the process of direct fieldwork is central to doing cultural anthropology. Unlike many other scientific endeavors, anthropological fieldwork inevitably has a powerful impact on the life of the practitioner. Spending a year or more living and working in an unfamiliar culture is bound to have life-altering consequences in some cases. The anthropologist is never quite the same after completing a fieldwork project (see DeVita 1992).

The anthropologist in the field is faced with a number of anxiety-producing situations that can be both stressful and growth inducing. In other words, both pains and gains are associated with doing anthropological fieldwork. For example, cultural anthropologists in the field rarely, if ever, follow their research design step-by-step in cookbook fashion. Despite the most meticulous research design and predeparture preparations, fieldwork is fraught with unanticipated difficulties. From day one, the fieldworker can expect to be surprised. Napoleon Chagnon's initial encounter with the Yanomamo Indians of Venezuela and Brazil was hardly what he had anticipated:

> I looked up and gasped when I saw a dozen burley, naked, sweaty, hideous men staring at us down the shafts of their drawn arrows! I am not ashamed to admit that had there been a diplomatic way out, I would have ended my fieldwork then and there.... I wondered why I ever decided to switch from physics and engineering in the first place. (1983:10–11, reprinted by permission.)

The initial desire to flee the fieldwork situation is more common than most anthropologists are willing to admit. And one does not have to travel to the remote parts of the world to feel that way. One American anthropology student who was preparing to do fieldwork among homeless people in Charlotte, North Carolina, experienced an initial rude awakening. During his first *hour* of fieldwork, while waiting to speak to the director of a homeless shelter, the budding anthropologist encountered a number of situations that made him question his sanity. In his own words,

> During the first five minutes of being in the shelter, a child tried to steal my knapsack. Both the homeless people in the waiting room and the staff kept looking at me with, what I can only describe as, disgust in their eyes. I overheard two Black men talking to each other. I couldn't for the life of me understand a word they were saying, although they seemed to be communicating just fine. Well, here it is—the old language barrier of anthropological fieldwork. So I decided to keep quiet and just listen and observe. Before long a White woman entered the waiting room with a 5-year-old boy, whereupon another woman yelled out, "We don't want that little rat in here." OK, I thought, we have a fight on our hands. But in fact, it turned out that the two women were friends.... Another small child approached me and pushed his head under my hand, as if he was a dog and wanted me to pat

his head in approval. I did. Then I noticed that all of the staff wore plastic gloves and only had physical contact with the homeless people when wearing them. I then decided that I had contracted head lice from the boy. My head started to itch, as if, oh I don't know, like I had lice or something. Despite the fact that I had just touched the child's head, I was convinced that I had head lice.... Then the director of the shelter came out to greet me. She was very cordial—perhaps she was trying to console me because she sensed that I had a head lice problem. Once in her office, I settled down somewhat and began to tell her about my research project, discussing theories and hypotheses as if I knew what I was talking about. But as we talked about research, my mind was on the lice in my head. Oh, to hell with anthropology. I'm going home to take a bath! (Frank Vagnone 1989, personal communication)

Sometimes cultural anthropologists in the field can be in life-threatening situations, not just uncomfortable ones. By conducting fieldwork in remote parts of the world, anthropologists expose themselves to dangers from the physical environment that can be fatal. Contagious disease, another major risk factor, has resulted in the serious illness or even death of anthropologists in the field. And, in certain situations, anthropologists are exposed to various forms of social violence, including civil wars, intergroup warfare, muggings, and other forms of crime. To illustrate, anthropologist Philippe Bourgois, who studied the drug culture of East Harlem, New York, witnessed shootings, muggings, bombings, machine gunnings, fire bombings, numerous fistfights, and was manhandled by New York City police who mistook him for a drug dealer. These risks, which can be fatal, make the conduct of fieldwork serious business. For those with higher "safety needs," you might want to consider becoming a historian who rarely has to stray from the safe, yet less interesting, stacks of the university library.

CULTURE SHOCK

Not all introductions to fieldwork are as unsettling as these, of course. But even anthropologists whose fieldwork experience is less traumatic undergo some level of stress caused by culture shock, the psychological disorientation caused by trying to adjust to major differences in lifestyles and living conditions. *Culture shock,* a term introduced by anthropologist Kalervo Oberg (1960), ranges from mild irritation to out-and-out panic. This general psychological stress occurs when the anthropologist tries to play the game of life with little or no understanding of the basic rules. The fieldworker, struggling to learn what is meaningful in the new culture, never really knows when she or he may be committing a serious social indiscretion that might severely jeopardize the entire fieldwork project.

When culture shock sets in, everything seems to go wrong. You often become irritated over minor inconveniences. The food is strange, people don't keep their appointments, no one seems to like you, everything seems so unhygienic, people don't look you in the eye, and on and on. Even though culture shock manifests itself in a number of symptoms, it is usually characterized by the following:

▶ A sense of confusion over how to behave
▶ A sense of surprise, even disgust, after realizing some of the features of the new culture
▶ A sense of loss of old familiar surroundings (such as friends, possessions, and ways of doing things)
▶ A sense of being rejected (or at least not accepted) by members of the new culture
▶ A sense of loss of self-esteem because you don't seem to be functioning very effectively
▶ A feeling of impotence at having so little control over the situation
▶ A sense of doubt when your own cultural values are brought into question.

Table 5-2 lists 16 symptoms of culture shock. One would hope that the training to become an anthropologist and the specific preparations for entering the field would help to avoid extreme culture shock. Nevertheless, every anthropologist should expect to suffer, to some extent, from the discomfort of culture shock. Generally, the negative effects of culture shock subside as time passes, but it is unlikely that they will go away completely. The very success or failure of an anthropological field project depends largely on how well the ethnographer can make the psychological adjustment to the new culture and overcome the often debilitating effects of culture shock.

Biculturalism

Not all of the consequences of fieldwork are negative. To be certain, culture shock is real and should not be taken lightly. Yet, despite the stress of culture shock—or perhaps because of it—the total immersion experience of fieldwork provides opportunities for personal growth and increased understanding. Spending weeks and months operating in a radically different culture can provide new insights into how the local people think, act, and feel. In the process of learning about another culture, however, we unavoidably learn a good deal about our own culture as well (see Gmelch 1994a). When we become bicultural, which can be a consequence of successful fieldwork, we develop a much broader view of human behavior. Richard Barrett captures the essence of this **bicultural perspective**, which he claims enables cultural anthropologists

to view the world through two or more cultural lenses at once. They can thus think and perceive in the categories of their own cultures, but are able to shift gears, so to speak, and view the same reality as it might be perceived by members of the societies they have studied. This intellectual biculturalism is extremely important to anthropologists. It makes them continually aware of alternative ways of doing things and prevents them from taking the customs of our own society too seriously. (1991:20–21)

·■ Recent Trends in ■· Ethnographic Fieldwork

THIS CHAPTER on ethnographic field research has taken an essentially scientific approach. We have explored the various stages of the ethnographic process as exemplified by the KKS. We have talked about generating hypotheses, dependent and independent variables, ways of maximizing the validity and reliability of the data, minimizing observer

TABLE 5-2		
Symptoms of Culture Shock		
Homesickness	Compulsive drinking	Hostility toward host nationals
Boredom	Irritability	Loss of ability to work effectively
Withdrawal (for example, spending excessive amounts of time reading, only seeing other Americans, and avoiding contact with host nationals)	Exaggerated cleanliness	Unexplainable fits of weeping
	Marital stress	Physical ailments (psychosomatic illnesses)
Need for excessive amounts of sleep	Family tension and conflict	
Compulsive eating	Chauvinistic excesses	
	Stereotyping of host nationals	

SOURCE: L. Robert Kohls, *Survival Kit for Overseas Living* (Yarmouth, ME: Intercultural Press, 1984), p. 65.

bias, and a fairly wide range of data-gathering techniques. The point of this chapter has been to demonstrate that cultural anthropology, like any scientific discipline, must strive toward objectivity by being sensitive to methodological issues.

Despite the quest for scientific objectivity, conducting ethnographic fieldwork is quite different from research in a chemistry or biology laboratory. To reflect the native's point of view, the observer must interact with her or his subjects, thereby introducing a powerful element of subjectivity. Nowhere is the coexistence of subjectivity and objectivity more evident than in the widely used data-gathering technique of participant-observation. Participation implies a certain level of emotional involvement in the lives of the people being studied. Making systematic observations, on the other hand, requires emotional detachment. Participant-observers are expected to be emotionally engaged participants while at the same time being dispassionate observers. Participant-observation, by its very nature, carries with it an internal source of tension, for it is incompatible to sympathize with those people whom you are trying to describe with scientific objectivity. Traditionally, most cultural anthropologists have resolved this objectivity/subjectivity tension by reporting their findings in scientific terms. That is, they would describe customs, norms, and other cultural features in general terms without discussing specific informants or their own interactions with them.

Since the 1970s, however, the postmodernists (see Chapter 4) have ushered in a new type of ethnography that has become known as *narrative ethnography*. Being less concerned with scientific objectivity, narrative ethnographers are interested in co-producing ethnographic knowledge by focusing on the interaction between themselves and their informants (Michrina and Richards 1996). These narrative ethnographers are no longer interested in producing descriptive accounts of another culture written with scientific detachment. Rather, their ethnographies are conscious reflections on how their own personalities and cultural influences combine with personal encounters with their informants to produce cultural data. According to Barbara Tedlock (1991:77–78),

> The world, in a narrative ethnography, is re-presented as perceived by a situated narrator, who is also present as a character in the story that reveals his own personality. This enables the reader to identify the consciousness which has selected and shaped the experiences within the text. . . . [N]arrative ethnographies focus . . . on the character and process of the ethnographic dialogue or encounter.

Thus, in the narrative ethnography the dialogue between ethnographer and informant becomes an integral part of the field experience as well as of the written ethnography.

The narrative approach to ethnography is most closely associated with the interpretative school of anthropology. To be certain, narrative ethnographies such as Ruth Behar's study of Esperanza (discussed in Chapter 4) are still the exception to the rule. Most ethnographers would agree that the narrative approach can be taken too far when we wind up learning more about the anthropologist than the focus culture. Indeed, the narrative approach has resulted in a scientific backlash, represented most recently by the appearance of Lawrence Kuznar's book *Reclaiming a Scientific Anthropology* (1996). Nevertheless, the emergence of narrative anthropology has stimulated a healthy debate among anthropologists as to whether anthropological fieldwork is an objective scientific enterprise or more of a dialogue or co-production between the ethnographer and the informant, and it has raised a number of important questions for the fieldworker, including, What is the best way to represent cultural reality?

STATISTICAL CROSS-CULTURAL COMPARISONS

During the first half of the twentieth century, anthropologists, following the lead of Boas in the United States and Malinowski in Britain, amassed considerable descriptive data on a wide variety of cultures throughout the world. Because of the many firsthand ethnographic field studies conducted by the students of Boas and Malinowski, by the end of World War II sufficient data existed to begin testing hypotheses and building theory inductively.

The emergence of statistical, cross-cultural comparative studies was made possible in the 1940s by George Peter Murdock and his colleagues at Yale University, who developed a coded data retrieval system known as the **Human Relations Area Files (HRAF).** The largest anthropological data bank in the world, HRAF has vast amounts of information organized according to over 300 different cultures and over 700 different cultural subject headings. The use of the simple coding system enables the cross-cultural researcher to access large quantities of data within minutes for the purpose of testing hypotheses and drawing statistical correlations.

The creation of HRAF has opened up the possibility for making statistical comparisons among large numbers of cultures. Murdock himself used HRAF as the basis for his groundbreaking book *Social Structure* (1949), in which he compiled correlations and generalizations on family and kinship organization. In the area of culture and personality, John Whiting and Irvin Child (1953) used HRAF as the database for their cross-cultural study of the relationship between child-rearing practices and adult attitudes toward illness. More recently, a host of studies using HRAF data have appeared in the literature, including studies on the adoption of agriculture (Pryor 1986), sexual division of labor (White et al. 1981), female political participation (Ross 1986), reproduction rituals (Paige and Paige 1981), and magico-religious practitioners (Winkelman 1987). Such cross-cultural studies are significant, for they allow us to test the universality of anthropological theories by using large numbers of ethnographic cases.

The HRAF data bank must be used carefully and in full recognition of some potential methodological pitfalls. For example, critics have noted the following:

▶ Much of the data contained in HRAF varies considerably in quality.
▶ The coverage is uneven, with a greater amount of material coming from non-Western cultures.
▶ Because the data describe a wide range of types of social systems (such as tribes, clans, nations, and ethnic groups), one can question whether the units of analysis are comparable.
▶ There is a problem determining the independence of individual cases, for if a cultural institution that is found in 10 different societies is traceable to a single source, should they all be considered independent units?
▶ There is a problem of functional unity: If, as the functionalists remind us, all parts of a culture are to some degree interconnected, how legitimate is it to pull a cultural trait from its original context and

= *This student is using the world's largest anthropological data bank, the Human Relations Area Files (HRAF), in its CD-ROM format.*

compare it to other cultural traits that have been similarly ripped from their contexts?

In the past several decades, however, largely through the efforts of Murdock and Raoul Naroll, most of these criticisms and objections to using HRAF for cross-cultural research have been adequately answered. Because many of these methodological shortcomings can now be overcome by thoughtful researchers, HRAF remains a powerful tool for testing universal theories and identifying causal relationships among cultural phenomena.

SUMMARY

1. Since the turn of the century, cultural anthropologists have conducted their research in a firsthand manner by means of direct fieldwork. Explicit discussion of how anthropologists actually do their fieldwork is a much more recent phenomenon, however.

2. A number of preparations must be made before any fieldwork experience is begun, including the securing of research funds, taking adequate health precautions such as immunizations, obtaining research

clearance from the host government, gaining proficiency in the local language, and attending to a host of personal matters, such as making provisions for accompanying family members, securing passports and visas, purchasing equipment, and making sure that one's affairs at home are in order.

3. Although every fieldwork project in cultural anthropology has its own unique character, all projects go through the same basic stages: selecting a research problem, formulating a research design, collecting the data, analyzing the data, and interpreting the data.

4. Because no two fieldwork experiences are identical, it is important that cultural anthropologists match the appropriate data-gathering techniques to their own fieldwork situations. Among the tools at the fieldworker's disposal are participant-observation, interviewing, ethnographic mapping, census taking, document analysis, the collection of genealogies, and photography.

5. Some general guidelines are applicable to most fieldwork situations. First, when attempting to work one's way into a small community, it is advisable to work one's way down, rather than up, the political hierarchy. Second, when introducing oneself to the local population, it is important to select a single role for oneself and use it consistently. Third, as a way of firmly establishing one's credibility with the local people, it is advisable to proceed slowly.

6. The use of the participant-observation technique has certain methodological advantages, including increasing rapport and being able to distinguish between real and normative behavior. Participant-observation is not without its methodological shortcomings, such as being time-consuming, posing problems of data comparability, presenting difficulties in recording data, and interfering with the very thing that is being studied.

7. Ethnographic interviewing, which is particularly useful for collecting both attitudinal and behavioral data, is of two basic types: unstructured and structured interviews. In unstructured interviews, interviewers ask open-ended questions and permit interviewees to respond at their own pace. In contrast, in structured interviews, interviewers ask the same questions of all respondents, in the same order, and under the same set of social conditions.

8. When cultural anthropologists conduct field research in cultures different from their own, they need to be personally flexible and should always expect the unexpected. Like anyone else trying to operate in an unfamiliar cultural setting, cultural anthropologists are susceptible to culture shock.

9. Since the 1980s, postmodernists have conducted fieldwork as a collaborative learning experience between themselves and their informants rather than as an objective, scientific discovery of how the culture works.

10. Largely through the efforts of Murdock, the Human Relations Area Files (HRAF)—the world's largest anthropological data bank—was developed for the purpose of testing hypotheses and building theory. The files include easily retrievable ethnographic data on over 300 different cultures organized according to more than 700 different subject headings.

KEY TERMS

analyzing data	Human Relations Area
attitudinal data	Files (HRAF)
behavioral data	independent variable
bicultural perspective	informant
census	interpreting data
collecting data	photography
dependent variable	proxemic analysis
documentary analysis	research clearance
ethnographic mapping	research design
event analysis	research proposal
fieldwork	sociometric tracking
genealogizing	structured interview
	unstructured interview

SUGGESTED READINGS

Agar, Michal H. *The Professional Stranger.* 2d ed. San Diego: Academic Press, 1996. An up-to-date consideration of a wide range of methodological issues facing anthropologists as they approach the twenty-first century. Drawing from his own extensive fieldwork experiences, Agar manages to integrate traditional notions of science with the more recent developments in narrative and interpretation.

Bernard, H. Russell. *Research Methods in Cultural Anthropology.* Newbury Park, CA: Sage, 1988. A thorough discussion of how to do cultural anthropological fieldwork. Drawing on a wide variety of examples from actual fieldwork situations, Bernard takes the student step-by-step through the procedures for preparing for the field, collecting data, and analyzing the findings.

DeVita, Philip R., ed. *The Naked Anthropologist: Tales from Around the World.* Belmont, CA: Wadsworth, 1992. A collection of very personal essays written by anthropologists about the agony and ecstasy of conducting fieldwork in many different parts of the world.

Fetterman, David M. *Ethnography: Step by Step.* Newbury Park, CA: Sage, 1989. A practical guide for doing ethnographic field research, this volume deals with such topics as participant-observation, sampling, interviewing, the use of technical equipment, analyzing data, and actually writing an ethnography.

Jackson, Bruce, and Edward Ives. *The World Observed: Reflections on the Fieldwork Process.* Urbana: University of Illinois Press, 1996. A collection of 16 essays by anthropologists, folklorists, and sociologists describing how the chaos of fieldwork comes into focus, how things eventually tend to make sense. The essays provide a glimpse, from several different perspectives, into how the fieldworker understands the data collected from ethnographic fieldwork.

Jorgensen, Danny L. *Participant Observation: A Methodology for Human Studies.* Thousand Oaks, CA: Sage, 1989. A practical handbook for the collection of anthropological data through the technique of participant-observation.

Michrina, Barry P., and Cherylanne Richards. *Person to Person: Fieldwork, Dialogue, and the Hermeneutic Method.* Albany: State University of New York Press, 1996. An introduction to qualitative methodology, this undergraduate guide discusses the basic differences between the scientific and the humanistic approaches to ethnographic fieldwork and argues strongly for the legitimacy of the latter.

Stocking, George W. *Observers Observed: Essays on Ethnographic Fieldwork.* Madison: University of Wisconsin Press, 1983. A volume comprising nine essays dealing with ethnographic fieldwork written by both anthropologists and historians. The essays by the historians offer a unique perspective on the participant-observation technique, which cultural anthropologists think of as distinctively their own.

Walcott, Harry F. *The Art of Fieldwork.* Walnut Creek, CA: AltaMira Press (Sage), 1995. By comparing anthropological fieldwork to the work of an artist, Walcott invites the reader to consider how fieldwork is both an artistic endeavor and a scientific one.

Wengle, John. *Ethnographers in the Field: The Psychology of Research.* Tuscaloosa: University of Alabama Press, 1988. A study of the psychological ramifications for cultural anthropologists of conducting participant-observation research in radically different cultures.

On the Net

1. Anthropologist Laura Zimmer Tamakoshi has developed an excellent web site that illustrates how she conducted fieldwork in Papua New Guinea. The site contains personal descriptions (complete with color photos) of such topics as preparation for the fieldwork experience, developing rapport with the local people, coping with culture shock, participating in the culture, taking field notes, and coming home again. Read over the material on this site to get a good feel for the types of challenges and rewards derived from anthropological fieldwork. You can find the site, entitled "Fieldwork: The Anthropologist in the Field," at the following URL:

http://www.truman.edu/academics/ss/faculty/tamakoshil/index.html

2. Assume that your employer has asked you to take a two-year assignment abroad. To increase your chances for success in your overseas assignment, you will need a lot of information in a hurry about your host country. Select a country where you would like to work for several years. Now start your Internet search for relevant *cultural* information that will enable you to make as smooth an adjustment as possible. Starting with any major search engine, locate as much cultural information about your host country and culture as you can. Then, write a several-page paper identifying the features of the host culture that will be most relevant to your making a satisfactory adjustment to working and living in the country.

3. Using any major search engine, type in the term "Human Relations Area Files". What can you learn about this vast anthropological data source that is not mentioned in the chapter?

Chapter Six

LANGUAGE

Like all humans, these West African women communicate both verbally (with language) and nonverbally (through gestures).

WHAT WE WILL LEARN:

▼

How does human language differ from forms of communication in other animals?

▼

How do children acquire language?

▼

How do languages change?

▼

Are some languages superior to others?

▼

What is the relationship between language and culture?

▼

How do people communicate without using words?

▼

Perhaps the most distinctive feature of being human is the capacity to create and use language and other symbolic forms of communication. It is hard to imagine how

culture could even exist without language. Such fundamental aspects of any culture as religion, family relationships, and the management of technology would be virtually impossible without a symbolic form of communication. Our very capacity to adapt to the physical environment—which involves identifying usable resources, developing ways of acquiring them, and finally forming groups to exploit them—is made possible by language. It is generally held that language is the major vehicle for human thought because our linguistic categories provide the basis for perception and concept formation. Moreover, it is largely through language that we pass on our cultural heritage from one generation to the next. In short, language is such an integral part of the human condition that it permeates everything we do.

•■ THE NATURE OF LANGUAGE ■•

LIKE SO MANY OTHERS that we think we understand, the term *language* is far more complex than we might imagine. Language, which is found in all cultures of the world, is a symbolic system of sounds that, when put together according to a certain set of rules, conveys meanings to its speakers. The meanings attached to any given word in all languages are totally **arbitrary.** That is, the word *cow* has no particular connection to the large bovine animal that the English language refers to as a cow. The word *cow* is a no more or less reasonable word for that animal than would be *kaflumpha, sporge,* or *four-pronged squirter.* The word *cow* does not look like a cow, sound like a cow, or have any particular physical connection to a cow. The only explanation for the use of the word is that somewhere during the evolution of the English language the word *cow* came to be used to refer to a large domesticated animal that gives an abundant quantity of milk. Other languages use totally different, and equally arbitrary, words to describe the very same animal.

DIVERSITY OF LANGUAGE

Given the very arbitrary nature of languages, it should come as no surprise that there is enormous linguistic diversity among human populations. Even though linguists do not agree on precisely how many discrete languages exist, a reasonable estimate would be 6,000 (Diamond 1993). The criterion used to establish such estimates is mutual unintelligibility. That is, linguists assume that if people can understand one another, they speak the same language; if they are unable to understand one another, they speak different languages. The application of this criterion is not as straightforward as it might appear, however, because there are differing degrees of intelligibility. Nevertheless, despite our inability to establish the precise number of discrete languages found in the world today, the amount of linguistic diversity is vast. (Figure 6-1 illustrates the world's major language families.)

Not only is there considerable variation in the number of languages of the world, but the size of the different language communities varies widely as well. It has been estimated (Katzner 1975) that 95 percent of the world's people speak fewer than 100 of the approximately 6,000 different languages. Mandarin alone accounts for about one in every five people on earth. When we add English, Hindi, Spanish, and Russian, the figure jumps to about 45 percent. Thus, the last 5 percent of the world's people speak thousands of discrete languages that have few speakers. Table 6-1 lists the major languages found in the world today.

Linguists today are particularly concerned about this last 5 percent of the world's languages, which are in danger of disappearing. The larger languages, which have both the power of the state and large numbers on their side, are

FIGURE 6-1

Major Language Families of the World

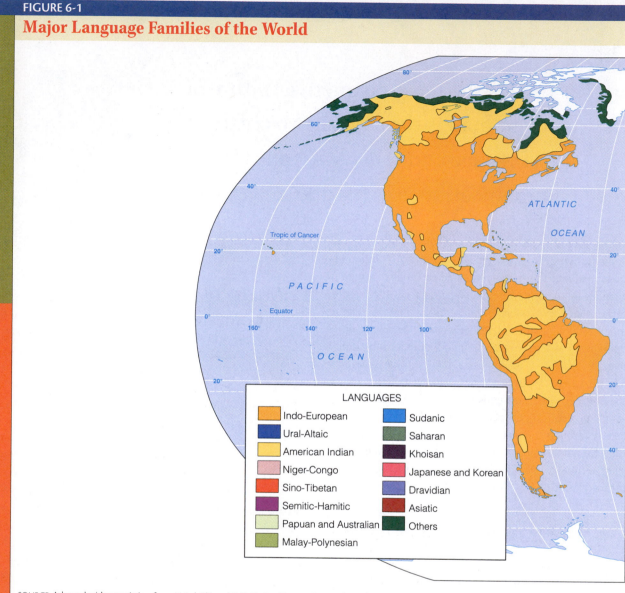

LANGUAGES

- Indo-European
- Ural-Altaic
- American Indian
- Niger-Congo
- Sino-Tibetan
- Semitic-Hamitic
- Papuan and Australian
- Malay-Polynesian
- Sudanic
- Saharan
- Khoisan
- Japanese and Korean
- Dravidian
- Asiatic
- Others

SOURCE: Adapted with permission from H. J. deBlij and P. O. Muller, *Human Geography: Culture, Society, and Space* (New York: Wiley, 1986), pp. 184–185.

in no danger of sliding into oblivion. But many linguists agree that at least half of those thousands of languages that have relatively few speakers will be extinct within a hundred years. If they do not die out altogether, they will become moribund—spoken only by a few older people and unknown to children. The revolutionary changes in high-speed transportation and communication in recent decades have turned many young people throughout the world to the languages found on television and the Internet. Moreover, the power of strong state governments can discourage the use of certain traditional languages, which may be used to identify those marked for genocide or re-

pression. Whatever the reasons, the world is losing a significant number of languages each year. The tragedy is that because every language has its own way of encoding and expressing human experience, an entire way of thinking is lost each time a language becomes extinct.

COMMUNICATION: HUMAN VERSUS NONHUMAN

Communication is certainly not unique to humans, for most animals have ways of sending and receiving messages. Various bird species use certain calls to commu-

nicate a desire to mate; honeybees communicate the distance and direction of sources of food very accurately through a series of body movements; certain antelope species give off a cry that warns of impending danger; even amoebae seem to send and receive crude messages chemically by discharging small amounts of carbon dioxide.

Communication among primates is considerably more complex. Certain nonhuman primate species, such as gorillas and chimpanzees, draw on a large number of modes of communication, including various calls as well as such nonverbal forms of communication as facial expressions, body movement, and gestures. Yet despite the complexity of communication patterns among nonhuman primates, these patterns differ from human patterns of communication in some significant ways. For example, because animal call systems are to a large extent genetically based, they are rigidly inflexible to the extent that each call always has the same form and conveys the same meaning.

Open and Closed Communication Systems

Chimpanzees make one sound when they have found a plentiful source of food, another when threatened, and a third when announcing their presence. Each of these three sounds is unique in both form and message. And each

TABLE 6-1

Major Languages of the World

LANGUAGE	PRIMARY COUNTRY	NUMBER OF FIRST-LANGUAGE SPEAKERS
Mandarin	China	885,000,000
Spanish	Spain	332,000,000
English	UK/USA	322,000,000
Bengali	Bangladesh	189,000,000
Hindi	India	182,000,000
Portuguese	Portugal	170,000,000
Russian	Russia	170,000,000
Japanese	Japan	125,000,000
German	Germany	98,000,000
Wu	China	77,175,000

SOURCE: Ethnologue, web site of the Summer Institute of Linguistics, 1999: *http://www.sil.org*

sound (call) is mutually exclusive. That is, the chimpanzee cannot combine elements of two or more calls in order to develop a new call. To this extent we speak of nonhuman forms of communication as being **closed systems of communication.** Humans, on the other hand, operate with languages that are **open systems of communication** because they are capable of sending messages that have never been sent before.

Language enables humans to send an infinite array of messages, including abstract ideas, highly technical information, and subtle shades of meaning. Starting with a limited number of sounds, human languages are capable of producing an infinite number of meanings by combining sounds and words into meanings that may have never been sent before. To illustrate, by combining a series of words in a certain order, we can convey a unique message that has, in all likelihood, never been previously uttered: "I think that the woman named Clela with the bright orange hair left her leather handbag in the 1951 Studebaker that was involved in a hit-and-run accident later in the day." This productive capacity of human language illustrates how efficient and flexible human communication can be.

To suggest, as has been done in the past, that the communication system of such nonhuman primates as chimps and gorillas is closed in contrast to the open system used by humans is perhaps an oversimplification. Some linguistic scholars (such as Noam Chomsky 1972) have posited that because human language is so radically different from other forms of animal communication, humans must be endowed with certain genetically based mental capacities found in no other species. As we have learned more about

the communication systems of nonhuman primates, however, a growing number of scholars have questioned this theory by claiming that certain species such as chimpanzees and gorillas have a latent capacity for language.

A major limitation to the development of language among gorillas and chimps is physical, for they do not possess the vocal equipment for speech. In an effort to circumvent this physical limitation, recent researchers have taught American Sign Language to chimpanzees and gorillas with some startling findings. In four years, Allen and Beatrice Gardner (1969) taught a chimp named Washoe to use 130 different signs. Of even greater significance is that Washoe was able to manipulate the signs in ways that previously had been thought possible only by humans. For example, Washoe was able to combine several signs to create a new word (having no sign for the word *duck*, she called it *waterbird*), thereby "opening up" her system of communication.

In another important research effort in nonhuman communication, a gorilla named Koko by age 4 was able to use over 250 different signs within a single hour and, like Washoe, was able to name new objects by combining several different signs. In addition, Koko was able to express her feelings and actually scored between 80 and 90 on a nonverbal IQ test.

These recent developments in communication studies among nonhuman primates suggest that chimps and gorillas have more advanced powers of reasoning than had been believed earlier. Some researchers have used this evidence to support the notion that chimpanzee and gorilla linguistic abilities differ from those of humans only in degree, not in kind. In other words, we should not think in terms of closed versus open systems of communication, but rather in terms of some systems being more open than others. Even if this is the case, however, it is important to remember that the degree of difference between human and nonhuman forms of communication remains immense.

Displacement

Human communication differs from other animal communication systems in at least two other important respects. One such feature of human language is its capacity to convey information about a thing or an event that is not present. This characteristic, known as **displacement,** enables humans to speak of purely hypothetical things, events that have happened in the past, and events that might happen in the future. In contrast to other animals, which communicate only about particular things that are

= *Even though this chimp has been trained to use American Sign language, the differences between his form of communication and human language is vast.*

in the present and in the immediate environment, through language humans are able to think abstractly. Another feature of human communication that distinguishes it from nonhuman forms of communication is that it is transmitted largely through tradition rather than through experience alone. Although our propensity (and our physical equipment) for language is biologically based, the specific language that any given person speaks is passed from one generation to another through the process of learning. Adults in a linguistic community who already know the language teach the language to the children.

•■ LANGUAGE ACQUISITION ■• AMONG CHILDREN

HOW IS IT that babies learn to speak? To be certain, they do not speak at birth. Nevertheless, after months of babbling and cooing, they begin to master the language spoken in their environment. Their random noises gradually become words, and within the first several years children begin to put words together in sentences to convey meaning. But language acquisition involves more than the mastery of a list of words, however long it may be. In order to speak a language, the child needs to master the system of grammatical rules with all of its complexities. For example, how does a child learn to put an -*s* on *cat* to make it plural but not on the word *fish?* Or how does an English-speaking child learn to put the adjective before the noun

rather than after the noun? How do children learn these *rules* of grammar? Clearly, the rules are not taught to 18-month-old children by adults as they would be in a high school English class. Somehow infants figure out the grammatical rules for themselves. And they do it in every human society at approximately the same age.

Some have suggested that language is acquired through imitation. That is, children hear, and then memorize, the words and sentences of those around them. This theory is at least partially valid, particularly in terms of the mastery of vocabulary. Because words tend to be arbitrary, there is no way that children can figure out what a word means simply by listening to the sound. So listening to a word over and over again eventually enables the child to attach a meaning to the word. Imitation of sounds also helps to explain the fact that children learn the specific language spoken in their immediate environment; that is, children raised in Copenhagen will learn to speak Danish whereas those raised in rural Kiambu (Kenya) will learn to speak Kikuyu.

Parents and child caretakers throughout the world modify their normal speech when talking to small children. Because young children do not understand the structure of the language, adults need to work harder to gain and keep the attention of children. Attention-getting devices found in most cultures involve such techniques as frequently using the child's name, using exclamations ("Look! A doggie!"), touching the child, and using a high-pitched

CROSS-CULTURAL MISCUE

AN IMPERFECT UNDERSTANDING of other languages has had some embarrassing consequences for North Americans engaging in international marketing. U.S. chicken entrepreneur Frank Purdue decided to translate one of his very successful advertising slogans into Spanish. Unfortunately, the new slogan didn't produce the desired results. The slogan "It takes a tough man to make a tender chicken" was translated into Spanish as "It takes a virile man to make a chicken affectionate." The Pepsi-Cola company, when attempting to use its catchy advertising slogan "Come alive with Pepsi" in Asia, learned that it was translated "Pepsi brings your dead ancestors back from the grave." And the Dairy Association's wildly successful U.S. ad campaign of "Got Milk?" had the unfortunate translation "Are you lactating?" when used in Mexico. Although all of these cross-cultural advertising blunders cause us to snicker, they can result in a loss of revenue and even product credibility.

voice. Once adults have the child's attention, adults will talk in simple sentences only about the here and now, rather than topics that deal with the past, the future, or things that are not in the child's immediate environment. They describe what the child is doing, or they talk about things that interest the child (like the furry kitten or a bright yellow banana). Operating on the assumption that some words are more difficult than others to understand, they avoid using abstractions such as truth, freedom, or the divine right of kings when talking to a 14-month-old. Parents in most cultures tend to exaggerate certain vowel sounds such as *ee ah,* and *oo* (for example, "Look at Mommy's pretty beeeeeeeeeds!"). Moreover, most languages have a form of baby talk used to help children grasp the meaning of words. To illustrate, baby talk falls into several recognizable categories: diminutive forms of animal names (horsie, kitty-cat, doggie); euphemisms for toilet functions (wee-wee or poo-poo); expressions for certain actions such as "bye-bye" or "night-night." And finally, adults often repeat themselves in their speech to small children. All of these modifications to normal adult speaking patterns are thought to assist children in acquiring their language.

Although imitating adults contributes to some language learning, it cannot explain why children and adults can produce totally new sentences. If all language learning involved imitating adult speech, then a speaker could produce a sentence only if he or she had heard it before. But we know that children are able to produce totally unique expressions. Largely through the research of linguist Noam Chomsky, we now believe that a child is genetically equipped to both reproduce all the sounds found in all languages as well as learn any system of grammar. Chomsky believes that language is more than the accumulation of words, sounds, and rules; rather, all languages share a limited set of organizing principles. Beneath the surface all humans are born with a blueprint or basic linguistic plan, which Chomsky calls *universal grammar.* When children from whatever part of the world are learning a language, they are not starting as completely blank slates but rather have an outline of a limited set of grammatical rules. Children listen to the language around them in order to determine which rules apply and which do not. They then add this grammatical rule to their growing number of rules. To illustrate, a child from an English-speaking family will observe that to change a word from the present to the past tense one adds an *-ed.* The rule certainly works when dealing with such verbs as *talk, walk,* and *climb.* This then becomes the child's general rule for past tense. As children are confronted with other verbs that do not conform to this rule (for instance, *eat/ate, hold/held, run/ran*), they must alter the rule or make an additional rule that accounts for the variations. The learning process, then, involves a constant editing of the grammatical rules until they eventually conform to that of adult speech. Along the way children have rejected the various principles or rules useful for other languages because they do not apply to their own language. Thus, as children learn to speak, they master a specific grammar system that has been imbedded in a universal grammar.

THE STRUCTURE OF LANGUAGE

EVERY LANGUAGE has a logical structure. When people encounter an unfamiliar language for the first time, they are confused and disoriented but after becoming familiar with the language, they eventually discover its rules and how the various parts are interrelated. All languages have rules and principles governing what sounds are to be used and how those sounds are to be combined to convey meanings. Human languages have two aspects of structure: a sound (or phonological) structure and a grammatical structure. **Phonology** involves the study of the basic building blocks of a language, units of sound called phonemes, and how these phonemes are combined. The study of grammar involves identifying recurring sequences of phonemes, called morphemes, the smallest units of speech that convey a meaning. The descriptive linguist, whose job is to make explicit the structure of any given language, studies both the sound system and the grammatical system of as many different human languages as possible.

PHONOLOGY

The initial step in describing any language is to determine the sounds that are used. Humans have the vocal apparatus to make an extraordinarily large number of sounds, but no single language uses all possible sounds. Instead, each language uses a finite number of sounds, called **phonemes,** which are the minimal units of sound that signal a difference in meaning. The English language contains sounds for 24 consonants, nine vowels, three semivowels, and some other sound features for a total of 46 phonemes. The number of phonemes in other languages varies from a low of about 15 to a high of 100.

Clearly, the 26 letters of the English alphabet do not correspond to the total inventory of phonemes in the English language. This is largely because English has a number of inconsistent features. For example, we pronounce the same word differently (as in the noun and verb forms of *lead*), and we have different spellings for some words that sound identical, such as *meet* and *meat.* To address this difficulty, linguists have developed the International Phonetic Alphabet, which takes into account all of the possible sound units (phonemes) found in all languages of the world.

The manner in which sounds are grouped into phonemes varies from one language to another. In English, for example, the sounds represented by *b* and *v* comprise two separate phonemes. Such a distinction is absolutely necessary if an English speaker is to differentiate between such words as *ban* and *van* or *bent* and *vent.* The Spanish language, however, does not distinguish between these two sounds. When the Spanish word *ver* (to see) is pronounced, it would be impossible for the English speaker to determine with absolute precision whether the word begins with a *v* or a *b.* Thus, whereas *v* and *b* are two distinct phonemes in English, they belong to the same sound class (or phoneme) in the Spanish language.

MORPHEMES

Sounds and phonemes, though linguistically significant, usually do not convey meaning in themselves. The phonemes *r, a,* and *t* taken by themselves convey no meaning whatsoever. But when combined, they can form the words *rat, tar,* and *art,* each of which conveys meaning. Thus, two or more phonemes can be combined to form a morpheme.

Even though some words are made up of a single morpheme, we should not equate **morphemes** with words. In our example, the words *rat, tar,* and *art,* each made up of a single morpheme, cannot be subdivided into smaller units of meaning. In these cases, the words are made up of a single morpheme. However, the majority of words in any language are made up of two or more morphemes. The word *rats,* for example, contains two morphemes, the root word *rat* and the plural suffix *-s,* which conveys the meaning of more than one. Similarly, the word *artists* contains three morphemes: the root word *art;* the suffix *-ist,* meaning one who engages in the process of doing art; and the plural suffix *-s.* Some of these morphemes, like *art, tar,* and *rat,* can occur in a language unattached. Because they can stand alone, they are called **free morphemes.** Other morphemes, such as the suffix *-ist,* cannot stand alone, for they have no meaning except when attached to other morphemes. These are called **bound morphemes** (Figure 6-2).

GRAMMAR

When people send linguistic messages by combining sounds into phonemes, phonemes into morphemes, and morphemes into words, they do so according to a highly complex set of rules. These rules, which are unique for each language, make up the **grammar** of the language and are well understood and followed by the speakers of that language. These grammatical systems, which constitute the formal structure of the language, consist of two parts: the rules governing how morphemes are formed into words (**morphology**) and the principles guiding how words are

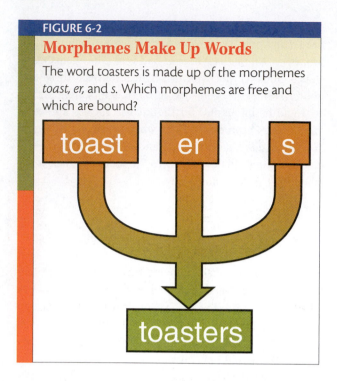

FIGURE 6-2

Morphemes Make Up Words

The word toasters is made up of the morphemes *toast, er,* and *s.* Which morphemes are free and which are bound?

arranged into phrases and sentences (**syntax**). In some languages, meanings are determined primarily by the way morphemes are combined to form words (morphological features), whereas in other languages meanings are determined primarily by the order of words in a sentence (syntactical features).

The distinction between morphology and syntax can be illustrated by looking at an example from the English language. From a grammatical point of view, the statement "Mary fix Tom phone" does not make much sense. The order of the words in the statement (the syntax) is correct, but clearly some revision in the way that the words themselves are formed (morphology) is required for the statement to make grammatical sense. For example, because the English language requires information about verb tense, we must specify whether Mary fixed, is fixing, or will fix the phone. The English grammar system also requires information about the number of phones and the nature of the relationship between the phone and Tom. To make this statement grammatical, we can add an *-ed* to fix, an *-s* to phone, and an *-'s* to Tom. The revised statement ("Mary fixed Tom's phones"), which is now grammatically correct, tells us that Mary has already fixed two or more phones that belong to Tom.

Whereas the English grammar system requires that tense, number, and relationship be specified, other language systems require other types of information. For example, in Latin, a noun must have the proper case ending

to indicate its role (such as subject or direct object) in the sentence. In some languages, such as Spanish, the ending on a noun determines the noun's gender (masculine or feminine). In the Navajo language, certain verbs such as "to handle" take different forms depending on the size and shape of the object being handled. Thus, every language has its own systematic way of ordering morphemes within a word to give linguistic meaning.

Syntax, on the other hand, is the aspect of grammar that governs the arrangement of words and phrases into sentences. In our original example ("Mary fix Tom phone"), the syntax is correct because the words are in the proper sequence. The statement would be totally meaningless if the words were ordered "fix Tom phone Mary," because the parts of speech are not in proper relationship to one another. Moreover, in English, adjectives generally precede the nouns they describe (such as "white horse"), whereas in Spanish adjectives generally follow the nouns they describe (such as "caballo blanco"). The order of the words, then, determines, at least in part, the meaning conveyed in any given language.

•■ LANGUAGE CHANGE ■•

WHEN LINGUISTS LOOK at the sound system or the structure of a language, they are engaging in **synchronic analysis** (that is, at a single point in time). However, like all other aspects of culture, language is not static but rather is constantly undergoing change. When linguists study how languages change over time, they are engaged in **diachronic analysis** (that is, through time). There are various ways that languages are studied diachronically. For example, linguists may study changes in a single language, such as changes from Old English to modern English. Or linguists can look at changes that have occurred in related languages (comparative linguistics). Thus historical linguists are interested in studying both the changes that have occurred in a single language through time as well as the historical relationship of languages to one another.

To better understand how a single language changes over time, we can look at certain versions of English over the past 600 years. Below are three different versions of the Lord's Prayer, one written in Middle English (about 1400), one in early modern English (1611), and a contemporary version:

Middle English (about 1400)

Oure fadir that art in heuene halowid be thi name, thi kyngdom come to, be thi wille don in erthe es in heuene, yeue to us this day oure bread ouir other substance, &

foryeue to us oure dettis, as we forgeuen to oure dettouris, & lede us not in temptacion: but belyuer us from yuel, amen.

Early Modern English (1611)

Our father which art in heaven, hallowed be thy Name. Thy kingdome come. Thy will be done, in earth, as it is in heaven. Giue vs this day our dayly bread. And forgiue vs our debts, as we forgiue our debters. And leade vs not into temptation, but deliuer vs from euill: For thine is the kingdome, and the power, and the glory, for euer, Amen.

Contemporary English

Our Father, who is in heaven, may your name be kept holy. May your kingdom come into being. May your will be followed on earth, just as it is in heaven. Give us this day our food for the day. And forgive us our offenses, just as we forgive those who have offended us. And do not bring us to the test. But free us from evil. For the kingdom, the power, and the glory are yours forever. Amen

As we can see from this example, the English language has changed in a number of aspects, including phonology, morphology, and syntax. Clearly spelling has changed, as in the cases of *erthe* to *earth* and *fadir* to *father*. Moreover, even the meanings of words change over time. In the earlier version the prayer speaks of forgiving our "debts" whereas in the more contemporary version the meaning changes to "offenses."

Historical linguistics seeks to discover not only how languages change, but also why they change. Although nineteenth-century linguists were less likely to ask questions of why, research in linguistic methods since the 1960s has enabled us to gain a better grasp of why languages change. To illustrate, we can take the everyday English word *good-bye*. The word originally appeared in the language approximately five hundred years ago as "God be with you." Linguists now suggest that the expression "God be with you" changed for two fundamental reasons. First, because it was considered blasphemy to utter the word *God* so casually, the use of *God* was changed to *good*, a word that had no taboo associated with it. And second, the substitution of *good* for *God* was likely because of its structural similarity to other greetings already in use, such as "good day" or "good evening." Thus, as Lyle Campbell (1999:6) suggests, these two reasons explain why the expression "God be with you" was merged into the single word *good-bye* and eventually that word has been shortened or abridged into *bye*.

Just as languages change from internal sources, they also change from external forces, or linguistic borrowing. It is generally thought that languages borrow from one another for two primary reasons: need and prestige. When a language community acquires a new cultural item such as a concept or a material object, it needs a word to describe it. This explains why different cultures have similar words referring to the same item such as automobiles, computers, and coffee. The other reason that words are borrowed from other languages is that they convey some measure of prestige to the speakers of the recipient language. To illustrate, the French word *cuisine* (from *kitchen*) was adopted into English because French food was considered more prestigious than English food during the period of French dominance (700–950 years ago).

Interestingly, the introduction of new words into a language parallels the events that shape that language community's history. In fact, knowing the history of a group of people, and particularly its relationships with other linguistic groups, is an excellent way of studying historical linguistics. Again, we can illustrate the history of changes in the English language by knowing something about early English history. For example, approximately 2,800 years ago the British Isles were settled by the Celts, which accounts for the original Celtic language. An initial introduction of Latin words was caused by Roman military forays 2,100 years ago. In the mid-fifth century, the German language was introduced when the Germans from mainland Europe defeated the Celts. More Latin words (for example, *pear, alter, school, chalice,* and *relic*) were introduced when England converted to Christianity around the sixth century. Such Scandinavian words as *sky, trust,* and *skirt* came into the English language as a direct result of the Scandinavian invasions between the ninth and eleventh centuries. A major period of word borrowing from the French language occurred after the Norman invasion (1066). More Latin and some Greek words were diffused into English during the times of Shakespeare and the European Renaissance. The era of British imperialism from the sixteenth to the nineteenth centuries—when the British were out to acquire spheres of influence outside of Europe—resulted in a number of new words (such as *safari, mogul,* and *pajama*) borrowed from Asia, India, and Africa. And the industrial revolution of the nineteenth century and the postindustrial information age of the late twentieth century have involved the incorporation of a large number of words into the English language, primarily of a technological nature.

Only slightly more than 60 percent of all English words used today are derived from Old English (Cipollone et al. 1998). In a survey of widely used English words, 38.3 percent of the words had their origins in other languages. The

French language, by far, has had the greatest lexical influence on English with more than 30 percent of all English words being derived from French. Approximately 3 percent of English words came from Latin, 1.7 percent from Scandinavian languages, and less than 1 percent from German and Dutch.

LANGUAGE FAMILIES

The study of historical linguistics dates back to the 1880s when Sir William Jones, a British scholar living in India, noticed the remarkable similarities between Sanskrit, an ancient Indian language, and classical Greek and Latin. Jones accounted for these similarities by suggesting that all three languages were descended from a common ancestral language. Because Jones was writing at the time when Darwin's notion of evolution was popular, it is not surprising that Jones assumed that languages evolve in much the same way as do biological organisms. Thus, Jones and the first generation of historical linguists suggested that languages had family trees. By comparing similar languages, linguists are able to identify their common features, which probably derive from an ancestral language or protolanguage. Thus, a **language family** is composed of all of the languages that derive from its common protolanguage. And in keeping with the family analogy, historical linguists use such terms as *mother, parent, sister,* and *daughter* languages. To illustrate, the English language is part of the family known as the Indo-European language family (see Figure 6-3). According to this figure, Germanic is the mother of English; French and Spanish (whose mother is Latin) are sister languages, whereas Russian, Bulgarian, and Polish share a common Slavic mother. Linguists generally agree that there are more than 250 different language families in the world today and about 6,000 distinct, mutually unintellible languages. Of these 250 language families, 150 are found in the Americas, 60 in New Guinea, 26 in Australia, 20 in Africa, and 37 in Europe and Asia.

Such diagrams of language families show the direction of linguistic change and how the various languages of a region are interconnected. They read very much like kinship diagrams (see Chapter 10) indicating the genealogical relationships between relatives. However, they can be misleading in their simplicity. Even though Figure 6-3 presents each language as a distinct, discrete entity, we should not assume that level of tidiness. Every language has both internal variations as well as ongoing relationships with nearby language communities. That is, all languages have internal dialects while at the same time sharing linguistic features with other languages. It is also misleading to assume that the splitting of a parent language into daughter languages occurs suddenly or abruptly. In reality, lan-

FIGURE 6-3

Proto Indo-European Languages

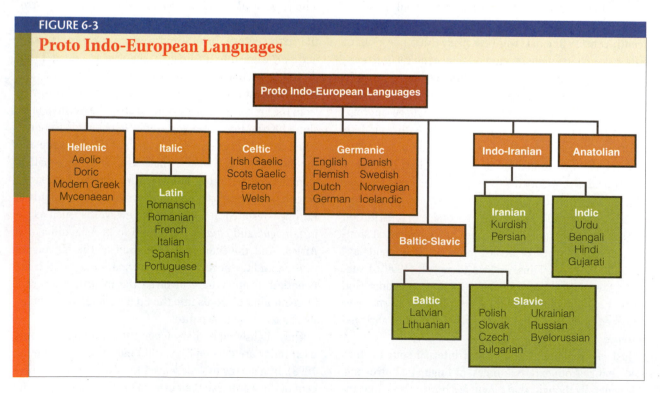

guages split apart very slowly, starting as dialects and then gradually establishing their own identity as a separate language. This gradual fission makes it very difficult to tell exactly when it is that a language becomes a separate entity.

•■ ARE SOME LANGUAGES ■• SUPERIOR TO OTHERS?

UNTIL THE START of the twentieth century, European linguists were convinced that Western languages were superior to all others in terms of elegance, efficiency, and beauty. It was generally assumed that small-scale, non-Western cultures characterized by simple technologies had equally simple languages. In short, preliterate people were thought to have primitive languages with a diminished capacity for expressing abstract ideas. Now, however, anthropological linguists, following the lead of Franz Boas, consider such a view untenable. Based on studies of American Indian languages, linguists have demonstrated time and again that people from technologically simple societies are no less capable of expressing a wide variety of abstract ideas than are people living in high-technology societies.

To illustrate this point, we can compare the English language with that of a traditionally technologically simple society: the Navajo people of the American Southwest. It is true that Navajo speakers are unable to make certain grammatical distinctions commonly made in English. For example, Navajo does not have separate noun forms for singular and plural (such as are found in English with the -s in *dogs* or the -*ren* in *children*); the third person pronoun is both singular and plural and gender nonspecific (it can be translated *he, she, it,* or *they,* depending on the context); and there are no adjectives, because the role of the adjective to describe nouns in English is played by the verb.

Although the Navajo language does not make the same grammatical distinctions as does the English language, in other areas it can express certain information with considerably more precision and efficiency than English. According to Peter Farb (1968:56), making a vague statement such as "I am going" is impossible in the Navajo language. Because of the structure of this language, the verb stem would include additional information on whether the person is going on foot, by horseback, in a wagon, by boat, or in an airplane. If the selected verb form indicates that the person is going on horseback, it is necessary to further differentiate by verb form whether the horse is walking, trotting, galloping, or running. Thus, in the Navajo language a great deal of information is conveyed in the single verb form that is selected to express the concept of going. To be certain, the grammatical systems of the English and Navajo languages are very different. The English language can convey all of the same information, but it requires many more words. Nevertheless, it is hardly reasonable to conclude that one is more efficient at expressing abstract ideas than the other.

•■ LANGUAGE AND CULTURE ■•

FOR THE CULTURAL ANTHROPOLOGIST, the study of language is important not only for the practical purpose of communicating while doing fieldwork but also because a close relationship exists between language and culture. It is widely accepted today that it would be difficult, if not impossible, to understand a culture without first understanding its language, and it would be equally impossible to understand a language outside its cultural context. For this reason, any effective language teacher will go beyond vocabulary and grammar by teaching students something about such topics as eating habits, values, and behavior patterns of native speakers. This important relationship between language and culture was recognized many decades ago by the father of modern American cultural anthropology, Franz Boas:

> The study of language must be considered as one of the most important branches of ethnological study, because, on the one hand, a thorough insight into ethnology cannot be gained without a practical knowledge of the language, and, on the other hand, the fundamental concepts illustrated by human languages are not distinct in kind from ethnological phenomena; and because, furthermore, the peculiar characteristics of language are clearly reflected in the views and customs of the peoples of the world. (1911:73)

HOW CULTURE INFLUENCES LANGUAGE

Although little research has been designed to explore how culture influences the grammatical system of a language, there is considerable evidence to demonstrate how culture affects vocabulary. As a general rule, the vocabulary found in any language tends to emphasize the words that are considered to be adaptively important in that culture. This notion, known as **cultural emphasis,** is reflected in the size and specialization of vocabulary.

In Standard American English, we find large numbers of words that refer to technological gadgetry (such as *tractor,*

APPLIED PERSPECTIVE
Applied Anthropology and Ebonics

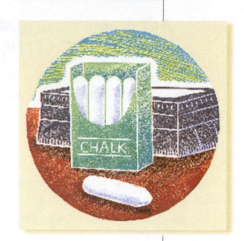

When language may have a bearing on the outcome of a court case, anthropologists (or more precisely, sociocultural linguists) may be brought in to give expert testimony. In 1979, a federal court in Ann Arbor, Michigan, concluded that Black students from a public elementary school were being denied their civil rights because they were not being taught to read, write, and speak Standard English as an alternative to their dialect of Black English Vernacular (BEV). The presiding judge ruled that because the school system failed to recognize and use BEV as the basis for teaching Standard English, the Black children were put at a disadvantage for succeeding in school and, consequently, in life (Chambers 1983).

This precedent-setting court decision rested on establishing the basic premise that BEV (now known as Ebonics) is a bona fide language. It was popularly held that the language of Black students was nothing more than slang, street talk, or a pathological form of Standard English. But, as William Labov, a sociolinguist from the University of Pennsylvania, was able to establish to the satisfaction of the court, BEV is a full-fledged linguistic system with its own grammatical rules, phonology, and semantics. In other words, Labov's testimony demonstrated that BEV is governed by linguistic rules rather than being the result of errors in Standard English; BEV is as capable of expressing a wide range of abstract and complex ideas as is Standard English; and the BEV spoken by children in Ann Arbor is the same as the BEV spoken in New York, Washington, Chicago, and Los Angeles.

On the basis of Labov's testimony, the federal court concluded that language is a vital link between a child and the education the child receives. Children who speak the same language as the language of instruction learn more effectively than those who speak a nonstandard version of the language of in-

---

microchip, and *intake valve*) and occupational specialties (such as *teacher, plumber, CPA,* and *pediatrician*) for the simple reason that technology and occupation are points of cultural emphasis in our culture. Thus, the English language helps North Americans adapt effectively to their culture by providing a vocabulary well suited for that culture. Other cultures have other areas of emphasis. Based on field research conducted in the 1880s, Franz Boas noted that people of the Arctic had large numbers of words for snow, ice, and seals, all three of which played a vital role in their adaptation to the environment and, indeed, in their sur-

vival. To illustrate, Boas reports that in addition to a general term for seal, the Inuit language contains specific words referring to a seal basking in the sun and a seal floating on a piece of ice, as well as a number of terms for seals of different age and sex.

The Nuer

A particularly good example of how culture influences language through the elaboration of vocabularies is provided by the Nuer, a pastoral people of the Sudan, whose daily preoccupation with cattle is reflected in their language

struction. It should be pointed out that the court did not rule that children had to be taught in BEV. Rather the court ordered that the local schools were to acknowledge the fact that language used at home and in the community can pose a barrier to student learning when teachers fail to recognize it, understand it, and incorporate it into their instructional methods.

Even though this court case is now more than two decades old, the controversy is hardly over. In 1996 the school board of Oakland, California, approved a resolution recognizing Ebonics as the primary language of the district's African American students. The public response, not only in Oakland but throughout the country, was instantaneous and almost universally negative. Everyone from the Reverend Jesse Jackson to White conservatives condemned the resolution as absolutely ridiculous. They argued that Black children needed to learn Standard English if they are to succeed in school and in the job market. Unfortunately, most of the public outcry missed the point. By recognizing Ebonics, the school board certainly wasn't saying that African American students should not be taught Standard English. On the contrary, the board was drawing on the very principles that Labov had fought for 17 years earlier. Their point was that the mastery of Standard English would be facilitated if the differences in Ebonics and Standard English were recognized and built into the educational program. The linguistic research conducted since Labov appeared in court in the late 1970s strongly suggests that Ebonic speakers learn Standard English more efficiently by using an approach that contrasts and compares the two languages.

QUESTIONS FOR FURTHER THOUGHT

1. Why did the judge in this court case rule that Black children were being placed at a disadvantage?
2. How was Labov able to argue that BEV was a bona fide language in its own right?
3. Why did the public outcry against Ebonics miss the point?
4. Of the various roles played by applied anthropologists that were discussed in Chapter 3, which best describes Labov's role in this case study?

(Evans-Pritchard 1940). The Nuer have a vast vocabulary used to describe and identify their cattle according to certain physical features such as color, markings, and horn configuration. The Nuer have 10 major color terms for describing cattle: *white* (*bor*), *black* (*car*), *brown* (*lual*), *chestnut* (*dol*), *tawny* (*yan*), *mouse-gray* (*lou*), *bay* (*thiang*), *sandy-gray* (*lith*), *blue and strawberry roan* (*yil*), and *chocolate* (*gwir*). When these color possibilities are merged with the many possible marking patterns, there are more than several hundred combinations. And when these several hundred possibilities are combined with terminology based on horn configuration, there are potentially thousands of ways of describing cattle with considerable precision in the Nuer language.

This highly complex system of terminology is directly related to the prominence of cattle in Nuer society. According to E. E. Evans-Pritchard (1940), cattle are used in a number of important ways. First, they serve a vital economic function in Nuer society (as they do in most other pastoral societies) by providing the people with milk, blood, and meat on certain occasions. Second, cows are used to create and maintain social relationships between

= *Although the Navajo and English languages have vastly different structures, these Navajo speakers can express abstract ideas every bit as effectively as native English speakers.*

people. For a Nuer marriage to be legitimate, cows must be transferred from the lineage of the groom to the lineage of the bride. Third, cows not only influence the relationship between people but also serve as a link with the people's dead ancestors. Cows are used as sacrificial animals to get the attention of ancestor ghosts; in fact, it is impossible to communicate with the dead without frequent references to cattle. Fourth, every Nuer man takes as one of his names the name of an ox given to him at birth or at his initiation. Men are often called by names that refer to the physical features of these oxen, and most age-mates prefer to be addressed by this ox-name. (For this reason, Evans-Pritchard [1940:18] notes that a Nuer genealogy sounds very much like an inventory of a family's cattle.) Finally, the names and traits of cows as well as the ox-names of men are often the subject of songs, poems, and stories. We could cite numerous other uses to which cattle are put, indicating their prominence within the Nuer culture. But suffice it to say that cattle are a dominant interest of the Nuer, or in Evans-Pritchard's own words,

> They are always talking about their beasts. I used sometimes to despair that I never discussed anything with the young men but livestock and girls, and even the subject of girls led inevitably to that of cattle. Start on whatever subject I would, and approach it from whatever angle, we would soon be speaking of cows and oxen, heifers and steers, rams and sheep, he-goats and she-goats, calves, and lambs, and kids. . . . Consequently he who lives among the Nuer and wishes to understand their social life must first master a vocabulary referring to cattle and to the life of the herd. (1940:18–19)

U.S. Example of Cultural Emphasis

In small-scale cultures such as the Inuit or the Nuer, where most people's lives revolve around hunting or herding, areas of cultural emphasis are quite obvious. In middle-class American culture, which tends to be more complex occupationally, it is not always easy to identify a single area of cultural emphasis. Nevertheless, sports tends to be one area of life in U.S. culture that can be shared by people from a wide variety of occupational or class backgrounds. Consequently, as Nancy Hickerson points out, we have many colloquialisms in American English that stem from the game of baseball, our national pastime:

- ► He made a grandstand play.
- ► She threw me a curve.
- ► She fielded my questions well.
- ► You're way off base.
- ► You're batting 1,000 (500, zero) so far.
- ► What are the ground rules?
- ► I want to touch all the bases.
- ► He went to bat for me.
- ► He has two strikes against him.
- ► That's way out in left field.
- ► He drives me up the wall.
- ► He's a team player (a clutch player).
- ► She's an oddball (screwball, foul ball).
- ► It's just a ballpark estimate. (1980:118)

HOW LANGUAGE INFLUENCES CULTURE

A major concern of linguistic anthropology since the 1930s has been the question of whether language influences or perhaps even determines culture. There is no consensus among ethnolinguists, but some have suggested that language is more than a symbolic inventory of experience and the physical world and that it actually shapes our thoughts and perceptions. This notion was stated in its most explicit form by Edward Sapir:

> The fact of the matter is that the real world is to a large extent unconsciously built up on the language habits of the group. No two languages are ever sufficiently similar to be considered as representing the same social reality. The worlds in which different societies live are distinct worlds, not merely the same world with different labels attached. (1929:214)

The Sapir–Whorf Hypothesis

Drawing on Sapir's original formulation, Benjamin Lee Whorf, a student of Sapir, conducted ethnolinguistic research among the Hopi Indians to determine whether different linguistic structures produced different ways of viewing the world. Whorf's observations convinced him that linguistic structure was in fact the causal variable for different views of the world. This notion that different cultures see the world differently because of their different linguistic categories has come to be known as the **Sapir–Whorf hypothesis.**

Both Sapir and Whorf were suggesting that language does influence the way people see the world. That is, language is more than a vehicle for communication; it actually establishes mental categories that predispose people to see things in a certain way. For example, if my language has a single word—*aunt*—that refers to my mother's sister, my father's sister, my mother's brother's wife, and my father's brother's wife, it is likely that I will perceive all of these family members as genealogically equivalent and consequently will behave toward them in essentially the same way. Thus, Sapir and Whorf would suggest that both perception and the resulting behavior are determined by the linguistic categories we use to group some things under one heading and other things under another heading.

TESTING THE HYPOTHESIS Since Sapir and Whorf's original formulation, a number of ethnolinguists have attempted to test the hypothesis. One study (Ervin-Tripp 1964) concluded that the very content of what is said by bilingual people varies according to which language is being spoken. Working with bilingual Japanese American women in San Francisco, Ervin-Tripp (1964:96) found that the responses to the same question given at different times by the same women varied significantly depending on the language used. To illustrate, when asked in English to finish the statement "Real friends should . . . ," the respondent answered, "be very frank"; when asked the same question in Japanese at a different time, she answered "help each other." Or, when asked, "When my wishes conflict with my family . . . ," the response in English was "I do what I want"; but in Japanese, the response was, "It is a time of great unhappiness." In other words, when the question was asked in Japanese, the bilingual respondent was more likely to give a "typical" Japanese response, and when questioned in English, she was more likely to give a "typical" American response. This is the kind of evidence that has been presented to support the validity of the Sapir–Whorf hypothesis because it strongly suggests that the language influences or channels perceptions as well as the content of verbal utterances.

One very creative attempt at testing the Sapir–Whorf hypothesis was conducted by Joseph Casagrande (1960), using a matched sample of Navajo-speaking children. Half

= *In certain bilingual populations, such as Japanese Americans, how a question is answered often depends on the language in which it is asked.*

of the sample, who spoke only Navajo, were matched on all significant sociocultural variables (such as religion, parental education, family income) with the other half, who spoke both Navajo and English. Because the groups were identical on all important variables except language, it would be logical to conclude that whatever perceptual differences emerged between the two groups could be attributed to language.

Having a thorough knowledge of the Navajo language, Casagrande understood that Navajo people, when speaking about an object, are required to choose among a number of different verb forms depending on the shape of the object. When asking a Navajo speaker to hand you an object, you use one verb form if the object is long and rigid like a stick and another verb form if it is long and flexible like a rope. Based on this Navajo linguistic feature, Casagrande hypothesized that children speaking only Navajo would be more likely to discriminate according to shape at an earlier age than the English-speaking children. English-speaking children would be more likely to discriminate according to other features such as size or color. This hypothesis was tested by having both groups of children participate in a number of tasks. The children were shown two objects (a yellow stick and a blue rope) and then asked to tell which of these two objects was most like a third object (a yellow rope). In other words, both groups of children were asked to categorize the yellow rope according to likeness with either the yellow stick or the blue rope. Casagrande found that the children who spoke only Navajo had a significantly greater tendency to categorize according to shape (yellow rope and blue rope) than the bilingual children, who were more likely to categorize according to color.

According to the Sapir–Whorf hypothesis, then, language establishes in our minds categories that force us to distinguish the things we consider similar from the things we consider different. In other words, language is a coercive force that causes people to see the world in a certain way. If this is the case, the speakers of different languages construct reality differently.

The power of language can also be seen in the way people use language to alter people's perceptions of various things. For example, language can be used to mislead by making things appear better than they actually are. Large organizations, such as corporations and branches of the federal government, are particularly adept at using euphemisms, forms of language used to conceal something unpleasant, bad, or inadequate. Companies no longer *fire* employees; rather, employees are *outplaced, released, dehired,* or *nonrenewed.* The corporate structures are *downsized, re-engineered,* or *revitalized.* Terms like *reducing redundancy* and *enhancing efficiency* are designed to conceal the fact that the company is having problems. Organizations such as the U.S. Armed Forces use such euphemisms as *tactical redeployment* to refer to a retreat of troops or a *preemptive strike* to disguise the fact that they attacked first. This type of language, designed to alter our perception of what is real, is called *doublespeak* by linguist William Lutz (1995:54):

> Doublespeak which calls cab drivers *urban transportation specialists,* elevator operators *members of the vertical transportation corps,* and automobile mechanics *automotive internists,* can be considered humorous and relatively harmless. However, doublespeak which calls a fire in a nuclear reactor building *rapid oxidation,* an explosion in a nuclear power plant an *energetic disassembly,* the illegal overthrow of a legitimate administration *destabilizing a government,* and lies *inoperative statements* is language which attempts to avoid responsibility, which attempts to make the bad seem good, the negative appear positive, something unpleasant appear attractive, and which seems to communicate but does not.

DRAWBACKS TO THE HYPOTHESIS The problem with the Sapir–Whorf hypothesis—and the reason that it remains a hypothesis rather than a widely accepted fact—is one of causation. Whorf and Sapir were linguistic determinists who posited that language determines culture. In fact, Sapir suggested that people are virtual prisoners of their language when he stated that "human beings . . . are very much at the mercy of the particular language which has become the medium of expression for their society" (1929:209). Others, taking the opposite position, have suggested that language simply reflects, rather than determines, culture. To be certain, language and culture influence each other in a number of important ways. Yet problems arise when attempting to demonstrate that language determines culture, or vice versa, in any definitive way. What does seem obvious, however, is that all people, being constantly bombarded with sensory stimuli, have developed filtering systems to bring order to all of these incoming sensations. Sapir and Whorf have suggested that the filtering system is language, which provides a set of lenses that highlight some perceptions and de-emphasize others. Whatever may be the precise effect of language on culture, the Sapir–Whorf hypothesis has served to focus attention on this important relationship. For an interesting discussion of the Sapir–Whorf hypothesis and how it applies to language use in the United States, see David Thomson (1994).

CROSS-CULTURAL MISCUE

DIFFICULTIES IN COMMUNICATION can arise even between two people who ostensibly speak the same language. Although both New Yorkers and Londoners speak English, there are enough differences between American English and British English to cause communication miscues. Speakers of English on opposite sides of the Atlantic often use different words to refer to the same thing. To illustrate, Londoners put their trash in a dust bin, not a garbage can; they take a lift, not an elevator; and they live in flats, not apartments. To further complicate matters, the same word used in England and the United States can convey very different meanings. For example, in England the word *homely* (as in the statement "I think your wife is very homely") means warm and friendly, not plain or ugly; for the British, the phrase "to table a motion" means to give an item a prominent place on the agenda rather than to postpone taking action on an item, as it means in the United States; and a rubber in British English is an eraser, not a condom. These are just a few of the linguistic pitfalls that North Americans and Brits may encounter when they attempt to communicate using their own versions of the "same" language.

LANGUAGE MIRRORS VALUES

In addition to reflecting its worldview, a language also reveals a culture's basic value structure. For example, the extent to which a culture values the individual, as compared to the group, is often reflected in its linguistic style. The value placed on the individual is deeply rooted in the North American psyche. Most North Americans start from the cultural assumption that the individual is supreme and not only can, but should, shape his or her own destiny. That individualism is highly valued in the United States and Canada can be seen throughout their cultures, from the love of the automobile as the preferred mode of transportation to a judicial system that goes as far as any in the world to protect the individual rights of the accused. Even when dealing with children North Americans try to provide them with a bedroom of their own, respect their individual right to privacy, and attempt to instill in them a sense of self-reliance and independence by encouraging them to solve their own problems.

Because of the close connection between language and culture, values (such as individualism in mainstream North America) are reflected in Standard American English. One such indicator of how our language reflects individualism is the number of words found in any American English dictionary that are compounded with the word *self*. To illustrate, one is likely to find in any Standard English dictionary no fewer than 150 such words, including *self-absorbed, self-appointed, self-centered, self-confidence, self-conscious, self-educated, self-image, self-regard,* and

self-supporting. This considerable list of English terms related to the individual is significantly larger than one found in a culture that places greater emphasis on corporate or group relationships.

In North America individual happiness is the highest good, whereas in such group-oriented cultures as Japan people strive for the good of the larger group such as the family, the community, or the whole society. Rather than stressing individual happiness, the Japanese are more concerned with justice (for group members) and righteousness (by group members). In Japan the "We" always comes before the "I"; the group is always more prominent than the individual. As John Condon (1984:9) reminds us, "If Descartes had been Japanese, he would have said, 'We think, therefore we are.'"

Group members in Japan don't want to stand out or assert their individuality because, according to the Japanese proverb, "The nail that sticks up gets hammered down." In contrast to North Americans, the emphasis in Japan is on fitting in, harmonizing, and avoiding open disagreement within the group. If one must disagree, it is usually done gently and very indirectly by using such passive expressions as "It is said that . . ." or "Some people think that. . . ." This type of linguistic construction enables one to express an opinion without having to be responsible for it in the event that others in the group disagree. One study of speech patterns among Japanese and American students (Shimonishi 1977) found that the Japanese students used the passive voice significantly more than did their American counterparts.

How language is used in Japan and North America both reflects and reinforces the value of group consciousness in Japan and individualism in North America. The goal of communication in Japan is to achieve consensus and promote harmony whereas in North America it is to demonstrate one's eloquence. Whereas language in Japan tends to be cooperative, polite, and conciliatory, language in Canada and the United States is often competitive, adversarial, confrontational, and aimed at making a point. The Japanese go to considerable length to avoid controversial issues that might be disruptive; North Americans seem to thrive on controversy, debate, argumentation, and provocation, as is evidenced by the use of the expression "Just for the sake of argument." Moreover, the Japanese play down individual eloquence in favor of being good listeners, a vital skill if group consensus is to be achieved. North Americans, in contrast, are not particularly effective listeners because they are too busy mentally preparing their personal responses rather than paying close attention to what is being said. Thus, these linguistic contrasts between North Americans and Japanese reflect their fundamentally different approaches to the cultural values of "groupness" and individualism.

The form of the English language that this U.S. teenager uses when speaking to her grandmother is quite different from the form she would use when talking to her peers.

•■ SOCIOLINGUISTICS ■•

ANTHROPOLOGICAL LINGUISTICS has devoted much of its time and energy to the study of languages as logical systems of knowledge and communication. Recently, however, linguists have taken a keen interest in how people actually speak to one another in any given society. Whereas earlier linguists tended to focus on uniform structures (morphology, phonology, and syntax), sociolinguists concentrate on variations in language use depending on the social situation or context in which the speaker is operating.

In much the same way that entire speech communities adapt their language to changing situations, so do the individuals in those speech communities. Bilingualism and multilingualism are obvious examples of the situational use of language. A Hispanic junior high school student in Miami, for example, may speak English in the classroom and Spanish at home. But often people who are monolingual speak different forms of the same language depending on the social situation. To illustrate, the language that a college sophomore might use with a roommate would be appreciably different from that used when talking to his grandparents; or the choice of expressions heard in a foot-

ball locker room would hardly be appropriate in a job interview. In short, what is said and how it is said are often influenced by such variables as the age, sex, and relative social status of the speakers. Whether we are talking about selectively using either totally different language or variations on the same language, the process is known as **code switching**.

The major focus of sociolinguistics is the relationship between language and social structure. What can we tell about the social relationships between two people from the language they use with each other? The analysis of terms of address can be particularly useful in this regard. Professor Green, for example, could be addressed as Dr. Green, Ma'am, Professor, Ms. Green, Elizabeth, Darling, Doc, Prof, or Beth, depending on who is doing the addressing. One would not expect that her mother or husband would refer to her as Ma'am or that her students would call her Beth. Instead we would expect that the term of address chosen would reflect appropriately the relative social status of the two parties. That is, in middle-class American society, the reciprocal use of first names indicates a friendly, informal relationship between equals; the reciprocal use of titles followed by last names indicates a more formal relationship between people of roughly the same status; and the nonreciprocal use of first names and titles is found among people of unequal social status. We would also expect that the same person might use different terms of address for Professor Green in different social situations. Her husband might call her Beth at a cocktail party, Darling when they are making love, and Elizabeth when engaged in an argument.

DIGLOSSIA

The situational use of language in complex speech communities has been studied by Charles Ferguson (1964), who coined the term **diglossia.** By this term, Ferguson was referring to a linguistic situation where two varieties of the same language (such as standard form, dialect, or pidgin) are spoken by the same person at different times and under different social circumstances.

Ferguson illustrates the concept of diglossia by citing examples from a number of linguistic communities throughout the world, including the use of classical or Koranic Arabic and local forms of Arabic in North Africa and the Middle East, the coexistence of standard German and Swiss German in Switzerland, and the use of both French and Haitian Creole in Haiti. In all of the speech communities where diglossia is found, there exists a long-standing connection between appreciably different linguistic varieties. Which form is used carries with it important cultural meanings. For example, in all cases of diglossia, one form of the language is considered to be high and the other low (Table 6-2). High forms of the language are associated with literacy, education, and, to some degree, religion. The high forms are usually found as part of religious services, political speeches in legislative bodies, university lectures, news broadcasts, and newspapers. Low forms are likely to be found in the marketplace, when giving instructions to subordinates, in conversations with friends and relatives, and in various forms of pop culture, such as folk literature, television and radio programs, cartoons, and graffiti.

It is generally agreed that high forms of the language are superior to low forms, and often the use of the high form is associated with the elite and the upwardly mobile. This general superiority of the high form is at least partially the result of its association with religion and the fact that much of the literature of the language is written in the high form.

Dialects

It is not at all uncommon for certain dialects in complex speech communities to be considered substandard or inferior to others. Such claims are made on social or political rather than linguistic grounds. That is, minority dialects are often assigned an inferior status by the majority for the purpose of maintaining the political, economic, and social subordination of the minority. People who are not from the South regard certain Southernisms such as "y'all" (as in the statement, "Y'all come by and see us now") as quaint and colorful regional expressions (at best) or inferior and inappropriate incursions into Standard American English (at worst). A more obvious example would be majority attitudes toward the nonstandard English dialect used by Black Americans in northern ghettos. Clearly, such usages as "You be goin home" or "Don't nobody go nowhere" will never be used by major network newscasters. Although such expressions are considered to be inferior by the speakers of Standard English, these forms demonstrate logically consistent grammatical patterns and in no way prevent the expression of complex or abstract ideas. Nonstandard English should not be viewed as simply a series of haphazard mistakes in Standard English. Rather it is a fully efficient language with its own unique set of grammatical rules that are consistently applied. Thus, in linguistic terms, the grammar and phonology of ghetto English are no less efficient than the language of the rich and powerful (see Hecht et al. 1993 and Rickford 1999).

Some linguists have suggested that during the last several decades of the twentieth century, regional dialects in the United States have become less noticeable because of mass media, increased geographic mobility, and differing immigration patterns. Another possible explanation is that because regional dialects or accents are associated with certain socioeconomic classes, they are often

TABLE 6-2

Diglossia

HIGH FORM	LOW FORM
Religious services	Marketplace
Political speeches	Instructions to subordinates
Legislative proceedings	Friendly conversations
University lectures	Folk literature
News broadcasts	Radio/TV programs
Newspapers	Cartoons
Poetry	Graffiti

SOURCE: Charles A. Ferguson, "Diglossia," in *Language in Culture and Society: A Reader in Linguistics*, ed. Dell Hynes (New York: Harper & Row, 1964), pp. 429–439.

dropped as people move up the social ladder. This seems to be the case with New Yorkese, the accent that the rest of the nation loves to hate. No matter where you are from, most people can recognize some of these classic New Yorkese expressions:

▶ Didja (did you) or dincha (didn't you) go to the park?
▶ I need to go to the terlet (toilet).
▶ I understand you had a baby goil (girl).
▶ You wanna cuppa (cup of) kawfee (coffee)?
▶ Hey, alla (all of) youze (you) guys, get ovuh heee (over here).

This last example of dropping the *r* sound in the word *here* is characteristic of New Yorkese. Several linguists have shown, however, that "*r*-lessness" is more common among lower-class than upper-class New Yorkers. William Labov (1972) conducted a series of spontaneous interviews with salespeople in three New York department stores: S. Klein's (a low-prestige store), Macy's (moderate prestige), and Saks Fifth Avenue (high prestige). Labov found that clerks in high-prestige stores were significantly more likely to pronounce their *r*'s than were clerks in low-prestige stores. The Labov study reminds us, first, that dialects can vary according to social class, and second, that these linguistic patterns are constantly changing. During the 1940s, for example, *r*-lessness was found widely in the speech of all New Yorkers. But over the course of the last half century, wealthy, fashionable, and upwardly mobile New Yorkers have modified their twang for social reasons. It is no coincidence that there are 28 listings for diction coaches in the Manhattan Yellow Pages.

LANGUAGE, NATIONALISM, AND ETHNIC IDENTITY

It should be recognized that language plays an important symbolic role in the development of national and ethnic identities. In some situations powerful political leaders or factions attempt to suppress local languages for the sake of standardization across a nation-state. The country of Tanzania is a case in point. When Tanzania became independent in the 1960s, its leaders were faced with the task of running a country that contained 120 mutually unintelligible languages. In addition, the country's boundaries were drawn quite arbitrarily by Europeans in the previous century. Faced with the very real challenge of administering a country with such linguistic diversity, the government, headed by President Julius Nyerere, adopted Swahili as the official national language. This entailed

Swahili becoming the language of instruction in schools, government bureaucracies, and parliament. Although Swahili (an Arabicized Bantu language) is no one's first language, it has served as a unifying lingua franca (common language) for the many linguistic communities that reside in Tanzania. To be certain, each linguistic group would have preferred to have had its own language declared the official language, but that decision early in its history as a sovereign nation enabled the country to standardize its national language and get on with the business of nation building.

In many other situations the establishment of official languages has not gone so smoothly. In an attempt to strengthen the power of the Spanish nation, the Franco government made a number of unsuccessful attempts to suppress the minority Basque and Catalan languages by forbidding them being spoken in public or appearing on signs or billboards. But people take their languages seriously, and they often became a rallying point for expressing one's cultural identity. Each time a strong national government tries to suppress a minority language or establish the majority language as the official one, it is likely that minority populations will strongly resist. The government of India, for example, has had to abort its several attempts to establish Hindi as the official language of India because of riots erupting in non–Hindi-speaking areas of the country.

Canada is experiencing bitter divisions that revolve around the issue of language policy in the French-speaking province of Quebec. In recent years the government of Quebec has passed laws that restrict the use of the English language as a medium of instruction in schools. The only way that an English-speaking student in Quebec can be taught in English is to have at least one parent who had been taught in English. Immigrant and French-speaking students in Quebec have been denied instruction in the English language since the early 1970s. The language laws have also restricted the use of English on signs and billboards within Quebec. The language laws, seen by many as discriminatory, have been challenged in the Supreme Court of Canada and have been brought before the UN Committee on Human Rights. The long-standing divisiveness over the language policy in Canada has led recently to a countrywide referendum on the separation of French-speaking Quebec from the rest of Canada. In its 1995 referendum, Canada managed to avoid having Quebec become an independent country by the narrowest of margins (the Separatists won 49.43 percent of the vote).

•■ NONVERBAL ■•
COMMUNICATION

TO COMPREHEND FULLY how people in any particular culture communicate, we must become familiar with their nonverbal forms of communication in addition to their language. **Nonverbal communication** is important because it both helps us interpret linguistic messages and often carries messages of its own. In fact, it has been suggested that up to 70 percent of all messages sent and received by humans are nonverbal in nature.

Like language, nonverbal forms of communication are learned and, as such, vary from one culture to another. Even though some nonverbal cues have the same meaning in different cultures, an enormous range of variation in nonverbal communication exists among cultures. In some cases, a certain message can be sent in a number of different ways by different cultures. For example, whereas in the United States we signify affirmation by nodding, the very same message is sent by throwing the head back in Ethiopia, by sharply thrusting the head forward among the Semang of Malaya, and by raising the eyebrows among the Dyaks of Borneo. Moreover, cross-cultural misunderstandings can occur when the same nonverbal cue has different meanings in different cultures. To illustrate, the hand gesture of making a circle with the thumb and forefinger, which means okay in the United States, signifies money in Japan, indicates worthlessness or zero in France, and is a sexual insult in parts of South America.

Humans communicate without words in a number of important ways, including hand gestures, facial expressions, eye contact, touching, space usage, scents, gait, and stance. A thorough discussion of these and other aspects of nonverbal communication, based on the recent literature, is beyond the scope of this textbook. A brief examination of three of the more salient types of nonverbal communication—hand gestures, eye contact, and touching—will help convey the importance of this form of human communication.

HAND GESTURES

Consider how many hand gestures we use every day. We cup our hand behind the ear as a nonverbal way of communicating that we cannot hear. We thumb our noses at those we don't like. We can thumb a ride on the side of the highway. We can wave hello or good-bye. We tell people to be quiet by holding our forefinger vertically against our lips. We give the peace sign by holding up our forefinger and middle finger. And we send a very different message when we flash half of the peace sign. Some of the hand gestures used widely in the United States are also used and understood in Europe, which should come as no surprise, given our strong European heritage. Nevertheless, as Desmond Morris and colleagues (1979) remind us, a number of nonverbal hand gestures used in western Europe have not been diffused across the Atlantic. For example, stroking the face between the cheekbones and the chin with the thumb and forefinger is a nonverbal way of saying "You look ill or thin" in the southern Mediterranean; pulling down on the lower eyelid with the forefinger means "Be alert" in parts of Spain, Italy, France, and Greece; and in Italy, pulling or flicking one's own earlobe is a way of calling into question a man's masculinity ("You are so effeminate that you should be wearing an earring").

POSTURE (BODY STANCE)

The way that people hold their bodies often communicates information about their social status, religious practices, feelings of submissiveness, desires to maintain social

= *The same gesture often carries different meanings in different languages. Beware! Don't do this in certain parts of South America. It doesn't mean "okay."*

APPLIED PERSPECTIVE

Anthropologist as Expert Witness

Although often described as a cultural and linguistic melting pot, the United States has always been the home of ethnically and linguistically diverse peoples. Most people living in the United States speak some English, but that in itself does not ensure smooth cross-cultural communication. One well-described case of cross-cultural misunderstanding occurred between six Bannock-Shoshoni Native American women from the Fort Hall reservation and officials at the Social Service Agency in Pocatello, Idaho (Joans 1984).

This breakdown in communication involved the issue of social service payments. The six Native American women were accused in court of withholding information from the agency and failing to report money they had received. To be eligible for supplemental security income (SSI), the women were required to report all forms of income. Several of the women had received several thousand dollars of rent money from small landholdings. They rented the land in January but were not paid until the following December, at which time they reported the income. The agency maintained that the money should have been reported as soon as the property was rented (January) rather than when the income was received. When agency officials learned of the unreported income, they stopped the SSI payments to the women and insisted that they return the money already paid to them. The women claimed that they did not understand the instructions, given in English, concerning the reporting of income. The agency claimed that the women knew full well about the regulations and simply chose to ignore them. When the case came to court, the central issue was whether the women understood what was expected of them.

Barbara Joans, a local anthropologist, was brought in to help resolve the issue. Because the verbal exchanges between the six women and the agency officials had been conducted in English, she would design a study that would

distance, and sexual intentions, to mention several areas. When communicating, people tend to orient their bodies toward others by assuming a certain stance or posture. A person can stand over another person, can kneel, or can "turn a cold shoulder," and in each case something different would be communicated by the body posture. The meaning attached to different body postures varies from one culture to another and is learned in the same way that other aspects of a culture are internalized. To illustrate this point, we can look at differences in body posture that people assume when relaxing. People in the United States,

for example, are sitters, whereas people in some rural parts of Mexico are squatters. This basic cultural difference has actually been used by the U.S. Border Patrol to identify illegal migrants. According to Larry Samovar and Richard Porter (1991), by flying surveillance planes at low altitudes over migrant worker camps in southern California, the border patrol can tell which groups of campers are squatting and which are sitting, the implication being that the squatters are the illegal aliens.

Perhaps one of the most visible and dramatic nonverbal messages sent by posture is that of submissiveness. Gen-

determine the extent to which the six Native American women understood the English language. To do this, she constructed a three-tiered English proficiency exam. Level one tested how well the women understood everyday questions such as, Where is the gas station? Are you too hot? How much is the loaf of bread? Level two tested how well the women understood jokes, double entendres, mixed meanings, and puns. The third level consisted of government/bureaucratic language dealing with such subjects as police operations and the workings of the town council.

The findings of this study demonstrated that the women all understood level one English, only one of the women could follow the conversation using level two English, and none of the six Native American women understood level three English. Over the course of three months, anthropologist Joans had frequent contact with the women in their homes, at the reservation trading post, in the lawyer's office, and in her own office. Based on this contact, Joans concluded that even though the women and the agency personnel all spoke English, they used the language very differently. On the basis of these findings, the judge ruled that, because of the difference in language usage, the women did not understand what was expected of them and thus were not responsible for returning the money. The judge added that in the future agency officials would have to use a Bannock-Shoshoni interpreter when they went to the reservation to describe program requirements. Thus, Joans used her knowledge of language usage, derived from anthropological research, to resolve a problem of miscommunication across cultures.

QUESTIONS FOR FURTHER THOUGHT

1. This case study revolves around a misunderstanding between Native Americans and government bureaucrats. Was this misunderstanding the result of cultural differences, class differences, or differences in power? Explain.
2. Is the United States more of a melting pot or a salad bowl? Explain.
3. When such culturally distinct groups as Native Americans come up against mainstream institutions, miscommunication often occurs. With what other social institutions (other than welfare agencies) could miscommunications occur with Native American populations?

erally, submissiveness is conveyed by making oneself appear smaller by lowering the body (crouching, cowering, or groveling). As part of their religious practices, some Christians kneel, Catholics genuflect, and Muslims kowtow, an extreme form of body lowering in which the forehead is brought to the ground. Nowhere is bowing more important to the process of communication today than in Japanese society. Bowing initiates interaction between two Japanese, it enhances and embellishes many parts of the ensuing conversation, and it is used to signal the end of a conversation. As an indication of how pervasive bowing is in contemporary Japan, some Japanese department stores employ people whose sole function is to bow to customers as they enter the store. In fact, bowing is so ingrained into the Japanese psyche that some Japanese actually bow to invisible partners at the other end of a telephone line.

TOUCHING

Touching is perhaps the most personal and intimate form of nonverbal communication. Humans communicate through touch in a variety of ways or for a variety of

= *Bowing is an important mode of nonverbal communication in Japan.*

purposes, including patting a person on the head or back, slapping, kissing, punching, stroking, embracing, tickling, shaking hands, and laying on hands. Every culture has a well-defined set of meanings connected with touching. That is, each culture defines who can touch whom, on what parts of the body, and under what circumstances.

Some cultures have been described as high-touch cultures, and others are low-touch. Some studies (Montagu 1972; Sheflen 1972; Mehrabian 1981) have suggested that eastern European, Jewish, and Arab cultures tend to be high-touch cultures, whereas northern European cultures such as German and Scandinavian cultures tend to be low touch. The difference between high- and low-touch cultures can be observed in public places, such as subways or elevators. For example, Londoners (from a low-touch culture) traveling in a crowded subway are likely to assume a rigid posture, studiously avoid eye contact, and refuse to even acknowledge the presence of other passengers. The French (from a high-touch culture), on the other hand, have no difficulty leaning and pressing against one another in a crowded Parisian subway.

SUMMARY

1. Language—and the capacity to use symbols— is perhaps the most distinctive hallmark of our humanity.

2. Although nonhumans also engage in communication, human communication systems are unique in several important respects. First, human communication systems are open; that is, they are capable of sending an infinite number of messages. Second, humans are the only animals not confined to the present, for they can speak of events that happened in the past or might happen in the future. Third, human communication is transmitted largely through tradition rather than experience alone.

3. Although imitating adult speech is partially responsible for childrens' acquisition of language, many linguists agree that all humans are born with a grammatical blueprint (Chomsky's universal grammar) that enables children to master their own specific grammatical system.

4. All human languages are structured in two ways. First, each language has a phonological structure comprising rules governing how sounds are combined to convey meanings. Second, each language has its own grammatical structure comprising the

principles governing how morphemes are formed into words (morphology) and how words are arranged into phrases and sentences (syntax).

5. Like other aspects of culture, languages change over time due to both internal and external sources. Historical linguists want to know not only how languages change but also why they change.

6. Despite considerable structural variations in the many languages of the world, there is no evidence to support the claim that some languages are less efficient at expressing abstract ideas than others.

7. Cultures can influence language to the extent that the vocabulary in any language tends to emphasize words that are adaptively important in that culture. Thus, the highly specialized vocabulary in American English relating to the automobile is directly related to the cultural emphasis that North Americans give to that particular part of their technology.

8. According to the Sapir–Whorf hypothesis, language is thought to influence perception. Language, according to Sapir and Whorf, not only is a system of communicating but also establishes mental categories that affect the way in which people conceptualize the real world.

9. Sociolinguists are interested in studying how people use language depending on the social situation or context in which they are operating.

10. As important as language is in human communication, the majority of human messages are sent and received without using words. Human nonverbal communication—which, like language, is learned and culturally variable—can be transmitted through facial expressions, gestures, eye contact, touching, and posture.

KEY TERMS

arbitrary nature of language
bound morphemes
closed systems of communication
code switching
cultural emphasis
diachronic analysis
diglossia
displacement
free morphemes
grammar
language family
morphemes
morphology
nonverbal communication
open systems of communication
phonemes
phonology
Sapir–Whorf hypothesis
synchronic analysis
syntax

SUGGESTED READINGS

Blount, Ben B. *Language, Culture, and Society: A Book of Readings.* 2d ed. Prospect Heights, IL: Waveland Press, 1995. A collection of two dozen readings dealing with a wide range of topics in anthropological linguistics including language and cognition, sociolinguistics, and the relationship between language and culture.

Farb, Peter. *Word Play: What Happens When People Talk.* New York: Knopf, 1974. A highly readable account of linguistics for the nonspecialist.

Fromkin, Victoria, and Robert Rodman. *An Introduction to Language.* New York: CBS College Publishing, 1993. A sprightly introduction to the field of anthropological linguistics.

Hecht, Michael L., Mary Jane Collier, and Sidney Ribeau. *African American Communication: Ethnic Identity and Cultural Interpretation.* Thousand Oaks, CA: Sage, 1993. This volume explores African American styles of communication, ethnic identity, language competence, and the relationship between African Americans and White Americans. The book is designed to help the reader better understand African American communication patterns in their proper cultural context.

Salzmann, Zdenek. *Language, Culture, and Society: An Introduction to Linguistic Anthropology.* Boulder, CO: Westview Press, 1993. A comprehensive, up-to-date introduction to anthropological linguistics, this textbook looks at phonology, the origins of language, the social context of language, nonverbal communication, and the ethnography of communications, among other topics.

Samovar, Larry A., and Richard E. Porter. *Communication Between Cultures.* Belmont, CA: Wadsworth, 1991. A clearly written introduction to the field of intercultural communication, a new field combining communication studies with sociocultural linguistics. The book not only shows how people from different cultures communicate in various ways but goes on to offer the reader specific strategies for improving cross-cultural communication.

Shaul, David, and N. Louanna Furbee. *Language and Culture.* Prospect Heights, IL: Waveland Press, 1997. An up-to-date treatment of the interrelationships of language and culture.

Trudgill, Peter, ed. *Applied Sociolinguistics.* London: Academic Press, 1984. A collection of nine essays by sociolinguists designed to demonstrate the range of real-world activities to which sociolinguistic data can be of interest, including education, psychology, the law, and the media.

Wardhaugh, Ronald. *An Introduction to Sociolinguistics.* Oxford: Blackwell, 1986. Designed as a beginning text in sociolinguistics, this volume deals with such topics as dialects and regional variations, speech communities, language change, gender differences, the relationship between language and culture, and language policy.

On the Net

1. The Summer Institute of Linguistics maintains an interesting web site filled with information about the different languages of the world:

http://www.sil.org

The Ethnologue database has information on thousands of different languages found in the world. Go to the section entitled "Language Name Index" and look up information on the Kikamba language. In what country is it spoken? How many speakers are there? What are several related languages? And what can you learn about the way of life of the speakers of this language?

2. In our very fast-paced world, it is not unlikely that during your career you will be asked to take a foreign assignment. In such an event, where would you turn to learn quickly at least some of the language of your host country? Select a language you would like to learn. By using any search engine, conduct a subject search on that language. What can you learn about the language from the Internet? Are there nearby language courses or schools of which you can take advantage? Are there self-instruction tutorials that you can take directly off the Internet?

3. The Center for Applied Linguistics is an organization devoted to developing effective educational practices for linguistic and cultural minority students. By using any major search engine, go to the center's web site:

http://www.cal.org/crede/

By browsing the different parts of the site, describe how the organization actually goes about applying linguistics to help in the educational process for linguistically and culturally different people.

LOG ON TO INFOTRAC COLLEGE EDITION and conduct a subject search of the topic nonverbal communication. Browse through the first 10 hits. What can you learn about different forms of nonverbal communication? What can you find about differences in nonverbal communication in other cultures? Write a one-page paper on cross-cultural differences in nonverbal communication.

Chapter Seven

GETTING FOOD

WHAT WE WILL LEARN:

▼

What are the different ways by which
societies get their food?

▼

How do technology and environment
influence food-getting strategies?

▼

How have humans adapted to their
environments over the ages?

▼

*A sheep herder from Israel
tending his flock.*

To survive, any culture needs to solve certain societal problems. As we pointed out in our discussion of cultural universals in Chapter 2, all societies must develop

systematic ways of controlling people's behavior, defending the group from outside forces, passing on the cultural traditions from generation to generation, mating, rearing children, and procuring food from the environment to meet their physical needs. Of these basic societal needs, the need to secure food from one's surroundings is the most critical. The human body can survive for as long as a week or so without water and perhaps up to a month without food. Unless a society can develop a systematic and regular way of getting food for its members, the population will die off.

Like other aspects of culture, food-getting strategies vary widely from one society to another. Nevertheless, it is possible to identify five major food-procurement categories found among the world's populations:

▶ *Food collection:* The systematic collection of wild vegetation, the hunting of animals, and fishing.
▶ *Horticulture:* A basic form of plant cultivation using simple tools and small plots of land and relying solely on human power.
▶ *Pastoralism:* Keeping of domesticated animals (such as cows, goats, and sheep) and using their products (such as milk, meat, and blood) as a major food source.
▶ *Agriculture:* A more productive form of cultivation than horticulture because of the use of animal power (such as horses, oxen) or mechanical power (tractors, reapers) and usually some form of irrigation.
▶ *Industrialization:* The production of food through complex machinery.

In this chapter we examine a number of different ways by which societies get their food, how food-getting strategies are influenced by technology and environment, and how humans adapt to a wide variety of environments. Such

means of livelihood as food collecting or nomadic pastoralism are often seen in the West as being backward, irrational, inefficient, and an obstacle to the development of modern economies. Starting from this ethnocentric perspective, many people in the industrialized world believe that foraging, small-scale farming, and nomadic pastoralism must be altered or obliterated as quickly as possible. Before concluding, however, that one particular means of livelihood is superior to all others, it is important to first look at the inherent logic in each food procurement system. When we do that, we are likely to see how that particular food-getting strategy is the most rational for that particular environment.

▪ ENVIRONMENT ▪ AND TECHNOLOGY

WHICH FOOD-GETTING STRATEGY is actually developed by any given culture depends, in large measure, on the culture's environment and technology. The relationship between physical environment and food-getting methods is not neat and tidy; that is, the earth cannot easily be divided into neat ecological zones, each with its own unique and mutually exclusive climate, soil composition, vegetation, and animal life. Nevertheless, geographers (such as James 1966) often divide the world's land surface into a number of categories, including grasslands, deserts, tropical forests, temperate forests, polar regions, and mountain habitats. Some of these environments are particularly hospitable to the extent that they support a number of modes of food acquisition. Others are more limiting in the types of adaptations they permit. Anthropologists generally agree that the environment does not determine food-getting patterns but rather sets broad limits on the possible alter-

Most anthropologists agree that the environment sets broad limits on the possible form that food-getting patterns may take. Cultures help people adapt to a number of generally inhospitable environments.

natives. For example, subsisting on horticulture in the polar region is not an ecological possibility, but a number of other alternatives are possible.

It is technology—a part of culture—that helps people adapt to their specific environment. In fact, the human species enjoys a tremendous adaptive advantage over all other species precisely because it has developed technological solutions to the problems of survival. In many cases, those cultures with complex technologies have gained greater control over their environments and their food supplies.

However, to suggest that such variations in technological adaptations exist is not to imply that societies with simple technologies are less intelligent or less able to cope with their environment. On the contrary, many societies with simple technologies adapt very ingeniously to their particular environment, and they do it without negative consequences to their environments. As John Collins reminds us,

Among some Eskimo groups, wolves are a menace—a dangerous environmental feature that must be dealt with. They could perhaps be hunted down and killed, but this involves danger as well as considerable expenditure of time and energy. So a simple yet ingenious device is employed. A sharp sliver of bone is curled into a springlike shape, and seal blubber is molded around it and permitted to freeze. This is then placed where it can be discovered by a hungry wolf, which, living up to its reputation, "wolfs it down." Later, as this "time bomb" is digested and the blubber disappears, the bone uncurls

and its sharp ends pierce the stomach of the wolf, causing internal bleeding and death. The job gets done! It is a simple yet fairly secure technique that involves an appreciation of the environment as well as wolf psychology and habits. (1975:235)

The specific mode of food getting, however, is influenced by the interaction of a people's environment with its technology. To illustrate, the extent to which a foraging society is able to procure food successfully depends on not only the sophistication of the society's tools but also the abundance of plant and animal life the environment provides. Similarly, the productivity of a society based on irrigation agriculture varies according to the society's technology as well as such environmental factors as the availability of water and the natural nutrients in the water. These environmental factors set an upper limit on the ultimate productivity of any given food-getting system and the size of the population it can support. Cultural ecologists call this limit the environment's **carrying capacity** (Glossow 1978).

A natural consequence of exceeding the carrying capacity is damage to the environment, such as killing off too much game or depleting the soil. Because of this carrying capacity, societies cannot easily increase their food-getting productivity. Thus, if a society is to survive, it must meet the fundamental need of producing or procuring enough food and water to keep its population alive. But beyond satisfying this basic minimal need of survival, societies also satisfy their idiosyncratic and quite arbitrary desires for certain types of food. To a certain degree, people regularly consume the foods that are found naturally (or can be produced) in their immediate environment. But often people go out of their way to acquire some special foods while avoiding other foods that may be both plentiful and nutritious.

Although early anthropologists wrote off such behavior as irrational and arbitrary, cultural ecologists in recent years have examined these peculiar behaviors more carefully and have found that they often make sense in terms of the energy expended versus the caloric value of the foods consumed. This theory—known as the **optimal foraging theory**—suggests that foragers will take the animals and plant species that tend to maximize their caloric return for the time they spend searching, killing, collecting, and preparing (see Smith 1983). In other words, when specific foraging strategies are examined in ethnographic detail, decisions to seek out one food source and not others turn out to be quite rational, for they are based on a generally accurate assessment of whether the search will be worth the effort. To illustrate, the Ache, a foraging group from Paraguay, prefer to hunt peccaries (wild pigs) rather than armadillos, even though armadillos are easier to find and easier to kill. This is, however, a rational decision because the peccaries produce considerably more calories of food per hour of hunting: 4,600 calories per hour for the peccaries as compared to only 1,800 calories for the armadillos (Hill et al. 1987).

•■ MAJOR FOOD-GETTING ■• STRATEGIES

THE FIVE FORMS of food procurement (food collection, horticulture, pastoralism, agriculture, and industrialization) are not mutually exclusive, for in most human societies we find more than one strategy. Where this is the case, however, one form usually predominates. Moreover, in each category we can expect to find considerable variations largely because of differences in environment, technology, and historical experiences. These five categories of food getting are explored in more detail in the following sections.

FOOD COLLECTION

Food collecting—as compared to food producing—involves the exploitation of wild plants and animals that already exist in the natural environment. People have been food collectors for the overwhelming majority of time that they have been on earth. It was not until the **neolithic rev-**olution—approximately 10,000 years ago—that humans for the first time produced their food by means of horticulture or animal husbandry. If we view the period of human prehistory as representing an hour in duration, then humans have been food collectors for all but the last 10 seconds! With the rise of food production, the incidence of food collecting has steadily declined, as George Murdock reminds us:

> Ten thousand years ago the entire population of the earth subsisted by hunting and gathering, as their ancestors had done since the dawn of culture. By the time of Christ, eight thousand years later, tillers and herders had replaced them over at least half of the earth. At the time of the discovery of the New World, only perhaps 15 per cent of the earth's surface was still occupied by hunters and gatherers, and this area has continued to decline at a progressive rate until the present day, when only a few isolated pockets survive. (1968:13)

Even though most societies have become food producers, a handful of societies in the world today (with a combined population of less than half a million people) are still food collectors. These few food-collecting societies vary widely in other cultural features and are to be found in a wide variety of environments (semideserts, tropical forests, and polar regions, among others). For example, some hunting-and-gathering societies such as the !Kung of the Kalahari Desert live in temporary encampments, have small-scale populations, do not store food, and are essentially egalitarian. At the other end of the spectrum are groups such as the Kwakiutl of the Canadian Pacific coast, who live in permanent settlements, have relatively dense populations, live on food reserves, and recognize marked distinctions in rank. Despite these considerable variations among contemporary food collectors, however, it is possible to make the following generalizations about most of them:

1. *Food-collecting societies have low population densities.* The reason for this is that food collection has built-in checks that prevent it from becoming a particularly efficient method for procuring large amounts of food. In other words, increased efficiency in the collection methods of these societies ultimately destroys their source of food.

2. *Food-collecting societies are usually nomadic or seminomadic rather than sedentary.* As a direct result of this continual geographic mobility, food-collecting peoples usually do not recognize individual land rights. By and large, food collectors move periodically from place to place in search of wild animals and

vegetation. Because game often migrates during the yearly cycle, hunters need to be sufficiently mobile to follow the game. Conversely, food producers such as cultivators tend to be more sedentary because of the large investment farmers usually have in their land. There are notable exceptions to both of these generalizations, however. Some food collectors, such as certain groups from the Canadian Pacific coast, live in particularly abundant environments that permit permanent settlements; some horticultural societies (such as the Bemba of Zambia) practice shifting cultivation and, for all practical purposes, are seminomadic.

3. *The basic social unit among food collectors is the family or band, a loose federation of families.* The typical type of social organization found among foragers is small groups of kinsmen that come together at certain times of the year. These small family bands tend to be highly flexible in membership, with various family members coming and going with considerable regularity. Social control revolves around family institutions rather than more formal political institutions, and, in fact, disputes can be avoided by group fission rather than fighting.

4. *Contemporary food-collecting peoples occupy the remote and marginally useful areas of the earth.* These areas include such places as the Alaskan tundra, the Kalahari Desert, the Australian outback, and the Ituru Forest of central Africa. It is reasonable to suggest that these food-gathering societies, with their simple levels of technology, have been forced into these marginal habitats by food producers, with their more dominating technologies.

The association of food collecting with an absence of social, political, and economic complexity is an accurate portrayal of contemporary foraging societies. With several notable exceptions (such as the Ainu of northern Japan and certain northwest coast Indian groups), most contemporary foraging societies are small-scale, unspecialized, egalitarian, and uncentralized. In recent years, however, archaeologists have pointed out that foraging societies in prehistoric times in all likelihood had considerably greater social complexity (see, for example, Price and Brown 1985).

In many societies that rely on both hunting game and collecting wild vegetable matter, the latter activity provides the greatest amount of food. Although hunting wild animals is both spectacular and highly prized, it has been suggested that the bulk of the diets of most food collectors consists of foods other than meat. For example, Richard Lee (1968) estimates that the !Kung of the Kalahari Desert derive between 60 and 80 percent of their diet by weight from vegetable sources. The near total absence of vegetable matter from the diet of the Arctic Inuit is the notable exception to this generalization.

Early anthropological accounts tended to portray food collectors as living precariously in a life-or-death struggle with the environment. In the 1960s, however, some anthropologists (Sahlins, Lee) suggested that certain food-gathering groups are well off despite inhabiting some very unproductive parts of the earth. The question of abundance within food-collecting societies became a topic of heated debate at a major conference of 75 scholars on "Man the Hunter" held in Chicago in 1966. In fact, Marshall Sahlins (1968) described foragers as representing the "original affluent society." Foragers, he argued, spent little time working, had all the food they needed, and enjoyed considerable leisure time. Although many scholars today would take issue with such a formulation, considerable evidence suggests that food collectors are capable of adapting to harsh environments with creativity and resourcefulness. Perhaps we can get a better idea of how foragers procure their food by examining two very different contemporary groups—the !Kung of present-day Namibia and the Inuit of the Arctic region—in greater detail.

The !Kung of the Kalahari Region

One of the best-studied food-collecting societies, the !Kung, inhabit the northwestern part of the Kalahari Desert, one of the least hospitable environments in the world. Inhabiting an area that is too dry to support either agriculture or the keeping of livestock, the !Kung are totally dependent on foraging for their food. Food-procuring activities are fairly rigidly divided between men and women. Women collect roots, nuts, fruits, and other edible vegetables, and men hunt medium and large animals. Although men and women spend roughly equivalent amounts of time on their food-procuring activities, women provide two to three times as much food by weight as men.

Even though the term *affluence* or *abundance* tends to be relative, Lee (1968) presents convincing evidence to suggest that the !Kung are not teetering on the brink of starvation. In fact, there are reasons to believe that the !Kung food-gathering techniques are both productive and reliable. For example, the !Kung's most important single food item is the mongongo nut, which accounts for about half of their diet. Nutritionally, the mongongo, which is found in abundance all year long, contains five times more

= *Despite popular misconceptions, foragers such as the !Kung of Namibia do not live on the brink of starvation.*

calories and 10 times more protein per cooked unit than cereal crops. Thus, quite apart from hunting, the !Kung have a highly nutritional food supply that is more reliable than cultivated foods. It is little wonder that the !Kung do not have a strong urge to take up agriculture when there are so many mongongo nuts available.

Another measure of the affluence of the !Kung is their selectivity in taking foods from the environment. If they were indeed on the brink of starvation, we would expect them to exploit every conceivable source of food. But in actual fact, only about one-third of the edible plant foods are eaten, and only 17 of the 223 local species of animals known to the !Kung are hunted regularly (Lee 1968).

Moreover, if the !Kung were in a life-or-death struggle with the natural environment, their survival rate and life expectancy would be low, infant mortality would be high, malnutrition would be rampant, and the elderly and infirm would be abandoned. This is hardly the demographic picture for the !Kung. Based on fieldwork conducted in the 1960s, Lee (1968) found that approximately 10 percent of

his sample population was 60 years of age or older, a percentage that was not substantially different from industrialized societies.

And finally, the !Kung's abundance of resources can be judged from the amount of time they devote to procuring food. Although food getting is the most important activity among the !Kung, the same is true for cultivators and pastoralists. Although the number of work hours varies from one food-collecting society to another, it appears that the !Kung, despite what might appear to be their harsh environment, are hardly overworked. Lee (1968) estimates that the average !Kung adult spends 12 to 19 hours per week in the pursuit of food. Usually, women can gather enough food in one day to feed their families for three days, leaving a good deal of time for such leisure activities as resting, visiting, entertaining visitors, and embroidering. Even though men tend to work more hours per week than women, they still have considerable leisure time for visiting, entertaining, and dancing.

The Inuit

Like the !Kung, the traditional Inuit of the Arctic region inhabit one of the least hospitable regions of the world. Living in a very delicate balance with their environment, the Inuit rely almost entirely on fishing and hunting of sea and land mammals. Plant life is so scarce that it plays a very minor role in their diet. Living in the barren Arctic and sub-Arctic regions stretching from Greenland in the east to Alaska in the west, the Inuit have had to adapt to a climate of bitterly cold temperatures, short summers, and a terrain almost totally devoid of vegetation. To adapt to such a harsh environment, the Inuit have developed a number of very creative survival strategies. (For much of the twentieth century, the term *Eskimo* has been used by Westerners, both scholars and nonscholars alike, to refer to the aboriginal peoples of Canada and Alaska. Because the term is not found in any of the indigenous languages, the people themselves prefer to be called *Inuit*.)

During the harsh winter months, when the sea is completely frozen over, the Inuit rely very heavily on seal hunting. The most efficient way of hunting seals under these winter conditions is in large hunting parties. To maximize their chances for successful seal hunting, the Inuit often organize themselves into large communities of up to 60 people from several distantly related extended families. During this time, social life is most intense, and various ceremonies are most likely to occur.

Under these frozen conditions seals maintain breathing holes in the ice. Inuit hunters station themselves at these breathing holes and wait patiently, sometimes for hours, for a seal to surface. When a seal appears the Inuit hunter thrusts his harpoon through the breathing hole through the head or neck of the seal. The head of the harpoon (which is attached to a line) separates from the shaft. As the seal attempts to swim away, the hunter pulls on the line until the animal can be brought to the surface, where it is then killed.

During the summer months when seals bask in the sun on top of the ice, the seal-hunting techniques change to include stalking. In order to get close enough to use a throwing harpoon, the hunter needs to get very close to the animal. Sometimes the stalking involves wearing light-colored clothing to blend into the snow and cloudy background. At other times, the hunter wears dark clothing and imitates the behavior of his prey. According to Norman Chance (1990:93), "By mimicking the animal's movements and timing his advance with the seal's short 'naps,' a capable hunter could approach within a few feet."

The most dramatic form of hunting, at least among the western Inuit, involves whaling, an activity that demands both courage and daring. Hunting whales using modern technology is dangerous enough but doing it with harpoons from small boats is even more so. Chance (1990:90) describes the hunt for bowhead whales among the peoples of northern Alaska:

> When a whale was sighted the boat crew launched the umiaq [skin-covered boats] and approached the animal in such a way that the bow of the boat could be placed on its back, or at least close enough for the harpooner to sink one or more of his toggle-headed harpoons into the thick skin. Attached to each harpoon were floats that other crew members quickly cast over the side. The purpose of these floats was not only to indicate the location of the whale, but also to slow it down during its attempts to sound or swim away. Once the whale had become exhausted, the crew could safely approach and the lancer begin his work. The aboriginal lance was ten to twelve feet long and tipped with a razor-sharp flint blade. To prevent the whale from sounding, the lancer severed the tendons controlling the whale's flukes and then probed deeply into its vital organs. As the wounded animal went into its death flurry, the crew retreated to a safe distance. The dead whale was then hauled onto the sea ice and butchered by the local village members.

Following the whaling season in April and May, the Inuit turn their attention to other forms of food collection. As the ice begins to break up, game becomes more plentiful, and the traditional Inuit hunts caribou with bows and arrows and fishes for salmon and trout with pronged spears. During these summer months, people tend to live in smaller groups, and their social interaction is less intense. Thus, the Inuit adapt to a difficult environment by organizing their economic and social lives around the availability of different types of game and the strategies required for hunting them. That is, large social and hunting groups that are more efficient for winter seal hunting split up during the summer into smaller groups that are more functional for fishing and hunting caribou.

Much of what we have described about traditional Inuit food-collection practices has changed over the last 40 years. Today most Inuit live in villages, hunt with guns rather than spears and harpoon, and use snowmobiles rather than dogsleds. Some live in houses with modern conveniences such as telephones and TVs, and a growing number of Inuit are engaged in wage employment. Even though they may eat some imported foods, most Inuit still engage in traditional hunting and fishing. Moreover, they have not abandoned their traditional system of food distribution, one that ensures that no one goes hungry. Today when someone bags a caribou, the local radio station is likely to broadcast the news so no one goes without.

As of April 1, 1999, the Inuit people became masters over their own land when the Canadian government created a new territory called Nunavut ("our land" in the Inuit language). The new territory is 1.2 million square miles, twice the size of Alaska, larger than all of western Europe, and comprising one-fifth of the entire Canadian landmass. Yet the total population for the vast territory is about 27,000, roughly the size of a small suburban commuter town on the outskirts of Toronto. The creation of this new territory will give the Inuit a measure of control over their own lives and an opportunity to preserve their traditional culture. Inuit culture over the years has been influenced by contact with the whaling industry, fur trappers, and even official government attempts to convert young Inuit by placing them in all-English language schools. Nevertheless, much of Inuit culture has remained intact, possibly because for much of the twentieth century the European-dominant Canadian government regarded the Inuit as so remote and insignificant in numbers that it didn't try to subdue them. Interestingly, unlike most other places in the world seeking self-determination, the Inuit were able to achieve theirs peacefully, without civil unrest or even lawsuits.

Unfortunately, not all relationships between foragers and people in the wider society are this cooperative. To illustrate, a contemporary group of Native Americans, the Makah of Neah Bay in the state of Washington, caused a firestorm of protest when in May 1999 they killed their first gray whale in more than 70 years. Environmental activists protested loudly, and according to a *Seattle Times* poll, 90 percent of the general public condemned the televised hunt (Montana 1999). But as tribal leaders pointed out, the Makah did not exercise their treaty rights to hunt gray whales for 70 years because non-Indian commercial hunters had greedily driven them to near extinction. Now that the whale population has recovered, the Makah were exercising their legal rights and their traditions in a responsible manner. In addition, even though the Makah had retained treaty rights to hunt whales during this 70-year hiatus, they chose to work through official channels, eventually receiving permission from the International Whaling Commission in 1997 to harvest up to four whales per year for five years. According to Billy Frank Jr., Chairman of the Northwest Indian Fisheries Commission, "What people saw on television was a living culture exercising a tradition. Just because it is a different tradition to most who live in Washington doesn't make it wrong, just different" (Montana 1999). However one feels about this issue, this recent incident provides an interesting look at a clash between the ancient traditions of a foraging people and the modern world.

These two ethnic groups—the !Kung and the Inuit—have been used consistently for the past several decades as classic examples of hunting-and-gathering societies. In fact, the !Kung have come to be regarded as the quintessential food collectors. Research since the 1980s, however, questions just how representative these two groups are of the world's food collectors. Today we are beginning to revise our view of food collectors as being clever "lay ecologists" who live in an affluent society. To illustrate, studies (Hawkes and O'Connell 1981; Hill et al. 1985) indicate that some foraging groups spend as much as seven or eight hours per day working in subsistence pursuits, not the 12 to 19 hours per week that Lee found to be typical for the !Kung. It also appears that a number of food-collecting groups experience seasonal fluctuations in their dietary intake; in fact, some are chronically undernourished (see, for example, Howell 1986 and Isaac 1990). Moreover, the idyllic, nonviolent existence attributed to foragers has in all likelihood been overstated, for they have been found fighting and raiding one another for food, revenge, or to defend territory (Ferguson 1984; Knauft 1987).

It is also important to keep in mind that although foragers occupy remote habitats, they have always had contact with nonforaging peoples. Today, food collectors do not live in a pristine, isolated world nor is there evidence to suggest that they did in the past. Instead, they are experiencing increased contact with a world of computers, civil wars, and World Bank–sponsored development projects. Many people from food-collecting societies have interacted for years with neighboring groups through trade, employment, and, in some cases, marriage. As Robert Kelly (1995:24–25) reminds us,

> The Penan of Borneo gather rattan today for the world market and probably traded with Chinese merchants at least as long ago as 900 A.D. . . . In Africa, many Bushmen were impressed into modern military forces because of their knowledge of bushlore. . . . African Pygmies were involved in the ivory trade long before Europeans penetrated the Ituri Forest. . . . In North America, Algonquians trapped beaver almost to extinction beginning in the early sixteenth century for the manufacture of hats and other goods in Europe. . . . Down under, Australian Aborigines traded with Macassans from the Celebes well before British colonization. . . . Virtually no hunter-gatherer in the tropical forest today lives without trading heavily with horticulturalists for carbohydrates, or eating government or missionary rations. . . . In brief, long before anthropologists arrived on the scene, hunter-gatherers had already been contacted, given diseases, shot at, traded with, employed and exploited by colonial powers, agriculturalists, and/or pastoralists.

These and many other examples of long-standing contact with the world of nonforagers has resulted in a wide variety of cultural patterns found among people who are generally classified as food collectors.

FOOD-PRODUCING SOCIETIES

Approximately 10,000 years ago, humans made a revolutionary transition from food collecting to food production (the domestication of plants and animals). For hundreds of thousands of years before this time, humans had subsisted exclusively on foraging. Then, for reasons that are still not altogether clear, humans began to cultivate crops and keep herds of animals as sources of food. For the first time, humans gained a measure of control over their food supply. That is, through tilling of the soil and animal husbandry, humans were able to produce food rather than having to rely solely on what nature produced for the environment. This shift from collecting to producing food, known as the neolithic revolution, occurred in several different areas of the world independently of one another. The earliest known plant and animal domestication occurred around 10,000 years ago in the so-called Fertile Crescent, including parts of Jordan, Israel, Syria, southern Turkey, northern Iraq, and western Iran. Other early centers of food pro-

CROSS-CULTURAL MISCUE

LIKE MANY AFRICAN CITIES, Nairobi, Kenya has experienced enormous population growth since the 1960s. A major problem facing urban planners in Kenya has been the question of providing adequate and affordable housing for the rapidly growing population. Nairobi's city council attempted to address this problem by constructing low-cost housing projects. However, the response of the African people to these new, clean, and spacious housing units was somewhat less than enthusiastic. These units—composed of a living room, dining room, kitchen, bathroom, and two bedrooms—were indistinguishable from those found in London or Los Angeles. Like their Western prototypes, those apartments built in Nairobi had the kitchen located next to the dining room with no more than an open portal separating the two rooms. Although this design feature works well in the United States, it violates a basic cultural value in East Africa—that is, that the preparation of food is viewed as an unclean activity. The idea of serving food to one's guests in a room that has a full view of the kitchen is considered rude and offensive. To place a doorless kitchen next to the dining room would be as inappropriate in East Africa as it would be to place a doorless bathroom next to the dining room in our own society. Thus, it is important that architects take into consideration the local cultural realities of the people for whom they are designing buildings.

duction had emerged in China by around 8,000 years ago, Thailand around 8,800 years ago, and sub-Saharan Africa around 5,000 years ago.

A number of theories have been suggested to explain why the neolithic revolution occurred. Although no definitive explanation has emerged, most archaeologists agree that the shift to food production was a response to certain environmental or demographic conditions, such as variations in rainfall or population pressures. It is reasonable to suggest that most of the early foragers did not rush to adopt **agriculture** because of its inherent superiority. Farming requires a greater expenditure of labor than does foraging, it involves more monotonous work, it provides less security, and it usually involves a less varied (and less interesting) diet. Rather than foragers purposefully choosing agriculture as a way of life, it is likely that food production came about because of the need to feed an increasing number of people who could not be sustained by foraging alone. As Jared Diamond (1987:66) has suggested, "farming could support many more people than hunting, albeit with a poorer quality of life."

Whatever the cause or causes may have been, there is little doubt of the monumental consequences of the neolithic revolution. What made the neolithic revolution so revolutionary was that it produced the world's first population explosion. Even though the early neolithic communities were small, they were far larger than any others in

human prehistory. Throughout the Near East, Egypt, and Europe, thousands of skeletal remains have been unearthed from the neolithic period (10,000 to 5,500 years ago) compared to only a few hundred for the entire paleolithic period, even though the paleolithic lasted hundreds of times longer than the neolithic.

Changes Resulting from Food Production

That food producing, as compared to food collecting, should result in a dramatic increase in population is not difficult to understand. As pointed out earlier, food collectors are subject to natural dietary limitations, for increased efficiency can ultimately destroy their source of food. Cultivators, however, can increase the food supply (and thus support larger populations) simply by sowing more seeds. Moreover, children are more useful economically for farmers and herders than they are for food collectors. Whereas children tend to be a burden for the hunter, for food producers they can be useful by weeding fields, scaring off birds or other small animals, and tending flocks at young ages. Population studies (Kasarda 1971; White 1973) have suggested that fertility rates tend to be higher in societies where children make an economic contribution.

Not only did populations become larger as a result of the neolithic revolution, they also became more sedentary. Whereas most food collectors must be mobile enough to follow migrating game, cultivators are more likely to invest their time and energy in a piece of land, develop the notion of property rights, and establish permanent settlements. In other words, a gradual settling-in process occurred as a result of the neolithic revolution. This is not meant to imply that all, or even most, people became tied to the land after the neolithic revolution. Many remained food collectors; some became nomadic or seminomadic pastoralists, and still others became shifting cultivators. Nevertheless, the neolithic (or food-producing) revolution initiated the gradual trend toward a more settled way of life.

The cultivation of crops also brought about other important, even revolutionary, cultural changes. For example, because farming is more efficient than food collecting, a single farmer can produce enough food to feed 10 people. This frees up nine people to engage in some activity other than food procurement. Thus, the neolithic revolution stimulated a greater division of labor. That is, people could for the first time become specialists, inventing and manufacturing the tools and machinery needed for a more complex social structure. Once some people were liberated from the food quest, they were able to develop new farm implements such as the plow, pottery storage containers, metallurgy, improved hunting and fishing technology, the wheel, and stone masonry. Without these and other inventions that resulted from an increase in labor specialization, it is unlikely that we would have ever reached the second revolution: the rise of civilization.

The multitude of changes brought about by the neolithic revolution cannot be overestimated. The introduction of agriculture and animal husbandry 10,000 years ago set humankind on a radically different evolutionary path. Although it enabled humans to move toward civilization (urban societies), the industrial revolution, and now the global information age, was not without its downside. Recent discoveries by paleopathologists (physical anthropologists who study disease among ancient peoples) suggest that early agriculture actually led to a decline in overall health as compared to foraging. To illustrate, skeletal remains of foragers from Greece and Turkey at the end of the ice age (approximately 12,000 years ago) indicate that the average height for men was 5 feet 9 inches and 5 feet 5 inches for women; but by 5,000 years ago the predominantly agricultural people from the same region were appreciably smaller (averaging 5 feet 3 inches for men and 5 feet 0 inches for women), indicating a nutritional decline. Moreover, the excavation of burial mounds in the Illinois and Ohio River valleys indicates a number of negative health consequences of a population that changed from foraging to maize cultivation in the twelfth century. For example, when compared to the foragers who preceded them, the maize farmers had a 50 percent increase in enamel defects caused by malnutrition, four times the incidence of iron deficiency anemia, and a 300 percent increase in bone lesions, indicative of infectious disease (Cohen and Armelagos 1984). With the onslaught of agriculture in the area, the average life expectancy dropped from 26 to 19 years.

There are several reasons why early farmers paid a high price for their newfound food-getting strategy. First, foragers generally had a better balanced diet (composed of both plants and animal proteins) than did early farmers who were often limited to one or several starchy crops. Second, if early farmers were dependent on a small number of crops, they ran the risk of serious malnutrition or even starvation if the crops should fail. And finally, the increased population densities caused by the neolithic revolution brought people into greater contact with one another and consequently made everyone more susceptible to both parasitic and infectious diseases.

Not only did food production have negative health consequences, it also had some dramatic social effects as well. The egalitarianism of foraging societies was rapidly replaced by increasing social inequality and all of the deleterious trappings, such as poverty, crime, war, aggression, and environmental degradation. Thus, even though we often glorify the introduction of agriculture as a defining moment in human evolution, it did certainly have some negative consequences.

Horticulture

Horticulture is the simplest type of farming that uses basic hand tools such as the hoe or digging stick rather than plows or other machinery driven by animals or machines. Because horticulturalists produce low yields, they generally do not have sufficient surpluses to allow them to develop extensive market systems. The land, which is usually cleared by hand, is neither irrigated nor enriched by the use of fertilizers. A major technique of horticulturalists is **shifting cultivation,** sometimes called **swidden cultivation** or the **slash and burn method.** This technique involves clearing the land by manually cutting down the growth, burning it, and planting in the burned area. Even though the ash residue serves as a fertilizer, the land is usually depleted within a year or two. The land is then allowed to lie fallow to restore its fertility, or it may be abandoned altogether. This technique of slash and burn cultivating can eventually destroy the environment, for if fields are not given sufficient time to fallow, the forests will be permanently replaced by grasslands.

The crops grown by horticulturalists can be divided into three categories: tree crops, seed crops, and root crops. Tree crops include bananas and plantains, figs, dates, and coconuts; major seed crops (which tend to be high in protein) are wheat, barley, corn, oats, sorghum, rice, and millet; main root crops (which tend to be high in starch and carbohydrates) include yams, arrowroots, taro, manioc, and potatoes. Because seed crops require a greater quantity of nutrients than root crops, seed cultivators need longer periods of time to fallow their fields. In some cases, this can have consequences for settlement patterns. That is, if seed cultivators do need a longer time to rejuvenate their fields, they may be less likely to live in permanent settlements than are root cultivators. However, even though swidden cultivation involves the shifting of fields, it does not necessarily follow that the cultivators also periodically shift their homes.

Many horticulturalists supplement their simple cultivation with other food-getting strategies. For example, some, such as the Yanomamo (Chagnon 1983), may engage in hunting and gathering; others, such as the Swazi (Kuper 1986), keep a variety of domesticated animals, including cows, goats, sheep, horses, donkeys, and pigs; still others (such as the Samoans) supplement their crops with protein derived from fishing.

At first glance it appears that slash and burn agriculture makes very poor use of the land. Because most land must be left fallow at any given time, the system of slash and burn cannot support the high densities of population that can be sustained by intensive agriculture. Although there are inherent limitations to the technique, slash and burn horticulturalists are often extremely adept at maximizing their resources. A number of slash and burn farmers produce quite abundant harvests of tropical forest products and do so without destroying the land. To illustrate, R. Jon McGee (1990) has shown that the Lacandon Maya of Chiapas, Mexico, disperse over 40 different crops throughout their cleared fields (milpas). By spreading their many crops over a milpa, the Lacandon are imitating both the diversity and the dispersal patterns found in the natural primary forest. According to McGee,

> In contrast to monocrop agriculture as practiced in the United States, the milpa attempts to maintain rather than replace the structure of the tropical rainforest ecosystem. In effect, the milpa is a portion of jungle where a greater

than normal population of food-producing crops has been concentrated. This concentration of food is aided by the fact that Lacandon farmers plant their milpas with crops that take advantage of different environmental niches within the same cleared area. For example, at ground level, hills of corn, beans, squash, and tomatoes are sown. A few meters above the surface grow tree crops such as bananas and oranges, and finally, subsurface root crops such as manioc and sweet potatoes are cultivated below the ground's surface. Thus, a Lacandon farmer achieves at least three levels of production from the same piece of land. (1990:36)

McGee points out that this form of slash and burn horticulture is quite efficient, for the typical Lacandon Mayan family can feed itself while working fewer than half the days in a year. Working in areas with vast areas of unused land, slash and burn horticulture can be a reasonably efficient form of food production. In the late 1990s, however, slash and burn horticulturalists were criticized by governments and environmental groups. Under normal rainfall conditions, the slash and burn technique destroys large tracts of both forests and grassland. But with the widespread droughts caused by El Niño in recent years, many of the fires for clearing land for crops have burned out of control. Huge clouds of smoke have recently spread over large areas of Brazil, Madagascar, Indonesia, and even east Texas, which has been in the path of slash and burning in Mexico. Major cities of Southeast Asia have experienced dangerous levels of air pollution due to fires raging out of control in Sarawak and Borneo. Under these dry conditions, the slash and burn horticultural technique has had disastrous consequences. Entire species of trees may be lost due to too frequent slash and burning, preventing the trees from regenerating their seeds. These uncontrolled fires have the additional negative effect of driving wildlife out of the forests. Moreover, the destruction of forests accelerates the rate of soil erosion, thereby reducing the long-term productivity of the land.

The Bemba

A specific example will help illustrate the practice of horticulture. Audrey Richards (1960) provides a particularly good case study with her writings on the Bemba of present-day Zambia (formerly Northern Rhodesia). The Bemba, like a number of other peoples in south central Africa, practice a type of shifting cultivation that involves clearing the land, burning the branches, and planting directly on the ash-fertilized soil without additional hoeing. Using the simplest technology (hoes and axes), the Bemba plant a fairly wide range of crops—including finger millet, bulrush millet, beans, cassava, and yams—but they rely most heavily on finger millet as their basic staple. Although predominantly horticultural, the Bemba do supplement their diet by some hunting, gathering, and fishing. The largest and most highly organized group politically in Zambia, the Bemba live in small, widely scattered, low-density communities comprising 30 to 50 huts.

Traditionally, Bemba society had a highly complex political system based on a set of chiefs whose authority rested on their alleged supernatural control over the land and the prosperity of the people. These supernatural powers were reinforced by the physical force that chiefs could exert over their subjects, whom they could kill, enslave, or sell. The power, status, and authority of the chiefs were based not on the accumulation of material wealth but rather on the amount of *service* they could extract from their subjects in terms of agricultural labor or military service. Interestingly, the marked status differences between chiefs (with their unchallenged authority) and commoners is not reflected in these people's diets. Although chiefs and their families may have a somewhat more regular supply of food, both rich and poor eat essentially the same types and quantities of food throughout the yearly cycle. Similarly, there are no appreciable differences in diet between Bemba men and Bemba women.

Because sparse rainfall at certain times of the year permits only one crop, a common feature of the Bemba diet is the alternation between scarcity and plenty. The harvest of finger millet, the mainstay of the Bemba diet, lasts only nine months (roughly from April through December). During the lean months of January through March, dramatic changes take place in village life. Because of the low energy levels, most activity—both leisure and work related—is reduced to a minimum. Given these alternating periods of feast and famine, it is not surprising that food and diet occupy a prominent place in Bemba culture. In much the same way that pastoralists often appear obsessed with their cattle, the Bemba tend to fixate on food. In fact, according to Richards, food and beer are the central topics of conversation among the Bemba:

> Any one who can follow the ordinary gossip of a Bemba village will be struck at once by the endless talk shouted from hut to hut as to what is about to be eaten, what has already been eaten, and what lies in store for the future, and this with an animation and a wealth of detail which would be thought quite unusual in this country. . . . The giving or receipt of food is a part of most economic transactions, and many come to represent a number of human relationships whether between different kinsmen or between subject and chief. . . . To speak of a chief is to mention before the end of the conversation his reputation for generosity or meanness in the giving of porridge and beer. To describe an attitude of any particular kinsman leads almost invariably to a comment, for instance, on the food in his granary, the numbers of relatives he supports, the share of meat he has asked for, or the amount of beer he contributed at the marriage of his daughter or the visit of an elder. In daily life the women, whether at work in the kitchen or sitting gossiping on their verandas at night, exchange interminable criticisms as to the way in which some particular dish of food has been divided, or the distribution of the four or five gourds of beer made at a brew. (1960:106)

Pastoralism

Like horticulture, **pastoralism** first appeared in the neolithic period. This form of food production involves the keeping of domesticated herd animals and is found in areas of the world that cannot support agriculture because of inadequate terrain, soils, or rainfall. However, these environments do provide sufficient vegetation to support livestock, provided the animals are able to graze over a large enough area. Thus, pastoralism is associated with geographic mobility, for herds must be moved periodically to exploit seasonal pastures (Barfield 1993).

Some anthropologists have differentiated between two types of movement patterns: transhumance and nomadism. With **transhumance,** some of the men in a pastoral society move their livestock seasonally to different pastures while the women, children, and the other men remain in permanent settlements. With **nomadism,** on the other hand, there are no permanent villages, and the whole social unit of men, women, and children moves the livestock to new pastures. But as Rada and Neville Dyson-Hudson have pointed out (1980), the enormous variations even within societies render such a distinction somewhat sterile. For example, following seven Karamojong herds over a two-year period, the Dyson-Hudsons found that "each herd owner moved in a totally different orbit, with one remaining sedentary for a full year and one grazing his herd over 500 square miles" (1980:18).

Even though anthropologists tend to lump pastoralists into a single food-getting category, pastoralism is not a unified phenomenon. For example, there are wide variations in the ways animals are herded. The principal herd animals are cattle in eastern and southern Africa, camels in North Africa and the Arabian Peninsula, reindeer in the sub-Arctic areas of eastern Europe and Siberia, yaks in the

Himalayan region, and various forms of mixed herding (including goats, sheep, and cattle) in a number of places in Europe and Asia. In addition to variations in the type of animals, a number of other social and environmental factors can influence the cultural patterns of pastoral people, including the availability of water and pasturage, the presence of diseases, the location and timing of markets, government restrictions, and the demands of other food-getting strategies (such as cultivation) that the pastoralists may practice.

A general characteristic of nomadic pastoralists is that they take advantage of seasonal variations in pasturage so as to maximize the food supply of their herds. The Kazaks of Eurasia, for example, keep their livestock at lower elevations during the winter, move to the foothills in the spring, and migrate to the high mountain pastures during the summer. Such seasonal movement provides optimal pasturage and avoids climatic extremes that could negatively affect the livestock. This willingness to move their animals at different times of the year avoids overgrazing and enables them to raise considerably more livestock than they could if they chose not to migrate.

The consensus among anthropologists is that pure pastoralists—that is, those who get all of their food from livestock—are either extremely rare or nonexistent. Because livestock alone cannot meet all of the nutritional needs of a population, most pastoralists need some grains to supplement their diets. Many pastoralists, therefore, either combine the keeping of livestock with some form of culti-

vation or maintain regular trade relations with neighboring agriculturalists. Moreover, the literature is filled with examples of nomadic pastoralists who produce crafts for sale or trade, occasionally work for the government, or drive trucks. Thus, many pastoralists have long engaged in nonpastoral activities, but they have always considered animal husbandry to be their normal, or certainly ideal, means of livelihood.

It is clear that in pastoral societies livestock play a vital economic role not only as a food source but also as a resource for other uses to which their products can be put. In addition to the obvious economic importance of meat, milk, and blood as food sources, cattle provide dung (used for fertilizer, house building, fuel), bone (used for tools and artifacts), skins (used for clothing), and urine (used as an antiseptic). But in addition to these important economic uses, there are a number of important noneconomic or **social functions of cattle.** Livestock often influence the social relationships among people in pastoral societies. To illustrate, an exchange of livestock between the families of the bride and the groom is required in many pastoral societies before a marriage can be legitimized. In the event of an assault or a homicide, in some societies livestock is used to compensate the victim's family as a way of restoring normal social relations. The sacrifice of livestock at the grave site of ancestor gods is a way in which people keep in touch with their gods. These and other social uses of cattle or other livestock should remind us that domesticated animals in pastoral societies not only serve as the major food

= *These Tibetan yak herders must move their animals periodically to ensure adequate pasturage.*

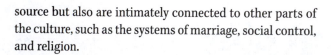

Traditional Pastoralists Become Cattle Ranchers

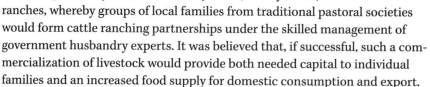

The Tanzanian Livestock Project is an excellent example of how the participation of a cultural anthropologist contributed to an economic development program in East Africa. The project, aimed at developing commercial beef ranching in Tanzania, involved a socioeconomic restructuring of pastoral economies. The objective of the program was to modify the largely subsistence nature of cattle keeping so that it would be more market oriented and produce more income. This was to be accomplished by the creation of Ujamaa ("familyhood") ranches, whereby groups of local families from traditional pastoral societies would form cattle ranching partnerships under the skilled management of government husbandry experts. It was believed that, if successful, such a commercialization of livestock would provide both needed capital to individual families and an increased food supply for domestic consumption and export.

Much to the credit of the project administrators, Priscilla Reining, a cultural anthropologist experienced with pastoral societies in northern Tanzania, was invited to participate in the appraisal of the project conducted by the World Bank. Reining was asked to assess a number of aspects of traditional culture that might have an impact on the formation of the proposed Ujamaa ranches, such as traditional sex roles, lines of authority, inheritance customs, value placed on age, and conceptions of property rights. Reining then had the difficult task of making recommendations on how to select program participants, how to organize the Ujamaa ranches, and what incentives to provide for participation.

source but also are intimately connected to other parts of the culture, such as the systems of marriage, social control, and religion.

SOMALI PASTORALISM The pastoral Somali of the Horn of East Africa are an excellent example of a pastoral society that engages in mixed herding. The Somali number over 2 million people in the Somali republic itself, with an additional million currently living in southeastern Ethiopia and northern Kenya. As in other pastoral societies, not only do livestock supply the bulk of the Somali's subsistence, but household composition and nomadic movements are dictated largely by environmental conditions and the seasonal needs of the herds.

Somali pastoralism is based on the keeping of sheep, goats, camels, cattle, donkeys, and horses. Sheep and goats contribute most to the Somali diet in the form of milk and meat. Camels provide some milk, but their main role in the Somali economy is to transport the collapsible huts during periods of migration. Zebu cattle, less common among the Somali, are used as a source of milk for domestic use and ultimately as an export commodity. Donkeys are used exclusively as beasts of burden, and horses, though scarce, serve as a means of rapid transportation and as a status symbol.

The physical environment of the Somali is anything but hospitable. Much of the terrain is semidesert, with sparse rainfall and intermittent vegetation. The Somali recognize

Based on her understanding of the traditional cultures of these pastoral peoples, Reining made a number of recommendations designed to mesh the program goals with the traditional cultural features. In addition, Reining was able to point out to the program administrators the multiple uses of cattle for the local herding peoples. As mentioned earlier, cows have a different meaning for East African pastoralists than they do for Texas beef ranchers. To be certain, cattle are important economic commodities, but for the Tanzanian pastoralist, they are also important socially in terms of prestige, friendship bonds, and the legitimization of marriages. Armed with this understanding, the program administrators came to realize that commercial ranching would not be accepted overnight. The success of the program depended on how well the social organization of the Ujamaa ranches provided appropriate alternatives for the many social uses of cattle found in the traditional cultures. Speaking of the anthropological contribution to the project, one administrator concluded the following:

> It appears unlikely that the team, without an anthropologist, could have seen all of the ramifications of the changes the project was proposing. The anthropological input was significant; it added depth and understanding to our reasons for supporting Ujamaa. (Husain 1976:78)

QUESTIONS FOR FURTHER THOUGHT

1. What was the major anthropological contribution to the Tanzanian Livestock Project?
2. In what ways do cattle have different significance for pastoralists in Tanzania and Texas beef ranchers?
3. Anthropologist Reining's role in this project was to demonstrate the social (noneconomic) importance of cattle and to suggest alternatives for taking these into consideration when planning a new livestock program. Should the job of anthropologists end with making suggestions, or should they also become involved in selecting and implementing the alternatives? Why?

three fairly distinct ecological zones that, depending on the season, provide differential quantities of the two resources absolutely essential to pastoralism: water and pasturage. Migration and temporary settlement take place in all three regions, depending on the four major seasons, two wet and two dry. Even under the best conditions, these three ecological zones are so harsh that, as I. M. Lewis concludes, "the line between survival and disaster is precariously narrow" (1965:329).

To maximize their resources as well as their adaptation to an unforgiving environment, Somali herders divide into two distinct grazing units. One unit is the nomadic hamlet, based on sheep and goats, that engages in migratory patterns designed to meet the regular watering needs of these important food-producing animals. Socially, these herding units consist of small groups of nuclear families related through the male line. Nomadic hamlets are not stable units, however, for men periodically attach their nuclear or polygynous families to a number of different groups of kin during any given season. On the average, nomadic hamlets contain three nuclear families but can involve more, particularly during times of warfare, when larger groups can provide greater security.

In contrast to the nomadic hamlet, the camel camp, containing only grazing camels, serves essentially as the training grounds where boys learn the skills of camel husbandry. Life in the camel camp is austere, especially during the dry season. The boys and men of the camel camp live predominantly on camel's milk, have no means of cooking, sleep out in the open, and spend large amounts of time driving their animals between water and pasturage. Unlike the hamlets, which may include a number of types of kin, the camel camps include only kin related through the male line, a distinction that reflects how the different types of livestock are viewed. Whereas sheep and goats are owned by individuals, camels are viewed as representing the wealth of the larger kin group—the lineage. Whereas goats and sheep are used primarily to meet individual dietary needs, camels are the principal currency in such important lineage transactions as bridewealth and blood compensation. Because of their different grazing requirements, the hamlets and the camel camps move independently of each other, being closer together during the wet seasons and more widely dispersed during the dry seasons.

In recent decades the pastoral Somali, like many other nomadic peoples, have been under pressure by their governments to give up their nomadic ways. Most governments are inherently suspicious of nomadism as a way of life because it doesn't fit neatly into national boundaries. Nomads are seen as unmodern, largely because they do not contribute to national economic development. Often governments justify their efforts to make nomads stay put on the basis that it is for their own good: Only if they are permanently settled can they receive proper education and medical care. But governments also have a need to know where all of their citizens are located so they can be taxed.

After the drought of 1974, the Somali government attempted to move over 100,000 camel herders into four villages on the coast of the Indian Ocean. The goal was to transform these nomadic camel keepers into small-scale farmers and fishermen. But, the keeping of livestock such as camels is far more than just a means of livelihood. In the case of the Somali people, camels are intertwined into the total fabric of their lives. To expect a Somali to willingly give up nomadic camel herding for farming is as probable as expecting the president of Ford Motor Company to become a social worker. Needless to say, this Somali relocation program—one designed to both change their way of life and make them sedentary—was not successful (Janzen 1994).

Agriculture

Agriculture (intensive cultivation) differs from horticulture in that agriculture relies on animal power and technology rather than on human power alone. Agriculture, a more recent phenomenon than horticulture, is characterized by the use of the plow, draft animals to pull the plow, fertilizers, irrigation, and other technological innovations that make intensive cultivation much more efficient than horticulture. A single cultivator using a horse-drawn plow, for example, not only can put a larger area of land under cultivation but also, because the plow digs deeper than the hoe or digging stick, unleashes more nutrients from the soil, thereby increasing the yield per acre. Animal fertiliz-

These Somali pastoralists live in a delicate balance with their semidesert environment.

CROSS-CULTURAL MISCUE

THE MASAI are a group of pastoralists (cattle herders) living in Kenya and Tanzania. In fact, they have so many cows that the environment cannot support them very well. As a result, the land is overgrazed, and the cows are rather scrawny and give little milk. With this in mind, the British colonial officials tried to get the Masai to reduce the size of their herds so that they would have healthier, fatter, and better milking cows. The British officials reasoned (correctly) that by reducing the number of cows, the Masai would actually have more milk and more beef in the long run. But the Masai strongly refused to reduce the size of their herds. The British concluded (this time incorrectly) that the Masai were simply too stupid to know any better.

The British officials failed to understand the basic value system of the Masai, a value system that is very different from their own. Unlike dairy farmers in the West, the Masai are not interested in maximizing the total quantity of milk given by their cows because they already have far more milk than they can drink, and they are not in the business of selling milk. For the Masai, cows are far more than simply sources of milk. Rather, cows are significant for social reasons. For example, cows are used to legalize marriages, to bond together friends, and to increase one's prestige. In short, the more cows the Masai have, the better off they are. They are not interested in having fat cows that give large quantities of milk. Instead, they are interested in the sheer number of cows, even if they are scrawny and poor milkers. Given such a value system, it would be as unreasonable for the Masai to voluntarily thin out their herds as it would be for us to exchange five old, wrinkled dollar bills for two new crisp dollar bills. From the Masai's perspective, it is the quantity, not the quality, of the cows that counts.

ers (from the excrement of the draft animals) permit land to be used year after year rather than having to remain fallow to restore its fertility naturally. Irrigation of fields that do not receive sufficient or consistent rainfall is another innovation contributing to the increased efficiency of intensive agriculture. Moreover, the invention of the wheel has been a boon to the intensive farmer in transportation, the water-raising wheel, and pottery making (storage vessels for surplus crops). Thus, through the application of technology, the intensive cultivator has access to a much greater supply of energy than is available to the horticulturalist.

This greater use of technology enables the agriculturalist to support many times more people per unit of land than the horticulturalist. There is a price for this greater productivity, however, because intensive agriculture requires a greater investment of both labor and capital. First, in terms of labor, agriculturalists must put in vast numbers of hours of hard work to prepare the land. In hilly areas, the land must be terraced and maintained, and irrigation systems may involve drilling wells, digging trenches, and building dikes. All of these activities increase the land's productivity enormously but are extremely labor intensive. Second, intensive agriculture, as compared to horticulture, requires a much higher investment of capital in terms of plows (which must be maintained), mechanical pumps (which can break down), and draft animals (which can become sick and die).

Agriculture, a more recent phenomenon than horticulture, is closely associated with both higher levels of productivity and more settled communities. In fact, not until early horticultural societies had developed into more intensive forms of agriculture could humankind develop civilizations (that is, urban societies). In other words, a fully efficient system of food production, brought about by intensive agriculture, is a necessary, if not sufficient, condition for the rise of civilization.

As farming became more intensive, the specialization of labor became more complex. Under a system of intensive agriculture, a single farmer could produce enough food for ten people; this increase in productivity meant that nine people could devote their time and energy to such

= *The use of draft animals, as practiced by this farmer from Hoi An, Vietnam, involves a more complex form of crop production than swidden farming.*

activities as manufacturing, education, public administration, writing, or inventing rather than the pursuit of food. Thus, the intensification of agriculture did not cause, but rather enabled, the development of a more complex division of labor. Societies became more stratified (that is, marked by greater class differences), political and religious hierarchies were established to manage the economic surpluses and mediate among the different socioeconomic classes, and eventually, state systems of government (complete with bureaucracies, written records, taxation, a military, and public works projects) were established. Although the relationship is not necessarily a causal one, these structural changes would not have occurred without the development of an efficient system of food production which agriculture provided.

Peasantry

With the intensification of agriculture and the rise of civilization came the development of the **peasantry.** Peasant farmers differ from American Indian horticulturalists, Polynesian fishing people, or East African herders in that they are not isolated or self-sufficient societies. Instead, peasants are tied to the larger unit (the city or state)—politically, religiously, and economically. More specifically, peasants are subject to the laws and controls of the state, are influenced by the urban-based religious hierarchies, and exchange their farm surpluses for goods produced in other parts of the state. Peasants usually make up a large percentage of the total population and provide most of the dietary needs of the city dwellers.

The intimate relationship peasants have with the cities and the state is succinctly stated by George Foster, who calls peasants "a peripheral but essential part of civilizations, producing the food that makes possible urban life, supporting the specialized classes of political and religious rulers and educated elite" (1967:7). Foster's statement is important because it reminds us that the relationship between the peasants and the state is hardly egalitarian. The

= *This terraced form of farming, as found in Indonesia, involves a long-term commitment to the land and a considerable expenditure of labor.*

peasants almost always occupy the lowest strata of society. Although they supply the rest of the society with its food, peasants have low social status, little political power, and scant material wealth. The more powerful urbanites, through the use of force or military power, often extract both labor and products from the peasants in the form of taxation, rent, or tribute.

Industrialized Food Getting

As we have seen, the domestication of plants and animals around 10,000 years ago expanded people's food-getting capacity geometrically from what it had been when they relied on hunting and gathering alone. Similarly, the intensification of agriculture brought about by the invention of the plow, irrigation, and fertilizing techniques had revolutionary consequences for food production. A third major revolution in our capacity to feed ourselves occurred several hundred years ago with the coming of the industrial revolution. **Industrialization** in food production relies on technological sources of energy rather than human or animal energy. Water and wind power (in the forms of waterwheels and windmills) were used in the early stages of the industrial period, but today industrialized agriculture uses motorized equipment such as tractors and combines. The science of chemistry has been applied to modern agriculture to produce fertilizers, pesticides, and herbicides, all of which increase agricultural productivity.

In addition to the quantum leaps in agricultural productivity in the past 200 years, technology has been applied with equally dramatic results to other areas of food production. For example, oceangoing fishing vessels harvest enormous quantities of fish from the seas, scientific breakthroughs in genetics and animal husbandry now produce increasingly larger supplies of meat and poultry, and a certain amount of food in the modern person's diet is actually manufactured or reconstituted.

Farmers operating in industrialized societies today have a wealth of new technology at their disposal to increase productivity. Like most other professions, industrialized farmers are now using the Internet for acquiring a wide range of agricultural information—from equipment sales to pesticide use to marketing opportunities. Moreover, new systems of gathering weather information are also helping farmers with crop management. Rather than individual farmers having to take weather measurements in their own orchards, fields, and vineyards, precise local information is now available on rainfall, temperature, humidity, and soil water content that comes directly to the farmer's own desktop computer. With such information at their fingertips, farmers are able to assess their risk and react quickly to protect their crops.

With industrialized farming becoming increasingly competitive, a small but growing number of farmers in North America are attempting to gain a competitive edge by using the very latest information technology. Thomas Friedman (1999) describes how some farmers are equipping their grain-harvesting combines with transmitters that allow a global positioning satellite (GPS) to track their exact position in their fields at any given point in time. This technology provides information on precisely how much grain is being harvested from each acre of land. Armed with such exact data on crop outputs, farmers can determine the precise crop variety, water level, and fertilizer that will produce the highest possible yield for each parcel of land. This high-tech solution to farm management is good for the environment because it uses fertilizer more economically, and it is good for the farmer because it increases the overall yield per unit of land. Thus, the information age is not just something that is transforming urban areas. Rather, it is having—and will continue to have—an important impact on rural, agricultural populations as well.

Food getting—and agriculture in particular—in contemporary industrialized societies has experienced some very noticeable changes since the late eighteenth century. Before the industrial revolution, agriculture was carried out primarily for subsistence; farmers produced crops for their own consumption rather than for sale. Today, however, agriculture is largely commercialized in that the overwhelming majority of food today is sold by food producers to nonproducers for some form of currency. Moreover, industrialized agriculture requires complex systems of market exchange because of its highly specialized nature.

Within the past several decades in the Western world, the trend toward commercialization of agriculture has seen its most dramatic expression in the rise of agribusiness—large-scale agricultural enterprises involving the latest technology and a sizable salaried workforce. The rise of agribusiness in recent years has been accompanied by the decline of mom-and-pop farms that drew mainly on family labor. As the number of family farms has declined and agriculture has become more highly mechanized, the developed world has witnessed a dramatic decrease in the percentage of the world's population that is engaged in food production.

Even though the industrialization of agriculture has produced farms of enormous size and productivity, these changes have not been without a very high cost. The

World's Drug Companies Rely on "Primitive Medicine"

Over the centuries indigenous peoples have accumulated vast amounts of scientific data that have relevance to the solution of contemporary societal problems. They have learned to use their knowledge of ocean currents to navigate long distances in the Pacific; they have cultivated numerous strains of crops useful to Western botanists; and they have exploited a wide variety of food sources without damaging their delicate ecosystems. However, much of this scientific knowledge is being lost as these indigenous peoples lose their land, their language, and their cultures.

The South American tropical rain forest is the home of about one-quarter (60,000) of all plant species on the planet. Of those, only a small fraction have been studied to determine their chemical properties or their therapeutic potential. In other words, there are tens of thousands of plant species in the Amazon jungle that could hold a key to solving a number of pressing medical problems, including AIDS and various forms of cancer. Western medical science is just beginning to realize that local tribal people know more about these plants and their healing properties than we do. Cultural anthropologists specializing in ethnobotany (the study of how tribal societies use local plant life) are now studying tribal pharmacology so that Western medicine can use this knowledge.

About one-quarter of all prescription drugs sold in the United States are derived from plants, and half of these come from the tropical rain forest of South America. Mark Plotkin (1995) estimates that people in the United States alone spend more than $6 billion per year on drugs derived from tropical plants. Among the many tropical plants used in Western medicine (which have been used to treat precisely the same maladies among indigenous rain forest cultures) are the following (Maybury-Lewis 1992:50):

Horse chestnuts	Anti-inflammatory
Lily of the valley	Heart stimulant
Common foxglove	Heart stimulant
Tumeric	Heart stimulant
May apple	Anticancer agent
Goldenseal	Astringent
Toothpick plant	Aid for breathing
Rattlebox	Antitumor agent

False hellebore	Tranquilizer
Yellow azalea	Tranquilizer
Quinine	Antimalarial
Cocoa	Diuretic
Kuntze	Diuretic

The pink-flowered periwinkle plant is an example of the impact tribal pharmacology has had on Western medicine. Although native to Madagascar, the pink-flowered periwinkle was transported throughout the tropical world by European explorers who valued it for its beautiful flowers. They did not realize that the plant had been used by native cultures of Asia, Africa, and the New World for its therapeutic properties. When researchers noticed that healers in Jamaica were using the plant to treat diabetes, they decided to test the chemical properties of periwinkle on rats. Due to the plant's ability to lower white blood cell counts, it is now used to treat leukemia, and an alkaloid, vinglastin, is used to treat lymphoma, tumors, and Hodgkin's disease.

Ethnobotanists such as Plotkin are collecting specimens of plant life that indigenous peoples of the rain forest have used for medicinal purposes. There are thousands of such species awaiting discovery by Western scientists. The important contribution that these cultural anthropologists are making is in the collection of the folk knowledge from the local medicinal practitioners as to how (and for what purposes) these medicines are used. The challenge is to collect this information before the rain forest, the traditional cultures, and their systems of drug use are lost forever. It is estimated that the rain forest is being destroyed at such an alarming rate that by the year 2000 10 percent of the rain forest's plant species will become extinct (Plotkin 1995). As David Maybury-Lewis (1992:49) has warned,

> What we are witnessing makes the burning of the library of Ancient Alexandria look insignificant by comparison. It is as if the greatest medical library in the world is burning faster than we can read its contents, which we have just begun to catalogue.

QUESTIONS FOR FURTHER THOUGHT

1. In addition to the medicinal properties of certain plants, what other things might the industrialized world learn from inhabitants of the rain forest?

2. Why are the Amazon rain forests disappearing so rapidly? What suggestions can you offer that would prevent the destruction of the rain forest and the cultures that inhabit it?

3. If anthropologists collect plants and knowledge from rain forest medical experts and then have them produced commercially by Western drug companies, should the local tribes benefit from the profits of the sale of these drugs?

machinery and technology needed to run modern-day agribusiness are expensive. Fuel costs to run the machinery are high. With the vast diversification of foods found in modern North American diets (oranges from Florida, cheese from Wisconsin, corn from Iowa, avocados from California, and coffee from Colombia), additional expenses are incurred for processing, transporting, and marketing food products. Moreover, large-scale agriculture has been responsible for considerable environmental destruction. For example, large-scale agriculture in various parts of the world has led to lowering of water tables, changes in the ecology of nearby bodies of surface water, the destruction of water fauna by pesticides, the pollution of aquifers by pesticides, salinization of soil from overirrigation, and air pollution from crop spraying. Moreover, large-scale commercial fishing has decimated fish stock throughout the world, and such commercial animal operations as hog farms in North Carolina have given us what are euphemistically called swine lagoons (man-made reservoirs filled with hog feces and urine), which have a nasty habit of breaking and dumping their contents into local rivers. The litany of the negative effects of agriculture is almost endless. In fact, one anthropologist (Diamond 1987) has described agriculture as "the worst mistake in the history of the human race."

•■ FOOD-COLLECTING ■• STRATEGIES AND SCIENCE

WHEN MOST WESTERNERS think about foragers, pastoralists, or horticulturalists, we tend to think of societies with minimal technology, inefficient means of survival, and little or no scientific rationality. But all of these so-called "primitive" means of livelihood require processing large amounts of information about the environment over long periods of time. Only through systematic observations over the long haul is it possible to see patterns and regularities. It is the generalizations made on the basis of these observations, resulting in scientific understanding, that enable indigenous peoples to adapt successfully to their environments. To illustrate, Inupiaq hunters of Alaska possess knowledge based on generations of systematic observations that are no less scientific than what we would expect from a trained zoologist. Ringed seals, they have found, can reliably forecast the weather by accurately predicting unexpected gales. Stable weather is in the forecast when the seals rise chest-high in the water with their noses pointing to the sky. But beware of a sudden storm when the seals surface briefly, with their heads low and their noses parallel to the water. Such scientific weather forecasting can be a matter of life or death for the Inupiaq hunter (Nelson 1993).

Systematic observations by horticulturalists have also led to important scientific discoveries that have enhanced their adaptation to their ecosystems. For example, Kayapo women of the Brazilian rain forest have discovered that foraging ants are positive influences in their gardens. Rather than wanting to destroy the pests, Kayapo women have found that the foraging ants actually protect their manioc and maize crops. Attracted by the manioc nectar, the ants eat the wild vines that would choke the crops. Thus, the ants not only weed the garden, they also fertilize it, for the decaying vines enrich the soil (Maybury-Lewis 1992).

Pastoralists, too, have developed certain canons of ecological wisdom by studying their environment with the same meticulousness found in the modern laboratory. Although government officials and development agencies have long criticized Gabra pastoralists of East Africa for overgrazing the landscape, they are beginning to realize that traditional Gabra scientific wisdom must be incorporated into development planning. For example, short-term overgrazing by Gabra cattle actually enhances the grass that eventually grows back. Western scientists (with the help of Gabra pastoral scientists) have now realized that the hoof pressure of the grazing animals activates nitrogen regeneration by crushing the grass (Maybury-Lewis 1992).

SUMMARY

1. If any culture is to survive, it must develop strategies and technologies for procuring or producing food from its environment. Though not mutually exclusive, five major food procurement categories are recognized by cultural anthropologists: food collecting (foraging), horticulture, pastoralism, agriculture, and industrialization.

2. The success of various food-getting strategies depends on the interaction between a society's technology and its environment. Although different environments present different limitations and pos-

sibilities, it is generally recognized that environments influence rather than determine food-getting practices. The level of technology that any society has at its disposal is a critical factor in adapting to and using the environment.

3. Carrying capacity is the limiting effect an environment has on a culture's productivity. If a culture exceeds its carrying capacity, permanent damage to the environment usually results.

4. Food collecting, the oldest form of food getting, relies on procuring foods that are naturally available in the environment. Approximately 10,000 years ago, people for the first time began to domesticate plants and animals. Since then the percentage of the world's population engaged in foraging has declined from 100 percent to a small fraction of 1 percent.

5. Compared to societies with other food-getting practices, foraging societies tend to have low-density populations, are nomadic or seminomadic, live in small social groups, and occupy remote, marginally useful areas of the world.

6. Foraging societies tend to be selective in terms of the plant and animal species they exploit in their habitats. Which species are actually exploited for food can be explained by the optimal foraging theory, a theory developed by cultural ecologists that suggests that foragers do not select arbitrarily but rather on the basis of maximizing their caloric intake for the amount of time and energy expended.

7. Horticulture, a form of small-scale plant cultivation relying on simple technology, produces low yields with little or no surpluses. Horticulture most often uses the slash and burn technique, a form of cultivation that involves clearing the land by burning it and then planting in the fertile ash residue.

8. Pastoralism, the keeping of domesticated livestock as a source of food, is usually practiced in areas of the world that are unable to support any type of cultivation. This food-getting strategy most often involves a nomadic or seminomadic way of life, small family-based communities, and regular contact with cultivators as a way of supplementing their diets.

9. Agriculture, a more recent phenomenon than horticulture, uses such technology as irrigation, fertiliz-

ers, and mechanized equipment to produce high yields and support large populations. Unlike horticulture, agriculture is usually associated with permanent settlements, cities, and high levels of labor specialization.

10. Industrialized food getting, which began several centuries ago, uses vastly more powerful sources of energy than had ever been used previously. It relies on high levels of technology (such as tractors and combines), a mobile labor force, and a complex system of markets.

KEY TERMS

agriculture
carrying capacity
food collecting
horticulture
industrialization
neolithic revolution
nomadism
optimal foraging theory

pastoralism
peasantry
shifting cultivation
slash and burn method
swidden cultivation
social functions of cattle
transhumance

SUGGESTED READINGS

Barfield, Thomas J. *The Nomadic Alternative.* Englewood Cliffs, NJ: Prentice-Hall, 1993. A historical and ethnographic discussion of pastoral societies in East Africa, the Middle East, and central Eurasia focusing on such topics as comparative social organization, relations with nonpastoral peoples, and the ecology of nomadic pastoralism.

Bates, Daniel. *Human Adaptive Strategies.* Boston: Allyn & Bacon, 1998. By drawing on a number of case studies, the author explores how cultures evolve within the context of their environments and how adaptive strategies influence other parts of the culture.

Evans-Pritchard, E. E. *The Nuer.* Oxford: Oxford University Press, 1940. A classic ethnography about a pastoral society of the Sudan showing the central role of cattle in the overall working of the society.

Harris, M., and E. B. Ross, eds. *Food and Evolution: Toward a Theory of Human Food Habits.* Philadelphia:

Temple University Press, 1987. A compendium of 24 essays by scholars from a number of disciplines explores why people in different parts of the world and at different periods of history eat the things they do. Perspectives from a wide range of academic disciplines are represented, including physical anthropology, psychology, archaeology, nutrition, and primatology.

Kelly, Robert L. *The Foraging Spectrum: Diversity in Hunter–Gatherer Lifeways.* Washington, DC: Smithsonian Institution Press, 1995. An excellent summary of the latest thinking on food-collecting cultures since the groundbreaking conference on "Man the Hunter" in 1968.

Kent, Susan, ed. *Cultural Diversity Among Twentieth-Century Foragers: An African Perspective.* Cambridge: Cambridge University Press, 1996. A collection of essays on various aspects of African foraging societies. Although foragers have been seen as culturally similar over the years, new research suggests greater diversity among foraging groups than has been acknowledged in the past.

Khazanov, Anatoly M. *Nomads and the Outside World.* 2d ed. Madison: University of Wisconsin Press, 1994. A newly revised and comprehensive study of nomadic pastoralism in a comparative perspective. Covering the major areas of the world where pastoralism is found, Khazanov looks at the nature of pastoralism from its earliest origins to modern times.

Lee, Richard B. *The Dobe !Kung.* New York: Holt, Rinehart & Winston, 1984. The basic ethnographic case study of the !Kung, foragers living in Botswana and Namibia, by one of the leading contemporary authorities on food-collecting societies.

Schrire, C., ed. *Past and Present in Hunter Gatherer Studies.* Orlando: Academic Press, 1984. A collection of 10 thoughtful essays on food-collecting societies by anthropologists who have worked with groups from southern Africa to Tasmania to the Philippines. The editor's aim in this work is to challenge the widely held notion that food-collecting societies have maintained their economic institutions through cultural isolation.

On the Net

1. As a way of learning more about foraging (hunting and gathering) societies, consult a web site entitled "Hunting and Gathering":

http://www.mc.maricopa.edu/academic/cult_sci/anthro/lost_tribes/hg_ag/index.html

This well-illustrated and attractive site, sponsored by Mesa Community College, provides excellent information on many of the topics discussed in this chapter, including foraging societies, pastoralists, the beginnings of agriculture, and the growth of sedentary lifeways. What can you learn from this site that supplements the knowledge gained from this chapter?

2. An excellent source of information on how the peoples of the world are feeding themselves is the web site provided by the Food and Agriculture Organization (FAO), a branch of the United Nations. Once on the FAO home page

http://www.fao.org

click on "FactFile". What can you learn from this site about world hunger and malnutrition? What is meant by the "feminization of agriculture" and where does it most frequently occur? How do developing countries and developed countries differ in terms of the mechanization of agriculture?

Chapter Eight

ECONOMICS

WHAT WE WILL LEARN:

▼

How do anthropologists study economic
systems cross-culturally?

▼

How are resources such as land and
property allocated in different cultures?

▼

What are the different principles
of distribution found in various
parts of the world?

▼

*A floating vegetable market in
Bangkok, Tailand.*

When we hear the word *economics*, a host of images comes to mind. We usually think of such things as money, supply and demand curves, lending and borrowing

money at some agreed-upon interest rate, factories with production schedules, labor negotiations, buying stocks and bonds, foreign exchange, and gross domestic product. Although these are all topics that one might expect to find in an economics textbook, they are not integral parts of all economic systems. Many small-scale cultures exist in the world that have no standardized currencies, stock markets, or factories. Nevertheless, all societies (whether small-scale or highly industrialized) face a common challenge: They all have at their disposal a limited amount of vital resources, such as land, livestock, machines, food, and labor. This simple fact of life requires all societies to plan carefully how to allocate scarce resources, produce needed commodities, distribute their products to all people, and develop efficient consumption patterns for their products so as to help people maximize their adaptation to the environment. In other words, every society, if it is to survive, must develop systems of production, distribution, and consumption.

•■ ECONOMICS AND ■• ECONOMIC ANTHROPOLOGY

THE SCIENCE of **economics** focuses on the three major areas of production, distribution, and consumption as observed in the industrialized world. The subdiscipline of **economic anthropology,** on the other hand, studies production, distribution, and consumption comparatively in all societies of the world, industrialized and nonindustrialized alike. The relationship between the formal science of economics and the subspecialty of economic anthropology has not always been a harmonious one. Formal economics has its philosophical roots in the study of Western, industrialized economies. As a result, much of formal economic theory is based on assumptions derived from observing

Western, industrialized societies. For example, economic theory is predicated on the assumption that the value of a particular commodity will increase as it becomes scarcer (the notion of supply and demand) or on the assumption that when exchanging goods and services, people naturally strive to maximize their material well-being and their profits. As we will see in this chapter, these basic assumptions are not found in all the cultures of the world.

Economists use their theories (based on these assumptions) to predict how people will make certain types of choices when producing or consuming commodities. Owners of a manufacturing plant, for example, are constantly faced with choices. Do they continue to manufacture only men's jockey shorts, or do they expand their product line to include underwear for women? Do they move some or all of their manufacturing facilities to Mexico, or do they keep them in North Carolina? Should they give their workers more benefits? Should they spend more of their profits on advertising? Should they invest more capital on machinery or on additional labor? Western economists assume that all of these questions will be answered in a rational way so as to maximize the company's profits. Similarly, Western economists assume that individuals as well as corporations are motivated by the desire to maximize their material well-being.

A long-standing debate between different schools of economics and anthropology has centered on the question of whether these and other assumptions that Western economists make about human behavior are indeed universal. How applicable are these economic theories to the understanding of small-scale, nonindustrialized societies? Are the differences between industrial and nonindustrial economies a matter of degree or a matter of kind? Some anthropologists contend that classic economic theories cannot be applied to the study of nonindustrialized soci-

= *Some Western economists assume that all people naturally seek to maximize their economic well-being, as has the owner of this BMW sport utility vehicle. Some economic anthropologists, however, argue that such an assumption does not hold true for all peoples of the world.*

eties. They argue that tribal or peasant societies, based as they are on subsistence, are different in kind from market economies found in the industrialized societies.

Whereas in Western societies production and consumption choices are made on the basis of maximization of profits, in nonindustrialized societies they often are based on quite different principles, such as reciprocity or redistribution. The principle of reciprocity (as in the biblical injunction to "Do unto others as you would have them do unto you") emphasizes the fair exchange of equivalent values and as such is in direct contrast to the principle of maximizing one's profits. Likewise, the principle of redistribution, found in many subsistence economies, discourages the accumulation of personal wealth by moving or redistributing goods from those who have to those who do not. Such principles as reciprocity and redistribution, with their emphasis on cooperation and generosity, are in stark contrast to the principle of maximization, which encourages individual accumulation and competition and consequently can lead to jealousy, hostility, and antagonism.

CROSS-CULTURAL EXAMINATION OF ECONOMIC SYSTEMS

A good deal of debate has taken place during the last half century over the extent to which the principles of classic economics can be useful for the study of all societies. Despite the substantial differences of economic systems found throughout the world—as well as the different theories used to analyze them—it is possible to examine economic systems cross-culturally along certain key dimensions:

1. *The regulation of resources:* How land, water, and natural resources are controlled and allocated.
2. *Production:* How material resources are converted into usable commodities.
3. *Exchange:* How the commodities, once produced, are distributed among the people of the society.

•■ THE ALLOCATION ■• OF NATURAL RESOURCES

EVERY SOCIETY has access to certain natural resources in its territorial environment, including land, animals, water, minerals, and plants. Even though the nature and amount of these resources vary widely from one group to another, every society has developed a set of rules governing the **allocation of resources** and how they can be used. For example, all groups have determined systematic ways for allocating land among their members. Hunters and gatherers must determine who can hunt animals and collect plants from which areas. Pastoralists need to have some orderly pattern for deciding access to pasturage and watering places. Agriculturalists must work out ways of acquiring, maintaining, and passing on rights to their farmland.

In our own society, where things are bought and sold in markets, most of the natural resources are privately owned. Pieces of land are surveyed, precise maps are drawn, and title deeds are granted to those who purchase a piece of property. Individual property rights are so highly valued in the United States that under certain circumstances, a property owner is justified in killing someone who is attempting to violate those property rights. Small pieces of land are usually held by individuals, and larger pieces of property are held collectively, either by governments (as in the case of roads, public buildings, and parks) or by private corporations on behalf of their shareholders.

To be certain, there are limitations on private property ownership in the United States. To illustrate, certain vital resources such as public utilities are either strongly regulated or owned outright by some agency of government; rights of eminent domain enable the government to force owners to sell their land for essential public projects; and zoning laws set certain limits on how property owners may use their land. Nevertheless, the system of resource allocation found in the United States is based on the general principle of private ownership, whereby an individual or a group of individuals have total or near total rights to a piece of property and consequently can do with it as they see fit.

Property rights are so strongly held in the United States (and other parts of the Western world) that some observers have suggested that humans have a genetically based territorial instinct that compels them to stake out and defend their turf (Ardrey 1968). However, the degree to which humans are territorial varies widely throughout the world. By and large, the notion of personal land ownership is absent in most societies that base their livelihood on food collecting, pastoralism, or horticulture. Let's examine how each of these types of societies deals with the question of access to land.

FOOD COLLECTORS

In most food-collecting societies, land is not owned, in the Western sense of the term, either individually or collectively. Food collectors have a number of compelling reasons to maintain flexible or open borders. First, because food collectors in most cases must follow the migratory patterns of animals, it makes little sense for people to tie themselves exclusively to a single piece of land. Second, claiming and defending a particular territory requires time, energy, and technology that many foraging peoples either do not have or choose not to expend. Third, territoriality can lead to conflict and warfare between

those claiming property rights and those who would violate those rights. Thus, for food-collecting societies, having flexible territorial boundaries (or none at all) is the most adaptive strategy.

Even though food collectors rarely engage in private ownership of land, there is some variation in the amount of communal control. At one extreme are the Inuit and the Hadza of Tanzania, two groups that have no real concept of trespassing whatsoever. They could go where they wanted, when they wanted, and were generally welcomed by other members of the society. The !Kung of the Kalahari area do recognize, to some degree, the association of certain territories with particular tribal bands, but it is not rigorously maintained. For example, members of one !Kung band are allowed to track a wounded animal into a neighbor's territory. Moreover, any !Kung can use the watering holes of any neighboring territory provided she or he seeks permission, which is always granted. This type of reciprocity, cooperation, and permissive use rights is adaptive in that it increases the chances of survival of all !Kung peoples. In a smaller number of societies, however, territorial boundaries between individual bands or extended families were maintained quite rigorously. Robert Kelly (1995) cites a number of examples from the ethnographic literature. To illustrate, certain native American groups living on the coast of southwestern Canada maintained exclusive rights to particular stretches of beaches. The food-collecting Maidu regularly patrolled their borders to guard against poachers and would claim as their own any animal shot by an outsider that died within its territory. The Vedda of India marked their hunting territory with small archers carved into tree trunks along the borders.

As a general rule, a food-collecting society will have open or flexible boundaries if animals are mobile and food and water supplies are unpredictable. Conversely, food collectors are more likely to live in permanent settlements and maintain greater control over land in the areas where food and water supplies are plentiful and predictable (Dyson-Hudson and Smith 1978).

PASTORALISTS

Like hunters and gatherers, nomadic or seminomadic pastoralists require extensive territory. For pastoralists to maintain their way of life, it is imperative that they have access to two vital resources for their livestock: water and pasturage. Depending on the local environment, the availability of these two resources may vary widely. In marginal environments where grass and water are at a premium, pastoralists need to range over wide territories and consequently require free access to land. In more environmentally friendly regions of the world where grass and water are more abundant, one is likely to find greater control over land and its resources. In any event, pastoral groups must work out arrangements among themselves and with nonpastoralists to gain access to certain pasturage.

Variations can be found, but corporate (that is, nonindividual) control of pastures is the general rule among pastoral peoples. At one extreme, there are pastoral societies whose entire territory is considered to belong to the society as a whole. In such societies (best represented by such East African groups as the Turkana, Jie, and Samburu), there are no fixed divisions of land that are used by different segments of the society. At the other extreme, we find societies in which the rights to use certain pastures are divided among certain segments of the society. These pastoral societies are most often found in the Eurasian steppes and in the Middle East. And in some pastoral societies the use of wells or natural watering sources is controlled, to some degree, by individuals or groups to the exclusion of others. However, as Anatoly Khazanov (1994) reminds us, the variations found in how pastoral societies allocate land and resources depend on a number of factors including ecological variables (such as climate and rainfall), types of animals herded, the size of the population relative to the land, and the relationship of the pastoralists to the wider society.

To avoid overgrazing and conflict, they may have to enter into agreements with other pastoralist families to share certain areas, or they may have to form contractual arrangements with sedentary cultivators to graze their animals on recently harvested fields. The pastoral Fulani of northern Nigeria, for example, although remaining removed from village life on an everyday basis, nevertheless have had to maintain special contacts with sedentary horticulturalists for rights of access to water and pastures. According to Derrick Stenning, "this has brought them into the orbit of the Muslim states of the western Sudan, in whose politics and wars they became involved principally to maintain or extend their pastoral opportunities" (1965:365).

HORTICULTURALISTS

In contrast to hunters and gatherers and most pastoralists, horticulturalists tend to live on land that is communally controlled, usually by an extended kinship group. Individual nuclear or polygynous families may be granted the use

of land by the extended family for growing crops, but the rights are limited. For example, the small family units usually retain their rights for as long as they work the land and are in good standing with the larger family. Because they do not own the land, however, they cannot dispose of it by selling it. They simply use it at the will of the larger group. Such a method of land allocation makes sense, given their farming technology. Because horticulturalists often are shifting cultivators, there would be no advantage to having claims of ownership over land that cannot be used permanently.

This communal type of land tenure is well illustrated by the Samoans of Polynesia. Under their traditional system, any piece of land belongs to the extended family that clears and plants it. Individual members of the extended family work the land under the authority of a *matai*, an elected family member who holds the title to the land on behalf of the entire group. The *matai*'s authority over the land depends on his meeting his responsibility to care for his extended family. If he does not, the family can remove his title. Any individual of the extended family group has undisputed rights to use the land provided he or she lives on the family land and serves and pays allegiance to the *matai* (see O'Meara 1990).

INTENSIVE AGRICULTURALISTS

In North America, and in most other parts of the industrialized world, resources such as land are allocated according to the principle of private individual ownership. Most English-speaking people have no difficulty understanding the concept of private ownership. When we say we "own" a piece of land the term *ownership* carries with it the implication that we have absolute and exclusive rights to it. We are able to sell it, give it away, rent it, or trade it for another piece of property, if we so choose. In other words, we have 100 percent rights to that piece of land. This association between private individual land ownership and intensive agriculture is at least partially due to the possibility of using the land year after year, thereby giving the land a permanent and continual value.

This concept of individual **property rights** is so entrenched in our thinking and our culture that we sometimes fail to realize that many other cultures do not share that principle with us. This cultural myopia led some early anthropologists to ask the wrong types of questions when they first encountered certain non-Western peoples. To illustrate, when studying a small group of East African horticulturalists who also kept cattle, some early anthropolo-

Is Nepotism Always Bad?

Social scientists often make distinctions between fundamentally different types of societies. One such distinction is between societies that are large, industrialized, highly differentiated, and stratified, and those that are small, nonindustrialized, egalitarian, and kinship oriented. Industrialized societies are characterized by bureaucracies in both government and business. People who operate in complex, bureaucratic organizations are expected to behave toward one another in an objective and straightforward manner, without regard to personal considerations. Social relations in these organizations are expected to be, in the words of sociologist Talcott Parsons (1951:62), universalistic. With **universalism,** the conduct between two people is to be determined by a universally applicable set of rules rather than personal status. Strong kinship ties and obligations have no place within a bureaucracy. Decisions such as who gets hired are to be determined by objective, universally applied criteria (examination results, previous job experience, educational background) rather than by such particularistic considerations as how the applicant is related to the personnel director.

Behavior patterns in small-scale, non-Western societies are essentially the logical opposites of those found in complex, bureaucratic societies. In many traditional societies, people relate to one another in particularistic, not universalistic terms. With **particularism,** people emphasize personal status relationships with one another, such as kinship connections or common ethnic affiliation. In very practical terms, a person is expected to show particular loyalty to a kinsman *because* that person is a kinsman. Thus, in societies that value loyalty between individuals, a person is likely to hire someone for a job because they have a special relationship (such as being cousins) rather than because of any universally applicable set of criteria (such as a high score on a standardized test).

In the developing world this basic value contrast between *particularism* and *universalism* can be seen most dramatically in urban areas. Rural migrants, with their particularistic values, come to cities seeking jobs in large corporations with bureaucratic norms of universalism. Western bureaucrats assume that new members of the workforce must shed their particularistic values, which they see as incompatible with bureaucratic structures. This notion was the starting point of an applied cultural research project conducted by Peter Blunt (1980) on workers in Nairobi, Kenya. Kenya is an excellent example of a developing country that, having experienced rapid urban growth during the twentieth century, has a workforce recruited largely from rural areas. Like other developing nations, Kenya has high unemployment, little affordable housing, and an urban population that is experiencing an increasing sense of powerlessness, exploitation, and alienation. Within this setting, Blunt wanted to examine hiring practices and organizational efficiency in several bureaucratic corporations. More specifically, he wanted to see whether workers in this part of the world with a particularistic (kinship or ethnic) orientation were incompatible with the more universalistic orientation of bureaucratic organizations.

Blunt conducted his research on two companies in Kenya that, contrary to conventional wisdom, recruited new workers on the basis of their kinship or ethnic relations with the present workers. In both situations the overwhelming majority of employees were from the same ethnic group, and many of them were related to one another. In one of the two companies the homogenization of the workforce took place rapidly over the course of a single year. At the beginning of the 12-month period, only a third of the employees were from the same ethnic group; a year later 95 percent were.

Blunt was interested in measuring the organizational efficiency both before and after the homogenization of this particular workforce. Contrary to our conventional wisdom about bureaucracies, Blunt found that ethnic/kinship homogenization, rather than damaging the organization, actually improved organizational efficiency. For example, turnover rates fell to less than half, customer complaints declined while the number of written commendations of workers by customers more than doubled, damage to company property was reduced 27 percent, and the number of poor performance warnings fell by 63 percent. Working with friends, relatives, or "people from home" enabled workers to cope more effectively with the alienation and loneliness so prevalent in cities. Moreover, the employee-recruiter felt a measure of satisfaction because he was now able to fulfill his kinship obligations.

Blunt's findings are significant because they remind us that theories that might be applicable in Chicago or Detroit are not necessarily relevant for other parts of the world. Multinational companies working in non-Western countries should take notice of the implications. Our Western idea of nepotism (allowing supervisors to hire kinfolk or fellow tribesmen) may actually maximize organizational efficiency in some situations even though the new recruit may have weaker skills than other candidates for the job. As one organizational theorist (Robinson 1984:101) put it, "In one's group, the insider may be more effective than the outsider with superior ability."

The lesson learned from Blunt's testing of these theories on bureaucracies is that corporate decision makers should not tie themselves to outdated notions of industrial organization. Instead, it would be beneficial to both the organization and its workforce to experiment with different organizational structures that take into account the realities of the local cultures.

QUESTIONS FOR FURTHER THOUGHT

1. In your own words, how would you distinguish between particularism and universalism?
2. Do you think that hiring on the basis of family connections would ever work at a company in your country? Why or why not?
3. What does this case study tell us about the wisdom of importing Western thinking into other parts of the world?

gists, using their own set of linguistic categories, asked what to them seemed to be a perfectly logical question: Who owns that brown cow over there? In actual fact, no one "owned" the cow in our sense of the term because no single individual had 100 percent rights to the beast. Instead, a number of people may have had limited rights and obligations to the brown cow. The man we see with the cow at the moment may have rights to milk the cow on Tuesdays and Thursdays, but someone else has rights to milk it on Mondays and Wednesdays. The cows are actually controlled by the larger kinship group (the lineage or extended family); the individual merely has limited rights to use the cow. This fundamental difference in property allocation is reflected in the local East African language of Swahili, which contains no word that would be comparable to the English word *own*. The closest Swahili speakers can come linguistically to conveying the notion of ownership is to use the word *nina*, which means literally "I am with."

This fundamentally different way of allocating property was at the heart of the 60-year dispute between the Kikuyu of Kenya and the British colonialists. The feud began with the alienation of Kikuyu land in the early 1900s and ended with the Mau Mau uprising of the 1950s. In a misguided attempt at economic development, the British colonial office encouraged British citizens to resettle in the Kikuyu highlands and start planting such marketable crops as tea and coffee. The colonial government thought it was respecting Kikuyu land rights by allocating only unused parcels of land to the European settlers. It was convenient for the government—pressured by a small but vocal settler population—to assume that all land not under cultivation was unoccupied and thus could be given to the European settlers. But in terms of Kikuyu perception, this land, although temporarily unoccupied, was hardly ownerless. Rather, because Kikuyu lineages (large extended families) controlled land and its inheritance, the land reverted to the surviving family members. Kikuyu lineages were more than just groups of kin; rather, they were corporate land-owning groups. Without land, the lineage lost its sense of unity. The land, which was the material symbol of lineage solidarity, was associated with an elaborate network of rights and obligations among kin. When a lineage lost control over its land, much more was at stake than the loss of a piece of property; it involved the suspension or drastic alteration of an entire set of social relationships. Had the British colonial government understood how the Kikuyu traditionally allocate land (their most valuable resource), much of the hostility between the British and the Kikuyu might have been avoided.

·■ PRODUCTION ■·

THE INITIAL STEP in meeting the material needs of any society is to establish a system of allocating the rights to resources to certain people. In very few situations, however, can resources be used by people in exactly the form they are found in nature. Animals must be butchered; grains must be ground and cooked; metal ores must be mined, smelted, combined with other chemical elements, and crafted before becoming tools; stones must be shaped before they can be put into the wall of a house. This process of obtaining goods from the natural environment and transforming them into usable objects is what economists call **production**.

All humans must meet certain fundamental material needs (such as food, water, and shelter), but how these needs are satisfied varies enormously from society to society. Some groups, such as the Siriono of eastern Bolivia, meet most of their material needs with goods procured from hunting and gathering. Others, such as the Masai and Samburu of East Africa, live essentially from the products of their livestock. Still others, such as people of the United States and certain western European nations, go well beyond meeting their basic physical needs through a complex system of technology and industrialization. How do we explain such diversity? Why is there such a vast range of systems of production? Why do two cultures inhabiting apparently similar environments develop substantially different systems of production?

The answer to these questions can be partially explained in economic terms. For example, why any society produces the things it does is determined, to some extent, by such economic factors as the accessibility of certain resources, the technology available for processing the resources, and the abundance of energy supplies. This is only part of the explanation, however, because cultural values also play a role in determining production. To illustrate, the Hadza of Tanzania are aware of the horticultural practices of their neighbors but choose not to engage in horticulture themselves for the simple reason that it involves too much effort for the anticipated yield. Also, in one form or another, most societies fail to exploit all of the resources at their disposal. Some societies living alongside bodies of water have strong prohibitions against eating fish. The Hindus in India, despite an abundance of cows, refuse to eat beef on religious grounds. The Inuit, even though they often experience food shortages, maintain a number of taboos against eating certain types of food. And, of course, people in the United States would never dream of routinely eating the flesh of dogs, cats, or rats, although these animals are a rich source of protein.

The apparent failure by some societies to exploit all of the resources at their disposal may not stem from irrationality or arbitrariness. As some cultural ecologists have shown convincingly, often there are good reasons for certain types of economic behavior, which at first glance might appear irrational. The sacred cow in Hindu India is a case in point. Even though the Indian population needs more protein in its diet, the Hindu religion prohibits the slaughter of cows and the eating of beef. This taboo has resulted in large numbers of half-starved cows cluttering the Indian landscape, disrupting traffic, and stealing food from marketplaces. But as Marvin Harris has demonstrated (1977, 1979), the taboo makes good economic sense because it prevents the use of cows for less cost-effective purposes. To raise cows as a source of food would be an expensive proposition, given the economic and ecological conditions found in India. Instead, cows are used as draft animals and for the products they provide, such as milk, fertilizer, and fuel (dung). The religious taboo, according to Harris, rather than being irrational, serves to regulate the system of production in a very effective way by having a positive effect on the carrying capacity of the land.

Units of production

Like other parts of culture, the way people go about producing is not haphazard or random but rather is systematic, organized, and patterned. Every society breaks up its members into some type of productive unit comprising people with specific tasks to perform. In industrialized societies such as our own, the productive unit is the private company that exists for the purpose of producing goods or services. These private firms range from small, individually owned retail operations to gigantic multinational corporations. Whatever the size and complexity, however, these private companies are made up of employees performing specific roles, all of which are needed to produce the goods and services that are then sold for a profit. The employees do not consume the products of the firm, but instead receive salaries, which they use to purchase the goods and services they need.

Production in the Household

In most nonindustrialized societies, the basic unit of production is the household. In these small-scale societies, most if not all of the goods and services consumed are produced by the members of the household. The household may be made up of a nuclear family (husband, wife, and children) or a more elaborate family structure containing married siblings, multiple wives, and more than two generations. In a typical horticultural society, household members produce most of what they consume; their work includes planting, tending, and harvesting the crops; building houses; procuring firewood and other fuels from the environment; making their own tools; keeping some livestock; making their own clothes; and producing various containers for storing and cooking foods. When a particular task is too complex to be carried out by a single household, larger groups of family members or neighbors usually join together to complete the task.

= *In Hindu India the cow is sacred and is never killed for food. This is an excellent example of how a religiously based food prohibition can be economically rational as well.*

Even though both the business firm and the household are units of production, there are significant structural differences between them. Whereas the business firm is primarily—if not exclusively—just a unit of production, the household performs a number of overlapping functions. When two male kinsmen who are part of the same household work side by side threshing wheat, it is very likely that they play a number of other roles together. For example, one man, because of his advanced age, may be a religious specialist; the other man, because of his leadership skills, may play an important political role in the extended family; and both men may enjoy spending their leisure time together drinking beer and telling stories. Thus, this productive unit of the household is the very same group that shares certain religious, political, and social activities.

A second structural difference between the business firm and the household is that the household is far more self-sufficient. In most cases, the members of the household in small-scale societies can satisfy their own material needs without having to go outside the group. People employed in a business firm, on the other hand, rely on a large number of people for their material well-being, including the butcher, the television repairer, the barber, the schoolteacher, the auto mechanic, and all of the thousands of people who make all of the things with which people surround themselves.

A third difference is that a business firm concentrates exclusively on its economic function and is therefore a more productive unit than the household. Because the family household is more than just a productive unit and must also be concerned with the emotional, social, psychological, and spiritual needs of its members, it is likely to use some of its resources in nonproductive ways. Consequently, the family-based household is less likely to use highly productive, progressive, or innovative methods than the business firm.

Division of labor

One very important aspect of the process of production is the allocation of tasks to be performed—that is, deciding which types of people will perform which categories of work. Every society, whether large or small, distinguishes, to some degree, between the work appropriate for men and women and for adults and children. Even though many societies have considerably more complex **divisions of labor,** all societies make distinctions on the basis of gender and age.

Gender Specialization

Although a number of roles (jobs) found in the world are played by both women and men, many others are associated with one gender or the other. For example, women generally tend crops, gather wild foods, care for children, prepare food, clean house, fetch water, and collect cooking fuel. Men, on the other hand, hunt, build houses, clear land for cultivation, herd large animals, fish, trap small animals, and serve as political functionaries. It is important to note that in many parts of the developing world today, men are migrating to the cities in search of wage employment and leaving most agriculturally related tasks to be carried out by women.

Several theories have been set forth to explain the very common, if not universal, division of labor by gender. One explanation is that because men have greater body mass and strength, they are better equipped physically to engage in hunting, warfare, and land clearing. A second argument is that women do the things they do because those tasks are compatible with child care. That is, unlike certain male tasks, such as hunting and warfare, women's tasks are more easily interrupted and can be accomplished without jeopardizing the child's safety and without having to leave home. A third explanation is that, in terms of reproduction, men tend to be more expendable than women. In other words, because women have more limited (and therefore more valuable) reproductive capacities, they are less likely to be required to engage in dangerous activities. For example, if men risk their lives hunting buffalo or whales, reproduction in the group will not suffer, provided that women continue to have access to men. To be certain, there are exceptions to these broad generalizations about what constitutes men's and women's work. In some parts of traditional Africa, for example, women are known to carry much heavier loads than men, work long hours in the fields, and even serve as warriors. Despite these exceptions, all three theories, when taken together, go a long way toward helping us understand this very common gender division of labor.

Yet along with these apparently rational theories, we must also note that men and women are often assigned roles because of the various social, political, and historical forces operating in individual societies. When these forces are inadequately understood, they can appear to be quite arbitrary. For example, although sewing clothes for the family is thought of as women's work in North America (most men have neither operated a sewing machine nor made a purchase in a fabric store), among the traditional

CROSS-CULTURAL MISCUE

WHILE MANAGING A PROJECT in Mexico City, you notice that one of your employees is particularly intelligent, successful, and diligent. Thinking he would make a great addition to the home office in Chicago, you offer him a job. Although your employee would receive a promotion, a large salary increase, and paid living expenses if he moves to Chicago, he declines your offer. You simply can't understand why he refuses the offer when it would be so beneficial to his career.

Many highly successful people in Mexico (and other parts of South America) do not make career decisions based primarily on their own self-interest, as is often the case north of the Rio Grande. In Mexico people tend to first consider the needs of their family or company before considering their own self-interest. Your offering a promotion and higher salary would not be the most compelling reason for taking a new position. Rather, your employee would think primarily about the interests of extended family members, many of whom probably would not want him to move. Then the employee would consider the interests of the local company, which probably needs him to continue working in Mexico City. What is best for the individual is not always the prime factor in deciding to take a new job.

Hopi of Arizona, it is the men who are the spinners, weavers, and tailors. Moreover, in our own society, women have been virtually excluded from a number of occupations (such as jockey, U.S. senator, and major league baseball umpire), even though men have no particular physiological advantage over women in performing these jobs.

Sometimes the division of labor by gender is so rigid that both men and women remain ignorant of the occupational skills of the opposite sex. This point is well illustrated by the Mixe Indians of Mexico, where men traditionally grew corn while women processed it for eating. According to Ralph Beals, Harry Hoijer, and Alan Beals,

Men received no training in the processing of maize and were incapable of surviving unless a woman was available to process the maize that the man produced. Although man's work involving the planting and raising of maize constituted a complicated technological process, it only represented one half of the food producing revolution. The other half, the processing of the crop, was equally complicated and time consuming. The processing involved removing the maize from the cob; boiling it with the proper amount of lime for a sufficient time to remove the hard outer shell and soften the kernel; grinding it on a flat stone slab until it reached the proper texture; working water into the dough; and shaping it between the palms until a flat cake of uniform thickness was formed. The cake was then cooked at the correct heat on a flat griddle, properly treated to prevent sticking. A Mixe woman with

a family of five would spend about six hours a day manufacturing tortillas. Under such circumstances it would be impossible for her to engage in the raising of the maize, just as it would be impossible for her husband to engage in the processing of the maize. (1977:348–350)

Age Specialization

In much the same way that societies divide labor on the basis of sex, they allocate tasks according to age. Because of their lack of knowledge and physical strength, children are often excluded from certain tasks. In our own society, where formal education routinely lasts through the late teens (and often beyond), young people generally do not engage in much productive work. By way of contrast, children in less industrialized societies usually become involved in work activities at a considerably earlier age. At the other end of the age continuum, the elderly, because of their waning physical strength, are often prohibited from engaging in certain tasks or are expected to engage in different activities from those they performed when they were younger. For example, according to C. W. M. Hart and Arnold Pilling (1960), old men among the Tiwi of North Australia give up the strenuous work of hunting in favor of staying at home to make hunting tools, such as spears and throwing sticks, for the younger men. Among the Abkhasians of Georgia, known for their longevity, the elderly do not retire, but the nature of their work becomes less

Are there any physical reasons why this job of umpiring a baseball game could not be done by a woman?

strenuous. Men in their 80s and 90s no longer are expected to plow fields but to continue doing light work like weeding; women of similar age stop working in fields and confine their chores to light housework, knitting, and feeding chickens (Benet 1976). Although normal adult work generally ceases during old age in these societies, the elderly do assume new roles dealing with spiritual matters. Moreover, because of their advanced years they take on the role of societal historians and advisors because they are the repositories of traditional wisdom. By way of contrast, the transition from being employed to being retired in the United States is considerably more abrupt. When most workers reach the age of 65, they usually receive a plaque or a certificate and cease their productive activity. Unlike the situation among the Tiwi and Abkhasians, when workers in the United States retire, they usually suffer a noticeable loss of prestige.

Labor Specialization

Labor specialization—another term for division of labor—is an important descriptive characteristic of any society. At one extreme, subsistence societies with low population densities and simple technologies are likely to have a division of labor based on little more than sex and age. Most men in these societies engage in essentially the same activities, and the same holds true for most women. If specialists do exist, they are usually part-timers engaged in political leadership, ceremonial activities, or specialized toolmaking. At the other extreme are industrialized soci-

eties, where most people are engaged in very specialized occupations, such as stockbroker, TV repairer, kindergarten teacher, janitor, CPA, or thoracic surgeon. One need only consult the yellow pages of the phone directory for any major city in the United States to get an idea of the vast diversity of specialized occupations in our own society. These two extremes should be viewed as the poles on a continuum of division of labor, between which all of the societies of the world could be placed.

One of the major consequences of the transition from hunting and gathering to plant and animal domestication (the neolithic revolution) has been the increasing amount of labor specialization in the world. Because agriculture is a far more efficient way of producing food than hunting and gathering, some people were freed up from the tasks of food production. Simple horticulture evolved into more complex forms of cultivation, which eventually led to the rise of civilizations (urban society).

With each advance in food-producing capacity came an increase in the complexity of labor specialization. This more complex division of labor is significant because the increase in specialized tasks provided a new basis for social solidarity. According to nineteenth-century French sociologist Emile Durkheim (1933), in highly specialized societies where people engage in complementary roles, social solidarity arises from their mutual dependence on one another. That is, teachers need to be on good terms with a butcher, a carpenter, and an auto mechanic because teachers are so highly specialized that they cannot procure meat on their own, build a wood deck, or fix a faulty carburetor. Durkheim calls the social solidarity resulting from this labor specialization and mutual interdependence **organic solidarity.** In contrast, societies with minimal division of labor also possess a form of solidarity, but of a different type. This type of solidarity, which Durkheim calls **mechanical solidarity,** is based on commonality of interests, social homogeneity, strict conformity, kinship, mutual affection, and tradition.

·■ DISTRIBUTION OF ■· GOODS AND SERVICES

ONCE GOODS HAVE BEEN PROCURED from the environment or produced, they need to get into people's hands. People often consume some of the commodities that they produce, but surpluses enter the society's system of exchange. Systems of exchange are essential for every economy, for they allow people to dispose of their surpluses and, at the same time, maximize the diversity of the goods and services consumed. As Karl Polanyi (1957) reminds us, goods and services are allocated in all societies according to three different modes of distribution: reciprocity, redistribution, and market exchange.

In the United States, most commodities are distributed according to a free-market exchange system based on the principle of each according to his or her capacity to pay. People receive money for their labor and then use that money to purchase the goods and services they need or want. In theory, at least, if people have the money, they can purchase a loaf of bread; if they don't, they can't. Even though this is the prevailing type, we can see examples of the other two modes operating in the United States as well. The principle of reciprocity operates, for example, when friends and relatives exchange gifts for birthdays, holidays, and other special occasions. We can see the principle of redistribution at work in the United States when people hand over a certain portion of their personal income to the government for taxes. Even though more than one mode of distribution can operate in any given society at a time, usually only one mode predominates. Let's examine each of these three modes of distribution in greater detail.

RECIPROCITY

Reciprocity is the exchange of goods and services of roughly equal value between two parties without the use of money. Economic anthropologists generally recognize three types of reciprocity, depending on the degree of closeness of the parties involved in the exchange: general-

ized reciprocity, balanced reciprocity, and negative reciprocity (Sahlins 1972).

Generalized Reciprocity

Generalized reciprocity, which is usually played out among family members or close friends, carries with it the highest level of moral obligation. It involves a form of gift giving without any expectation of immediate return. Generalized reciprocity is perhaps best illustrated by the type of giving that takes place between parents and children in our own society. Parents usually give (or at least try to give) the children as much as they can while their children are growing up: food, toys, a set of encyclopedias, a room of their own, and the like. In fact, this providing of goods and services for children often continues after the children become adults. For example, parents may provide babysitting services, a downpayment on a first home, or a subsidized vacation for their adult children.

In most cases, parents provide for their children materially without the expectation that their children will repay them at any time in the future. Because of the intimate bonds between parents and children, parents usually provide for their children out of a sense of love, obligation, and social responsibility. In reality, this sense of love and obligation usually becomes a two-way street, for children usually come to the assistance of their elderly parents when the parents become too old to care for themselves. Thus, even in this most generalized form of reciprocity, the exchange of goods and services often balances out over the long run.

Even though generalized reciprocity is found in our own society, it is not the predominant form of exchange, as it is in smaller-scale societies, where the primary unit of economic organization is the nuclear or extended family and where material resources may be unpredictable and uncertain. An exchange system based primarily on generalized reciprocity is common among food collectors and indeed contributes to their very survival.

In most foraging societies, when a large animal such as a bushbuck is killed, the hunter keeps enough for his own immediate family and distributes the rest to his more distant relatives. With no refrigeration or other way of preserving meat, it would make little sense for the hunter to hoard all of the meat himself, for it would spoil before it could be eaten. Instead, sharing with others becomes the expected norm. And, of course, given the uncertainty of hunting, sharing your kill today would entitle you to share someone else's kill tomorrow. Such an economic strategy helps all family members sustain themselves by providing

CROSS-CULTURAL MISCUE

ALTHOUGH THE PRACTICE of exchanging gifts is found in most societies, the meanings attached to gift giving vary widely from society to society. In some societies gifts may be given in a fairly altruistic manner—that is, nothing is expected in return. More often, however, gift giving is used to create and strengthen social bonds between people, and as such, some type of gift is expected in return. Lee Cronk provides us with an interesting cross-cultural misunderstanding arising from different notions of gift giving between European settlers in America and Native Americans during the eighteenth century:

> [The] Englishman newly arrived in America is welcomed to an Indian lodge with the present of a pipe. Thinking the pipe a wonderful artifact, he takes it home and sets it on his mantelpiece. When he later learns that the Indians expect to have the pipe back, as a gesture of goodwill, he is shocked by what he views as their short-lived generosity. The newcomer did not realize that, to the natives, the point of the gift was not to provide an interesting trinket but to inaugurate a friendly relationship that would be maintained through a series of mutual exchanges. Thus, his failure to reciprocate appeared not only rude and thoughtless but downright hostile. "White man keeping" was as offensive to native Americans as "Indian giving" was to settlers. (1989:2–4)

a fairly steady supply of meat despite the inconsistent success of most individual hunters. In such societies generosity is perhaps the highest ideal, and hoarding and stinginess are seen as being extremely antisocial.

We should not think of generalized reciprocity as being motivated totally by altruism. For all people who live at a subsistence level, maintaining reciprocal exchange relationships is vital to their economic self-interest. At subsistence levels, a person is more dependent on others for her or his material security. In the absence of worker's compensation, unemployment insurance, and bank loans, people must rely on others when their crops fail or they become too sick to hunt. Subsistence farmers, for example, might not survive without occasional help from their relatives, friends, and neighbors. A farmer may need extra seeds for planting, help with fixing a roof, or extra cash

In hunting-and-gathering societies such as the !Kung of the Kalahari region, food is frequently distributed along kinship lines.

to pay for a child's school fees. The best way of ensuring that these needs will be met is to respond quickly and unselfishly to the requests of others for similar types of assistance.

Although we don't always recognize it, reciprocal gift giving in our own society takes a number of different forms. Either consciously or unconsciously, we often give gifts with the expectation of getting something in return. We may expect gratitude, acceptance, friendship, or obligation rather than a material item. For example, why do we send wedding invitations to our friends? Is it solely for the sake of sharing with them the joy of the ceremony? When we give our brother a birthday present, would we not be hurt or disappointed if he did not reciprocate on our birthday? And do Western industrialized nations give millions of dollars in foreign aid to less industrialized nations totally out of a sense of altruism and generosity? Or are the donor nations looking for something in return, such as access to natural resources, political cooperation, or prestige? Thus, it appears that in all societies, including our own, gifts almost always come with strings attached.

After having lived in Kandoka village in Papua New Guinea on several different occasions, anthropologist David Counts (1995:95–98) learned several important lessons about life in a society that practices reciprocity:

> First, in a society where food is shared or gifted as part of social life, you may not buy it with money.... [Second,] never refuse a gift, and never fail to return a gift. If you cannot use it, you can always give it to someone else.... [Third,] where reciprocity is the rule and gifts are the idiom, you cannot demand a gift, just as you cannot refuse a request.

Balanced Reciprocity

Balanced reciprocity is a form of exchange involving the expectation that goods and services of equivalent value will be returned within a specified period of time. In contrast to generalized reciprocity, balanced reciprocity involves more formal relationships, greater social distance, and a strong obligation to repay the original gift. The repayment in balanced reciprocity does not have to be immediate, for, as Marcel Mauss (1954) has suggested, any attempt to repay the debt too quickly can be seen as an unwillingness to be obligated to one's trading partner.

A major economic motivation of balanced reciprocity is to exchange surplus goods and services for those that are in short supply. Shortfalls and surpluses can result from different levels of technology, environmental variations, or different production capacities. But whatever the cause, balanced reciprocity enables both parties in the exchange to maximize their consumption. The Indians of Oaxaca, Mexico, exemplify balanced reciprocity in the exchange of both goods and services. According to social custom, a man is expected to sponsor at least one fiesta celebrating a major saint's day. Such events, involving an elaborate amount of food, beverages, and entertainment, almost always are beyond the capacity of a man to provide by himself. Consequently, the man solicits the help of his relatives, friends, and neighbors, thereby mortgaging his future surpluses. Those who help out expect to be repaid in equivalent amounts when sponsoring a similar fiesta.

THE SEMANG In some cases of balanced reciprocity, people go to considerable lengths to maintain the relationship. For example, the Semang of the Malay Peninsula engage in a form of **silent trade,** whereby they studiously avoid any face-to-face contact with their trading partners. The Semang leave their products collected from the forest at an agreed-upon location near the village of their trading partners. They return at a later time to receive the commodities (usually salt, beads, and tools) left in exchange. By avoiding social contact, both the Semang and their exchange partners eliminate the risk of jeopardizing the relationship by haggling or arguing over equivalencies (Service 1966).

THE KULA RING Perhaps the most widely analyzed case of balanced reciprocity is the **kula ring** found among the Trobriand Islanders off the coast of New Guinea. First described by Bronislav Malinowski (1922), the kula involves an elaborate and highly ritualized exchange of shell bracelets and shell necklaces that pass (in opposite directions) between a ring of islands. The necklaces move in a clockwise direction and the bracelets move counterclockwise. Many of these shell objects have become well known for their beauty, the noble deeds of their former owners, and the great distances they have traveled. Their main significance is as symbols of the reciprocal relationships between trading partners. These partnerships are often maintained for long periods of time.

The Trobriand Islanders and their neighbors have fairly diversified systems of production with considerable labor specialization. They produce garden crops such as yams and taro, are skilled at fishing, build oceanworthy boats, raise pigs, and produce a wide range of crafts, including dishes, pots, baskets, and jewelry. When trading partners meet, they exchange shell necklaces for shell bracelets according to a set of ceremonial rituals. Then, for the next several days, they also exchange many of their everyday commodities, such as yams, boats, pigs, fish, and craft items.

The shell necklaces and bracelets have no particular monetary value, yet they are indispensable, for they symbolize each partner's good faith and willingness to maintain the longevity of the trading relationship. Trading partners must avoid at all costs any attempt to gain an advantage in the exchange. Generosity and honor are the order of the day. Whoever receives a generous gift is expected to reciprocate.

This very complex system of trade found among the Trobriand Islanders has been surrounded with ritual and ceremony. Individuals are under a strong obligation to pass on the shell objects they receive to other partners in the chain. After a number of years, these bracelets and necklaces will eventually return to their island of origin and from there continue on the cycle once again. Thus, the continual exchange of bracelets and necklaces ties together a number of islands, some of which are great distances from one another.

= *Necklaces and bracelets from the Trobriand Islands.*

Because the ceremonial exchange of shell objects has always been accompanied by the exchange of everyday, practical commodities, the kula ring has clearly functioned as an effective, albeit complicated, system of exchange of goods. Yet, the kula ring is more than just an economic institution. Because there are no all-encompassing political institutions to maintain peace among all of these islands, the maintenance of cordial relationships between trading partners no doubt serves as a peacekeeping mechanism. Moreover, the kula ring also plays an important sociocultural role by creating and maintaining long-term social relationships and by fostering the traditional myths, folklore, and history associated with the circulating shell bracelets and necklaces.

Negative Reciprocity

Negative reciprocity is a form of exchange between equals in which the parties attempt to take advantage of each other. It is based on the principle of trying to get something for nothing or to get the better of the deal. Involving the most impersonal (possibly even hostile) social relations, negative reciprocity can take the form of hard bargaining, cheating, or out-and-out theft. In this form of reciprocity, the sense of altruism and social obligation is at its lowest, and the desire for personal gain is the greatest. Because negative reciprocity is incompatible with close, harmonious relations, it is most often practiced against strangers and enemies.

REDISTRIBUTION

Another principle of exchange is **redistribution,** whereby goods are given to a central authority and then given back to the people in a new pattern. The process of redistribution involves two distinct stages: an inward flow of goods and services to a social center, followed by an outward dispersal of these goods and services back to society. Although redistribution is found in some form in all societies, it is most common in societies that have political hierarchies.

Redistribution can take a number of different forms. In its simplest form, we can see redistribution operating within large families, where family members give their agricultural surpluses to a family head, who in turn stores them and reallocates them back to the individual family members as needed. In complex societies with state systems of government, such as our own, taxation is a form of redistribution. That is, we give a certain percentage of our earnings to the government in exchange for certain goods and services, such as roads, education, and public health

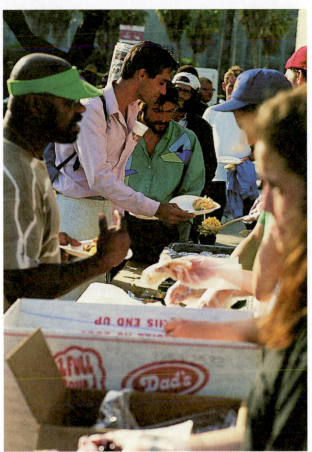

= *In North America, individuals and organizations help redistribute goods and services from the "haves" to the "have-nots." Here volunteers work in a soup kitchen to feed the homeless.*

projects. The giving of gifts to charitable institutions (such as the Salvation Army or Goodwill) can also involve a form of redistribution because the gifts are usually given to the poor or homeless.

Tribute

In some societies without standardized currency, tribal chiefs are given a portion of food and other material goods by their constituents. Some of these food items are then given back to the people in the form of a feast. Such a system of redistribution—known as **tribute**—serves several important social functions at once. In addition to serving as a mechanism for dispensing goods within a society, it is a way of affirming both the political power of the chief and the value of solidarity among the people.

A good illustration of tribute can be seen in traditional Nyoro, a society with a state system of government from Uganda (Taylor 1962). Even though most goods and services were dispersed within the family or local village,

some redistribution followed feudal lines. The rank and file often gave gifts of beer, grain, labor, and livestock to the king and to various levels of chiefs. The king and chiefs in return gave gifts to their trusted followers and servants. These gifts might have included livestock, slaves, or pieces of land. Among the Nyoro, the major criterion for redistribution was, by and large, loyalty to the political hierarchy. Consequently, the king and the chiefs had no particular incentive to make an equitable redistribution or to see that the commoners received in return something roughly equivalent to what they donated.

Equitable distribution is rarely found in most situations where tribute is given. Instead, the chiefs, headmen, and other high-status people invariably come out ahead. For example, among the Fijian Islanders of Moala, somewhat larger quantities and higher quality goods usually went to the chiefs and people of high status; leaders among the Hottentots in southern Africa often took the best portions of meat at the communal feasts; and according to Jesuit accounts, important Huron chiefs in North America always took the large share of furs at ritual redistributions. As Laura Betzig (1988:49) describes it, the redistributor "seems inclined to skim the fat off the top."

Big Men/Feast-Givers

In less centralized societies that do not have formal chiefs, redistribution is carried out by economic entrepreneurs whom anthropologists call **big men.** Unlike chiefs, who usually inherit their leadership roles, big men are self-made leaders who are able to convince their relatives and neighbors to contribute surplus goods for the sake of communitywide feasting. Big men are found widely throughout Melanesia and New Guinea. By using verbal coercion and setting an example of diligence, they persuade their followers to contribute excess food to provide lavish feasts for the followers of other big men. The status of a local big man—and of his followers—increases in direct proportion to the size of the feast, his generosity, and hospitality. Big men of the South Pacific distinguish themselves from ordinary men by their verbal persuasiveness, generosity, eloquence, diligence, and physical fitness. Unlike chiefs, who are usually not producers themselves, big men work hard to produce surpluses and encourage their followers to do so as well, all for the sake of giving it away. In fact, because generosity is the essence of being a big man, many big men often consume less food than ordinary people in order to save it for the feasts.

The many studies on big men during the first half of the twentieth century described exclusively males playing

= *Big men, such as this one from Papua New Guinea, play a major role in the redistribution of goods within their societies.*

these roles. However, there is a growing body of evidence to suggest that there are also big women in Melanesia. Anthropologist Maria Lepowsky (1990) found that on the island of Vanatinai (located in the southeastern part of Papua New Guinea) there are *giagia* (singular *gia*), a gender neutral term that simply means "giver." These *giagia*, who are both men and women, are successful in accumulating and then redistributing ceremonial goods and in hosting mortuary feasts for their kin and neighbors. Although these *giagia* conform very closely to the ideal type of big man as described by the early ethnographers, the major difference is that they are "big persons," not just big men. In some parts of the Pacific such as in the Trobriand Islands, women have their own sphere of exchange of goods and products (yams and skirts) that they have produced by their own labor. But on Vanatinai, Lepowsky (1990:37) found "that women and men exchanged valuables with exchange partners of both sexes and compete with each other to obtain the same types of valuables. . . . Any individual, male or female, may choose to exert the ex-

tra effort to go beyond the minimum contributions to the mortuary feasts expected of every adult. He or she accumulates ceremonial valuables and other goods in order to give them away in acts of public generosity." Under this system it is possible for a woman to be more prominent and influential than her husband owing to her greater ability to acquire and redistribute valuables. Although there are, in fact, more big men than big women in Vanatinai, there are some women that are far more active and successful at exchanging goods than most men.

Bridewealth

In addition to tribute and big manship, several other social institutions also function to allocate material goods according to the principles of redistribution and reciprocity. Because some of these social institutions perform functions other than economic ones, we often overlook their economic or distributive functions. One such social institution (discussed in detail in Chapter 9) is **bridewealth**, which involves the transfer of valuable commodities (often livestock) from the groom's lineage to the bride's lineage as a precondition for marriage.

Even though bridewealth performs a number of noneconomic or social functions—such as legalizing marriages, legitimizing children, creating bonds between two groups of relatives, and reducing divorce—it also serves as a mechanism for maintaining the roughly equitable distribution of goods within a society. Because lineages are the giving and receiving groups and are made up of a relatively equal number of men and women, the practice of bridewealth ensures that all people will have access to the valued commodities. That is, no lineage is likely to get a monopoly on the goods because each group must pay out a certain number of cows when marrying off a son while receiving a roughly equivalent number of cows when marrying off a daughter. Even though the amounts paid may differ depending on the social status of the bride's lineage, all lineages have access to some of the material goods of the society.

Potlatch

Still another customary practice that serves as a mechanism of redistribution is the **potlatch** found among certain Native Americans of the Northwest Coast (Jonaitis 1991). Perhaps the best-known example of the potlatch was found among the Kwakiutl Indians of British Columbia, for whom social ranking was of great importance (see Rohner and Rohner 1970). Potlatches were ceremonies in which chiefs or prominent men publicly announced certain hereditary rights, privileges, and high social status within their communities. Such claims were always accompanied by elaborate feasting and gift giving provided by the person giving the potlatch. In fact, at a potlatch, the host would either give away or destroy all of his personal possessions, which could include such articles as food, boats, blankets, pots, fish oil, elaborately engraved copper shields, and various manufactured goods.

Marvin Harris (1990:89) provides a glimpse into how a Kwakiutl potlatch worked:

> The host chief and his followers arranged in neat piles the wealth that was to be given away. The visitors stared at their host sullenly as he pranced up and down, boasting about how much he was about to give them. As he counted out the boxes of fish oil, baskets full of berries, and piles of blankets, he commented derisively on the poverty of his rivals. Laden with gifts, the guests finally were free to paddle back to their own village. Stung to the quick, the guest chief and his followers vowed to get even. This could only be achieved by inviting their rivals to a return potlatch and obliging them to accept even greater amounts of valuables than they had given away.

The number of guests present and the magnitude of the personal property given away were a measure of the prestige of the host. The more the host could give away, the stronger would be his claim to high social status. In a sense the gifts given at a potlatch served as payment to the guests for serving as witnesses to the host's generosity. In addition to serving as a way of allocating social status, the potlatch was an important mechanism for the dispersal of material goods, for each time a person was a guest at a potlatch, she or he would return home with material goods.

Potlatches, which were widely practiced during the nineteenth century, fell into disfavor with the Canadian government, which saw them as shamefully wasteful. Despite potlatches being declared illegal by the Canadian government, they have not ceased to exist as we begin the new millennium. Owing to their illegal status, they went underground for a number of decades, but the laws have since elapsed, and the potlatch is today making somewhat of a resurgence. In May 1999, the *Christian Science Monitor* reported a potlatch held by the Makah people (who live in the northwestern part of Washington State) in honor of the revival of their centuries-old whale hunting tradition (Porterfield 1999). People from a number of neighboring Native American groups—including the Tulalip, Hoh, Quinault, and Yakima—attended the week-long celebration, which included traditional costumes, food, dancing, and, of course, gift giving.

MARKET EXCHANGE

The third major form of distribution is based on the principle of **market exchange,** whereby goods and services are bought and sold, often through the use of a standardized currency. In market exchange systems, the value of any particular good or service is determined by the market principle of supply and demand. Market exchange tends to be somewhat less personal than exchanges based on reciprocity or redistribution, which often involve ties of kinship, friendship, or political relationships. In this respect, market exchanges are predominantly economic in nature because people are more interested in maximizing their profits than in maintaining a long-term relationship or demonstrating their political allegiance to a chief or leader.

Market exchange systems are most likely to be found in sedentary societies that produce appreciable surpluses and have a complex division of labor. Societies with very simple technologies, such as food collectors, are likely to have no surpluses or such small ones that they can be disposed of quite simply by reciprocity or redistribution. The amount of labor specialization in a society also contributes to a market exchange system, for an increase in the division of labor brings with it a proliferation of specialized commodities and an increased dependency on market exchange.

Standardized Currency

A commonly found trait of market economies is the use of **standardized currency** for the exchange of goods and services. Money can be defined as a generally accepted medium of exchange that also measures the value of a particular item. Money is significant because it is a highly flexible medium of exchange. As the range of exchangeable goods becomes wider, it becomes more difficult to find another person who has exactly what you want and wants something you have to give. Because money (standard currency) is recognizable, long-lasting, portable, and divisible, it becomes an efficient medium of exchange in complex economies. The anthropological literature suggests that money is most often found in those societies with high levels of economic development.

Market economies do not always involve money, however. In some small-scale societies, for example, market exchanges may be based on **barter:** the exchange of one good or service for another without using a standardized form of currency. In a bartering situation, a metalsmith may exchange a plow blade for several bushels of wheat, or an artist and a migrant laborer may swap a piece of

APPLIED PERSPECTIVE
Anthropology and Market Research

As we have pointed out, all economies, wherever they may be found, involve systematic ways of producing goods, distributing them, and then using those goods to satisfy basic human and societal needs. Anthropologists traditionally have studied consumption patterns as part of their analyses of economies. Recently, the business world has discovered that anthropologists' insights can be helpful, particularly in the area of new product development.

In recent years, anthropologists have become increasingly important players in the market research industry. Market research is aimed at learning how and why people use certain products or fail to do so. Manufacturers need this information so they can modify their products in ways that will make them more attractive to consumers. During the 1980s, anthropologist Steve Barnett served as senior vice president of Planmetrics Cultural Analysis Group, a market research firm in New York that studied consumer behavior through direct observations (see Baba 1986). Many market researchers gather data by interviewing people randomly in shopping malls, but Barnett and his associates used a number of innovative techniques designed to learn what people actually do rather than what they say they do. To illustrate, in order to learn more about dishwashing practices in the United States, Barnett put videocameras in people's kitchens for a period of three weeks. The information gathered by this direct observational research enabled Procter and Gamble to alter its television commercials to bring them more into line with actual dishwashing behavior.

More recently, studying consumer habits at close range has become popular in the high-tech arena, where the time pressures, stakes, and failure rates for

sculpture for three days of labor. Even in the highly complex market economy found in the United States, we find bartering institutions that facilitate the wholesale bartering of goods and services between large corporations. By turning over part of its surplus to a bartering corporation, a company that manufactures office furniture can exchange its surplus furniture for items it may need (such as air conditioners, automobile tires, or computers). In the United States and Canada, an increasing number of people (such as artists, therapists, and other freelance suppliers) are creating an underground economy by using bartering as a way of avoiding paying taxes on goods and services.

The major prerequisite of a market exchange is not whether the exchange is based on currency or barter but rather that the value (or price) of any good or service is determined by the market principle of supply and demand. That is, we can consider an exchange to be based on the market principle when a pig can be exchanged for 10 bushels of corn when pigs are scarce but bring only four bushels of corn when pigs are plentiful.

Variety of Markets

The extent to which markets are responsible for the distribution of goods and services in any given society varies widely throughout the world. The market economy of

new products are high. Anthropologist John Sherry, who years ago studied communications technology among the Navajo, is now a member of a team of design ethnographers with Intel Corporation. Their purpose is to learn as much as possible (by using anthropological methods) about how people work and use high-tech tools so that Intel can design more efficient tools in the future. Anthropologists are trained to patiently observe human behavior for hours on end while recording those behaviors in minute detail. And, Intel (along with other high-tech firms like IBM, Hewlett-Packard, Motorola, AT&T, and Xerox) is betting that useful insights will emerge from those minute details.

To illustrate this application of anthropology, Sherry and his fellow design ethnographers spend large amounts of time hanging out in teenagers' bedrooms. (Takahashi 1998:B1). They talked to over a hundred teenagers, analyzed still photos, and studied hours of videos that catalogued how their bedrooms were used. The team concluded that teenagers would like to be able to send photos to one another by transmitting images over telephone lines that would enter a friend's computer and then be displayed in a bedside electronic picture frame. In all likelihood, it will not be long before such a product hits the market. This type of market research, which draws on traditional anthropological techniques and concerns, provides us with an excellent example of how cultural anthropology is being applied to careers in the private sector.

QUESTIONS FOR FURTHER THOUGHT

1. Why have anthropologists become so important to the market research industry in recent years?
2. What major data-gathering techniques could be used by anthropologists to assist in market research?
3. How many different subcultural groups in your society can you identify that should be researched before marketing a product such as a light beer? What do you know about these groups that might affect how an advertising campaign might be structured?

the United States, with its vast network of commercial interests and consumer products, represents one extreme. There is virtually nothing that cannot be bought or sold in our highly complex markets. In some of our markets (such as supermarkets, shops, and retail stores), buyers and sellers interact with one another in close proximity to the goods. But other types of markets in the United States are highly impersonal because the buyers and sellers have no personal interaction. For example, stock markets, bond markets, and commodities markets are all conducted electronically (through brokers), with buyers and sellers having no face-to-face contact with one another. Beginning in the late 1990s an increasing number of goods and services

(everything from books, CDs, and household items from Amazon.com to personal banking with Bank of America) have been marketed over the Internet. Such markets, which exist for the sole purpose of buying and selling, serve an exclusively economic function and fulfill no social functions.

At the opposite extreme are certain small-scale economies that have little labor specialization, small surpluses, and a limited range of goods and services exchanged in markets. Many of the material needs of a household are met by the productive activities of its members. Whatever surpluses exist are brought to market for sale or exchange; the profits are used to purchase other goods or to pay taxes. In such societies, the actual location of the market is important because many social functions are performed in addition to the economic exchange of goods and services. In traditional West Africa, for example, the market is the place where buyers and sellers meet to exchange their surplus goods. But it may also be the place where a man will go to meet his friend, settle a dispute, watch dancing, hear music, pay respects to an important chief, have a marriage negotiated, get caught up on the latest news, or see some distant relatives.

Societies with well-developed market economies have always struggled with the question of how much to rely on the forces of the market or on the government to regulate the economy. Free markets and governments represent different modes that can be used to determine what goods and services will be available and, consequently, what the population will consume. Historically, the United States, perhaps as much as any country in the world, has relied on the free enterprise system for economic decision making. By and large, the U.S. economy is based on the principle that prices are set by market forces as buyers and sellers vie with one another in a changing balance of supply and demand. Motivated by what Western economists call enlightened self-interest, decisions to produce goods and services are made on the basis of the public's desire or willingness to purchase them. A number of other countries during the twentieth century have opted for more state-controlled economies, where the government (not impersonal market forces) determines what will be produced and how much it will cost. The collapse of the former Soviet Union in the 1980s exposed many of the liabilities of relying too heavily on government bureaucracies for making basic economic decisions. Nevertheless, every economy is a blend of both government control and free markets. Even in its heyday, the Soviet economy relied heavily on free markets, particularly with domestic farm products; and at different times, the U.S. economy has experimented with varying levels of government control. The controversy arises when attempting to determine just what that blend should be.

Supporters of the free-market economy during the 1990s point to the collapse of the Soviet Union as a vindication of the free-market system. Those enamored with a free-market economy point to a number of inefficient government enterprises such as the U.S. Postal Service and Amtrak. Calling for a minimum of government regulation, they claim that the forces of the free market are most likely to produce the highest quality of goods and services. But supporters of more government regulation argue that an uncontrolled free-market economy is certainly not in the public interest for several reasons. First, they claim that markets are not likely to produce low-profit products, which are needed by the poor. Because building low-income housing is not likely to generate large profits, builders operating in a free-market economy will choose to build middle- and upper-class housing instead. If governments had not intervened to either build or subsidize low-income housing, the poor would have even fewer places to live. Second, capitalistic, free-market economies lead to increased social stratification where the rich get richer and the poor get poorer. And third, critics argue that unregulated market economies can lead to a number of negative tendencies, including price gouging by monopolistic companies, disregard for dangerous working conditions, rampant inflation, and harm to consumers because of faulty products. Although most people prefer some economic regulation, what the balance should be continues to be debated throughout North America and the rest of the world.

Globalization of World Markets

Since the end of the Cold War in the late 1980s, world markets have experienced dramatic changes. This process, known as **globalization,** essentially involves the spread of free-market economies to all parts of the world. The basic idea behind globalization is that economies will be healthier and growth will occur more rapidly if we allow market forces to rule and if we open up all economies to free trade and competition. This involves lowering tariff barriers (or eliminating them altogether), deregulating the economy, and privatizing services formerly provided by governments. With the disintegration of the former Soviet Union in the late 1980s, the world has witnessed a stunning proliferation of free trade, opening up of markets, and heightened competition. The European Economic Union (EEU) and NAFTA (North American Free Trade Agreement) are good examples of this process of globalization. And with the advent of e-commerce, anyone with a good product, a computer, a telephone, access to the Internet, a web site, and a Federal Express or UPS account will be able to become a potentially successful entrepreneur. The global revolution has encouraged the participation of large numbers of new players in the markets. It is now possible to enter the world marketplace virtually overnight, with very little capital outlay, and become a global competitor by the next afternoon.

SUMMARY

1. The study of economic anthropology involves a theoretical debate between those who believe the concepts of Western economics are appropriate for the study of all economic systems and those who do not.

2. Economic anthropology involves examining how resources are allocated, converted into usable commodities, and distributed.

3. Whereas property rights to land are strongly held in the U.S., in most food-collecting societies land is not owned either individually or collectively. The extent to which people have free access to land in pastoral societies depends on local environmental conditions, with free access to land found in environments where water and pasturage are scarce. Land rights are more rigidly controlled among horticulturalists and agriculturalists than among foragers and pastoralists.

4. People in some parts of the world do not share most North Americans' notion of property ownership. Instead of owning something in our sense of the word, people have limited rights and obligations to a particular object.

5. Every society, to one degree or another, allocates tasks according to gender. Because the same type of activity (such as weaving) may be associated with the opposite gender in different cultures, the division of labor by gender is sometimes seen as arbitrary.

6. The amount of specialization (division of labor) varies from society to society. Based on the extent of division of labor, French sociologist Durkheim distinguished between two different types of societies: those based on mechanical solidarity and those based on organic solidarity. According to Durkheim, societies with a minimum of labor specialization are held together by mechanical solidarity, which is based on a commonality of interests, whereas highly specialized societies are held together by organic solidarity, which is based on mutual interdependence.

7. Goods and services are distributed according to three different modes: reciprocity, redistribution, and market exchange. Reciprocity is the exchange of goods and services of roughly equal value between two trading partners; redistribution, found most commonly in societies with political bureaucracies, is a form of exchange whereby goods and services are given to a central authority and then reallocated to the people according to a new pattern; market exchange systems involve the use of standardized currencies to buy and sell goods and services.

8. Economic anthropologists generally recognize three types of reciprocity depending upon the degree of closeness of the parties: generalized reciprocity involves giving a gift without any expectation of immediate return; balanced reciprocity involves the exchange of goods and services with the expectation that equivalent value will be returned within a specific period of time; and negative reciprocity involves the exchange of goods and services between equals in which the parties try to gain an advantage.

9. Whereas reciprocity is essentially the exchange of goods and services between two partners, redistribution involves a social center from which goods are distributed. The institutions of tribute paid to an African chief, bridewealth, and the potlatch found among the Native Americans of the Northwest Coast are all examples of redistribution.

10. Market exchange, based on standardized currencies, tends to be less personal than either reciprocity or redistribution because people in such an exchange are interested primarily in maximizing their profits. As a general rule, the more labor specialization in a society, the more complex the system of market exchange.

11. Societies with self-developed market economies have to decide to what extent they will allow free markets or the government to control the economy.

KEY TERMS

allocation of resources	mechanical solidarity
balanced reciprocity	negative reciprocity
barter	organic solidarity
big men	particularism
bridewealth	potlatch
division of labor	production
economic anthropology	property rights
economics	reciprocity
generalized reciprocity	redistribution
globalization	silent trade
kula ring	standardized currency
labor specialization	tribute
market exchange	universalism

SUGGESTED READINGS

Douglas, Mary, and Baron Isherwood. *The World of Goods: Toward an Anthropology of Consumption.* New York: Norton, 1979. A study of theories of consumption examined from a cross-cultural perspective.

Gudeman, Stephen, ed. *Economic Anthropology.* Northampton, MA: Edward Elgar, 1999. An impressive collection of essays highlighting the differences and convergences between economists and anthropologists from 1922 until the present.

Jonaitis, Alldona, ed. *Chiefly Feasts: The Enduring Kwakiutl Potlatch.* Seattle: University of Washington Press, 1991. A handsomely illustrated coffee table book that combines photography of the art and material culture of the Kwakuitl of southwestern Canada with five essays describing the meanings, history, and contemporary form of the potlatch.

Malinowski, Bronislav. *Argonauts of the Western Pacific.* New York: Dutton, 1922. A classic ethnography based on four years of uninterrupted fieldwork in which Malinowski describes in detail the kula exchange system found among the Trobriand Islanders.

Ortiz, Sutti, and Susan Lees, eds. *Understanding Economic Process.* Lanham, MD: University Press of America, 1992. The essays in this volume, presented at the tenth annual meeting of the Society for Economic Anthropology, represent a 10-year review of the central issues in economic studies of market and nonmarket societies.

Plattner, Stuart, ed. *Economic Anthropology.* Stanford, CA: Stanford University Press, 1989. This compilation of articles in the field of economic anthropology covers the traditional topics of economic behavior in all of the different types of economic systems from foraging societies, through horticultural and agricultural societies, to industrialized societies. It also deals with contemporary issues such as the informal economy, sex roles, and urban economic systems.

Pryor, F. L. *The Origins of the Economy: A Comparative Study of Distribution in Primitive and Peasant Economies.* New York: Academic Press, 1977. An empirical approach to the cross-cultural study of distribution systems in primitive and peasant economies.

Wilk, Richard. *Economies and Culture: Foundations of Economic Anthropology.* Boulder, CO: Westview Press, 1996. Examines a number of questions such as whether people are inherently greedy or generous and whether markets should be viewed as promoting equality and prosperity or poverty and mean-spiritedness. Wilk makes the point that an anthropological perspective is most useful for getting to the answers to these universal questions.

On the Net

The nature of markets in the world is changing very rapidly. Just several decades ago, it was expected that the buyer and the seller of most goods and services would have some face-to-face contact. Today, however, it is possible to buy things over the phone, through mail-order catalogues, and via fax. Moreover, within the last several years it has become possible to order a wide range of goods and services almost instantaneously over the Internet. To really appreciate how widely the Internet is now used for marketing goods and services, use any major search engine (Alta Vista, Yahoo) to identify how you can find and order the following items:

1. A book of photographs by William Wegman
2. Tickets to your favorite professional sports team
3. A Doberman pinscher puppy
4. A Roger Maris baseball card
5. A glass sculpture by Dante Marioni

LOG ON TO INFOTRAC COLLEGE EDITION. Conduct a subject search of articles on the topic of *either* potlatch, kula ring, or big men. What can you learn about your topic that was not mentioned in the book?

Chapter Nine

MARRIAGE AND THE FAMILY

A Korean couple in traditional dress.

WHAT WE WILL LEARN:

▼

Is the family found universally in all cultures?

▼

What functions do family and marriage systems perform?

▼

How do we explain the fact that all societies have some notion of incest?

▼

What different types of economic considerations are associated with marriage in the world's contemporary societies?

▼

In what ways do societies regulate whom a person can or cannot marry?

▼

In all known societies, people recognize a certain number of relatives who make up the basic social group generally called the family. This is not to imply, however, that

all societies view the family in the same way. In fact, humans have developed a wide variety of types of families. To most middle-class North Americans, the family includes a husband and a wife and their children. To an East African herdsman, the family might include several hundred kin related through both blood and marriage. Among the Hopi, the family would be made up of a woman and her husband and their unmarried sons and married daughters, along with the daughters' husbands and children. This chapter examines the variety of family types found throughout the world and the process of marriage that is responsible for the formation of families.

•■ MARRIAGE AND THE FAMILY: ■• SOME DEFINITIONS

EVEN THOUGH we use the terms *family* and *marriage* routinely, their meanings are ambiguous. Because social scientists and laypeople alike use these terms indiscriminately, it will be helpful to define them in more detail. A *family* is a social unit characterized by economic cooperation, the management of reproduction and child rearing, and common residence. It includes both male and female adults who maintain a socially approved sexual relationship. Family members, both adults and children, recognize certain rights and obligations toward one another. The family is distinct from the institution of *marriage,* which we can define as a series of customs formalizing the relationship between male and female adults within the family. Marriage is a socially approved union between a man and a woman that regulates the sexual and economic rights and obligations between them. Marriage usually involves an explicit contract or understanding and is entered into with the assumption that it will be a permanent arrangement.

Although our definition of marriage holds true for most situations found in the world, it is not universally inclusive of all marital arrangements. Because our definition defines marriage as establishing legitimate relationships between men and women, it tends to assume that all marriages are heterosexual. However, some cultures recognize marriages of men to men and women to women as being legitimate. Indeed, in certain industrialized countries (such as Canada and the Netherlands), same-sex relationships are recognized as legal and, consequently, are protected under the law in the same way as heterosexual unions. In parts of West Africa successful women merchants, who may already be married to a husband, will take a wife to help with the domestic duties while she is at work (Amadiume 1987). Moreover, among the Nandi of Kenya, a woman can marry a woman (female husband) when her father has only daughters and no male heirs. Under such conditions the female husband arranges for a male consort to father children biologically for her bride. Among the Cheyennes of the Great Plains, warriors were permitted to take male transvestites as second wives (Hoebel 1960).

SEXUAL UNION

As with any term, the definition of marriage often must be qualified. Marriage, according to our definition, is a socially legitimate sexual union. When a man and a woman are married, it is implied that they are having a sexual relationship or that the society permits them to have one if they desire it. Although this is generally true, we should bear in mind that this social legitimacy is not absolute, for there may be specified periods during which sexual relations with one's spouse may be taboo. To illustrate, in many societies, sexual relations between spouses must be suspended during periods of menstruation and pregnancy. After a child is born, women in many societies are expected to observe a **postpartum sex taboo,** lasting in some cases until the child is weaned, which can be as long as several years. As William Stephens has suggested, "there may be other sex taboos in honor of special occasions: before a hunting trip, before and after a war expedition, when the crops are harvested, or during various times of religious significance" (1963:10). Given this wide range of occasions where sex with one's spouse is illegitimate, it is possible that in some societies, husbands and wives will be prevented from having sexual relations for a significant segment of their married lives.

PERMANENCE

A second qualification to our definition relates to the permanence of the marital union. Often, as part of the marriage vows recited in Western weddings, spouses pledge to live together in matrimony "until death do us part." Even though it is difficult to ascertain a person's precise intentions or expectations when entering a marriage, an abundance of data suggests that the permanence of marriage varies widely, and in no societies do all marriages last until death. For example, recent statistics indicate that more than one of every two marriages in the United States ends in divorce. Impermanent marriages can also be found in smaller-scale societies. Dorothea Leighton and Clyde Kluckhohn report that they often encountered Navajo men who had "six or seven different wives in succession" (1948:83). In short, when dealing with the permanence of marriage, there is always a discrepancy between ideal expectations and actual behavior.

COMMON RESIDENCE

A qualifying statement must also be added about the notion that family members share a common residence. Although family members usually do live together, there are some obvious definitional problems. If we define "sharing a common residence" as living under the same roof, a long list of exceptions can be cited. In Western society, dependent children sometimes live away from home at boarding schools and colleges. Additionally, in this age of high-speed transportation and communication, it is possible for a husband and wife to live and work in two different cities and see each other only on weekends. On a more global scale, 94 of the 240 African societies listed in George Murdock's *Ethnographic Atlas* (1967) are characterized by wives and their children living in separate houses from the husband. In some non-Western societies, adolescent boys live with their peers apart from their families; and in some cases, such as the Nyakyusa (Wilson 1960), adolescent boys have not only their own houses but their own villages. In each of these examples, family membership and participation are not dependent on living under the same roof.

Thus, as we are beginning to see, the terms *marriage* and *family* are not easy to define. For years, anthropologists have attempted to arrive at definitions of these terms that will cover all known societies. Anthropologists have often debated whether families and the institution of marriage are universals. The Nayar of southern India are an interesting case. According to some (Gough 1959), they did not have marriage in the conventional sense of the term. Although pubescent Nayar girls took a ritual husband in a public ceremony, the husband took no responsibility for the woman after the ceremony, and often he never saw her again. Instead of cohabitating with her "husband," the Nayar bride continued to live with her mother, mother's sister, and mother's brother while being visited over the years by other "husbands." The bride's family retained full responsibility for the woman and whatever children she bore during her lifetime. Thus, it appears that the Nayar do not have marriage according to our definition in that there is no economic cooperation, regulation of sexual activity, cohabitation, or expectation of permanency.

•■ MARRIAGE AND THE FAMILY: ■• FUNCTIONS

WHETHER OR NOT marriage is a cultural universal found in all societies depends on the level of abstraction in our definitions. Without entering into that debate here, suffice it to say that the formation of families through marriage serves several important functions for the societies in which the families operate. One social benefit that marriage provides is the creation of fairly stable relationships between men and women that regulate sexual mating and reproduction. Because humans are continually sexually receptive, and (in the absence of contraceptives) sexual activity usually leads to reproduction, it is imperative that societies create and maintain unions that will regulate mating, reproduction, and child rearing in a socially approved manner.

A second social benefit of marriage is that it provides a mechanism for regulating the sexual division of labor that exists to some extent in all societies. For reasons that are both biological and cultural, men in all societies perform some tasks, and women perform others. To maximize the chances of survival, it is important for a society to

= *The family, such as this one in Mexico, provides a structured environment that supports and meets the needs of children.*

arrange the exchange of goods and services between men and women. Marriage usually brings about domestic relationships that facilitate the exchange of these goods and services.

Third, marriage creates a set of family relationships that can provide for the material, educational, and emotional needs of children for a long period of time. Unlike most other animal species, human children depend on adults for the first decade or more of their lives for their nourishment, shelter, and protection. Moreover, human children require adults to provide the many years of cultural learning needed to develop into fully functioning members of the society. Even though it is possible for children to be reared largely outside a family (as is done on the kibbutzim of Israel), in most societies marriage creates a set of family relationships that provide the material, educational, and emotional support children need for their eventual maturity.

•■ MATE SELECTION: ■•
WHO IS OUT OF BOUNDS?

EVERY SOCIETY known to anthropology has established for itself rules regulating mating (sexual intercourse). The most common form of prohibition is mating with certain types of kin who are defined by the society as being inappropriate sexual partners. The prohibition on mating with certain categories of relatives is known as the **incest taboo.** Following the lead of Robin Fox (1967), it is important

to distinguish between sexual relations and marriage. Incest taboos are prohibitions against having sexual relations with certain categories of kin. This is not exactly the same thing as rules prohibiting marrying certain kin. Although incest taboos and rules prohibiting marrying certain kin often coincide with each other (that is, those who are forbidden to have sex are also forbidden to marry), it cannot be assumed that they always coincide.

The most universal form of incest taboo involves mating between members of the immediate (nuclear) family —that is, mothers and sons, fathers and daughters, and brothers and sisters—although there are several notable yet limited exceptions. For political, religious, or economic reasons, members of the royal families among the ancient Egyptians, Incas, and Hawaiians were permitted to mate with and marry their siblings, although this practice did not extend to the ordinary members of those societies. The incest taboo invariably extends beyond the scope of the immediate or nuclear family, however. In a number of states in the United States, people are forbidden by law from mating with the children of their parents' siblings (that is, first cousins). In some non-Western societies, the incest taboo may extend to large numbers of people on one side of the family but not on the other. And in still other societies, a man is permitted (even encouraged) to mate with and marry the daughter of his mother's brother (a cross cousin and a first cousin) but is strictly prohibited from doing so with the daughter of his mother's sister (also a first cousin but a parallel cousin). Thus, although it seems

The Anthropological Study of Skid Row

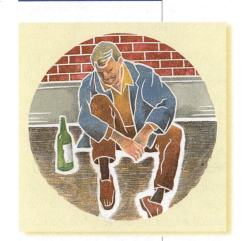

*I*n the social science literature the term *skid row men* refers to indigents who regularly consume inexpensive alcoholic beverages as a way of life, are frequently picked up by the police for public drunkenness, and find themselves repeatedly in "detox" centers. According to most studies (Parsons 1951; Rooney 1961; Spradley 1970), the skid row men have lost all significant involvement with their kinsmen. They are, in short, men without families and men who do not want families.

This general perception that skid row men do not maintain their family ties may be more the result of failing to investigate this aspect of their lives than a true measure of reality. Prompted by such a possibility, Merrill Singer (1985) decided to conduct ethnographic interviews with 28 skid row men who had been admitted to an alcohol detoxification center in Washington, DC. The interview schedule, composed of 100 open-ended questions, was designed to collect information on family background, drinking history, current lifestyle, and social networks. Singer reasoned that if, in fact, these skid row men do maintain kinship ties, then it might be possible to use these kinship links as part of the strategy for therapeutic intervention.

Interestingly, the data revealed that this sample of skid row men maintained fairly regular contact with relatives. Specifically, 93 percent of the men both stayed in regular contact with, and felt emotionally close to, at least one kinsman; 90 percent received nonmaterial aid from relatives; and 86 percent received material assistance from kinsmen. Despite numerous disappointments caused by the alcoholics' inability to stay out of trouble, ties with certain kin (mostly female) were both persistent and emotionally laden. The skid row men were found to both respect and care for their supportive kin.

Based on these findings from the ethnographic interviews, Singer concluded that these female supportive kinsmen may be an important link in the alcoholic rehabilitation programs for skid row men. Some of the men interviewed stated that some of their kinsmen had not given up on them and would be willing to participate in family therapy. Because there is general agreement in the therapeutic community that successful alcoholic rehabilitation requires the involvement of caring significant others, these findings encourage the use of family therapy for the treatment of skid row alcoholics.

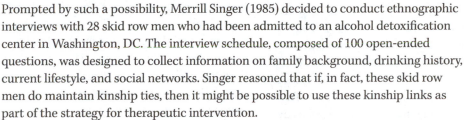

QUESTIONS FOR FURTHER THOUGHT

1. What are some other terms that refer to the same population as those from skid row?
2. In what practical ways can kinship ties be used to help in the therapeutic intervention of those living on skid row?
3. Why do you think most of the relatives with whom the skid row men maintained contact were women and not men?

clear that every society has incest taboos, the relatives that make up the incestuous group vary from one society to another. Given that incest taboos are universally found throughout the world, anthropologists have long been interested in explaining their origins and persistence. A number of possible explanations have been set forth.

NATURAL AVERSION THEORY

One such theory, which was popular about a hundred years ago, rests on the somewhat unsatisfying concept that there is a natural aversion to sexual intercourse among those who have grown up together. Although any natural (or genetically produced) aversion to having sexual relations within the nuclear family is rejected today, there is some evidence to suggest that such an aversion may be developed. For example, according to Yohina Talmon (1964), sexual attraction between Israelis reared on the same **kibbutz** is extremely rare, a phenomenon attributed by the kibbutz members themselves to the fact that they had grown up together. Another study (Wolf 1968) of an unusual marital practice in Taiwan, whereby infant girls are given to families with sons to be their future brides, found that these marriages were characterized by higher rates of infidelity and sexual difficulties and fewer children. Thus, it appears that in at least some situations, people who have grown up together and have naturally experienced high levels of familiarity have little sexual interest in each other. Nevertheless, this familiarity theory does not appear to be a particularly convincing explanation for the existence of the incest taboo.

If familiarity does lead to sexual aversion and avoidance, how do we explain why incest does occur with considerable regularity throughout the world? Indeed, in our own society, it has been estimated that 10 to 14 percent of children under 18 years of age have been involved in incestuous relationships (Whelehan 1985). In short, the familiarity theory does not explain why we even need a strongly sanctioned incest taboo if people already have a natural aversion to incest.

INBREEDING THEORY

Another theory that attempts to explain the existence of the incest taboo focuses on the potentially deleterious effects of inbreeding on the family. This inbreeding theory, proposed first in the late nineteenth century, holds that mating between close kin, who are likely to carry the same harmful recessive genes, tends to produce a higher incidence of genetic defects (which results in an increased sus-

ceptibility to disease and higher mortality rates). This theory was later discredited because it was argued that sharing the same recessive genes could produce adaptive advantages as well as disadvantages. However, recent genetic studies have given greater credence to the older theory that inbreeding does lead to some harmful consequences for human populations. Conversely, outbreeding, which occurs in human populations with strong incest taboos, has a number of positive genetic consequences. According to Bernard Campbell (1979), these include increases in genetic variation, a reduction in lethal recessive traits, improved health, and lower rates of mortality.

Even though it is generally agreed today that inbreeding is genetically harmful to human populations, the question still remains whether prehistoric people understood this fact. After all, the science of Mendelian genetics did not become established until the start of the twentieth century. However, it is not necessary for early people to have recognized the adaptive advantages of avoiding inbreeding through an incest taboo. Rather, the incest taboo could have persisted through time for the simple reason that it was adaptively advantageous. That is, groups that practiced the incest taboo would have more surviving children than societies without the incest taboo. Thus, this greater reproductive success would explain, if not the origins of the incest taboo, at least why it has become a cultural universal.

FAMILY DISRUPTION THEORY

Whereas the inbreeding theory focuses on the biological consequences of incest, a third theory centers on its negative social consequences. This theory, which is most closely linked with Bronislaw Malinowski (1927), holds that mating between a mother and son, father and daughter, or brother and sister would create such intense jealousies within the nuclear family that the family would not be able to function as a unit of economic cooperation and socialization. For example, if adolescents were permitted to satisfy their sexual urges within the nuclear family unit, fathers and sons and mothers and daughters would be competing with one another, and, consequently, normal family role relationships would be seriously disrupted. The incest taboo, according to this theory, originated as a mechanism to repress the desire to satisfy one's sexual urges within the family.

In addition to causing disruption among nuclear family members through sexual competition, incest creates the further problem of **role ambiguity**. For example, if a child is born from the union of a mother and her son, the child's father will also be the child's half-brother, the child's mother will also be the child's grandmother, and the child's half sister will also be the child's aunt. These are just some of the bizarre roles created by such an incestuous union. Because different family roles, such as brother and father, carry with them vastly different rights, obligations, and behavioral expectations, the child will have great difficulty deciding how to behave toward his or her immediate family members. Does the child treat the male who biologically fathered him or her as a father or as a brother? How does the child deal with the woman from whose womb he or she sprung—as a mother or a grandmother? Thus, the incest taboo can be viewed as a mechanism that prevents this type of role ambiguity or confusion.

THEORY OF EXPANDING SOCIAL ALLIANCES

Incest avoidance can also be explained in terms of positive social advantages for societies that practice it. By forcing people to marry out of their immediate family, the incest taboo functions to create a wider network of interfamily alliances, thereby enhancing cooperation, social cohesion, and survival. Each time one of your close relatives mates with a person from another family, it creates a new set of relationships with whom your family is less likely to become hostile. This theory, first set forth by Edward Tylor (1889) and later developed by Claude Lévi-Strauss (1969), holds that it makes little sense to mate with someone from one's own group with whom one already has good relations. Instead, there is more to be gained, both biologically and socially, by expanding one's networks outward. Not only does mating outside one's own group create a more peaceful society by increasing the number of allies, but it also creates a larger gene pool, which has a greater survival advantage than a smaller gene pool.

The extent to which wider social alliances are created by requiring people to mate and marry outside the family is illustrated by a study of Rani Khera, a village in northern India. In a survey of the village population (Lewis 1955), it was found that the 226 married women residing in the village had come from approximately 200 separate villages and that roughly the same number of village daughters married out. Thus, the village of Rani Khera was linked through marriage to hundreds of other northern Indian villages. In fact, this pattern of mating and marrying outside one's own group (created out of a desire to avoid incest) is an important factor integrating Indian society.

= *A bride and groom in Lapland, Norway.*

•■ MATE SELECTION: ■• WHOM SHOULD YOU MARRY?

AS WE HAVE SEEN, every society has the notion of incest that defines a set of kin with whom a person is to avoid marriage and sexual intimacy. In no society is it permissible to mate with one's parents or siblings (that is, within the nuclear family), and in most cases the restricted group of kin is considerably wider. Beyond this notion of incest, people in all societies are faced with rules either restricting one's choice of marriage partners or strongly encouraging the selection of other people as highly desirable mates. These are known as rules of **exogamy** (marrying outside of a certain group) and **endogamy** (marrying within a certain group).

RULES OF EXOGAMY

Because of the universality of the incest taboo, all societies to one degree or another have rules for marrying outside a certain group of kin. These are known as rules of exogamy.

In societies such as the United States, which are not based on the principle of unilineal descent groups, the exogamous group extends only slightly beyond the nuclear family. It is considered either illegal or immoral to marry one's first cousin and, in some cases, one's second cousin, but beyond that one can marry other more distant relatives with only mild disapproval. In societies that are based on unilineal descent groups, however, the exogamous group is usually the lineage, which can include many hundreds of people, or even the clan, which can include thousands of people who are unmarriageable. Thus, when viewed cross-culturally, rules of exogamy based on kinship do not appear to be based on genealogical proximity.

RULES OF ENDOGAMY

In contrast to exogamy, which requires marriage outside one's own group, the rule of endogamy requires a person to select a mate from within one's own group. Hindu castes found in traditional India are strongly endogamous, believing that to marry below one's caste would result in serious ritual pollution. Caste endogamy is also found in a somewhat less rigid form among the Rwanda and Banyankole of eastern Central Africa. In addition to being applied to caste, endogamy can be applied to other social units, such as the village or local community, as was the case among the Incas of Peru, or to racial groups, as has been practiced in the Republic of South Africa for much of the twentieth century.

Even though there are no strongly sanctioned legal rules of endogamy in the United States, there is a certain amount of marrying within one's own group based on class, ethnicity, religion, and race. This general de facto endogamy found in the United States results from the fact that people do not have frequent social contacts with people from different backgrounds. Upper-middle-class children, for example, tend to grow up in the suburbs, take golf and tennis lessons at the country club, and attend schools designed to prepare students for college. By contrast, many lower-class children grow up in urban housing projects, play basketball in public playgrounds, and attend schools with low expectations for college attendance. This general social segregation by class, coupled with parental and peer pressure to "marry your own kind," results in a high level of endogamy in many complex Western societies such as our own.

It should be noted that rules of exogamy and rules of endogamy are not opposites or mutually exclusive. Indeed, they can coexist in the same society provided the endoga-

mous group is larger than the exogamous group. For example, it is quite possible to have an endogamous ethnic group (that is, one must marry within one's ethnic group) while at the same time having exogamous lineages (that is, one must marry outside one's own lineage).

ARRANGED MARRIAGES

In Western societies, with their strong emphasis on individualism, mate selection is largely a decision made jointly by the prospective bride and groom. Aimed at satisfying the emotional and sexual needs of the individual, the choice of mates in Western society is based on such factors as physical attractiveness, emotional compatibility, and romantic love. Even though absolute freedom of choice is constrained by such factors as social class, ethnicity, religion, and race, individuals in most contemporary Western societies are free to marry whomever they please.

In many societies, however, the interests of the families are so strong that marriages are arranged. Negotiations are handled by family members of the prospective bride and groom, and for all practical purposes, the decision of whom one will marry is made by one's parents or other influential family members. In certain cultures, such as parts of traditional Japan, India, and China, future marriage partners are betrothed while they are still children. In one extreme example—the Tiwi of North Australia—females are betrothed or promised as future wives *before* they are born (Hart and Pilling 1960). Because the Tiwi believe that females are liable to become impregnated by spirits at any time, the only sensible precaution against unmarried mothers is to betroth female babies before birth or as soon as they are born.

All such cases of **arranged marriage,** wherever they may be found, are based on the cultural assumption that because marriage is a union of two kin groups rather than merely two individuals, it is far too significant an institution to be based on something as frivolous as physical attractiveness or romantic love.

Arranged marriages are often found in societies with elaborate social hierarchies, perhaps the best example of which is Hindu India. Indeed, the maintenance of the caste system in India depends largely on a system of arranged marriages. As William Goode reminds us,

> Maintenance of caste was too important a matter to be left to the young, who might well fall prey to the temptations of love and thus ignore caste requirements. To prevent any serious opposition, youngsters were married early enough to ensure that they could not acquire any

= *For people in some parts of the world, such as India, mate selection is often not decided by the bride and groom.*

resources with which to oppose adult decisions. The joint family, in turn, offered an organization which could absorb a young couple who could not yet make their own living. . . . This pattern of marriage has always been common among the nobility, but in India it developed not only among the wealthy, who could afford early marriages and whose unions might mark an alliance between two families, but also among the poor, who had nothing to share but their debts. (1963:208)

Arranged marriages in India are further reinforced by other traditional Indian values. Fathers, it was traditionally held, sinned by failing to marry off their daughters before puberty. Indeed, both parents in India shared the common belief that they were responsible for any sin the daughter might commit because of a late marriage. For centuries, Hindu civilization, with its heritage of eroticism expressed in the sexual cult of Tantricism, has viewed women as lustful beings who tempt men with their sexual favors. Thus, a girl had to be married at an early age to protect both herself and the men who might become sinners. And, if girls were to become brides before reaching adolescence, they could hardly be trusted to select their own husbands. Prompted by this belief, in certain parts of India girls marry at a very young age. According to a government survey of 5,000 women in Rajastan in northern India, more than half were married before they were 15 years old, and of these, 14 percent married before they were 10 and 3 percent before they were 5. Even though the Indian govern-

ment passed a law in 1978 setting a minimum age of marriage for females at 18, the law has been largely unenforced.

Anthropologist Serena Nanda (1992) reminds us that arranging marriages in India is serious business and should not be taken frivolously. In addition to making certain that a mate is selected from one's own caste, parents must be careful to arrange marriages for their children that take into consideration such factors as level of education, physical attractiveness, compatibility with future in-laws, and level of maturity. Requiring seriousness, hard work, and patience, arranging marriages may take years to bring about, as one of Nanda's Indian informants explains:

> This is too serious a business. If a mistake is made we have not only ruined the life of our son or daughter, but we have spoiled the reputation of our family as well. And, that will make it much harder for their brothers and sisters to get married. (1992:142)

Even though mate selection in North America generally is a matter of individual choice, many singles are not opposed to seeking help. As we begin the new millennium, there are dozens of web sites devoted to matchmaking, including such alluring sites as "Cupid's Network," "Authoritative Matchmaker," and "Match.com." For those who need assistance in finding a mate along the Information Superhighway, Jodie Gould and Lisa Skriloff have written a handbook, largely for women, entitled *Men Are from Cyberspace*, which offers advice on making the leap from mouse to spouse. Now, according to Alex Kuczynski (1999), even Wall Street has its own matchmaker. Fast-track financial types with little time to look for Mr. or Ms. Right can hire Janis Spindel, a New York City "romantic headhunter." Even though the notion of traditional matchmaking is antiquated, it somehow fits in very nicely with the pressures of the modern business world. Particularly when financial markets have been active (as they have for most of the 1990s), investment bankers, managing directors, corporate lawyers, and other financial high rollers simply don't have time to find a mate. So for $10,000, Spindel offers a dozen dates over the course of a year. Having brokered 294 monogamous relationships and 70 marriages, Spindel says this about her personal service business: "Who wants to look around all the time when you can hire me, your own personal shopper"(Kuczynski 1999:11).

PREFERENTIAL COUSIN MARRIAGE

A somewhat less coercive influence on mate selection than arranged marriages is found in societies that specify a preference for choosing certain categories of relatives as marriage partners. A common form of preferred marriage is **preferential cousin marriage,** which is practiced in one form or another in most of the major regions of the world. Unlike our own kinship system, kinship systems based on lineages distinguish between two different types of first cousins: cross cousins and parallel cousins. This distinction rests on the gender of the parents of the cousin. **Cross cousins** are children of siblings of the opposite sex—that is, one's mother's brothers' children and one's father's sisters' children. **Parallel cousins,** on the other hand, are children of siblings of the same sex (the children of one's mother's sisters and one's father's brothers). In societies that make such a distinction, parallel cousins, who are considered family members, are called "brother" and "sister" and thus are excluded as potential marriage partners. However, because one's cross cousins are not thought of as family members, they are considered by some societies as not just permissible marriage partners but actually preferred ones.

The most common form of preferential cousin marriage is between cross cousins because it functions to strengthen and maintain ties between kin groups established by the marriages that took place in the preceding generation. That is, under such a system of cross cousin marriage, a man originally would marry a woman from an unrelated family, and then their son would marry his mother's brother's daughter (cross cousin) in the next generation. Thus, because a man's wife and his son's wife come from the same family, the ties between the two families tend to be solidified. In this respect, cross cousin marriage functions to maintain ties between groups in much the same way that exogamy does. The major difference is that exogamy encourages the formation of ties with a large number of kinship groups, whereas preferential cross cousin marriage solidifies the relationship between a more limited number of kin groups over a number of generations.

A much less common form of cousin marriage is between parallel cousins, the child of one's mother's sister or father's brother (Murphy and Kasdan 1959). Found among some Arabic-speaking societies of the Middle East and North Africa, it involves the marriage of a man to his father's brother's daughter. Because parallel cousins belong to the same group, such a practice can prevent the fragmentation of family property.

THE LEVIRATE AND SORORATE

Individual choice also tends to be limited by another form of mate selection that requires a person to marry the husband or wife of deceased kin. The **levirate** is the custom whereby a widow is expected to marry the brother (or some close male relative) of her dead husband. Usually, any children fathered by the woman's new husband are considered to belong legally to the dead brother rather than to the actual genitor. Such a custom serves as a form of social security for the widow and her children and preserves the rights of the husband's family to her sexuality and future children. The levirate, practiced in a wide variety of societies found in Oceania, Asia, Africa, and India, is closely associated with placing high value on having male heirs. Hindu men, for example, needed sons to perform certain family ceremonies, and ancient Hebrews placed a high value on sons so that a man's lineage would not die out. In both cases, men were under great pressure to marry their dead brothers' widows.

The **sororate,** which comes into play when a wife dies, is the practice of a widower's marrying the sister (or some close female relative) of his deceased wife. If the deceased spouse has no sibling, the family of the deceased is under a general obligation to supply some equivalent relative as a substitute. For example, in some societies that practice the sororate, a widower may be given as a substitute wife the daughter of his deceased wife's brother.

CROSS-CULTURAL MISCUE

TONY MANZA, a high-level sales executive with a Canadian office furniture company, was in Kuwait trying to land a large contract with the Kuwaiti government. Having received an introduction from a mutual friend, Manza made an appointment with Mr. Mansour, the chief purchasing agent for the government. In his preparation for the trip, Manza had been told to expect to engage in a good deal of "small talk" before actually getting down to business. So Manza and Mansour chatted about the weather, golf, and Tony's flight from Toronto. Then, quite surprisingly, Mansour inquired about Manza's 70-year-old father. Without giving it much thought, Manza responded by saying that his father was doing fine but that the last time he had seen him four months ago in the nursing home, he had lost some weight. From that point onward, Mansour's attitude changed abruptly from warm and gracious to cool and aloof. Manza never did get the contract he was after.

Although Manza thought he was giving Mansour a straightforward answer, his response from Mansour's perspective made Tony an undesirable business partner. Coming from a society that places very high value on family relationships, Mansour considered putting one's own father into a nursing home (to be cared for by total strangers) to be inhumane. If Manza could not be relied upon to take care of his own father, he surely could not be trusted to fulfill his obligations in a business relationship.

•■ NUMBER OF SPOUSES ■•

IN MUCH THE SAME WAY that societies have rules regulating whom one may or may not marry, they have rules specifying how many mates a person may or should have. Cultural anthropologists have identified three major types of marriage based on the number of spouses permitted: **monogamy** (the marriage of one man to one woman at a time), **polygyny** (the marriage of a man to two or more women at a time), and **polyandry** (the marriage of a woman to two or more men at a time).

MONOGAMY

The practice of having only one spouse at a time is so widespread and rigidly adhered to in the United States that most people would have great difficulty imagining any other marital alternative. We are so accustomed to thinking of marriage as an exclusive relationship between husband and wife that for most North Americans, the notion of sharing a spouse is unthinkable. Any person who chooses to take more than one marriage partner at a time is in direct violation of conventional norms, religious standards, and the law and, if caught, will probably be fined or sent to jail.

So ingrained is this concept of monogamy in Western society that we often associate it with the highest standards of civilization, while associating plural marriage with social backwardness and depravity. Interestingly, many societies that practice monogamy circumvent the notion of lifelong partnerships by either permitting extramarital affairs (provided they are conducted discreetly) or practicing **serial monogamy** (taking a number of different spouses one after another rather than at the same time). In fact, serial monogamy is very common in the United States, Canada, and much of western Europe.

POLYGYNY

Even though monogamy is widely practiced in the United States and generally in the Western world, the overwhelming majority of world cultures do not share our values about the inherent virtue of monogamy. According to Murdock's *World Ethnographic Sample,* approximately seven out of every 10 cultures of the world permit the practice of polygyny. In fact, in most of the major regions of the world, polygyny is the preferred form of marriage. It was practiced widely in traditional India and China and remains a preferred form of marriage throughout Asia, Africa, and the Middle East. There is also evidence to support the idea

= *A Yao tribal chief from Laos is pictured here with his two wives.*

that polygyny played a significant role in our own Western background by virtue of the numerous references to polygyny in the Old Testament of the Bible.

Many Westerners, steeped in a tradition of monogamy, interpreted the very existence of polygyny as having its basis in the male sex drive. Because they presumed that men had a stronger sex drive than women, polygyny was seen as a mechanism for men to satisfy themselves at the expense of women. This interpretation is flawed on a number of counts. First, there is little hard evidence to suggest that the sex drive is innately stronger for men than for women. Moreover, if men were interested in increasing their sexual options, it is not likely that they would choose multiple wives as a way of solving the problem. Instead, they would resort to multiple extramarital liaisons, which would be far less complicated than taking on the responsibilities of multiple wives.

To suggest that approximately 70 percent of the world's cultures practice polygyny is not tantamount to saying that 70 percent of the world's population practices polygyny. We must bear in mind that many of the cultures that practice polygyny are small-scale societies with small pop-

ulations. Moreover, even in polygynous societies, the majority of men at any given time still have only one wife. Even in societies where polygyny is most intensively practiced, we would not expect to find more than 35 to 40 percent of the men actually having two or more wives. Polygyny in these societies is the preferred, not the usual, form of marriage. It is something for which men strive but only some attain. Just as the ideal of becoming a millionaire is usually not realized in the United States, so too in polygynous societies, only some men actually practice polygyny.

There are a number of reasons why most men in polygynous societies never acquire more than one wife. First, marriage in many polygynous societies requires the approval (and financial support) of large numbers of kinsmen, and this support is not always easy to obtain. Second, in some polygynous societies it is considered inappropriate for men of low rank to seek additional wives, thereby restricting a certain segment of the males in the society to monogamy. And third, being the head of a polygynous household, which invariably carries with it high prestige, is hard work. The management of two or more wives and their children within a household requires strong administrative skills, particularly if relations between the wives are not congenial. A recent study of polygyny among the present-day Zulu of South Africa (Moller and Welch 1990) indicates that Zulu men tend to opt for monogamy over polygyny for the additional reasons that they are under increasing pressure to accept the socially dominant values of South African Whites, and the dominant White Christian churches have opposed polygyny militantly. In short, most men in polygynous societies, for a variety of reasons, have neither the inclination, family power base, nor social skills needed to achieve the high status of being a polygynist.

Economic Status of Women in Polygynous Societies

The rate of polygyny varies quite widely from one part of the world to another. A critical factor influencing the incidence of polygyny is the extent to which women are seen as economic assets (where they do the majority of labor) or liabilities (where men do the majority of work). To illustrate, in such areas of the world as sub-Saharan Africa where women are assets, it has been estimated (Dorjahn 1959) that the mean rate of polygyny is approximately 35 percent, ranging from a low of 25 percent (!Kung) to a high of 43 percent (Guinea Coast). Conversely, in societies where women are an economic liability (such as among the Inuit, where only about 5 percent of the men practice polygyny), few men can afford the luxury of additional wives (Linton 1936).

Sex Ratio in Polygynous Societies

For polygyny to work, a society must solve the very practical problem of the sex ratio. In most human populations, the number of men and women is roughly equal. The question therefore arises: Where do the excess women who are needed to support a system of polygyny come from? It is theoretically possible that the sex ratio could swing in favor of females if males were killed off in warfare, if women were captured from other societies, or if the society practiced male infanticide. All of these quite radical solutions may account for a small part of the excess of women needed for a polygynous marriage system in some societies.

More commonly, this numerical discrepancy is alleviated quite simply by postponing the age at which men can marry. That is, if females can marry from age 14 on and males are prohibited from marrying until age 26, a surplus of marriageable women always exists in the marriage pool. In some traditional societies, such as the Swazi of southern Africa, young adult men were required by their regimental organizations (that is, age groups) to remain unmarried until the inauguration of the next regiment. Generally, this meant that men were not free to marry until their mid- to late 20s. Because women were able to marry in their teens, the Swazi society had solved the numerical dilemma presented by polygyny by simply requiring men to marry later in life than women.

Advantages of Polygyny

Having two or more wives in a polygynous society is usually seen as a mark of prestige or high status. In highly stratified kingdoms, polygyny is one of the privileges of royalty and aristocrats, as was the case with the late King Sobhuza of Swaziland, who, it was estimated, had well over a hundred wives. In societies that are stratified more on age than on political structure, such as the Azande of the Sudan and the Kikuyu of Kenya, polygyny is a symbol of prestige for older men. Whether aristocrat or commoner, however, having multiple wives means wealth, power, and high status for both the polygynous husband and the wives and children. That is, a man's status increases when he takes additional wives, and a woman's status increases when her husband takes additional wives. For this reason, women in some African societies actually urge their husbands to take more wives. Clearly, these African women do not want to be married to a nobody.

The old anthropological literature (written before the 1970s) gave the impression that women in polygynous societies generally favored polygyny over monogamy. However, such a conclusion was to some extent the result of male bias because the majority of ethnographers for the first half of the twentieth century were men. As Philip Kilbride (1997:284) suggests,

> There is evidence that women, in fact, do traditionally value polygyny. There is also evidence that suggests that men value it even more. There is also strong evidence that modernizing or westernizing women most likely value it not at all.

Sometimes multiple wives are taken because they are viewed by the society as economic and political assets. Each wife not only contributes to the household's goods and services but also produces more children, who are valuable economic and political resources. The Siuai of the Solomon Islands provide an excellent example of how having multiple wives can be an economic advantage for the polygynous husband. Pigs are perhaps the most prized possession of Siuai adults. According to Douglas Oliver, "To shout at a person 'you have no pigs' is to offer him an insult" (1955:348). Women are particularly valuable in the raising of pigs, for the more wives, the more hands to work in the garden, the more pig food, and, consequently, the more pigs. Oliver continues,

> It is by no mere accident that polygynous households average more pigs than monogamous ones. Informants stated explicitly that some men married second and third wives in order to enlarge their gardens and increase their herds. . . . Opisa of Turunom did not even trouble to move his second wife from her village to his own. She, a woman twenty years his senior, simply remained at her own home and tended two of his pigs. (1955:352–353)

Competition Among Wives

Despite the advantages just discussed, living in a polygynous household has drawbacks. Even though men desire multiple wives, they recognize the potential pitfalls. The major problem is jealousy among the wives, who often compete for the husband's attention, sexual favors, and household resources. In fact, in some African societies, the word for *co-wife* is derived from the root word for *jealousy*. As related here, jealousy and dissension among wives are common among the Gusii of western Kenya:

> Each wife tends to be the husband's darling when she is the latest, and to maintain that position until he marries again. . . . This tendency in itself causes jealousy among

the wives. In addition, any inequality in the distribution of gifts or money, or in the number of children born and died, or the amount of education received by the children, adds to the jealousy and hatred. A woman who becomes barren or whose children die almost always believes that her co-wife has achieved this through witchcraft or poisoning. She may then attempt retaliation. (LeVine quoted in Stephens 1963:57)

Even though competition among wives in polygynous societies can be a threat to domestic tranquility, there are several ways to minimize the friction. First, some societies practice a form of polygyny called *sororal polygyny*, where a man marries two or more sisters. It is possible that sisters, who have had to resolve issues of jealousy revolving around their parents' attention, are less likely to be jealous of one another when they become wives. Second, wives in many polygynous societies are given their own separate living quarters. As Paul Bohannan and Philip Curtin (1988) remind us, because women may have more difficulty sharing their kitchens than their husbands, jealousy can be minimized by giving each wife her own personal space. Third, dissension is lessened if the rights and obligations among the wives are clearly understood. Fourth, potential conflict among wives can be reduced by establishing a hierarchy among the wives. Because the senior wife often exerts considerable authority over more junior wives, she can run a fairly smooth household by adjudicating the various complaints of the other wives.

Not only can the jealousies among wives be regulated, but some ethnographic reports from polygynous societies reveal considerable harmony and cooperation among the wives. Elenore Smith Bowen (1964:127–128) relates the story of Ava, a Tiv woman who was the senior of five wives:

The women were fast friends. Indeed it was Ava who had picked out all the others. She saved up forty or fifty shillings every few years, searched out an industrious girl of congenial character, then brought her home and presented her to her husband: "Here is your new wife." Ava's husband always welcomed her additions to his household and he always set to work to pay the rest of the bride-wealth, for he knew perfectly well that Ava always picked hard-working, healthy, handsome, steady women who wouldn't run away.

Although North America is adamantly monogamous, the practice of having more than one wife at a time does exist, particularly in the state of Utah. Although the Mormon church outlawed polygyny in 1890, the practice persists on a small scale, and, in fact, has experienced a resurgence over the last 30 years. Officially, polygyny remains a felony in Utah, but because it is considered benign, it is no longer prosecuted. Although accurate statistics on the incidence of polygyny in the United States are not available, it is estimated that as many as 30,000 people practice polygyny. Some Mormons practice polygyny today because of its deep-seated religious significance. Others practice it because it provides considerable social security, particularly for women. But, whatever the motivation, there are growing numbers of middle-class polygynists in parts of the United States. Some of the polygynist homesteads in this subculture are quite elaborate. The *Charlotte Observer* (Williams 1998) ran a picture of one such home: a 35,000 square foot structure with 37 bathrooms and 31 bedrooms, which housed a wealthy Mormon fundamentalist, his 10 wives, and 28 children!

POLYANDRY

Polyandry involves the marriage of a woman to two or more men at a time. A much rarer form of plural marriage, polyandry is found in less than 1 percent of the societies of the world, most notably in Tibet, Nepal, and India. Polyandry can be fraternal (where the husbands are brothers) or nonfraternal.

Perhaps the best-known case of polyandry is found among the Toda of southern India, who practice the fraternal variety. When a woman marries a man, she also becomes the wife of all of his brothers, including even those who have not yet been born. Marriage privileges rotate among the brothers. Even though all of the brothers live together with the wife in a single household, there is little competition or sexual jealousy. Whenever a brother is with the wife, he places his cloak and staff at the door as a sign not to disturb him. When the wife becomes pregnant, paternity is not necessarily ascribed to the biological father (genitor) but is determined by a ceremony that establishes a social father (pater), usually the oldest brother. After the birth of two or three children, however, another brother is chosen as the social father for all children born to the woman thereafter.

Toda society is characterized by a shortage of females brought about by the traditional practice of female infanticide, and this shortage of women may be one of the reasons for the existence of polyandry among the Toda. Because of the influence of both the Indian government and Christian missionaries, however, female infanticide has largely disappeared today, the male–female sex ratio has become essentially balanced, and polyandry among the Toda is, for all practical purposes, a thing of the past.

In addition to explaining the existence of polyandry by the shortage of women, there are certain economic factors to consider. According to William Stephens (1963), senior husbands among the wealthier families in Marquesans society recruited junior husbands as a way of augmenting the manpower of the household. It has also been suggested (Goldstein 1987) that Tibetan serfs practice polyandry as a solution to the problem of land shortage. To prevent the division of small plots of land among their sons, brothers could keep the family land intact by marrying one woman. By marrying one woman, two or more brothers are able to preserve the family resources; that is, if all of the sons split up to form their own monogamous households, the family would rapidly multiply and the family land would rapidly fragment. In such a monogamous situation, the only way to prevent this rapid fragmentation of family land is to practice primogeniture (all land is inherited by the oldest son only). Such a system, though keeping the land intact, does so at the expense of creating many landless male offspring. In contrast, the practice of fraternal polyandry does not split up the family land but rather maintains a steady ratio of land to people.

•◼ ECONOMIC CONSIDERATIONS ◼• OF MARRIAGE

MOST SOCIETIES view marriage as a binding contract between at least the husband and wife and, in many cases, between their respective families. Such a contract includes the transfer of certain rights between the parties involved—rights of sexual access, legal rights to children, and rights of the spouses to each other's economic goods and services. Often the transfer of rights is accompanied by the transfer of some type of economic consideration. These transactions, which may take place either before or after the marriage, can be divided into five categories: bridewealth, bride service, dowry, woman exchange, and reciprocal exchange.

BRIDEWEALTH

Bridewealth is the compensation given upon marriage by the family of the groom to the family of the bride. According to Murdock's *World Ethnographic Sample* (reported in Stephens 1963:211), approximately 46 percent of all societies give substantial bridewealth payment as a normal part of the marriage process. Although bridewealth is practiced in most regions of the world, it is perhaps most widely found in Africa, where it is estimated (Murdock 1967) that 82 percent of the societies require the payment of bridewealth; most of the remaining 18 percent practice either token bridewealth or **bride service** (providing labor, rather than goods, to the bride's family).

Bridewealth is paid in a wide variety of currencies, but in almost all cases, the commodity used for payment is highly valued in the society. For example, reindeer are given as bridewealth by the reindeer-herding Chukchee, horses by the equestrian Cheyenne of the Central Plains, sheep by the sheep-herding Navajo, and cattle by the pastoral Masai, Samburu, and Nuer of eastern Africa. In other societies, marriage payments take the form of blankets (Kwakiutl), pigs (Alor), mats (Fiji), shell money (Kurtachi), spears (Somali), loincloths (Toda), and even the plumes of the bird of paradise (Siane).

Just as the commodities used in bridewealth transactions vary considerably, so does the amount of the trans-

CROSS-CULTURAL MISCUE

BROOKS (1990) relates an incident of intercultural misunderstanding that occurred recently in Saudi Arabia between a North American woman and her local Saudi landlord. The woman, the wife of a U.S. Marine chaplain stationed in Saudi Arabia, was at home when the landlord arrived with several workmen to make repairs. Upon entering, the landlord passed the American woman but never spoke to her or even acknowledged her presence. The chaplain's wife thought that the landlord's behavior was extremely rude.

Actually, according to Saudi culture, the landlord was treating her with the utmost respect and politeness. He did not want to invade her privacy by speaking to her without her husband being present. As Brooks explains, "He was honoring her the best way he knew how."

action. To illustrate, an indigent Nandi of Kenya, under certain circumstances, can obtain a bride with no more than a promise to transfer one animal to the bride's father. A suitor from the Jie tribe of Uganda, on the other hand, normally transfers 50 head of cattle and 100 head of small stock (sheep and goats) to the bride's family before the marriage becomes official. Large amounts of bridewealth, as found among the Jie, are significant for several reasons. First, the economic stakes are so high that the bride and groom are under enormous pressure to make the marriage work. Second, large bridewealth payments tend to make the system of negotiations between the two families more flexible and, consequently, more cordial. When the bridewealth is low, the addition or subtraction of one item becomes highly critical and is likely to create hard feelings between the two families.

Not only do bridewealth payments vary between different cultures, but variations also exist within a single cultural group. In a study of bridewealth payments among the Kipsigis of western Kenya, Monique Mulder (1988) found that intragroup variations depended on several key factors. First, high bridewealth is given for brides who mature early and are plump because such women are thought to have greater reproductive success. Second, lower bridewealth is given for women who have given birth previously. And third, women whose natal homes are far away from their marital homes command higher bridewealth because they spend less time in their own mother's household and

therefore are more available for domestic chores in their husband's household.

The meaning of bridewealth has been widely debated by scholars and nonscholars for much of the twentieth century. Early Christian missionaries, viewing the practice of bridewealth as a form of wife purchase, argued that it was denigrating to women and repugnant to the Christian ideal of marriage. Many colonial administrators, taking a more legalistic perspective, saw bridewealth as a symbol of the inferior legal status of women in traditional societies. Both of these negative interpretations of bridewealth led to a number of vigorous yet unsuccessful attempts to stamp out the practice.

Less concerned with moral or legal issues, cultural anthropologists saw the institution of bridewealth as a rational and comprehensible part of traditional systems of marriage. Rejecting the interpretation that bridewealth was equivalent to wife purchase, anthropologists tended to concentrate on how the institution operated within the total cultural context of which it was a part. Given such a perspective, cultural anthropologists identified a number of important functions that the institution of bridewealth performed for the well-being of the society. For example, bridewealth was seen as security or insurance for the good treatment of the wife, as a mechanism to stabilize marriage by reducing the possibility of divorce, as a form of compensation to the bride's lineage for the loss of her economic potential and her childbearing capacity, as a symbol

= *Among the Shilluk of the Sudan, cows are used as the medium of exchange in marriage transactions.*

of the union between two large groups of kin, as a mechanism to legitimize traditional marriages in much the same way that a marriage license legitimizes Western marriages, as the transference of rights over children from the mother's family to the father's family, and as the acquisition by the husband of uxorial (wifely) rights over the bride.

To avoid the economic implications of "wife purchase," E. E. Evans-Pritchard (1940) suggested that the term *bridewealth* be substituted for the term *bride price,* and Alfred Radcliffe-Brown (1950:47) used the word *prestation,* a term with even fewer economic connotations. Although a much-needed corrective to the earlier interpretations of bridewealth as wife purchase, much of the anthropological literature has overlooked the very real economic significance of bridewealth. It was not until near the end of the colonial period that Robert Gray (1960) reminded social scientists that it was legitimate to view bridewealth as an integral part of the local exchange system and that in many traditional societies, wives are dealt with in much the same way as other commodities. It is now generally held that a comprehensive understanding of the practice of bridewealth is impossible without recognizing its economic as well as its noneconomic functions.

Since the mid-1980s a number of studies in different parts of the world have documented the monetization of bridewealth (that is, the use of money as the medium of exchange). The transition from subsistence-based economies to cash-based economies has had a profound effect in recent times on traditional bridewealth practices and on the institution of marriage itself. As we have pointed out in this section, traditional bridewealth was an exchange of (often valuable) commodities from the groom's lineage to the bride's lineage. Because traditional bridewealth is a matter of solidifying long-term ties between two entire lineages, the actual pair to be married did not benefit directly from the exchange. However, when bridewealth becomes tied to cash payments that individual prospective grooms are able to earn on the open market, the close interdependence of family members (and their sanctioning of the marriage) becomes much less important. Today a growing number of wage earners in societies that practiced traditional bridewealth are becoming independent of their kinship group when it comes time to get married.

This monetization of bridewealth in Oceania is particularly well described in a recent edited volume called *The Business of Marriage* (Marksbury 1993). Contributing authors show how people from Panam, the Fiji Islands, and Papua New Guinea are viewing marriage increasingly as a financial transaction. This transition of bridewealth from being symbolic of alliances between kin groups to more commercial in nature is having a number of important consequences on the entire marital process. According to Richard Marksbury (1993), people are postponing getting married until a later age, marriage payments are being used more for personal fulfillment rather than being redistributed among a wide range of kin, men are incurring serious debts in their attempts to meet their payments, marriages are becoming less stable, and traditional husband–wife roles are changing.

Whatever the medium of exchange may be, bridewealth is still widely practiced today in certain parts of the world. In the 1970s this author conducted a study of changing patterns of bridewealth among the Kikuyu of East Africa and found that the traditional practice of bridewealth had survived amazingly well in the face of significant forces of change. More than two decades later, Bert Adams and Edward Mburugu (1994), studying a sample of 297 Kikuyu interviewees, reported that over 90 percent claimed that bridewealth was still being paid. Interestingly, neither educational level nor long-standing urban residence seemed to reduce the likelihood or amount of bridewealth. These data are consistent with studies of bridewealth in other parts of Africa (Ferraro 1983; Mwamwenda and Monyooe 1997), which indicate similar resilience of bridewealth in rapidly changing societies.

BRIDE SERVICE

In societies with considerable material wealth, marriage considerations take the form of bridewealth and, as we have seen, are paid in various forms of commodities. But because many small-scale, particularly nomadic, societies cannot accumulate capital goods, men often give their labor to the bride's family instead of material goods in exchange for wives. This practice, known as bride service, is found in approximately 14 percent of the societies listed in Murdock's *World Ethnographic Sample.*

In some cases, bride service is practiced to the exclusion of property transfer; in other cases, it is a temporary condition, and the transfer of some property is expected at a later date. When a man marries under a system of bride service, he often moves in with his bride's family, works or hunts for them, and serves a probationary period of several weeks to several years. This custom is similar to that practiced by Jacob of the Old Testament (Genesis, Chapter 29), who served his mother's brother (Laban) for his two wives, Leah and her sister Rachel. In some cases where bride service is found, other members of the groom's family, in addition to the groom himself, may be expected to give service, and this work may be done not only for the bride's parents but also for her other close relatives, as is the case with the Taita of Kenya (Harris 1972).

DOWRY

In contrast to bridewealth, a **dowry** involves a transfer of goods or money in the opposite direction, from the bride's family to the groom or to the groom's family. The dowry is always provided by the bride or the bride's family, but the recipient of the goods varies from one culture to another. In some societies, the dowry was given to the groom, who then had varying rights to dispose of it. In rural Ireland, it was given to the father of the groom in compensation for land, which the groom's father subsequently bequeathed to the bride and groom. The dowry was then used, wholly or in part, by the groom's father to pay the dowry of the groom's sister.

More often than not, the dowry was not given to the husband but was something that the bride brought with her into the marriage. In traditional society in Cyprus the dowry often consisted of a house or other valuable property. If the husband mistreated his wife or if the marriage ended in divorce, the woman was entitled to take the dowry with her. The dowry in this sense, very much like bridewealth, functioned to stabilize the marriage by providing a strong economic incentive not to break up.

The dowry is not very widely practiced throughout the world. Less than 3 percent of the societies in Murdock's sample actually practice it. It is confined to Eurasia, most notably in medieval and renaissance Europe and in northern India.

In certain European countries, where it is still practiced to some extent today, substantial dowry payments have been used as a means of upward mobility, that is, as a way to marry a daughter into a higher status family. Around the beginning of the twentieth century, a number of daughters of wealthy U.S. industrialists entered into mutually beneficial marriage alliances with European nobles who were falling upon hard economic times. The U.S. heiresses brought a substantial dowry to the marriage in exchange for a title.

Even though bridewealth is the usual form of marriage payment in Africa, there are several instances where the direction of payment is in the opposite direction. One such case is found among the Nilo-Hamitic Barabaig of Tanzania. Although a small number of goods are given to the bride's kin group, her family confers on her a dowry of two

to 40 head of large stock, depending on their means. These dowry cattle, which often outnumber the cattle held originally by the groom, are kept in trust as inheritance cattle for the bride's sons and as dowry cattle for the bride's daughters. Because the Barabaig are patrilocal, the wife and her dowry cattle reside at the husband's homestead. Even though the husband has nominal control over the herd, he still must ask his wife's permission to dispose of any of the cattle, for technically the herd belongs to his wife's father. Until the herd is finally redistributed among their own children, it will remain a source of friction between the husband and wife because the very existence of such a dowry gives the wife considerable economic leverage in her marital relations.

WOMAN EXCHANGE

Another way of legitimizing marriage by means of economic considerations is the practice of **woman exchange,** whereby two men exchange sisters or daughters as wives for themselves, their sons, or their brothers. This practice, which is limited to a small number of societies in Africa and the Pacific, is found in less than 3 percent of the world's societies. According to Edward Winter (1956), woman exchange was the primary means by which marriages were legitimized among the traditional Bwamba of Uganda. Such a system suffers from a considerable disadvantage: The exchange of one woman for another allows little room for individual variation. Bwamba women differ, as do women elsewhere, in terms of age, beauty, and procreative powers. Bwamba men prefer young, attractive, industrious, and fertile women. The exchange system cannot accommodate variations in these qualities.

In a system using conventional material objects such as bridewealth cattle, a man's preference may be reflected to a certain degree by the quality and quantity of his gifts. We should also bear in mind that the system of woman exchange has different implications for the distribution of women (especially in polygynous societies) than does a system using more conventional objects of exchange. Under the latter system, it is the wealthy man in the society who is able to obtain a large number of wives, whereas under the exchange system, the number of wives a man can obtain is limited to the number of sisters and daughters at his disposal.

RECIPROCAL EXCHANGE

Reciprocal exchange is found in approximately 6 percent of the societies listed in Murdock's *Ethnographic Atlas,* most prominently in the Pacific region and among traditional Native Americans. It involves the roughly equal exchange of gifts between the families of both the bride and the groom. Such a custom was practiced by the traditional Vugusu people of western Kenya, who exchanged a large variety of items between a sizable number of people from both families. According to Gunter Wagner, the gifts made and the expenses incurred were basically reciprocal, with only "a slight preponderance on the bride's side" (1949: 423). The variety of the reciprocal gift giving and the number of people involved in Vugusu society tend to emphasize the generally valid tenet that marriages in many parts of the world are conceived not simply as a union between a man and a woman but rather as an alliance between two families.

•■ RESIDENCE PATTERNS: WHERE ■• DO WIVES AND HUSBANDS LIVE?

IN ADDITION to establishing regulations for mate selection, the number of spouses one can have, and the types of economic considerations that must be attended to, societies set guidelines regarding where couples will live when they marry. When two people marry in North American society, it is customary for the couple to take up residence in a place of their own, apart from the relatives of either spouse. This residence pattern is known as *neolocal residence* (that is, a new place). As natural as this may appear to us, by global standards it is a rare type of residence pattern, practiced in only about 5 percent of the societies of the world. The remaining societies prescribe that newlyweds will live with or close to relatives of the wife or the husband.

One question facing these societies is, Which children stay at home when they marry, and which ones leave? Also, of those who leave, with which relative are they expected to reside? Although these questions can be answered in a number of ways, most residence patterns fall into one of five patterns (percentages based on tabulations from Murdock's *Ethnographic Atlas* [1967]):

Patrilocal residence: The married couple lives with or near the relatives of the husband's father (69 percent of the societies).

Matrilocal residence: The married couple lives with or near the relatives of the wife (13 percent of the societies).

Avunculocal residence: The married couple lives with or near the husband's mother's brother (4 percent of the societies).

Ambilocal (bilocal) residence: The married couple has a choice of living with either the relatives of the wife or the relatives of the husband (9 percent of the societies).

Neolocal residence: The married couple forms an independent place of residence away from the relatives of either spouse (5 percent of the societies).

To a significant degree, residence patterns have an effect on the types of kinship systems (discussed in Chapter 10) found in any society. For example, there is a reasonably close correlation between patrilocal residence and patrilineal descent (tracing one's important relatives through the father's side) and between matrilocal residence and matrilineal descent (tracing one's important relatives through the mother's side). To be certain, residence patterns do not determine kinship ideology, but social interaction between certain categories of kin can be facilitated if those kin reside (and play out their lives) in close proximity to one another.

It should be kept in mind that these five residence patterns, like most other aspects of culture, are ideal types. Consequently, how people actually behave—that is, where they reside—doesn't always conform precisely to these ideals. Sometimes, normative patterns of residence are altered or interrupted by events such as famines or epidemics that force newlyweds to reside in areas that will maximize their chances for survival or their economic security. To illustrate, during the Depression years of the 1930s, the normal neolocal pattern of residence in the United States was disrupted when many young married adults moved in with one set of parents to save money. And, because of the high cost of living for young adults during the 1990s, the same pattern may be developing again.

•■ FAMILY STRUCTURE ■•

CULTURAL ANTHROPOLOGISTS have identified two fundamentally different types of family structure: the nuclear family and the extended family. The **nuclear family** is based on marital ties, and the **extended family**, a much larger social unit, is based on blood ties among three or more generations of kin.

THE NUCLEAR FAMILY

Consisting of husband and wife and their children, the nuclear family is a two-generation family formed around the conjugal or marital union. Even though the nuclear family to some degree is part of a larger family structure, it

APPLIED PERSPECTIVE

Hawaiian Children at School and at Home

A basic premise of educational anthropology is that the cultural patterns students bring with them into the classroom must be taken into account if these students are to be successfully integrated into the culture of the school. This is precisely the objective that educational anthropologist Cathie Jordan brought to her work with the Kamehameha Elementary Education Program (KEEP), a privately funded educational research effort designed to develop more effective methods for teaching Hawaiian children in the public schools.

For decades children of Hawaiian ancestry, particularly those from low-income families, have been chronic underachievers in the public school system. Classroom teachers often describe Hawaiian children as lazy, uncooperative, uninvolved, and disinterested in school. Differences do exist between their dialect, known as Hawaiian Creole English, and the Standard English used by teachers, but the linguistic differences are minimal. Thus, Cathie Jordan and her colleagues at KEEP needed to look beyond linguistic differences to find an explanation for why Hawaiian children were not succeeding in school. Accordingly, KEEP focused on the wider Hawaiian culture—particularly interaction patterns within the family—in order to discover learning skills the children had developed at home that could be used and built upon in the classroom.

When dealing with parents and siblings at home, Hawaiian children behave very differently than when interacting with teachers and classmates. From a very early age, Hawaiian children contribute significantly to the everyday work of the household. Tasks that all children are expected to perform regularly include cleaning, cooking, laundry, yard work, caring for younger siblings, and (for male siblings) earning cash from outside employment. Working together in cooperative sibling groups, brothers and sisters organize their own household work routines with only minimal supervision from parents. Young children learn to perform their household tasks by observing their older siblings and adults. And, according to Jordan and her colleagues (1992:6), these chores

remains an autonomous and independent unit. That is, the everyday needs of economic support, child care, and social interaction are met within the nuclear family itself rather than by a wider set of relatives. In societies based on the nuclear family, it is customary for married couples to live apart from both sets of parents (neolocal residence). The married couple is also not particularly obliged or expected to care for their aging parents in their own home. Gener-

ally, parents are not actively involved in mate selection for their children, in no way legitimize the marriages of their children, and have no control over whether their children remain married.

The nuclear family is most likely to be found in societies with the greatest amount of geographic mobility. This certainly is the case in the United States and Canada, which currently have both considerable geographic mobility and are performed willingly within a "context of strong values of helping, cooperation, and contributing to the family."

The paradox facing KEEP was, How could children be so cooperative and responsible at home and yet so disengaged and lazy in school? A comparison of the home and school cultures revealed some major structural differences. When a mother wants her children to do a job around the house, she makes that known and then allows the children to organize how it will get done. In other words, she hands over the responsibility of the job to the children. In contrast, the classroom is almost totally teacher dominated. The teacher makes the assignments, sets the rules, and manages the resources of the classroom. Children are controlled by the classroom rather than being responsible for it. Once these cultural differences between home and school were revealed by anthropological fieldwork, the educational anthropologist was able to suggest some changes for improving student involvement in school. The solution was fairly straightforward: Have teachers run their classrooms in much the same way as Hawaiian mothers run their households. Specifically, teachers should minimize verbal instructions, withdraw from direct supervision, and allow students to take responsibility for organizing and assigning specific tasks. When these changes were made, Hawaiian students became more actively involved in their own education, and consequently their achievement levels improved.

Here, then, is an example of how educational anthropologists can apply their findings to improve the learning environment for Hawaiian children. Interestingly, this case of applied anthropology did not follow the traditional solution to problems of minority education, which involves trying to change the child's family culture to make it conform to the culture of the classroom. Rather, Jordan and her colleagues at KEEP solved the problem by modifying the culture of the classroom to conform to the skills, abilities, and behaviors that the Hawaiian students brought with them from their family culture.

QUESTIONS FOR FURTHER THOUGHT

1. What is educational anthropology?
2. Can you think of any subcultural groups living in your town or region whose family patterns should be studied by the public school systems that are responsible for educating their children?
3. What other types of educational problems might applied anthropologists be able to solve?

the ideal of the nuclear family. During much of our early history, the extended family—tied to the land and working on the family farm—was the rule rather than the exception. Today, however, the family farm—housing parents, grandparents, aunts, uncles, cousins, and siblings—is a thing of the past. Now, in response to the forces of industrialization, most adults move to wherever they can find suitable employment. Because one's profession largely determines where one will live, adults in the United States and Canada often live considerable distances from their parents or other nonnuclear family members.

In addition to being found in such highly industrialized societies as our own, the nuclear family is found in certain societies located at the other end of the technological spectrum. In certain foraging societies residing in environments where resources are meager (such as the Inuit of northern Canada and the Shoshone of Utah and Nevada), the nuclear family is the basic food-collecting unit. These nuclear families remain highly independent foraging groups that fend for themselves. Even though they cannot expect help from the outside in an emergency, they have developed a family structure that is well adapted to a highly mobile life. Thus, both U.S. society and some small-scale food-collecting societies have adopted the nuclear family pattern because of their need to maintain a high degree of geographic mobility.

Although the independent nuclear family has been the ideal in the United States for much of the twentieth century, significant changes have occurred in recent years. According to the U.S. Census, less than one in three households consists of the nuclear family (parents and one or more children), a sharp decline from earlier decades. The other two-thirds of the U.S. households are made up of married couples without children, single adults, single parents, unmarried couples, roommates, extended family members, or adult siblings. As Conrad Kottak (1987) has suggested, these changing patterns of family life have been reflected in a number of television sitcoms. For example, during the 1950s the family was depicted by Ozzie and Harriet Nelson and their sons, David and Ricky, and by Ward and June Cleaver and their sons, Wally and the Beaver. Within the last several years, however, an increasing number of TV shows have featured alternative living arrangements such as roommates, single adults, working mothers, and single parents. In fact, some of the most popular TV sitcoms in recent years feature characters who are neither related to nor living with one another (such as *Seinfeld, Friends,* and *Ally McBeal*).

There are several explanations for the decline of the nuclear family in the United States as we begin the twenty-first century. First, as more and more women complete higher education and enter the job market, they are more likely to delay marrying and having children. Second, the increasing cost of maintaining a middle-class household that includes the parents, children, a three- or four-bedroom house, a cocker spaniel, and a car or two has caused some couples to opt for remaining childless altogether. Third, the ever-increasing divorce rate in the United States has contributed to the increase in nonnuclear families in recent decades.

THE EXTENDED FAMILY

In societies based on extended families, blood ties are more important than ties of marriage. Extended families consist of two or more families that are linked by blood ties. Most commonly, this takes the form of a married couple living with one or more of their married children in a single household or homestead and under the authority of a family head. Such extended families, which are based on parent–child linkages, can be either patrilineal (comprising a man, his sons, and the sons' wives and children) or matrilineal (comprising a woman, her daughters, and her daughters' husbands and children). It is also possible for extended families to be linked through sibling ties rather than parent–child ties, such as extended families consisting of two or more married brothers and their wives and children. According to Murdock's *Ethnographic Atlas* (1967), approximately 46 percent of the 862 societies listed have some type of extended family organization.

When a couple marries in a society with extended families, there is little sense that the newlyweds are establishing a separate and distinct family unit. In the case of a patrilineal extended family, the young couple takes up residence in the homestead of the husband's father, and the husband continues to work for his father, who also runs the household. Moreover, most of the personal property in the household is not owned by the newlyweds but is controlled by the husband's father. In the event that the extended family is large, it may be headed by two or more powerful male elders who run the family in much the same way that a board of directors runs a corporation. Eventually, the father (or other male elders) will die or retire, allowing younger men to assume positions of leadership and power within the extended family. Unlike the nuclear family, which lasts only one generation, the extended family is a continuous unit that can last an indefinite number of generations. As old people die off, they are replaced through the birth of new members.

It is important to point out that in extended family systems, marriage is viewed more as bringing a daughter into the family than acquiring a wife. In other words, a man's obligations of obedience to his father and loyalty to his brothers are far more important than his relationship to his wife. When a woman marries into an extended family, she most often comes under the control of her mother-in-law, who allocates chores and supervises her domestic activities.

In some extended family systems, the conjugal relationship is suppressed to such an extent that contact between husband and wife is kept to a minimum. Among the Rajputs of northern India, for example, spouses are not allowed to talk to each other in the presence of family elders. Public displays of affection between spouses are considered reprehensible; in fact, a husband is not permitted to

= *An extended family gathering in Grinagar, in the Kashmir region of India.*

show open concern for his wife's welfare. Some societies take such severe measures to subordinate the husband–wife relationship because it is feared that a man's feelings for his wife could interfere with his obligations to his own blood relatives.

Why do so many societies in the world have extended families? There is some indication that extended families are more likely to be found in certain types of economies than others. As previously mentioned, economies based on either foraging or wage employment (which require considerable geographic mobility) are more likely to be associated with nuclear than with extended families. In addition, a rough correlation exists between extended family systems and an agricultural way of life. Several logical explanations have been suggested for this correlation. First, extended families provide large numbers of workers, who are necessary for success in both farm production and the marketing of surpluses. Second, in farm economics, where cultivated land is valuable, an extended family system prevents the land from being continually subdivided into smaller and less productive plots. As an alternative explanation, Burton Pasternak, Carol Ember, and Melvin Ember (1976) have suggested that extended family systems develop in response to what they call "incompatible activity requirements." That is, extended families are likely to prevail in societies where there is a lack of man- and woman-power to simultaneously carry out subsistence and domestic tasks.

Modern-Day Family Structure

Most Western social thinkers over the past century have been in general agreement concerning the long-term effects of urbanization and modernization on the family. In general, they see a progressive nuclearization of the family in the face of modernization. This position is perhaps most eloquently presented by William Goode, who has stated that industrialization and urbanization have brought about "fewer kinship ties with distant relatives and a greater emphasis on the 'nuclear' family unit of couple and children" (1963:1). Although in many parts of the world we can observe the association between modernization and fewer extended kinship ties, there are a number of exceptions, most notably in certain developing countries. To illustrate, in the Kenya Kinship Study (KKS) discussed in Chapter 5, no significant differences were found in the extended family interaction between rural Kikuyu and Kikuyu living in Nairobi. This retention of extended family ties in this urban, industrialized setting could be explained by several relevant economic factors. First, the combination of a fiercely competitive job market and few or no employment benefits (such as workers' compensation, retirement, and unemployment insurance) means that the average urban worker has little job security. Second, despite the creation of freehold land tenure in Kenya in recent years, land inheritance still generally takes place within the extended family.

= *Typically, when two people marry in the United States, they live in a home of their own apart from relatives of either spouse.*

Urban workers who sever ties with their rural-based extended kin relinquish their rights to inherit land, which for many remains the only haven from the insecurities of urban employment.

Interestingly, we do not need to focus on developing countries to find the retention of extended kin ties in urban, industrialized areas. For example, Carol Stack (1975) and Jagna Sharff (1981) have shown how urban Blacks in the United States use extended kinship ties as a strategy for coping with poverty. Moreover, at least one immigrant group in the United States—the Vietnamese—has used modern technology to help maintain and strengthen its traditional family values. Jesse Nash (1988) reports that immigrant Vietnamese families routinely rent Chinese-made films (dubbed in Vietnamese) for their VCRs. Whereas most films and TV programming in the United States tend to glorify the individual, Chinese films tend to emphasize the traditional Confucian value of family loyalty.

For at least the first half of the twentieth century, popular opinion (buttressed by the Judeo-Christian tradition) upheld a fairly uniform notion of what form the typical U.S. family should take. The natural family, according to this view, was a nuclear family consisting of two monogamous heterosexual parents (the breadwinning male and the female homemaker) with their children. In the past five decades, however, this so-called typical family has become harder to find. In fact, there is no longer a "typical family" in the United States. According to census data for 1990, fewer than 27 percent of all families in the United States are made up of married couples with children under 18 years of age. Moreover, even fewer (approximately 20 percent) of all U.S. families fit the typical model with the breadwinning husband and the homemaking wife. As we begin the twenty-first century, nearly three out of every four families are atypical in that they are headed by a female single parent, a male single parent, unmarried partners, or childless or post–child-rearing couples. There are also stepfamilies, extended families, homosexual families, and communal families, all of which are accepted alternative family forms.

SUMMARY

1. Because of the vast ethnographic variations found in the world, the terms *family* and *marriage* are not easy to define. Recognizing the difficulties inherent in such definitions, the family is a social unit, the members of which cooperate economically, manage reproduction and child rearing, and most often live together. Marriage, the process by which families are formed, is a socially approved union between male and female adults.

2. The formation of families through the process of marriage serves several important social functions by reducing competition for spouses, regulating the sexual division of labor, and meeting the material, educational, and emotional needs of children.

3. Every culture has a set of rules (incest taboos) regulating which categories of kin are inappropriate partners for sexual intercourse. A number of explanations have been suggested for this universal incest taboo, including the natural aversion theory, the inbreeding theory, the family disruption theory, and the theory of expanding social alliances.

4. Cultures restrict the choice of marriage partners by such practices as exogamy, endogamy, arranged marriages, preferential cousin marriage, the levirate, and the sororate.

5. All societies have rules governing the number of spouses a person can have. Societies tend to emphasize either monogamy (one spouse at a time), polygyny (a man marrying more than one wife at a time), or polyandry (a woman marrying more than one husband at a time).

6. In many societies, marriages involve the transfer of some type of economic consideration in exchange for rights of sexual access, legal rights over children, and rights to each other's property. These economic considerations involve such practices as bridewealth, bride service, dowry, woman exchange, and reciprocal exchange.

7. All societies have guidelines regarding where a married couple should live after they marry. Residence patterns fall into five different categories. The couple can live with or near the relatives of the husband's father (patrilocal), the wife's relatives (matrilocal), the husband's mother's brother (avunculocal), the relatives of either the wife or the husband (ambilocal), or the husband and wife can form a completely new residence of their own.

8. Cultural anthropologists distinguish between two types of family structure: the nuclear family, comprising the wife, husband, and children; and the extended family, a much larger social unit, comprising relatives from three or more generations.

KEY TERMS

ambilocal (bilocal) residence	bride service
arranged marriage	cross cousins
avunculocal residence	dowry
	endogamy

exogamy	polyandry
extended family	polygyny
incest taboo	postpartum sex taboo
kibbutz	preferential cousin marriage
levirate	reciprocal exchange
matrilocal residence	role ambiguity
monogamy	serial monogamy
neolocal residence	sororate
nuclear family	woman exchange
parallel cousins	
patrilocal residence	

SUGGESTED READINGS

Coontz, Stephanie, Maya Parson, and Gabrielle Raley, eds. *American Families: A Multicultural Reader.* New York: Routledge, 1999. This collection of essays shows the considerable diversity in family forms, gender roles, values, and parenting practices found in the United States.

Fox, Robin. *Kinship and Marriage: An Anthropological Perspective.* Baltimore: Penguin Books, 1968. An excellent introduction to the cross-cultural study of marriage, particularly exogamous systems.

Goody, Jack, and S. J. Tambiah. *Bridewealth and Dowry.* Cambridge: Cambridge University Press, 1973. These two forms of marriage transactions are analyzed in the context of Africa, where bridewealth predominates, and Asia, where dowry is the most common practice.

Hart, C. W. M., Arnold Pilling, and Jane C. Goodale. *The Tiwi of North Australia.* 3d ed. New York: Holt, Rinehart & Winston, 1988. A fascinating ethnographic account of the Tiwi of Melville Island (off the northern coast of Australia), who practice an extreme form of polygyny, whereby all females are always married and males spend much of their lives competing for the society's major status symbol: wives.

Kendall, Laurel. *Getting Married in Korea: Of Gender, Morality, and Modernity.* Berkeley: University of California Press, 1996. An in-depth, ethnographic examination of what it takes to get married in contemporary Korea, including such topics as courtship, the exchange of goods between families, and the ceremony itself.

Mair, Lucy. *Marriage.* Baltimore: Penguin Books, 1971. Drawing on data from a wide variety of non-Western societies, the author examines the functions, regulations, symbolic rituals, and economic considerations of marriage.

Marksbury, Richard A. *The Business of Marriage: Transformations in Oceanic Matrimony.* Pittsburgh: University of Pittsburgh Press, 1993. Eleven Oceania scholars examine the changes taking place in marriage institutions among Pacific Island peoples brought about by colonization, urbanization, and the changeover from a subsistence to a monetary economy.

Stephens, William N. *The Family in Cross Cultural Perspective.* New York: Holt, Rinehart & Winston, 1963. Citing literature from all over the world, this cross-cultural study of marriage and the family examines such topics as the universality of the family, plural marriage, mate selection, sexual restrictions, divorce, and conjugal roles.

Weston, Kath. *Families We Choose: Lesbians, Gays, Kinship.* New York: Columbia University Press, 1991. This award-winning book, based on participant-observation and in-depth interviews in the San Francisco area, examines gay and lesbian families in a historical perspective.

On the Net

Starting with any search engine, conduct a subject search for the name Brian Schwimmer, an anthropologist who has developed an interactive tutorial entitled "Kinship and Social Organization." Click on the section of the tutorial titled "Marriage Systems" and answer the following questions:

1. What is the difference between exogamy and endogamy?
2. In reference to marriage, what are the three ranges of social distance mentioned in this tutorial?
3. How many ranges of social distance are found in Yanomamo society? What are they?
4. What is the difference between cross cousins and parallel cousins?
5. What is meant by "avunculocal residence"?

As was discussed in this chapter, people in the Western world, although not generally favoring arranged marriages, often get some help in finding Mr. or Ms. Right. Using any search engine, conduct a subject search for "matchmaker" and answer the following questions:

1. Roughly how many different web sites did you find that offer matchmaking services for single people?
2. How many of these sites specialize in finding a specific type of partner, such as Christians, Russians, or vegetarians?
3. Select any one site and describe the services provided and the procedures one follows to find the perfect "soul mate."

Chapter Ten

KINSHIP AND DESCENT

Sibundoy Indian family from Columbia.

WHAT WE WILL LEARN:

▼

Why have cultural anthropologists spent so much time studying kinship?

▼

What are the various functions of descent groups?

▼

What are the different ways in which cultures categorize kin?

▼

Why is it important to know something about the kinship systems in other cultures?

▼

It has been said many times that humans are social animals. Even though other species display certain social features (such as baboons living in permanent troops),

what sets humans apart from the rest of the animal world is the complexity of their social organization. People live in groups to a much greater degree than any other species. Individuals play specific social roles, have different statuses, and form patterned relationships with other group members.

Human social groups are formed on the basis of a number of factors, including occupation, kinship, social class, sex, age, ethnic affiliation, education, and religion. In most small-scale, nonindustrialized societies, social organization is based largely on kinship affiliation. That is, kinship is the basis for group membership, and most of an individual's social life is played out with other kin. By way of contrast, social relationships in industrialized societies are based on other factors, such as profession, neighborhood, or common interests, and to a lesser degree kinship. Although different societies give different weights to these different factors, kinship is without question the single most important factor contributing to social structure. In other words, how people interact with one another in all societies is influenced by how they are related to one another. Even in the United States, where kinship ties are sometimes overshadowed by nonkinship ties, relations among kin are usually more long term, intense, and emotionally laden than are relations with nonkin.

•■ KINSHIP DEFINED ■•

KINSHIP REFERS TO the relationships—found in all societies—that are based on blood or marriage. Those people to whom we are related through birth or blood are our **consanguineal relatives;** those to whom we are related through marriage are our **affinal relatives.** Each society has a well-understood system of defining relationships between these different types of relatives. Every society, in

other words, defines the nature of kinship interaction by determining which kin are more socially important than others, the terms used to classify various types of kin, and the expected forms of behavior between them. Although the systems vary significantly from one society to another, one thing is certain: Relationships based on blood and marriage are culturally recognized by all societies.

Sometimes kinship terms are used with people who are not related by either blood or marriage. This usage, known as **fictive kinship,** can take a number of different forms. For example, the process of adoption creates a set of relationships between the adoptive parents and child that have all of the expectations of relationships that are based on descent or marriage. Often, close friends of the family are referred to as aunt or uncle, even though they have no biological or marital relationship. College fraternities and sororities and some churches use kinship terminology (such as brothers and sisters) to refer to their members. Members of the Black community in the United States often refer to one another as brother and sister. And, of course, the godparent–godchild relationship, which carries with it all sorts of kinship obligations, often involves people who do not share blood or marriage connections. These examples should remind us that it is possible to have kinshiplike relationships (complete with well-understood rights and obligations) without having an actual biological or marital connection.

In the United States the biological meaning of kinship is very powerful. This is particularly true when determining legal parenthood. For example, surrogate mothers who have borne children for wealthy women have had some success in the courts in reclaiming those children purely on the basis of being the natural (biological) mother. And biological fathers who have abandoned their families have returned to claim custody of their children solely on the basis of biological paternity. In some parts of the world, however, the *social* component of kinship is given far more weight than in the United States. For the Zumbagua of highland Ecuador, parenthood is not established solely and automatically on the basis of either giving birth or impregnating a woman. Rather, it involves a relationship that must be *achieved* over a relatively long period of time. According to Mary Weismantel (1995:697):

> Among the Zumbagua, if the biological father's role ends after conception, or if the mother's role ends shortly after birth, these biological parents have a very weak claim to parenthood should they re-enter the child's life at a later time. Thus, the Zumbagua notion of parenthood involves *working* at nurturing the child over a number of years; mere conception or childbirth alone does not, in and of itself, give a man or a woman the right to claim parenthood of a child.

Since cultural anthropologists began conducting fieldwork, they appear to have spent a disproportionate amount of time and energy describing kinship systems. Not only have they devoted more time to studying kinship systems than any other single topic, but they have spent more time than other social scientists have on kinship systems. The reason cultural anthropologists spend so much time on what Malinowski called "kinship algebra" is related to the type of societies they have traditionally studied. Cultural anthropology, though interested in all societies of the world, has in actual practice tended to concentrate on small-scale societies where kinship relations tend to be all-encompassing. In highly urbanized, techno-logical societies, such as those studied most often by sociologists, few social relationships are based on kinship. In the United States, for example, social relationships that are essentially political, economic, recreational, or religious are usually not played out with our kin. In contrast, in small-scale, non-Western, preliterate, and technologically simple societies, kinship is at the heart of the social structure. Whom a person marries, where he or she lives, and from whom a person inherits property and status all depend on the person's place within the kinship system. In such societies, it might not be an exaggeration to say that kinship relations are tantamount to social relations.

•■ CULTURAL RULES ■• REGARDING KINSHIP

TO BE CERTAIN, all kinship systems are founded on biological connections. Family and kinship groups would not exist if men and women did not mate and have children. However, kinship systems involve more than biological relationships. Rather, each society classifies its kin according to a set of cultural rules that may or may not account for biological factors. For example, according to our own kinship system, we refer to both our father's brother and our father's sister's husband as uncles even though the former is a blood relative and the latter is not. In many societies, a man refers to his father's brother and his mother's brother (both blood relatives) by different terms and is expected to behave very differently toward the two. This distinction between the biological and cultural dimensions of kinship

= *Cultural anthropologists generally have studied societies in which kinship activities play a very important role. This farmer's family from Anhul, China, includes three generations.*

can be seen in U.S. society when we refer to our adopted children as sons and daughters (with all of the rights and obligations that biological children have), even though they have no genetic connection. Thus, as we can see, the way that different societies sort and categorize kinship relationships is as much a matter of culture as it is a matter of biology.

FUNCTIONS OF KINSHIP SYSTEMS

ALL KINSHIP SYSTEMS, wherever they may be found, serve two important functions for the well-being of the total society. First, by its **vertical function,** a kinship system provides social continuity by binding together a number of successive generations. Kinship systems are most directly involved with the passing of education, tradition, property, and political office from one generation to the next. Second, kinship systems tend to solidify or tie together a society horizontally (that is, across a single generation) through the process of marriage. Because kinship systems define the local kin groups outside of which people must take a spouse, it forces groups to enter into alliances with other kinship groups, thereby creating solidarity within a much larger society. This **horizontal func-**

tion of kinship was perhaps best illustrated by the case of the late King Sobhuza II of Swaziland, who solidified his entire kingdom by taking a wife from virtually every non-royal lineage in the country.

USING KINSHIP DIAGRAMS

ALTHOUGH KINSHIP systems are found in every society, how any particular society defines the relationships between kin varies widely from one group to another. In different societies, people with the same biological connection may be defined differently, labeled differently, and expected to behave differently toward one another. And, as we shall see, societies can choose from a vast array of possibilities. Before trying to sort out the complexities of different kinship systems, it would be helpful to introduce a form of shorthand used by cultural anthropologists in analyzing kinship systems.

As a way of simplifying kinship systems, anthropologists use kinship diagrams rather than relying on verbal explanations alone. In this standardized notational system, all kinship diagrams are viewed from a central point of reference (called **EGO**), the person from whose point of view we are tracing the relationship. All kinship diagrams use the symbols found in Figure 10-1.

FIGURE 10-1

Kinship Diagram Symbols

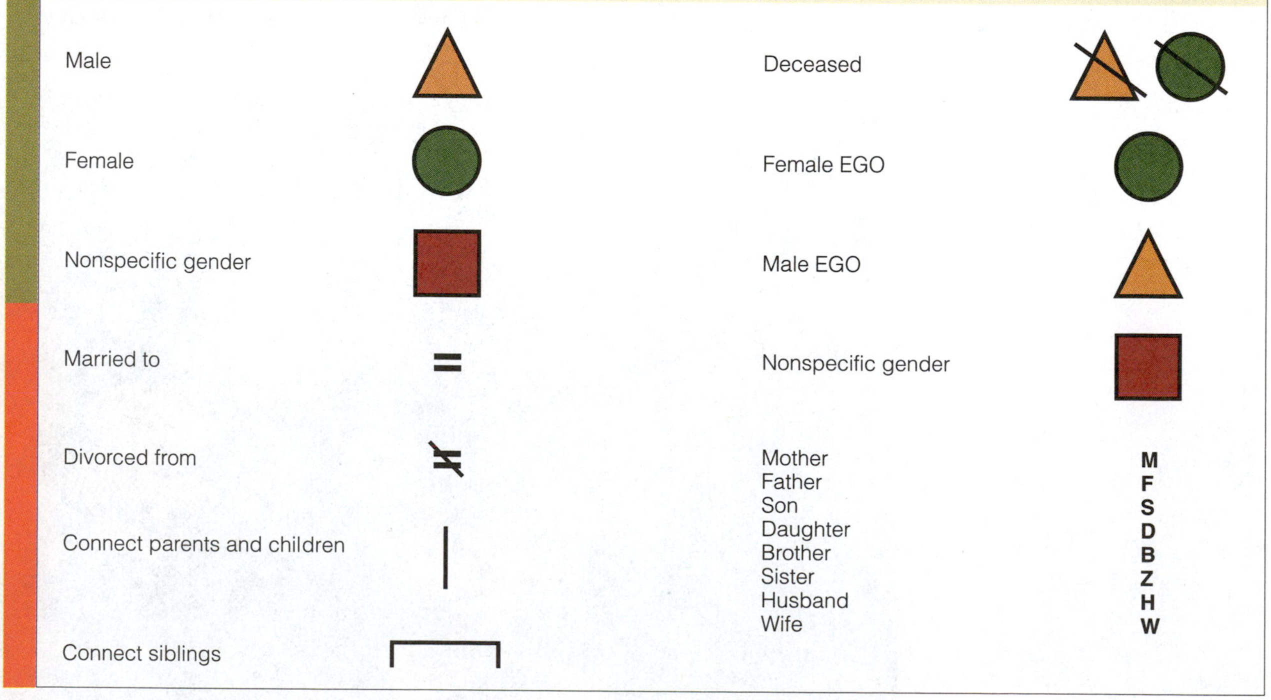

Male	△	Deceased	△̸ ⊘
Female	●	Female EGO	●
Nonspecific gender	■	Male EGO	△
Married to	=	Nonspecific gender	■
Divorced from	≠	Mother	M
Connect parents and children	|	Father	F
		Son	S
		Daughter	D
		Brother	B
		Sister	Z
		Husband	H
Connect siblings	⊓	Wife	W

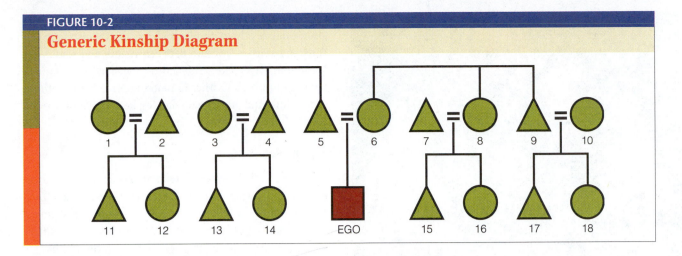

FIGURE 10-2

Generic Kinship Diagram

Starting with our point of reference (EGO) and using the symbols, it is possible to construct a hypothetical family diagram as in Figure 10-2. If we start with EGO as our point of reference, we can refer to all of the people in the diagram in the following way:

1. Father's sister (FZ)
2. Father's sister's husband (FZH)
3. Father's brother's wife (FBW)
4. Father's brother (FB)
5. Father (F)
6. Mother (M)
7. Mother's sister's husband (MZH)
8. Mother's sister (MZ)
9. Mother's brother (MB)
10. Mother's brother's wife (MBW)
11. Father's sister's son (FZS)
12. Father's sister's daughter (FZD)
13. Father's brother's son (FBS)
14. Father's brother's daughter (FBD)
15. Mother's sister's son (MZS)
16. Mother's sister's daughter (MZD)
17. Mother's brother's son (MBS)
18. Mother's brother's daughter (MBD)

•■ PRINCIPLES OF KINSHIP ■• CLASSIFICATION

NO KINSHIP SYSTEM in the world uses a different term of reference for every single relative. Instead, all kinship systems group relatives into certain categories, refer to them by the same term, and expect to behave toward them in a similar fashion. How a particular society categorizes relatives depends on which principles of classification are used. Various kinship systems use a number of principles to group certain relatives together while separating others, as discussed in the following subsections.

GENERATION

In some kinship systems—our own being a good example—distinctions between kin depend on generation. Mothers, fathers, and their siblings are always found in the first ascending generation, immediately above EGO; sons, daughters, nieces, and nephews are always one generation below EGO in the first descending generation; grandmothers and grandfathers are always two generations above EGO, and so forth. Although this seems like the natural thing to do, some societies have kinship systems that do not confine a kin category to a single generation. It is possible, for example, to find the same kin category in three or four different generations. The Haida of British Columbia use the same kinship term to refer to one's father's sister, father's sister's daughter, and the daughter of the father's sister's daughter.

SEX OR GENDER

Some kinship systems group certain kin together because of common gender (Collier and Yanagisako 1987). In our English system, such kin categories as brother, father, father's brother, son, and grandfather are always males; sister, mother, mother's sister, daughter, and grandmother are always females. The one area where we do not distinguish on the basis of gender is at the cousin level (but, then, the consistent application of a particular principle is not required). Even though this principle of gender operates at most levels of our own system, it is hardly universally applicable. In other words, some societies allow for the possibility of both males and females occupying a single kin category.

= *One function of kinship systems is to bind together a number of successive generations, as with this man, his daughter, and his granddaughter.*

LINEALITY VERSUS COLLATERALITY

Lineality refers to kin related in a single line, such as son, father, grandfather. **Collaterality,** on the other hand, refers to kin related through a linking relative, such as the relationship between EGO and his or her parents' siblings. Whereas the principle of lineality distinguishes between father and father's brother, the principle of collaterality does not. That is, in some societies, EGO uses the term *father* to refer to both his or her father and his or her father's brother; similarly, EGO's mother and her sisters may be referred to by the single term *mother.*

CONSANGUINEAL VERSUS AFFINAL KIN

Some societies make distinctions in kinship categories based on whether people are related by blood (consanguineal kin) or through marriage (affinal kin). Our own kinship system uses this principle of classification at some levels but not at others. To illustrate, we distinguish between sons and sons-in-law and between sisters and sisters-in-law. But in EGO's parents' generation, we fail to distinguish between mother's brother (a blood relative) and mother's sister's husband (an affinal relative), both of whom we call uncle.

RELATIVE AGE

In certain kinship systems, relative age serves as a criterion for separating different types of relatives. In such societies, a man will have one kinship term for younger brother and another term for older brother. These different terms based on relative age carry with them different behavioral expectations, for often a man is expected to act toward his older brother with deference and respect while behaving much more informally toward his younger brother.

SEX OF THE CONNECTING RELATIVE

Some societies distinguish between different categories of kin based on the sex of the connecting (or intervening) relative. To illustrate, a mother's brother's daughter (18) and a mother's sister's daughter (16), who are both called cousins in our system, are given two different kinship terms. Similarly, a father's brother's daughter (14) and a father's sister's daughter (12) are given different kinship terms. One category of cousins (12 and 18) is called cross cousins and the other (14 and 16) is called parallel cousins. According to this principle, these first cousins are considered to be different by virtue of the sex of their parents.

SOCIAL CONDITION

Distinctions among kin categories can also be made based on a person's general life condition. According to this criterion, different kinship terms would be used for a married brother and a bachelor brother or for a living aunt and one who is deceased.

SIDE OF THE FAMILY

A final principle has to do with using different kin terms for EGO's mother's side of the family and EGO's father's side of the family. The kinship system used in the United States makes no such distinction, for we have aunts, uncles, cousins, and grandparents on both sides of our family. In societies that use this principle of classification, a mother's brother would be given a different term of reference than a father's brother.

CROSS-CULTURAL MISCUE

MEDICAL ANTHROPOLOGIST Geri-Ann Galanti (1991) tells of a tragic incident that resulted from a U.S. physician working in Saudi Arabia failing to understand the culture of one of his patients. An 18-year-old Bedouin girl from a remote village was brought into the hospital with a gunshot wound in the pelvis. When the doctors took X-rays to determine the extent of the girl's injury, they discovered, much to their surprise, that she was pregnant. Because Bedouin girls receive no sex education, the girl was unaware that she was pregnant.

Three doctors were involved in the case: an American neurosurgeon who had worked in the region for several years, a European gynecologist who had worked in the Middle East for a decade, and a young internist from the United States who had just arrived to the area. They all realized that the girl's pregnancy presented a real problem because tribal custom punishes out-of-wedlock pregnancies with death.

In order to save the girl's life, the physicians decided to send the girl to Europe for a secret abortion, telling her parents that her gunshot wound needed special treatment available only in Europe. The young American physician was very hesitant to make such a recommendation, but the other two doctors, more experienced in Middle Eastern cultures, convinced him of the seriousness of the situation. They explained that a pregnant unmarried girl was a terrible slur on the reputation of the men of the family, who were responsible for her protection. Her pregnancy was a sure sign that they had not done their job. The only way that the family could restore its honor was to put the girl to death.

The young American reluctantly agreed not to tell the parents, but at the last minute changed his mind because he could not be deceitful. He decided to tell the girl's father as she was being wheeled to the airplane. The father immediately grabbed the girl off the stretcher, rushed her to his car, and drove away. Several weeks later the hospital staff learned that the girl had been killed by the family. The family honor had been restored. But the ethnocentric internist had a nervous breakdown and returned to the United States.

THE FORMATION OF DESCENT GROUPS

AS WE HAVE SEEN, kinship systems play an important role in helping people sort out how they should behave toward various relatives. In anthropological terms, **kinship systems** encompass all of the blood and marriage relationships that help people distinguish among different categories of kin, create rights and obligations among kin, and serve as the basis for the formation of certain types of kin groups.

Anthropologists also use the narrower term **descent** to refer to the rules a culture uses to establish affiliations with one's parents. These rules of descent often provide the basis for the formation of social groups. These social groups, which are called descent groups, are collections of relatives (usually lineal descendants of a common ancestor) who live out their lives in close proximity to one another.

In societies that have descent groups, the group plays a central role in the lives of its members. Descent group members have a strong sense of identity, often share communally held property, provide economic assistance to one another, and engage in mutual civic and religious ceremonies. In addition, descent groups function in other ways by serving as a mechanism for inheriting property and political office, controlling behavior, regulating marriages, and structuring primary political units.

Rules of descent can be divided into two distinct types. The first is unilineal descent, whereby people trace their ancestry through either the mother's line or the father's line, but not both. Unilineal groups that trace their descent through the mother's line are called matrilineal descent groups; those tracing their descent through the father's line are called patrilineal descent groups. The second type of descent is known as cognatic (or nonunilineal) descent, which includes double descent, ambilineal descent, and bilateral descent. Because descent is traced in mainstream North America according to the bilateral principle, many Westerners have difficulty understanding unilineal kinship systems.

UNILINEAL DESCENT GROUPS

Approximately 60 percent of all kinship systems found in the world are based on the unilineal principle. **Unilineal descent** groups are particularly adaptive because they are clear-cut, unambiguous social units. Because a person becomes a member of a unilineal descent group by birth, there is no confusion as to who is a group member and who is not. For societies that rely on kinship groups to perform most of their social functions (such as marriage, dispute settlement, or religious ceremonies), unilineal descent groups, with their clear-cut membership, provide a social organization with unambiguous roles and statuses. Because it is clear to which group one belongs, a person has no questions about her or his rights of inheritance, prestige, and social roles.

Patrilineal Descent Groups

Of the two types of unilineal descent groups, **patrilineal descent** is by far the most common. Patrilineal descent groups are found on all of the major continents and in a wide range of societies, including certain food-collecting Native American groups, some East African farmers and pastoralists, the Nagas of India, the Kapauku Papuans of the New Guinea Highlands, and the traditional Chinese. In societies with patrilineal descent groups, a person is related through the father, father's father, and so forth. In other words, a man, his own children, his brother's children (but not his sister's children), and his son's children (but not his daughter's children) are all members of the same descent group. Females must marry outside their own patrilineages, and the children a woman bears belong to the husband's lineage rather than to her own. The principle of patrilineal descent is illustrated in Figure 10-3.

Matrilineal Descent Groups

In a matrilineal kinship system, a person belongs to the mother's group. A **matrilineal descent** group comprises a woman, her siblings, her own children, her sisters' children, and her daughters' children. Matrilineal descent

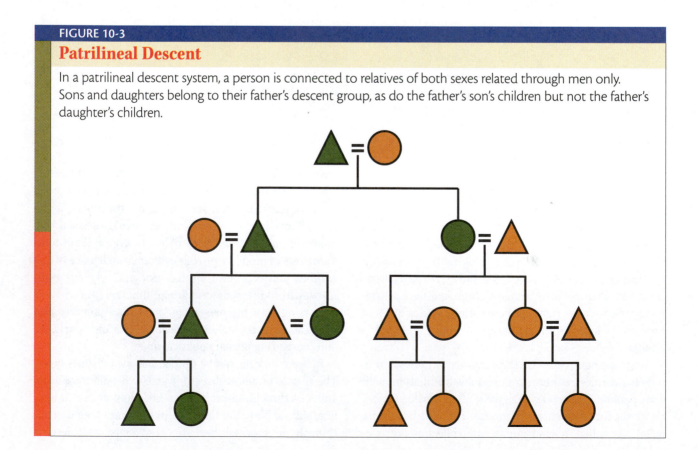

FIGURE 10-3

Patrilineal Descent

In a patrilineal descent system, a person is connected to relatives of both sexes related through men only. Sons and daughters belong to their father's descent group, as do the father's son's children but not the father's daughter's children.

= *This Kikuyu family of Kenya has a patrilineal descent system.*

groups make up about 15 percent of the unilineal descent groups found among contemporary societies. They are found in a number of areas of the world, including some Native Americans (such as Navajo, Cherokee, and Iroquois), the Truk and Trobrianders of the Pacific, and the Bemba, Ashanti, and Yao of Africa.

It is important not to confuse matrilineal descent with **matriarchy,** a situation known only in myth, whereby women have greater authority and decision-making prerogatives than men. In most cases where matrilineal descent is practiced, men retain the lion's share of power and authority. Political offices are held by men, and it is men, not women, who control property. In matrilineal societies, both property and political office pass from one man to another but through a woman. To illustrate, whereas in a patrilineal society a man passes his property and hereditary political office to his own son, in a matrilineal society property and office pass from a man to his sister's son. In fact, in a matrilineal society, the most important male relationship a man has is with his sister's son (or mother's brother). The principle of matrilineal descent is illustrated in Figure 10-4.

Types of Unilineal Descent Groups

Anthropologists recognize different types of kinship groups that are based on the unilineal principle. Categorized according to increasing levels of inclusiveness, the four major types of descent groups are lineages, clans, phratries, and moieties. These four types of unilineal descent groups can form an organizational hierarchy, with moieties comprising two or more phratries, phratries comprising two or more clans, and clans comprising two or more lineages. All societies may not have all four types of groups, but some can.

LINEAGES Lineages are unilineal descent groups of up to approximately 10 generations in depth; their members can trace their ancestry back (step-by-step) to a common founder. When descent is traced through the male line, the groups are known as patrilineages; when traced through the female line, they are known as matrilineages.

Sometimes lineages undergo a process known as **segmentation,** a subdivision into smaller units depending on the social situation. This process can occur when antagonisms arise among lineage members. For example, a lineage can be divided into two secondary lineages, divided again into tertiary lineages, and further subdivided into minimal lineages. These minimal lineages may be only three or four generations in depth. Such a segmentation process is diagrammed in Figure 10-5.

At certain times and under certain social situations, different segments compete with one another, but at other times they are allied. In Figure 10-5, because all of the minimal lineages are autonomous, normally (a) and (b) do not have a lot to do with each other. But if (d) becomes involved in a dispute with (b), then (a) is likely to ally itself with (b) because of their common ancestry with (1). However, if (d) has a conflict with (f), it is likely that (a), (b), and (c) would all come to the defense of (d) because

FIGURE 10-4

Matrilineal Descent

In a matrilineal descent system, a person is connected to kin of both sexes related through women only. Sons and daughters belong to their mother's descent group, as do the mother's daughers' children but not the mother's sons' children.

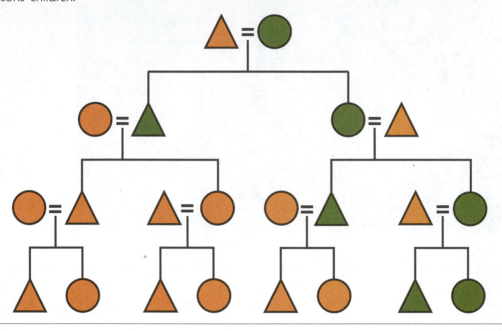

FIGURE 10-5

Lineage Segmentation

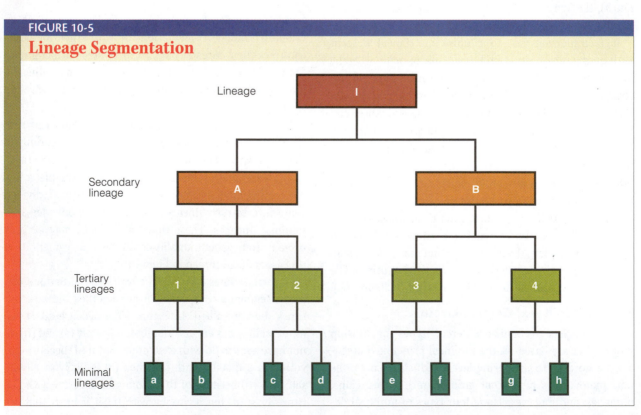

of their common genealogical connection to (A). It is also likely that (a) through (h) will all come together on certain ritual occasions to acknowledge their common relationship to (I). Thus, sublineages are allied with one another at some times and in conflict with one another at other times.

CLANS Clans are another type of unilineal descent group. A clan is a group of kin usually comprising 10 or more generations whose members believe they are all related to a common ancestor but are unable to trace that genealogical connection step-by-step. When clans and lineages are found together, the clan is usually made up of a number of different lineages. Depending on which line is emphasized, the clan can be either a matriclan or a patriclan.

In some societies, clans are close-knit groups, very much like lineages, whose members have a high degree of interaction with one another. More commonly, however, clan members are widely dispersed geographically and rarely get together for clanwide activities. Unlike lineages, which serve as corporate, functioning groups, clans tend to be larger and more loosely structured categories with which people identify. Often, clans are associated with animals or plants (that is, totems) that provide a focal point for group identity.

PHRATRIES At the next order of magnitude are **phratries**, unilineal descent groups composed of two or more clans. In societies in which phratries are found, the actual connections among the various clans usually are not recognized. Generally, phratries are rare, and, when they are found, they do not serve important social functions. Although phratries have been significant social, political, and religious groups in some cases, such as traditional Aztec society, this is the exception rather than the rule.

MOIETIES In some cases, societies are divided into two unilineal descent groups called **moieties** (a term derived from the French word for *half*). In societies that have only two clans, the clans and the moieties are identical to each other. But when moieties are made up of more than two clans (as is usually the case), the moiety is the larger unit.

Moieties are an excellent example of social reciprocity. For example, if a society is made up of two large exogamous moieties, each moiety provides the other group with its marriage partners. Moreover, moiety affiliation has been used for seating arrangements at ceremonial occasions or for sports competitions. Among the Seneca Indians, one moiety performs mourning rituals for the other. Thus, although moieties can play important roles in the society, they are not a part of the political structure in the same way as are lineages or clans.

The Corporate Nature of Unilineal Descent Groups

One feature of all unilineal descent groups—whether we are talking about lineages, clans, phratries, or moieties—is that they clearly define who is a member and who is not. These collective kinship groups also endure over time. Even though individual members are born into the group and leave it by dying, the unilineal descent group continues on. Because of their unambiguous membership and continuity, unilineal descent groups are good examples of corporate entities that play a powerful role in the lives of the individual members.

We can cite a number of indicators of the corporate nature of unilineal descent groups. First, such unilineal groups as lineages often shape a person's identity in significant ways. When a stranger asks the simple question, "Who are you?" some lineage members will probably respond, "I am a member of such and such a lineage," rather than "I am John Smith." Lineage members, in other words, see themselves first and foremost as members of the kinship group rather than as individuals. Second, unilineal descent groups regulate marriage to the extent that large numbers of kin on both the bride's and the groom's side of the family must give their approval before the marriage can take place. Third, property (such as land and livestock) is usually regulated by the descent group, rather than being controlled by the individual. The group allocates specific pieces of property to individual members for their use but only because they are kin members in good standing. Fourth, even the criminal justice system in unilineal societies has a strong corporate focus. For example, if a member of lineage (a) assaults a member of lineage (q), the entire lineage (q) will seek compensation from or revenge on lineage (a). The assaulter would not be held solely accountable for her or his individual actions, but rather the group (the lineage or clan) would be culpable.

The corporate nature of unilineal descent groups is no better illustrated than in the strong bonds of obligations that exist among members. The kinship group provides a firm base of security and protection for its individual members. If crops fail, an individual can always turn to her or his unilineal descent group members for assistance; in the event of any threat from outsiders, a person should expect support and protection from members of her or his own descent group. The strength of these bonds of obligation

APPLIED PERSPECTIVE

Agricultural Development in West Africa

For decades, agricultural development has been a high priority for sub-Saharan Africa and other parts of the developing world. Nevertheless, many agricultural development programs have suffered from a noticeable blindspot: an imperfect understanding of the basic agricultural unit, namely the African family. One such agricultural development project that suffered from this blindspot was the Guinea Agricultural Capacity and Training Project conducted in the West African country of Guinea. Sponsored by USAID, the project was a five-year, $4.9 million project designed to improve farm production by training agricultural researchers, extension workers, and administrators.

As originally conceived, the project involved three main building activities: an agricultural laboratory, additional teaching facilities at the agricultural college, and a research substation and demonstration farm, all equipped with American technology. The original program designers assumed that agricultural productivity would be increased by improving the quality of research and the training of agricultural extension personnel. Assuming that U.S. technology would transform the rural areas, they did not think it necessary to understand the local cultures.

Within its first several years, it was apparent that the project had some serious problems. The construction of the three facilities was running nearly two years behind schedule, projected costs had tripled to $15 million, and it had become clear that plans for using these facilities were very inadequate. To address this problem of inadequate planning, USAID appointed a team made up of an anthropologist (Robert Hecht), an economist, and an agronomist to study the program and make recommendations for change.

The team concluded that the most glaring weakness of the project was that it totally ignored the cultural realities of the small farmers in Guinea. Relying too heavily on technology to solve all problems, the original planners saw no reason to understand the rural cultural features. They had neither consulted the farmers, provided for their participation in the program, nor sought feedback from them.

To gain a better understanding of the problems facing the original project design, Hecht needed to gather data on the social and economic features of the local Malinke peasants. On the basis of a number of village visits and ethnographic interviews, Hecht (1986) made some significant findings about the Malinke family and kinship system:

1. The average household is large (approximately nine people), in part because of the high incidence of polygyny and in part because of the complex patrilineal kinship structure. These large kinship-based households have important implications for the project because of their potential for extended forms of economic cooperation among lineage members (such as forming producer groups or building communal fertilizer storage facilities).

2. Because land in Malinke society is controlled by corporate lineages, a household had rights to land only by virtue of its membership in a patrilineal lineage. Rank among lineages in the village determined the allocation of land, with chiefly and higher-status lineages controlling more land than commoner lineages. Even within lineages, elders had more and better land than heads of more junior households. Given this hierarchy within the land tenure system, Hecht recommended that the revised project should "be sensitive to the needs of those at the bottom of the distribution hierarchy, who possessed the smallest plots and least fertile land" (1986:22).

3. Most farm labor (which was not based on wages) among the Malinke was supplied largely by household members and supplemented by other kin outside the household.

The basic picture that emerged from Hecht's research was one of a kinship-based production system based on land controlled by corporate lineages and a workforce recruited along kinship lines. Only after this connection between the kinship and the agricultural systems had been understood, could changes be made in this multimillion-dollar USAID project.

The traditional anthropological data-gathering techniques of household surveys, interviews, and participant-observation yielded the type of sociocultural data necessary for designing a workable program. As Hecht reminds us, anthropology's holistic approach, coupled with its emphasis on learning from the local population, provided important information that helped turn a potential disaster into a viable program of agricultural development.

QUESTIONS FOR FURTHER THOUGHT

1. What basic assumptions had the original planners made that were erroneous and contributed to the near collapse of the project?
2. What data-gathering techniques did Hecht use in his applied anthropological research? Were these methods appropriate for the problem under investigation?
3. What is meant by the term *corporate lineage*? How was an understanding of this term instrumental in contributing to the success of the development project?

depends on the closeness of the ties. Mutual assistance is likely to be taken very seriously among lineage members, less so among clan members, and not very seriously at the phratry or moiety level.

COGNATIC (NONUNILINEAL) DESCENT GROUPS

Approximately 40 percent of the world's societies have kinship systems that are not based on the unilineal principle. Anthropologists call these **cognatic descent** or nonunilineal descent groups and classify them into three basic types: double descent, ambilineal descent, and bilateral descent.

Double Descent

Some societies practice a form of **double descent** (or double unilineal descent), whereby kinship is traced both matrilineally and patrilineally. In such societies, an individual belongs to both the mother's and the father's lineage. Descent under such a system is matrilineal for some purposes and patrilineal for others. For example, movable property such as small livestock or agricultural produce may be inherited from the mother's side of the family, whereas nonmovable property such as land may be inherited from the father's side.

Double descent is rare; only about 5 percent of the world's cultures practice it. One such culture, the Yako of Nigeria, has been particularly well described by Daryll Forde (1967). For the Yako, both matrilineality and patrilineality are important principles of kinship. Among the traditional Yako, cooperation in everyday domestic life is strongest among members of the patriclan for the obvious reason that they live with or near one another. Resources such as land, forest products, and trees as well as membership in men's associations are inherited by patrilineal descent.

The mother's line is also important, even though matriclan members do not live in close proximity to one another. Because the Yako believe strongly that all life stems from the mother, a mother's children are honor-bound to help one another and maintain peaceful and harmonious relations among themselves. Certain movable property, such as livestock and currency, passes from one matriclan member to another. Moreover, matriclans supervise funeral ceremonies and are responsible for providing part of the bridewealth payment. Thus, as the Yako well illustrate, in a double descent system the patrilineal groups and the matrilineal groups are active in different spheres of the culture.

Ambilineal Descent

In societies that practice **ambilineal descent,** parents have a choice of affiliating their children with either kinship group. Unlike unilineal systems, which restrict one's membership to either the mother's or the father's group, ambilineal systems are more flexible because they allow for individual choice concerning group affiliation. The range of choice varies from one ambilineal system to another. In some cases, the parents are expected to choose the group with which their children eventually affiliate. Other systems allow the individual to move continuously through life from one group to another, provided he or she affiliates with one descent group at a time. Still other systems permit the overlapping of membership with a number of groups at the same time. This flexibility does not come without a price, however. As a general rule, the greater the flexibility concerning membership, the weaker the group's loyalties, cohesiveness, and impact on the lives of its members.

Bilateral Descent

In societies that practice **bilateral descent,** such as our own, a person is related equally to both the mother's and the father's side of the family. A bilateral system tends to be symmetrical to the extent that what happens on one side of the kinship diagram also happens on the other side. In other words, the grandparents, aunts, uncles, and cousins are treated equally on both sides of the family. In unilineal systems, a person is affiliated with a large number of kin over many generations but only on one side of the family. By way of contrast, bilateral systems create links from both sides of the family but usually include only close kin from a small number of generations.

The kinship group recognized in a bilateral system is known as the **kindred:** a group of closely related relatives connected through both parents to one living relative (or to EGO). Unlike unilineal descent, which forms discrete, mutually exclusive groups, bilateral systems give rise to the situation in which no two individuals (except siblings) have the same kindred. The kindred is not a group at all but rather a network of relatives.

Unlike the lineage or the clan, the kindred has no founding ancestor, precise boundaries, or continuity over time. In short, because kindreds are not corporate groups, they cannot perform the same types of functions—such as joint ownership of property, common economic activities, regulation of marriage, or mutual assistance—as unilineal groups. To be certain, an individual can mobilize some members of his or her kindred to perform some of these tasks, but the kindred does not function as a corporate entity. This type of loosely structured network of relatives works particularly well in a society like our own that highly values personal independence and geographic mobility.

·■ SIX BASIC SYSTEMS ■·
OF CLASSIFICATION

EVERY SOCIETY has a coherent system of labeling various types of kin. In any given system, certain categories of kin are grouped together under a single category, whereas others are separated into distinct categories. In our own society, we group together under the general heading of "aunt" our mother's sisters, father's sisters, mother's brothers' wives, and father's brothers' wives. Similarly, we lump together under the heading of "uncle" our father's brothers, mother's brothers, father's sisters' husbands and mother's sisters' husbands. In contrast, other societies might have separate terms for all eight of these categories of kin. Whatever system of classification is used, however, cultural anthropologists have found them to be both internally logical and consistently applied. Even though individual societies may have their own variations, six basic classification systems have been identified: Eskimo, Hawaiian, Iroquois, Omaha, Crow, and Sudanese (Figure 10-6).

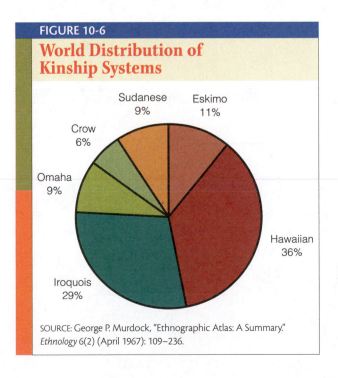

FIGURE 10-6

World Distribution of Kinship Systems

Sudanese 9%
Eskimo 11%
Crow 6%
Omaha 9%
Hawaiian 36%
Iroquois 29%

SOURCE: George P. Murdock, "Ethnographic Atlas: A Summary." *Ethnology* 6(2) (April 1967): 109–236.

ESKIMO SYSTEM

Found in approximately one-tenth of the world's societies, the **Eskimo system** of kinship classification (Figure 10-7) is associated with bilateral descent. The major feature of this system is that it emphasizes the nuclear family by using separate terms (such as mother, father, sister, brother) that are not used outside the nuclear family. Beyond the nuclear family, many other relatives (such as aunts, uncles, and cousins) are lumped together. This emphasis on the nuclear family is related to the fact that societies using the Eskimo system lack large descent groups such as lineages and clans. Moreover, the Eskimo system is most likely to be found in societies (such as U.S. society and certain food-collecting societies) where economic conditions favor an independent nuclear family.

HAWAIIAN SYSTEM

Found in approximately a third of the societies in the world, the **Hawaiian system** (Figure 10-8) uses a single term for all relatives of the same sex and generation. To illustrate, a person's mother, mother's sister, and father's sister are all referred to by the single term *mother*. In EGO's own generation, the only distinction is one based on sex so that male cousins are equated with brothers and female cousins are equated with sisters. The Hawaiian system, which uses the least number of terms, is often associated with ambilineal descent, which permits a person to affiliate with either the mother's or the father's kin. The Hawaiian system is found in societies that submerge the nuclear family into a larger kin group to the extent that nuclear family members are roughly equivalent in importance to more distant kin.

IROQUOIS SYSTEM

In the **Iroquois system** (Figure 10-9), EGO's father and father's brother are called by the same term, and EGO's mother's brother is called by a different term. Likewise, EGO's mother and mother's sister are lumped together under one term, and a different term is used for EGO's father's sister. Thus, a basic distinction of classification is made between the sex of one's parents' siblings (that is, mother's brothers and sisters and father's brothers and sisters). At EGO's own generation, EGO's own siblings are given the same term as the parallel cousins (children of one's mother's sister or father's brother), and different terms are used for cross cousins (children of one's mother's brother or father's sister). Thus, the terminological distinction made between cross and parallel cousins is logical,

FIGURE 10-7
Eskimo Kinship System

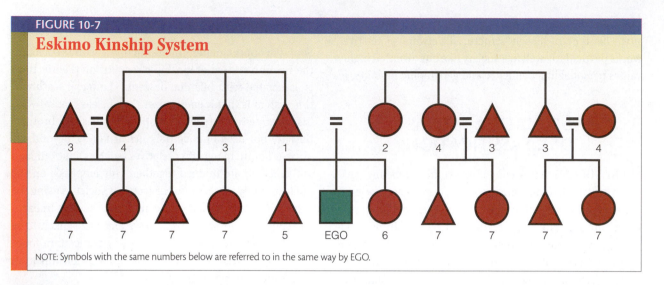

NOTE: Symbols with the same numbers below are referred to in the same way by EGO.

FIGURE 10-8
Hawaiian Kinship System

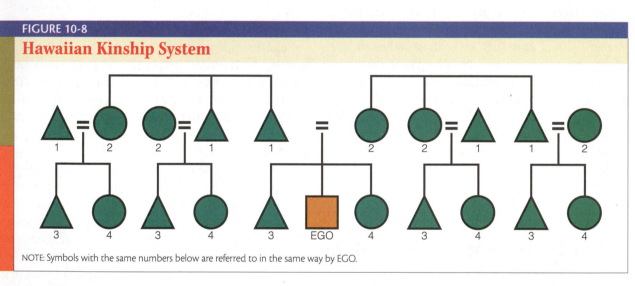

NOTE: Symbols with the same numbers below are referred to in the same way by EGO.

FIGURE 10-9
Iroquois Kinship System

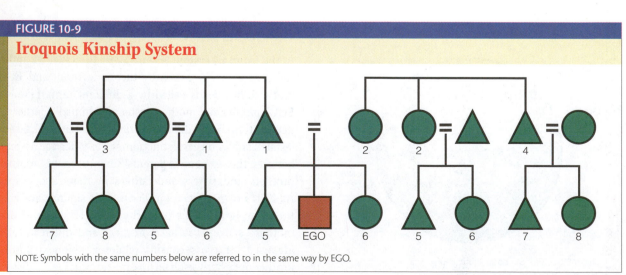

NOTE: Symbols with the same numbers below are referred to in the same way by EGO.

CROSS-CULTURAL MISCUE

UNDERSTANDING KINSHIP SYSTEMS in other cultures can have very practical repercussions on how effectively we do our jobs. Anthropologist Clyde Kluckhohn, who spent much of his career studying the Navajo Indians of the American Southwest, tells of an intelligent and successful Chicago public schoolteacher who was teaching in a Navajo reservation school. When he asked how her Navajo students compared to her Chicago students, she responded that she was puzzled by the apparent bizarre behavior of several of her Navajo students. She told Kluckhohn,

The other night we had a dance in the high school. I saw a boy who is one of the best students in my English class standing off by himself. So I took him over to a pretty girl and told them to dance. But they just stood there with their heads down. They wouldn't even say anything. (1949:19–20)

What appeared to the teacher to be strange behavior can make sense only if we first understand several features of Navajo culture—features that are radically different from the culture of a White middle-class schoolteacher from Chicago. First, the type of dancing that the teacher expected of these two Navajo teenagers is considered quite promiscuous by Navajo standards. Whereas middle-class North Americans attach little, if any, sexual meaning to the type of bodily contact involved in ballroom dancing, the Navajo think it highly inappropriate for adults of the opposite sex to move around the dance floor in a semi-embrace with the fronts of their bodies touching.

And second, according to the Navajo kinship system, which is made up of exogamous clans, the incest taboo applies as strictly to all clan members as it does to members of one's own nuclear family. Unfortunately—and quite unbeknownst to the teacher—the Navajo boy and girl the teacher had chosen were members of the same clan and, as such, were strictly forbidden from engaging in the public display of intimacy implied in Western-style dancing.

As Kluckhohn suggested, the humiliation these two Navajo youngsters must have experienced would have been roughly equivalent to the embarrassment the teacher would have felt had the manager of a crowded hotel asked her to share a bed with her adult brother. Here, then, was a poignant and needless miscommunication that was the direct result of the teacher's not understanding the nature of the kinship system of her students.

---

given the distinction made between the siblings of EGO's parents. The Iroquois system emphasizes the importance of unilineal descent groups by distinguishing between members of one's own lineage and those belonging to other lineages.

OMAHA SYSTEM

Whereas the Iroquois system reflects the importance of unilineal descent groups, the **Omaha system** (Figure 10-10) is more specific in that it emphasizes patrilineal descent. Under this system, EGO's father and father's brother

are called by the same term, and EGO's mother and mother's sister are also called by the same term. Equivalent terms are used for both parallel cousins and siblings, but separate terms are used for cross cousins. This pattern is internally consistent because if EGO calls some men and women "father" and "mother," it follows logically that EGO should also call their children "brothers" and "sisters."

On the mother's side of the family, there is a merging of generations. In other words, similar terms are used for people in different generations. Because our own Eskimo system always uses separate terms for people in different generations, the type of generation merging found in the Omaha system seems somewhat strange to many Westerners. To illustrate this merging of generations, all men regardless of age or generation who are part of EGO's mother's patrilineage are called mother's brother. This can be seen in Figure 10-10 with the cases of EGO's mother's brother (4) and EGO's mother's brother's son (4). In addition, similar kinship terms (2) are used for EGO's mother, mother's sister, and mother's brother's daughter.

That merging of generations does not occur on EGO's father's side of the family is a reflection of the greater importance of the father's patrilineage. That is, EGO's father and father's brothers are lumped together as a separate category from other males in the patrilineage because paternal uncles have the same level of authority over EGO as does EGO's biological father. This lumping together of several generations on the mother's side is indicative of the fact that EGO's connection to his or her mother's lineage is less important than to his or her father's lineage.

CROW SYSTEM

By concentrating on matrilineal rather than patrilineal descent, the **Crow system** of kinship classification (Figure 10-11) is the mirror image of the Omaha system. The

---

FIGURE 10-10

Omaha Kinship System

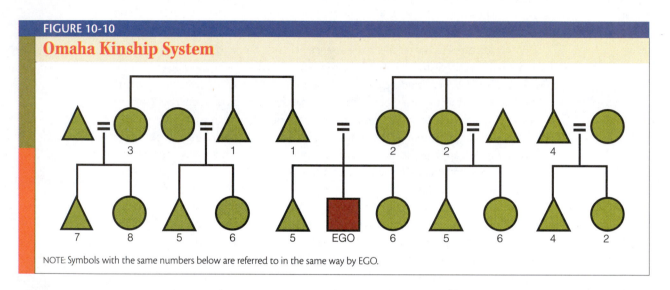

NOTE: Symbols with the same numbers below are referred to in the same way by EGO.

FIGURE 10-11

Crow Kinship System

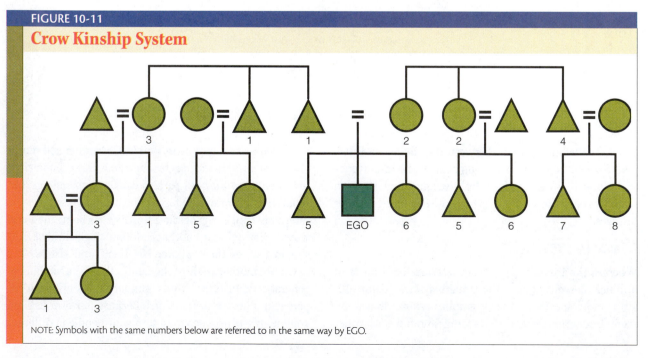

NOTE: Symbols with the same numbers below are referred to in the same way by EGO.

Crow and Omaha systems are similar in that both use similar terms for EGO's father and father's brother, EGO's mother and mother's sister, and EGO's siblings and parallel cousins. But because of its less important nature, the father's side of the family merges generations. That is, all males in the father's line, regardless of generation, are combined under a single term (1), as are all women in that line (3). However, on EGO's mother's side of the family, which is the important descent group, generational distinctions are recognized.

Sudanese System

The **Sudanese system** (Figure 10-12), which is named after the region in Africa where it is found, is the most descriptive (particularistic) system because it makes the largest number of terminological distinctions. For instance, under such a system, separate terms are used for mother's brother, mother's sister, father's brother, and father's sister as well as their male and female children. As shown in Figure 10-12, EGO has eight different types of first cousins. This highly precise system, which is generally associated with patrilineal descent, is found in some societies that have considerable differences in wealth, occupation, and social status. A possible explanation for this is that the Sudanese system permits the recognition of socioeconomic differences.

•■ KINSHIP AND ■• THE MODERN WORLD

THIS CHAPTER looked at the basic features of kinship systems in all of their various forms. By necessity our discussion (complete with mathematically precise diagrams)

has been simplified. Many of the generalizations concerning kinship systems and relationships are never that neat and tidy in real life. There are also exceptions to the rules and aberrant forms of individual behavior found in any system. Moreover, kinship systems are constantly experiencing changes through contact with external forces such as industrializing economies, colonization and decolonization, missionary intrusions, and cultural diffusion in general.

Of all aspects of human societies, kinship systems are the most intimate, intense, and long-lasting set of social relationships. Based as they are on birth and marriage, they create social ties that are often close and emotional. Kinship groups often involve strong bonds of obligations, security for their members, and moral coercion to adhere to social norms. We cannot assume, however, that these well-integrated kinship groups remain unchanged in the face of external pressures such as urban migration, poverty, unemployment, and a host of other hardships.

Anthropologist Nancy Scheper-Hughes (1989) has documented how one essential feature of all kinship systems, the mother–infant bond, has been altered among poor women living in a shantytown in Brazil. Conducting fieldwork in the sugar plantation area of northeast Brazil, Scheper-Hughes described this area's vast array of social problems. Life expectancy is only about 40 years, largely because of the high incidence of infant mortality. Children are at high risk of death due to lack of access to breastfeeding, poor diets, and inadequate child care. Single mothers are the norm in this shantytown. Wages for these single mothers are extremely low, sometimes less than a dollar a day. Mother–infant contact is minimal because babies cannot be taken to work, nor can mothers carry

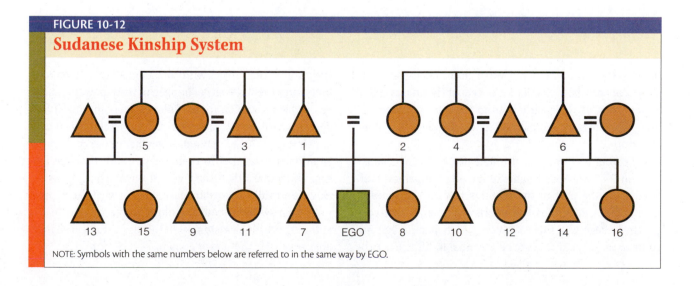

FIGURE 10-12

Sudanese Kinship System

NOTE: Symbols with the same numbers below are referred to in the same way by EGO.

APPLIED PERSPECTIVE

Anthropology and Court-Ordered Child Custody

*I*t has been estimated (Tischler 1990) that approximately one out of every two marriages contracted at the present time in the United States will eventually end in divorce. The breakup of a marriage can have devastating effects on the lives of children. This is particularly true in those divorces that involve bitter custody disputes. As a general rule, the more intransigent the disputants, the more harmful will be the effects on the children (as well as the parents' own adjustment process of restructuring their lives). The prevalence of divorce in the United States in recent decades, and the custody disputes that frequently follow, led one anthropologist, Linda Girdner, to focus her research efforts on the policies and practices relating to custody disputes among divorcing parents.

Girdner's original research examined the relationship between legal customs in child custody cases and the norms and symbols about gender and family in the United States. The research was designed to answer such questions as, What are the legal rules guiding decisions in custody cases? What does it mean to be a mother or a father in the United States? What codes of behavior are expected of "fit parents"? During the course of conducting this research, Girdner collected a good deal of descriptive data on the American kinship system, gender roles, and parenting, as well as how this information relates to child custody policy and practices. The fieldwork took place during 1978 and 1979 in the circuit and family courts in a large suburban county in the eastern part of the United States. Data-gathering techniques involved in-

them to the river where they wash clothes because of the danger of parasitic infections. Consequently, infants spend a good deal of their early lives in the care of older siblings, who are reluctant babysitters, or are simply left alone at home.

Following an outbreak of infant deaths in the shantytown in 1965, Scheper-Hughes observed an apparent indifference on the part of the mothers toward the death of their infants. After nearly a quarter of a century of conducting research in this shantytown, Scheper-Hughes has come to see what appears to be maternal indifference to be

the result of their living with continuous high infant mortality rates in conditions of hunger, poverty, powerlessness, and economic exploitation. Under such conditions, infant deaths have come to be expected. As a psychological coping strategy, mothers do not allow themselves to become emotionally attached to their infants until they are reasonably certain that they will survive. Thus, Scheper-Hughes provides a poignant case study of what can happen to kinship systems—and the mother–infant bond that is at the heart of such systems—in the face of radical change, abject poverty, and powerlessness.

formal interviews with judges, attorneys, parents, and witnesses; systematic observations of "court culture"; and the examination of court records.

Utilizing the results from 18 months of anthropological research, Girdner was trained as a family mediator, practiced family mediation for two years at a divorce clinic, and then participated in the development and implementation of a court-ordered custody mediation program in Illinois. Thus, over several years, Girdner's initial role as a researcher became intertwined with the practitioner role. Based on her formal anthropological research and her experience as a custody mediator, Girdner put her knowledge and experience to use by helping to develop a custody mediation program with the local community and the state. Her utilization efforts, which lasted from 1981 to 1987, involved three phases: an education phase consisting of classroom teaching, presentations and workshops for professionals and presentations to the lay public; a developmental phase consisting of serving as an advisor to the Family Law Section of the Illinois State Bar Association, which eventually formulated a statewide set of standards for custody mediation; and an implementation phase, which involved training, developing public awareness, and program evaluation. Girdner's critical involvement in research and practice relating to child custody issues illustrates quite dramatically how anthropological methods and insights into the U.S. kinship system can be useful for the amelioration of social problems.

QUESTIONS FOR FURTHER THOUGHT

1. Of the various roles that anthropologists play (discussed in Chapter 3), what role would you say best describes Girdner's activities?
2. Why is it so important for custody cases to be mediated peacefully rather than being fought out in court proceedings?
3. When trying to determine if a parent is fit, what criteria do you think courts in the United States use?

SUMMARY

1. Although kinship relations are more important in some societies than others, kinship is the single most important aspect of social structure for all societies. Kinship is based on both consanguineal (blood) relationships and affinal (marriage) relationships. Most societies recognize some type of fictive kinship, whereby kinship terms and obligations are applied to nonkin.

2. Kinship has both a biological and a cultural dimension. This is the reason some categories of relatives include some people who have biological connections and others who do not.

3. A fundamental feature of all kinship systems is that they group relatives into certain categories, call them by the same name, and expect to behave toward them in similar ways. How a particular culture categorizes its relatives varies according to different principles of classification. These principles are

based on such criteria as generation, gender, lineality, consanguineality, relative age, sex of the connecting relative, social condition, and side of the family.

4. Many societies have sets of rules, called rules of descent, that affiliate people with different sets of kin. Patrilineal descent affiliates a person with the kin group of the father, matrilineal descent affiliates a person with the kin group of the mother, and ambilineal descent permits an individual to affiliate with either the mother's or the father's kin group.

5. Patrilineal descent groups, which are more common than matrilineal, are found in most areas of the world. In a patrilineal system, a man's children belong to his lineage, as do the children of his son, but not the children of his daughter. Women marry outside their own lineage.

6. In matrilineal systems, a woman's children are affiliated with her lineage, not her husband's. Because the mother's brother is the social father of the woman's children, the relations between husband and wife in a matrilineal system tend to be more fragile than in patrilineal societies.

7. In societies that trace their descent unilineally (through a single line), people recognize that they belong to a particular unilineal descent group or series of groups. These different levels of kinship organization include lineages (a set of kin who can trace their ancestry back through known links), clans (a unilineal group claiming descent but unable to trace all of the genealogical links), phratries (groups of related clans), and moieties (two halves of a society related by descent).

8. Bilateral descent, which is found predominantly among foraging and industrialized societies, traces one's important relatives on both the mother's and the father's side of the family. Bilateral systems, which are symmetrical, result in the formation of kindreds, which are more like loose kinship networks than permanent corporate functioning groups.

9. There are six primary types of kinship systems based on how the society distinguishes different categories of relatives: Eskimo, Hawaiian, Iroquois, Omaha, Crow, and Sudanese.

KEY TERMS

affinal relatives
ambilineal descent
bilateral descent
clans
cognatic descent
collaterality
consanguineal relatives
Crow system
descent
double descent
EGO
Eskimo system
fictive kinship
Hawaiian system
horizontal function
  of kinship
Iroquois system
kindred
kinship system
lineages
lineality
matriarchy
matrilineal descent
moieties
Omaha system
patrilineal descent
phratries
segmentation
Sudanese system
unilineal descent
vertical function of kinship

SUGGESTED READINGS

Collier, Jane F., and J. Yanagisako, eds. *Gender and Kinship: Essays Toward a Unified Analysis.* Stanford, CA: Stanford University Press, 1987. Starting from the assumption that intracultural kinship patterns can vary according to gender, this collection of articles makes a significant contribution to the analysis of the relationship between kinship and gender.

Fox, Robin. *Kinship and Marriage.* Baltimore: Penguin Books, 1967. An excellent introduction to a broad and complex field of cultural anthropology written for serious students and laypeople alike. Fox not only brings together a number of different theories to explain the workings of different types of systems but also suggests some interesting theories of his own on the question of incest.

Murdock, George P. *Social Structure.* New York: Macmillan, 1949. A classic cross-cultural study of variations in such aspects of social structure as family, marriage, the incest taboo, and the regulation of sexual behavior.

Parkin, Robert. *Kinship: An Introduction to Basic Concepts.* Malden, MA: Blackwell, 1997. A comprehensive introduction to the anthropology of kinship that deals with both theoretical and fieldwork issues.

Pasternak, Burton. *Introduction to Kinship and Social Organization.* Englewood Cliffs, NJ: Prentice-Hall, 1976. A brief introduction to the cross-cultural study of family and kinship written for the beginning student.

Radcliffe-Brown, A. R., and D. Forde, eds. *African Systems of Kinship and Marriage.* London: Oxford University Press, 1950. A collection of nine essays by British social anthropologists on kinship and marriage systems in sub-Saharan Africa. Radcliffe-Brown's 85-page introduction, although somewhat dated, remains one of the best summaries of the literature on kinship and marriage in the non-Western world.

Schusky, Ernest. *Manual for Kinship Analysis.* 2d ed. Lanham, MD: University Press of America, 1982. A short text designed to give beginning anthropology students a clear statement of some of the essential features of kinship systems. By including a number of student activities, Schusky introduces the student to concepts of kinship logically and sequentially.

On the Net

Go to the same web site you visited for the Internet exercise in Chapter 9: Brian Schwimmer's interactive tutorial "Kinship and Social Organization." Start the tutorial and answer the following questions:

1. How does the author distinguish between matrilineal, patrilineal, and bilateral kinship systems?
2. Are the kinship symbols used in the tutorial different from those used in your textbook?
3. What is the difference between consanguineal and affinal relations?
4. In such matrilineal societies as the Ashanti kingdom of West Africa, who is the heir to the throne?

Chapter Eleven

SEX AND GENDER

What it means to be male or female in Tahiti is quite different from what it means in the United States.

WHAT WE WILL LEARN:

▼

To what extent does biology influence maleness and femaleness?

▼

Are males dominant over females in all societies?

▼

How similar are gender roles throughout the world?

▼

Do women and men in the same culture speak differently?

▼

How can extreme gender ideology lead to the exploitation of women?

▼

One need not be a particularly keen observer of humanity to recognize that men and women differ physically in a number of important ways. Men on average are taller and have considerably greater body mass than women. There are noticeable differences between men and women in their sex organs, breast size, hormonal levels, body hair, and muscle/fat ratios. With their larger hearts and lungs and greater muscle mass, men have greater physical strength. Moreover, men and women differ genetically, with women having two X chromosomes and men having an X and a Y chromosome. Unlike humans, some animals (such as mice and pigeons) manifest no obvious sexual differences between males and females. Because of these significant physiological differences, we say that humans are **sexually dimorphic.**

Most researchers can agree on the physiological (genetically based) differences between men and women, but there is considerably less agreement on the extent to which these differences actually cause differences in behavior or in the way men and women are treated in society. As is the case with so many other aspects of behavior, the nature–nurture debate is operating in the area of behavioral differences between men and women. In other words, do men and women behave differently because of their genetic predisposition or because of their culture? During the twentieth century, ethnographers have shown that the definition of femaleness and maleness varies widely from society to society. Because of this considerable cultural variability in behaviors and attitudes between the sexes, most anthropologists now prefer to speak of gender differences rather that sex differences. For purposes of this chapter, we can use Alice Schlegel's (1990:23) definition of **gender,** which she defines as "the way members of the two sexes are perceived, evaluated, and expected to behave."

Although the use of the term *gender* acknowledges the role that culture plays, it is not always possible to determine the extent to which culture or biology determines differences in behaviors or attitudes between the sexes. What we can say, however, is that biological differences influence (or set broad limits on) social definitions of maleness or femaleness to varying degrees. To illustrate, the fact that only women can give birth provides a basis for developing a set of attitudes and behaviors for women that are maternal, supportive, and nurturing. Likewise, because of their greater body mass, men may be defined as inherently strong, courageous, aggressive, and warlike. Nevertheless, many different social definitions of **masculinity** and **femininity** can be found throughout the world.

Margaret Mead's (1950; originally published 1935) classic study of sex and temperament in three New Guinea cultures illustrates the range of gender variation found among the Arapesh, Mundugumor, and Tchambuli. Mead found that among the Arapesh, both men and women were cooperative, nonaggressive, and responsive to the needs of others—all traits that most Westerners would consider to be feminine. In contrast, both genders among the Mundugumor were expected to be fierce, ruthless, and aggressive. Among the Tchambuli, there was a complete reversal of the male–female temperaments found in our own society; that is, women were the dominant, impersonal partners who were aggressive food providers, whereas the males were less responsible, more emotionally dependent, more preoccupied with art, and spent more time on their hairdos and gossiping about the opposite sex. Mead argued that if those temperaments that we regard as feminine (that is, nurturing, maternal, and passive) can be held as a masculine ideal in one group and can be banned for both sexes in another, then we no longer have a basis for saying that masculinity and femininity are biologically based. Although Mead's work has been criticized in recent years for its subjectivity, it nevertheless demonstrates the enormous variability in gender roles across cultures.

More recently, we saw radically different views of masculinity and femininity during the 1999 Women's World Cup Soccer Championships. Throughout the championships matches, the U.S. Women's Soccer Team attracted spectacular crowds in the stadium and an enormous amount of attention on television, in the press, and with a whole series of TV commercials. The U.S. women were talented, quick, disciplined, and tough, both mentally and physically. Players like Mia Hamm and Brandi Chastain were the idols of tens of thousands of young girls and women who aspired to become world-class athletes. And throughout all of the hype and excitement of winning the World Cup, there were few if any comments about how these women were compromising their femininity. Their success on the soccer field, in other words, in no way diminished them as women in the eyes of the nation. By way of contrast, the women on Brazil's soccer team (where men's soccer is revered) are viewed by their own countrymen with suspicion more than with adoration. In Brazil,

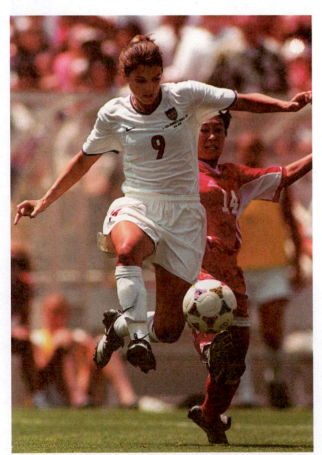

= *Soccer star Mia Hamm and her teammates on the U.S. World Cup Team have helped redefine the nature of femininity in the United States.*

soccer, defined as a masculine sport, is associated with physical confrontation, dominance, conflict, and control. Women, on the other hand, are idolized as delicate objects and consequently are seen as incapable of performing in such high contact sports. The general Brazilian public assumes that any woman who plays a highly competitive sport such as soccer has compromised her femininity. How these two female soccer teams are seen in their own countries illustrates the very significant role that culture plays in defining masculinity and femininity.

Cross-cultural studies further complicate our understanding of gender. In the United States, we generally envision only two genders, male and female, leaving no room for other gender alternatives such as hermaphrodites or androgynous individuals. Westerners, uncomfortable with these ambiguous gender identities, tend to explain them away by categorizing them as pathological, illegitimate, and perhaps even criminal. However, some cultures not only accommodate the ambiguities of these gender alternatives, but see them as legitimate or, in some cases, as powerful. One stunning example is the male/female Hijra role found in Hindu India.

The notion of a combined male/female role is a major theme in Hindu art, religion, and mythology. For example, androgynous people and impersonators of the opposite sex are found widely in Hindu mythology among both humans and their deities. These same themes are played out in parts of contemporary India. For example, according to Serena Nanda (1990:20–21),

> In Tamil Nadu, in South India, an important festival takes place in which hijras, identifying with Krishna, become wives, and then widows, of the male deity Koothandavar.... For this festival, men who have made vows to Koothandavar dress as women and go through a marriage ceremony with him. The priest performs the marriage, tying on the traditional wedding necklace. After 1 day, the deity is carried to a burial ground. There, all of those who have "married" him remove their wedding necklaces, cry and beat their breasts, and remove the flowers from their hair, as a widow does in mourning for her husband. Hijras participate by the thousands in this festival, coming from all over India. They dress in their best clothes and jewelry and ritually reaffirm their identification with Krishna, who changes his form from male to female.

The Hijra of Hindu India are significant because they provide an example of a society that tolerates a wider definition of gender than is found in our own society. The Hijra, who undergo an emasculation rite, present themselves as being "like women," or female impersonators.

They do not function sexually as men, claim to have no sexual feelings for women, dress in women's clothing, adopt womens' hairstyles, and even walk and carry themselves as women do. Clearly, Hijra are neither male nor female in the conventional sense of the term. But rather than being viewed as social deviants who should be discouraged, the Hijra are seen as a special, even sacred, gender group.

·■ HUMAN SEXUALITY ■·

EVEN THOUGH cultural anthropology has the reputation of concerning itself with documenting the exotic sexual practices of non-Western people, in actual fact the discipline of anthropology has not been interested in **human sexuality** until quite recently. Indeed, the subject of human sexuality was not formally recognized until 1961, when the AAA held a plenary session on the topic at its national meetings. To be certain, a number of anthropologists had documented exotic sexual practices, usually as part of general ethnographies, but before the 1960s there had been relatively little research on comparative human sexuality. Within the last three decades, however, anthropologists have become more interested in the theoretical aspects of human sexuality. Perhaps the most fundamental generalization that has emerged in recent decades is that human sexuality varies widely from culture to culture. In other words, we find enormous variations throughout the world in terms of sexual behaviors permitted or encouraged before marriage, outside marriage, and within marriage.

Although no society fails to regulate sexual conduct, some societies are permissive and others are more restrictive. Some cultures have very serious sanctions against premarital sex and others treat it much more casually. Among the more sexually restricted cultures are the traditional Cheyenne Indians of the American Plains, whose women were legendary for their chastity. When adolescent Cheyenne girls began to attract the attention of suitors, they were constantly chaperoned by aunts to ensure total abstinence from sexual behavior. The courting process was long and timid, often lasting five years before the couple could marry. Adolescent boys and girls had little or no contact, and young men were taught to suppress their sexual impulses, a Cheyenne value that they took with them into marriage. Premarital and extramarital sex were extremely rare among the Cheyenne, and when they occurred, they were met with powerful social sanctions (Hoebel 1960).

Another example of a society with limited sexual expression is the Dani of New Guinea. Whereas the Cheyenne were socialized to avoid intimate sexual displays from early childhood and deviants were punished, the Dani appear to be disinterested in sexual behavior. According to Karl Heider (1979), the Dani practice a five-year period of **postpartum sexual abstinence.** That is, husband and wife abstain from any sexual activity for five years after the birth of a child. Although all societies practice some form of abstinence after the birth of a child, usually it lasts for several weeks or several months; in some societies, however, it lasts until the child is weaned, which may take several years. Most North Americans, who feel that they must keep pace with the reported national average of 2.7 times per week, find Heider's claim hard to believe. After questioning his informants in a number of different ways, however, Heider found no contrary evidence. Not only do the Dani practice these long periods of abstinence, but they appear to have no other sexual outlets such as **extramarital activity** or homosexuality. Nor are Dani adults particularly stressed out by these five-year abstinences. Although Dani sexual restraint does not derive from awesome sanctions designed to punish the deviant, Dani people seem to learn in subtle ways that low sexual expressiveness is normal. As hard as it may be for Westerners to believe, the Dani simply have a low **sex drive.**

At the other extreme from such groups as the Cheyenne and the Dani are societies in which people are expected to have a great deal of sexual experience before marriage. Among such Oceanian societies as the Trobrianders, the Tikopia, and the Mangaians of Polynesia, premarital sex is not only permitted but encouraged; indeed, it is viewed as a necessary preparatory step for marriage. Young boys and girls in these societies receive sex education at an early age and are given permission to experiment during their adolescent years. Premarital lovers are encouraged, and in some societies in the Pacific, trial marriages are actually permitted.

The Mangaians of central Polynesia provide an interesting case of a society that draws a dichotomy between the public and private domains. This society is characterized by near total segregation of men and women in their public lives. Around the age of 4 or 5, boys and girls separate into gender-defined groups that will identify them for the rest of their lives. Brothers and sisters, husbands and wives, old men and old women, and female and male lovers have very little social contact in their everyday lives. Nevertheless, in their private lives, away from the public eye, men and women engage in sexual behavior that is both frequent and intense. Sexual intercourse is a principal concern for both Mangaian men and women, a concern that

CROSS-CULTURAL MISCUE

SOMETIMES OUR CULTURE can get us into trouble despite our best intentions. While conducting ethnographic fieldwork among the Kikuyu of Kenya in the 1970s, this author became involved in an embarrassing incident that he could not seem to prevent (Ferraro 1998:82):

Even before going to Kenya I had known through ethnographic readings that Kikuyu men routinely held hands with their close personal friends. After several months of living and working with Kikuyu, I was walking through a village in Kiambu District with a local headman who had become a key informant and a close personal acquaintance. As we walked side by side my friend took my hand in his. Within less than 30 seconds my palm was perspiring all over his. Despite the fact that I knew cognitively that this was a perfectly legitimate Kikuyu gesture of friendship, my own cultural values (that is, that "real men" don't hold hands) were so ingrained that it was impossible for me not to communicate to my friend that I was very uncomfortable.

---

is backed up by a detailed knowledge of the technical/biological aspects of sex. According to ethnographer Donald Marshall (1971:110), "the average Mangaian youth has fully as detailed a knowledge—perhaps more—of the gross anatomy of the penis and the vagina as does a European physician."

Like the Mangaians, the !Kung of southwestern Africa believe that sexual activity is a very natural, and indeed essential, part of life. !Kung adolescents are permitted to engage in both **heterosexual** and **homosexual** play, and discreet extramarital sexual activity is condoned. Conversations between women about their sexual exploits are commonplace, as is sexually explicit joking between men and women. According to Marjorie Shostak (1983:31), sexual activity is considered essential for good mental and physical health, for as one female informant put it, "If a girl grows up without learning to enjoy sex, her mind doesn't develop normally . . . and if a woman doesn't have sex her thoughts get ruined and she is always angry."

•■ GENDER ROLES ■•

AS MENTIONED in Chapter 8, all societies make some distinctions between what men are expected to do and what women are expected to do. In some cases **gender roles** are rigidly defined, but in others men's and women's roles overlap considerably. Yet despite the universality (and some variation) of division of labor by gender, the cultures of the world are noticeably uniform in the way they divide tasks between women and men. To illustrate, in most cases men engage in warfare, trap small animals, work with hard sub-

stances such as wood and stone, clear land, build houses, and fish. Women, on the other hand, tend crops, gather wild fruits and plants, prepare food, care for children, collect firewood, clean house, launder clothing, and carry water. In addition, a number of tasks are performed by both men and women. These include tending small domesticated animals, making crafts (pottery, baskets, and the like), milking animals, planting and harvesting crops, and collecting shellfish.

Some of these gender-specific roles (such as hunting for men and child care for women) are very closely associated with one gender or the other. For example, Murdock's *Ethnographic Atlas* (1967) classifies hunting as an exclusively male activity in over 99 percent of the societies listed; the remaining 1 percent are described as societies in which both males and females hunt, but "males do appreciably more than females." On the other side of the equation, child care is an overwhelmingly female activity, although in some cases men do make minor contributions. That such activities as hunting and child care are so thoroughly gender-specific requires some explanation.

A number of theories have been set forth to explain this very common division of labor by gender. One explanation is that because men have greater body mass and strength, they are better equipped to engage in such physical activities as hunting, warfare, and land clearing. To be certain, this explanation has a certain underlying logic, for men are better equipped physically than women to lift heavy loads, run fast, and fight ferociously. Proponents of this theory would argue that men are more likely than women to have the traits needed to be an efficient hunter (strength, speed, and endurance). Like any theory, however, this biological theory does not constitute a total explanation. There are some notable exceptions to the general rule that men engage in roles demanding maximum physical strength. To illustrate, in certain parts of East Africa, women routinely carry enormous loads of firewood on their backs for long distances. Not only is this a normative practice, but among some groups a woman's femininity is directly related to the size of the load she is able to carry. Also, among the foraging Agta of the Philippines, hunting is not exclusively a male activity; women hunt regularly. According to Frances Dahlberg (1981:12),

> Hunting is not confined to the oldest daughters in families without sons, young widows, deserted wives, or unusually vigorous personalities. . . . Agta women do not hunt only in cooperation with men (as do Mbuti women in net hunting) nor do they hunt only in the absence of men (as do Chipewyan women). . . . The Agta do not restrict any type of food collecting to one sex. Hunters, both female and male, begin hunting when their stamina and ability make it worthwhile and cease when they lose strength. . . . Each hunter uses techniques that work for her or for him; hunting techniques are not sex typed.

Although these exceptions do not invalidate the general rule, some have argued (Burton et al. 1977) that the division of labor by gender is more the result of constraints stemming from childbirth and infant care than it is from differences in strength.

This brings us to a second argument often used to explain this nearly universal type of gender division of labor:

Women do the things they do because those tasks are compatible with pregnancy, breastfeeding, and child care. Unlike certain male tasks, such as hunting and warfare, women's tasks can be accomplished without jeopardizing their own and their children's safety and without having to stray too far from home. This theory suggests that pregnant women would be at a marked disadvantage in running after game, lactating mothers would need to interrupt their tracking/hunting activities several times a day to nurse their children, and, given the danger involved in hunting, small children accompanying their mothers would not be safe. Judith Brown (1970) was the first to hypothesize that women tend to concentrate on tasks that are compatible with child care (that is, nursing and looking after children). Such tasks tend to be monotonous and require little concentration, can be interrupted without reducing efficient performance, provide for the safety of small children, and can be performed in or near the home.

Although this theory is sensible and no doubt can account for some of the division of labor by gender, it doesn't tell the whole story. A number of ethnographic studies from around the world since the late 1970s have seriously questioned this connection between female reproductive/child-care roles and the division of labor. To illustrate, some researchers (Burton et al. 1977) have argued that although pregnancy and breastfeeding do limit work roles for women, a woman's economic (work) obligations may take precedence over child-care considerations. In other words, a woman may make alternative child-care arrangements in order to engage in some type of work outside the

= *Do the greater size and weight of this Asmat male from Irian Jaya (Indonesia) provide an advantage in hunting?*

home. This can be seen in parts of the preindustrial world, where women leave their small children in the care of older siblings or other adults and, in the United States, where working mothers leave their infants at professional day care centers. In addition, others (Raphael and Davis 1985) have shown how women purposefully choose supplemental feeding rather than breastfeeding for their children because of work considerations.

•■ GENDER STRATIFICATION ■•

IT IS GENERALLY recognized that the status of women varies from one society to another. In some societies, women are in a clearly subordinate position in their social relationships with men. In other societies, the relationships between the genders are more egalitarian. Social scientists would generally agree that **gender stratification** exists to some degree in all societies, but there is considerably less agreement as to how one measures the status of men and women because gender stratification involves a number of different components that may vary independently of one another. It is now recognized that there are a number of important indicators of women's status, including economic, power, prestige, autonomy, and ideological dimensions. To illustrate, when considering the relative status of women in any society, one needs to look at the roles played by women, the value society places on their contributions, their legal rights, whether and to what degree they are expected to be deferential to men, their economic independence, and the degree to which they decide on the major events of their lives such as marriage, profession, and conception. The multidimensional nature of women's status was illustrated by Martin Whyte's (1978) comparative study of 93 societies, which identified 52 status dimensions found in the anthropological literature. Interestingly, all of these status dimensions varied independently of one another. In other words, no single cluster or complex of variables of women's status varied consistently from culture to culture. To illustrate, women in certain West African societies, because of their influence in the marketplace, may have an appreciable amount of economic independence, but they nevertheless remain subordinate to their husbands in most other respects. Thus, determining the status of women is difficult because it is not a unidimensional phenomenon.

Another difficulty in ascertaining the status of women is that it is not static. In some societies, the relative status of men and women fluctuates along with political changes. To illustrate, during the reign of the Shah of Iran, women's roles kept pace with modernization. During the 1960s and 1970s, increasingly large numbers of Iranian women abandoned the rules of **purdah** (domestic seclusion and veiling), obtained higher education, and gained entry to traditionally male professional roles. With the return of the religious and cultural fundamentalism under the Ayatollah Khomeini, however, women have returned to the veil and resumed more traditional female roles. Moreover, in a less dramatic fashion, the relative status of women in the United States has undergone some significant changes over the last several generations in terms of job opportunities and legal rights.

Yet another complicating factor in determining the status of women is the relative age of women in any given society. The Tiwi of North Australia are an interesting case in point. In this polygynous society, the accumulation of wives was a man's single most important measure of power and prestige. As C. Hart, Arnold Pilling, and Jane Goodale (1988:58) describe it, daughters, sisters, and mothers were for men "the main currency of the influence struggle, the main 'trumps' in the endless bridge game." Men would give their own daughters to other men in exchange for their daughters as future brides. An influential man could gain control of his sisters and his widowed mother as "chips" in his never-ending quest for additional wives for himself. Some observers have seen women in Tiwi society as nothing more than chattel—pieces of property with few rights of their own. This was generally the case with younger women because daughters were subordinate to the wishes of their fathers and wives were controlled by their husbands. But as widowed mothers or sisters, they could not be manipulated, or even coerced, by their sons or brothers. A son who wished to give his widowed mother or sister to a political ally needed her full consent and collaboration. Hart, Pilling, and Goodale (1988:59) go on to say:

> Young girls thus had no bargaining power but young widows had a good deal. . . . Thus, for women, as for men, age and political skill were the crucial factors in determining their position. . . . Not as independent operators, but as behind-the-scenes allies of their sons and brothers, Tiwi mothers and sisters enjoyed much more essential freedom in their own careers as often-remarried widows than would appear at first sight in a culture that ostensibly treated all women as currency in the political careers of the men.

Muslim societies in the Middle East are among the most highly stratified along gender lines. Nearly 4,000 years ago, the Code of Hammurabi firmly established the legal subordination of women. Although by the seventh century Mu-

= *In some societies, women are excluded from certain areas that are "for men only," such as this all-men's bar in Perth, Australia.*

hammad set forth rules protecting the rights of women, women's rights were never intended to be equal to men's rights. Moreover, in recent centuries, these rules have come to be interpreted to mean that women should be confined to the domestic realm and almost totally isolated from the public sphere of power. Today, in many of the small towns in Iraq, Iran, and Syria, women have very low status. Many women, particularly those from upper-class families, adhere to the strict rules of purdah. If they must leave the seclusion of the family compound, as many poor and middle-class Arab women must do to help support the family by working, they must obtain their husband's permission and cover themselves from head to toe in black, cloaklike garments. At mealtimes men are served first and the women eat the leftovers from the men's plates. Women have essentially no economic autonomy and legally are viewed as being under the authority of their husbands and fathers. Given the seclusion expected of Arab women and the strict insistence on virginity at marriage, women in the Muslim world have little or no control over their bodies or their sexuality, but no such restrictions apply to men.

In contrast to the marked status distinctions between the sexes found in traditional Middle Eastern cultures, the relationship between men and women in some foraging societies tends to be more egalitarian. For example, Colin Turnbull (1981) reports a good deal of mutual respect between the sexes among the Mbuti Pygmies of Central Africa, particularly among elders of the group. Adult Mbuti call their parents "tata" (elders) without distin-

guishing by gender. Mbuti men and women see themselves as equals in all respects but one: Women have the enormously important power of giving birth. This equation of womanhood with motherhood, which affords Mbuti women high status, is played out through a number of rituals in their everyday lives. Even their natural habitat (the forest), which is considered to be both sacred and supreme, is often called "mother." Moreover, Mbuti women choose their own mates, determine their own daily activities, and exercise considerable power as social critics.

In such food-collecting societies, the roles performed by men and women are very different, but their relative statuses are not. Such sexual equality is not surprising, however, for marked status differences of any type are rare in foraging societies. Because constant migration inhibits the accumulation of property, foraging societies tend to have very little private property, and sharp status distinctions are minimized for both men and women.

Although it is possible to identify societies where gender distinctions are kept to a minimum, the overwhelming evidence suggests that in many critical areas of life women are subordinate to men. To be certain, from time to time women in various cultures have wielded considerable power, but there is no ethnographic or archaeological evidence to support the notion that matriarchy—rule or domination of women over men—exists anywhere in the world or, for that matter, ever has existed (Bamberger 1974). Rather, what we find is that women, to one degree or another, are excluded from the major centers of

In many Islamic societies, women have relatively few rights and prerogatives.

economic and political power and control. Moreover, the roles women play as mothers and wives invariably carry with them fewer prerogatives and lower prestige than male roles. Even in egalitarian societies, it is headmen, not headwomen, who make such important decisions as how to allocate resources or whether to wage war against a neighboring group. Although we do find reigning queens in the world today, they are usually temporary holders of regal power. Less than 4 percent of the independent nations of the world have female heads of state (Women's International Network News, 2000:80), a clear indication of the worldwide subordination of women in terms of political power. Although to speak of **universal male dominance** is an oversimplification, the evidence does suggest a general gender asymmetry among most cultures of the world in the expression of power and influence.

Even a cursory examination of statistics on the status of women reveals what one social scientist (Smith 1995:237) has called the "Apartheid of gender." In terms of education, women throughout the world have made some progress toward equal educational enrollment, but huge gaps remain. Two-thirds of all the illiterate people in the world today are women. More than 70 percent of women age 25 and above in sub-Saharan Africa, southern Asia, and western Asia are illiterate. There are more illiterate women than men in every major region of the world. Even though world literacy has been on the rise in recent decades, it has risen faster for men than for women, thereby widening the gender gap.

Sometimes gender bias in the field of education can be very subtle. According to a report conducted by the AAUW (American Association of University Women), girls in the United States are shortchanged in the classroom because they are given less attention by their teachers than boys receive (Mincer 1994). This gender bias, the study found, undermines the girls' confidence and self-esteem and often discourages them from taking additional math and science courses. Because of its subtle nature, this form of gender bias does not receive a lot of attention. Nevertheless, it is important to note that girls on average are ahead of boys when they enter elementary school, but they graduate behind boys in nearly every subject area. The AAUW study concluded that this slippage was due primarily to the loss of female self-esteem caused by systematic gender bias in the schools.

The percentage of women in the world's workforce has increased in the last several decades, due largely to necessity. However, the world's women, particularly in developing countries, are concentrated in the lowest-paid occupations and receive less pay and fewer benefits than men. Women are also more likely to work part-time, have less seniority, and occupy positions with little or no upward mobility. Moreover, an increasing number of women in Asia, Africa, and South America are being pushed into the informal economy: small-scale, self-employed trading of goods and services. Some of the activities associated with the informal economy—such as street vending, beer brewing, and prostitution—are outside the law.

In addition to education and employment, a third area in which the world's women have not fared well is reproductive health. Although most women in the developed world control the number of children they have, in some parts of the world there is pressure to have large numbers of children, and these women on average have four to five children. In certain countries with particularly high birthrates (such as Malawi, Yemen, Ethiopia, and the Ivory Coast), the average woman has more than seven children in her lifetime (MacFarquhar 1994). Pregnant women in developing countries face a number of risks, including malnutrition and a lack of trained medical personnel to deal with high-risk pregnancies. In fact, it has been estimated that pregnant women in developing countries are 80 to 600 times more likely to die of complications of pregnancy and birthing than are women in the industrialized world.

Women of the world are also at a disadvantage in terms of finance. According to World Bank estimates, 90 percent of the more than half-billion women living in poverty around the world do not have access to credit. Small loans to women of $100 would go a long way in helping women to start their own small businesses, which could substantially improve their economic conditions. But both private lenders and aid organizations, by and large, have not made even this level of credit available to women. A notable exception has been the Grameen Bank in Bangladesh, the world's best-known micro-lender, which for more than two decades has made small business loans to the poorest segments of Bangladesh society. By 1995 the Grameen Bank had made over 2 million loans, many of them to women in subsistence farming and craft occupations, who used the modest loans to turn their operations into viable businesses. Extending this type of credit to impoverished women has proven to be an excellent investment for several reasons. First, World Bank data show that women repay their loans in 98 percent of the cases, as compared to 60 to 70 percent for men. And second, the World Bank has found that credit given to women has a greater impact on the welfare of the family because women tend to spend their money on better nutrition and education for their children—areas given lower priority by male borrowers (Kaslow 1995).

Thus, it is clear that women throughout the world continue to carry a heavy burden of inequality. Although they make up half of the world's population, women do approximately two-thirds of the work, earn one-tenth of the world's income, and own less than 1 percent of the world's property. And even in the wake of political and economic advances, women in many parts of the world are falling further behind their male counterparts. For example, the recent collapse of the former Soviet Union has taken a particularly heavy toll on women, who have lost their jobs at a much higher rate than men. It is estimated that 70 percent of those laid off in the first two years following the fall of Russian communism were women. The double-digit annual economic growth in the People's Republic of China is being driven largely by women, who make up the bulk of sweatshop laborers. Recently, Islamic fundamentalists in the Middle East have become increasingly militant in crusading against women's rights (MacFarquhar 1994).

This **sexual asymmetry** is often evident in the forms of language spoken by men and women. Sometimes the linguistic distinctions between men and women are reflected in vocabulary. Some languages have pairs of words (called doublets) that carry the same meaning, but men use one word and women the other. To illustrate, among the Island Carib of the West Indies, men use the word *kunobu* to mean "rain" and women use the word *kuyu* (Hickerson 1980). Among the Merina in Madagascar (Keenan 1974), for example, speech patterns associated with men, which are indirect, allusive, and formal, are considered respectable and sophisticated. Merina women, on the other hand, are thought to be ignorant of the subtleties of sophisticated speech and, consequently, are considered to be inferior. Moreover, submissiveness and lack of social power can be observed in female speech patterns in the United States in terms of intonation, loudness, and assertiveness. To illustrate, women in the United States have a less forceful style of speaking than men in that they use a greater number of qualifiers (such as "It may be just my opinion but . . ."). Also, many U.S. women soften the impact of a declarative statement by ending it with a question such as " . . . wouldn't you agree?" (Kramer 1974).

These linguistic gender differences in the United States (called **genderlects**) have been the subject of a best-selling book by Deborah Tannen (1990), who claims that women and men in the United States have different linguistic styles and communication goals. Women engage in "rapport-talk" and men use "report-talk." Rapport-talk characteristic of women seeks to establish connections, negotiate relationships, and reach agreement. Women's speech tends to be cooperative in character in that women acknowledge one another's contributions and engage in more active listening. Report-talk, in contrast, is a male mode of discourse that is more competitive. Men's conversations are less social and more individualistic and aim at controlling the flow of talk. In cross-sex conversations, men tend to dominate women by talking more, interrupting women more often, and focusing the conversation on the topics of their own choice.

Julia Wood (1994) has suggested that these basic speech differences between men and women in the United States are, at least in part, the result of the childhood games that girls and boys play. Girls when growing up tend to play

APPLIED PERSPECTIVE
Using Family Planning Clinics in Ecuador

For the past several decades, many development experts have identified high birthrates as the major obstacle to economic development. No matter how successful programs in health, education, and agriculture may be, any gains will be offset if the society is experiencing high annual population growth. Consequently, many international development organizations have given top priority to programs designed to slow population growth through family planning.

A common method of evaluating the success of family planning programs is by measuring the extent to which people actually use them. A number of significant factors may affect whether women initially attend (or return to) family planning clinics, including the women's attitudes toward contraception, the quality of the interaction with staff members, and the length of time they must wait to see a doctor. Susan Scrimshaw (1976), an applied anthropologist studying family planning clinics in Ecuador, identified another significant factor—women's modesty—that had important implications for how women felt about attending family planning clinics.

Using traditional anthropological methods, Scrimshaw collected data on 65 families living in Guayaquil, Ecuador, a tropical port city of approximately 1 million people. Scrimshaw found that small girls in Guayaquil—as in South America generally—are taught the virtues of modesty at a very early age. Even though boys are often seen without pants until the age of 4 or 5, little girls always have their genitals covered. Because girls usually reach puberty without any prior knowledge of menstruation, their first menstruation is both frightening and embarrassing. In general, Scrimshaw found that girls and women in Guayaquil do not have very positive attitudes about their bodies, their sexuality, or such natural bodily processes as menstruation, all of which are associated with the word *verguenza* (shame or embarrassment). Given this strong sense of modesty about their bodies, their sexuality, and reproduction, it is not surprising that these Ecuadorian women would feel uncomfortable even talking about contraceptives, let alone submitting to gynecological examinations.

Scrimshaw also conducted a survey on the use of family planning clinics among 2,936 women. She found that although 74 percent of the women questioned wanted more information on birth control methods, only 20 percent of them had actually taken the initiative to obtain the information, and less than 5 percent of the women surveyed had ever been to a family planning clinic. When the women who had attended were asked why they never returned, nearly half (48 percent) had been influenced by verguenza.

Information gained through participant-observation at a number of these family planning clinics helped explain why women were so reluctant to return to the clinics. Screening questions were asked by an intake worker, usually within earshot of other patients. Doctors gave patients very little explanatory information while requesting a large amount of information from them, much of which was never used. The clinics provided no private place for women to undress and did not supply the women with gowns, nor were the women properly draped during their physical exams. Even for women in the United States, who are usually afforded these courtesies, gynecological exams are often uncomfortable and embarrassing. Submitting to a physical exam under conditions of minimal privacy, however, was even more difficult for these Ecuadorian women because of their strong cultural emphasis on feminine modesty.

On the basis of these findings on women's modesty, Scrimshaw (1976:177–178) made the following practical recommendations for maximizing the utility of family planning clinics in Guayaquil:

1. *Discreetness:* Women in clinics should not be interviewed within the hearing of anyone but the parties directly involved. Questions should be kept to a minimum.

2. *Privacy:* Wherever possible, a woman should be given privacy to undress. The examining room should ensure security and privacy.

3. *Awareness of modesty:* A drape should be provided for a woman's legs.

4. *Talk during the examination:* Talking during the examination both between the doctor and other staff and between the doctor and the patient should be confined to the examination. Trivial talk should be avoided.

5. *Frequency of visits to the clinic and examination:* Many clinics require monthly visits for examinations and supplies. In most cases, such frequent examinations are unnecessary, and supplies can be picked up every three months.

6. *Male versus female physicians:* All women questioned said they preferred female physicians. Thus, women doctors need to be actively recruited.

These types of recommendations can be useful to those in charge of administering family planning clinics in Ecuador. None of the proposed changes alone will make or break a family planning program, but this case study does point up the need for the clinical staff to understand and acknowledge the modesty of Ecuadorian women and the role that cultural anthropologists can play in bringing this important social value to the attention of the clinical staff.

QUESTIONS FOR FURTHER THOUGHT

1. In what ways can applied anthropologists contribute to family planning programs in developing nations?
2. How does female modesty (*verguenza*) in Guayaquil shape attitudes about birth control clinics and gynecological examinations?
3. Do you think that the gender of the researcher studying family planning clinics affects the type of information gathered?

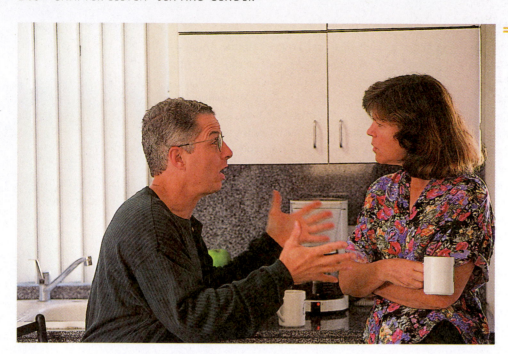

= *In what ways do the communication styles of men and women differ in the United States?*

games that are cooperative, collaborative, and inclusive. There is little incentive to outdo others, and there is a strong inclination to be sensitive to others' feelings. Boys, on the other hand, are expected to assert themselves, establish their leadership, and win. By focusing on outcomes, boys' games encourage participants to solve problems, achieve goals (such as scoring a touchdown), and generally "make things happen." Because of these differences in childhood games and socialization, Wood finds that women talk for the purpose of building and supplementing rapport with others, but men use talk to assert themselves; women use self-disclosure as a way of learning about others, but men tend to avoid self-disclosure; women's discourse strives for equality in social relationships, but men's discourse attempts to establish status and power; women often match experiences with others for the sake of showing understanding and empathy ("I know how you feel"), but men match experiences for the sake of gaining attention ("I can top that"); and finally, women show their support by expressing their understanding, but men show their support by giving advice or wanting to solve a problem.

•■ GENDER IDEOLOGY ■•

THIS UNIVERSAL male dominance is buttressed by a **gender ideology,** which we can define as a system of thoughts and values that legitimize gender roles, statuses, and customary behavior. In religion, women are often excluded

categorically by gender ideology from holding major leadership roles or participating in certain types of ceremonies. In some African societies, men's physical well-being is thought to be jeopardized by contact with a woman's menstrual discharge. In Bangladesh and in other Muslim cultures, men are associated with the right side and women are associated with the left side, a dichotomy that also denotes purity–pollution, good–bad, and authority–submission. Even in the area of food production, foods procured by men (such as meat from the hunt) are often more highly valued than those procured by women (such as roots or berries), even though the latter foods are the major source of nutrition. In many parts of the world, women are treated legally as minors in that they are unable to obtain a driver's license, bank account, passport, or even a birth control device without the consent of their husbands or fathers. One particularly effective ideological mechanism for keeping women in a subordinate position is found among the Luo of western Kenya whose creation myth (no doubt originated and perpetuated by men) blames women for committing the original sins that resulted in the curse of work for men.

In many parts of the world the devaluation of women starts early in life. The birth of a son is often cause for rejoicing, but the birth of a daughter is met with silence. In a number of patrilineal societies boys are more highly valued because they will contribute to the longevity of the lineage, whereas their sisters will produce children for their husband's lineage. Because parents often assume that sons will provide for them in their old age, they are much more likely to give sons preferential treatment for education and careers. Because girls are not likely to support their parents later in life, they are more often denied access to schooling, medical facilities, and nutritious diets. There are some rare societies that prefer female children (found in East Africa, Pakistan, and New Guinea), but the dominant trend is toward male-biased parental favoritism.

These are just some of the values reported in the ethnographic literature that legitimize the subordination of women. Nevertheless, we need to ask whether women in societies with such powerful gender ideologies actually buy into the ideologies. In other words, do they accept these ideological justifications for their subjugation? Because so many ethnographic reports were based on male testimony given to male ethnographers, it is likely that women, if their opinions were solicited, would describe themselves quite differently than they are portrayed in the ethnographic literature. Within the last several decades, a number of studies (Strathern 1984; Kirsch 1985; Errington and Gewertz 1987) have been written from the perspective of female informants; they demonstrate how distorted our interpretations of gender ideology have been.

An example of this distortion is provided by Thomas Buckley (1993), who has shown how our own Western view of menstruation and pollution has led to a very one-sided view of the culture of the Yurok Indians of California. Early ethnographic accounts of the Yurok suggested that menstruating women had to seclude themselves as a way of protecting men from the pollution of menstrual blood. Buckley's study of Yurok women, however, gives a very different interpretation of female seclusion during menstruation. Yurok women went into seclusion for a 10-day period not because they saw themselves as unclean or polluting, but because they were at the height of their power. Because this was a time of meditation, introspection, and personal growth, they did not want to be distracted by mundane tasks or concerns of the opposite sex. Rather, women were taught to be proud of their menstrual cycle and were expected to accumulate spiritual energy by meditating about the mysteries of life. Thus, for Yurok women menstruation was a highly positive part of their lives. As Buckley (1993:135) describes it, "The blood that flows serves to 'purify' the woman, preparing her for spiritual accomplishment."

In another study, Alma Gottlieb (1990) illustrates how the correlation between menstrual fluids and pollution is an oversimplification of the ethnographic facts. Based on research among the Beng of the Ivory Coast, Gottlieb shows that the Beng do not hold the classic analogy of equating men with purity and females with pollution. Rather,

> In some contexts Beng women are indeed polluting, while in others they can prevent or even counteract pollution. In still other situations, men and women are equally, and mutually, polluting. In short, Beng women as a category are no more fully defined by pollution than are men as a category.

Thus, Gottlieb's research shows that simple equations of women with pollution fail to take into account the complexity of gender ideologies.

Still another study that illustrates the complexity of gender ideology was conducted by Sandra Barnes (1990) among Yoruba women in Lagos, Nigeria. Female subordination among the Yoruba can best be described as contextual or situational. That is, women subordinate themselves in some contexts by showing great deference to their husbands, male family elders, employers, and public officials, but in other situations (such as market activity) they are independent, assertive, and powerful. Thus, we see a basic paradox in Yoruba society: Although female subordination is clearly the norm, particularly in family affairs, it is widely held that women can, and even should, strive for powerful positions in the world of economics and politics. Barnes explains the apparent paradox in terms of home ownership. Because of their success in the markets, women are able to attain high status through home ownership, and once they become homeowners, they are able to cross over into the realm of politics and public affairs. As Barnes (1990:276–277) concludes, "[home] ownership must be seen as a threshold for women in their desire to gain economic independence and security, because once they reach this point they automatically gain the rights to move further into the domain of public affairs."

These and many other studies in recent years have raised interesting theoretical and methodological questions. For example, to what degree have our male-dominated ethnographies of the past shaped our views of those cultures? Much of this research has challenged the prevailing views on the nature of gender inequality and has called into question such concepts as universal male dominance. Buckley has shown that Yurok women, unlike Yurok men, interpret menstrual periods as times of great personal power, not as periods of ritual pollution. Gottlieb demonstrates that pollution is not associated exclusively with women among the Beng of West Africa but that both genders can be polluting and that in some contexts women can counteract pollution. Barnes shows how women in

= *Although they assume a subordinate position in their family lives, some African women are able to maintain considerable power, authority, and autonomy by virtue of their economic activities, as with this vegetable vendor in Ethiopia.*

Lagos, Nigeria, although dependent on men for security, nevertheless seek and often gain power and authority through property ownership.

Because traditional ethnographies have tended to be conducted by male anthropologists who concentrate on male informants, the women's perspective has often been absent. Nowhere is this more evident than in the Middle East where women are secluded and protected from the wider society. To most Westerners, the veil is a symbol of repression, representing extreme restrictions, coercion, immobility, and degradation. However, in such Middle Eastern countries as Saudi Arabia, there will be well-educated computer experts and business professionals found behind the veil. Many of these women look at the veil not in terms of what it denies them but rather in terms of the demands that it makes on the men in the society. For many Saudi women, both educated and uneducated alike, the veil is a symbol of safety, security, protection, and privacy, which they would not necessarily choose to abandon.

All of these recent studies, written from a woman's perspective, are important because they serve as a long overdue corrective to the male gender bias found in many of our ethnographies. They also serve as a reminder that gender issues are far more complex than one might think by looking at a society only from a male perspective. Nevertheless, these new studies, although providing a richer and more accurate description of reality, should not obscure the fact that in most societies men still enjoy the majority of power, prestige, and influence.

•■ EXPLOITATION CAUSED ■• BY GENDER IDEOLOGY

IN SOME PARTS of the world, gender ideology is so extremely male biased that females can suffer dire consequences. In certain parts of the world, there are large numbers of females who are missing in census counts. It has been estimated (MacFarquhar 1994) that the countries of China and India together have 75 million fewer females than would be expected. In most countries, including the United States and Canada, women slightly outnumber the men. But in India and China, where there is a strong gender bias against females, the sex ratio strongly favors males. The discrepancy in census counts is caused by females receiving less adequate nutrition and medical care, selective abortions, or, as is the case in China, the underreporting or hiding of female births.

A particularly malignant manifestation of **male gender bias** in North India is **female infanticide,** which involves outright killing of female children. Sons are much more desirable than daughters because they are considered economic assets. They are needed for farming, are more likely to be wage employed, are the recipients of marriage dowry, and because they don't leave home when they marry, they can support the parents in their later years.

Yet, there are also less direct and immediate forms of female child abuse, such as sustained **nutritional deprivation,** which, if not fatal, can retard learning, physical development, or social adjustment. Barbara Miller (1993) found considerable evidence of this less direct form of gender exploitation. For example, the sex ratio of children being admitted to hospitals is at least two to one in favor of boys, an imbalance caused by the sex-selective child-care practices of the parents. Betty Cowan and Jasbir Dhanoa (1983) examined a large sample of **infant mortality** cases in Ludhiana District in North India and found that 85 percent of all deaths between 7 and 36 months were female. They also found that the prevalence of malnutrition for children between the ages of 1 and 3 was more than three times as high for females as it was for males. Moreover, there is evidence (Ramanamma and Bambawale 1980) of sex-selective abortion. For 700 pregnant women applying for prenatal sex determination in a North Indian hospital, 250 fetuses were determined to be male and 450 fetuses were female; all of the male fetuses were kept to term but 430 of the 450 female fetuses were aborted. All of these studies indicate how an extreme gender ideology can lead to a lethal form of gender exploitation.

Yet another form of extreme gender bias involves **honor killings** of women practiced in a number of countries of the Middle East as well as in India and Pakistan. As illustrated in the Cross-Cultural Miscue in Chapter 10, the men of a traditional family believe that a woman's purity is the most important part of the family's reputation. If it is even rumored that a daughter has lost her virginity or has had an extramarital affair, the family as a group will be shamed. An unchaste woman is considered worse than a murderer because she doesn't merely affect a single victim but her entire family. And it is believed that the only way for the family to restore its honor and avoid being shunned by the rest of the community is to kill the daughter. Even though some governments in Arabic states have taken a stand against honor killings, the practice remains widespread because an unchaste woman is seen as a threat. In traditional communities, where this belief is the norm, the girl's family will be ostracized. Her sisters will be considered unfit for marriage, and her brothers will be taunted in the streets and will have their manhood questioned. Because honor killings are often disguised to look like accidents, and because of the general reluctance in traditional societies to blow the whistle on the killer, it is very difficult to determine the number of honor killings that occur each year. According to one source (Jehl 1999), there were over 400 such killings in 1997 in the country of Yemen (population of 16 million). Whatever the number, however, this particular practice of honor killings places the entire burden of maintaining the family's honor on the woman, rather than punishing the man who also played a part in the loss of the girl's virginity.

A particularly graphic form of gender exploitation is **female genital mutilation** found in large parts of Africa.

■ *Because of gender ideology, this boy in Ragasthan, India, is more likely to receive medical attention than his sister.*

UNICEF estimates that as many as 130 million women living in Africa today have had their childhood or early adolescence interrupted by a traumatic operation in which the clitoris is partially or completely removed. And, despite efforts to convince people to give up the practice, approximately 6,000 girls are subjected to the operation each day. According to Amnesty International estimates, the African countries of Egypt, Eritrea, Ethiopia, Mali, and Somalia have an incidence of female genital mutilation of over 90 percent (Hecht 1998). In some cases this procedure is followed by a partial removal of the labia, which are then sewn together to almost totally close the entrance to the vagina. These operations are typically performed with crude and unsterile instruments, without the benefit of anesthesia, and with little or no protection against infection.

Although the World Health Organization has unanimously condemned the practice as dangerous and medically indefensible, the practice continues throughout much of sub-Saharan Africa. In fact, women themselves perform the operations, and young girls are often coerced into submission by their own mothers and grandmothers. Traditionalists justify the practice for a number of reasons, including the preservation of a girl's chastity (and, thus, the family's honor), cleanliness, curbing of a girl's sexual desires, reduction of rape, and proper socialization of young girls to become responsible women (Boddy 1989; Lightfoot-Klein 1989). To be certain, female genital mutilation is a highly controversial contemporary issue. Even though we can find certain explanations for its continuation, the fact remains that millions of girls are being subjected to pain, infection, and death to an extent that their brothers are not. Thus, this female genital mutilation illustrates how extreme gender ideology can lead to differential levels of subjugation between men and women.

Widespread female infanticide, abuse, and mutilation in other non-Western cultures are deeply disturbing and shocking, but we should not assume that equally appalling gender-based violence does not occur in our own culture. Both physical violence, in the form of wife-battering and homicide, and sexual assault against women are pervasive

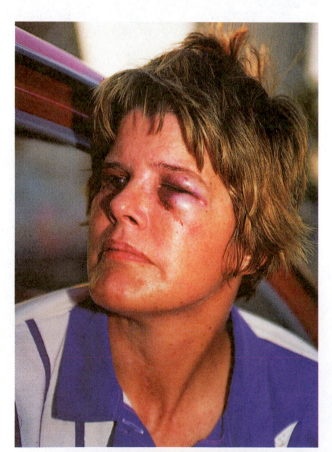

= *Physical violence against women, the result of gender ideology, continues to be a problem in the United States.*

and direct consequences of extreme gender ideology. Sexual and physical violence against women has been, and continues to be, a serious problem in the United States. In 1990, police received reports on more than 100,000 attempted or completed sexual assaults on women and girls (U.S. Department of Justice 1990). However, according to a study conducted by the National Center for Victims of Crime (Kilpatrick et al. 1992), because of serious underreporting of sexual assault, the rate in the United States was more than six times higher than was actually reported.

From a cross-cultural perspective, it is clear that domestic violence against women exists in all parts of the world. For example, the United Nations (1995) cites studies from around the world on the most pervasive form of gender-based violence: abuse by a husband or intimate partner. Survey results indicate that the percentage of women who have been physically assaulted by an intimate partner ranged from a low of 17 percent in New Zealand, to 28 percent in the United States, to as high as 60 percent in Sri Lanka, Ecuador, and Tanzania. We need not cite any additional statistics to illustrate that male-biased gender ideologies can have negative, and often lethal, consequences for the subordinate gender.

•■ GENDER IN ■• THE UNITED STATES

WHEN WE THINK of traditional gender roles in the United States, two words usually come to mind: **breadwinner** and **housewife.** According to this traditional view, males, who are often characterized as logical, competitive, goal oriented, and unemotional, were responsible for the economic support and protection of the family. Females, on the other hand, with their warm, caring, and sensitive natures, were expected to restrict themselves to child rearing and domestic activities. However, this traditional view of gender roles in the United States was valid only for a relatively brief period in our nation's history, from roughly 1860 through the 1950s. Kingsley Davis and Wilbert Moore (1988:73) have called the period between 1860 and 1920 the "heyday of the breadwinner system"; they identify 1890 as its peak because less than 3 percent of native-born married women in the United States worked outside the home at that time. Before industrialization, pioneer women were fully productive members of the rural homestead.

With the rise of industrialization in the late nineteenth century, the nation's economy shifted from agriculture to manufacturing. This rapid industrialization was revolutionary because it tended to separate work life from family life. Unlike work on the family farm, factory work could not be easily combined with child rearing and domestic tasks. As women became more confined to the home, their direct contribution to economic production decreased. As men's and women's spheres were separated, the terms *breadwinner* and *housewife* became entrenched in our vocabulary. Interestingly, we maintained this view of separate spheres for men and women well into the twentieth century even though forces for change that eroded those separate spheres were under way by the early 1900s.

It is true that men entered the workforce in greater numbers than women during the twentieth century, but we must not assume that women did not also make significant contributions to factory production. This is particularly true of poor and working-class women, minority women, immigrant women, and single mothers. The entry of women into the workforce was facilitated by a number of factors. First, as industrialization became more complex, more clerical workers were needed, and most of them were women. Second, as infant mortality rates fell, women bore fewer children, thereby increasing the number of years they could work outside the home. Third, many women gravitated toward the textile industry because they were thought to possess greater manual dexterity than men and therefore to be more adept at sewing clothes. Fourth, the rising rate of divorce has forced many women to support themselves and their children without the financial aid of a spouse. Fifth, the development of the baby bottle enabled many women to work outside the home without jeopardizing the nutritional needs of their infants. And, finally, periodic economic downturns have driven an increasing number of women to join the workforce because two salaries are often needed to make ends meet.

Today, both men and women are in the paid labor force, with approximately 76 percent of men and 57 percent of women participating. One demographic feature that must be mentioned, however, is that the nature of the women working outside the home has changed dramatically over the past 30 years. That is, the percentage of working women between the ages of 25 and 54 has increased appreciably from 50 percent in 1970 to 76 percent in 1995 (Spain and Bianchi 1996). It is important to point out that employed married women, particularly those with children, carry a **double workload** by being both wage employed and primarily responsible for housework and child care (Renzetti and Curran 1992).

Another characteristic of the wage sector of the U.S. economy is that there is a high rate of **occupational segre-**gation along gender lines. According to the U.S. Bureau of Labor (1990), women in the United States are typically concentrated in certain lower-paying jobs. For example, in such occupations as secretary, day-care worker, and check-out clerk, more than 99 percent are women, and women make up 96 percent of nurses, 83 percent of librarians, and 71 percent of teachers. At the other end of the spectrum, women make up only 1 percent of corporate CEOs, 6 percent of partners in private law firms, and 8 percent of state and federal judges. In addition, men tend to dominate the supervisory positions, even in areas where a majority of workers are women. Despite these data illustrating occupational segregation, in the last several decades women have made considerable inroads into high-status professions. According to Richard Morin and Megan Rosenfeld (1998), between 1983 and 1996 the percentage of female judges and lawyers had doubled to 29 percent while the percentage of female physicians increased from 16 to 26 percent. Moreover, approximately three out of every 10 professional athletes are female, nearly a 100 percent increase since the mid-1980s.

Not only are jobs segregated by gender in the United States, but men are better paid for their efforts. Wages for full-time female employees are only 70 percent of wages for full-time male employees. And although this is up from 61 percent three decades ago, the gap between male and female earnings remains wide. To illustrate, female clerical workers in the United States earn only 64 cents for every dollar earned by a male clerical worker. For sales workers, the gender discrepancy is even more pronounced, with women earning only 57 cents on the dollar (Faludi 1991). At the upper end of the occupational scale, female executives make less than two-thirds what their male counterparts earn (Pennar 1991). Regardless of which data are used, women earn less than men. Many of the jobs that are predominantly female are low-paying jobs with low upward mobility. But even in professions that require high levels of training and education—such as teaching, library science, and nursing—women earn less than their male counterparts.

Although an increasing number of women are entering professions such as law, medicine, and engineering that require advanced education, occupations associated with low prestige and income still have high proportions of women. Moreover, a logical extension of this is the phenomenon known as the **feminization of poverty**. For example, more than half of all female-headed families with children are living below the poverty line—a poverty rate that is approximately four times higher than the poverty

CROSS-CULTURAL MISCUE

TERESA, A SOPHOMORE at the University of Minnesota, shared a suite in the dorm with Yoko, an exchange student from the most prestigious university in Tokyo. Within the first several weeks, both girls became fast friends. They were both economics majors, enjoyed many of the same leisure interests, and shared some fairly progressive ideas about women's rights. On their way back from the cafeteria, Teresa asked Yoko what she planned to do after graduation. Much to Teresa's surprise, Yoko said that she planned to be a secretary for one of Japan's large multinational companies. Surely Yoko was too bright and well educated to waste her time on a mere secretarial job!

Teresa concluded that either Yoko was selling herself short vocationally or that Japan must be a terribly sexist society. In actual fact there was another explanation that Teresa failed to realize. The word *secretary* has different meanings in Japan and in the United States. For Teresa, the word *secretary* meant a clerk or typist. What Yoko had in mind, however, was more along the lines of a well-paid executive administrative assistant with a high level of responsibility.

rate for male-centered families. The feminization of poverty is particularly acute when we look at minorities. Whereas 45 percent of the White female-headed families live in poverty, approximately 70 percent of African Americans and Hispanics are officially living in poverty. There are a number of factors contributing to the feminization of poverty not only in America but throughout the world. These include the continued involvement of women in low-paying jobs; the additional responsibilities for child rearing, which many men do not have; the relative dearth of women in political or policymaking positions; and limited access to education, skills training, financial credit, and health care.

Despite the significant inequities that exist within the workforce in the United States, a recent national survey reports that men and women have declared a ceasefire in the battle between the sexes that raged for the last 40 years. Rather than blaming one another, both men and women face a new common enemy—lack of time, stress, and the pressure of living in the high-speed information age. Ac-

cording to a survey conducted in 1997 by the *Washington Post*, the Kaiser Family Foundation, and Harvard University, a majority of men and women agreed that although greater opportunities for women in the workplace has enriched both sexes, it has put additional strains on marriages, child rearing, and the pursuit of a satisfying life. To be certain, the survey revealed some significant differences in gender perspectives. For example, men are more likely to support increases in defense spending, value more highly an active sex life, and spend more time thinking about career success; women, on the other hand, are more likely to be religious, support public education and health care, and value close personal relationships. Yet, despite these differences, both women and men, rather than blaming each other for their life's problems, share a sense of their anxieties and confusions as to how to cope with the escalating pressures of everyday life. As Morin and Rosenfeld (1998; A1) put it, "the politics of resentment have become the politics of fatigue."

SUMMARY

1. The word *gender* refers to the way members of the two sexes are perceived, evaluated, and expected to behave. Although biology sets broad limits on gen-

der definitions, there is a wide range of ideas about what it means to be feminine or masculine, as Margaret Mead demonstrated in her classic study of sex and temperament in New Guinea.

2. There are considerable differences in degrees of permissiveness, but all societies regulate the sexual conduct of their members. Some societies, such as the Cheyenne Indians of the American Plains, are very restrictive, whereas others, such as the Mangaians of Polynesia, not only permit but actually encourage frequent and intense sexual activity between men and women.

3. In very general terms, there is considerable uniformity in sex roles found throughout the world. For example, men engage in warfare, clear land, hunt and trap animals, build houses, fish, and work with hard substances; women tend crops, prepare food, collect firewood, clean house, launder clothes, and carry water.

4. The status of women is multidimensional, involving such aspects as the division of labor, the value placed on women's contributions, economic autonomy, social and political power, legal rights, levels of deference, and the extent to which women control the everyday events of their lives.

5. Muslim societies of the Middle East are among the most highly stratified along gender lines. At the other extreme, certain foraging societies, such as the Mbuti Pygmies of Central Africa, take the most egalitarian (or least stratified) approach to men and women. Although these represent the two extremes of the status of women in the world, it is clear that in most critical areas women tend to be subordinate to men in just about all societies of the world.

6. Gender ideology is used in most societies to justify this universal male dominance. Deeply rooted values about the superiority of men, the ritual impurity of women, and the preeminence of men's work are often used to justify the subjugation of women. However, it has been demonstrated in recent years that women do not perceive themselves in the same ways that they are portrayed in these (largely male) gender ideologies.

7. In some societies, gender ideologies become so extreme that females suffer serious negative consequences such as female infanticide, female nutritional deprivation, honor killings, female genital mutilation, rape, and spouse abuse.

8. Although the words *breadwinner* and *housewife* accurately described the middle-class American household around the beginning of the twentieth century, the separate spheres implied by these two terms have been more myth than reality. In fact, over the past four decades the number of women in the United States working outside the home has increased dramatically.

9. The economy of the United States is characterized by a high rate of occupational segregation along gender lines. Not only are occupations gender segregated, but women tend to earn considerably less than men. Moreover, there has been a trend in recent decades toward the feminization of poverty.

KEY TERMS

breadwinner	housewife
double workload	human sexuality
extramarital activity	infant mortality
female genital mutilation	male gender bias
female infanticide	masculinity
femininity	nutritional deprivation
feminization of poverty	occupational segregation
gender	postpartum sexual
gender ideology	abstinence
genderlects	purdah
gender roles	sex drive
gender stratification	sexual asymmetry
heterosexual	sexual dimorphism
homosexual	universal male dominance
honor killings	

SUGGESTED READINGS

Bonvillain, Nancy. *Women and Men: Cultural Constructs of Gender.* 2d ed. Upper Saddle River, NJ: Prentice-Hall, 1998. This recent book examines gender roles cross-culturally in societies ranging from foraging countries to industrialized states.

Brettell, Caroline B., and Carolyn Sargent. *Gender in Cross Cultural Perspective.* 2d ed. Englewood Cliffs, NJ: Prentice-Hall, 1997. A collection of 46 articles written by anthropologists on such aspects of gender as inequity, sexuality, and division of labor. Each major section of the volume is prefaced by a substantive essay written by the editors.

Caplan, Pat, ed. *The Cultural Construction of Sexuality.* London: Tavistock, 1987. This collection of essays examines the relationship between sex, gender, and sexuality in a wide variety of cultures, ranging from Britain, the United States, and Italy in the West to Kenya, Jamaica, and Fiji in the developing world.

di Leonardo, Micaela, ed. *Gender at the Crossroads of Knowledge: Feminist Anthropology in the Postmodern Era.* Berkeley: University of California Press, 1991. An up-to-date collection of essays that discusses the current thinking in feminist anthropology. In addition to a substantial introductory essay by the editor, the 12 articles deal with such topics as language and gender, feminism in primate studies, women in technological development, and the sexual division of labor.

Kahne, Hilda, and Janet Z. Giele, eds. *Women's Work and Women's Lives: The Continuing Struggle Worldwide.* Boulder, CO: Westview Press, 1992. A provocative set of essays examining women and paid employment in both developing and industrialized societies. The volume explores women's social status in different cultures and provides valuable data on pay equity, work schedules, and the informal economy.

Mencher, Joan P., and Anne Okongwu, eds. *Where Did All the Men Go?: Female Headed/Female Supported Households in Cross Cultural Perspective.* Boulder, CO: Westview Press, 1993. This collection of essays looks at the rising number of female-headed households and the increasing povertization of mothers and their children in different parts of the world. Specifically, the volume examines contributing factors to this worldwide phenomenon, coping strategies that women have developed, and policy recommendations for addressing the issue.

Nanda, Serena. *Gender Diversity: Cross Cultural Variations.* Prospect Heights, IL: Waveland Press, 2000. Readable yet scholarly selections dealing with the cultural construction of sex and gender.

Renzetti, Clair M., and Daniel Curran. *Women, Men, and Society.* 2d ed. Boston: Allyn & Bacon, 1992. A thorough and up-to-date examination of gender issues in the United States, written by sociologists.

Sanday, Peggy Reeves, and Ruth G. Goodenough, eds. *Beyond the Second Sex: New Directions in the Anthropology of Gender.* Philadelphia: University of Pennsylvania Press, 1990. A recent volume of articles that reexamine traditional notions of gender by avoiding preconceived theories. Societies dealt with in this volume include the Mende of Sierra Leone, the Bedouins of Egypt, the Mendi of Papua New Guinea, and the United States.

Spain, Daphne, and Suzanne Bianchi. *Balancing Act: Motherhood, Marriage, and Employment Among American Women.* New York: Russell Sage Foundation, 1996. By using a wide range of census and survey data, this study examines how American women balance their careers with their roles as wives and mothers.

Suggs, David N., and Andrew Miracle, eds. *Culture and Human Sexuality: A Reader.* Pacific Grove, CA: Brooks Cole, 1993. A collection of articles on human sexuality, this volume contains case studies and more theoretical essays from a number of cultures in various parts of the world. Topics include sex and the nature of humanity, sexual practices, sexual orientations, and the relationships between culture and sexually transmitted diseases.

Tannen, Deborah. *You Just Don't Understand: Women and Men in Conversation.* New York: Morrow, 1990. While drawing heavily on recent scholarly research, this highly readable discussion of the sociolinguistics of gender shows how men's and women's patterns and styles of speaking are substantially different.

Womack, Mari, and Judith Marti. *The Other Fifty Percent: Multicultural Perspectives on Gender Relations.* Prospect Heights, IL: Waveland Press, 1993. Drawing on case studies from Asia, Africa, Europe, and the Americas, this collection of articles examines gender as it plays out in marriage, economics, religion, and politics.

On the Net

1. Using any search engine, find the home page entitled "Gender in Development: UNDP." What is meant by the term *gender mainstreaming*? Go to the section of the site called "Gender Good Practice." Select any single case study (from any part of the world) and describe its essential features in no more than 250 words.

2. This chapter has mentioned the general gender discrimination that exists in North America as well as in other parts of the world. It would be interesting to see what our legislators are doing about this problem in the United States and Canada. For U.S. students, consult the home page of the United States Senate:

http://www.senate.gov

Canadian students can do the same by consulting the home page of the Canadian Parliament:

http://www.parl.gc.ca

Select a woman from the directory of U.S. senators or the directory of Canadian MPs. Find as much information on this female legislator as possible concerning the topic of eliminating discrimination against women in the workplace. Read her speeches and public statements that are part of her own home page. Once you have familiarized yourself with this legislator's public positions, write her a letter via e-mail asking her what specific pieces of legislation she is sponsoring or supporting that will help eliminate or minimize gender discrimination in the workplace.

Chapter Twelve

POLITICAL ORGANIZATION AND SOCIAL CONTROL

A West African chief of high status.

WHAT WE WILL LEARN:

▼

What are the different types of political organization?

▼

What are the various theories concerning the origins of the state?

▼

In the absence of kings, presidents, legislatures, and bureaucracies, how is social order maintained in stateless societies?

▼

What are the causes of war?

▼

As mentioned in the discussion of cultural universals in Chapter 2, all societies, if they are to remain viable over time, must maintain social order.

Every society must develop a set of customs and procedures for making and enforcing decisions, resolving disputes, and regulating the behavior of its members. Every society must make collective decisions about its environment and its relations with other societies and about the eventuality of disruptive or destructive behavior on the part of its members. These topics generally are discussed under such headings as *political organization, law, power, authority, social control,* and *conflict resolution.* While exploring all of these subjects, this chapter deals with the cultural arrangements by which societies maintain social order, minimize the chances of disruption, and cope with whatever disruptions do occur (Vincent 1990; McGlynn and Tuden 1991).

When most North Americans think of politics or political structure, a number of familiar images come to mind, such as the following:

▶ Political leaders such as presidents, governors, mayors, or commissioners.
▶ Complex bureaucracies employing thousands of civil servants.
▶ Legislative bodies ranging from the smallest town council to the U.S. Congress.
▶ Formal judicial institutions that comprise municipal, state, and federal courts.
▶ Such law enforcement bodies as police departments, national guard units, and the armed forces.
▶ Political parties, nominating conventions, and secret ballot voting.

All of these are mechanisms that our own society uses for making and enforcing political decisions as well as coordinating and regulating people's behavior. Many societies in the world have none of these things—no elected officials, legislatures, formal elections, armies, or bureaucracies. We should not conclude from this, however, that such societies do not have some form of political organization, if by political organization we mean a set of customary procedures that accomplish decision making, conflict resolution, and social control.

•■ TYPES OF POLITICAL ■• ORGANIZATION

POLITICAL ORGANIZATION can be found in all societies, but the degree of specialized and formal mechanisms varies considerably from one society to another. Societies differ in their political organization based on three important dimensions:

▶ The extent to which political institutions are distinct from other aspects of the social structure; that is, in some societies, political structures are barely distinguishable from economic, kinship, or religious structures.
▶ The extent to which **authority** is concentrated into specific political roles.
▶ The level of **political integration** (that is, the size of the territorial group that comes under the control of the political structure).

These three dimensions are the basis for the classification of societies (following Service, 1978) into four fundamentally different types of political structure: band societies, tribal societies, chiefdoms, and state societies. Although societies do not all fit neatly into one or another of these categories, this fourfold scheme is useful to help us understand how different societies administer themselves and maintain social order.

Although our discussion of all four types of political organization are written using the "ethnographic present," we need to remember that there are no pure bands, tribes, or chiefdoms in the world today. Rather, today these non-state forms of political organization have had more complex state political systems superimposed over them.

BAND SOCIETIES

The least complex form of political arrangement is the band, characterized by small and usually nomadic populations of food collectors. Although the size of a band can range anywhere from 20 to several hundred individuals, most bands number between 30 and 50 people. The actual size of particular bands is directly related to food-gathering methods; that is, the more food a band has at its disposal, the larger the number of people it can support. Although bands may be loosely associated with a specific territory, they have little or no concept of individual property ownership and place a high value on sharing, cooperation, and reciprocity. **Band societies** have very little role specialization and are highly egalitarian in that few differences in status and wealth can be observed. Because this form of political organization is so closely associated with a foraging technology, it is generally thought to be the oldest form of political organization.

Band societies have a number of traits in common with one another. First, band societies have the least amount of political integration; that is, the various bands (each comprising 50 or so people) are independent of one another and are not part of a larger political structure. The integration that does exist is based largely on ties of kinship and marriage. All of the bands found in any particular culture are bound by a common language and general cultural features. However, they do not all pay political allegiance to any overall authority.

Second, in band societies political decisions are often embedded in the wider social structure. Because bands are composed of kin, it is difficult to distinguish between purely political decisions and those that we would recognize as family, economic, or religious decisions. Political life, in other words, is simply one part of social life.

Third, leadership roles in band societies tend to be very informal. In band societies, there are no specialized political roles or leaders with designated authority. Instead, leaders in foraging societies are often, but not always, older men respected for their experience, wisdom, good judgment, and knowledge of hunting. Most decisions are made through discussions by the adult men. The headman can persuade and give advice but has no power to impose his will on the group. The headman often gives advice on such matters as migratory movements, but he has no perma-

nent authority. If his advice proves to be wrong or unpopular, the group members will look to another person to be headman. Band leadership, then, stems not so much from power but rather from the recognized personal traits admired by the others in the group.

The !Kung of the Kalahari exemplify a band society with a headman. Although the position of headman is hereditary, the actual authority of the headman is quite limited. The headman coordinates the movement of his people and usually walks at the head of the group. He chooses the sites of new encampments and has first pick of location for his own house site. But beyond these limited perks of office, the !Kung headman receives no other rewards. He is in no way responsible for organizing hunting parties, making artifacts, or negotiating marriage arrangements. These activities fall to the individual members of the band. The headman is not expected to be a judge of his people. Moreover, his material possessions are no greater than any other person's. As Lorna Marshall so aptly put it when referring to the !Kung headman, "He carries his own load and is as thin as the rest" (1965:267).

TRIBAL SOCIETIES

Whereas band societies are usually associated with food collecting, **tribal societies** are found most often among food producers (horticulturalists and pastoralists). Because plant and animal domestication is far more productive than foraging, tribal societies tend to have populations that are larger, denser, and somewhat more sedentary in nature. Tribal societies are similar to band societies in several important respects. They are both egalitarian to the extent that there are no marked differences in status, rank, power, and wealth. In addition, tribal societies, like bands, have local leaders but do not have centralized leadership.

The major difference between tribes and bands is that tribal societies have certain **pan-tribal mechanisms** that cut across and integrate all of the local segments of the tribe into a larger whole. These mechanisms include such tribal associations as clans, age grades, or secret societies. Pan-tribal associations function to unite the tribe against external threats. These integrating forces are not permanent political fixtures, however. Most often the local units of a tribe operate autonomously, for the integrating mechanisms come into play only when an external threat arises. When the threat is eliminated, the local units return to their autonomous state. Even though these pan-tribal mechanisms may be transitory, they nevertheless provide

Tribal societies, such as the Samburu of Kenya, have certain pan-tribal mechanisms, such as clans and age organizations, that serve to integrate the tribe as a whole.

wider political integration in certain situations than would ever be possible in band societies.

In many tribal societies, the kinship unit known as the clan serves as a pan-tribal mechanism of political integration. The *clan* is defined as a group of kin who consider themselves to be descended from a common ancestor, even though individual clan members cannot trace, step-by-step, their connection to the clan founder. Clan elders, though not holding formal political offices, usually manage the affairs of their clans (settling disputes between clan members, for example) and represent their clans in dealings with other clans.

Another form of pan-tribal association based on kinship that is found in tribal societies is the *segmentary lineage system* (discussed in Chapter 10). Though less common than tribal societies based on clans, those based on segmentary lineage systems are instructive because they demonstrate the shifting or ephemeral nature of the political structure in tribal societies. In a segmentary system, individuals belong to a series of different descent units (corresponding to different genealogical levels) that function in different social contexts.

The most basic or local unit is the minimal lineage, comprising three to five generations. Members of a minimal lineage usually live together, consider themselves to be the closest of kin, and generally engage in everyday activities together. Minimal lineages, which tend to be politically independent, form a hierarchy of genealogical units. For example, minimal lineages make up minor lineages, minor lineages coalesce into major lineages, and major lineages form maximal lineages. When a dispute occurs between individuals of different segments, people are expected to side with the disputant to whom they are most closely related. Thus, people who act as a unit in one context merge into larger aggregates in other social situations. This process of lineage segmentation means that segments will unite when confronted by a wider group. In the words of John Middleton and David Tait,

> A segment that in one situation is independent finds that it and its former competitors are merged together as subordinate segments in the internal administrative organization of a wider overall segment that includes them both. This wider segment is in turn in external competitive relations with other similar segments, and there may be an entire series of such segments. (1958:6–7)

It is important to keep in mind that these various segments—minimal, minor, major, and maximal lineages—are not groups but rather alliance networks that are activated only under certain circumstances. This process tends to deflect hostilities away from competing kin and toward an outside or more distant enemy. Such a level of political organization is effective for the mobilization of a military force either to defend the entire tribe from outside forces or for expanding into the territories of weaker societies.

The pastoral Nuer of the southern Sudan are a good example of a tribal form of political organization (Evans-Pritchard 1940). The Nuer, who number approximately

APPLIED PERSPECTIVE
Are the Poarch Creek a Tribe?

*I*n the early 1970s, cultural anthropologist Anthony Paredes began his studies of the Poarch Creek, an obscure cultural group of American Indians located in southern Alabama and numbering about 500 people (1992). As a student of ethnohistory and social change, Paredes was interested in studying how the Poarch Creek had managed to maintain their Indian identity in the face of considerable intermarriage with non-Indians and the virtual disappearance of their language and culture. During the course of his initial investigations, which used the ethnographic methods of interviewing and participant-observation, Paredes learned that since the 1940s the Poarch Creek community had actually been pursuing ways of overcoming such long-standing problems as poverty, underemployment, poor education, and poor health. One very effective way of addressing these problems was to petition the federal government to become an officially recognized Indian tribe. If the Poarch Creek community was successful in its petition, it would be eligible for economic support from a number of government agencies.

Although the Poarch Creek had begun petitioning for federal recognition before Paredes entered the community, the research (both ethnographic and archival) that Paredes conducted turned out to have a very practical use in addition to its scholarly value. The research was highly instrumental in the group's eventually successful petition for official recognition. To be successful in their claim, the Poarch Creek needed to demonstrate that they had maintained a continuous existence as a political unit with viable leadership that had authority over its members. A critical problem was the conspicuous information gap in the late 1800s. There were sufficient historical records of government dealings with the Poarch Creek during the first half of the nineteenth century and ample evidence of more recent times gained through ethnographic interviewing with living tribal members. The challenge facing Paredes was to fill in the historical record of the late-nineteenth and early-twentieth centuries through a combination of archival research and ethnographic/ethnohistorical methods.

300,000 people, have no centralized government and no government functionaries with coercive authority. Of course, there are influential men, but their influence stems more from their personal traits than from the force of elected or inherited office. The Nuer, who are highly egalitarian, do not readily accept authority beyond the elders of the family. Social control among the Nuer is maintained by segmentary lineages in that close kin are expected to come to the assistance of one another against more distantly related people.

CHIEFDOMS

As we have seen, in band and tribal societies local groups are economically and politically autonomous, authority is uncentralized, and populations tend to be generally egalitarian. Moreover, roles are unspecialized, populations are

In the early 1980s, Paredes was hired by the tribal council to conduct research in the National Archives in Washington, DC, and in the state archives in Montgomery, Alabama. Paredes helped reconstruct periods of tribal history by gathering bits and pieces of information from various government records including homestead files, obituaries, court cases, and various types of government correspondences. By locating historical materials, he was able to support, confirm, and amplify much of the data he had gained from interviewing his older tribal informants. In his own words, Paredes (1992:218) was "able to combine disparate bits of seemingly trivial information with data from ethnographic fieldwork to confirm informants' recollections and cast new light on community organization and leadership in an earlier era."

Thus, what started out as a general scholarly inquiry into the recent history of the Poarch Creek Indians turned out to have important practical implications. The information collected by anthropologist Paredes was used to buttress the tribe's petition to the Bureau of Indian Affairs (BIA) for official recognition by the federal government. This petition for official recognition, which met with success in 1984, has had far-reaching benefits for the Poarch Creek community. Within the first two years of being officially recognized, the tribal community received approximately $2 million from the BIA, the Indian Health Service, and other federal agencies for the purpose of supporting tribal government operations, a health center, education, a housing project, and law enforcement. With the help of a federally secured loan, the tribe has purchased a motel on a nearby interstate highway. According to Paredes, the tribe has become one of the major employers in the county. Thus, the scholarly research of one anthropologist, initially aimed at reconstructing the history of the Poarch Creek Indians of Alabama, turned out to have a very significant impact on the revitalization of this group of Native Americans.

QUESTIONS FOR FURTHER THOUGHT

1. Why was it important for the Poarch Creek community to receive official federal recognition?
2. Would recognition have been possible without the anthropological research conducted by Paredes?
3. How would you characterize the applied anthropological role that Paredes played in this case study?

small, and economies are largely subsistent in nature. But as societies become more complex—with larger and more specialized populations, more sophisticated technology, and growing surpluses—their need for more formal and permanent political structures increases. In such societies, known as **chiefdoms,** political authority is likely to reside with a single individual, acting alone or in conjunction with an advisory council.

Chiefdoms differ from bands and tribes in that chiefdoms integrate a number of local communities in a more formal and permanent way. Unlike bands and tribes, chiefdoms are made up of local communities that are not equal but rather differ from one another in terms of rank and status. Based on their genealogical proximity to the chiefs, nobles and commoners hold different levels of prestige and power. Chiefships are often hereditary, and the chief and his or her immediate kin constitute a social and political elite. Rarely are chiefdoms totally unified politically under a single chief; more often, they are composed of several political units, each headed by a chief.

Chiefdoms also differ from tribes and bands in that chiefs are centralized and permanent officials with higher rank, power, and authority than others in the society. Unlike band or tribal headmen or headwomen, chiefs usually have considerable power, authority, and, in some cases, wealth. Internal social disruptions are minimized in a chiefdom because the chief usually has authority to make judgments, punish wrongdoers, and settle disputes. Chiefs usually have the authority to distribute land to loyal subjects, recruit people into military service, and recruit laborers for public works projects. Chiefly authority is usually reinforced by certain alleged supernatural powers. Polynesian chiefs, for example, were believed to possess the supernatural power of *mana*, which lent a special type of credence to their authority.

Chiefs are also intimately related to the economic activities of their subjects through the redistributive system of economics (see Chapter 8). Subjects give food surpluses to the chief (not uncommonly at the chief's insistence), which are then redistributed by the chief through communal feasts and doles. This system of redistribution through a chief serves the obvious economic function of ensuring that no people in the society go hungry. It also serves the important political function of providing the people with a mechanism for expressing their loyalty and support for the chief.

Within the past 120 years, a number of societies with no former tradition of chiefs have had chiefships imposed on them by some of the European colonial powers. As the European nations created their colonial empires during the nineteenth century, they created chiefs (or altered the nature of traditional chiefs) to facilitate administering local populations. For example, the British created chiefs for their own administrative convenience among chiefless societies in Nigeria, Kenya, and Australia. These new chiefs —who were given salaries and high-sounding titles such as "Paramount Chief"—were selected primarily on the basis of their willingness to work with the colonial administration rather than any particular popularity among their own people. In some cases, these new chiefs were held in contempt by their own people because they were collaborators with the colonial governments, which were often viewed as repressive and coercive.

The precolonial Hawaiian political system of the eighteenth century embodied the features of a typical chiefdom. According to Elman Service (1975), Hawaiian society, covering eight islands, was layered into three basic social strata. At the apex of the social hierarchy were the *ali'i*, major chiefs believed to be direct descendants of the gods; their close relatives often served as advisors or bureaucrats under them. The second echelon, known as the *konohiki*, were less important chiefs who were often distant relatives of the ali'i. And finally, the great majority of people were commoners, known as *maka'ainana*. Because there was little or no intermarriage among these three strata, the society was castelike. But because the *ali'i* had certain priestly functions by virtue of their connection with the gods, Hawaiian society was a theocracy as well.

The Hawaiian economy during the precolonial period was based on intensive agriculture (taro, breadfruit, yams, and coconuts) with extensive irrigation. Because of their control over the allocation of water, the major chiefs and their subordinates wielded considerable power and authority over the general population. In addition, chiefs were in control of communal labor, artisans, and gathering people for war. Hawaiian chiefs could also bring considerable coercive power to bear on disputants to encourage them to settle their quarrels, although in actual practice most disputes were settled through collective action. In summary, the precolonial Hawaiian political system, according to Service,

> was a theocracy, held together by an ideology that justified and sanctified the rule of the hereditary aristocracy, buttressed by age-old custom and etiquette. Such a system is in some contrast to a primitive state, which, although it attempts to rule ideologically and customarily, has had to erect the additional support of a monopoly of force with a legal structure that administers the force. (1975:154)

STATE SYSTEMS

The **state system of government** is the most formal and most complex form of political organization. A state can be defined as a hierarchical form of political organization that governs many communities within a large geographic area. States possess the power to collect taxes, can recruit labor for armies and civilian public works projects, and have a monopoly on the right to use force. They are large bureaucratic organizations made up of permanent institutions with legislative, administrative, and judicial functions. Whereas bands and tribes have political structures based on kinship, state systems of government organize their power on a suprakinship basis. That is, a person's membership in a state is based on his or her place of residence and

State systems of government are characterized by a high degree of role specialization and a hierarchical organization. Many of these specialized political roles are played out in parliament buildings such as this one in Ottowa, Canada.

citizenship rather than on kinship affiliation. Over the past several thousand years, state systems of government have taken various forms, including Greek city-states; the far-reaching Roman Empire; certain traditional African states such as Bunyoro, Buganda, and the Swazi; theocratic states such as ancient Egypt; and such modern nation-states as Germany, Japan, Canada, and the United States.

The authority of the state rests on two important foundations. First, the state holds the exclusive right to use force and physical coercion. Any act of violence not expressly permitted by the state is illegal and, consequently, punishable by the state. Thus, state governments make written laws, administer them through various levels of the bureaucracy, and enforce them through such mechanisms as police forces, armies, and national guards. The state needs to be continuously vigilant against threats both from within and from without to usurp its power through rebellions and revolutions. Second, the state maintains its authority by means of ideology. For the state to maintain its power over the long run, there must be a philosophical understanding among the citizenry that the state has the legitimate right to govern. In the absence of such an ideology, it is often difficult for the state to maintain its authority by means of coercion alone.

State systems of government, which first appeared about 5,500 years ago, are associated with civilizations. Thus, they are found in societies with complex socioeconomic characteristics. For example, state systems of government are supported by intensive agriculture, which is required to support a large number of bureaucrats who are not producing food. This fully efficient food production system gives rise to cities, considerable labor specialization, and a complex system of internal distribution and foreign trade. Because the considerable surpluses produced by intensive agriculture are not distributed equally among all segments of the population, state societies are stratified. That is, such forms of wealth as land and capital tend to be concentrated in the hands of an elite, who often use their superior wealth and power to control the rest of the population. Moreover, the fairly complex laws and regulations needed to control a large and heterogeneous population give rise to the need for some type of writing, record keeping, and weights and measures.

State systems of government are characterized by a large number of **specialized political roles.** Many people are required to carry out very specific tasks such as law enforcement, tax collection, dispute settlement, recruitment of labor, and protection from outside invasions. These political/administrative functionaries are highly specialized and work full time to the extent that they do not engage in food-producing activities. These permanent political functionaries, like the society itself, are highly stratified or hierarchical. At the apex of the administrative pyramid are those with the greatest power—kings, presidents, prime ministers, governors, and legislators—who enact laws and establish policies. Below them are descending echelons of bureaucrats responsible for the day-to-day administration of the state. As is the case in our own form of government, each level of the bureaucracy is responsible to the level immediately above it.

In recent times the word *state* has often been combined with the word *nation* to form the entity called a *nation-state*. Although these two words are often used interchangeably in everyday conversation, they are two quite distinct concepts. A **nation** is a group of people who share

= *Even though these people live in the nation-state of Tanzania, they tend to identify themselves more as members of an ethnic group than as Tanzanians.*

a common symbolic identity, culture, history, and often, religion. A **state,** on the other hand, is a particular type of political structure distinct from a band, tribal society, or chiefdom. When combined, the term *nation-state* refers to a group of people sharing a common cultural background and unified by a political structure that they all consider to be legitimate.

Although this is a fairly tidy definition, few of the nearly 200 so-called nation-states in the world today actually fit the definition. This is largely because few such entities actually have populations with homogeneous cultural identities. For example, the country of Great Britain, which has been in existence for centuries, comprises England, Wales, Ireland, and Scotland. We sometimes refer to Great Britain as England, but the Welsh, Irish, and Scots clearly do not regard themselves as English in terms of language, tradition, or ethnicity. The collapse of the Soviet Union in recent years has given rise to a dozen new nation-states including Belarus, Ukraine, Georgia, Azerbaijan, and Moldova. And, of course, many of the newly independent African nation-states represented in the United Nations since the 1960s have enormous ethnic heterogeneity. To illustrate, the country of Tanzania comprises approximately 120 different ethnic groups, all of which speak languages that are mutually unintelligible. Thus, even after more than three decades of living in a nation-state, the people of Tanzania tend to identify themselves more as Masai, Wazaramo, or Wachagga than as Tanzanians.

VARIATIONS IN POLITICAL STRUCTURES

The preceding sections have looked at four fundamentally different types of political systems. Such a fourfold scheme, although recognized by other anthropologists, is not universally accepted. For example, in a classic study of political systems in Africa, Meyer Fortes and E. E. Evans-Pritchard (1940) distinguish between only two types of structures: state systems and **acephalous** (headless) **soci-**

CROSS-CULTURAL MISCUE

EVEN WORLD LEADERS sometimes send unintentional nonverbal messages. As his motorcade passed a group of protesters in Canberra, Australia, in 1992, U.S. President George Bush held up his middle and forefingers with the back of his hand toward the protesters. He thought that he was giving the "V for victory" gesture but failed to realize that in Australia that hand gesture is the same as holding up the middle finger in the United States.

eties. Others (Cohen and Eames 1982) recognize three major forms of political structure: simple, intermediate, and complex. Such differences in the way various ethnologists have conceptualized political structures should serve as a reminder that all of these schemes are ideal types. That is, all of the societies in the world cannot be fit neatly into one box or another. Instead of discrete categories, in reality there is a continuum with bands (the simplest forms) at one extreme and states (the most complex forms) at the other. Thus, whether we use two, three, or four major categories of political organization, we should bear in mind that all political systems found in the world vary along a continuum on a number of important dimensions. To illustrate, as we move from bands through tribes and chiefdoms to states, gradations occur, as shown in Figure 12-1. These variations in political structures are accompanied by corresponding variations in other aspects of the cultures, as shown in Figure 12-2.

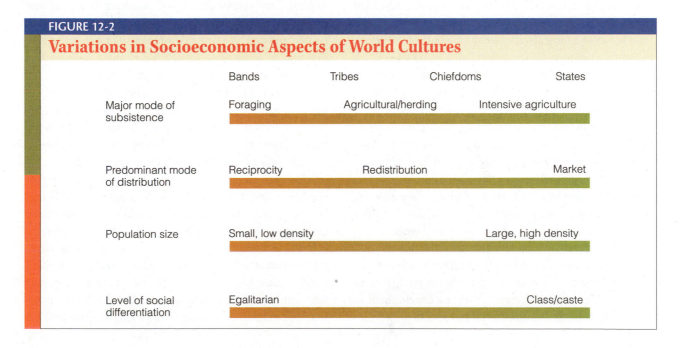

FIGURE 12-1

Variations in Political Aspects of World Cultures

	Bands	Tribes	Chiefdoms	States
Degree to which political institutions are distinct from kinship	Indistinguishable			Distinct
Level of political integration	Local group			Many groups
Specialized political roles	Informal leadership			Highly specialized
	Temporary			Permanent
Degree of political coerciveness	Little/none			Complete

FIGURE 12-2

Variations in Socioeconomic Aspects of World Cultures

	Bands	Tribes	Chiefdoms	States
Major mode of subsistence	Foraging	Agricultural/herding	Intensive agriculture	
Predominant mode of distribution	Reciprocity	Redistribution		Market
Population size	Small, low density			Large, high density
Level of social differentiation	Egalitarian			Class/caste

For the overwhelming majority of their existence, humans have lived in small food-collecting bands characterized by little or no political integration and few, if any, specialized political roles. Not until the neolithic revolution (domestication of plants and animals) occurred approximately 10,000 years ago were socioeconomic forces unleashed that permitted the formation of larger, more complex sociopolitical systems. With the new food-producing technologies brought in with the neolithic revolution, populations have become larger and more heterogeneous, and as a result, political organizations have become increasingly complex and centralized. Today, state systems of government predominate in the world, whereas small-scale band societies account for a very small (and decreasing) percentage of the world's societies.

Although the rise of state systems of government was clearly a significant development, there is little consensus on why these complex forms of government emerged. By examining both ancient and contemporary societies, anthropologists and social philosophers have developed a number of explanations as to why some societies have developed state systems whereas others have not. Explanations for the rise of the state hinge on the question of what induces people to surrender at least a portion of their autonomy to the power and control of the state. Some theories suggest that people purposefully and voluntarily gave up their sovereignty because of the perceived benefits. That is, these theorists reason that the limited loss of autonomy was outweighed by the benefits people derived from their integration into a wider political structure. These benefits included greater protection from hostile outside forces, more effective means of conflict resolution, and the opportunity for increased food production.

A good example of this **voluntaristic theory of state formation** was put forth by archaeologist V. Gordon Childe. According to Childe (1936), the introduction and development of intensive agriculture (stimulated by the introduction of the plow, irrigation, metallurgy, and draft animals) during the neolithic period created food surpluses. These food surpluses, in turn, freed up a certain segment of the population from tasks of food production, allowing them to engage in a wide variety of new occupational roles, such as weavers, traders, potters, and metalworkers. This dramatic increase in occupational specialization necessitated a wider form of political integration to mediate between and protect the varied special interest groups and to provide the economic superstructure to enable them to work in an efficient and complementary fashion.

Another voluntaristic explanation of the emergence of the state is the **hydraulic theory of state formation,** suggested by Karl Wittfogel. According to this theory (Wittfogel 1957), small-scale irrigation farmers in arid or semiarid areas eventually came to see certain economic advantages to surrendering their autonomy and merging their small communities into a larger political entity capable of large-scale irrigation. Even though archaeological evidence indicates that certain states (such as China, Mexico, and Mesopotamia) developed before the introduction of large-scale irrigation, centralized political governments do appear to be functional for agricultural systems dependent on irrigation.

Still another theory of state origins, set forth by Robert Carneiro (1970), suggests that the existence of the state is the direct result of warfare. Offering a **coercive theory of state formation,** Carneiro holds that "force, and not enlightened self interest, is the mechanism by which political evolution has led, step by step, from autonomous villages to the state" (1970:217). Carneiro elaborates that although warfare is the mechanism of state formation, it operates only under certain environmental conditions—namely, in areas that have limited agricultural land for expanding populations. To illustrate his theory, Carneiro uses the case of the Inca state that developed in the narrow valleys of the Peruvian coast, which were geographically circumscribed in that the valleys faced the ocean, backed up to the mountains, and were flanked on either end by deserts. As populations grew in this region, there was no land into which to expand. Land pressure increased, resulting in intense land competition and eventually warfare. Increasingly more centralized political units developed to conduct the warfare and to administer subjugated peoples. Villages that lost wars became subjugated populations, whereas the victors headed up increasingly larger and more complex warring political units. Carneiro (1970) claims that similar political evolution occurred in other parts of the world characterized by circumscribed agricultural land such as the Nile Valley, Mesopotamia, and the Indus Valley.

Whatever caused the rise of state systems of government—and there were, no doubt, a number of different causes in different parts of the world—state systems of government have certainly changed over the millennia. One major change, particularly evident during the twentieth century, has been the democratization of many nation-states. During much of the twentieth century, governments could (and many did) control the flow of information available to the citizenry, thereby severely limiting popular participation in government. People were given only that information that the government deemed necessary. As long as governments could control the content of newspapers and radio and television broadcasts, the citizenry was prevented from hearing alternative views and opinions. Since the early 1990s, however, with the widespread use of the Internet, governments can no longer control the flow of information. This free flow of information is perhaps the biggest threat to despotic nation-states. To illustrate, Thomas Friedman (1999) reminds us that during the 1980s, *Pravda,* the official government newspaper of the Soviet Union, published pictures of food lines in New York City as an indicator of poverty in the capitalistic West. In actual fact these food lines turned out to be New Yorkers waiting in line to purchase their designer pastries and coffee at Zabar's, a fashionable, upscale food store on the Upper West Side of Manhattan! Such blatant campaigns of misinformation are no longer possible with the relatively free access of information over the Internet. Because information is no longer filtered by the government-controlled media, power is beginning to pass from potentially repressive governments to the general citizenry.

In those nation-states with relatively unencumbered access to the Internet, the information revolution in general—and the Internet specifically—is significantly impacting the political and electoral processes. As we approach the 2000 presidential elections, politicians have access to computer-generated mailing lists. They can become much more efficient in campaign fundraising by using certain computer programs that can identify potential donors on the basis of large databases. The Internet is a cost-effective way of disseminating information about their candidacy as well as recruiting and mobilizing their supporters. In the past, an election could be (and usually was) decided by the number and effectiveness of the TV commercials a candidate could purchase. Such a system clearly worked to the advantage of those candidates with the most money. With widespread accessibility of the Internet, however, candidates can get their message across for a fraction of the cost of television ads. Thus, it is possible that the most successful candidates in the future will be those with the most creative web masters. And if the recent past is an accurate indicator, the Internet will have an important influence on future elections. According to a postelectoral survey conducted after the 1996 elections, approximately 9 percent of the U.S. electorate (over 8 million voters) indicated that their choice of candidates was influenced by information from the Internet (Henschen

and Sidlow, 1999). As its use becomes even more widespread, the Internet will be even more influential in the electoral process.

•■ SOCIAL CONTROL ■•

AS THE PREVIOUS SECTION explained, political structures vary from very informal structures such as bands at one extreme to highly complex state systems of government at the other extreme. Whatever form of political organization is found in a society, it must inevitably address the issue of **social control.** In other words, every society must ensure that most of the people behave themselves in appropriate ways most of the time. Statelike societies, such as our own, have a wide variety of formalized mechanisms that function to keep people's behavior in line, including written laws, judges, bureaucracies, prisons, electric chairs, and police forces. At the other extreme, small-scale band societies, such as the Inuit or !Kung, have no centralized political authority but nevertheless maintain social order among their members quite effectively through informal mechanisms of social control. In fact, people deviate from acceptable behavior considerably less in most band societies than in societies with more elaborate and complex forms of political organization.

Every society has defined what are normal, proper, or expected ways of behaving. These expectations, known as **social norms,** serve as behavioral guidelines and help the society work smoothly. To be certain, social norms are not adhered to perfectly, and, in fact, there is always a certain level of deviance from them (see Freilich et al. 1990). But most people in any given society abide by them most of the time. Moreover, social norms take a number of different forms—ranging from etiquette to formal laws. Some norms are taken more seriously than others. On one hand, all societies have certain social expectations of what is proper, but such behavior is not rigidly enforced. To illustrate, although it is customary in the United States for people to shake hands when being introduced, a person's refusal to shake hands does not constitute a serious violation of social norms. The person who does not follow this rule of etiquette might be considered rude but would not be arrested or executed. At the other extreme, certain social norms (such as grand larceny or murder) are taken very seriously because they are considered absolutely necessary for the survival of the society.

Social scientists use the term **deviance** to refer to the violation of social norms. However, it is important to keep in mind that deviance is relative. Whatever people in one culture consider to be a deviant act is not necessarily considered to be a deviant act by people in other cultures. In other words, it is not the act itself but rather how people define the act that determines whether it is deviant. To illustrate, suicide among middle-class North Americans is considered to be unacceptable under any conditions. In traditional Japan, however, the practice of *hara-kiri,* committing ritual suicide by disembowelment, was considered in traditional times the honorable thing to do for a disgraced nobleman. Thus, whereas ritual suicide was normative for the Japanese nobleman, it is considered very deviant by the standards of a businessperson in Montreal or Miami.

All social norms, whether trivial or serious, are sanctioned. That is, societies develop patterned or institutionalized ways of encouraging people to conform to the norms. These **sanctions** are both positive and negative, for people are rewarded for behaving in socially acceptable ways and punished for violating the norms. **Positive sanctions** range from a smile of approval to being awarded the Congressional Medal of Honor. **Negative sanctions** include everything from a frown of disapproval to corporal punishment.

Social sanctions may also be formal or informal, depending on whether a formal law (legal statute) has been violated. To illustrate, if a woman in a restaurant is talking in a voice that can be easily overheard by people at nearby tables, she will probably receive stares from the other diners. But if she starts yelling at the top of her lungs in the restaurant, she will probably be arrested for disturbing the peace or disorderly conduct. The difference, of course, is that in the first case the woman wasn't breaking the law, but in the second case she was. Figure 12-3 illustrates a continuum of the formal–informal dimension of social norms and sanctions in U.S. society.

Just as the types of social norms found in any society vary, so do the mechanisms used to encourage people to adhere to those norms. For most North Americans, the most obvious forms of social control are the formal or institutionalized ones. When asked why we tend to behave ourselves, we would probably think of formal laws, police forces, courts, and prisons. We don't rob the local convenience store, in other words, because if caught, we are likely to go to prison.

Most of our "proper" behavior is probably caused by less formal, and perhaps less obvious, mechanisms of social control. In band and tribal societies that lack centralized authority, informal mechanisms of social control may be all that exists. The remainder of this chapter looks at the informal mechanisms of social control so characteristic of band and tribal societies and at more formal institutions aimed primarily at social control, some of which involve

= *The recognition by the state of meritorious conduct serves as a positive sanction.*

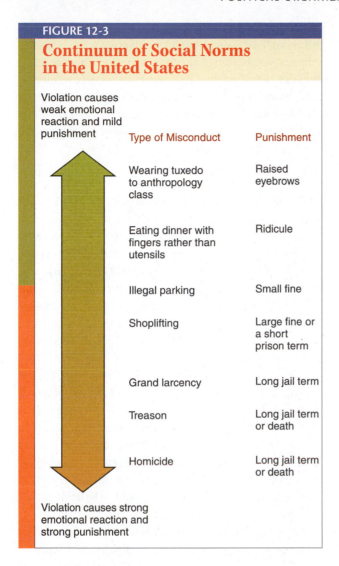

FIGURE 12-3

Continuum of Social Norms in the United States

Violation causes weak emotional reaction and mild punishment

Type of Misconduct	Punishment
Wearing tuxedo to anthropology class	Raised eyebrows
Eating dinner with fingers rather than utensils	Ridicule
Illegal parking	Small fine
Shoplifting	Large fine or a short prison term
Grand larceny	Long jail term
Treason	Long jail term or death
Homicide	Long jail term or death

Violation causes strong emotional reaction and strong punishment

laws and adjudicating bodies. It should be emphasized, however, that this distinction between formal and informal mechanisms should in no way imply that informal means of social control exist only in band and tribal societies. Although societies with complex political organizations (state societies in particular) are best known for written laws and courts, they also rely on an appreciable number of informal mechanisms of social control.

INFORMAL MEANS OF SOCIAL CONTROL

Compared to complex state organizations, bands and tribes have little in the way that appears to be governmental in the Western sense of the term. They include very low levels of political integration, few (if any) specialized political roles, and little **political coerciveness.** These small-scale political systems have been called acephalous (that is, headless) or "tribes without rulers" (Middleton and Tait

1958). In the absence of formal government structures, how do these acephalous societies maintain social order? The following subsections examine a number of informal mechanisms of social control that not only operate in acephalous societies but in many cases also operate in more complex societies.

Socialization

Every society, if it is to survive, must pass on its social norms from one generation to another. It seems obvious that people cannot conform to the social norms unless they are taught them. Thus, all societies have some system of **socialization,** which involves teaching the young what the norms are as well as teaching that these norms—because they are inherently proper—should not be violated. People learn their social norms with a certain degree of moral compulsion. We learn, for example, that in North America people wear clothes in public and that we should as well. Usually, we internalize our social norms so effectively that we would never consider violating them. Some social norms—such as not appearing nude in public—are so thoroughly ingrained in us through socialization that the thought of violating them would be distasteful and embarrassing. Other social norms do not have the same level of moral intensity, such as driving within the speed limit or maintaining good oral hygiene. But as a general rule, when people learn their norms, they are at the same time internalizing the moral necessity to obey them.

Public Opinion

One of the most compelling reasons for not violating the social norms is **public opinion** or social pressure. In general, people from all parts of the world wish to be accepted by the other members of their society. Most people fear being rejected or talked about by their friends or neighbors. This strong desire to win the approval of other members of one's society is summed up in such comments as, "Don't do that! What will the neighbors think?" Of course, it is impossible to determine how many people are deterred from violating the social norms because of fear of negative public opinion. At the same time, we can cite many examples of how societies use social pressure very deliberately to keep people in line. Indeed, gossip, ostracism, rumor, sarcasm, and derision are all powerful corrective measures for reforming social behavior. For example, city and county governments in the United States print the names of tax delinquents in the local newspaper in an attempt to embarrass them into paying their taxes. In colonial America, the stock and pillory was an excellent example of how the society used public opinion to control people's behavior. Someone who was caught breaking the social norms (such as committing adultery or stealing) was confined to the stock and pillory, which, not coincidentally, was always located right in the center of town. Even though long confinements in the stock and pillory were physically very uncomfortable, the realization that all of your friends, relatives, and neighbors would see you and know of your crime was by far the greater punishment.

In some societies, when someone strays too far from acceptable behavior, the group takes very explicit steps to indelibly brand the person as a deviant. The character Hester Prynne from Hawthorne's *Scarlet Letter* had a large red *A* sewn to her dress to identify her as an adulteress to the rest of the community. Military officers found guilty in a court marshall are often ceremoniously stripped of their insignia of rank in a public display of humiliation. Harold Garfinkle (1956) has used the term **degradation ceremonies** to refer to these formal societal mechanisms to publicly humiliate a deviant.

The deliberate use of social pressure to maintain social control is particularly important and, in some cases, quite dramatic in acephalous societies. A case in point is the custom of the duel found in Tiwi society of North Australia (Hart and Pilling 1960). Men in traditional Tiwi society achieve power and status by amassing large numbers of wives. Under such conditions of intense polygyny, all females are married or betrothed before or at birth, but men do not take their first wives until their late 30s or early 40s. Thus, at any given moment in time, all women are married to older men.

If a younger Tiwi male (say, one in his 20s) is to have any intimate relations with a Tiwi woman, it must, by definition, be with an older man's wife. When this occurs, the older man challenges the young adulterer to a duel, which, like the use of the stock and pillory, is always public. All the people in the community (men, women, and children) form a circle in an open field, surrounding the older man and the accused adulterer. With the entire community watching, the older man throws spears at the younger man, along with a string of verbal insults. The younger man is expected to submit himself to this verbal harangue while sidestepping the spears. But before the event can end, the younger man must allow one of the spears to strike him, it is hoped in a nonvulnerable place.

The key to understanding the Tiwi duel is its public nature. Even though the guilty party suffers some physical punishment (the superficial wound), the real punishment is the public disapproval of the younger man's behavior by all of the onlookers. The Tiwi duel, in other words, is an institutionalized form of public humiliation whereby public opinion is mobilized in an attempt to reform unacceptable behavior. The Tiwi duel is a particularly effective mechanism of social control because it not only helps to reform the behavior of the accused but also serves as a reminder to all of the other members of the community who might want to violate the social norms.

Corporate Lineages

Corporate lineages play a dominant role in most small-scale (acephalous) societies. Members of corporate lineages (who can number in the hundreds) often live, work, play, and pray together. Property is controlled by the lineage, people derive their primary identity from the group, and even religion (in the form of ancestor worship) is a lineage matter. Acting like a small corporation, the lineage has a powerful impact on the everyday lives of its members and can exert considerable pressure on people to conform to the social norms.

One means by which corporate lineages exert control over its members is economic. All important property, such as land and livestock, is controlled by the elders of the corporate lineage. Often property is allocated on the basis of conformity to societal norms. Those who behave as the society expects them to behave are likely to receive the best plots of land and use of the best livestock. Conversely, those who violate social norms are likely to be denied these valuable economic resources.

Corporate lineages, to some degree, also act as mechanisms of social control because of their scale. Corporate lineages serve as localized communities, numbering from several hundred to several thousand relatives. Because members of the lineage have frequent and intense interaction with one another on a daily basis, it is virtually impossible for anyone to maintain her or his anonymity. People's lives are played out in such close proximity to one another that everyone knows what everyone else is doing. To illustrate, a man who wants to engage in socially inappropriate behavior (such as having an extramarital affair) would think twice because it would be difficult, if not impossible, to keep it a secret. By way of contrast, it is considerably easier to have an extramarital affair and remain undetected in a large city. Thus, the small-scale nature of corporate lineage communities tends to inhibit social deviance because it is much more difficult to get away with it.

The way roles are structured in corporate lineage societies also contributes to social control. In terms of role structure, corporate lineages have what Talcott Parsons and Edward Shils (1952) call "diffuse roles." People play social roles in a number of different domains, such as kinship, economic, political, ritual/religious, and recreational roles. A role is diffuse when it ranges over two or more of these domains. For example, a diffuse role structure occurs when a man's grandfather (kinship role) is also his teacher (educational role), his priest (religious role), the local chief (political role), and his hunting partner (economic role). The man, in other words, has a number of overlapping roles; he is playing roles from a number of different domains with the same person. In contrast, roles in large-scale, complex societies such as our own tend to be segmented or narrowly defined so that single roles are played out with one person at a time. People in corporate lineage societies (with diffuse or overlapping roles) have a built-in incentive not to violate the social norms, for to do so would have very serious consequences. If the man in the preceding illustration offends his grandfather, he is not only negatively affecting his kinship domain but is also affecting the educational, economic, political, and religious domains.

Marriage in corporate lineage societies tends to be highly collective. That is, marriage in such societies is regarded primarily as an alliance between two lineages—that of the bride and that of the groom—and only secondarily as a union between individuals. In many cases, the marriage is legitimized by bridewealth (the transfer of property, often livestock, from the kin group of the groom to the kin group of the bride). When a man wants to get married, he cannot pay the bridewealth himself because he does not have personal control over property. Like the rest of his relatives, he has limited rights and obligations to such pieces of property as cattle. If marriage cattle are to be transferred from one lineage to another, a group decision must be made. For example, if eight cows must be given to the prospective bride's family before the marriage can be legitimate, the prospective groom must convince a number of his kin to give up their limited use of cows. If the prospective groom has a reputation for violating the social norms, it is likely that the permission to transfer the cows will be withheld. Thus, the members of a corporate lineage, through their collective capacity to control marriage, have considerable power to coerce people into appropriate behavior.

Supernatural Belief Systems

A powerful mechanism of social control in acephalous societies is **supernatural belief systems**—belief in supernatural forces such as gods, witches, and sorcerers. People will refrain from antisocial behavior if they believe that some supernatural (suprahuman) force will punish them for it. Of course, it is impossible to determine how many norms are not violated because people fear supernatural retribution, but we have to assume that the belief in supernatural sanctions acts as a deterrent to some degree. Nor is it necessary to prove that the gods, for example, will punish the social deviants. If people believe that "god will get them" for doing something wrong, the belief itself is usually enough to discourage the deviant behavior. This is certainly the case in Western religions (Judeo-Christian), which teach about atonement for one's sins, Judgment Day, and heaven and hell. In small-scale societies there are other forms of supernatural belief systems (such as ancestor worship, witchcraft, and sorcery), which are equally effective social mechanisms for controlling peoples' behavior.

ANCESTOR WORSHIP **Ancestor worship** is a form of supernatural belief that serves as an effective means of social control in some acephalous societies. In such societies, dead ancestors are considered fully functioning members of the descent group. In fact, the death of a respected elder marks that person's elevation in status to supernatural being rather than his or her departure from the group. Respect for the ancestor-gods is often demonstrated by

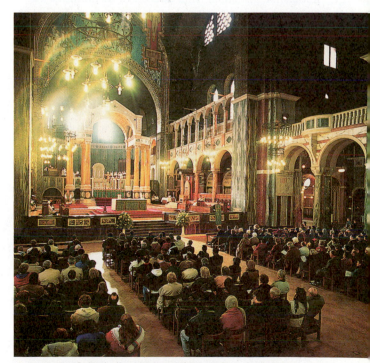

= *Many people, including these worshippers from a Western Christian church, tend to conform to social norms out of a strong belief in supernatural forces.*

sacrifices and proper behavior, for which the living members are believed to be rewarded or punished, depending on how well they meet these obligations.

The Lugbara society of Uganda provides a good example of ancestor worship. According to John Middleton (1965), the well-being of the entire kinship group is ensured only if people behave in socially appropriate ways. The Lugbara believe that personal and group tragedies are a direct result of the transgression of certain social norms, such as showing disrespect to living and dead elders, adultery, incest, assault, or homicide.

The Lugbara generally believe that the ancestor-gods inflict with illness the living kin who endanger the well-being of the lineage by committing any of these offenses. Sickness of any type is explained in terms of ancestral displeasure with the conduct of the living. Thus, sickness (resulting from sin) is followed by either ghost invocation or ghostly vengeance. In **ghost invocation,** a living man—typically an elder—calls forth the wrath of the ancestor-gods against the sinner. **Ghostly vengeance** is the belief that ancestor-gods inflict sickness on their own without having to be invoked.

Whether ancestral ghosts in traditional Lugbara society were directly responsible for sickness among the living is perhaps of greater interest to the theologian than to the anthropologist. What is of interest to the anthropologist, however, is the effects of the belief on the behavior of the living, for it is the belief that has implications for social control rather than its ability to undergo scientific verification. Such rites as ghostly invocation give regular expression to fears of supernatural retribution, which in turn control, or at least influence, a person's conduct.

WITCHCRAFT The belief in **witchcraft,** which is common in acephalous societies, also functions to control people's behavior by discouraging socially deviant behavior. In many societies where witchcraft is practiced, people reject the idea that misfortunes are the result of natural causes. If crops fail or large numbers of people die, the usual explanation is that someone has been practicing witchcraft. In societies that believe in witchcraft, a deviant runs the risk of being labeled a witch, and fear of being accused of witchcraft strongly encourages conformity. For example, in colonial America, nonconformists, freethinkers, and others who didn't conform to expected behavioral norms were driven from their communities for allegedly being witches. Jean La Fontaine notes the way witchcraft serves as a mechanism of social control among the Bantu-speaking Bagisu of East Africa:

Witchcraft beliefs act as a form of social control in discouraging behavior that is socially unacceptable. In Bagisu the eccentric is branded a witch. . . . Children grow up with the realization that the stigma of nonconformity is dangerous; too great a departure from the norms of everyday conduct will attract the suspicion of others and lead to isolation and eventual destruction. (1963:217)

Often a witch is identified by a ritual specialist, called a **shaman,** who is believed to have clairvoyant powers. By putting him- or herself into an altered state of consciousness, the shaman reveals the name of the witch who is causing the bad things to happen. The community then takes action, sometimes murder, to rid itself of the troublemaker. Although it might appear, particularly to Westerners who do not generally believe in witchcraft, that innocent people can be falsely accused and punished for being witches, the shaman does not act arbitrarily or capriciously. Even though shamans do make indictments by virtue of their alleged supernatural powers, they are heavily influenced by public opinion. Long before making an accusation of witchcraft, the shaman will have gathered opinions about the suspected culprit from members of the community. In most cases the accused will be unpopular, have a history of disputes with neighbors, and have a weak network of kinsmen. In many respects the shaman collects a good deal of information, makes some informed deductions, and ultimately expresses the will of the community. In effect, the job of the shaman in identifying the witch is as much social as it is supernatural.

Age Organizations

In some acephalous societies, **age organizations** serve as effective means of social control. Societies with age organizations have distinct groups of people passing periodically through distinct age categories (Figure 12-4). This involves the basic distinction that cultural anthropologists make between age sets and age grades. An **age set** is a group of people (usually men) initiated during a periodic ceremony and having a strong sense of group identity with one another. An age set lasts from its inception, usually when most members are late adolescents, until its last member has died. Age sets pass (as a group) through successive categories, called **age grades,** such as warriors, elders, or various subdivisions of these grades. Each age grade is associated with a well-understood set of social roles (that is, they perform exclusive functions) and statuses (that is, higher prestige is associated with increasing age). To illustrate this distinction further, an age set is analogous to a group of students who go through

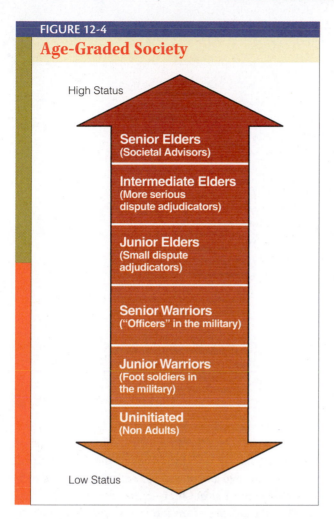

FIGURE 12-4

Age-Graded Society

High Status

Senior Elders
(Societal Advisors)

Intermediate Elders
(More serious
dispute adjudicators)

Junior Elders
(Small dispute
adjudicators)

Senior Warriors
("Officers" in the military)

Junior Warriors
(Foot soldiers in
the military)

Uninitiated
(Non Adults)

Low Status

passage are almost always preceded by intense periods of training in the norms and values of the society. These periods of intense socialization teach the soon-to-become adults not only the expected behaviors but also why the behaviors should be followed and the penalties for deviation.

Third, the bonds of camaraderie that exist among members of the same age set are usually so strong that age sets tend to take on the characteristics of a corporate group. Age-set members who have experienced their initiation ceremonies together support one another throughout the remainder of their lives in much the same way as do members of the same lineage.

Unlike lineages, age sets are neither self-perpetuating nor property owning, but they exert the same type of pressure to conform on their members as lineages do on theirs.

FORMAL MEANS OF SOCIAL CONTROL

As previously noted, all societies use informal mechanisms of social control to some degree. Western cultures rely heavily on such mechanisms as socialization, public opinion, and supernatural sanctions to encourage people to maintain social order by behaving appropriately. Often these informal mechanisms of social control are not sufficient to maintain the desired level of conformity to the norms. The violation of social norms often results in disputes among people in the society. When such disputes become violent conflicts (such as theft, assault, or homicide), we call them crimes. Because societies face the possibility of violent conflict erupting among their members, they need to develop explicit mechanisms to address and, it is hoped, resolve the conflicts.

Although no society in the world is immune from **crime,** the incidence of crime varies considerably from society to society. It appears that crime is more likely to occur in large, heterogeneous, stratified societies than in small-scale societies. For example, the crime rate in U.S. cities is approximately 10 times as high as in rural areas. Several logical arguments support these findings. First, as mentioned in the discussion of corporate lineages, people in small-scale societies have little or no anonymity, which makes getting away with a crime more difficult. Second, because people in small-scale societies know most of the other people, they are more likely to be concerned with negative public opinion. Third, the heterogeneous character of populations in large-scale, complex societies means that there will be a number of groups with different, and probably conflicting, interests. Finally, the fact that large-scale societies are almost always stratified into classes or

college together. The academic grades through which they pass—that is, freshman through senior—are comparable to the age grades. Thus, we can speak of a particular age set occupying the senior warrior grade at a particular moment.

Age organizations control behavior in a number of significant ways. First, because age organizations establish a clear set of roles and statuses, they are particularly effective as channels for the distribution of authority. Because men of every age grade have well-defined and well-understood roles, there is little room for infringing on the authority or domain of others. There is little incentive, in other words, to try to usurp the authority of those above you for the simple reason that if you live long enough, you will eventually have that authority by virtue of your own advanced age.

Second, individuals enter the age-set system at the lowest echelon through the process of initiation. These rites of

CROSS-CULTURAL MISCUE

HAND GESTURES, like other forms of nonverbal communication, can change the meaning of our words as well as carry meanings totally by themselves. Unless we understand the meanings attached to certain hand gestures in different cultures, we are likely to send and receive unintended messages when dealing with people from other cultures. When two ordinary citizens from two different cultures miscommunicate through hand gestures, the result can be embarrassment or hard feelings. When a country's leader sends an unintended message, however, it can lead to an international incident. This was dramatically illustrated with the now famous clapsed-hands-over-the-head gesture used by Soviet Premier Khrushchev when visiting the United States in the 1960s. This gesture, which for Russians is a sign of international brotherhood, was interpreted by most Americans as an arrogant gesture usually used by prizefighters after defeating an opponent. This cross-cultural *faux pas* did little to improve U.S.–Soviet relations during the height of the Cold War.

castes means that certain segments (that is, the lower strata) of the population may feel blocked from upward mobility and consequently may be more likely to want to violate the rights of those in the more privileged strata.

Song Duels

Just as societies differ in terms of the incidence of crime, they also differ in the way they handle disputes and crimes. One example of a formal mechanism for resolving disputes was found among the Inuit of Canada, Alaska, and Greenland. Because the Inuit had little property because of their nomadic way of life, conflicts rarely arose over violation of property rights. However, disputes often arose between men over the issue of wife stealing. A man would attempt to steal the wife of a more prominent man as a way of elevating his own standing within the community.

A common way of resolving wife stealing among the Inuit was to murder the wife stealer. In fact, Knud Rasmussen (1927) found that all of the men he studied had been a party to a murder, either as the murderer or as an accessory, and invariably these murders stemmed from allegations of wife stealing. However, there were alternative resolutions to disputes over wife stealing. One alternative was to challenge the alleged wife stealer to a **song duel,** a derisive song contest, which was fought with song and lyrics rather than with weapons. The plaintiff and defendant, appearing in a public setting, would chide each other with abusive songs especially composed for the occasion. The contestant who received the loudest applause emerged the winner of this "curse by verse" song duel. In-

terestingly, the resolution of the conflict was based not on a determination of guilt or innocence but on one's verbal dexterity.

Intermediaries

Some societies use **intermediaries** to help resolve serious conflicts. The Nuer of the African Sudan are a case in point (Evans-Pritchard 1940). Even though the Nuer political system is informal and uncentralized, one role in the society—the **Leopard-skin Chief**—is, to a degree, institutionalized. In the absence of any formal system of law courts to punish serious crimes such as murder, the Leopard-skin Chief serves as a mediator between the victim's family and the family of the murderer. When a homicide occurs, the murderer, fearing the vengeance of the victim's family, takes sanctuary in the home of the Leopard-skin Chief. In an attempt to prevent an all-out feud, the Leopard-skin Chief attempts to negotiate a settlement between the two families. His role is to work out an equitable settlement between the two families whereby the murderer's family will compensate the victim's family with some form of property settlement (say, 40 head of cattle) for the loss of one of its members. These animals will be used as bridewealth for the lineage to obtain a wife for one of its members. It is thought that the sons from such a marriage will fill the void left by the murder victim.

If either side becomes too unyielding, the Leopard-skin Chief can threaten to curse the offending party. The Leopard-skin Chief does not decide the case, however. Rather, he is only an intermediary, with no authority to determine guilt or force a settlement between the parties. Intervening on behalf of the public interest, he uses his personal and supernatural influence to bring the disputing parties to some type of agreed-upon settlement of their dispute.

Moots: Informal Courts

Found in many African societies, moots serve as a highly effective mechanism for conflict resolution. **Moots** are informal airings of disputes involving kinsmen and friends of the litigants. These adjudicating bodies are ad hoc, with considerable variation in composition from case to case. Moots generally deal with the resolution of domestic disputes such as mistreating a spouse, disagreements over inheritance, or the nonpayment of debts owed to kin or neighbors.

Anthropologist James Gibbs (1963) describes in considerable detail the moot system as found among the Kpelle, a Mande-speaking group of rice cultivators living in Liberia and Guinea. Gibbs found that moots differ from the more formal court system that is administered by district chiefs in Kpelle society. First, unlike the more formal court system, moots are held in the homes of the complainant rather than in public places. Second, all parties concerned (elders, litigants, witnesses, and spectators) sit very close to one another in a random and mixed fashion. This is in marked contrast to more formalized courts, which physically separate the plaintiff, the defendant, and the judge. Third, because the range of relevance in moots is very broad, the airing of grievances is more complete than in formal courts of law. Fourth, whereas in formal courts the judge controls the conduct of the proceedings, in moots the investigation is more in the hands of the disputants themselves. Fifth, moots do not attempt to blame one party unilaterally but rather attribute fault in the dispute to both parties. Finally, the sanctions imposed by the moot are not so severe that the losing party has grounds for a new grudge against the other party. The party found to be at fault is assessed a small fine, is expected to give the wronged party a token gift, and is required to make a public apology.

Unlike more formal court systems—including those found in our own society—moots do not separate the guilty party from society by incarceration. Just the opposite is true. Moots attempt to reintegrate the guilty party back into the community, restore normal social relations between disputing parties, and achieve reconciliation without bitterness and acrimony. The ritualized apology given by the guilty party symbolizes the consensual nature of the resolution and its emphasis on healing the community rather than simply punishing the wrongdoer.

Oaths and Ordeals

Another way of resolving conflicts—particularly when law enforcement agencies (such as governments) are not especially strong—is through religiously sanctioned methods such as oaths and ordeals. An **oath** is a formal declaration to some supernatural force that what you are saying is truthful or that you are innocent. Although they can take many different forms, oaths almost always are accompanied by a ritual act, such as smoking a peace pipe, signing a loyalty document, or swearing upon the Bible (as in our courts of law). Because some believe that to swear a false oath could lead to supernatural retribution, oaths can be effective in determining guilt or innocence.

An **ordeal** is a means of determining guilt by submitting the accused to a dangerous test. If the person passes the test, it is believed that a higher supernatural force has determined the party's innocence; if he or she fails, the gods have signaled the party's guilt. Ordeal by drinking poison was found among the Ashanti in West Africa. If the accused vomited after drinking a poison concoction, the person was considered innocent; if the accused didn't vomit, he or she died and was therefore considered guilty.

It has been suggested (Roberts 1967; Meek 1972) that oaths and ordeals are most likely to be found in complex societies where the political leadership lacks the power to enforce judicial decisions; consequently, the leaders must rely on supernaturally sanctioned mechanisms such as oaths and ordeals to make certain that people will obey. Where political leaders wield greater power, oaths and ordeals are no longer needed.

Courts and Codified Law

A characteristic of state systems of government is that they possess a monopoly on the use of force. Through a system of codified laws, the state both forbids individuals from using force and determines how it will use force to require citizens to do some things and prevent them from doing others. These laws, which are usually in written form, are established by legislative bodies, interpreted by judicial bodies, and enforced by administrators. When legal prescriptions are violated, the state has the authority, through its courts and law enforcement agencies, to fine, imprison, or even execute the wrongdoer. To suggest that the state has a monopoly on the use of force does not mean that only the government uses force. State systems of government

Transforming New Guinea Customary Law Into a National Legal System

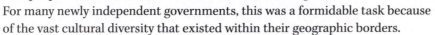

As a general rule, when Western governments administered their colonies during the nineteenth and twentieth centuries, they invariably imposed on local populations their own Western legal systems, which were often at odds with the local customary laws. As the colonial period came to an end during the 1960s and 1970s, many newly independent governments were faced with the need to develop a new national legal system that would be based on the customs and traditions of their own people rather than on those of the former colonial powers. For many newly independent governments, this was a formidable task because of the vast cultural diversity that existed within their geographic borders.

One such former colony was the country of Papua New Guinea, which won its independence in 1975. Papua New Guinea had a population of 3.5 million people who spoke approximately 750 mutually unintelligible languages and had at least as many customary legal systems (Scaglion 1987). Thus, the Papua New Guinea government was faced with the gargantuan twofold task of identifying the legal principles of these diverse customary legal systems and reconciling them into a new statewide legal system. To accomplish these tasks, the parliament established a Law Reform Commission, which, shortly after its own creation, sponsored the Customary Law Project. Headed by legal anthropologist Richard Scaglion, this project was designed to conduct research on local customary law so as to determine how and to what extent it might serve as the basis for a national legal system (Scaglion 1987).

As project director, Scaglion supervised a small cadre of local university students, who were fluent in the local languages and cultures. It was their job to collect original conflict case studies from which principles of customary law could be extracted. The primary data-gathering technique used in this project was the case method of legal anthropology first made popular by K. Llewellyn and E. A. Hoebel (1941) and later refined by Laura Nader (Nader and Todd 1978). The local student researchers collected approximately 600 detailed case

are constantly having to deal with unauthorized uses of force, such as crime (violent disputes between individuals or groups), **rebellion** (attempts to displace the people in power), and **revolution** (attempts to overthrow the entire system of government).

The system of codified laws used to resolve disputes and maintain social order in complex societies is distinct from other types of social norms. Legal anthropologist E. Adam-

son Hoebel (1972) has identified three basic features of **law.** Although his definition of law goes beyond the type of law found in Western societies, it certainly holds true for that type of law as well. First, law involves the legitimate use of physical coercion. Law without the force to punish or deprive is no law at all, although in most cases force is not necessary because the very threat of force or compulsion acts as a sufficient deterrent to antisocial behavior.

studies from all parts of the country; the case studies constituted a legal database that the Law Reform Commission could use for its unification of customary law.

The collection of these detailed case studies made two very important practical contributions to the emerging legal system in Papua New Guinea. First, this legal data bank on customary law and legal principles was immediately useful to lawyers. The computerized retrieval system of case studies was a great help to lawyers in searching out legal precedents for their ongoing court cases.

The second major contribution of the Customary Law Project was that it helped to identify, and subsequently alleviate, certain problems arising from a conflict between customary law and the existing national legal system. Family law was one such area. To be specific, under customary marriage practices, polygyny was a perfectly permissible alternative, but it was strictly forbidden under existing statutory law. Drawing on the legal data bank of case studies, the Law Reform Commission, in conjunction with the legislative and judicial branches of the government, drafted a family bill that formally recognized the legality of customary marriages and provided for polygyny under certain conditions. Thus, new legislation was introduced into the parliament that incorporated elements of customary law into the national system.

Although the implementation phase of the Customary Law Project (that is, the creation of the original data bank of case studies) has been completed, the research on additional case studies is ongoing. With an ever-increasing number of case studies from customary law, practicing lawyers will continue to have access to customary legal precedents relevant to the cases they are arguing in court. In addition, those responsible for the more long-term process of national legal reform will continue to draw on the anthropological concepts, data, and methods established by the Customary Law Project under the direction of legal anthropologist Richard Scaglion.

QUESTIONS FOR FURTHER THOUGHT

1. Why was the government of Papua New Guinea faced with the particularly difficult dilemma of developing a national legal system?
2. What was the purpose of the Customary Law Project?
3. How would you describe the anthropological contribution that Scaglion made to the Customary Law Project?

But when it is needed, a true legal system can draw on the legitimate use of force. Second, legal systems allocate official authority to privileged people who are able to use coercion legitimately. Third, law is based on regularity and a certain amount of predictability. That is, because laws build on precedents, new laws are based on old ones. This regularity and predictability eliminate much of the whim and capriciousness from the law.

Legal systems in complex societies such as our own have different objectives than systems of conflict resolution found in other societies. The objective of the Nuer Leopard-skin Chief and the Kpelle moots, for example, was to compensate the victim and to reestablish harmony among the disputants and, consequently, peace within the community. Law enforcement and conflict resolution in complex societies, in contrast, tend to emphasize punishment

= *By means of codified laws, state systems of government maintain a monopoly on the use of force.*

of the wrongdoer, which often takes the form of incarceration or, in some cases, death. In other words, it is not aimed at either compensating the victim or reintegrating the offender back into the community. This emphasis on punishment in complex societies is understandable in that lawbreakers pose a particular threat to the authority of the government officials. Unless serious offenders are punished or separated from the rest of society, they are likely to threaten the very legitimacy of political and legal authority.

Warfare

Just as societies have ways of regulating the social relationships of people within their own society, they also have mechanisms for managing external relationships with other groups, be they states, tribes, bands, clans, or lineages. One such mechanism of social control outside one's own group or society is **warfare**, which we can define as systematic, organized, and institutionalized fighting between different groups. People will be less willing to engage in antisocial or aggressive behavior if that behavior might bring about an attack by outside forces. As with most other aspects of culture, there is enormous cultural variability in terms of the extent to which societies use warfare, or other forms of large-scale violence, as a way of resolving conflicts and controlling peoples' behavior. In some small-scale societies, warfare as we know it is virtually nonexistent; at the other end of the spectrum are societies like the United States, which participated in World War II at a cost of hundreds of thousands of lives and nearly $3 trillion.

It is often stated that warfare has been around as long as there have been people. Although it is probably true that violence has occurred on occasions throughout human history, warfare has only been a human activity since the neolithic period, starting about 10,000 years ago. Most prehistorians agree that warfare, as we know it, was unknown before the invention of food production techniques. Prior to food production, foraging societies had little motivation for engaging in warfare. We can cite a number of compelling reasons why foraging societies were not warlike: First, they had no centralized governments that could finance and coordinate the relatively large numbers of people needed for military campaigns. Second, the absence of food surpluses precluded prolonged combat. Third, because foraging societies did not control land or territorial boundaries, one of the major motivations of warfare simply did not exist. And fourth, because foraging societies are small-scale (usually composed of exagamous bands), they are not likely to become hostile toward other bands into which one's own relatives have married.

With the coming of food production 10,000 years ago, populations became more sedentary, people began to claim rights over specific pieces of land, and the world experienced its first population explosion. If farmers and pastoralists, by the very nature of their means of livelihood, experience significant population growth and land scarcity, they are more likely to resort to warfare as a solution to the problem of increasing resource depletion. They will, in other words, resort to warfare to procure rights to other peoples' land and scarce resources.

Even though small-scale warfare was a possibility 10,000 years ago, war increased in scale with the rise of civilizations (state societies) 5,500 years ago. The formation of large, hierarchically organized states allowed the creation of significant military organizations. In fact, some have argued that state systems of government could not exist without powerful armies to both protect and control their populations. Since those early states, which arose more than 5,000 years ago, the sophistication of military organization and technology has increased steadily over the centuries. And particularly the twentieth century has witnessed an incredible escalation in the power of warfare throughout the world. Not only does humankind now possess the technological capacity to totally annihilate itself within a matter of hours, but warfare during the past century, in part due to that technology, has resulted in the killing of large segments of civilian populations. Today, in other words, modern warfare is likely to produce more civilian than military casualties.

For decades anthropologists and other social scientists have been fascinated with the question, What causes war? To address this question, a number of anthropologists over the past 30 years have examined the Yanomamo peoples of the Amazon region of Brazil and Venezuela. Although these people have been in the news recently because they are threatened by the worst abuses of economic "development," they have been of interest to anthropologists because of their institutionalized form of warfare and their reputation for fierceness. Napoleon Chagnon, who has written a best-selling ethnography of the Yanomamo, has attempted to explain their system of warfare on the basis of their acephalous political structure and their competition over women (1983, 1992). Marvin Harris (1979, 1984), a cultural materialist (see Chapter 4), has offered a materialist explanation, namely that Yanomamo warfare is the result of shortages of protein. The most recent entry into the debate is anthropologist Brian Ferguson (1995), who claims that the Yanomamo go to war over metal tools. Despite the popular view that the Yanomamo are isolated rain forest dwellers untouched by the outside world, Ferguson documents their relatively long-standing contact with modern society and, consequently, their exposure to and desire for metal tools. By drawing on a number of other ethnographic studies, Ferguson shows how warfare increases directly with the scarcity of metal tools. In other words, Yanomamo are more likely to go to war when their highly valued metal tools are in short supply.

Thus, we have three anthropologists attempting to explain Yanomamo warfare using three different sets of causal factors. Chagnon, taking the most emic view, ascribes Yanomamo warfare to social structure—namely their acephalous (headless) political structure and the competition for women. Harris and Ferguson suggest that the major reason for going to war is a shortage of either protein or metal tools. That three competent scholars can come up with three different primary causes for Yano-

mamo warfare illustrates the complexity of trying to understand warfare. In all likelihood, all three sets of causal factors are valid to some degree. But warfare among the Yanomamo is a multidimensional phenomenon. Any attempt to explain why Yanomamo go to war by using any single factor will be like trying to explain the motion of an airplane exclusively in terms of the power of its engine while ignoring other factors such as wind speed, altitude, the design and weight of the aircraft, and the skill of the pilot.

When trying to search for the causes of war in general, the task becomes even more daunting. When considering warfare (for all time) in both small-scale societies and modern nation-states, we can identify several general factors that contribute to warfare. These include:

- ▶ *Social problems:* When internal social problems exist, political leaders may turn the society's frustrations toward another group. The outsiders may be portrayed as having more than their share of scarce resources or even as causing the social problems. It matters little if this type of blaming is justified; what is important is that people are convinced that other groups are the cause of their problems. When that happens, one group can declare war on another. This factor is illustrated when Yanomamo go to war with neighboring villages over scarce metal tools or when Adolph Hitler moved his troops into neighboring European countries to acquire more "living room" for the German people.

- ▶ *Perceived threats:* In some cases societies will go to war when they feel that their security or well-being is in jeopardy. The people of North Vietnam during the 1960s were willing to wage war because they felt that their security was threatened by the long-term influence of the French and Americans in the southern part of Vietnam. The Americans, on the other hand, felt, either rightly or wrongly, that Vietnam, and indeed all of Asia, was being threatened by the presence of a godless, communist regime; if South Vietnam fell to the communists, it would start a domino effect that would eventually threaten the entire free world.

- ▶ *Political motivations:* Sometimes governments will wage war for the purpose of furthering their own political objectives. The brief wars (or "military actions") that the United States initiated in Haiti, Grenada, and Somalia were motivated by the desire to show sufficient power to enforce its political will.

▶ *Moral objectives:* It is difficult to think of any war in human history that has been waged without a shred of moral urgency. Even when wars are waged primarily for political or economic reasons, those who commit their soldiers to battle will justify their actions on some moral grounds. Europeans waged the Crusades against the Islamic infidels because they were convinced that God was on their side. Interestingly, if we read accounts of those same wars written by Islamic historians, it is the European Christians who were the godless bad guys. Both sides justified waging wars for generations on the basis of moral correctness. Somewhat closer to home, the United States waged a short but expensive war against Iraq in 1991, ostensibly on the moral grounds of stopping Saddam Hussein's aggression into Kuwait, even though a primary motivation was to protect the U.S. oil interests in the region.

SUMMARY

1. All societies have political systems that function to manage public affairs, maintain social order, and resolve conflict. The study of political organization involves such topics as the allocation of political roles, levels of political integration, concentrations of power and authority, mechanisms of social control, and means for resolving conflict.

2. Political anthropologists generally recognize four fundamentally different levels of political organization based on levels of political integration and the degree of specialized political roles: bands, tribes, chiefdoms, and states.

3. Societies based on bands have the least amount of political integration and role specialization. They are most often found in foraging societies and are associated with low population densities, distribution systems based on reciprocity, and egalitarian social relations.

4. Tribal organizations are most commonly found among horticulturalists and pastoralists. With larger and more sedentary populations than are found in band societies, tribally based societies have certain pan-tribal mechanisms that cut across a number of local segments and integrate them into a larger whole.

5. At the next level of complexity are chiefdoms, which involve a more formal and permanent political structure than is found in tribal societies. Political authority in chiefdoms rests with a single individual, either acting alone or with the advice of a council. Most chiefdoms, which tend to have quite distinct social ranks, rely on feasting and tribute as a major way of distributing goods.

6. State systems—with the greatest amount of political integration and role specialization—are associated with intensive agriculture, market economies, urbanization, and complex social stratification. States, which first appeared about 5,500 years ago, have a monopoly on the use of force and can make and enforce laws, collect taxes, and recruit labor for military service and public works projects.

7. Theories put forth to explain the rise of state systems of government have centered on the question of why people surrender some of their autonomy to the power and authority of the state. Some theories (such as those of Childe and Wittfogel) suggest that people voluntarily gave up their autonomy in exchange for certain perceived benefits such as protection, more effective means of conflict resolution, and greater food productivity. Other explanations, such as that offered by Carneiro, hold that states developed as a result of warfare and coercion rather than voluntary self-interest.

8. In the absence of formal mechanisms of government, many band and tribal societies maintain social control by means of a number of informal mechanisms such as socialization, public opinion, corporate lineages, supernatural sanctions, and age organizations.

9. In addition to using informal means of social control, societies control behavior by more formal mechanisms whose major function is maintaining social order and resolving conflicts. These mecha-

nisms include verbal competition, intermediaries, councils of elders, oaths, ordeals, formal court systems, and warfare.

10. A society will go to war when it (a) blames another society for its own social problems, (b) believes that it is threatened, (c) wants to further its own ends, or (d) is defending a moral position.

KEY TERMS

acephalous societies	oath
age grades	ordeal
age organizations	pan-tribal mechanisms
age set	political coerciveness
ancestor worship	political integration
authority	positive sanctions
band societies	public opinion
chiefdoms	rebellion
coercive theory of state formation	revolution
corporate lineages	sanctions
crime	shaman
degradation ceremonies	social control
deviance	socialization
ghost invocation	social norms
ghostly vengeance	song duel
hydraulic theory of state formation	specialized political roles
	state
intermediaries	state system of government
law	supernatural belief systems
Leopard-skin Chief	tribal societies
moots	voluntaristic theory
nation	of state formation
negative sanctions	warfare
	witchcraft

SUGGESTED READINGS

Cohen, Ronald, and Elman R. Service, eds. *Origins of the State: The Anthropology of Political Evolution.* Philadelphia: Institute for the Study of Human Issues, 1978. A collection of essays on how and why state systems of government have evolved, written by such noted political anthropologists as Morton Fried, Elman Service, and Robert Carneiro. An excellent introductory essay is written by one of the editors, Ronald Cohen.

Ferguson, Brian. *Yanomami Warfare: A Political History.* Santa Fe: School of American Research Press, 1995. A recent analysis of warfare among the Yanomamo of Venezuela and Brazil that reevaluates the interpretations of the causes of warfare previously offered by Napoleon Chagnon and Marvin Harris.

Fried, M. H. *The Evolution of Political Society: An Essay in Political Anthropology.* New York: Random House, 1967. A classic work in the field of political anthropology setting forth the fourfold typology of political organization—egalitarian societies, rank societies, stratified societies, and states—that has been widely used as a model for classifying different types of sociopolitical systems.

Haas, Jonathan. *The Anthropology of War.* Cambridge: Cambridge University Press, 1990. This edited volume explores such issues as the origins, causes, effects, and persistence of war in nonstate societies.

Kuper, Hilda. *The Swazi: A South African Kingdom.* 2d ed. New York: Holt, Rinehart & Winston, 1986. An excellent short monograph on the dual monarchy of the Swazis from traditional times up to the recent present.

McGlynn, Frank, and Arthur Tuden, eds. *Anthropological Approaches to Political Behavior.* Pittsburgh: University of Pittsburgh Press, 1991. A collection of 16 essays that highlight the major theoretical concerns of political anthropology. These articles deal with such topics as conflict resolution, leadership, ideology, and authority among small-scale societies in Africa, Latin America, Europe, and Oceania.

Mair, Lucy. *Primitive Government.* Baltimore: Penguin Books, 1962. A regional study of traditional political systems in East Africa ranging from such minimal governments as the Nuer to the more complex interlacustrine Bantu kingdoms, which include the Ganda, Soga, Nyoro, and Ankole.

Meggitt, Mervyn. *Blood Is Their Argument.* Palo Alto, CA: Mayfield, 1977. An ethnographic study of warfare among the Mae Enga tribesmen of New Guinea, which explores the modes of clan warfare, the reasons for fighting, the outcomes of the conflicts, and methods for establishing peace.

Ross, Marc Howard. *The Management of Conflict: Interpretations and Interests in Comparative Perspective*. New Haven, CT: Yale University Press, 1996. A cross-cultural analysis of constructive conflict management that draws examples from such diverse settings as a public housing dispute in New York City, warfare in postcolonial highlands of New Guinea, and the Camp David peace accords.

Vincent, Joan. *Anthropology and Politics: Vision, Traditions, and Trends*. Tucson: University of Arizona Press, 1990. This encyclopedic work traces the history of political anthropology from the 1870s through the present by examining the questions political anthropologists have asked, the ethnographies they wrote, and the conclusions they reached. The book contains a 76-page bibliography on political anthropology.

On the Net

State systems of government are complex organizations with many branches and many layers. In the United States, the federal government is divided into three major branches: the legislative, the executive, and the judicial. The legislature makes the laws, the executive branch administers the laws, and the judiciary interprets the laws. Perhaps the most poorly understood branch of the U.S. government is the judiciary.

To learn more about how the federal judiciary operates, start with the Yahoo search engine. Click on "government," then "law," then "federal," and then "federal courts." Now go to "United States Federal Judiciary" and then click on the section titled "About the U.S. Courts." Then go to "Understanding the Federal Courts" and click on "structure." Examine the various descriptions of the federal district courts, courts of appeals, and the Supreme Court. Describe the path a civil case takes as it works its way through the federal system. Now do the same for a criminal case. Write a one-page paper on what you learned from this exercise.

LOG ON TO INFOTRAC COLLEGE EDITION to do a subject search for Nuu-chah-nulth or Nootka, an ethnic group residing on Vancouver Island in British Columbia. Or conduct an author or title search for an article written in the fall 1998 issue of *Ethnology* by Michael Harkin entitled "Whales, Chiefs, and Giants: An Exploration into Nuu-chah-nulth Political Thought." It is an excellent article on the ideology of chieftainship among this Northwest Coast people. Read the article and write a one-page paper on the characteristics of a good chief among the Nuu-chah-nulth.

Chapter Thirteen

SOCIAL STRATIFICATION

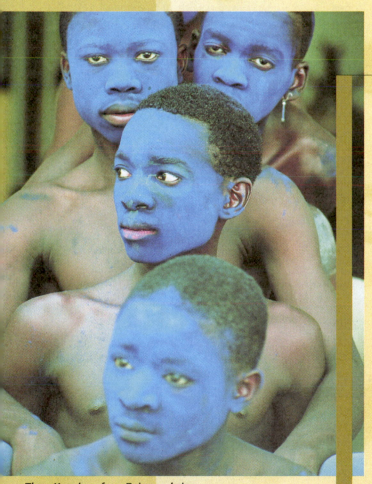

These Kota boys from Zaire are being initiated into adulthood. The blue faces symbolize the end of their childhood, blue being the color of death.

WHAT WE WILL LEARN:

▼

To what extent do the societies of the world vary in terms of the equitable distribution of power, prestige, and wealth?

▼

How do class systems differ from caste systems?

▼

What are the different ways of interpreting systems of social stratification?

▼

O ne important difference between the societies of the world is the degree to which individuals in any given society have equal access to wealth, power, and prestige.

To one degree or another, all people are socially differentiated on the basis of such criteria as physical appearance, ethnicity, profession, family background, sex, ideology, age, or skill in performing certain kinds of economic or political roles. Societies confer a larger share of the rewards (that is, wealth, power, and prestige) on those possessing the most admired characteristics. Scholars generally agree that all complex societies are *stratified*—that is, the societies make distinctions among certain groups or categories of people that are hierarchically ranked relative to one another. However, many anthropologists do not find systems of social stratification in the simpler societies of the world in the sense of a clear-cut division of the society into hierarchically ranked strata; even these societies, however, have role and status differences.

•■ DIMENSIONS OF ■•
SOCIAL INEQUALITY

MAX WEBER (1946) has delineated three basic criteria used for measuring levels of social inequality: wealth, power, and prestige. First, people are distinguished from one another by the extent to which they have accumulated economic resources, or their **wealth.** The forms that wealth may take vary from one society to the next. For the Mexican farmer, wealth resides in the land; for the Samburu of East Africa, a man's wealth is measured by the number of cows he has; and in the United States, most people equate their wealth with income earned in wages, property, stocks, bonds, equity in a home, or other resources that have a cash value.

The extent of economic inequality varies from one society to the next. In some societies, such as that of the Pygmies, there are virtually no differences in wealth. In terms of their material possessions and well being, all people in

egalitarian societies are virtually indistinguishable from one another. By way of contrast, enormous differences in wealth exist in certain capitalistic societies such as the United States. The range of wealth in the United States runs from the unemployed father who sells his blood several times a month to feed his children at one end of the spectrum to Bill Gates, chairman of Microsoft, who in his 40s had a total net worth approaching $100 billion (that's *billion,* not *million!*) at the other. Economists Paul Samuelson and William Nordhaus (1989:644) capture the magnitude of the economic inequities in the United States: "If we made an income pyramid out of a child's blocks, with each layer portraying $500 of income, the peak would be far higher than Mount Everest, but most people would be within a few feet of the ground."

A second dimension of social inequality, according to Weber, is **power,** which he defined as the ability to achieve one's goals and objectives even against the will of others. Power, to be certain, is often closely correlated with wealth, for economic success, particularly in Western societies, increases the chances of gaining power. Nevertheless, wealth and power do not always overlap. In certain parts of the world, power can be based on factors other than wealth, such as the possession of specialized knowledge or eloquence as a speaker. In such cases, the wealth or material possessions of the powerful and the not-so-powerful may not differ.

Where does power reside in the United States? According to our democratic ideology, power is in the hands of the people. We all exercise our power by voting for our political representatives, who see to it that our will is carried out. Although this is how it works in theory, in real life the picture is quite different. Some social scientists (Hellinger and Judd 1991) have suggested that this ideology is no more than a democratic façade that conceals the fact

■ *With a personal net worth approaching $100 billion, Microsoft chairman Bill Gates represents the upper level of wealth in the United States and the world.*

from one culture to another. For example, among certain traditional Native American groups, warriors on horseback held high prestige; in certain age-graded societies, such as the Samburu of Kenya, old men were accorded the highest prestige; and in the United States, high prestige is closely associated with certain professions.

Research indicates that occupations in the United States carry different levels of prestige and that those rankings have remained remarkably stable throughout much of the twentieth century (Counts 1925; National Opinion Research Center 1947; Hodge et al. 1964; Coleman and Rainwater 1978; Nakao and Treas 1990). That is, the occupations that ranked high in the 1950s still rank high in the 21st century. Not surprisingly, physicians, corporate presidents, scientists, and top-ranking government officials enjoy high levels of occupational prestige, whereas garbage collectors, shoe shiners, and street sweepers are at the low end of the prestige scale. Essentially there are four factors that separate the occupations at the top from those at the bottom. The occupations at the top end are higher paying, require more education, offer greater autonomy (less supervision), and require more abstract thinking and less physical labor.

It is interesting to note that occupational rankings in the United States are surprisingly consistent with rankings from other parts of the world. To illustrate, in all countries where ranking has been conducted, college professors are ranked higher than nurses, nurses higher than electricians, and electricians higher than janitors (Treiman 1977).

It should be kept in mind that although wealth, power, and prestige are often interrelated, they can also operate independently of one another. To illustrate, it is possible to possess both power and wealth while having little prestige, as is the case with leaders of organized crime. Some people, such as classical pianists, may be highly esteemed for their musical virtuosity yet have modest wealth and little power or influence over people. And, odd as it may seem to Westerners, people in some societies (such as the Kwakiutl of British Columbia) acquire high prestige by actually destroying or giving away all of their personal possessions (refer to the discussion of the potlatch in Chapter 8).

that the real power resides with an unofficial power elite. As early as the 1950s, C. Wright Mills (1956) insisted that power was concentrated in the hands of a power elite. Since then William Domhoff (1990) has arrived at a similar conclusion. The power elite share many of the same values, belong to the same clubs, sit on the same boards of directors, are graduates of the same schools, and even vacation at the same resorts. They are the owners and managers of major corporations, advisors to governments, and members of commissions and agencies. They give large sums of money to the fine arts, contribute heavily to their favorite political candidates, and are often on a first-name basis with the political establishment. According to Mills and Domhoff, the concentration of real power in the hands of an elite in the United States has been a constant for the past 50 years.

The third dimension of social stratification, according to Weber's formulation, is **prestige:** the social esteem, respect, or admiration that a society confers on people. Because favorable social evaluation is based on the norms and values of a particular group, sources of prestige vary

▪■ TYPES OF SOCIETIES ■▪

FOLLOWING THE LEAD of Morton Fried (1967), most anthropologists distinguish three types of societies based on levels of social inequality: egalitarian, rank, and stratified societies. Egalitarian societies have few or no groups that have greater access to wealth, power, or prestige; they are usually found among food collectors, have economies based on reciprocity, and have little or no political role specialization. In rank societies, certain groups enjoy higher prestige, even though power and wealth are equally distributed; they are usually found among chiefdoms, have economies based on redistribution, and exhibit limited political role specialization. Stratified societies illustrate the greatest degree of social inequality in terms of all three forms of social rewards (wealth, power, and prestige). They are found in industrialized societies, have market economies, and are associated with state systems of government. Rather than thinking of these three types of societies as discrete and mutually exclusive, it is more accurate to view them as points on a continuum, ranging from egalitarian societies (the least amount of social inequality) to stratified societies (the greatest degree of social inequality).

EGALITARIAN SOCIETIES

In **egalitarian societies,** which are located at the low end of the inequality continuum, no individual or group has appreciably more wealth, power, or prestige than any other. Of course, even in the most egalitarian societies, personal differences in certain skills are acknowledged. Some people are more skilled than others at hunting, others may be recognized as particularly adept at crafts, and still others may be well known and respected for their skills at settling disputes. Even though certain individuals in an egalitarian society may be highly esteemed, they are not able to transform their special skills into wealth or power. No matter how much or how little respect an individual in an egalitarian society may have, he or she is neither denied the right to practice a certain profession nor subject to the control of others. Moreover, whatever esteem an individual manages to accrue is not transferable to his or her heirs.

In an egalitarian society, the number of high-status positions for which people must compete is not fixed. According to Fried, "there are as many positions of prestige in any given age–sex grade as there are persons capable of filling them" (1967:33). The esteem gained by being a highly skilled dancer is given to as many individuals in the society as there are good dancers. If 15 people are highly skilled dancers this year, all 15 will receive high status. If next year there are 24 skilled dancers, all 24 will be so recognized. Thus, the number of high-status positions in an egalitarian society is constantly changing to reflect the number of qualified candidates. In other words, everyone,

depending on her or his personal skill level, has equal access to positions of esteem and respect.

Egalitarian societies are found most readily among geographically mobile food collectors such as the !Kung of the Kalahari region, the Inuit, and the Hadza of Tanzania. There are a number of logical reasons why unequal access to wealth, power, and prestige would be discouraged among nomadic foragers. First, the very nature of a nomadic existence inhibits the accumulation of large quantities of personal possessions. Second, because foragers do not hold claims to territory, individuals can forage in whatever areas they please. If someone wants to exercise control over others, they can choose to live in some other territory. Finally, food collectors tend to be egalitarian because sharing tends to maximize their chances for adaptation. When a hunter kills a large animal, he is unlikely to try to keep the entire carcass for himself, given the lack of refrigeration. Rather, it makes much more sense for the hunter to share the meat with the expectation that others will share their kills with him. In fact, foraging societies, with economies based on the principle of generalized reciprocity, place a high value on sharing. Generosity in such societies is expected, and attempts to accumulate possessions, power, or prestige are ridiculed.

Often, egalitarian societies are transformed considerably when they come into contact with highly stratified (statelike) societies. Sometimes this transformation from egalitarian to nonegalitarian society is the result of normal cultural diffusion. Often it occurs because such a change meets the needs of colonial governments. For example, during the early part of the twentieth century, the British colonial government in Kenya created, for its own administrative convenience, local chiefs among the Kikuyu, a traditionally egalitarian people with no history of any type of chief. Although the colonial government thought it was creating new high-status positions, the Kikuyu people themselves adhered to their egalitarian ideals and refused to recognize the legitimacy of these new government-appointed chiefs.

RANK SOCIETIES

Rank societies have unequal access to prestige or status but not unequal access to wealth or power. In rank societies, there is usually a fixed number of high-status positions, which only certain individuals are able to occupy. The others are systematically excluded regardless of their personal skills, wisdom, industriousness, or other personal

= *Band societies, such as the !Kung, tend to be highly egalitarian.*

traits. Such high-prestige positions as chief—which are largely hereditary in nature—establish a ranking system that distinguishes among various levels of prestige and esteem. In fact, kinship plays an important role in rank societies. Because some clans or lineages may be considered aristocratic, their members qualify for certain titles or high-status positions. Other kin groups are rank ordered according to their genealogical proximity to the aristocratic kin groups. Thus, the number of high-status positions in ranked societies is limited, and the major criterion for allocating such positions is genealogical.

Even though the chiefs in a rank society possess great prestige and privilege, they generally do not accumulate great wealth, for their basic standard of living is not noticeably different from that of an ordinary person. Chiefs usually receive gifts of tribute from members of other kin groups, but they never keep them for their personal use. Instead, they give them all away through the process of redistribution (refer to Chapter 8). In many rank societies,

chiefs are considered to own the land but not in the Western sense of the term. The chief certainly has no power to keep anyone from using the land. The chief may control land to the extent that he encourages people not to neglect either the land or their obligation to contribute to the chief's tribute. But the chief has no real power or control over the land. He maintains his privileged position as chief not by virtue of his capacity to impose his will on others but rather by virtue of his generosity.

Examples of rank societies are found in most areas of the world, but most prominently in Oceania and among Native Americans of the Northwest Coast. In fact, for reasons that are not fully understood, some strikingly similar cultural traits are found in parts of Polynesia and among Native Americans residing in a narrow coastal region between northern California and southern Alaska. These cultural similarities are particularly noticeable in the area of status ranking. One such group that exemplifies a rank society is the Nootka of British Columbia (Service 1978). Like a number of ethnic groups in the American Northwest, the Nootka, a hunting-and-fishing society, live in an area so abundant in food resources (such as big game, wild edible plants, waterfowl, and fish) that their standard of living is comparable to societies that practice horticulture and animal husbandry.

Social ranking among the Nootka is closely related to the principle of kinship proximity. People are ranked within families according to the principle of primogeniture. Position, privileges, and titles pass from a man to his eldest son. All younger sons are of little social importance because they are not in direct line to inherit anything from the father. Furthermore, in much the same way that individuals are ranked within the family, lineages are graded according to the birth order (or genealogical proximity) of the founding ancestors of each lineage. Nootka society does not comprise clearly marked social strata but rather a large number of individual status positions ranked relative to one another. Thus, no two individuals have the exact same status.

Differential status takes a number of forms in Nootka society. First, the most visible symbol separating people of different rank is clothing. As a general rule, the higher the social position, the more ornate a person's dress. More specifically, wearing ornaments of teeth and shells or robes trimmed with the fur of sea otters is the exclusive privilege of chiefs. Second, an individual's status is directly linked to the bestowal of certain hereditary titles that are the names of important ancestors. Third, social position is expressed economically in terms of the amount of tribute (in surplus goods) a chief receives from the lower-ranked individuals who acknowledge his higher status. The receipt of tribute in no way enhances the personal wealth of the chief, for he redistributes the surplus goods back to the society in the form of elaborate feasts and ceremonies. Finally, social rank is determined by one's success in potlatch ceremonies, wherein prominent men compete with one another to see who can give away the largest quantities of material goods, such as food, blankets, and oil. Unlike Western societies, which equate high status with the accumulation of material wealth, the Nootka confer high status on those who can give away the greatest quantities of material goods. Even though potlatch ceremonies function to distribute needed material goods throughout the society, they also serve as a mechanism for validating rank.

STRATIFIED SOCIETIES

Unlike rank societies, which are unequal only in terms of prestige, **stratified societies** are characterized by considerable inequality in all forms of social rewards (power, wealth, and prestige). The political, economic, and social inequality in stratified societies is both permanent and formally recognized by the members of the society. Some people—and entire groups of people—have little or no access to the basic resources of the society. Various groups in stratified societies, then, are noticeably different in social position, wealth, lifestyle, access to power, and standard of living. The unequal access to rewards found in stratified societies is generally inheritable from one generation to the next.

Although distinctions in wealth, power, and prestige began to appear in the early neolithic period (approximately 10,000 years ago), true stratified societies are closely associated with the rise of civilization approximately 5,500 years ago. A basic prerequisite for civilization is a population with a high degree of role specialization. As societies become more specialized, the system of social stratification also becomes more complex. Different occupations or economic interest groups do not have the same access to wealth, power, and prestige but rather are ranked relative to one another. As a general rule, the greater the role specialization, the more complex the system of stratification.

Class Versus Caste

Social scientists generally recognize two different types of stratified societies: those based on class and those based on caste. The key to understanding this fundamental distinction is **social mobility**. In **class** systems, a certain amount of upward and downward social mobility exists. In other words, an individual can change his or her social position dramatically within a lifetime. An individual, through diligence, intelligence, and good luck, could go from rags to riches; conversely, a person born to millionaire parents could wind up as a homeless street person (Newman 1988). **Caste** societies, on the other hand, have no social mobility. Membership in a caste is determined by birth and lasts throughout one's lifetime. Whereas members of a class society are able to elevate their social position by marrying into a higher class, caste systems are strictly endogamous (allowing marriages only within one's own caste).

Another important distinction is how statuses (positions) within each type of society are allocated. Class systems are associated with an **achieved status** whereas caste systems are associated with an **ascribed status.** Achieved statuses are those that the individual chooses or at least has some control over. An achieved status is one that a person has as a result of her or his personal effort, such as graduating from college, marrying someone, or taking a particular job. In contrast, a person is born into an ascribed status and has no control over it. Statuses based on such criteria as sex, race, or age are examples of ascribed statuses, which are found mainly in caste societies.

It is important to bear in mind that stratified societies cannot all be divided neatly into either class or caste systems. In general, class systems are open to the extent that they are based on achieved statuses and permit considerable social mobility, and caste systems tend to be closed in that they are based on ascribed statuses and allow little or no social mobility, either up or down. Having made these conceptual distinctions, however, we must also realize that in the real world, class and caste systems overlap. In other words, most stratified societies contain elements of both class and caste. Rather than think in either–or terms, we should think in terms of polarities on the ends of a continuum. There are no societies that have either absolute mobility (perfect class systems) or a total lack of mobility (perfect caste systems). Rather, all stratified societies found in the world fall somewhere between these two ideal polarities, depending on the amount of social mobility permitted in each.

CLASS SOCIETIES Even though the boundaries between social strata in a class society are not rigidly drawn, social inequalities nevertheless exist. A social class is a segment of a population whose members share similar lifestyles

CROSS-CULTURAL MISCUE

TOM HOLMES, a high-ranking official in an American-based company, had been his company's chief architect of a joint venture with a Japanese company. After months of meetings, Holmes and his Japanese counterpart, Mr. Hayashi, were sitting down with their two teams to review the details of the joint venture. Both teams had worked hard to bring about a relationship that Holmes believed to be satisfactory to both companies. Over the months Holmes and Hayashi had developed a good working relationship, and both men were optimistic about the venture upon which their companies were about to embark. In fact, Holmes was so pleased with the draft proposal that he had invited his boss, vice president Frank Mistretta, to be present at this final review meeting.

Once the meeting started, however, Holmes's optimism began to wane. He found himself doing all of the talking, while Hayashi and his team remained silent. Holmes wondered what had gone wrong. Now that everything had been worked out, were the Japanese changing their minds? After about 45 minutes, Holmes called for a recess. Looking very frustrated, Holmes took Hayashi aside and asked him, "What's wrong? I thought we agreed on all of the details of our proposal. This meeting was simply to review the details to make certain everything was in place. But you are not saying anything. Are there parts of the proposal you are having difficulty with? I just don't understand!"

In actual fact, the Japanese team had not changed its position on the proposal. Hayashi was still in agreement with all of the details that the two sides had agreed upon. The problem for the Japanese was the presence of Holmes's boss, Mistretta. During the months of negotiations Holmes and Hayashi, and their respective teams, were of equal status. Thus, they could speak with each other openly as equals. But the introduction of Mistretta into the equation changed things dramatically for the Japanese. Because Mistretta was of obviously higher status than any of the Japanese, Hayashi and his team were reluctant to speak. Tom had invited his boss as a way of showing commitment to the proposed partnership with the Japanese. Unfortunately, for the very status-conscious Japanese, Mistretta's presence at the meeting was seen as intimidating.

and levels of wealth, power, and prestige. The United States is a good example of a class society (Table 13-1). In some areas of the United States, such as coal-mining towns in Appalachia, there may be only two classes: the haves and the have-nots. More often, however, social scientists have identified five (or more) social classes: upper, upper middle, lower middle, working, and lower (Bensman and Vidich 1987; Vanneman and Cannon 1987; Sullivan and Thompson 1990).

The *upper class* in the United States, comprising approximately 3 percent of the population, consists of old wealth (Carnegies, Rockefellers), those who have recently made fortunes (**nouveau riche**), and top government and judicial officials who, despite modest wealth, wield considerable power. The ownership of the means of production by the upper class affords them the power over jobs for the

rest of society. Moreover, their control of the media largely shapes the nation's consciousness. Primarily because of the rapid development of the global economy, the number of people in the United States with worth of over a million dollars has increased dramatically in recent decades. Whereas there were 13,000 millionaires in 1945, that number jumped to more than 1.5 million by 1990, more than a hundredfold increase (Philips 1991).

The *upper middle class*, comprising about 14 percent of the U.S. population, is made up of business and professional people with high incomes and modest amounts of overall wealth. This is the class that is most shaped by education. Nearly all members of the upper middle class are college educated, and many have postgraduate degrees. These people are professionals (such as doctors and lawyers), own their own businesses, or manage the

TABLE 13-1

U.S. Class Structure

CLASS	INCOME	EDUCATION	OCCUPATION	%
Upper class	$500,000+	Prestige universities	CEOs, investors, top government officers	3
Upper middle class	$90,000+	Top colleges and postgraduate	Upper managers, professionals	14
Lower middle class	$40,000	High school and some college	Lower managers, teachers, civil servants	30
Working class	$30,000	High school	Clerical, sales, factory	30
Working poor	$18,000	Some high school	Low-paying service jobs, laborers	20
Underclass	Under $10,000	Some high school	Unemployed	3

corporations owned by members of the upper class. They have secure economic positions, almost always send their children to college, drive new automobiles, and are likely to be active in civic organizations and local politics.

The *lower middle class*, constituting approximately 30 percent of the population, is made up of hardworking people of modest income, such as small entrepreneurs, teachers, nurses, civil servants, and lower-level managers. People in this class make a modest income, enjoy relative security (threatened occasionally by rising taxes and inflation), and have the potential for upward social mobility. Though sometimes indistinguishable from the working class, the lower middle class generally has slightly higher income and more prestige.

Comprising approximately 30 percent of the population, the *working class* (blue collar and some white collar) occupations tend to be fairly routine, closely supervised, and usually require no more than a high school education. These occupations include factory workers, sales clerks, construction workers, office workers, and appliance repairpersons. Because of their lack of higher educa-

tion, social mobility among the working class is possible but not likely. Vulnerable to downturns in the economy, working-class people are subject to layoffs during recessions and justifiably feel threatened by our increasingly globalizing economy, in which many jobs are going to workers abroad.

The *working poor,* about 20 percent of the population, barely earn a living at unskilled, low-paying, often temporary jobs with little security and frequently no benefits. They tend to be undereducated, and even though some may have completed high school, some are functionally illiterate. They live from paycheck to paycheck, often depend on food stamps, and have little or no savings as a safety net. Members of the working poor are often just a layoff away from living on the streets or in a homeless shelter.

The *underclass* occupies the lowest sector of U.S. society. Some have suggested that the underclass actually represents the people who are beneath the class structure, a type of castelike group that has little or no chance of ever making it to the first rung of the social ladder. The underclass are unemployed (or severely underem-

In stratified societies different groups, ranging from the homeless to the upper class, have different levels of power, prestige, and wealth.

ployed), are homeless, and often suffer from substance abuse and in some cases mental illness. They are almost always confined to blighted urban areas plagued by violence, gangs, and drugs.

During the 1990s, the American economy experienced the longest peacetime expansion in history. Unemployment was lower than it had been in decades, interest rates were low, consumer confidence was high, and the stock market (Dow Jones) had gone from 2810 in January 1990 to nearly 11,000 by 2000. Conventional wisdom would suggest that with such unparalleled growth, the gap between those at the bottom and those at the top would narrow. Yet, ironically, despite all of the economic hoopla, wealth has become increasingly more *unequal* over the past quarter of a century. The wealthy, in other words, have become wealthier, while everyone else has become relatively worse off than they were. According to Chuck Collins, Betsy Leondar-Wright, and Holly Sklar (1999), financial security for the majority of Americans has become more elusive over the past several decades. After adjusting for inflation, the net worth of the top 1 percent of U.S. households increased by 17 percent between 1983 and 1995. The bottom 40 percent lost a startling 80 percent of their net wealth, falling from $4,400 in 1983 to a mere $900 in 1995. The middle fifth, roughly equivalent to the lower middle class, lost 11 percent of their net worth over this same period. The average American worker during this time of unprecedented economic growth has less income (when adjusted for inflation) than he or she did during the Nixon administration. It was only the upper 5 percent of American households that experienced a net gain during this period. In fact, that same upper 5 percent of American households now controls approximately 60 percent of all household wealth.

This increasing disparity over the past several decades has been the result of a combination of a number of factors. Many Americans claim that the major culprit is the globalization of world economies, which has had the effect of moving many jobs to other countries. But there have been a number of other causes as well. For example, the influence of labor unions, which traditionally have fought for higher wages for U.S. workers, has declined in recent years. The rising number of single-parent households has also led to the overall lowering of average household income. In addition, unskilled laborers have suffered from the decline in the real value of the minimum wage as well as from competition from immigrant workers. Moreover, the gap between the haves and the have-nots widened due to the substantial tax cuts during the Reagan years,

Although we like to think that there is a good deal of upward social mobility in the United States, how likely is it that this youngster growing up in the South Bronx, New York, will gain entry into the upper class?

which had the effect of helping the wealthy far more than the rest of the population.

Our national mythology includes the belief that a good deal of social mobility exists in the United States. After all, there are no formal or legal barriers to equality, and we all grow up believing that it is possible for anyone (or at least, any White male) to become president of the United States. Although it is possible to cite a number of contemporary Americans who have attained great wealth, power, and prestige from modest beginnings, studies of social class in the United States have shown that most people remain in the class into which they are born and marry within that class as well.

In many cases, a child's physical and social environment greatly influence her or his life's chances and identification with a particular class. To illustrate, the son of a school janitor in Philadelphia living in a lower-class

APPLIED PERSPECTIVE
Anthropology and Architecture

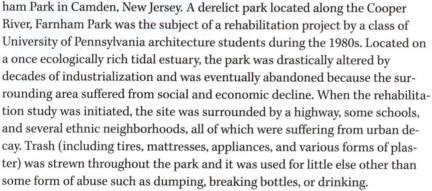

A basic premise of this chapter is that, to one degree or another, all societies are segmented into groups that have different access to wealth, power, and prestige. In such societies as the United States, various groups differ appreciably in terms of their access to power, social position, lifestyles, and standards of living. These segments of U.S. society, which are called classes, often display marked differences in life experiences, educational backgrounds, and values.

Anthropologist Setha Low (1981), a professor of landscape architecture at the University of Pennsylvania, put this basic principle into operation when planning the restoration of Farnham Park in Camden, New Jersey. A derelict park located along the Cooper River, Farnham Park was the subject of a rehabilitation project by a class of University of Pennsylvania architecture students during the 1980s. Located on a once ecologically rich tidal estuary, the park was drastically altered by decades of industrialization and was eventually abandoned because the surrounding area suffered from social and economic decline. When the rehabilitation study was initiated, the site was surrounded by a highway, some schools, and several ethnic neighborhoods, all of which were suffering from urban decay. Trash (including tires, mattresses, appliances, and various forms of plaster) was strewn throughout the park and it was used for little else other than some form of abuse such as dumping, breaking bottles, or drinking.

Once the city expressed an interest in restoring the park, a number of important design questions emerged. What does the city, and particularly this neighborhood, need in the way of a park? The design team attempted to answer this question by conducting a comprehensive research project using anthropological data-gathering strategies, including participant-observation, ethnographic interviewing, and social mapping. Data were gathered on the values and behavior patterns of local residents, their current use of the space, their perception of problems, their past memories of the area, and their preferences for a park for the future.

A significant part of the data collection for this project involved the identification of the dominant values and cultural features of the major social constituencies. In other words, who were the major players who had an interest in the rehabilitation of the park? The research team identified six interest groups:

neighborhood will spend his formative years playing in crowded public playgrounds, working at the grocery store after school, and generally hanging out with kids from the neighborhood. The son of a bank president, on the other hand, also living in Philadelphia, will attend a fashionable prep school, take tennis lessons at the country club, and drive his own car. When the two youths finish high school, the janitor's son will probably not continue his education, whereas the banker's son will go off to a good college, perhaps follow that with law school, and then land a high-

1. The parkside residents, who wanted a nice, quiet park for families to picnic.
2. The unemployed youth and teenagers, who hung out on the basketball courts.
3. The teachers and administrators from nearby schools, who wanted the park to be restored as a nature center for educational purposes.
4. The young children, who wanted to use the gym equipment but were reluctant to do so because they were afraid of the older children.
5. Members of the city government, who would finance the improvement to the park.
6. The county government officials, who would finance the ongoing maintenance of the park.

Each group was asked to prepare a sketch plan of the proposed park that reflected their own values, interests, and needs. These plans were then analyzed by the research team, which tried to identify points of commonality among the constituencies. Agreement was found on the following elements: the restoration of the dike that would stabilize the size of the pond; the creation of a large grassy area; the maintenance of a wildlife area; the provision of picnic tables; the creation of sports fields; the encouragement of fishing and other passive water sports; the provision of special skills equipment; the creation of a cultural activities center; and the inclusion of biking, walking, and jogging trails. Once the team was able to identify elements that appealed to all constituencies, they were able to start the design phase of the park rehabilitation project.

This is another example of the utility of cultural knowledge. In this case, an understanding of the norms, values, and behavior patterns of different subcultures in a community can help landscape architects design public parks. The use of anthropological methods such as social mapping, participant-observation, and ethnographic interviewing can provide an essential form of data that must be wedded to the aesthetic principles of architectural design. This anthropological approach to designing public places serves to remind architects that the perceptions, values, and interests of the user groups must be taken into account if the end product is to be functional.

QUESTIONS FOR FURTHER THOUGHT

1. In what ways can anthropologists be valuable employees of an architectural firm?
2. How can cultural knowledge contribute to the style and function of architectural design?
3. Would the restoration of the park have been successful (even possible) without the input of the major neighborhood groups? Why?

paying job. Even though it is possible that the janitor's son could go to Harvard Law School and become upwardly mobile, such a scenario is not very likely.

Members of the same social class share not only similar economic levels but also similar experiences, educational backgrounds, political views, memberships in organizations, occupations, and values. In addition, studies of social class have shown, not surprisingly, that members of a social class tend to associate more often with one another than with people in other classes. In other words, a person's life chances, though not determined, are very much influenced by that person's social class.

Caste Societies

In contrast, societies based on caste rank their members according to birth. Membership in castes is unchangeable, people in different castes are segregated from one another, social mobility is virtually nonexistent, and marriage between castes is strictly prohibited. Castes, which are usually associated with specific occupations, are ranked hierarchically.

Caste societies, wherever they may be found, have a number of characteristics in common. First, caste membership is directly related to such economic issues as occupation, workloads, and control of valuable resources. The higher castes have a monopoly on certain occupations, control the allocation of resources to favor themselves, and avoid engaging in difficult or low-status work. In short, the higher castes have more and do less. Second, members of the same caste share the same social status, largely because of their strong sense of caste identity, residential and social segregation from other castes, and uniformity of lifestyles. Third, caste exclusiveness is further enhanced because each caste has its own set of secret rituals, which tend to intensify group awareness. Fourth, the higher castes are generally most interested in maintaining the caste system for the obvious reason that they benefit from it the most.

HINDU CASTE SYSTEM Caste societies can be found in a number of regions of the world, such as among the Rwandans in Central Africa, but the best-known—and certainly the best-described—example of the caste system is in Hindu India. Hinduism's sacred Sanskrit texts rank all people into one of four categories, called *varnas*, which are associated with certain occupations. Even though local villagers may not always agree as to who belongs to which *varna*, most people accept the *varna* categories as fundamentally essential elements of their society.

According to a Hindu myth of origin (see Mandelbaum 1970), the four major *varnas* originated from the body of primeval man. The highest caste, the Brahmins (priests and scholars), came from his mouth, the Kshatriyas (warriors) emanated from his arms, the Vaishyas (tradesmen) came from his thighs, and the Shudras (cultivators and servants) sprang from his feet. Each of these four castes is hierarchically ranked according to its ritual purity. Below these four castes—and technically outside the caste system—is still another category, called the Untouchables or, literally, outcastes. The Untouchables, who are confined to the lowest and most menial types of work, such as cleaning latrines or leatherworking, are considered so impure that members of the four legitimate castes must avoid all contact with them.

Ideally, all of Hindu India is hierarchically ranked according to these four basic castes. In actual practice, however, each of these four categories is further subdivided and stratified. To add to the complexity of the Indian caste system, the order in which these subcastes are ranked varies from one region to another. These local subgroups, known as *jati*, are local family groups that are strictly endogamous. All members of a *jati*, who share a common social status, are expected to behave in ways appropriate for that *jati*. A person's *jati* commands his or her strongest loyalties, serves as a source of social support, and provides the primary basis for personal identity. Thus, the *jati* serves as the important social entity in traditional Hindu society. The members of each *jati* maintain its corporateness in two ways: through egalitarian socializing with members of their own *jati* and by scrupulously avoiding any type of egalitarian socializing (such as marriage or sharing of food) with members of other *jati*. Although the

= *In India the Untouchables, who must refrain from having social contact with members of the four major castes, are relegated to the most menial occupations.*

jati were originally linked to traditional occupations, that is no longer the case. For instance, today most members of the traditional leatherworker caste are landless laborers.

Even though the prohibitions against social intercourse among castes are as rigidly defined as anywhere in the world, the amount of interdependence among local castes should not be overlooked. This interdependence is largely economic in nature rather than social. Like any society with a complex economy, India has an elaborate division of labor. In fact, one of the basic features of caste in India is that each *jati* is associated with its own traditional occupation that provides goods or services for the rest of the society. Certain lower-caste *jati* (such as barbers, potters, and leatherworkers) provide vital services for the upper echelon (landowning) castes from whom they receive food and animal products. For the economy to work, lower castes sell their services to the upper castes in exchange for goods. Thus, despite the very high level of social segregation between the castes in India, there is considerable economic interrelatedness, particularly at the village level.

An important tenet of Hindu religious teachings is *reincarnation,* the notion that at death a person's soul is reborn in an endless sequence of new forms. The caste into which a person is born is considered to be her or his duty and responsibility for that lifetime. Hindu scripture teaches that the good life involves living according to the prescriptions of the person's caste. Members of higher castes must do everything possible to retain their ritual purity by avoiding any type of intimate interaction with members of lower castes; correspondingly, members of lower castes must refrain from polluting higher castes. It is taught that those who violate their caste prescription will come back in a lower caste or, if the transgression is sufficiently serious, in a nonhuman form. Hindu scripture is very explicit about the consequences of violating prescribed caste behaviors. For example, the Brahmin who steals the gold of another Brahmin will be reincarnated in the next thousand lives as a snake, a spider, or a lizard. That's a powerful sanction! In other words, it is believed that people's caste status is determined by how they behaved in former lives and that their present behavior determines their caste status in future lives.

Even though the Indian government has attempted to discourage it, the caste system still plays an important role in the lives of most contemporary Indians. The author of the Indian constitution in 1950, B. R. Ambedkar, himself an Untouchable, tried to eliminate some of the worst features of the caste system by making it a criminal offense to discriminate against Untouchables. He also established the world's first affirmative action program by establishing quotas for the Untouchables (and other underprivileged groups) for proportional representation in the parliament, government jobs, and education. And, in 1997 India elected its first president, K. R. Narayanan, from among the ranks of the Untouchable caste.

Nevertheless, even though caste inequities have been explicitly prohibited by the constitution, India has a long way to go before the injustices of the past are eliminated. Politics in contemporary India are becoming increasingly caste oriented. Lower-caste politicians promise to protect the lower castes; middle-caste politicians promise to look after their own; and the upper-caste Brahmins in recent years are becoming increasingly defensive because they can no longer count on those lower castes whose servitude they had always taken for granted. As the demands of the Untouchables and other lower castes have increased recently, there has been a rise in caste-related violence. Disputes over jobs, wages, land ownership, and water rights often flare up into open conflict. Caste violence over the issue of affirmative action in higher education has recently broken out at a leading medical school in India where students claim to have been beaten by upper-caste students who oppose the admission of those from lower castes (Lloyd 1999).

·■ RACIAL AND ETHNIC ■· STRATIFICATION

THE DISCIPLINE of anthropology has as its primary goal to study the extraordinary physical and cultural diversity found among the world's population. This vast physical and cultural diversity is also of great interest to the peoples themselves because human relationships are often shaped by the differences, either real or imagined, between groups or subgroups of people. To one degree or another, all societies differentiate among their members, and these differences can become the basis for social inequalities. People are often characterized on the basis of their distinctive physical characteristics or their learned cultural traits. Those sharing similar physical traits are often defined as belonging to the same *race,* and those sharing similar cultural characteristics are said to belong to the same **ethnic group.**

Throughout history, and in many parts of the world, racial and ethnic differences have led to inequality, discrimination, antagonism, and, in some cases, violence. Each day we read in the newspaper about racial or ethnic conflict in various parts of the world: the Irish Republican Army bombings in England, the ethnic cleansing in Bosnia, terrorist attacks on Palestinians and Jews in Israel, and long-standing ethnic antagonisms between the Japanese and Koreans. Much closer to home we have racial rioting in Los Angeles, ethnic gang wars in our cities, and widespread resentment that recent immigrants from Southeast Asia are taking so many places in our best universities. So even in the United States—a country constitutionally and legally committed to social equality—physical (racial) or cultural (ethnic) differences still greatly affect relations between groups and their relative positions in the social hierarchy.

The terms *race* and *ethnicity* are sometimes used synonymously in everyday speech, but to anthropologists they have very different meanings. Technically, a *race* is an interbreeding population whose members share a greater number of traits with one another than they do with people outside the group. During the first half of the twentieth century, physical anthropologists devoted considerable effort to dividing the world's populations into racial categories based on shared physical traits. They carefully measured such traits as hair color and texture, eye color and shape, thickness of lips, breadth of the nose, body stature, and skin color, among others. But when the measuring frenzy was over, what did we really have? Depending on who was doing the categorizing, some racial typologies had hundreds of categories (that is, "races") and others had as few as three (Mongoloid, Caucasoid, and Negroid).

Race, then, is no more than a statistical statement about the occurrence of physical traits. When people who share a large number of biological traits intermarry, it is likely (but by no means certain) that they will have offspring who share those traits. When two blond-haired, blue-eyed Norwegians mate and have children, those children are statistically more likely to look like Scandinavians than like Nigerians. Similarly, when we cross two Chihuahuas, the offspring are more likely to look like Chihuahuas than Great Danes. Based on our knowledge of genetics, we know that there are no pure races because recessive traits are not lost but can reappear in future generations. Because different populations have been interbreeding for thousands of years, a continuum of human physical types has resulted.

A major problem with racial classifications is that the schemes differ depending on the traits on which they are based. That is, it would be possible to put all of the world's people into a number of different categories based on skin color. But if those same people were categorized according to body stature, many people would be assigned to different categories. Each physical trait is biologically determined by distinct genes that vary independently of one another. Therefore, having a particular color of hair in no way determines what your eye color will be. All physical anthropologists who have attempted to classify people according to race have arbitrarily selected the traits they have used. For example, instead of using skin color or blood type, we could classify people according to their earlobe structure (attached or detached earlobes), which is also a genetically determined physical trait. Although no one ever has, we could divide the world's population into two major races: those with attached earlobes and those with detached earlobes. Then, also quite arbi-

= *Although the concept of race has little scientific significance, it is extremely important socially.*

trarily, we could assert that people with attached earlobes (like your author) are clearly more intelligent than those with detached earlobes. Furthermore, they are of better character and are more likely to practice good personal hygiene. Moreover, we could then insist that we don't want people with detached earlobes living in our neighborhoods, going to our schools, or marrying our daughters. That stand would make as much scientific sense as basing such a position on any other physical characteristic, such as skin color.

As a scientific concept, then, race is not terribly significant, for it gives us very little insight into human behavior. Nevertheless, because of the way people interpret physical differences, race is important socially. That is, it makes little difference that beliefs about race have no scientific basis. Race relations and stratification based on race are affected by people's beliefs, not necessarily by scientific facts. If people define a situation as real, then it will be real

for them, and it will have very real consequences. The consequences of people's beliefs can be very powerful. All too often in human history, groups have separated themselves according to physical differences. They soon decide that physically different people are inferior and then use that belief to exclude, exploit, or brutalize them.

Whereas *race* refers to physical traits, *ethnicity* refers to cultural traits that are passed on from generation to generation. These cultural traits may include religion, dietary practices, language, humor, clothing, cultural heritage, folklore, national origins, and a shared ancestry and social experience. Members of an ethnic group perceive themselves as sharing these (and perhaps other) cultural characteristics. Moreover, ethnic group members have a sense of ethnic identity whereby they define themselves and members of their group as "us" and everyone else as "them." Because of their cultural homogeneity, ethnic groups tend to cut across socioeconomic lines.

CROSS-CULTURAL MISCUE

THE SCENE is a classroom in an inner-city elementary school in Richmond, Virginia. Pedro, the 9-year-old son of a recent immigrant family from Puerto Rico, leaves his seat to sharpen his pencil. When the teacher, Ms. Harkins, asks Pedro where he is going, Pedro casts his eyes downward and tries to explain that he was going to the pencil sharpener. Ms. Harkins, thinking that Pedro has something to hide by not looking her in the eye, becomes so annoyed with him that she lifts up his chin and says, "Look at me when I'm talking to you!" Pedro cannot understand what he did wrong that made his teacher so angry.

This unfortunate scenario—played out all too often in our multicultural schools—is a classic example of how cross-cultural communication can be short-circuited. This needless escalation of ill will between student and teacher could have been avoided if Ms. Harkins had understood several fundamental features of Pedro's Puerto Rican culture.

First, relations between teachers and students in Puerto Rico are more formal than they are in the United States. Moreover, one's position in the social hierarchy is taken more seriously in Puerto Rico than it is in the United States. As a result, Puerto Rican students learn from an early age that they are expected to show the utmost respect and deference to authority figures such as teachers. And, second, Ms. Harkin failed to understand how Puerto Rican children express deference and respect to high-status people. In Ms. Harkin's culture, the student is expected to maintain a high level of eye contact with the teacher as a sign of respect. But in Puerto Rico, Pedro learned that eye contact has the opposite meaning—that to avoid eye contact is a sign of respect for high-status people, such as teachers, priests, grandparents, and adults in general. Thus, Pedro was trying to show the greatest respect for his teacher by avoiding eye contact, but Ms. Harkins mistook his downcast eyes as a sign of disrespect or disinterest. This cross-cultural misunderstanding—stemming from a lack of knowledge about other cultures—affected student–teacher rapport.

In some cases certain groups are both racially and ethnically distinct from their neighbors. For example, some Native Americans, such as the Zuni, have very distinctive physical features and also identify themselves strongly with their native language, political organizations, family networks, and cultural practices. Other groups, such as Italian Americans and Greek Americans, may look alike but form their own distinctive (and usually exclusive) social clubs and social networks.

■· RACE AND ETHNICITY ■·
IN THE UNITED STATES

FOR MUCH of the twentieth century, the United States has been described as a large melting pot in which people from many cultural backgrounds were fused into a homogeneous American nationality. However, this idea of mass cultural amalgamation has not been realized. Although significant numbers of individuals have broken out of their ethnic patterns, ethnic groups remain. To illustrate, large numbers of Asian Americans (Chinese, Japanese, Vietnamese) live in California; Hispanics in Miami, Los Angeles, Chicago, and New York; Arabic-speaking peoples in Detroit; Amish in Pennsylvania and Indiana; and hundreds of Native American groups throughout North America. In fact, the United States has experienced a revival of ethnic consciousness in recent decades, particularly in urban areas. We often hear about ethnic neighborhoods, ethnic

foods, and various ethnic studies programs at universities. Thus, the notion of the melting pot appears to be more of a metaphor than a reality. Perhaps we should think of contemporary American society less as a melting pot and more as a salad bowl, in which the individual ethnic groups are mixed together but retain their own distinctiveness and identity.

As we begin the twenty-first century, the fastest-growing ethnic group in the United States is really not an ethnic group at all. Referred to by the catch-all term *Hispanics,* this rapidly growing segment of the U.S. population is composed of a number of different subcultural groups that share a common language. In a recent article, Linda Robinson (1998) describes 17 different Hispanic subcultures within the continental United States. Some have lived in the United States for generations whereas the majority have immigrated from Central and South America more recently. Coming from more than 20 different countries, many Hispanics cannot agree on what they would like to be called. Some want to be called by their former nationality (for example, Cubans, Mexicans, Guatemalans), whereas others prefer the term *Latino.*

However we may choose to classify them, collectively they are changing the face of the country and having an enormous impact on the nation's economy, politics, entertainment, and educational systems. The Latino population during the decade of the 1990s has grown 38 percent as compared to 9 percent for the overall population. It is es-

= *Many ethnic groups, such as Hispanics in New York City, maintain their own distinct neighborhood and sense of cultural identity even though they have lived in the United States for generations.*

timated that by the year 2005, they will replace African Americans as the largest minority group and that by 2050, they will represent one-quarter of the total U.S. population (Chambers 1999).

Not only do they have numbers, but many Hispanics are making their mark on all aspects of U.S. culture. Young Americans of all types are dancing to salsa music, buying CDs recorded by Jennifer Lopez and Ricky Martin, and cheering for their favorite Major League Baseball players with names like Sosa, Ramirez, and Conseco. Yet, not everyone in the United States has been willing to embrace this rapidly growing Latino presence. In California, which has the largest number of Latinos of any state, voters supported several initiatives that would deny schooling and social services to undocumented immigrants and would eliminate bilingual education programs in the schools.

This backlash is based on a number of myths about the Hispanic population. First, because of the widespread use of Spanish on signs in cities like Los Angeles and Miami, many people assume that Hispanics do not speak English or have no desire to learn it. But the rate of learning English for Hispanic immigrants is approximately the same as for other immigrant groups, and, in fact, one-third of Latinos living in Los Angeles speak only English. Second, Hispanics are sometimes viewed (erroneously) as not fully participating in the economy. However, Mexicans and Central Americans have a labor force participation rate of 62 percent, which exceeds the Anglo rate and far exceeds that of African Americans. Hispanics generally are found doing the jobs that other Americans refuse to do: harvesting crops, making beds, landscaping, and construction-related work such as house framing, roofing, and masonry. They have the diligence and enterprise, coupled with strong family ties, that characterized the Irish, Italians, and Poles during the early 1900s. And third, many non-Hispanic Americans view recent migrants as "short-timers" who are interested only in making enough money to return home. But when asked in a national survey if they planned to stay permanently in the United States, more than 90 percent of the legal immigrants said yes (Pachon 1998). To be certain, some immigrants do return home, and others continue to send sizable portions of their income to relatives back home. But, like their European counterparts a century earlier, the great majority of Mexicans and Central Americans plant their roots and commit to becoming citizens. And once that occurs, it is not long before they move to the suburbs, register as Republicans, and join the country club.

FORMS OF INTERGROUP RELATIONS

Some racial and ethnic groups live together in peace and with a large degree of social equality. In most situations, however, racial and ethnic groups tend to engage in varying levels of conflict and inequality. How racial and ethnic groups relate to one another can be viewed as a continuum ranging from cooperation to outright hostility. George Simpson and J. Milton Yinger (1985) have identified six major forms of interracial and interethnic relations, which become less humane as you move from number one to number six:

1. *Pluralism:* In this situation, two or more groups live in harmony with one another while retaining their own ethnic heritage, pride, and identity. Swiss society—composed of Germans, Swiss Germans, French, and Italians living together peacefully, if not always amicably—is a good example of a pluralistic society. However, not all situations are as harmonious as the multicultural country of Switzerland. Present-day Canada is an excellent example of a multicultural society that is experiencing a number of challenges to its national cohesion by French separatists who want to assert their cultural uniqueness. A truly multicultural society has been realized when there is no longer a single dominant ethnic or racial group.

2. *Assimilation:* **Assimilation** occurs when a racial or ethnic minority is absorbed into the wider society. The many Asian and Pacific ethnic groups that have peacefully and voluntarily assimilated themselves into Hawaiian society over the past several centuries are an example. Assimilation involves several different forms, which usually progress in sequential stages. The first stage of assimilation is cultural, whereby minority group members gradually surrender their own cultural features (such as language, values, and behaviors) while accepting those of the dominant group. The second form is social assimilation, where minority group members join into secondary and eventually primary group relationships (such as churches, unions, and neighborhood associations) with members of the mainstream. The final stage of assimilation involves physical integration through intermarriage, whereby the biological distinctions between the minority and the majority groups gradually decline or disappear.

3. *Legal protection of minorities:* In societies where racial and ethnic groups are hostile toward one

APPLIED PERSPECTIVE
Diabetes Among Mexican Americans

*I*t has been found that non–insulin-dependent diabetes mellitus (NIDDM), a serious health problem in the United States, is particularly prevalent among minority populations. Medical researchers have found that Mexican Americans are two to three times more likely to suffer from diabetes than are non-Hispanic Whites. Factors accounting for this higher incidence among Mexican Americans include a genetic predisposition, culture, geography, and a number of variables associated with low socioeconomic status (such as income, access to health facilities, and literacy).

Diabetes is not curable. Rather, it must be managed over the course of the patient's lifetime. To manage diabetes, patients need to take medication in the proper doses, exercise regularly, and adhere to a healthy diet. A major problem in the treatment of NIDDM is that patients often fail to follow through on recommended treatment behaviors. Noncompliance with prescribed treatment behaviors is particularly high among Mexican Americans.

Medical anthropologist Linda Hunt, along with her colleagues Jacqueline Pugh and Miguel Valenzuela, wanted to know more about the factors influencing self-care among Mexican American patients with NIDDM so they could develop recommendations to improve intervention strategies (1995). Hunt and her colleagues conducted open-ended interviews with 51 Mexican American patients with NIDDM in San Antonio and Laredo, Texas. Their findings showed that none of the patients in the sample followed the recommended treatment exactly. However, it wasn't because of disinterest or ignorance. Rather, they were adapting their self-care behavior to the social realities of their everyday lives, making choices based on two important sociocultural factors: (1) their limited financial resources and (2) their desire to conduct "normal" social relationships. Let us look at each of these factors.

Because all interviewees were low-income patients, their diabetes imposed several hardships on them. Many felt too sick to work, thereby reducing their income; the cost of treatment, despite the clinics' sliding fee scales, was still a major financial burden; and the cost of changing their diets usually involved substituting more expensive foods (such as fresh fruits and vegetables) for the things that they normally ate. Because of their limited finances, patients would conserve resources not by discontinuing a certain treatment (such as taking medication or testing for blood sugar level) but rather by doing it less often than prescribed.

The second factor that influenced decisions about self-care was a desire on the part of both men and women to "feel normal" by continuing in the same roles as they had before they developed diabetes. Because many women play the role of caregivers within their families, those who have sick relatives at home find it impossible to get out of the house to get the proper exercise. Moreover, female patients with diabetes find it very difficult to cook food for their families that they themselves are not allowed to eat. Men found it particularly difficult to change their eating habits because they desired to maintain their masculine image, to be "able to make their own decisions about what to eat and drink, and able to participate, as any other man, in the usual social events like parties or watching football, which often involve drinking alcohol." Thus, for both men and women, having to alter one's usual roles and behavior was seen as interfering with their normal social life.

Understanding the social and cultural realities of Mexican Americans, the researchers could recommend improved intervention strategies. Rather than blaming the patients for failed treatments, the researchers appreciated the patients' limited finances and were able to come up with some creative solutions. It was possible to cut the cost of self-treatment without sacrificing quality. For example, Hunt and her colleagues suggested such cost-cutting strategies as establishing safe procedures for reusing syringes, using phone follow-up to replace some of the clinic visits, and formulating ways of reducing the cost of the foods needed for a healthy diet. There were also recommendations that took into account the need of patients to maintain normal social relationships. To illustrate, people who feel pressure to eat and drink inappropriate things at social events need culturally acceptable strategies for turning down food or decreasing the amount they eat. In some cases, the solution may be as simple as getting people to use different language when describing food. As Hunt and her colleagues have suggested, "the concept of a 'diabetic diet' could be replaced by pointing out that it is really just a 'healthy diet' for everyone."

Hunt's research suggests that clinicians, particularly when working with culturally different patients, need to understand why people make certain choices concerning their self-care treatment. Rather than assuming that ignorance or indifference is the cause of poor outcomes, clinicians need to explore what patients are doing and why they are doing it. Only by entering into a continuing dialogue with culturally different patients can clinicians help them make the most medically appropriate choices for managing their illness.

QUESTIONS FOR FURTHER THOUGHT

1. Why did none of the Mexican American patients in Hunt's study strictly follow the prescribed self-care behaviors?
2. Can you think of other reasons why it might be more difficult for low-income Mexican Americans to get regular exercise than it would be for upper-middle-class people living in the suburbs?
3. From what you know about proper self-care behavior for diabetes, can you identify other ethnic groups in your area of the country that would have similar difficulties adhering to prescribed forms of self-care?

another, the government may step in to legally protect the minority group. In Great Britain the Race Relations Act makes it a criminal offense for anyone to express publicly any sentiments that might lead to racial or ethnic hostility. In the United States, three constitutional amendments (the 13th, 14th, and 15th), several civil rights laws, and a number of executive directives have provided legislative and administrative protection to minorities over the past decades. The recent passage of the Native Title Bill in Australia guarantees a number of territorial rights to the country's indigenous population (a mere two centuries after European settlers drove them off their ancestral land!). None of these pieces of legislation have given equal citizenship to minority groups, but they have provided a measure of security against some of the more blatant forms of prejudice and discrimination.

4. *Population transfer:* One solution to intergroup conflict is **population transfer,** which involves the physical removal of a minority group to another location. The forced relocation of 16,000 Cherokee Indians from North Carolina to Oklahoma in 1838 is a case in point. A more recent example from the United States, although a temporary situation, was the forced relocation of thousands of Japanese Americans into internment camps during World War II. Unfortunately, this particular form of intergroup relationship has been played out in a number of different places in the world in recent years. To illustrate, tens of thousands of Vietnamese people have fled Cambodia to Vietnam to avoid being killed by the Cambodian government. Large numbers of ethnic Tutsi from Rwanda have fled to Zaire, Tanzania, and Uganda to avoid persecution by the majority Hutu government. Often these population transfers cause enormous hardships both for those being moved and for the local people into whose territories they are arriving.

5. *Long-term subjugation:* In some parts of the world, racial and ethnic minorities have been politically, economically, and socially repressed for indefinite periods of time. Until the recent changes in the mid-1990s, the repression of Blacks under the apartheid system in the Republic of South Africa was an example of the long-term institutionalized (legal) repression of one ethnic and racial group by another. Separate and unequal facilities (schools, restrooms, housing) and strict legalized segregation were government policy in South Africa for much of the twentieth century. The White population (13 percent) controlled the best 87 percent of the land, whereas the non-Whites (87 percent) lived on the worst 13 percent of the land. The situation that until recently existed in South Africa was just slightly better than slavery for the non-White population.

6. *Genocide:* Sometimes the symbols of race and ethnicity can be so powerful that they can cause people to engage in **genocide:** mass annihilation of groups of people. The most notorious example, of course, is Adolph Hitler, who during World War II sent over 6 million people (Jews, Gypsies, Slavs, homosexuals, and others he considered to be subhuman) to be killed in death camps. Unfortunately, there are many other examples of genocide from around the world that, although involving fewer deaths, are just as inhumane. To illustrate, in what used to be Yugoslavia, Serbian forces under the leadership of President Slobodan Milosevic engaged in what has been euphemistically called ethnic cleansing, in which Muslims and Croats were murdered by the thou-

= *Serbian leader Slobodan Molosevic is accused of a form of genocide euphemistically called ethnic cleansing, in which thousands of Muslims and Croats were murdered or brutalized.*

sands, and many more were raped and brutalized. And in 1994, in a very purposeful attempt at genocide, the Hutu extremists in Rwanda massacred an estimated million Tutsi. Although widely condemned by most people in the world, genocide is still used as a way to gain political advantage.

It is important to note that these ways of classifying racial and ethnic relations are not mutually exclusive. More than one classification can exist in a society at the same time.

•■ THEORIES OF STRATIFICATION ■•

THE INEQUITABLE DISTRIBUTION of wealth, power, and prestige appears to be a fundamental characteristic of most societies, particularly those with complex, highly differentiated economies. Some modern societies—such as the former Soviet Union, the People's Republic of China, and Albania—have attempted to become classless by eliminating all vestiges of inequality. But even in these societies, high-ranking government officials have been far more generously rewarded than the workers.

The basic question is, Why is inequality a nearly universal trait of social life? The debate among social scientists, which at times has been heated, revolves around two conflicting positions, which are based on different philosophical assumptions and have distinct political implications. The more conservative position, the **functional theory,** holds that social inequality exists because it is necessary for the maintenance of society. The more liberal **conflict theory** explains social inequality as the result of benefits derived by the upper classes who use their power and privilege to exploit those below them.

THE FUNCTIONALIST INTERPRETATION

By stressing the integrative nature of social systems, functional anthropologists argue that stratification exists because it contributes to the overall well-being of the society. According to Kingsley Davis and Wilbert Moore (1945), complex societies, if they are to survive, depend on the performance of a wide variety of jobs, some of which are more important than others because they require specialized education, talent, and hard work. If people are to make the sacrifices necessary to perform these vital jobs, they must be adequately rewarded. For example, because the skills of a physician are in greater demand by our society than are those of a garbage collector, the rewards (money and prestige) are much greater for the physician. Functionalists ar-

gue that these differential rewards are necessary if societies are to recruit the best-trained and most highly skilled people for these highly valued positions. If physicians and garbage collectors received the same pay and social status, few people would opt to become physicians. Thus, according to the functionalist interpretation, social stratification is necessary or functional for the society because it serves as a mechanism for allocating rewards and motivating the best people to fill the key jobs in the society.

Although the functionalist view seems quite plausible, it has weaknesses. First, some critics of the functionalist position point out that stratified societies do not always give the greatest rewards to those filling the most vital positions. Rock singers, baseball players, and movie stars often make many times more money than teachers, pediatricians, or U.S. Supreme Court justices. Second, the functionalists do not recognize the barriers that stratification systems put in the way of certain segments of the society, such as members of low-prestige and low-power groups. Ethnic and racial minorities, women, and the poor do not always have equal opportunities to compete because they are too poor or have the wrong accent, skin color, or gender. Third, the functionalist position can be called into question because it tends to make a fundamentally ethnocentric assumption. That is, the functionalists assume that people in all societies are motivated by the desire to maximize their wealth, power, and prestige. In actual fact, however, a number of societies emphasize the equitable distribution of social rewards rather than rewarding individuals for amassing as much as possible for themselves.

THE CONFLICT THEORY INTERPRETATION

Whereas the functionalist view starts with the assumption of social order, stability, and integration, conflict theorists assume that the natural tendency of all societies is toward change and conflict. According to this theory, stratification exists because the people occupying the upper levels of the hierarchy are willing and able to use their wealth, power, and prestige to exploit those below them. The upper strata maintain their dominance through the use of force or the threat of force and by convincing the oppressed of the value of continuing the system. Thus, those at the top use their wealth, power, and prestige to maintain—perhaps even increase—their privileged position.

This conflict theory of social stratification is derived largely from the late-nineteenth-century writings of Karl Marx, who, unlike the functionalists, did not view stratification systems as either desirable or inevitable. Believing that economic forces are the main factors shaping a society, Marx (1909) viewed history as a constant class struggle between the haves and the have-nots. Writing during the latter stages of the industrial revolution in Europe, Marx saw the classic struggle occurring between the **bourgeoisie** (those who owned the means of production) and the **proletariat** (the working class who exchanged their labor for wages).

Because of their control of the means of production, the small bourgeoisie exert significant influence over the larger working class. By controlling such institutions as schools, factories, government, and the media, the bourgeoisie can convince the workers that the existing distribution of power and wealth (that is, the status quo) is preferable and that anyone can be successful if only he or she works hard enough. Thus, according to the classic Marxist view, the bourgeoisie create a false consciousness among the workers by leading them to believe that if they are not successful, it is because they have not worked hard enough rather than because their opportunities for advancement were blocked by the powerful upper class.

As long as the workers accept this ideology legitimizing the status quo, the inequities of the stratification system will continue to exist. Believing that class conflict is inevitable, Marx predicted that eventually the proletariat would recognize both the extent of their own exploitation and their collective power to change it. When the workers develop a class consciousness, they will revolt against the existing social order, replace capitalism with communism, and eliminate scarcity, social classes, and inequality.

FUNCTIONALISTS VERSUS CONFLICT THEORISTS

Functionalists and conflict theorists—with their radically different interpretations of social inequality—have been locking horns for years. Functionalists hold that systems of stratification exist and are necessary because they benefit the societies of which they are a part. Conflict theorists, on the other hand, claim that systems of stratification exist because they help the people at the top (that is, the wealthy and powerful) maintain their privileged position. The functionalist position emphasizes the positive benefits of social stratification for the total society. Conflict theorists draw our attention to such negative aspects as the unjust nature of stratification systems and how that inherent unfairness can lead to rebellions, revolts, and high crime rates.

Although there is truth in both of these interpretations, neither theory can be used exclusively to explain the existence of all types of stratification systems. Functionalists are correct to point out that open class systems, for example, are integrative to the extent that they promote constructive endeavor that is beneficial to the society as a whole. Yet, once established, these class systems often become self-perpetuating, with those at the top striving to maintain their superior positions at the expense of the lower classes. At the same time, the underclasses—through political mobilization, revitalization movements, and even violent revolutions—seek to free themselves from deprivation and exploitation. In short, functional integration is real, but so is conflict.

Not only do the functionalist and conflict theories represent two contrasting interpretations of social inequality, but they also have radically different policy implications for modern society. The functionalist view carries with it the implication that social stratification systems should be maintained because the best-qualified people, through the competitive process, will be motivated to fill the top positions. In contrast, the view of conflict theorists implies that social inequality should be minimized or eliminated because many people in the lower strata never have a chance to develop their full potential. Thus, the functionalist position would want the government to take no action (such as welfare programs or a progressive income tax) that would redistribute wealth, power, or prestige. Conflict theorists would call for exactly the opposite course of action, arguing that eliminating barriers to social mobility would unleash the hidden brilliance of those currently living in the underclasses.

SUMMARY

1. Social ranking is an important feature found to one degree or another in all societies. The degree to which societies distribute wealth, power, and prestige on an equitable basis can be used to distinguish among three different types of societies. Egalitarian societies are unstratified in that they allocate wealth, power, and prestige fairly equally. In rank societies, which are partially stratified, people have equal access to power and wealth but not to prestige. The most completely stratified societies are those based on classes or castes that have unequal access to wealth, power, and prestige.

2. Stratified societies, which are associated with the rise of civilization, range from open class societies, which permit high social mobility, to more rigid caste societies, which allow for little or no social mobility. Class societies are associated with achieved status, the positions that the individual can choose or at least have some control over. Caste societies, on the other hand, are based on ascribed statuses into which one is born and cannot change.

3. The United States is often cited as a prime example of a class society with maximum mobility. Although our national credo includes a belief in the possibility of going from rags to riches, most people in the United States remain in the class into which they are born because social environment has an appreciable effect on a person's life chances.

4. Hindu India is often cited as the most extreme form of caste society found in the world. Social boundaries among castes are strictly maintained by caste endogamy and strongly held notions of ritual purity and pollution.

5. Race is a classification of people based on physical traits, whereas ethnicity is a scheme based on cultural characteristics. Although the concept of race is not particularly meaningful from a scientific standpoint, it is important because people's ideas of racial differences have led to very powerful systems of stratification and discrimination.

6. There are two conflicting interpretations of social stratification. The functionalist theory emphasizes the integrative nature of stratification systems by pointing out how class systems contribute to the overall well-being of a society by encouraging constructive endeavor. Conflict theorists believe that stratification systems exist because the upper classes strive to maintain their superior position at the expense of the lower classes.

KEY TERMS

achieved status	conflict theory
ascribed status	egalitarian societies
assimilation	ethnic group
bourgeoisie	functional theory
caste	genocide
class	*jati*
nouveau riche	rank societies
population transfer	social mobility
power	stratified societies
prestige	*varnas*
proletariat	wealth

SUGGESTED READINGS

Beeghley, Leonard. *The Structure of Social Stratification in the United States.* 2d ed. Boston: Allyn & Bacon, 1996. An up-to-date discussion of social class in the United States that is both theoretically informed and statistically rich. In addition to examining all classes up and down the social ladder, Beeghley also deals with the issues of gender, racial, and ethnic inequalities.

Bernardi, Bernardo. *Age Class Systems: Social Institutions and Policies Based on Age.* New York: Cambridge University Press, 1985. Drawing on ethnographic data largely from Africa, the author defines the characteristics of age class systems, their geographic distribution, and various anthropological approaches to their study.

Berreman, Gerald D., and Kathleen M. Zaretsky, eds. *Social Inequality: Comparative and Development Approaches.* New York: Academic Press, 1981. A collection of 15 essays on the topic of social inequality that attempts to treat the subject comparatively across a wide range of cultures, comparatively over time, and within the appropriate sociocultural context.

Domhoff, G. William. *Who Rules America?* 3rd ed. Mountain View, CA: Mayfield, 1998. Using a power elite model, Domhoff argues that power in the United States is in the hands of an elite composed of corporate CEOs, political leaders, and military leaders, all of whom are intimately interconnected.

Fried, Morton. *The Evolution of Political Society.* New York: Random House, 1967. A widely quoted work that examines three fundamentally different types of societies (egalitarian, rank, and stratified) and how they relate to the political structure.

Lenski, Gerhard E. *Power and Privilege: A Theory of Social Stratification.* New York: McGraw-Hill, 1966. A wide-ranging analysis of human inequality that takes the reader through centuries and to all parts of the world. As the title of his first chapter indicates, Lenski asks the fundamental question of stratification studies: Who gets what and why? He then proceeds to answer the question by drawing liberally on anthropological, historical, and sociological data.

Newman, Katherine S. *Declining Fortunes: The Withering of the American Dream.* New York: Basic Books, 1993. Anthropologist Newman sheds new light on downward mobility and the politics of resentment among baby boomers in the United States. After the Great Depression of the 1930s, many Americans took prosperity for granted, but the economic realities of the 1980s and 1990s have prevented many from realizing those dreams of prosperity.

Romanucci-Ross, Lola. *Ethnic Identity: Creation, Conflict, and Accommodation.* 3rd ed. Walnut Creek, CA: AltaMira Press, 1995. This reader includes a number of articles showing how ethnic identity is related to language, nationalism, religion, and localism in such locations as former Yugoslavia, Sri Lanka, Southeast Asia, and Latino communities in the United States.

Schlegel, Alice, ed. *Sexual Stratification: A Cross Cultural View.* New York: Columbia University Press, 1977. A series of essays on the status of women in different societies.

On the Net

1. A problem that is becoming increasingly widespread in North America is that of homelessness, particularly in urban areas. Partly because homelessness is on the increase, many people have a poor understanding of the dimensions of the problem. Using the search engine of your choice, conduct a subject search on homelessness. You will find a web site titled "54 Ways You Can Help the Homeless" by Rabbi Charles A. Kroloff. Which of the 54 ways do you think are the most realistic? Can you suggest any others?

2. As part of your subject search on homelessness, find a site called "Homeless in America." According to the data found on this site, how many people in the United States are homeless? What are the major causes of homelessness?

3. Conduct a subject search for a site called "United for a Fair Economy." Go to the section of the site entitled "Shifting Fortunes: The Perils of the Growing American Wealth Gap (1999)." Read over the "overview" section and write a one-page summary on the growing wealth gap in the United States.

4. While still on the "United for a Fair Economy" site, visit the section entitled "The Racial Wealth Gap: Left Out of the Boom." What data are provided to suggest that racial minorities have not gained economically during the relatively good economic years of the 1990s?

Chapter Fourteen

SUPERNATURAL BELIEFS

WHAT WE WILL LEARN:

▼

What is religion?

▼

What functions does religion play for both the individual and the society as a whole?

▼

What different forms does religion take among the societies of the world?

▼

What role does religion play in the process of culture change?

▼

Indian woman in prayer.

Modern anthropologists have devoted considerable attention to the analysis of religion since they began to make direct field observations of peoples of the world.

Although twentieth-century anthropologists have not always agreed on how to interpret different religious systems, all would agree that the many religious practices found throughout the world vary widely from one another as well as from our own. These religious systems might involve sacrificing animals to ancestor gods, using a form of divination called ordeals to determine a person's guilt or innocence, or submitting oneself to extraordinary levels of pain as a way of communicating directly with the deities (Lehmann and Myers 1993).

·■ DEFINING RELIGION ■·

THE FORMS OF RELIGION vary enormously, but they are all alike to the extent that they are founded on a belief in the supernatural. For our purposes in this chapter, we shall define **religion** as a set of beliefs and patterned behaviors concerned with supernatural beings and forces. Because human societies are faced with a series of important life problems that cannot all be resolved through the application of science and technology, they attempt to overcome these human limitations by manipulating supernatural forces.

Anthropologists have long observed that all societies have a recognizable set of beliefs and behaviors that can be called religious. According to George Peter Murdock's widely quoted list of cultural universals (1945), all societies have religious rituals that propitiate supernatural forces, sets of beliefs concerning what we would call the soul, and notions about life after death. To be sure, non-religious people can be found in all societies. But when we claim that religion (or a belief in the supernatural) is universal, we are referring to a cultural phenomenon rather than an individual one. For example, we can find individuals in the Western world who do not believe personally in such supernatural forces as deities, ghosts, demons, or spirits. Nevertheless, these people are part of a society that has a set of religious beliefs and practices to which many (perhaps a majority) of the population adhere.

Because religion, in whatever form it may be found, is often taken very seriously and passionately by its adherents, there is a natural tendency for people to see their own religion as the best while viewing all others as inferior. Westerners often use science, logic, and empirical evidence (for example, through the study of biblical texts) to bolster and justify their own religious practices. Nevertheless, science and logic are not adequate to either establish the inherent validity of Western religious beliefs or to demonstrate that non-Western religions are false. In other words, no religion is able to demonstrate conclusively that its deities can work more miracles per unit of time than can those of other religions, although some certainly try. The central issue for anthropologists is not to determine which religion is better or more correct but rather to identify the various religious beliefs in the world as well as how they function, to what extent they are held, and the degree to which they affect human behavior.

PROBLEMS OF DEFINING RELIGION

Despite this rather facile definition of religion, we should hasten to point out that there is no universal agreement among anthropologists as to how to distinguish between religious and nonreligious phenomena. The problem lies in the fact that religion in some societies is so thoroughly embedded in the total social structure that often it is difficult to distinguish the religious from economic, political, or kinship behavior. To illustrate, when a Kikuyu elder sacrifices a goat at the grave of an ancestor god, is he engaging in religious behavior (he is calling for the ancestor god to intervene in the affairs of the living), economic behavior (the meat of the sacrificed animal will be distributed to and eaten by members of the kinship group), or kinship behavior (kin will have a chance to express their group solidarity at the ceremonial event)?

Such a ritual sacrifice is all of these at the same time. In highly specialized societies, such as our own, people tend to divide human behavior into what, at least for them, are logical categories: social, economic, political, religious, educational, and recreational, for example. Because many small-scale, less specialized societies do not divide human behavior into categories used in Western society, it is often difficult for Westerners to recognize the aspects of human behavior that they think of as religious.

Another difficulty in defining religion and the supernatural is that different societies have different ways of distinguishing between the natural world and the supernatural world. In our own society, we reserve the term *supernatural* for phenomena we cannot explain through reason or science. Other societies, however, do not dichotomize the world into either natural or supernatural explanations. For example, the Nyoro of Uganda have a word for *sorcery* that means "to injure another person by the secret use of harmful medicines or techniques" (Beattie 1960:73). Sorcery in Nyoro society can take a number of different forms. Placing a person's body substances (such as pieces of hair or fingernail clippings) in an animal horn and putting the horn on the roof of the person's house with the intention of causing that person harm is an act of sorcery in Nyoro society, but so is putting poison into an enemy's food or drink.

Given our own Western dichotomy between the natural and the supernatural, we would interpret these two acts as substantially different in nature. We would interpret the first act as an attempt to harm another person by the use of magic. If the intended victim dies, our own Western law courts would never hold the perpetrator culpable, for the simple reason that it could not be proven scientifically that placing the magical substances on the roof was the cause of the death. However, Westerners would view the poisoning as premeditated murder because it could be determined scientifically (that is, through an autopsy) that the poison did cause the person to die. This illustration should remind us that not all societies share our Western definition of supernatural. It is precisely because of this difference in viewing the natural and supernatural worlds that

Westerners have so much difficulty understanding non-Western religions, which they usually label as irrational or contradictory.

RELIGION AND MAGIC

Anthropologists studying supernatural beliefs cross-culturally have long been fascinated by the relationship between religion and magic. Whereas some anthropologists have emphasized the differences between these two phenomena, others have concentrated on the similarities. It is important to examine both the similarities and the differences because even though religion and magic can be found operating separately, most often they are found in some combined or compound form.

Religion and magic share certain features. Because both are systems of supernatural belief, they are nonrational; that is, they are not susceptible to scientific verification. In other words, whether religious or magical practices actually work cannot be empirically demonstrated. Rather, such practices must be accepted as a matter of faith. Moreover, both religion and magic are practiced—at least in part—as a way of coping with the anxieties, ambiguities, and frustrations of everyday life.

On the other hand, magic and religion differ in a number of important respects. First, religion deals with the major issues of human existence, such as the meaning of life, death, and one's spiritual relationship with deities. In contrast, magic is directed toward specific, immediate problems, such as curing an illness, bringing rain, or ensuring safety on a long journey. Second, religion uses prayer and sacrifices to appeal to or petition supernatural powers for assistance. Magical practitioners, on the other hand, believe they can control or manipulate nature or other people by their own efforts. Third, religion by and large tends to be a group activity whereas magic is more individually oriented. Fourth, whereas religion is usually practiced at a specified time, magic is practiced irregularly in response to specific and immediate problems. Fifth, religion usually involves officially recognized functionaries such as priests, whereas magic may be performed by a wide variety of practitioners who may or may not be recognized within the community as having supernatural powers.

Despite these five differences, in actual practice elements of religion and magic are often found together. In any religion, for example, there is a fine line—some would argue, no line at all—between praying for God's help and coercing or manipulating a situation to bring about a

= *A traditional healer from Jamaica uses supernatural powers.*

desired outcome. Also, it is not at all unusual for a person to use elements of both religion and magic simultaneously. To illustrate, a soldier about to enter combat may ask the gods for protection through prayer while carrying a lucky rabbit's foot (a magical charm).

Magic involves the manipulation of supernatural forces for the purpose of intervening in a wide range of human activities and natural events. The ritualistic use of magic can be found in some societies to ensure the presence of game animals, to bring rain, to cure or prevent illness, or to protect oneself from misfortune. Magic, however, can also be (and often is) directed to cause evil. In some societies it is believed that certain people called witches or sorcerers use supernatural powers to bring harm to people. Because these forms of "negative magic" hold such fascination for Westerners, it is instructive to examine them in greater detail.

SORCERY AND WITCHCRAFT

Although the terms *witchcraft* and *sorcery* are sometimes used synonymously, cultural anthropologists generally distinguish between them. As practiced in a wide variety of societies throughout the world, *witchcraft* is an inborn, involuntary, and often unconscious capacity to cause harm to other people. On the other hand, **sorcery**, which often involves the use of materials, potions, and medicines, is the deliberate use of supernatural powers to bring about harm. Some societies have specialized practitioners of sorcery, but in other societies sorcery can be practiced by anyone. Because sorcery involves the use of certain physical substances, the evidence for its existence is more easily found. Witchcraft, by contrast, is virtually impossible to prove or disprove because of the absence of any visible evidence of its existence.

Whereas sorcery involves the use of material substances to cause harm to people, witchcraft, it is thought, relies solely on psychic power (that is, thoughts and emotions). In other words, witches can turn their anger and hatred into evil deeds simply by thinking evil thoughts. How witches are conceptualized varies widely from society to society, but, in all cases, witches are viewed negatively. Witches, who are viewed universally as antisocial, are generally seen as being unable to control the human impulses that normal members of society are expected to keep in check. They have insatiable appetites for food, uncontrollable hatred, and perverted sexual desires. The Mandari believe that witches dance on their victims' graves. The Lugbara of Uganda speak of witches who dance naked, which for them is the ultimate social outrage. The Ganda and Nyoro of Uganda believe in witches who eat corpses. Among the Kaguru of Tanzania, witches are believed to walk upside-down, devour human flesh, commit incest, and in general fail to recognize the rules and constraints of normal society. In many parts of the world, witches are associated with the night, which separates them from normal people, who go about their business during the daytime. Moreover, witches are often associated with certain animals, such as bats, rats, snakes, lizards, or leopards, which may be black in color, dangerous, and nocturnal.

Sorcerers are generally believed to direct their malevolence purposefully against those they dislike, fear, or envy rather than acting randomly or capriciously. In any given society, hostile relations can occur between people who have some relationship to each other—such as outsiders who marry into a local village, rivals for a father's inheritance, wives in a polygynous household, men who are competing for a political office, or even rivals in competitive sports. People are therefore likely to attribute their own personal misfortune to the sorcery of some rival who might gain from harming them. Thus, accusations of sorcery are patterned to the extent that they reflect the con-

CROSS-CULTURAL MISCUE

WHILE ON A RECENT trip to Taipei, Matt Erskine had made plans to have dinner with his former college roommate John, who is Taiwanese. After catching up on each other's lives, Matt learned that John was about to leave his present job to start his own consulting business. However, before launching the new business, John told Matt that he must wait until the telephone company granted him the proper telephone number. Given all of the work he had done to get his new business started, Matt thought that having the proper telephone number was a minor obstacle that need not delay the opening of the business. But John insisted that he could not start his new enterprise until he had the right telephone number. Matt got the impression that John, perhaps fearful of taking risks, was using the telephone number as a lame excuse for not launching the business. But Matt misinterpreted this situation because he failed to understand some basic features of contemporary culture in Taiwan.

Despite their great economic leap into the global economy, many Taiwanese still retain a good deal of their beliefs in supernatural forces. This is particularly true about certain numbers. Some primary numbers, associated with very negative things such as death or excrement, are to be avoided at all costs. Other numbers, associated with positive things such as money, growth, and wealth, should be used in house addresses, license plates, and telephone numbers. In Taiwan the telephone company receives many requests for numbers that include the lucky numbers, leaving those with unlucky numbers unused. Thus, John believed strongly that unless he got a telephone number with lucky numbers in it, his business would be doomed from the start.

flicts, rivalries, and antagonisms that already exist among the people in any given society.

Although witchcraft and sorcery are usually associated with small-scale societies in the non-Western world, they are also found in highly industrialized parts of the world such as the United States, Canada, and a number of western European countries. Although they take a number of different forms, the basic distinction found in the Western world is between the forms of magic used for beneficial purposes and those used for malevolent purposes. Though considerably more complex, this basic distinction is best exemplified by modern-day witches (who put their beliefs to good ends) and Satanists (who use their magic for evil purposes).

Contemporary Western witches, who use their supernatural powers for good purposes, call their belief system **wicca,** a term meaning "witch," derived from Old English. Practiced largely in urban areas, witchcraft, like more orthodox religions, involves worship as a central part of its activities. Although it is possible for both men and women to practice witchcraft, in North American cities most practitioners are women, and wicca has an unmistakable matriarchal character. Local organizations of witches, called covens, are often presided over by high priestesses, symbolic representations of the mother goddess. Some covens consider themselves fertility cults, and some actually involve sexual intercourse as part of their initiation. Although this has attracted a good deal of interest in the news media, the wiccas emphasize fertility, not sexuality.

Wicca may involve the practice of magic, which is defined as bringing about changes by concentrating on one's *natural* powers. It is important to note that wiccans do not see their magical powers as supernatural. Wiccans use certain tools such as visualizations, spells, chants, and meditation to focus their inner powers to bring about a desired change. Practitioners of modern witchcraft claim that their early pre-Christian ancestors possessed these natural magical powers, but they were subsequently lost when they were forced to go underground by the Roman Catholic church. As a neo-pagan movement, contemporary wiccans view themselves as rediscovering these ancient lost magical powers.

In recent decades Europe and North America have experienced a gradual decline in memberships in ecclesiastical, institutionalized religions. At the same time, there has been an increase in religious pluralism, particularly

■ *The Reverend High Priestess Gypsy Ravish and her husband, Reverend High Priest Richard Ravish, both of Salem, Massachusetts, conduct a ritual of male and female union performed with a blade and chalice.*

among such esoteric forms of spirituality as witchcraft. In late 1999, this author, conducting a simple subject search on the Yahoo search engine, located 140 separate wiccan web sites. The Internet bookseller Amazon.com had sold 285 books on the wiccan movement and 1,255 books on the general topic of witchcraft by the end of 1999. The general sales of books on the practice of contemporary witchcraft have increased appreciably in the last decade. According to one publisher, although there are no blockbuster bestsellers, sales of wiccan books have increased from 3,000 or 4,000 copies a year in the late 1980s to as many as 40,000 copies by the late 1990s. Moreover, the long-term success of the wiccan movement would seem to be assured because many of the books being sold today are targeting the teenage market. Whereas many readers of witchcraft books during the 1980s were baby boomers looking for alternative forms of spirituality, today the major share of the growing market are young women in their teens (Carvajal 1998).

Contemporary witches see themselves as very different from **Satanists,** who worship the Judeo-Christian devil. Satanists view themselves as the antithesis of Christians, in league with the devil. Interestingly enough, it has been suggested that modern Satanism is a direct outgrowth of the Christian churches' strong stance against witchcraft. According to Marcello Truzzi (1993:402), "The inquisitors so impressed some individuals with the fantastic and blasphemous picture of Satanism that they apparently decided that they would rather reign in hell than serve in heaven."

Edward Moody presents evidence of a group of Satanists in San Francisco that uses evil magic to curse their enemies. Members are taught to "hate your enemies with a whole heart, and if a man smite you on one cheek, SMASH him on the other" (Moody 1993:236). If the group discovers that someone has harmed or hurt one of its members, the entire cult will ritually curse the perpetrator. In one case, which Moody personally witnessed, a man who allegedly slandered the name of the cult was given the most serious form of magical curse—the ritualistic casting of the death rune—the sole purpose of which is death and total destruction. When the death rune is cast, the victim's name is written in blood on a special parchment, and a lamb's-wool figurine is made to represent the victim. Then, according to Moody's account, in "an orgy of aggression . . . the lamb's-wool figure . . . was stabbed by all members of the congregation, hacked to pieces with a sword, shot with a small calibre pistol, and then burned."

After several weeks, the victim of the ritual entered the hospital with a bleeding ulcer and, when released, left the San Francisco area permanently. Did the curse result in the bleeding ulcer? Of course, the Satanic cult claimed a resounding victory for black magic. Even though the victim was suffering from hypertension and had had problems with ulcers before, it is possible that his knowledge of the curse could have precipitated the bleeding ulcer and his hasty departure from the San Francisco area.

The anthropologist is not particularly interested in determining whether the Satanic curse actually had its intended outcome. What is important to the anthropologist is that this is a dramatic example of how some people, even in industrialized societies, use sorcery or witchcraft to explain events in their lives.

Whether we are talking about the practice of witchcraft or Satanism in traditional or modern industrialized societies, there is no evidence that these forms of supernatural belief are dying out. In fact, some have suggested that they have been on the rise in recent years (see Singer and Benassi 1981; Truzzi 1993). Interest in such forms of belief fluctuates over time, but it serves as an accurate barometer of social strain and dislocation, rebellion against tradition, and the search for alternative systems for explaining the unexplainable. That is, those who become devil-worshippers are really searching for ways of coping with the strains and stresses of everyday life. Recognizing that they have dark, evil forces within themselves, those who embrace Satanism are seeking to either control those evil forces or be released from them. They come to these modern cults with anxiety and unsolved problems. Witchcraft and Satanism, like other belief systems, can be empowering in that they offer a sense of control, provide an explanation for personal failure and inadequacy, and allow the individual social acceptance into a group.

•■ MYTHS ■•

EVERY SOCIETY, from the smallest band society to the most complex industrial society, has a sacred literature called myth that states certain religious truths. **Myths,** embodying a specific worldview, contain stories of the gods, their origins, their activities, and the moral injunctions they teach. Unlike magic or witchcraft, myths serve to explain the large questions surrounding human existence such as why we are here. Myths not only have an explanatory function, but they also validate some of the essential beliefs, values, and behavior patterns of a culture. That is, a culture's mythology is closely connected to its moral and social order. It is important to point out that myths need not have any basis in historical fact. Although there may be elements of history in myth (and vice versa), the importance of myth from an anthropological perspective is that the narrative reflects, supports, and legitimizes patterns of thought and behavior.

A common form of myth is the myth of origin, which provides answers to questions about how things began. Often, these myths tell of the origins of the gods themselves, their adventures, and how they went about creating both humans and the natural environment. Some myths, which can be told in either sacred or profane settings, describe how various gods (or divinely inspired humans) brought about the existence of important cultural features such as government, fire, or agriculture. Another type of myth, known as a trickster myth, is less serious in tone but carries important messages. These often humorous myths serve at least two functions, as Anthony Wallace (1966: 57–58) reminds us:

> In trickster myths the successive triumphs and misadventures of an anthropomorphized animal—a raven,

a rabbit, or a coyote, for instance—are told in such a way that not only the historical origins of certain features of the world are accounted for, but also a moral is conveyed: the dangers of pride, the risk of gluttony, the perils of boastfulness.

•■ FUNCTIONS OF RELIGION ■•

ANTHROPOLOGICAL STUDIES of religion are no longer dominated by the search for origins. More recent studies have focused on how religious systems function for both the individual and the society as a whole. Because religious systems are so universal, it is generally held that they must fill a number of important needs at both personal and societal levels.

Anthropologists have always been fascinated by the origins of religion, but until recently, the lack of written records and archaeological evidence has made the subject highly speculative. Within the last several decades, however, archaeological evidence has given us a more complete picture of the early origins of religion. Arthur Lehmann and James Myers (1985) remind us that the tools, weapons, and artifacts found in neanderthal graves (dating back about 100,000 years) have led anthropologists to conclude that these early people believed in an afterlife. Even more recently, the study of paleolithic art (Lewis-Williams and Dowson 1988) has made a strong case for suggesting that symbolic representations that are religious in nature may have appeared as early as 200,000 to 300,000 years ago.

As anthropologists turned away from searching for the origins of religion, they became increasingly interested in a closely related question: How can we explain the universal existence of religion? This question has become all the more intriguing, particularly in light of the very elusive nature of religion. As far as we can tell, every society has some system of supernatural belief. Yet it is impossible to prove beyond a reasonable doubt that any supernatural powers (such as gods, witches, angels, or devils) actually exist. Moreover, it should be obvious to most religious practitioners that supernatural powers don't always work as effectively as the practitioners think they should. For example, we pray to God for the recovery of a sick friend, but the friend dies nevertheless; a ritual specialist conducts a rain dance, but it still doesn't rain; or the living relatives sacrifice a goat at the grave site of the ancestor god but still are not spared the ravages of the drought. Although supernatural beings and forces may not always perform their expected functions (that is, bring about supernatural events), they do perform less obvious functions for both the individual and the society as a whole. These latent functions, as they would be called by Robert Merton (1957), fall into two broad categories: social and psychological.

SOCIAL FUNCTIONS OF RELIGION

One of the most popular explanations for the universality of religion is that it performs a number of important functions for the overall well-being of the society of which it is a part. Let's consider three such social functions of religion: social control, conflict resolution, and intensifying group solidarity.

Social Control

One very important social function of religion is that it serves as a mechanism of social control. Through a series of both positive and negative sanctions, religion tends to maintain social order by encouraging socially acceptable behavior and discouraging socially inappropriate behavior. Every religion, regardless of the form it takes, is an ethical system that prescribes proper ways of behaving. When social sanctions (rewards and punishments) are backed with supernatural authority, they are bound to become more compelling. Biblical texts, for example, are very explicit about the consequences of violating the Ten Commandments. Because of their strong belief in ghostly vengeance, the Lugbara of Uganda scrupulously avoid engaging in any antisocial behavior that would provoke the wrath of the ancestral gods. As mentioned in the chapter on social stratification, Hindus in India believe that violating prescribed caste expectations will jeopardize their position in future reincarnations.

From an anthropological perspective, it is irrelevant whether these supernatural forces really do reward good behavior and punish bad behavior. Rather than concern themselves with whether and to what extent supernatural forces work the way they are thought to, anthropologists are interested in whether and to what extent people actually *believe* in the power of the supernatural forces. After all, it is the *belief* in the power of the supernatural sanctions that determines the level of conformity to socially prescribed behavior.

Conflict Resolution

Another social function of religion is the role that it plays in reducing stress and frustrations that often lead to social conflict. In some societies, for example, natural calamities such as epidemics or famines are attributed to the evil deeds of people in other villages or regions. By concentrating on certain religious rituals designed to protect themselves against any more outside malevolence, people avoid the potential disruptiveness to their own society that might occur if they take out their frustrations on the evildoers. Moreover, disenfranchised or powerless people in stratified societies sometimes use religion as a way of diffusing their anger and hostility that might otherwise be directed against the total social system. To illustrate, in his study of separatist Christian churches in the Republic of South Africa, Bengt Sundkler (1961) showed how small groups of Black South Africans—who until recently were systematically excluded from the power structure by apartheid—created the illusion of power by manipulating their own set of religious symbols and forming their own unique churches. By providing an alternative power structure, these breakaway Christian churches served to reduce conflict in South Africa by diverting resentment away from the wider power structure.

Sundkler's interpretation of separatist churches in South Africa is very similar to Marx's nineteenth-century interpretation of religion as the opium of the people. As an economic determinist, Marx claimed that religion, like other institutions, reflects the underlying modes of production in the society. The purpose of religion, according to Marx, was to preserve the economic superstructure that allowed the upper classes (bourgeoisie) to exploit the working classes (proletariat). By focusing people's attention on the prospects of the eternal bliss found in heaven, religion diverts their attention away from the misery of their lives in the here and now. In other words, religion blinds working people to the fact that they are being exploited by the ruling class. As long as the working class focuses on the afterlife, they are not likely to heed Marx's advice to revolt against their oppressors. Thus, religion serves as a societal mechanism to reduce conflict between differing economic subgroups.

Group Solidarity

A third social function of religion is that in a number of important ways, it intensifies the group solidarity of those who practice it. Religion enables people to express their common identity in an emotionally charged environment. Powerful social bonds are often created among people who share the experiences of religious beliefs, practices, and rituals. Because every religion or supernatural belief system contains its own unique structural features, those who practice it will share in its mysteries, whereas those who

— *Widespread participation in communal ceremonies, such as this funeral procession in Bali in Indonesia, serves to intensify the group solidarity of all those community members in attendance.*

do not will be excluded. In short, religion strengthens a person's sense of group identity and belonging. And, of course, as people come together for common religious experiences, they often engage in a number of other non-religious activities as well, which further strengthens the sense of social solidarity.

Psychological Functions of Religion

In addition to serving the well-being of the society, religion functions psychologically for the benefit of the individual. Anthropologists have identified two fundamentally different types of psychological functions of religion: a cognitive function, whereby religion provides an intellectual framework for explaining parts of our world that we don't under-

stand, and an emotional function, whereby religion helps to reduce anxiety by prescribing some straightforward ways of coping with stress.

Cognitive Function

In terms of its cognitive/intellectual function, religion is psychologically comforting because it helps us explain the unexplainable. Every society faces a number of imponderable questions that have no definitive logical answers: When did life begin? Why do bad things happen to good people? What happens to us when we die? Even in societies like our own—where we have, or think we have, many scientific answers—many questions remain unanswered. A medical pathologist may be able to explain to the parents of a child who has died of malaria that the cause of death was a bite by an infected anopheles mosquito. But that same pathologist cannot explain to the grieving parents why the mosquito bit their child and not the child next door. Religion can provide satisfying answers to such questions because the answers are based on supernatural authority.

Unlike any other life-form, humans have a highly developed urge for understanding themselves and the world around them. But because human understanding of the universe is so imperfect, religion provides a framework for giving meaning to the events and experiences that cannot be explained in any other way. Religion assures its believers that the world is meaningful, that events happen for a reason, that there is order in the universe, and that apparent injustices will eventually be rectified. Humans have difficulty whenever unexplained phenomena contradict their cultural worldview. One of the functions of religion, then, is to enable people to maintain their worldview even when events occur that seem to contradict it.

Emotional Function

The emotional function of religion is to help individuals cope with the anxieties often accompanying illness, accidents, deaths, and other misfortunes. Because people never have complete control over the circumstances of their lives, they often turn to religious ritual in an attempt to maximize control through supernatural means. In fact, the less control people feel they have over their own lives, the more religion they are likely to practice. The fear of facing a frightening situation can be at least partially overcome by believing that supernatural beings will intervene on one's behalf; shame and guilt may be reduced by becoming pious in the face of the deities; and during times of bereavement, religion can provide a source of emotional strength.

Anthropology and the U.S. Supreme Court

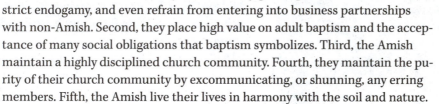

Anyone traveling through rural Pennsylvania, Indiana, or Ohio is likely to see bearded men in black hats driving horse-drawn buggies and women wearing long dresses reminiscent of the nineteenth century. These people, seemingly so out of place in today's modern world, are the Old Order Amish, one of the oldest and most visible minorities in the United States. Amish society is characterized by several cultural themes to which they strongly adhere. First, they strive to separate themselves from the world to the extent that they avoid worldly goods, practice strict endogamy, and even refrain from entering into business partnerships with non-Amish. Second, they place high value on adult baptism and the acceptance of many social obligations that baptism symbolizes. Third, the Amish maintain a highly disciplined church community. Fourth, they maintain the purity of their church community by excommunicating, or shunning, any erring members. Fifth, the Amish live their lives in harmony with the soil and nature.

In the early 1970s, the Amish were involved in a legal battle with the state of Wisconsin that went all the way to the U.S. Supreme Court. The central issue revolved around whether the state's compulsory education law violated the free exercise of religion of the Amish. Holding the religious belief that their church communities should be separate from the world, the Amish raise their children to be members of a self-sufficient community that rejects many of the values and physical trappings of mainstream U.S. society. The Amish argue that if they are required to send their children to public high schools, their self-sufficient church communities would be destroyed in a generation or two.

In its landmark decision in *Wisconsin v. Yoder,* the U.S. Supreme Court ruled that for the state to require Amish parents to send their children to public school beyond the eighth grade was a violation of their constitutional rights. By agreeing with the Amish argument, the Court exempted the Amish from compliance with the state's compulsory education law on the grounds of their religious beliefs. In rendering its decision, the Court drew heavily upon the tes-

People perform religious rituals as a way of invoking supernatural beings to control the forces over which they feel they have no control. This takes a number of different forms throughout the world. To illustrate, the Trobriand Islanders perform a series of magico-religious rituals for protection before a long voyage; to protect their gardens, men in parts of New Guinea put a series of leaves across their fences because they believe that the leaves will paralyze the arms and legs of any thief who raids the garden; and in Nairobi, Kenya, some professional soccer teams reportedly hire their own ritual specialists to bewitch their opponents. In addition to providing greater peace of mind, such religious practices may actually have a positive indirect effect on the events they are intended to influence.

timony of John Hostetler, an anthropologist who served as an expert witness at the lower-level court proceedings. In fact, as one observer (Rosen) commented,

> A close reading of the Supreme Court opinion clearly demonstrates that the anthropological testimony in this case may well have been indispensable to the Court's assertion that enforcement of the school attendance law would have had an unusually harsh effect on the entire community of Amish people. (nd:20)

Hostetler argued that to require Amish teenagers to attend high schools that fostered such radically different social and religious values would subject them to great psychological harm. The conflicting values between mainstream schools and Amish church communities would cause considerable alienation between Amish parents and their children. Central to Hostetler's argument is the anthropological theory of the integrated nature of a culture. Hostetler was able to convince the Court that Amish culture is an organic whole, the parts of which are intimately interconnected. More specifically, he pointed out the close interconnection between Amish religion and the Amish people's daily communal life.

Basing much of its decision on Hostetler's anthropological testimony, the Court concluded:

> Aided by a history of three centuries as an identifiable religious sect and a long history as a successful and self-sufficient segment of American society, the Amish in this case have convincingly demonstrated the sincerity of their religious beliefs, the interrelationship of belief with their mode of life, the vital role that belief and daily conduct play in the continued survival of Old Order Amish communities and their religious organization, and the hazards presented by the State's enforcement of a statute generally valid to others.

Because of the closeness of fit between Hostetler's testimony and the Court's decision, it seems safe to conclude that this landmark case might well have had a different outcome had Hostetler not used his anthropological insights as an expert witness.

QUESTIONS FOR FURTHER THOUGHT

1. In what ways is Amish society different from mainstream U.S. society?
2. What is the anthropological theory concerning the integrated nature of a culture, and how does it apply to this case study?
3. What social function of religion (discussed earlier in this chapter) would have been disrupted had this case been decided differently?

For example, even if their witchcraft doesn't work, football players in Kenya are likely to play more confidently if they believe they have a supernatural advantage. This ability to act with confidence is a major psychological function of religion.

Although most North Americans think of themselves as highly scientific, on many occasions we too use supernatural forces to ensure that our activities will have a successful outcome. For example, anthropologist George Gmelch (1994b) shows us how professional baseball players use ritual to try to control the uncertainty of a game:

> To control uncertainty Chicago White Sox shortstop Ozzie Guillen doesn't wash his underclothes after a good game. The Boston Red Sox's Wade Boggs eats chicken

before every game (that's 162 meals of chicken per year). Ex–San Francisco Giant pitcher Ron Bryant added a new stick of bubble gum to the collection in his bulging back pocket after each game he won. Jim Ohms, my teammate on the Daytona Beach Islanders in 1966, used to put another penny in the pouch of his supporter after each win. Clanging against the hard plastic genital cup, the pennies made an audible sound as the pitcher ran the bases toward the end of a winning season.

In some cases, Western governments will use non-Western spiritual practices when it is politically expedient to do so. In 1998 the Transit Authority of Portland, Oregon, proudly unveiled its light rail system, featuring the Washington Park Station, which, at 260 feet below ground, was the deepest subway station in the United States. However, members of local Asian communities in Portland were appalled because the tunnel ran under a cemetery, which, they claimed, disturbed the spirits of the dead and created a dangerous situation for the train riders. In fact, several above-ground traffic accidents were cited by the Asian groups as having been caused by the angry spirits of the dead. In response to these very real concerns of the Asian community, Transit Authority officials brought in a group of Lao Buddhist monks who performed rituals to appease the dead spirits. Even though transit officials were ribbed for allowing these Eastern rituals to be performed in the subway tunnel, they did ease the minds of local Asians and restored their confidence in the local transit system (D'Antoni and Heard, 1998).

•■ TYPES OF RELIGIOUS ■• ORGANIZATION

LIKE OTHER ASPECTS of culture, religion takes a wide variety of forms throughout the world. To bring some measure of order to this vast diversity, it is helpful to develop a typology of religious systems based on certain elements of commonality. One commonly used system of classification, suggested by Anthony Wallace, is based on the level of specialization of the religious personnel who conduct the rituals and ceremonies. Wallace (1966) identified four principal patterns of religious organization based on what he calls cults. Wallace uses the term *cult* in a general sense to refer to forms of religion that have their own set of beliefs, rituals, and goals. The four forms of religious organization he has identified are individualistic cults, shamanistic cults, communal cults, and ecclesiastical cults. According to Wallace's typology, these cults form a scale. Societies with ecclesiastical cults also contain communal, shamanistic, and individualistic cults; those with a communal form also contain shamanistic and individualistic cults; and those with shamanistic cults also contain individualistic cults. Although it is possible that societies with only individualistic cults could have existed in earlier times, there are no contemporary examples of such religious systems.

Wallace's four types correspond roughly to different levels of socioeconomic organization. That is, in a very general way, individualistic and shamanistic cults are usually associated with food-collecting societies, communal cults are usually found in horticultural and pastoral societies, and ecclesiastical cults are characteristic of highly complex industrialized economies. We should bear in mind, however, that this association between forms of religious organization and socioeconomic types is only approximate at best, for there are some notable exceptions. For example, certain American Plains Indians and some aboriginal Australians had communal forms of religion even though they were food collectors and lived in bands. See Table 14-1 for a summary of the characteristics of the different religious organizations.

INDIVIDUALISTIC CULTS

Individualistic cults have no religious specialists and represent the most basic level of religious structure according to Wallace's typology. Each person has a relationship with one or more supernatural beings whenever he or she has a

TABLE 14-1			
Characteristics of Different Religious Organizations			
	ROLE SPECIALIZATION	SUBSISTENCE PATTERN	EXAMPLE
Individualistic	No role specialization	Food collector	Crow vision quest
Shamanistic	Part-time specialization	Food collector/pastoralism/horticulture	Tungus shamanism
Communal	Groups perform rites for community	Horticulture/pastoralism	Totemistic rituals
Ecclesiastical	Full-time specialization in hierarchy	Industrialism	Christianity and Buddhism

SOURCE: Adapted from Anthony F. C. Wallace, *Religion: An Anthropological View.* New York: Random House, 1966.

need for control or protection. Because individualistic cults do not make distinctions between specialists and laypersons, all people are their own specialists; or as Marvin Harris (1991) has put it, these cults are a type of do-it-yourself religion. Even though no known societies rely exclusively on the individualistic form of religion, some small-scale band societies practice it as a predominant mode.

The **vision quest**, a ritual found among a number of traditional Plains Indian cultures, is an excellent example of an individualistic cult. During traditional times, it was expected that through visions, people would establish a special relationship with a spirit that would provide them with knowledge, power, and protection. Sometimes these visions came to people through dreams or when they were by themselves. More often, however, the individual had to purposefully seek out the visions through such means as fasting, bodily mutilation, smoking hallucinogenic substances, and spending time alone in an isolated place.

A person would go on a vision quest if he or she wanted special power (to excel as a warrior, for example) or knowledge (to gain insight into a future course of action, for example). A Crow warrior would go to a place that was thought to be frequented by supernatural spirits. Here he would strip off his clothes, smoke, and abstain from drinking and eating. He might even chop off part of a finger or engage in other types of self-inflicted torture for the sake of getting the spirits' attention. In some cases the vision seekers never did receive a vision, but Crow vision seekers often did.

Crow visions took a variety of forms but usually had several elements in common. First, the visions usually came in the form of a spirit animal, such as a bison, eagle, or snake. Second, the vision seeker gained some special knowledge or power. Third, the vision often appeared on the fourth day of the quest, four being a sacred number for the Crow. Finally, the animal spirit would adopt the quester by functioning as his or her own protector spirit.

It is important to bear in mind that for the Crow the vision quest was a normal way of dealing with the stresses and strains of everyday life. Robert Lowie reminds us of the wide range of problems that were addressed in Crow vision quests:

> The young man who has been jilted goes off at once to fast in loneliness, praying for supernatural succor. An elk spirit may come and teach him a tune on a flute, as a means of luring the maiden back. The young man plays his tune, ensnares the haughty girl, and turns her away in disgrace, thus regaining his self-respect. Similarly, a wretched orphan who has been mocked by a young man

of family hastens to the mountains to be blessed by some being, through whose favor he gains glory and loot on a raid, and can then turn the tables on his tormentor. A woman big with child fasts and in a vision sees a weed which she subsequently harvests and through which she ensures a painless delivery. A gambler who has lost all his property retrieves his fortune through a revelation; and by the same technique a sorrowing kinsman identifies the slayers of his beloved relative and kills them. These are all typical instances, amply documented in personal recollections of informants and in traditional lore, showing the intrusion of religion into the frustrations of everyday living. (1963:537)

SHAMANISTIC CULTS

In addition to having individualistic cults, all contemporary societies also operate at the shamanistic level. Shamans are part-time religious specialists who are thought to have supernatural powers by virtue of birth, training, or inspiration. These powers are used for healing, divining, and telling fortunes during times of stress, usually in exchange for gifts or fees. **Shamanistic cults** represent the simplest form of religious division of labor, for, as Wallace reminds us, "the shaman in his religious role is a specialist; and his clients in their relation to him are laymen" (1966: 86). The term *shaman*, derived from the Tungus-speaking peoples of Siberia (Service 1978), encompasses a number of different types of specialists found throughout the world, including medicine men and women, diviners, spiritualists, palm readers, and magicians.

Shamans are generally believed to have access to supernatural spirits that they contact on behalf of their clients. The reputation of a particular shaman often rests on the power of the shaman's spirit helpers and her or his ability to contact them at will. Shamans contact their spirits while in an altered state of consciousness brought on by smoking, taking drugs, rhythmic drumming, chanting, or monotonous dancing. Once in a trance, the shaman, possessed with a spirit helper, becomes a medium or spokesperson for that spirit. While possessed, the shaman may perspire, breathe heavily, take on a different voice, and generally lose control over his or her own body. In this respect, traditional shamans found in non-Western societies are not appreciably different from professional channelers in the United States who speak on behalf of spirits for their paying clients.

How an individual actually becomes a shaman varies from society to society. In some societies, it is possible to become a shaman by having a particularly vivid or powerful vision in which spirits enter the body. In other societies,

= *A Mayan shaman from Mexico prays with the help of a crucifix.*

one can become a shaman by serving as an apprentice under a practicing shaman. Among the Tungus of Siberia, mentally unstable people who often experience bouts of hysteria are the most likely candidates for shamanism because hysterical people are thought to be the closest to the spirit world (Service 1978). In societies that regularly use hallucinogenic drugs, almost any person can achieve the altered state of consciousness needed for the practice of shamanism. For example, Michael Harner (1973) reports that among the Jivaro Indians of the Ecuadorian Amazon who use hallucinogenics widely and have a strong desire to contact the supernatural world, about one in four men is a shaman.

As practiced by the Reindeer Tungus of Siberia, shamans are people who have the power to control various spirits, can prevent those spirits from causing harm, and, on occasions, can serve as a medium for those spirits (Service 1978). Tungus shamans—who can be either men or women—use special paraphernalia, such as elaborate costumes, a brass mirror, and a tambourine. The rhythmic beating of the tambourine is used to induce a trance in the shaman and to produce a receptive state of consciousness on the part of the onlookers. The shaman, possessed by the rhythmic drumming, journeys into the spirit world to perform certain functions for individual clients or the group as a whole. These functions may include determining the cause of a person's illness, finding a lost object, conferring special powers in a conflict, or predicting future events. Shamanism among the Tungus does not involve the power

to cure a particular illness but rather only determines the cause of the malady. In this respect, the shaman is a medical diagnostician rather than a healer.

Interestingly, shamanism experienced a resurgence in post–Soviet Siberia during the 1990s. Due largely to the economic hard times experienced by Russians since the collapse of socialism, local peoples of Siberia are seeking comfort in shamanism and other forms of traditional worship. Cold, hungry, and jobless, many Siberians are turning to traditional means of livelihood (hunting and fishing) for their material needs and, at the same time, turning to the old ways of the shaman for spiritual and psychological comfort. At a time when the world is increasingly embracing the Internet and cell phones, globalization seems to be passing by the descendants of the Tungus, who are again turning to their traditional ways (Matloff 1998).

COMMUNAL CULTS

Communal cults—which involve a more elaborate set of beliefs and rituals—operate at a still higher level of organizational complexity. Groups of ordinary people (organized around clans, lineages, age groups, or secret societies) conduct religious rites and ceremonies for the larger community. These rites, which are performed only occasionally or periodically by nonspecialists, are considered to be absolutely vital to the well-being of both individuals and the society as a whole. Even though these ceremonies may include such specialists as shamans, orators, or magicians, the primary responsibility for the success of the ceremonies lies primarily with the nonspecialists, who at the conclusion of the ceremony return to their everyday activities. Examples of communal cults are the ancestral ceremonies among the traditional Chinese, puberty rites found in sub-Saharan African societies, and totemic rituals practiced by aboriginal peoples of Australia.

Communal rituals fall into two broad categories: *rites of passage,* which celebrate the transition of a person from one social status to another, and *rites of solidarity,* which are public rituals serving to foster group identity and group goals and having very explicit and immediate objectives, such as calling upon the supernatural beings/forces to increase fertility or prevent misfortune. Let's look at these two types of communal cults in greater detail.

Rites of Passage

Rites of passage are ceremonies that mark a change in a person's social position. These ritualistic ceremonies, which have religious significance, help both individuals and the society deal with important life changes, such as birth, puberty, marriage, and death. Rites of passage are more than ways of recognizing certain transitions in a person's life, however. When a person marries, for example, he or she not only takes on a new status but also creates an entire complex of new relationships. Rites of passage, then, are important public rituals that recognize a wider set of altered social relationships.

According to Arnold Van Gennep (1960), all rites of passage, in whatever culture they may be found, tend to have three distinct ritual phases: separation, transition, and incorporation. The first phase—separation—is characterized by the stripping away of the old status. In cases of puberty rites, for example, childhood is ritually or symbolically killed by pricking the initiate's navel with a spear. In the second phase, the individual is in an in-between stage, cut off from the old status but not yet integrated into the new status. Because this transition stage is associated with danger and ambiguity, it often involves the endurance of certain unpleasant ordeals as well as the removal of the individual from normal, everyday life for a certain period of time. The third and final phase involves the ritual incorporation of the individual into the new status. Ethnographic data from all over the world have supported Van Gennep's claim that all rites of passage involve these three discrete phases.

These three ritual phases are well demonstrated in the rites of adulthood practiced by the Kikuyu of Kenya, who initiate both girls and boys (Middleton and Kershaw 1965).

The Kikuyu, like other traditional East African societies, practice initiation ceremonies as a way of ensuring that children will be converted into morally and socially responsible adults. Despite some regional variations, the Kikuyu initiation rite includes certain rituals that conform to Van Gennep's threefold scheme.

Kikuyu initiation into adulthood involves a physical operation—circumcision for males and clitoridectomy for women. Days before the physical operation, the initiates go through a number of rituals designed to separate them from society and their old status and place them in close relationship to god. First, the initiates are adopted by an elder man and his wife; this event symbolically separates them from their own parents. Second, the initiates spend the night before the circumcision singing and dancing in an effort to solicit the guidance and protection of the ancestral gods. Third, the initiates have their heads shaved and anointed, symbolizing the loss of the old status. And finally, they are sprayed with a mixture of honey, milk, and medicine by their adoptive parents in another separation ritual, which John Middleton and Greet Kershaw (1965) call the ceremony of parting.

As Van Gennep's theory suggests, the second (transition) phase of the Kikuyu initiation ceremony is a marginal phase filled with danger and ambiguity. The initiates undergo the dramatic and traumatic circumcision or clitoridectomy as a vivid symbolization of their soon-to-be assumed responsibility as adults. Both male and female initiates are physically and emotionally supported during the operation by their sponsors, who cover them with cloaks as soon as the operation is completed. Afterward, the initiates spend four to nine days in seclusion in temporary huts (*kiganda*), where they are expected to recover from the operation and reflect upon their impending status as adults.

The third and final phase of Kikuyu initiation rituals involves the incorporation of the initiate (with his or her new status) back into the society as a whole. At the end of the seclusion period, the new male adults have certain ceremonial plants put into the large loops in their earlobes (a form of body mutilation practiced during childhood), symbolizing their newly acquired status as adult men. This phase of incorporation (or reintegration) involves other rituals as well. The men symbolically put an end to their transition stage by burning their *kiganda;* their heads are again shaved; they return home to be anointed by their parents, who soon thereafter engage in ritual intercourse; they ritually discard their initiation clothing; and they are given warrior paraphernalia. Once these incorporation rituals have been completed, the young people become full adults with all of the rights and responsibilities that go along with their new status.

Rites of Solidarity

The other type of communal cult is directed toward the welfare of the community rather than the individual. These **rites of solidarity** permit a wider social participation in the shared concerns of the community than is found in societies with predominantly shamanistic cults. A good example of a cult that fosters group solidarity is the ancestral cult, found widely throughout the world. Ancestral cults are based on the assumption that after death, a person's soul continues to interact with and affect the lives of her or his living descendants. In other words, when people die, they are not buried and forgotten but rather are elevated to

= *This Asmat man from Irian Jaya is wearing around his neck the skull of a dead ancestor, which is believed to have the supernatural power to protect the wearer.*

the status of ancestor ghost or god. Because these ghosts, who are viewed as the official guardians of the social and moral order, have supernatural powers, the living descendants practice certain communal rituals designed to induce the ancestor ghosts to protect them, favor them, or at least not harm them.

Like many of their neighboring cultures in northern Ghana, the Sisala believe that the ancestor ghosts are the guardians of the moral order. All members of Sisala lineages are subject to the authority of the lineage elders. Because the elders are the most important living members of the group, they are responsible for overseeing the interests and harmony of the entire group. Though responsible for group morality, the elders have no direct authority to punish violators. The Sisala believe that the primary activity of the ancestor ghosts is to punish living lineage members who violate behavioral norms. To be specific, ancestor ghosts are thought to take vengeance on any living members who steal from their lineage mates, fight with their kin, or generally fail to live up to their family duties and responsibilities. Eugene Mendonsa (1985:218–219) describes a specific case that graphically illustrates the power of ancestral cults among the Sisala:

> At Tuorojang in Tumu there was a young man named Cedu. He caught a goat that was for the ancestor of his house (*dia*), and killed it to sell the meat. When the day came for the sacrifice, the elders searched for the goat so they could kill it at the *lele* shrine. They could not find it, and asked to know who might have caught the goat. They could not decide who had taken the goat, so they caught another and used it for the sacrifice instead. During the sacrifice, the elders begged the ancestors to forgive them for not sacrificing the proper goat. The elders asked the ancestors to find and punish the thief. After the sacrifice, when all the elders had gone to their various houses, they heard that Cedu had died. They summoned a diviner to determine the cause of death, and found that Cedu had been the thief. The ancestors had killed him because he was the person who stole the goat which belonged to the ancestors.

This case illustrates the Sisala's belief in the power of the ancestor ghosts to protect the moral order. When a breach of the normative order occurs, the elders conduct a communal ritual petitioning the ghost to punish the wrongdoer. As with other aspects of religion, the anthropologist is not concerned with whether the diviner was correct in determining that Cedu died because he stole the goat. Instead, the anthropologist is interested in the communal ritual and its immediate social effects: It served to restore

CROSS-CULTURAL MISCUE

INATTENTION TO FOREIGN CULTURES can result in some costly blunders when working in the international business arena. Alison Lanier, an international business consultant, tells of one U.S. executive who paid a very high price for ignoring the culture of his international business partners:

> A top-level, high-priced vice president had been in and out of Bahrain many times, where liquor is permitted. He finally was sent to neighboring Qatar (on the Arabian Gulf) to conclude a monumental negotiation that had taken endless months to work out. Confident of success, he slipped two miniatures of brandy in his briefcase, planning to celebrate quietly with his colleague after the ceremony. Result: not only was he deported immediately on arrival by a zealous customs man in that strictly Moslem country, but the firm was also "disinvited" and ordered never to return. The Qatari attitude was that this man had tried to flout a deeply held religious conviction; neither he nor his firm, therefore, was considered "suitable" for a major contract. (1979:160–161)

social harmony within the lineage and served as a warning to others who might be thinking of stealing from their lineage members.

ECCLESIASTICAL CULTS

The most complex form of religious organization according to Wallace is the **ecclesiastical cult,** which is found in societies with state systems of government. Examples of ecclesiastical cults can be found in societies with a pantheon of several high gods (such as traditional Aztec, Incas, Greeks, or Egyptians) or in those with essentially monotheistic religions, such as Hinduism, Buddhism, Christianity, Judaism, or Islam (see Figure 14-1). Ecclesiastical cults are characterized by full-time professional clergy, who are formally elected or appointed and devote all or most of their time performing priestly functions. Unlike shamans who conduct rituals during times of crisis or when their services are needed, these full-time priests conduct rituals that occur at regular intervals.

In addition, these priests are organized into a hierarchical or bureaucratic organization under the control of a centralized church or temple. Often, but not always, these clerical bureaucracies are either controlled by the central government or closely associated with it. In many ecclesiastical cults, the prevailing myths and beliefs are used to support the supremacy of the ruling class. In fact, it is not unusual for the priests to be part of that ruling class. Because of this close association between the priesthood and the politicoeconomic institutions, women have not tradi-

tionally played very active roles as priests. This is another important difference between priests and shamans, for at least as many women as men are practicing shamanism throughout the world. Even in modern complex societies, women are particularly active as mystics, channelers, palm readers, astrologers, and clairvoyants.

In societies with ecclesiastical cults, a clearly understood distinction exists between laypersons and priests. Laypersons are primarily responsible for supporting the church through their labor and their financial contributions. The priests are responsible for conducting the religious rituals on behalf of the lay population, either individually or in groups. Whereas the priests serve as active ritual managers, the lay population participates in ritual in a generally passive fashion. Because the members of the lay population have little control over religion, they become spiritually dependent on the priests for their ritual/supernatural well-being.

Although ecclesiastical cults have enormous control over people's lives, they certainly have not wiped out other forms of religion. Eskimos who have converted to Christianity, for example, may continue to consult a shaman when ill; Africans from Tanzania often still worship their ancestors although being practicing Roman Catholics; and in our own society, many people have no difficulty consulting a palmist, a psychic, or an astrologer even though they adhere to one of the large, worldwide, monotheistic religions.

We certainly do not need to go very far from home to see examples of ecclesiastical organizations. The United

FIGURE 14-1

Major Religions of the World

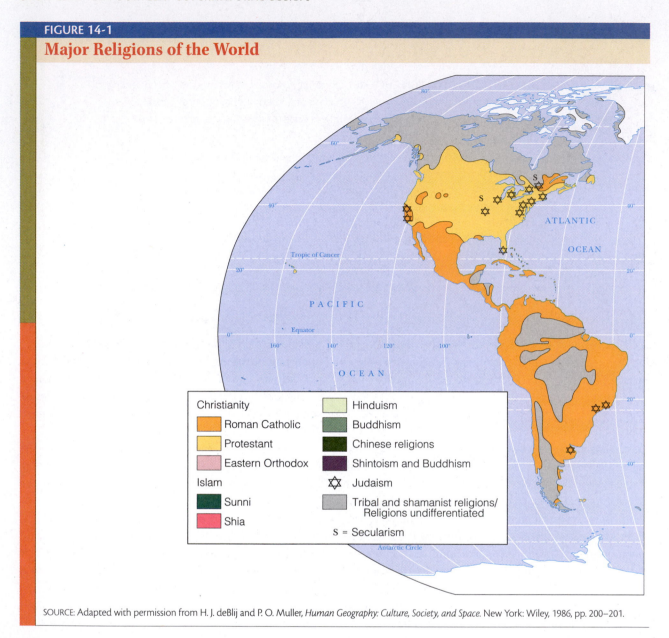

Christianity
- Roman Catholic
- Protestant
- Eastern Orthodox

Islam
- Sunni
- Shia

Hinduism
Buddhism
Chinese religions
Shintoism and Buddhism
✡ Judaism
Tribal and shamanist religions/
Religions undifferentiated

s = Secularism

SOURCE: Adapted with permission from H. J. deBlij and P. O. Muller, *Human Geography: Culture, Society, and Space.* New York: Wiley, 1986, pp. 200–201.

States, for example, has hundreds of religious denominations and approximately a quarter of a million separate congregations. Most people in the United States think they understand the nature of religious institutions around them, but there are probably more myths and stereotypes about religion than about any other area of American life. Most people would be surprised to learn that church membership in the United States has grown, not declined, steadily over the last several hundred years. According to Roger Finke and Roger Stark (1992), only 17 percent of the population in 1776 claimed church membership; by the start of the Civil War it had grown to 37 percent; by the

mid-1920s, it had leaped to 58 percent; and by 1993, 69 percent claimed church affiliation.

North Americans also tend to think of their society as being much more secular than religious. But when compared to other industrialized nations, the United States places a very high value on organized religion. A 1981 Gallup Poll found that 57 percent of the U.S. population acknowledged affiliation with a church or religious organization as compared to 22 percent of British, 15 percent of Spaniards, 13 percent of West Germans, and only 5 percent of Italians.

In addition, people in the United States tend to harbor misconceptions concerning the ethnic affiliations of

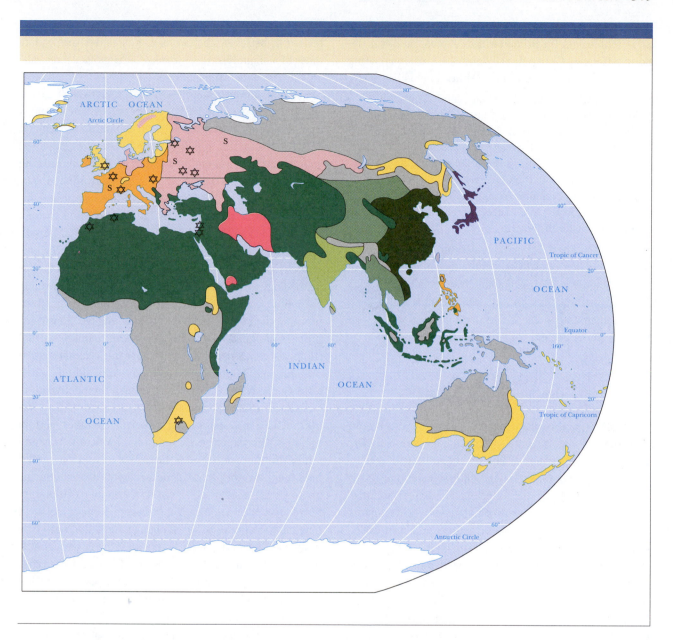

certain religious groups residing within their borders. As Barry Kosmin and Seymour Lachman (1993) have reported from their extensive survey of religion in America, most Americans of Irish descent are not Catholic, and most Asian Americans are Christian; in addition, most American Muslims are not Arabic, and most Arab Americans are not Islamic.

Globalization of World Religions

In much the same way that markets have been globalizing over the past decade, the revolution in information and communications has had far-reaching effects on the various ecclesiastical religions of the world. For much of the twentieth century, most North Americans identifying with a particular religion adhered to a fairly straightforward set of religious beliefs and practices. People practiced Islam, Christianity, Buddhism, or Judaism, and it was relatively easy to predict what set of beliefs they held. As we begin the new millennium, however, many people are practicing a hodgepodge of beliefs. It has been reported (Lamont-Brown 1999) that as many as 40 million people in Japan are now practicing "new religions," which involve blending of the two major religions in Japan (Buddhism and Shintoism) with elements of Confucianism, shamanism, animism, ancestor worship, Protestantism, and Catholicism. Traditional world religions, and even denominations of Christian religions, are cross-pollinating at a rapid rate. As one observer (Miller 1999:1) has noted,

> Jews flirt with Hinduism, Catholics study Taoism, and Methodists discuss whether to make the Passover seder an official part of worship. Rabbi Zalman Schachter-Shalomi, a prominent Jewish scholar, is also a Sufi sheik, and James Ishmael Ford, a Unitarian minister in Arizona, is a Zen sensei, or master. The melding of Judaism with Buddhism has become so commonplace that marketers who sell spiritual books, videotapes and lecture series have a name for it: "JewBu."

It is difficult to tell if this cross-fertilization of religious beliefs and practices will be a short-term phenomenon or a more long-term, and permanent, transition of the world's ecclesiastical religions. In any event, it is causing a fairly serious dilemma for the leaders of world religions who see this as a threat to their very identity.

·■ RELIGION AND ■· SOCIAL CHANGE

BY LOOKING at the various functions of religion, it is quite clear that religion is a conservative force within a society. In a general sense religions support the status quo by keeping people in line through supernatural sanctions, relieving social conflict, and providing explanations for unfortunate events. Moreover, some of the major world religions, through both philosophical convictions and political interpretations, have tended to retard social change. To illustrate, orthodox Hindu beliefs, based on the notion that one's present condition in life is based on deeds from past lives, has the effect of making people so fatalistic that they accept their present situations as unchangeable. Such a worldview is not likely to bring about major revolutions, or even minor initiatives for change. Likewise, on a number of issues facing the world's population, Catholicism has taken highly conservative policy positions. For example, the 1968 papal decree by Pope Paul VI opposing all forms of artificial birth control makes it very difficult for developing nations to bring their high population growth under control. Conservative Muslims in a number of countries have taken a strong stand against the introduction of new values and behaviors, particularly from the Western world. For example, the Islamic government of Bangladesh issued a warrant for the arrest of feminist writer Taslima Nasreen for blasphemy because of her statement that the Koran (Islamic holy book) needs to be revised to better protect women. Nasreen's writings, like those of Salman Rushdie, provoked a religious decree calling for her death (Weiner 1994).

Religion, however, has also played a major role in global social change over the past several decades. For example, the Catholic church, allied with the Solidarity Movement, played a pivotal role in bringing about the downfall of the communist government in Poland in 1989. By burning themselves alive on the streets of Saigon during the 1960s, Buddhist priests in Vietnam played a powerful role in stimulating antiwar sentiments in the United States, which eventually led to the withdrawal of U.S. troops. In South America during the 1970s and 1980s, a militant form of Catholicism known as **liberation theology** merged Catholic theology with an activism for social justice for the poor. Catholic priests and nuns, often without the support or approval of their own church authorities, engaged in various projects designed to help the poor raise themselves from the lowest echelons of society. Because these liberation theologians were often at odds with government and church officials, many lost their lives because of their activism.

Under certain circumstances, religion can play an important role in transforming a society. At times, certain societies have experienced such high levels of stress and strain that the conservative functions of religion cannot hold them together. Instead, new religions or sects spring up to create a new social order. A number of different terms have been used in the literature to describe these new religious forces of social change, including **nativistic movements,** found among American Indians; **cargo cults,** found in Melanesia; the **separatist Christian churches** of southern Africa; **mahdist movements** in the Muslim world; and **millenarian movements** found in Christian areas of the world.

All of these religious movements, with their aim of breathing new life and purpose into the society, are called **revitalization movements** by Anthony Wallace (1966). The common thread running through them is that they tend to occur during times of cultural stress brought about by rapid change, foreign domination, and perceived deprivation. Because these three conditions are often, but not always, associated with colonialism, many revitalization movements have appeared in societies that have been under colonial domination.

Although recognizing considerable differences in the details surrounding various revitalization movements, Wallace (1966) suggests that most follow a fairly uniform process. Starting from the state of equilibrium (in which change occurs, although slowly, and individual stress levels are tolerable), a society is pushed out of equilibrium by such forces as conquest and social domination. These conditions lower the self-esteem of an increasing number of individuals and place them under intolerable stress. People become disillusioned, and the culture becomes disorganized (with higher crime rates and a general increase in antisocial behavior, for example). When the social fabric deteriorates sufficiently, revitalization movements are likely to appear in an effort to bring about a more satisfying society. Some movements call for a return to the better days of the past; others seek to establish a completely new social order.

Revitalization movements have been found in many parts of the world, but nowhere have they been more widespread and better documented than among Native American groups. The tragic suffering of American Indians since their earliest contact with Europeans has resulted in a number of revitalization movements, including the movement among the Seneca Indians headed by Handsome Lake, several versions of the Ghost Dance, and the Peyote cults found among the Plains Indians. In recent decades, these religious revitalization movements have been replaced by more secular/political efforts to reclaim Indian land, resources, and dignity through legal action, political activism, and civil disobedience.

One of the earliest Native American revitalization movements was started by Handsome Lake (Parker 1913; Deardorff 1951). By the year 1800, the Seneca Indians of New York State had fallen upon hard times. They had lost much of their land to Whites, who held them in contempt because they were on the losing side of the French and Indian War. The Seneca were confined to reservations, and their numbers had been severely reduced by such European diseases as measles and smallpox. Once a proud nation of warriors, hunters, and traders, the Seneca by the start of the nineteenth century were defeated, dehumanized, and demoralized. Alcoholism became rampant, and conflicts and accusations of witchcraft increased.

From this state of cultural disorganization came a prophet—Handsome Lake—who was visited by God in a vision and told to stop drinking and start a new revitalizing religion. The deity warned that the Seneca would suffer a great catastrophe (such as fire, destruction, and death) if they did not mend their ways. Most of the prescriptions set down by Handsome Lake constituted a new set of moral principles and rules of behavior. Followers of the new reli-

gious movement were expected to stay sober, be peaceful, and lead pure and upright lives.

Handsome Lake instituted a number of other important cultural changes as well. For example, he urged his followers to adopt European agricultural practices involving both men and women working in the fields. In terms of the Seneca family, he emphasized the priority of the conjugal unit of man and wife over the matrilineage. Divorce, which had always been common in traditional Seneca society, was no longer permitted. Thus, Handsome Lake's revitalization movement led to far-reaching cultural changes. The Seneca became models of sobriety, their family structure was altered, they initiated new farming practices, and they changed the traditional division of labor between men and women.

REVITALIZATION IN THE AGE OF GLOBALIZATION

The last several hundred years have witnessed a number of religious revitalization movements, but it is also possible to find such movements in today's world of cell phones, space travel, and the Internet. In the late 1990s, the economy of Indonesia, due largely to the widespread corruption of the Suharto government, went into major crisis. Banks failed, companies went bankrupt, unemployment soared, and there was a mass exodus of foreign investment from the country. The general Indonesian population, suffering from widespread poverty even before the financial meltdown, experienced extreme hardship and economic stress.

In this environment of economic crisis, Indonesia's Muhammadiyah Islamic organization is emerging as a new form of religious revitalization. According to Habib Chirzin, a leading figure in the organization, Islam is the answer to Indonesia's crisis. The decades of the 1980s and 1990s saw the Indonesian economy grow rapidly, due largely to foreign investment. But the rapid economic growth caused many people (and their government) to lose their moral compass. The result was that corruption and cronyism became the order of the day. The Muhammadiyah, which has approximately 30 million members, wants to reinstate the basic principles of Islam—devotion to God and community self-help—as the most effective way of recovering from the economic crisis that is gripping its people. The organization—which operates 130 universities, 13,000 schools, and 750 medical clinics—is beginning to re-energize its communities by encouraging a number of local self-help initiatives, including health-care

= *In countries such as Iraq, the notion of religious nationalism makes no attempt to separate church and state.*

programs, food kitchens, child care, and job programs. By focusing on education and encouraging people to help themselves and one another, they are revitalizing the basic principles of Islam and, at the same time, building a broader base of economic development that is less dependent on foreign capital and less susceptible to government cronyism (Fuller 1999).

An extremely significant trend in global religion today is what is called **religious nationalism.** This movement, which can be found in countries that represent a number of different religious traditions, rejects the idea that religion and government should be separate. Instead, religious nationalism calls for an absolute merging of traditional religious beliefs into government institutions and leaders. With the collapse of the former Soviet Union and the communist bloc, many nations are beginning to reject the secular solutions that were so prevalent during the Cold War years. Instead, they are increasingly embracing a fundamentalist religious state that does not tolerate nonbelievers.

Nowhere is religious nationalism more evident than in the Middle East. Islamic nationalism—perhaps the most visible form of religious nationalism—combines fundamentalist religious orthodoxy with contemporary political institutions. In the late 1970s the pro-American Shah of Iran was overthrown by the fundamentalist Islamic revolution headed by Ayatollah Khomeini. That revolution, condemning the United States as the "great Satan," has spread throughout other parts of the Islamic world. This form of religious nationalism rejects individual freedom of expression and political choice so highly valued in the West. Islamic nationalism also represents a rejection of the often-exploitive government and economic systems (such as capitalism and democracy) that Middle Eastern peoples have endured over the decades. At the very least this Islamic nationalism represents an attempt to draw on their own religious, cultural, and political ideas to forge their way into the twenty-first century. Some have suggested that a new Cold War may emerge that will pit these religious nationalists against the Western democratic countries.

SUMMARY

1. Although all cultures have supernatural beliefs, the forms the beliefs take vary widely from society to society. It is often difficult to define supernatural belief systems cross-culturally because different societies have different ways of distinguishing between the natural and the supernatural.

2. The anthropological study of religion does not attempt to determine which religions are better than others or which gods are able to work the most miracles per unit of time. Rather, cultural anthropolo-

gists concentrate on describing the various systems of religious belief, how they function, and the degree to which they influence human behavior.

3. Religion differs from magic in that religion deals with big issues such as life, death, and God, whereas magic deals with more immediate and specific problems. Whereas religion asks for help through prayer, magic is a direct attempt to control and manipulate supernatural forces.

4. Witchcraft and sorcery are two types of supernatural belief systems that cause harm to people. Whereas sorcery involves the deliberate attempt to cause people misfortune through the use of certain material substances, witchcraft is an inborn and generally involuntary capacity to work evil.

5. Religion performs certain social functions. It enhances the overall well-being of the society by serving as a mechanism of social control, helping to reduce the stress and frustrations that often lead to social conflict, and intensifying group solidarity.

6. Religion also performs certain psychological functions by providing emotional comfort by helping to explain the unexplainable and helping a person cope with the stress and anxiety often accompanying illness or misfortune.

7. Following the scheme suggested by Wallace, there are four distinctive patterns of religious organization: individualistic cults, shamanistic cults, communal cults, and ecclesiastical cults. These four types of religion vary roughly with increasing levels of socioeconomic complexity; individualistic cults are associated with food-collecting societies and ecclesiastical cults are found in highly industrialized societies.

8. The most basic level of religious organization is the individualistic cult, characterized by an absence of religious specialists. The vision quest practiced by certain North American Indian cultures is an example of an individualistic cult.

9. Shamanistic cults involve the least complex form of religious division of labor. Shamans are part-time religious specialists who, it is believed, help or cure their clients by intervening with the supernatural powers while in an altered state of consciousness.

10. Communal cults involve groups of ordinary people who conduct religious ceremonies for the well-being of the community. Examples of communal cults are the rites of passage (such as circumcision ceremonies) found widely throughout sub-Saharan Africa and the ancestral cults that function to foster group solidarity among members of a kinship group.

11. Ecclesiastical cults, which are found in societies with state systems of government, are characterized by full-time professional clergy who are usually organized into a hierarchy.

12. Revitalization movements—religious movements aimed at bringing new life and energy into a society—usually occur when societies are experiencing rapid culture change, foreign domination, or perceived deprivation. Revitalization movements have taken a number of different forms, including nativistic movements, cargo cults, and millenarian movements.

13. Religion has played an important role in global social change through liberation theology (whereby Catholic priests and nuns work for social reform and justice for the poor) and religious nationalism (whereby religious beliefs are merged with government institutions).

KEY TERMS

cargo cults
communal cults
ecclesiastical cults
individualistic cults
liberation theology
magic
mahdist movements
millenarian movements
myths
nativistic movements
religion

religious nationalism
revitalization movements
rites of passage
rites of solidarity
Satanists
separatist Christian churches
shamanistic cults
sorcery
vision quest
wicca

SUGGESTED READINGS

Kamenetz, Rodger. *The Jew in the Lotus.* San Fransisco: Harper, 1995. Illustrating the trend of theological borrowing among practitioners of world religions,

Kamenetz takes the reader on his personal journey of a Jew who finds spiritual renewal in the Buddhism of the Dalai Lama.

Kosmin, Barry A., and Seymour P. Lachman. *One Nation Under God: Religion in Contemporary American Society.* New York: Crown, 1993. Based on one of the most extensive surveys ever attempted on religion in the United States, this study provides substantial amounts of statistical data and also explodes a number of widely held myths about the practice of religion in a country that is "paradoxically among the most religious and the most secular on earth."

Lattas, Andrew. *Cultures of Secrecy: Reinventing Race in Bush Kaliai Cargo Cults.* Madison: University of Wisconsin Press, 1998. By taking an ethnographic approach, Lattas explores one form of religious revitalization movement, the cargo cults, by showing how the Kaliai of Papua New Guinea have blended their traditional myths with imported folklore and Christian stories.

Lehmann, Arthur C., and James E. Myers, eds. *Magic, Witchcraft, and Religion.* 3d ed. Palo Alto, CA: Mayfield, 1993. Now in its third edition, this reader is an excellent collection of essays on supernatural belief systems. The essays are scholarly, representative of the field of religious anthropology, and understandable by university undergraduates.

Lewis, I. M. *Ecstatic Religion: A Study of Shamanism and Spirit Possession.* 2d ed. London: Routledge, 1989. Discussing the sociocultural aspects of shamanism in Africa, Asia, and South America, Haitian voodooism, and Christian mysticism, Lewis argues that spiritual possession is nearly a universal phenomenon.

Morris, Brian. *Anthropological Studies of Religion: An Introductory Text.* New York: Cambridge University Press, 1987. A good, readable introduction to the study of supernatural belief systems from a cross-cultural perspective.

Pandian, Jacob. *Culture, Religion, and the Sacred Self: A Critical Introduction to the Anthropological Study of Religion.* Englewood Cliffs, NJ: Prentice-Hall, 1991. A small but comprehensive discussion of the scope and objectives of the anthropological study of religion. Through the cross-cultural analysis of shamanism, myth, religious movements, and ritual, Pandian offers the reader an interpretation of the relationship between supernatural beliefs and the cultural formation of the self.

Sanders, Andrew. *A Deed Without a Name: The Witch in Society and History.* Oxford: Berg, 1995. A comprehensive yet readable study of witchcraft drawing on contemporary and historical case studies from medieval Europe to African tribal societies to contemporary North America. The author suggests that the process of labeling witches is similar in all societies, both now and in the past.

Wallace, Anthony F. C. *Religion: An Anthropological View.* New York: Random House, 1966. An old yet still valuable analysis of the anthropology of religion that discusses some general theories, the structure, goals, functions, and ritual processes of religion from a cross-cultural perspective.

On the Net

1. Shamans and shamanism are usually associated with small-scale, non-Western societies, but shamanism is also found in the industrialized world. Conduct an Internet subject search on the topic of shamanism. As strange as it may seem, many contemporary shamans have their own web sites. What can you learn from these web sites about the practice of shamanism in the Western, industrialized world?

2. Melanesia in the southwest Pacific has experienced a number of revitalization movements that collectively are called cargo cults. Using any search engine, conduct a subject search on cargo cults on the Internet. One particularly good site is the Jon Frum home page, which describes a particular cargo cult located in Vanuatu. Write a one-page paper (written for someone who has never had a course in anthropology) describing the general features of cargo cults.

Chapter Fifteen

ART

Ethnomusicologists would be interested in studying both the music of this folk orchestra in Tadzhik of the former Soviet Union and how it reflects the wider culture of which it is a part.

WHAT WE WILL LEARN:

▼

How do anthropologists define the arts?

▼

What are the various functions
of art in society?

▼

How do music and dance reflect
other aspects of a culture?

▼

Artistic expression is one of the most distinctive human characteristics. No group of people known to cultural anthropologists spends all of its time

in the utilitarian pursuit of meeting its basic survival needs. In other words, people do not hunt, grow crops, make tools, and build houses purely for the sake of sustaining themselves and others. After their survival needs are met, all cultures, even technologically simple ones, decorate their storage containers, paint their houses, embroider their clothing, and add aesthetically pleasing designs to their tools. They compose songs, tell riddles, dance creatively, paint pictures, make films, and carve masks. All of these endeavors reflect the human urge to express oneself and take pleasure from aesthetics. It would be hard to imagine a society without art, music, dance, and poetry. As the study of cultural anthropology reminds us, artistic expression is found in every society, and aesthetic pleasure is felt by all members of humankind (see Coote and Shelton 1992).

•■ WHAT IS ART? ■•

FOR CENTURIES, people from a wide range of perspectives—including philosophers, anthropologists, politicians, art historians, and professional artists themselves —have proposed definitions of art. As George Mills has suggested, "definitions (of art) vary with the purposes of the definers" (1957:77). To illustrate, the artist might define art in terms of the creative process, the politician's definition would emphasize the communicative aspects of art that could mobilize public opinion, the art historian or knowledgeable collector would focus on the emotional response that art produces, and the cultural anthropologist might define art in terms of the role or function it plays in religious ceremonies. Nevertheless, despite these diverse definitions, any definition of art, if it is to have any cross-cultural applicability, must include certain basic elements:

1. The artistic process should be creative, playful, and enjoyable and need not be concerned with the practicality or usefulness of the object being produced.
2. From the perspective of the consumer, art should produce some type of emotional response, either positive or negative.
3. Art should be **transformational.** An event from nature, such as a cheetah running at full speed, may be aesthetically pleasing in that it evokes a strong emotional response, but it is not art. It becomes art only when someone transforms the image into a painting, dance, song, or poem.
4. Art should communicate information by being representational. In other words, once the object of art is transformed, it should make a symbolic statement about what is being portrayed.
5. Art implies that the artist has developed a certain level of technical skill not shared equally by all people in a society. Some people have more highly developed skills than others because of the interplay of individual interests and opportunities with genetically based acuities.

Centuries of continual debate by reasonable people have failed to produce a universally agreed-upon definition of art. Though not presuming to propose a universal definition, it will be useful, for purposes of this chapter, to suggest a working definition of art based on the five elements just listed. *Art,* then, is both the process and the products of applying certain skills to any activity that transforms matter, sound, or motion into a form that is deemed aesthetically meaningful to people in a society.

By using these five features, we can include a wide variety of types of artistic activities in our definition of art. In all societies people apply imagination, creativity, and technical skills to transform matter, sound, and movement into works of art. The various types of artistic expression include the graphic or plastic arts—such as painting, carving, weaving, sculpture, and basket making; the creative manipulation of sounds and words in such artistic forms as music, poetry, and folklore; and the application of skill and creativity to body movement that gives rise to dance. It should be pointed out that these three neatly defined categories of artistic expression sometimes include forms that are not familiar to Westerners. Westerners usually think of graphic and plastic arts as including such media as painting, sculpture, and ceramics, but in the non-Western world people may also include the Nubians' elaborate body decoration (Faris 1972), Navajo sand painting (Witherspoon 1977), and the Eskimos' body tattooing (Birket-Smith 1959). Moreover, sometimes activities that in our own society have no particular artistic content are elevated to an art form in other societies. The Japanese tea ceremony is an excellent case in point.

Every society has a set of standards that distinguish between good art and bad art or between more and less satisfying aesthetic experiences. In some societies, such as our own, what constitutes good art is determined largely by a professional art establishment comprising art critics, museum and conservatory personnel, professors of art, and others who generally make their living in the arts. Although other societies may not have professional art establishments, their artistic standards tend to be more democratic in that they are maintained by the general public. Thus, the decoration on a vase, the rhythm of a song, the communicative power of a dance, or the imagery of a painting are subject to the evaluation of artists and nonartists alike.

•■ DIFFERENCES IN ART FORMS ■•

AS CHAPTER 2 POINTED out, the term *primitive* has fallen out of fashion when referring to societies that are radically different from our own. When associated with art, however, the term has had greater staying power. Despite numerous attempts by some art historians and anthropologists to disassociate themselves from the term, it still retains some legitimacy. This reluctance to eliminate the use of *primitive* was expressed in H. W. Janson's *History of Art:*

> Primitive is a somewhat unfortunate word. . . . Still, no other single term will serve us better. Let us continue, then, to use primitive as a convenient label for a way of life that has passed through the Neolithic Revolution but shows no signs of evolving in the direction of "historic" civilizations. (1986:35)

= *Elaborate body decoration is an important form of artistic expression in South Kordofan in the African country of Sudan.*

Despite such attempts by art historians to perpetuate the use of the term *primitive*, it is not used in this book because of its misleading connotations of both inferiority and evolutionary sequencing. Instead, the term *small-scale* is used to describe egalitarian societies with small populations, simple technologies, and little labor specialization.

Having disposed of the term *primitive*, we can now proceed to look at some of the major differences in art forms between small-scale and complex societies (this discussion is developed in much fuller detail by Anderson 1990). One difference stems from the general lifestyles and settlement patterns found in these logically opposite types of societies. Because small-scale societies tend to be foragers, pastoralists, or shifting cultivators with nomadic or seminomadic residence patterns, the art found in these societies must be highly portable. It is not reasonable to expect people who are often on the move to develop an art tradition comprising large works of art such as larger-than-life sculptures or large painted canvases. Instead, art in small-scale societies is limited to forms that people leave behind on rock walls or cliffs or forms that they can take with them easily, such as performing arts (song, dance, and storytelling); body decoration, such as jewelry, body painting, tattooing, and scarification; and artistic decorations on practical artifacts such as weapons, clothing, and food containers.

= *In complex societies, artistic standards are defined by full-time specialists such as philosophers, curators, professors of art, and art critics, many of whom are associated with such institutions as the Art Institute of Chicago.*

Another significant difference between the art of small-scale societies and complex societies stems from their different levels of social differentiation (that is, labor specialization). As societies began to develop increasingly more specialized roles following the neolithic revolution (about 10,000 years ago), some segments of the population were freed from the everyday pursuits of food getting. The subsequent rise of civilizations was accompanied by the emergence of full-time specialists, such as philosophers, intellectuals, literati, and aesthetic critics, whose energies were directed, among other things, at distinguishing between good art and bad art. The standards of aesthetic judgment have become much more explicit and elaborately defined by specialists in more complex societies. To be certain, aesthetic standards exist in small-scale societies, but they are less elaborate, more implicit, and more widely diffused throughout the entire population.

A third major contrast arises from differences in the division of labor. As a general rule, as societies become more specialized, they also become more highly stratified into classes with different levels of power, prestige, and wealth. The aesthetic critics responsible for establishing artistic standards in complex societies are invariably members of the upper classes or are employed by them. Thus, art in complex societies becomes associated with the elite. Not only are the standard setters often members of the elite, but art in complex societies often is owned and controlled by the upper classes. Moreover, in some complex societies, art both glorifies and serves the interests of the upper classes. In contrast, because small-scale societies are egalitarian, art tends to be more democratic in that all people have roughly equal access to it.

In addition to these three fundamental differences between art in small-scale and complex societies, we often see art in small-scale societies embedded to a greater degree in other aspects of the culture. To be certain, we can observe connections between art and, say, religion in our own society. But in small-scale societies art is even more permeated into other areas of culture. In fact, because art is such an integral part of the total culture, many small-scale societies do not even have a word for art. That is, because art permeates all aspects of peoples' lives, they do not think of art as something separate and distinct. One such example, sand painting as practiced in Navajo culture, is as much religion, myth, and healing as it is art. According to Dorothy Lee, Navajo sand paintings are created as part of a ceremony that

> brings into harmony with the universal order one who finds himself in discord with it. . . . Every line and shape

= *The art form of sand painting among the Navajo of New Mexico is intimately connected to the traditional systems of healing and religion.*

and color, every relationship of form, is the visible manifestation of myth, ritual and religious belief. The making of the painting is accompanied with a series of sacred songs sung over a sick person. . . . When the ceremonial is over, the painting is over too; it is destroyed; it has fulfilled its function. (1993:13)

In some parts of the world, it is possible to see how the political system of a society can be reflected in its art. Anthropologist Christopher Steiner (1990) has shown how one form of artistic expression—body decoration—reflects the different political structures in Melanesia and Polynesia. As mentioned in Chapter 8, a prominent form of political leadership in Melanesia is big men. In the absence of permanent political offices or hierarchies, big men earn their authority by working hard to attract a large number of followers. Because big men can lose their followers, the system of political leadership in Melanesia is a very fluid one, always subject to change. In Polynesia, on the other hand, leadership is based on centralized chiefdoms with permanent (usually hereditary) authority. The differences in political structure of these societies are reflected in their forms of bodily adornment. Melanesians decorate their bodies with paints—a temporary medium that can be washed away or lost in much the same way that a big man can lose his high status if he loses support of his followers. By way of contrast, Polynesians use tattoos, a permanent form of body art, reflecting the more centralized and permanent nature of political authority. Thus, to distinguish themselves from commoners, Polynesian chiefs use tattoos, a particularly appropriate form of body decoration that reflects the high status of their hereditary offices.

•■ THE FUNCTIONS OF ART ■•

TO GAIN A FULLER understanding of art, we must move beyond our working definition to an examination of the roles art plays for both people and societies. The very fact that artistic expression is found in every known society suggests that it functions in some important ways in human life. The two different approaches to functionalism taken by Malinowski and Radcliffe-Brown can be instructive for our analysis of the functions of art. As mentioned in Chapter 4, Malinowski tended to emphasize how various cultural elements function for the psychological well-being of the individual. Radcliffe-Brown, in contrast, stressed how a cultural element functions to contribute to the well-being or continuity of the society. Although we will examine the various functions of art for both the individual and society, it should be pointed out that in terms of the analysis of art, Radcliffe-Brown's more structural approach has been the more fruitful.

EMOTIONAL GRATIFICATION FOR THE INDIVIDUAL

Quite apart from whatever benefits art may have for the total society, it is generally agreed that art is a source of personal gratification for both the artist and the viewer. It

CROSS-CULTURAL MISCUE

AS AN ART MAJOR at a Canadian university, George Burgess has invited Kamau, his Kenyan roommate, to his family home in Toronto for the Christmas holidays. While in the downtown area, George suggests that they go to the local art museum to see a new exhibition of abstract expressionists from the 1940s. While looking at an abstract painting by Jackson Pollock, Kamau asked George what it means. George threw up his hands and said cheerfully, "That is the beauty of abstract art; it can mean anything you want it to mean." Kamau looked puzzled and answered tersely, "Then why did he make it?" George could not understand why Kamau didn't appreciate this classic piece of abstract expressionism.

George did not realize that different cultures have different ideas about what art is and what function it should perform. Art in Kenya, and in many parts of Africa, is much more public in nature than it is in North America. African artists tend to emphasize both conveying a message to the audience and demonstrating the function of the piece of art for the life of the community. In contrast, the Western artistic tradition that George was studying at the university places much more importance on the individual expressiveness and creativity of the artist. This cross-cultural misunderstanding occurred because Kamau failed to appreciate the highly individualistic nature of the artist in Western society, and George failed to understand the African tradition of the artist explicitly communicating to the audience.

would be hard to imagine a world in which people engaged only in pursuits that contributed to their basic survival needs. Although most people devote the lion's share of their time and energy to meeting those needs, it is equally true that all people derive some level of enjoyment from art because it provides at least a temporary break from those practical (and often stressful) pursuits. After the crops have been harvested, the African horticulturalist has time to dance, tell stories, and derive pleasure from making or viewing pieces of art. Likewise, as a diversion from their workaday lives, many Westerners seek gratification by attending a play, a concert, or a museum. No doubt, it was this personal gratification one derives from art that prompted Richard Selzer to comment that "art . . . is necessary only in that without it life would be unbearable" (1979:196).

The psychologically beneficial functions of art can be examined from two perspectives: that of the artist and that of the beholder. For the artist, the expression of art permits the release of emotional energy in a very concrete or visible way—that is, by painting, sculpting, writing a play, or performing an interpretive dance. Artists, at least in the Western world, are viewed as living with a creative tension that, when released, results in a work of art. This release of creative energy also brings pleasure to the artist to the extent

that she or he derives satisfaction from both the mastery of techniques and the product itself.

From the perspective of the viewer, art can evoke pleasurable emotional responses in several important ways. For example, works of art can portray events, people, or deities that conjure up positive emotions. The symbols used in a work of art can arouse a positive emotional response. The viewer can receive pleasure by being dazzled by the artist's virtuosity. These pleasurable responses can contribute to the mental well-being of art viewers by providing a necessary balance with the stresses in their everyday lives.

However, it is also possible for art to have the opposite effect by eliciting negative emotions. The artistic process, if not successful from the artist's point of view, can result in increased frustrations and tension. Moreover, any art form is capable of eliciting disturbing or even painful emotions that can lead to psychological discomfort for the viewer.

ART CONTRIBUTES TO SOCIAL INTEGRATION

In addition to whatever positive roles it may play for the individual, art functions to help sustain the longevity of the society in which it is found. Again, as functionalist anthropologists remind us, art is connected to other parts of the social system. One need only walk into a church, a synagogue, or a temple (or any other place of worship) to see the relationship between art and religion. Moreover, art has been used in many societies to evoke positive sentiments for systems of government and individual political leaders. This section explores some of the ways that art functions to contribute to the maintenance and longevity of a society.

Through various symbols, art, in whatever form it may take, communicates a good deal about the values, beliefs, and ideologies of the culture of which it is a part. The art forms found in any given society reflect the major cultural themes and concerns of the society. To illustrate, prominent breasts on female figures are a major theme in much of the wood sculpture from West Africa. This dominant theme reflects a very important social value in those West African societies: the social importance of having children. Somewhat closer to our own cultural traditions, much of the art in Renaissance Europe reflected many of the religious themes central to Christianity. Thus, certain forms of graphic arts function to help integrate the society by making the dominant cultural themes, values, and beliefs more visible. By expressing these cultural themes in a very tangible way, art ultimately functions to strengthen the existing culture by reinforcing those cultural themes.

The intimate interconnectedness of art and religious life is well illustrated in Bali (Indonesia), a culture with a long and rich tradition of dance and music. The large number of ceremonies that occur annually on the Bali-Hindu calendar involve elaborate displays and performances designed to attract the gods and please the people. Various life cycle events such as birth and funerals are celebrated by special orchestras with music and dance. Some musical instruments, thought to be the gift of the gods, are considered so sacred that they can only be displayed, not actually played. According to one Balinese expert,

> Music and dance are spiritual musts. The arts are an invitation for the gods to come down and join the people. There is a very physical contact with the unseen, with the ancestors . . . which makes the people in the village very happy. (Charle 1999:28)

Other forms of art, such as music, also help to strengthen and reinforce both social bonds and cultural themes. For example, cultural values are passed on from generation to generation using the media of song and dance. As part of the intense education in African bush schools, various forms of dance are used to teach proper adult attitudes and behaviors to those preparing for initiation. The role of mu-

Much of the art found in Western churches, such as this one in Linz, Austria, reflects the basic themes of Christianity.

sic as a mechanism of education is well illustrated by Bert, Ernie, Kermit, and the other characters of *Sesame Street,* who sing about such values as cooperation, acceptable forms of conflict resolution, the fun of learning, and race relations. Music also can be used to solidify a group of people. Any history of warfare would be woefully incomplete without some mention of the role that martial music played to rally the people together against the common enemy.

SOCIAL CONTROL

A popular perception of artists and their works in the Western world is that they are visionary, nonconformist, and often anti-establishment. Although this is often the case in contemporary Western societies, much art found in other societies (and indeed in our own Western tradition in past centuries) functions to reinforce the existing sociocultural system. For example, art can help instill important cultural values in younger generations, coerce people to behave in socially appropriate ways, and buttress the inequalities of the stratification system within a society. We will briefly examine several ways that the arts can contribute to the status quo.

First, art can serve as a mechanism of social control. Art historians generally recognize that art has a strong religious base, but they have been less cognizant of the role art plays in other cultural domains. A notable exception has been Roy Sieber (1962), an art historian who has demonstrated how wooden masks serve as agents of social control in several tribal groups in northeastern Liberia. It was generally believed by the Mano, for example, that the god-spirit mask embodied the spiritual forces that actually control human behavior. The death of a high-status man was marked by carving a wooden death mask in his honor. A crude portrait of the deceased, the death mask was thought to be the ultimate resting place of the man's spirit.

Through the medium of these pieces of art, the spirits were thought to be able to intervene in the affairs of the living. Specifically, the masks played an important role in the administration of justice. When a dispute arose or a crime was committed, the case was brought before a council of wise and influential men who reviewed the facts and arrived at a tentative decision. This decision was then confirmed (and given supernatural force) by one of the judges, who wore the death mask, concealing his own identity. Thus, in addition to whatever other functions these artis-

tically carved masks may play among the Mano, they serve as mechanisms of social control and conflict resolution.

Art also plays an important role in controlling behavior in more complex societies. In highly stratified societies, state governments sponsor art for the sake of instilling obedience and maintaining the status quo. In some of the early civilizations, for example, state-sponsored monumental architecture, such as pyramids, ziggurats, and cathedrals, was a visual representation of the astonishing power of both the gods and the rulers. Most people living in these state societies would think twice before breaking either secular or religious rules when faced with the awesome power and authority represented in these magnificent works of art.

PRESERVING OR CHALLENGING THE STATUS QUO

By serving as a symbol for social status, art also contributes to the preservation of the status quo. To one degree or another, all societies make distinctions between different levels of power and prestige. As societies become more highly specialized, systems of stratification become more complex, and the gap between the haves and the have-nots becomes wider. Power is expressed in a number of different ways throughout the world, including the use of physical force, the control over political decisions, and the accumulation of valuable resources. One particularly convincing way to display one's power is symbolically through the control of valuable items in the society. The accumulation of practical objects such as tools would not be a particularly good symbol of high prestige because everyone has some and because one hardly needs an overabundance of everyday practical objects to meet one's own needs. The accumulation of art objects, however, is much more likely to serve as a symbol of high prestige because art objects are unique, not commonly found throughout the society, and often priceless.

This association of art with status symbols is seen in many societies with ranked populations. For example, virtually all of the art in ancient Egyptian civilizations was the personal property of the pharaohs. The high status of the hereditary king of the Ashanti of present-day Ghana is symbolized by a wide variety of artistic objects, the most important of which is the Golden Stool. In the Western world, many public art galleries are filled with impressive personal collections donated by powerful, high-status members of society (Getty, Hirshhorn, and Rockefeller, among others).

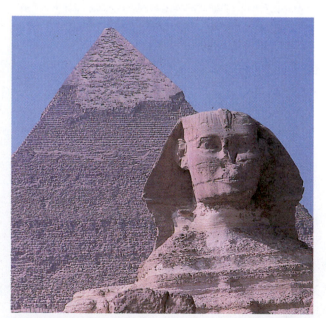

= *This monumental piece of art—the Sphinx—was designed to evoke positive feelings about the ancient Egyptian government and the pharaohs responsible for its creation.*

Not only is art a force for preserving the status quo, it is often used in just the opposite way, as a vehicle of protest, resistance, and even revolution. There are a number of instances of artists who, through their own artistic media, attempted to raise the consciousness of their oppressed countrymen in order to bring about changes in the political and social structure. For example, Marjorie Agosin (1987) documented the case of the Chilean *arpilleristas* who told the story of political oppression on scraps of cloth. These courageous artists were considered such a threat to the established government that they were eventually banned in their own country. Also in Chile during the Pinochet regime, local artists painted murals in the cover of night depicting scenes of government oppression, only to have them removed by the military police the next morning.

Perhaps one of the most influential forms of art used for social change is what has come to be known as **liberation theater.** Based on the philosophies of Franz Fanon, Eric Fromm, and Paulo Freire, among others, liberation theater was started in the 1960s by Augusto Boal in Peru. Boal was one of the first to suggest that effective political theater (used to bring about change) should not focus on the plot, the dialogue, or the quality of acting, but rather on the involvement of the audience in the *creation* and the *performance* of the play itself. Boal developed the now-legendary method that he called the liberation theater workshop. Working with experienced theater people, oppressed people from local communities participate in workshops that may last for several days. Through a series of experiential techniques they are exposed to the language of theater, such as body movement. Participants are then invited to write their own scenarios portraying oppression from their own lives, which are then acted out by professional actors. Just the oppressive scenario is acted out, not the resolution. After seeing the scenario played out, participants are then asked to offer possible resolutions to the scenarios, and if they wish, they may play it out themselves by taking the role of the actor. Thus, through the medium of theater, Boal was training locally oppressed people to assume the protagonist role, offer solutions to the situation, and discuss strategies for change. As Boal (1979:122) himself wrote, "The theater is not revolutionary in itself, but it is surely a rehearsal for the revolution."

In his discussion of liberation theater in Asia, Eugene Van Erven (1992) described an action-oriented example of liberation theater on the Island of Mindanao in the Philippines. In 1985 the artists from the local liberation theater group gathered about a hundred men and women in a local gymnasium for a three-day theatrical workshop. Workshop participants, drawn from the local poor, were instructed in the areas of creative body movement and symbolic choreography; visual artists taught them how to make masks from readily available materials; and, working with trained actors, workshop participants wrote a play based on their own experiences of exploitation. Armed with a new (theatrical) way of expressing themselves, participants began to compose their own songs, painted murals and banners, and fleshed out the dramatic scenes they

= *Art auction at Christie's in London. Because many pieces of Western art bring high prices, they can serve as very visible symbols of social status for the upper class.*

had improvised on the previous day. At the end of the day, they spontaneously marched out of the gymnasium, waving their banners, singing their songs, and performing their skits on street corners. They attracted a crowd of several thousand that followed them to several government offices, which were subsequently picketed for an entire week (Van Erven 1992).

As we have seen, art can be used to both preserve and to challenge the status quo. In some cases, works of art can be the focal point of controversy between those who would defend, as opposed to those who would oppose, the existing thinking in a society. To illustrate, in 1999 the Brooklyn Museum of Art in New York (a publicly supported facility) organized a major art show entitled "Sensation: Young British Artists from the Saatchi Collection." Although the show contained a number of controversial (anti-establishment) works of art, there was one in particular that caught the eye of New York City Mayor Rudolph Giuliani: a painting entitled "The Holy Virgin Mary" by Chris Ofili, who used elephant dung as one of his materials. Mayor Guiliani, a Roman Catholic, was so outraged by the painting that he threatened to cut all New York City funding to the Brooklyn museum unless the show was cancelled. The museum filed suit against the mayor in federal court on First Amendment grounds; the Mayor's office filed a countersuit against the museum. Both opponents and supporters of the exhibit held demonstrations in front of the museum. And, because of the controversy, the attendance at the public opening was considerably larger than expected.

Clearly the battle lines were drawn between those who would preserve the traditional image of the Virgin Mary (status quo) and those who would encourage alternative depictions. Of course, this art controversy is much more complicated than simply a struggle between artistic conservatives and liberals. None of the major players in this controversy would back down because they all stood to benefit from it. The New York City mayor, who at the time was running for a Senate seat from New York, took an indignant stand against this "sick art" because he was trying to appeal to the largely conservative voters in upstate New York. The director of the Brooklyn Museum of Art, Arnold Lehman, could afford to take a strong position on the freedom of artistic expression because the controversy brought large numbers of visitors to his museum. The wealthy collector, Charles Saatchi, who owned the works of art on display, no doubt profited from the controversy because the publicity of the exhibition increased the value of the art. Even the gallery owners, who contributed to the

cost of underwriting the controversial show, stood to profit because they represented many of the artists whose works increased in value because of the controversy. Thus, this scenario not only illustrates how art can be at the focal point between defenders and challengers of the status quo; it also illustrates how intimately art can be related to other areas of a culture—namely, politics and economics.

GRAPHIC AND PLASTIC ARTS

GRAPHIC AND PLASTIC ARTS include a number of forms of expression and a wide variety of skills. Although the Western notion of **graphic** and **plastic arts** usually refers to painting, sculpture, printmaking, and architecture, the anthropological definition also includes such art forms as weaving, embroidery, tailoring, jewelry making, and tattooing and other forms of body decoration. In some societies one form of art, such as wood carving, may be highly developed, and others, such as painting or metalworking, may be nonexistent. The analysis of these art forms is further complicated because different cultures use different materials and technologies depending, in part, on what materials are available locally. Whereas Native Americans of the Northwest Coast are well known for their carvings of wood, other cultures may use horn, bone, ivory, or soapstone. In some small-scale societies, the nature of people's ceramic art is determined by the availability of locally found clays. Often the level of technology influences whether a culture uses metals such as gold, silver, and bronze in its art traditions.

CROSS-CULTURAL VARIATIONS

Not only do different art traditions draw on different materials, techniques, and media, but the nature of the creative process can also vary cross-culturally. To illustrate, in the Western tradition, the practice of commissioning a piece of art is quite common. For a fee, portrait artists use their creative talents to paint realistic (and usually flattering) likenesses of their prominent clients. However, it is not likely that a client could commission an Eskimo artist to carve a walrus from a piece of ivory. According to the Eskimo notion of the creative process, that would be much too willful, even heavy-handed. Whereas the Western artist is solely responsible for painting the canvas or molding the clay in a total act of will, the Eskimo carver never forces the ivory into any uncharacteristic shapes. The Eskimo artist does not create but rather helps to liberate what is already in the piece of ivory. Edmund Carpenter describes the Eskimo's notion of the role of the artist:

As the carver holds the unworked ivory lightly in his hand, turning it this way and that, he whispers, "Who are you! Who hides there!" And then: "Ah, Seal!" He rarely sets out to carve, say, a seal, but picks up the ivory, examines it to find its hidden form and, if that's not immediately apparent, carves aimlessly until he sees it, humming or chanting as he works. Then he brings it out: Seal, hidden, emerges. It was always there: he did not create it, he released it; he helped it step forth. (1973:59)

Of all of the various forms of art found in the world, the graphic and plastic arts have received the greatest amount of attention from cultural anthropologists. This is understandable because until recently the analysis of the plastic and graphic arts was the most manageable. Until the recent development of such data-gathering technology as sound recorders, motion pictures, and videotape recorders, the analysis of music and dance was difficult. The graphic and plastic arts, however, are very physical and can be removed from their cultural contexts, displayed in museums, and compared with ease. Moreover, a painting or a sculpture has a permanence of form not found in music, dance, or drama.

•■ MUSIC ■•

WE OFTEN HEAR the expression "music is the universal language." By this people mean that even if two people do not speak each other's language, they can at least appreciate music together. But like so many popular sayings, this one is only partially true. Although all people do have the same physiological mechanisms for hearing, what a person actually hears is influenced by his or her culture. Westerners tend to miss much of the richness of Javanese or Sri Lankan music because they have not been conditioned to hear it. Whenever we encounter a piece of non-Western music, we hear it (process it) in terms of our own culturally influenced set of musical categories involving scale, melody, pitch, harmony, and rhythm. And because those categories are defined differently from culture to culture, the appreciation of music across cultures is not always ensured. To illustrate this point, Mark Slobin and Jeff Titon tell a story about a famous Asian musician who attended a symphony concert in Europe during the mid-nineteenth century:

> Although he was a virtuoso musician in his own country, he had never heard a performance of western music. The story goes that after the concert he was asked how he liked it. "Very well," he replied. Not satisfied with this answer, his host asked (through an interpreter) what part he liked best. "The first part," he said. "Oh, you enjoyed the first movement?" "No, before that!" To the stranger, the best part of the performance was the tuning-up period. (1984:1)

ETHNOMUSICOLOGY

The cross-cultural study of music is known as **ethnomusicology,** a new field involving the cooperative efforts of both anthropologists and musicologists (Nettl and Bohlman 1991). Though still not a well-defined field of study, ethnomusicology has made rapid progress lately because of the

■ *A traditional musician from Bhutan.*

APPLIED PERSPECTIVE

A Pottery Renaissance

Abasic theme running through this textbook is that cultural anthropology is not just a discipline for those interested in curious and esoteric facts but rather is eminently practical. When perusing museums exhibiting Native American arts and crafts, we frequently concentrate on one of two things: (1) certain artistic issues (such as design features, skills of the artist, use of colors) or (2) the cultural/historical significance of the objects. That such objects should be aesthetically appealing or educational is sufficient reason for anthropologists to collect and display them in museums. However, sometimes these traditional forms of art, such as pottery, can have far-reaching impacts on the lives of contemporary peoples. Such was the case at the Tewa pueblo of San Ildefonso in northern New Mexico.

According to William Whitman (1963), in 1907 the School of American Research, under the direction of E. L. Hewett, initiated a series of archaeological excavations of the ancient ruins of the Pajarito Plateau. The workers employed in the dig were all local Tewa Indians from San Ildefonso. The Tewa laborers—and particularly the women who periodically visited the site—took a keen interest in the pottery vessels being unearthed from the ruins. Some of the women, who were themselves local potters, held lively discussions of the ancient pottery styles and designs that had died out during the first century after the Spanish conquest. Within several years it had become apparent that the contemporary potters were attempting to emulate the excellent quality of the ancient vessels. Gradually, the local potters began to improve the quality of their wares. Realizing the importance of the process, the staff at the School of

recent developments in high-quality recording equipment needed for basic data gathering. Slobin and Titon (1984) have identified four major concerns of ethnomusicology:

1. *Ideas about music:* How does a culture distinguish between music and nonmusic? What functions does music play for the society? Is music viewed as beneficial or harmful to the society? What constitutes beautiful music? On what occasions should music be played?

2. *Social structure of music:* What are the social relationships between musicians? How does a society distinguish between various musicians on the basis of such criteria as age, gender, race, ethnicity, or education?

3. *Characteristics of the music itself:* How does the style of music in different cultures vary (scale, melody,

harmony, timing)? What different musical genres are found in a society (lullaby, sea chantey, hard rock, and so on)? What is the nature of musical texts (words)? How is music composed? How is music learned and transmitted?

4. *Material culture of music:* What is the nature of the musical instruments found in a culture? Who makes musical instruments and how are they distributed? How are the musical tastes reflected in the instruments used?

As these areas of interest indicate, ethnomusicology is concerned with both the structure and techniques of music and the interconnections between music and other parts of the culture. Yet, during the course of cross-cultural

American Research became directly involved by encouraging the women to incorporate the ancient artistic features into their own work. Staff from the school brought pieces of ancient pottery (as well as photographs of pieces in the museum) to the local Tewa potters.

In 1915 Hewett was put in charge of the displays of Indian culture at the Panama-California Exposition. As part of that exhibit, several women potters from San Ildefonso demonstrated their techniques before large audiences. Because of that experience and exposure, these local potters came to realize that their work—which by now had incorporated a number of traditional features—could bring infinitely higher prices from tourists than they had ever imagined.

Over the next several decades, the quality of the pottery of San Ildefonso, as it became infused with the ancient styles, improved. Equally important, this revitalization of ancient ceramics had profound economic and social consequences for the Tewa pueblo. By the late 1930s, pottery had become the major source of income in the pueblo. This revitalized pottery industry provided many people with a reasonable income, enabled them to purchase a wide variety of consumer items, send their children to college, and gain some measure of financial independence. Moreover, this craft revitalization enabled the Tewa to rediscover and reassert their past cultural identity. Thus, in this case, the efforts of anthropologists to reconstruct the ancient past had the additional consequences of breathing new life into the work of native artists, providing desired economic development, and creating a resurgence of ethnic pride in the process.

QUESTIONS FOR FURTHER THOUGHT

1. What role did anthropology play in positively affecting a local group of people?
2. What were some of the beneficial consequences for the people of San Ildefonso?
3. Are there examples from other cultures where the findings of anthropologists have been used to rejuvenate a local craft industry?

studies of music, ethnomusicologists have been torn between two approaches. At one extreme, they have searched for musical universals—elements found in all musical traditions. At the opposite extreme, they have been interested in demonstrating the considerable diversity found throughout the world. Bruno Nettl describes this tension:

In the heart of the ethnomusicologist there are two strings: one that attests to the universal character of music, to the fact that music is indeed something that all cultures have or appear to have . . . and one responsive to the enormous variety of existing cultures. (1980:3)

All ethnomusicologists—whether their background is in music or cultural anthropology—are interested in the study of music in its cultural context. Alan Lomax and his colleagues (1968) conducted one of the most extensive studies of the relationship between music and other parts of culture. Specifically, Lomax found some broad correlations between various aspects of music and a culture's level of subsistence. Foraging societies were found to have fundamentally different types of music, song, and dance than more complex producers. By dividing a worldwide sample of cultures into five different levels of subsistence complexity, Lomax found some significant correlations. For example, differences emerged between egalitarian, small-scale societies with simple subsistence economies and large-scale, stratified societies with complex systems of production (see Table 15-1).

TABLE 15-1	
Comparison of Music from Egalitarian Societies and Stratified Societies	
EGALITARIAN SOCIETIES WITH SIMPLE ECONOMICS	STRATIFIED SOCIETIES WITH COMPLEX PRODUCTION SYSTEMS
Repetitious texts	Nonrepetitious texts
Slurred articulation	Precise articulation
Little solo singing	Solo singing
Wide melodic intervals	Narrow melodic intervals
Nonelaborate songs (no embellishments)	Elaborate songs (embellishments)
Few instruments	Large number of instruments
Singing in unison	Singing in simultaneously produced intervals

These are just some of the dimensions of music that Lomax was able to relate to different types of subsistence. This monumental study, which required large samples and extensive coding of cultural material, was open to criticism on methodological grounds. The difficulties involved in such an approach help explain why ethnomusicology has made considerably greater gains in the analysis of musical sound than in the study of the cultural context of music. Nevertheless, the efforts of Lomax and his associates represent an important attempt to show how music is related to other parts of culture.

DANCE

DANCE HAS BEEN DEFINED as purposeful and intentionally rhythmical nonverbal body movements that are culturally patterned and have aesthetic value (Hanna 1979:19). Although **dance** is found in all known societies, the forms it takes and the meanings attached to it vary widely from society to society. In some societies, dance involves enormous energy and body movement, whereas in other societies it is much more restrained and subtle. Because the variety of postures and movements the human body can make is vast, which body parts are active and which postures are assumed differ from one dance tradition to another. In some African societies (such as the Ubakala of Nigeria), drums are a necessary part of dance, whereas in others (such as the Zulu) they are not. Dancing alone is the expected form in some societies, but in others it is customary for groups to dance in circles, lines, or other formations.

FUNCTIONS OF DANCE

As with other forms of artistic expression, the functions of dance are culturally variable. Dance is likely to function in a number of different ways both between and within societies. Dance often performs several functions simultaneously within a society, but some functions are more prominent than others. To illustrate, dance can function *psychologically* by helping people cope more effectively with tensions and aggressive feelings; *politically* by expressing political values and attitudes, showing allegiance to political leaders, and controlling behavior; *religiously* by various methods of communicating with supernatural forces; *socially* by articulating and reinforcing relationships between members of the society; and *educationally* by passing on the cultural traditions, values, and beliefs from one generation to the next.

DANCE AND OTHER ASPECTS OF A CULTURE

Lomax and his colleagues (1968) demonstrated quite graphically how dance is connected to other aspects of a culture. Specifically, their research shows how dance reflects and reinforces work patterns. By examining over 200 films, they were able to find a number of similarities between work styles and dance styles. The Netsilik Eskimos (Inuit) provide an interesting—and not atypical—example. For the Netsilik, dancing consists of solo performances that take place during the winter in a large communal igloo. Lomax describes the dance in considerable detail:

> One after another, the greatest hunters stand up before the group, a large flat drum covered with sealskin in the left hand, a short, club-like drumstick in the other. Over to the side sit a cluster of women chanting away as the hunter drums, sings, and dances. The performer remains in place holding the wide stance used by these Eskimos when they walk through ice and snow or stand in the icy waters fishing. Each stroke of the short drumstick goes diagonally down and across to hit the lower edge of the drum and turn the drumhead. On the backstroke it strikes the other edge, reversing the motion which is then carried through by a twist of the left forearm. The power and solidity of the action is emphasized by the

= *Indonesian women dance at a cremation ceremony in Bali.*

downward drive of the body into slightly bent knees on the downstroke and the force of trunk rising as the knees straighten to give full support to the arm on the upstroke. The dance consists largely of these repeated swift and strong diagonal right arm movements down across the body. (1968:226–227. Copyright by AAAS. Reprinted with permission of the publisher.)

Many of the motions found in Netsilik dance are the very ones that are necessary for successful hunting in an Arctic environment, as Lomax describes:

> A look at Eskimo seal hunting or salmon fishing shows this same posture and pattern of movement in use—a harpooning, hooking movement. The salmon-fisher stands hip deep in the clear waters of the weir, thrusting his spear down and across, lifting the speared fish clear of the water, twisting it off the barb, and threading it on the cord at his waist in a series of swift, strong, straight, angular movements tied together by powerful rotations of the forearm. At the seal hole on the ice pack, where the hunter may wait in complete stillness during the five frozen hours before the nose of the seal appears, there is

time for only one thrust of the spear: a miss spoils a day's hunting in subarctic temperature. His harpoon, then, flies in a lightning stroke, diagonally down across the chest. (1968:226–227. Copyright by AAAS. Reprinted with permission of the publisher.)

We can see thus that the stylistic movements found in Netsilik dance are essentially identical to those found in their everyday hunting activities. The qualities of a good hunter—speed, strength, accuracy, and endurance—are portrayed and glorified in dance. In other words, as part of their leisure activity, Inuit hunters, through the medium of dance, redramatize the essentials of the everyday subsistence activities that are so crucial for their survival.

▪◾ VERBAL ARTS ◾▪

CREATIVE FORMS of expression using words are found in all societies of the world. In Western societies—which place a great deal of emphasis on the written form—one might immediately think of the common literary genres of the novel, the short story, and poetry. Western societies also have a strong tradition of unwritten verbal arts, which are often subsumed under the general heading of **folklore.** In preliterate societies these unwritten forms are the only type of verbal art. Although the term *folklore* is a part of everyday vocabulary, it has eluded a precise definition. Alan Dundes has attempted to define folklore by listing a considerable number of forms that it might take. Recognizing that this is only a partial listing, Dundes includes the following:

> Myths, legends, folktales, jokes, proverbs, riddles, chants, charms, teases, toasts, tongue-twisters, and greeting and leave-taking formulas (e.g., see you later alligator). It also includes folk custom, folk dance, folk drama (and mime), folk art, folk belief (or superstition), folk medicine, folk instrumental music (e.g., fiddle tunes), folksongs (lullabies, ballads), folk speech (e.g., slang), folk similes (e.g., blind as a bat), folk metaphors (e.g., to paint the town red), and names (e.g., nicknames and place names). Folk poetry ranges from oral epics to autograph-book verse, epitaphs, latrinalia (writing on the walls of public bathrooms), limericks, ball-bouncing rhymes, finger and toe rhymes, dandling rhymes (to bounce the children on the knee), counting-out rhymes (to determine who will be "it" in games), and nursery rhymes. The list of folklore forms also contains games; gestures; symbols; prayers (e.g., graces); practical jokes; folk etymologies; food recipes; quilt and embroidery designs; . . . street vendors' cries; and even the traditional conventional sounds used to summon animals or to give them commands. (1965:2)

CROSS-CULTURAL MISCUE

SOME ANTHROPOLOGISTS (Geertz 1973) have suggested that various forms of game playing in a culture can be considered an art form. It has been argued that such games as baseball or football could be considered a kind of art because they involve performances that combine the experiences of the performers and the audience. If we follow this line of thought, we can look at the "art of baseball" as it is performed in North America and in Japan.

In recent decades, an increasing number of Major League Baseball players from North America have signed contracts to play in Japan. Many unsuspecting American ballplayers think that if they can pitch, field, or hit a baseball effectively at home, they will be equally successful playing in the Japanese league. Although America's pastime is played according to the same rules in Japan, the values, attitudes, and behaviors surrounding the game are worlds apart.

At the heart of the differences between baseball in these two cultures is the concept of *wa*, translated as "group harmony" (Whiting 1979). Baseball players in the United States—not unlike people in other sectors of American life—emphasize individual achievement. American ballplayers are constantly vying with one another for the most impressive set of statistics. Those with the best stats can demand the highest salaries. If management fails to meet their demands, the better players are likely to refuse to show up for spring training.

In contrast, Japanese ballplayers are expected to put the interest of their team above their own personal interests. Because it is assumed that the Japanese manager is always right, any disagreement with a manager's decision is a serious disruption of the team's *wa*. In the Japanese view, *wa* is the most important factor in having a winning team.

Robert Whiting documents a number of cases of North American ballplayers who had considerable difficulty adjusting to the radically different behavior expected on Japanese teams. Many Western ballplayers, despite their own personal success on the field, often found themselves being traded because their very individualistic (and typically American) behavior was seen as damaging the team's *wa*. The American players who have been successful in Japan have understood the importance of *wa*. Thus, if they want to perform well in the art of baseball, even these high-priced professional athletes will need to understand cultural differences.

This list is neither comprehensive nor exhaustive, but it does give us some idea of the wide range of verbal arts that have been, or could be, studied by cultural anthropologists. Even though we could focus on any of these forms of verbal art, our discussion concentrates on the forms that have received the greatest amount of attention: myths and folktales.

MYTHS

As mentioned in Chapter 14, myths are specific types of narratives that involve supernatural beings and are designed to explain some of the really big issues of human existence, such as where we came from, why we are here, and how we account for the things in our world. In other words, they are stories of our search for significance, meaning, and truth.

The relationship between the artistic expressions of myth and other aspects of a culture is well illustrated by the myths of creation found among the Yanomamo of Venezuela and Brazil. According to Napoleon Chagnon (1983), the Yanomamo have two separate creation myths: one for men and one for women. Both myths illustrate two fundamental themes of Yanomamo culture: fierceness and sexuality. According to the myth of male creation, one of the early ancestors shot the moon god in the stomach with an arrow. The blood that dripped from the wound onto the ground turned into fierce men. The blood that was the thickest on the ground turned into the most ferocious men, and the blood that was more spread out turned into men who engaged in more controlled violence. Nevertheless, the fierceness of the Yanomamo people today is seen as a direct result of the early violence described in the male creation myth.

According to the other creation myth, which attempts to account for the beginning of Yanomamo women, the men created from the blood of the moon god were without female mates. While collecting vines, one of the men noticed that the vine had a wabu fruit attached to it. Thinking that the fruit looked like what a woman should look like, he threw it to the ground, and it immediately turned into a woman. The other men in the group, struck with intense feelings of lust, began copulating frantically with the woman. Afterward the men brought the woman to the village, where she copulated with all of the other men of the village. Eventually, she gave birth to a series of daughters, from whom descended all other Yanomamo women. This highly sexual account of the creation of women is certainly consistent with everyday Yanomamo life, for as Chagnon reminds us, "Much of their humor, insulting, fighting, storytelling, and conceptions about humans revolve around sexual themes" (1983:94).

It is generally thought in the Western world that myths, such as those of the Yanomamo, are symptomatic of small-scale, non-Western, preliterate peoples. The entire history of Western civilization, particularly since the Enlightenment, has witnessed what Belden Lane (1989) has described as a demythologization—a steady rejection of myth and illusion as we "progress" toward science, rationality, and critical insight.

Yet even the highly reason-oriented West is not without its mythology. How else can we account for the enormous popularity in recent years of the works of Joseph Campbell on mythology, the proliferation of seminars and books based on Jungian psychology, and such futuristic mythological figures as Luke Skywalker and Obi-Wan Kenobi? We continue to learn a great deal about living from myths, and indeed much of our scientific Western culture has been molded by the power of myth, an art form that continues to have relevance for both Western and non-Western societies alike.

Folktales

In contrast to myths, **folktales** (or legends) are more secular in nature, have no particular basis in history, and exist largely for the purposes of entertainment. Like myths,

folktales are instructive, although they lack the largely sacred content of myths. Because most folktales have a moral, they play an important role in socialization. Particularly in societies without writing, folktales can be significant in revealing socially appropriate behavior. The heroes and heroines who triumph in folktales do so because of their admirable behavior and character traits. Conversely, people who behave in socially inappropriate ways almost always get their comeuppance. To illustrate, tales with very strong social messages are told to Dahomean children in West Africa around a fire (Herskovits 1967). Usually held at the compound of an elder, these storytelling sessions are designed to entertain, provide moral instruction for children, and develop the children's storytelling skills by encouraging them to tell tales of their own. Despite the very different settings, a storytelling session among traditional Dahomeans is quite similar to parents reading "Jack and the Beanstalk" or "Cinderella" to their children in front of the fireplace.

Folktales can be seen as an art form from two perspectives. Like written works of literature, folktales are creative expressions that can be analyzed in terms of plot, character development, and structure, even though the original author or authors may have been long forgotten. In much the same way that literary critics have analyzed the structure and meaning of Western literature (such as poetry and prose), the literary and artistic structure of folklore in

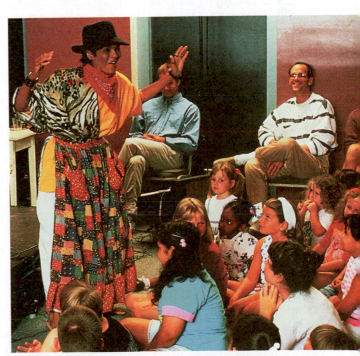

= *Folktales are told to children of all cultures, including our own.*

APPLIED PERSPECTIVE
Cursing in Verse

The Persian Gulf conflict, precipitated by the Iraqi invasion of Kuwait in August 1990, resulted in the most massive mobilization of military personnel and conventional weapons in history. High casualty rates and massive destruction of property were suffered by both Kuwait and Iraq. Moreover, massive divisions and realignments were made among the various states in the Arab world. The Western press concentrated on the military and diplomatic maneuverings in the conflict, but there was actually another war being waged—a propaganda war—between the principal Arabic players in the conflict: Iraq, Kuwait, and Saudi Arabia.

According to Ehud Ya'ari and Ina Friedman (1991), for the months before the Allied bombing, the two sides in the conflict used an archaic rhetorical art form to trade insults over the airwaves. This traditional genre, known as **hija,** has biblical precedents in the episodes where warriors (such as Goliath) loudly ridiculed their adversaries while boasting of their own power. This ancient Semitic tradition was based on the assumption that warriors could acquire supernatural power by insulting their opponents in rhyme or, as Ya'ari and Friedman (1991:22) have put it, "cursing in verse." For centuries, the most highly esteemed poets in the Arabic literary tradition have been those with a flair for offensive and vitriolic insults. This *hija* rhetorical art form has its own format, meters, and rhyming patterns. Classic *hija* starts with boastful self-praise and then moves into a series of abusive insults.

Unknown to most Westerners, there was a revival of *hija* rhetoric immediately after the Iraqi invasion of Kuwait in August 1990. Without commercial interruption, Saudi, Iraqi, and Kuwaiti (in exile) television broadcast hours of *hija* poetry, praising the justness of their own cause and lambasting the opposition. Interestingly, many of the subtleties of this ancient artistic form of rhyming put-down are not widely understood by the viewing public. The poems are highly ambiguous, even to those well-educated in classic Arabic, because conventionally *hija* poets choose words, phrases, and metaphors that have been out of general use for centuries. Even though the use of such an archaic and es-

both complex and small-scale societies can be analyzed. For example, Dell Hymes (1977) has demonstrated how the folklore narratives of the Native American Chinooka people of Oregon and Washington was highly organized in terms of lines, verses, stanzas, scenes, and acts. According to Hymes,

A set of discourse features differentiates narratives into verses. Within these verses, lines are differentiated, com-

monly by distinct verbs. . . . The verses themselves are grouped, commonly in threes and fives. These groupings constitute "stanzas" and, where elaboration of stanzas is such as to require a distinction, "scenes." In extended narratives, scenes themselves are organized in terms of a series of "acts." (1977:431)

The elaborative structures of these folk narratives allow us to regard them and similar texts as legitimate works of art.

oteric art form would seem to dilute its effectiveness as a propaganda device, the messages were not lost on the general public. Although many of the subtleties escaped the average citizen, the general messages came through on a gut level. The verses, intoned with dramatic cadence, conjured up heroic images of one's own leaders and Satanic images of the opposition's leaders.

The content of the *hija* poetry flowing over the airwaves was often vicious. With the buildup of Allied troops—some of whom were women—in Saudi Arabia before the outbreak of hostilities, the Iraqi *hija* poets took the Saudis to task for "hiding behind the skirts of women," a scathing insult to Arab masculinity. Not to be outdone, Saudi *hija* poets constructed their own vitriolic verse berating Iraqi leader Saddam Hussein for attacking his enemies at night and for being a contemptible neighbor. Specifically, Hussein was portrayed as an ungrateful neighbor who repudiated the help he had received in his earlier struggles with Iran. Moreover, the Saudi *hija* poets delivered the ultimate putdown to Hussein by denouncing him as a Jew.

The significance of the recent revival of *hija* rhetoric goes beyond its role as a patriotic mechanism or as a popular form of entertainment. As Ya'ari and Friedman have suggested, these *hija* recitations "provide channels for a kind of offbeat diplomacy by which more messages are transmitted across the lines than through conventional diplomatic means" (1991:24). In other words, the ebb and flow of the conflict can be assessed by analyzing the strength of the verbal venom coming from each camp. Provided one understands the art form, these quasi-news programs may be an even more accurate barometer of contemporary political and diplomatic relations than official newscasts or press releases. Even though U.S. intelligence may not have drawn on this artistic form of poetry as a source of information, reportedly both Saddam Hussein and King Fahd of Saudi Arabia received daily intelligence summaries of what the opposition poets were saying.

QUESTIONS FOR FURTHER THOUGHT

1. How would you define *hija* and how was it used by Iraq, Kuwait, and Saudi Arabia during the Gulf War?
2. Are there art forms in your culture that can give people from other countries a better understanding of the political climate?
3. Has Canada or the United States ever used art in the media as a propaganda device? To what ends?

In addition to the artistic structure, artistry is present in the telling and retelling of folktales. Even though the basic elements of the original tale cannot be changed, the tale teller retains the right to embellish and dramatize the story as he or she sees fit. The rhythm of the storyteller's utterances, the dramatic emotions expressed, and the use of nonverbal gestures all possess an artistic content of their own. Chagnon reminds us that in Yanomamo folklore a certain amount of artistry is in the telling:

Some of the characters in Yanomamo myths are downright hilarious, and some of the things they did are funny, ribald, and extremely entertaining to the Yanomamo, who listen to men telling mythical stories or chanting episodes of mythical sagas as they prance around the village, tripping out on hallucinogens, adding comical twists and nuances to the sidesplitting delight of their audiences. Everybody knows what Iwariwa did, and that part cannot be changed. But how he did it, what minor gestures and comments he made, or how much it hurt or pleased him as he did it is subject to some considerable poetic license, and it is this that is entertaining and amusing to the listener. (1983:93. Copyright, reprinted by permission of the publisher.)

•■ ART: CONTINUITY ■• AND CHANGE

LIKE ALL OTHER ASPECTS of culture, the various forms of expressive arts (graphic and plastic arts, music, dance, verbal arts) are subject to both internal and external forces of change. Anyone who has ever taken a course in the history of twentieth-century American art, for example, will know that unique schools of painting (with their own distinctive styles, materials, and themes) emerge, become prominent, and eventually die out and become part of history. To illustrate, the ashcan school (Edward Hopper, Arthur Davies) from 1908–1918 featured scenes of urban realism; the 1920s and 1930s witnessed the Art Deco style characterized by straight lines and slender forms; abstract expressionists during the 1940s such as Jackson Pollock and Willem de Kooning emphasized spontaneous personal expression over more conventional artistic values; minimalism, popular in the 1950s, emphasized pure, simple, and reduced forms; and, finally, the pop art of Andy Warhol and Roy Lichtenstein used images of mass media, advertising, and popular culture in ironic ways. In the early centuries of American art, painting styles and approaches were relatively stable, often lasting a number of decades. In the absence of high-speed transportation and communication technology, different artistic traditions were not able to diffuse very rapidly. The twentieth century, however, has witnessed many more changes than occurred in the two previous centuries.

As we begin the new millennium, the possibilities for quick and widespread cultural diffusion, and the accompanying cross-fertilization of artistic traditions, are increasing. Art exhibits today travel around the world rather than remaining in galleries or museums for centuries on end as they did in the past. Similarly, in the area of music, both rock stars and symphony orchestras go on world tours, performing in front of audiences all over the globe. It is not unusual today for Celine Dion to perform in South Africa, the Chicago Symphony to perform in Bangkok, or the Dixie Chicks to perform in Copenhagen. And, it is not just Western music that is being exported and diffused to other parts of the world; there is considerable flow in the opposite direction. In recent years we have seen recording artist Paul Simon collaborate with Ladysmith Black Mambazo, a singing group from South Africa, or Sting record fusion music with Cheb Mami from Algeria. As part of its marketing campaign for the 2000 Olympic Games in Sydney, Bank of America, the largest bank in the United States, has sponsored a multicity tour of Australian aboriginal musicians. And if the world population cannot see foreign musicians in live concert, they can always order their music CDs over the Internet from Barnes & Noble or Amazon.com. Thus, pure art forms, either Western or non-Western, will become increasingly difficult to find as the world becomes more interdependent.

The collaboration between recording artist Paul Simon and the South African singing group Ladysmith Black Mambazo is an example of the globalization of artistic styles and traditions.

Many cultures that, just several years ago, were relatively isolated, are today linked to the rest of the world through mass media, tourism, and the Internet. Some social scientists fear that today's fiercely competitive consumerism will quickly obliterate the various artistic traditions of many small-scale societies. As younger generations are exposed to different art forms from other parts of the world, there may not be a sufficient number of people to carry on the traditional art forms. Young people from Bolivia, for example, may be so enamored with Elton John or Gloria Estefan that they will lose interest in learning how to play the traditional flute. To be certain, there is reason to be concerned that traditional art forms in small-scale societies may be globalized out of existence.

As was mentioned earlier in this chapter, the island of Bali in Indonesia has had a long and rich tradition of the performing arts that permeates the everyday lives of its citizens. Dance and music in Bali are interwoven into the total fabric of Balinese culture. Participation in the arts is so widespread in Bali that some observers have suggested that everyone in Bali is an artist. Although this is perhaps overstating the case, it would not be an exaggeration to say that most Balinese are influenced by the traditional forms of music and dance in Bali. And because Bali has become a mecca of tourism in recent decades, it is feared that much of this traditional dance and music will be cheapened, or changed beyond recognition, by making it available to tourists. Expressing such fears more than a century ago, some nineteenth-century Dutch colonialists proposed making Bali an artistic museum so as to preserve its traditional art forms. Sukarno, the first president of Indonesia, considered Bali to be the center of Indonesian culture and took specific steps during his administration to protect it from tourism.

Although the vulgarization of these art forms would be disastrous, there is reason to believe that (perhaps *because* of its interconnectedness to other parts of the culture) these Balinese art forms have traditional resilience and staying power. Despite the fact that Bali is now the home of world-class hotels and its own Club Med, Balinese artists have always had a capacity to absorb features of other artistic traditions and make them their own. According to local legend, some elaborate (and sacred) musical instruments were introduced into Balinese society by foreign sailors as early as 1,200 years ago. This propensity to incorporate outside artistic themes and techniques into their own Balinese traditions is further explained by Indonesianist Suzanne Charle (1999:28):

> The *kecak* dance—the "classic" monkey dance in which scores of men chant the syncopated rhythm—was, in fact, commissioned by Walter Spies, a German artist who lived here in the 1930s and based his dance on older Balinese forms. In turn, his *kecak* has been reworked time and again, most recently as "Body Cak," a wildly popular collaboration between . . . the director of the arts college and Keith Terry, a California artist.

In addition to this knack for collaboration, present-day Balinese are making deliberate efforts to preserve their traditional arts. In precolonial times, Indonesian art was nurtured and sponsored by the royal palaces. After the ruling elites were deposed in 1949, traditional art forms, although somewhat repressed, survived the socialist regime of Sukarno and the chilling effects of the anticommunist government of Suharto. Today, art supporters in Bali are purposely stepping up to ensure the survival of traditional art forms. Private art dealers are using their own money to fund public museums; world-class dancers, who have performed all over the world, are spending their retirement years teaching young children the intricacies of Balinese dance; and professors from the College of Indonesian Arts are documenting the rural dances that were near extinction, while their students are actually going to these remote regions of the country to study with the local dance masters. Thus, owing to both considerable flexibility and a strong desire to maintain their aesthetic traditions, it appears that traditional arts in Bali will remain intact well into the future.

SUMMARY

1. Although there is no universal definition of art, for purposes of this chapter we have defined art as the process and products of applying certain skills to any activity that transforms matter, sound, or motion into a form that is deemed aesthetically meaningful to people in a society. The creative process of making art should be enjoyable, produce an emotional response, be transformational, convey a message, and involve a certain level of skill on the part of the artist.

2. The forms of artistic expression discussed in this chapter include the graphic and plastic arts (such as painting, carving, and weaving), music, dance, and verbal art (such as myth and folklore).

3. Rather than using the term *primitive* to refer to certain types of art, we use the term *small-scale*, which refers to essentially egalitarian societies with small populations, simple technology, no written language, and little labor specialization. In contrast to the art found in small-scale societies, the art of more complex societies is more permanent, has more elaborate and explicit standards of evaluation, and is associated with the elite.

4. Art contributes to the well-being of both the individual and the society. For the individual, art provides emotional gratification to both the artist and the beholder. From the social perspective, various forms of art strengthen and reinforce both social bonds and cultural themes, act as a mechanism of social control, and serve as a symbol of high status particularly in complex societies.

5. The study by ethnomusicologist Alan Lomax suggests that the music traditions found in small-scale societies differ from those of more complex societies in that the former are characterized by more repetitive texts, slurred articulation, little solo singing, nonembellished songs, few instruments, and singing in unison.

6. Verbal art includes myths and folktales. Myths tend to involve supernatural beings whereas folktales are more secular in nature. Like other forms of art, the verbal arts are intimately connected to other aspects of a culture, as illustrated by the Yanomamo myth of creation.

KEY TERMS

dance	*hija*
ethnomusicology	liberation theater
folklore	plastic arts
folktales	transformational
graphic arts	

SUGGESTED READINGS

Anderson, Richard L. *Calliope's Sisters: A Comparative Study of Philosophies of Art.* Englewood Cliffs, NJ: Prentice-Hall, 1990. This jargon-free study provides a unique look at the aesthetics in 10 major culture areas of the world, including the San, the Eskimos, the Aztecs, the Japanese, and the Western world. The philosophies of art from the 10 culture areas are used to make comparative statements about the nature of art, its origins, and its role in human affairs.

Berlo, Janet, and Lee Wilson. *Arts of Africa, Oceania, and the Americas: Selected Readings.* Englewood Cliffs, NJ: Prentice-Hall, 1993. A recent collection of 24 original articles written on a wide range of artistic forms from Africa, Oceania, and the Americas.

Coote, Jeremy, and Anthony Shelton, eds. *Anthropology, Art, and Aesthetics.* Oxford: Clarendon Press, 1992. A scholarly collection of writings on how anthropologists treat art and aesthetics, this recent volume contains articles on a wide range of topics from a number of different parts of the world, including Oceania, Mexico, the southern Sudan, and Australia. Prefacing these substantive (culture-specific) articles is a more general piece by Raymond Firth that discusses the changing relationship between art and anthropology over the past 60 years.

Dissanayake, Ellen. *Home Aesthetics: Where Art Comes from and Why.* Seattle: University of Washington Press, 1995. A thought-provoking book that argues that art was central to human evolutionary adaptation. Drawing on her experiences in a number of different parts of the world, the author shows how song, dance, drama, and the visual arts help people define their cognitive world.

Dundes, Alan. *Folklore Matters.* Knoxville: University of Tennessee Press, 1989. A collection of essays written by one of the leading figures in the study of folklore. Of particular relevance are the essays on folklore and identity and how anthropologists use the comparative method in the study of folklore.

Garland Encyclopedia of World Music. Hamden, CT: Garland, 1999. A 10-volume set of encyclopedias dealing with music from all parts of the world, ethnic groups, and traditional cultures written by eminent ethnomusicologists. An extraordinarily complete set of reference books on music.

Hatcher, Evelyn P. *Art as Culture.* 2d ed. Westport, CT: Bergin and Garvey, 1999. An excellent introduction to the field of anthropology and art, this book looks at the correlation between the level of complexity of a culture and its art forms.

Hanna, Judith L. *To Dance Is Human: A Theory of Non-verbal Communication.* Austin: University of Texas Press, 1979. A comprehensive ethnological treatment of dance as a significant part of culture. It is particularly strong in drawing on various forms of dance throughout the world to illustrate how this artistic form functions within religious, political, and social institutions.

Lomax, Alan. *Folk Song Style and Culture.* Washington, DC: American Association for the Advancement of Science, 1968. A classic study of musical styles around the world and how they relate to other aspects of culture.

Maquet, Jacque. *The Aesthetic Experience: An Anthropologist Looks at the Visual Arts.* New Haven, CT: Yale University Press, 1986. A French anthropologist looks at what is universal about art and how it differs in the many cultures of the world.

Nettl, Bruno, and Philip V. Bohlman, eds. *Comparative Musicology and Anthropology of Music.* Chicago: University of Chicago Press, 1991. A collection of writings discussing a wide range of issues in the study of the anthropology of music by some of the leading scholars in the field.

Titon, Jeff Todd, et al. *Worlds of Music: An Introduction to the Music of the World's Peoples.* New York: Simon & Schuster, 1996. An introductory survey of music in various parts of the world including Native America, Africa, Indonesia, eastern Europe, Japan, and India. The book contains a number of case studies written by ethnomusicologists with first-hand knowledge of the music and culture of a number of peoples of the world.

On the Net

1. Starting with Yahoo, click on "Arts and Humanities" and then "Cultures and Groups." You will find a list of approximately 45 countries. Select a country that you have a particular interest in by clicking on it. By browsing through the various sites, what can you learn about the artistic tradition of that country? What forms of art are most prominent? What connections can you find between this country's art forms and other parts of the culture? After considering these questions write a two-page paper on the art of this country.

2. Glass sculptural art, a relatively new art form, has developed in the United States and Canada over the last 30 years. One of the up-and-coming glass artists in the United States today is Dante Marioni. Using the name "Dante Marioni," conduct a search on the Internet to see if you can locate any of his art for sale. By which gallery is he represented? Select a piece of Marioni's glass sculpture that you find appealing. How would you describe this piece of sculpture? How much does it cost?

Chapter Sixteen

CULTURAL CHANGE

A traditional geisha in Kyoto, Japan, makes the point that some things change while others remain the same.

WHAT WE WILL LEARN:

▼

How do cultures change?

▼

What are some obstacles to cultural change?

▼

How do cities differ from noncities?

▼

Do economic development programs always benefit the people of developing countries?

▼

What is globalization, and how does it affect the cultures of the world?

▼

In a very real sense, any ethnographic description of a specific group of people is like a snapshot at one particular time. If the ethnographer conducts a restudy of the

same group five years later, it is likely that a number of cultural features will have changed. Some cultures (usually small-scale, preliterate, and technologically simple societies) tend to change slowly. Modern, complex, highly industrialized societies tend to change much more rapidly. Whatever the rate of change, however, we can bank on one thing when dealing with cultures: Nothing is as constant as change.

If we require proof of this basic maxim, we need only turn to the republished (1969) 1902 edition of the Sears, Roebuck catalogue. Glancing through the pages, one is struck by the vast changes that have taken place in our material culture since the turn of the century. Because of its comprehensiveness, the catalogue, in the words of Cleveland Amory, "mirrors the dreams and needs of Americans at a time when life was less complex than it is today" (1969: Introduction). In other words, it provides a near total inventory of our material culture at the turn of the century. Today many items in the 1902 catalogue—such as horse-drawn plows, patent medicines, and hightop leather shoes —can be found only in museums. Other items in the 1902 edition still exist as part of our material culture but in drastically altered form, such as sewing machines, windmills, men's toupees, and lawn mowers.

We can learn much about the attitudes and values of our turn-of-the-century ancestors from the material goods these people surrounded themselves with. For example, the catalogue advertised a substantial number of books on palmistry, astrology, and hypnotism. Many were "self-help" books that came in very handy in rural areas. Nearly a quarter of the book section was devoted to family Bibles. Another dramatic measure of the magnitude of changes that have occurred in U.S. culture is the three-page section devoted to the advertisement of corsets and bustles, designed to rearrange or accentuate certain features of the female anatomy. On nearly every page of the catalogue, we are reminded of the vast cultural changes, both material and nonmaterial, that have occurred in U.S. society since the early 1900s.

As mentioned in Chapter 2, it is generally recognized that cultures change as a result of both internal and external forces. Cultures change from internal mechanisms such as inventions or innovations, and cultures change from external mechanisms through the process of cultural diffusion or borrowing. Although diffusion is responsible for the greatest amount of cultural change, it is important to examine both processes of change in greater detail.

•■ INVENTIONS/INNOVATIONS ■•

ANY NEW THING, idea, or behavior pattern that emerges from within the society is an **invention**. Some inventions are very deliberate and purposeful; others are unconscious and unintentional. Ralph Linton, one of the most prominent scholars of cultural change in the twentieth century, has suggested that over the long run, the unconscious inventor has had a greater impact on cultural change than has the conscious inventor. The unconscious or accidental inventor contributes to cultural change without being driven by an unmet societal need or even realizing that she or he is making a contribution. As Linton put it, "Their inventions are, as a rule, of little individual importance, but they loom large in the aggregate" (1936:311).

These numerous unintentional inventors often go unnoticed and unrewarded, even though they may be making a very significant cumulative contribution to their culture. Yet, it is the deliberate, intentional inventor who tends to receive the greatest rewards and recognition. From our own recent history, Eli Whitney was sufficiently motivated to invent the cotton gin by the need to produce more cotton,

Jonas Salk discovered the polio vaccine to eradicate a crippling disease, and hundreds of other inventors have come up with new gadgets and ideas because they wanted to do something better or more efficiently.

There is a good deal of truth in the adage "Necessity is the mother of invention." Often, an invention develops because there is a pressing need for it. Linton (1936) relates the case of an invention that occurred around the turn of the century on the island of Hiva Oa. A man from the neighboring Gilbert Islands took up residence on Hiva Oa, married a local woman, and became a fisherman. It soon became apparent to him, however, that theft of outrigger canoes was rampant on the island. Motivated by the desire to avoid having his own boat stolen, he invented a new type of outrigger canoe with a detachable outrigger. By removing the outrigger assemblage, he could leave the canoe on the beach unattended. Within a short time, this new detachable outrigger almost totally replaced the previous model because there was a perceived need for this particular invention.

For years, social scientists have tried to discover which people tend to become inventors or innovators. (It should be pointed out that *innovation* and *invention* are not synonymous, for it is possible to be an innovator without being an inventor. Innovators are the first people to adopt or use a new thing or idea.) Why do some people invent new things, ideas, and behavior patterns, whereas most do not? And once something is invented, which people are most likely to adopt the invention? A number of interesting theories have been set forth. Some (Tarde 1903; Smith 1976; Rogers 1983) have suggested that both inventors and innovators tend to be **marginal people** living on the fringes of society. Not bound by tradition or convention, these marginal people can see problems and their solutions with a fresh perspective. Louise Spindler summed up this position when she noted that "Innovators are often 'marginal men,' who are, for a variety of reasons, somewhat divorced from the core of their culture and thus more free to create" (1984:15).

Everett Rogers's (1983) research suggests that innovators and early adopters are most likely to come from upper-class, wealthy, and well-educated segments of society. He goes on to speak of a basic paradox whereby the people who most need the benefits of an innovation are generally the least likely to adopt it. Rogers illustrates this paradox by looking at the adoption of contraception in developing countries. Citing his own research, Rogers (1973) notes that elite families, which already had small numbers of children, were the most receptive to adopting contraceptives, whereas lower-status (poorer) families, which averaged between five and six children, were the most resistant.

Other theorists tend to take a more psychological approach by looking at the effects of child rearing on innovative personalities. Everett Hagen (1962), for example, holds that innovators are most likely to come from families with excessively demanding fathers or from families with weak fathers and nurturing mothers. In his classic studies on achievement, David McClelland (1960) found that early training in the mastery of certain skills often leads to entrepreneurial success. As interesting as many of these theories are, we still do not have a very definitive understanding as to why some people are innovators and others are not. An idea may appear to be sound, a technological invention may appear to be efficient, or a new behavior may appear to make sense, and yet it will not be adopted by a particular group of people. The problem, of course, is that there are a multitude of variables—some social, some cultural, and others psychological—and some are operating in some situations but not in others.

·■ DIFFUSION ■·

IN ADDITION to changing through inventions and discoveries, cultures change through the process of *cultural diffusion:* the spreading of a thing, an idea, or a behavior pattern from one culture to another. As important as inventions and discoveries are to cultural change, the total number of inventions in any given society is generally quite small. In fact, Linton (1936) estimates that no more than 10 percent of all of the cultural items found in any culture—including our own—originated in that culture. If every culture had to rely solely on its own inventions, human progress over the centuries would indeed be slow. Cultures have developed as rapidly as they have precisely because the process of diffusion has enabled humans to pool their creative/inventive resources.

GENERAL PATTERNS OF DIFFUSION

Because diffusion plays such a prominent role in cultural change, it is appropriate to examine this process in some detail. Even though cultural diffusion varies from situation to situation, a number of generalizations about the process are worth mentioning.

Selectivity

The process of diffusion is selective in nature. When two cultures come into contact, not every cultural item is exchanged with another. If that were the case, there would be no cultural differences in the world today. Rather, only a small number of cultural elements are ever diffused from one culture to another. Which cultural item is accepted depends largely on the item's utility and compatibility with already existing cultural traits. For example, it is not very likely that men's hair dyes designed to "get out the gray" will diffuse into parts of rural Africa where a person's status is elevated with advancing years. Similarly, most people in the United States have resisted adopting the metric system because they see no particular advantage to taking the time and effort to learn it.

According to Rogers (1983), the speed with which an innovation is adopted—or whether it is adopted at all—usually is affected by whether it is seen to be superior to what already exists, it is consistent with existing cultural patterns, it is easily understood, it can be tested on a trial basis, and its benefits are clearly visible. This process of selective diffusion is evident in the area of religious ideas and practices. As mentioned in Chapter 14, in recent years a number of religions have experienced cross-pollination of ideas. One of the more popular Eastern religions in North America today is Buddhism. In many parts of the United States, Christians and Jews of all varieties are forming *sanghas,* or small communities, for the purpose of practicing Buddhist meditation. Even though the number of Jews and Christians engaging in certain Buddhist practices does not exceed a million people, the numbers are not insignificant. Most of them, however, have not embraced Buddhism totally. Most do not adhere to the complex and esoteric Buddhist theology but instead focus more on certain techniques that aid concentration and relieve stress. For example, from Zen Buddhism, practiced most in Japan and China, North American adherents have taken meditation, breathing, and stilling the mind, whereas from Tibetan Buddhism they have adopted visualization and chanting. In a world that is becoming increasingly fast-paced and stressful, it is not surprising that Westerners are turning to those aspects of Buddhism that stimulate spirituality as well as provide relief from the hassles of everyday life. Thus, by accepting some aspects of Buddhism but not others, a growing number of Westerners serve to remind us that diffusion is indeed a selective process.

Reciprocity

Diffusion is a two-way process. We should not assume that cultural items diffuse only from technologically complex societies to simpler societies. The anthropological record from many parts of the world clearly shows that cultural traits are diffused in both directions. European contact

= *Items of material culture are more likely to be diffused than are ideas or behavior patterns. Here one aspect of U.S. culture—the golden arches of McDonald's—has been diffused to Tokyo, Japan.*

with Native Americans is a case in point. Even though Europeans introduced much of their culture to Native Americans, they nevertheless received a number of cultural features in return, including articles of clothing such as ponchos, parkas, and moccasins; medicines such as quinine, anesthetics, and laxatives; and food items such as corn, beans, squash, yams, and the so-called Irish potato.

Modification

Once a cultural element is accepted into a new culture, it may undergo changes in form or function. Pizza is a good example of how a cultural item can change form as it diffuses. Pizza, which diffused from Italy to the United States in the late nineteenth century, has been modified in a number of significant ways to conform to American tastes. It is likely that its Italian originators would hardly recognize a pizza made on French bread, English muffins, or pita bread and topped with pineapple, tuna fish, or jalapeño peppers.

Sometimes the reinterpretation process involves a change in the way an item is used. While living in Kenya, this writer observed a stunning example of functional reinterpretation. The Masai of Kenya and Tanzania practice the custom of piercing their earlobes and enlarging the hole by inserting increasingly larger round pieces of wood until a loop of skin is formed. Rather than using pieces of round wood for this purpose, one group of Masai was observed using Eveready flashlight batteries obtained from the United States. In this case, the form of the batteries was the same, but the function was definitely reinterpreted.

Likelihood

Some parts of culture are more likely to be diffused than others. As a general rule, items of material culture are more likely candidates for diffusion than are ideas or behavior patterns. For example, a traditional farmer in Senegal is more likely to be convinced of the advantages of a bulldozer over a shovel for moving dirt than he is of substituting Buddhism for his form of ancestor worship.

Variables

There is reason to believe that diffusion is also affected by a number of important variables: the duration and intensity of contact, the degree of cultural integration, and the similarities between the donor and recipient cultures. Although we know a good deal about the process of diffusion, social scientists still are not able to predict with certainty when and where diffusion will take place.

•■ ACCULTURATION ■•

THE CONCEPTS of diffusion and acculturation have some things in common; in fact, **acculturation** is a special type of diffusion that takes place as a result of sustained contact between two societies, one of which is subordinate to the other. Thus, both diffusion and acculturation involve cultural change as a result of contact with another group. But whereas diffusion involves a single trait or a complex of traits, acculturation involves the widespread reorganization of one or both cultures over a short period of time. Both the dominant and subordinate culture may experience changes, but the subordinate culture always changes most dramatically. Acculturation can have a variety of consequences. The subordinate culture could become extinct, it could be incorporated as a distinct subculture of the dominant group, or it could be assimilated (blended) into the dominant group. But whatever form it may take, acculturation is the forced borrowing under conditions of external pressure.

The extent of the external pressure put on a subordinate culture varies considerably from one acculturation situation to another. Some cultural anthropologists (such as Mead 1956) have described situations of acculturation in which the less dominant culture freely chooses to emulate the culture of the more dominant society. At the other extreme we find examples of excessive coercion, such as the Spanish conquest of Mexico, which involved the brutal exploitation of the local population by both the Spanish government and the Spanish church (see Beals et al. 1977 for more details).

We should bear in mind that not all anthropologists agree on how to interpret the levels of coercion to which subordinate peoples are subjected. Some anthropologists (Diamond 1960; Bodley 1982) feel strongly that there is no such thing as voluntary acculturation. They hold that there are simply different degrees of force and coercion. As Stanley Diamond has stated, "Acculturation has always been a matter of conquest . . . refugees from the foundering groups may adopt the standards of the more potent society in order to survive as individuals. But these are conscripts of civilization, not volunteers" (1960:vi).

At the "free choice" end of the spectrum are the Manus of the South Pacific as described by Margaret Mead (1956). When Mead first studied the Manus in the late 1920s, the people lived in stilt houses over the lagoons, had no writing, wore simple grass skirts, and lived in extended family groups. When she returned to restudy the Manus in the 1950s, Mead found a culture that was actively and intentionally seeking education and a place in the modern world. During that intervening quarter of a century, the Manus had been exposed to hundreds of thousands of American soldiers who passed through the Admiralty Islands during World War II. They had been exposed to large doses of American technology as well. The American armed forces built roads, houses, and runways with the help of Manus labor. Mead claims that the Manus emulated the Americans not only because the Americans had an impressive array of technology but also because they treated the Manus with greater respect than had earlier contacts. So complete was the transformation in a mere quarter of a century that Mead spoke of the Manus as having given up their old lives for new ones.

Whereas most previous studies of rapid cultural change were quick to point up the deleterious effects on the affected culture, Mead's restudy of the Manus suggests that rapid cultural change doesn't have to be disruptive. Mead claimed that if the local people were willing participants in the change, the disruptive effects of change would be minimal, however rapidly the change may come. Even though Mead may have overestimated the Manus' willingness to participate in the acculturation process and underestimated the disruptive effects on their lives, this nevertheless serves as an excellent example of acculturation without much coercion.

Sometimes people voluntarily become acculturated because they believe that the adoption of certain technologies or behaviors will increase their adaptation to the environment. A case in point is the extensive cultural change that resulted from the rapid adoption of snowmobiles by the reindeer-herding Skolt Lapps of Finland. According to Pertti Pelto (1973), the first snowmobile was introduced into Finland in 1962, and nine years later 58 of the 70 families under study owned at least one snowmobile.

Traditional Lapp culture had always placed considerable emphasis on transportation systems and mobility. The seminomadic Skolt Lapps had adapted to their environment by maintaining two separate households: their nucleated villages inhabited during the winter and their calving and fishing ground, which they inhabited during the spring. From these seasonal homesteads, the Lapp herders traveled intensively, rounding up their herds. The concern with transportation as a key to successful adaptation was expressed in songs and folklore, in recreational activities (such as reindeer races), and in courting and marriage rituals. As Pelto reports, "Personal mobility, it was told to me again and again, is a main characteristic of the successful reindeer man: 'You have to be able to get around'" (1973:55). Thus, it is not difficult to understand the fascination that the Skolt Lapps had with the snowmobile: It provided them with a technological quantum leap in efficient mobility. In the process of adopting the snowmobile to reindeer herding, however, the Skolt Lapps experienced far-reaching changes in both their technology and their sociocultural patterns.

•■ LINKED CHANGES ■•

CHAPTER 2 INTRODUCED the concept that cultures are more than the sum of their parts. Rather, cultures are systematic wholes, the parts of which are interconnected. If cultures were, in fact, integrated wholes, it would follow that a change in one part of the culture is likely to bring about changes in other parts. In other words, most changes that occur in cultures are **linked changes.** The introduction of a single technological innovation, for example, may well set off a series of changes in other parts of the culture. This proposition can be illustrated by looking at one such

innovation—television—which was introduced into U.S. society during the 1950s. When the TV set, a part of our technological system, replaced the radio as the major form of electronic communication in U.S. households, it had far-reaching consequences for other nontechnological parts of the culture, such as the family system, the political process, and our religious institutions.

Without question, the advent of television has altered the nature of the American family. Before television became widespread, dinnertime provided an occasion for family members to have face-to-face interaction with one another. With the coming of television and the TV dinner, however, parents and children began spending dinnertime interacting with the "electronic Cyclops" rather than with one another. Campaign politics has never been the same since the arrival of television. Whereas Truman and Dewey conducted their presidential campaigns largely from the back of a railroad car in 1948, subsequent candidates were brought into our homes via television advertisements and televised debates. Today's candidates for public office need to be as attentive to such variables as lighting, clothing, and makeup as they are to the substantive issues in the campaign. In the area of organized religion, evangelicalism has been greatly enhanced by television. One can legitimately question whether Billy Graham would have such a lucrative ministry, Oral Roberts would have a university named after him, or Jim Bakker would have served time in federal prison if television did not exist.

•■ OBSTACLES TO CULTURAL CHANGE ■•

IN EVERY CULTURE there are always two opposing sets of forces: those promoting the status quo and those promoting change. At certain times, the forces of conservatism are in control, but at other times, the forces of change are in ascendancy. These two sets of forces are really two sides of the same coin. People are motivated to change their culture by a host of factors, including the desire for prestige, economic gain, or a new, more efficient way of solving a problem. There are also certain barriers to cultural change that are important to understand, particularly if one works as a change agent. Some of the more prominent change-retarding factors are discussed in the following sections.

CULTURAL BOUNDARY MAINTENANCE

An important mechanism for preventing cultural change is the creation and maintenance of cultural boundaries that keep people separate from other groups. Sometimes

Environmental Impact Study

*I*n the early 1970s, a group of urban residents in Charlotte, North Carolina, brought a class action suit against all parties involved in building a highway through their neighborhood. Because the highway in question was part of the U.S. interstate highway system, the defendants in the case were the municipal government of Charlotte, the North Carolina Department of Transportation, and the U.S. Department of Transportation. Because much of the highway construction had already been completed at the time the lawsuit was filed, the plaintiffs were not asking the court to stop the construction permanently. However, they did claim that the construction of a major six-lane interstate highway through their neighborhood was having serious negative consequences. In particular, the suit charged that all three levels of government, in violation of federal law, had failed to conduct an environmental impact study on the neighborhood. On these grounds, the presiding judge ordered that all further construction on the highway be halted until an environmental impact study was conducted to determine the negative effects the highway was having on the lives of local residents and to make recommendations for helping to alleviate some of the more serious consequences.

At the request of the attorneys for the plaintiffs and with the approval of the court, an urban anthropologist was hired to conduct a short-term environmental impact study on the project's effects on the community. Because work was totally halted (and people were temporarily out of work) until the study was completed, the court impressed upon this newly recruited applied anthropologist that time was of the essence. Unlike more conventional anthropological field studies, which can take a year or longer, this study was expected to take no longer than several weeks to complete.

Despite the time constraints, some traditional anthropological data-gathering methods were used. Using maps from the planning commission, it was possible to reconstruct the transportation flow between different parts of the neighborhood before the highway construction and determine how that flow had been disrupted. Extensive interviews were conducted with members of the community association, local entrepreneurs, and randomly selected neighborhood residents. And finally, the old anthropological standby—participant-observation—was used to actually observe the movement of people at certain key times, such as early-morning rush hour, late-afternoon rush hour, and Sunday mornings, when people went to church.

Based on people's comments and personal observations, it became clear that the construction of a multilane highway through the center of the neighborhood had significantly disrupted the lives of the residents. A change in the people's physical environment had affected other parts of their culture and lifestyles.

The most damaging impact on the neighborhood had to do with the way people got around to take care of their everyday affairs, such as going to school, doing their grocery shopping, and attending their neighborhood churches. Because this was a low-income neighborhood (somehow planners never seem to build highways through the high-rent districts!), the majority of people did not own cars, relying instead on public bus transportation. Because people's lives for the most part were played out in the neighborhood itself, they had used a number of well-traveled pedestrian routes. The highway cut off most of these routes. Now a person who lived on one side of the highway had no way of walking to the other side to shop or attend church. For those with automobiles, the construction of the highway made car travel within the neighborhood somewhat less convenient. But for the majority of people who relied on walking, the transportation patterns were disrupted almost completely.

Based on these findings, two recommendations were made to the court. First, because the only vehicular bridge spanning the highway had no provisions for pedestrian traffic, it was recommended that the builders add sidewalks, curb ramps for bicycles and baby carriages, traffic lights, and other amenities that would enable pedestrians to walk in safety. The second recommendation was to construct a separate pedestrian bridge over another part of the highway that would link part of the residential area with the neighborhood elementary school. This would add a second avenue for pedestrians to link up with both halves of the community as well as provide a traffic-free passageway for elementary schoolchildren. The court accepted both recommendations and required the defendants to carry them out as a precondition for the resumption of construction.

Here, then, is yet another example of how anthropological data and insights can be used to solve a particular societal problem. This short-term anthropological research project started with a fundamental idea about cultural change. That is, a change in one part of the system is likely to bring about changes in other parts of the system. Through conventional field techniques (albeit for a short period of time), the anthropologist was able to document the degree to which a change in the people's material culture (that is, the system of roads and pathways) affected their everyday patterns of transportation and social interaction. Once the sociocultural problems were identified, it was possible to make recommendations that would at least soften the negative impact of the highway construction on the lives of the local residents.

QUESTIONS FOR FURTHER THOUGHT

1. What negative consequences could the building of a six-lane highway have on the inhabitants of the neighborhood through which it runs?
2. Why do you think that most development projects in North American cities are planned in low-income neighborhoods?
3. What other types of societal problems can be solved by the research findings of urban anthropologists?

these boundaries are physical to the extent that most or all of the people live in one geographic area while excluding those who are not in the group. The more physically isolated a group is, the less susceptible it is to cultural diffusion. A culture does not need to be physically remote from other cultures, however, to avoid, or at least retard, cultural change. Rather, a culture can maintain its distinctiveness by imposing certain cultural boundaries that strengthen and glorify its own cultural traditions and discourage cultural borrowing from other groups. Aspects of culture such as language, eating habits, clothing, folklore, and humor are used to both emphasize a culture's uniqueness and to exclude outsiders.

Language

Perhaps no other part of culture is more unique to a group than its language. As discussed in Chapter 6, language is more than merely a system for sending and receiving messages. It is also highly reflective of a people's ethos or worldview. In other words, language is an embodiment of the people's values. If a group of people want to remain culturally separate, the way to do it is to use their own language exclusively, forbid the use of other languages, and discourage outsiders from speaking their language. Perhaps the most dramatic expression of linguistic exclusiveness takes the form of battles revolving around national language policy. The selection of Hindi in India or Swahili in Tanzania as a national language can be seen as an attempt to assert a particular cultural tradition while excluding others. Closer to home, the Quebec language law and the recent referendum on establishing a French-speaking state are also examples of the use of language as a mechanism of cultural boundary maintenance.

Clothing

In large part because of its high visibility, clothing is another important symbol of group identity used to distinguish "us" from "them." To maintain their own unique cultural identity, people (particularly when away from home) are likely to wear their own ethnic or national dress. Africans wearing brightly colored kenti cloth, Chinese wearing Mao jackets, or American bikers wearing black leather jackets are all examples of expressions of cultural uniqueness. Sometimes feelings run high about the meanings conveyed by ethnic dress. For example, a man from the Swiss–German section of Switzerland who was married to a German woman refused to allow his 7 year-old son (who was half German) to wear *lederhosen,* a distinctive type of leather pants from southern Germany, because he wanted to make sure that everyone knew his son was Swiss and not German (personal communication).

Eating Styles

Eating customs are another critical dimension of ethnicity that can serve as a cultural barrier to contact with other groups. In most cultures, if not all, eating is a highly social activity. What foods are eaten, in what manner, how often, and particularly with whom are all factors that vary from one culture to another. Every culture uses the sharing of food in one way or another to maintain social ties and group solidarity. A good illustration is Hindu India, where people are strictly forbidden from eating with members of

= *The sharing of food and eating habits are a cultural barrier to contact with other cultural groups.*

other castes. In some societies, the communal aspects of eating are emphasized to a far greater degree than they are in the United States. For example, Amharic speakers from Ethiopia not only eat food from a common basket but on special social occasions will actually put the food into one another's mouths rather than in their own. Moreover, by creating and maintaining certain food taboos, cultures set themselves apart from other cultures that do not recognize such prohibitions.

RELATIVE VALUES

Sometimes people resist changes in their culture because the proposed change is not compatible with the existing value system. Change agents (such as overseas development workers, Peace Corps volunteers, or missionaries) often fail to understand why some people are so resistant to certain changes and don't seem to comprehend the advantages of the change. People from a particular culture may refuse to participate in an agricultural improvement project not because they do not understand the likely outcome of the project but because the change would bring about a situation that would be less desirable (according to their values) than the status quo.

An illustration of resistance to change caused by relative values occurred in Kenya in the early 1970s. Because of shortfalls in the maize production for several years running, the government, which controlled the sale of all maize meal in the country, decided to alleviate the shortage by mixing 10 percent wheat flour with 90 percent maize meal. Government officials reasoned that the ground wheat (obtained free from foreign assistance programs abroad) would make their dwindling maize supply last longer and avoid shortages in the retail stores. But the population reacted strongly against the government's attempt to dilute their basic staple (maize meal), which is used to make *ugali,* a porridge eaten at most meals. It seems that the maize meal mixed with 10 percent wheat had a somewhat different taste and consistency than 100 percent maize meal. As it turned out, according to the local value system, the quality of their maize meal was more important than the quantity. In other words, the people in Kenya were willing to put up with some degree of food shortages, provided the usual quality of their primary food source was not sacrificed.

Another example of relative values serving as a barrier to cultural change comes from South America (Ferraro 1998). A U.S. timber company harvesting wood in a remote area of the rain forest was experiencing difficulties recruiting labor from among the local Indian communities. In an attempt to attract laborers away from its main competitor (a German company), the U.S. firm invested heavily in housing for its employees, offered considerably higher wages than its competitor, and guaranteed the workers a 40-hour workweek (the Germans paid their workers by the hour). Yet despite these economic advantages, the majority of workers continued to work for the German firm. The explanation for this apparent irrational behavior on the part of the Indian workforce is that what might be of value to workers in Detroit is not what appeals to Indian workers in the South American rain forest. For the Indian workers, flexibility of their time was more important than housing or high wages. Under the system used by the German firm, which paid an hourly wage rather than a 40-hour per week salary, the workers were able to take time off for their festivals and ceremonies without fear of losing their jobs.

CULTURES AS ORGANIC WHOLES

The functional interrelatedness of the parts of culture—as discussed in the preceding section—serves as a conservative force discouraging people from cultural change. After a number of generations of adapting to their environments, many small-scale societies are in a state of equilibrium. That is, solutions to most societal problems have been worked out (albeit imperfectly), and a balance of social relationships has been established between various members of the group. To change one part of such a culture is likely to threaten existing social and economic relationships. To illustrate, Alan Beals (1962) cites the case of Gopalpur, a village in South India, which for centuries has used farming techniques that do not produce great yields. The use of modern technology, pesticides, chemical fertilizers, and more modern irrigation systems would, in all likelihood, result in increased agricultural productivity. But by adopting new farming techniques, the local farmer would jeopardize some significant social and economic relationships. As Beals put it:

> At every step, the farmer wishing to improve his agricultural practices must weigh the claims of the new method against the known economic and social benefits of the traditional method. To purchase improved agricultural equipment, the farmer must sever his traditional relationship with the Blacksmith and Carpenter. This is more than an economic relationship. Not only are the Carpenter and Blacksmith neighbors and friends, but they have religious functions that make their presence essential on such occasions as births, marriage, and death. (1962:79)

As Beals demonstrates, accepting changes in one part of a culture (such as agricultural technology) is likely to bring about undesirable changes in other parts of the culture (such as social and religious relationships). By refusing to adopt new farming technology, the rural farmer is not necessarily reacting in an ultraconservative way but rather is responding very sensibly.

•■ URBANIZATION AND CHANGE ■•

ALTHOUGH CITIES have existed for more than 5,000 years, the acceleration of **urbanization** over the past century has been staggering. In 1900 there were only 16 cities in the world with a population of a million or more people. A mere 90 years later there were 276 such cities. Looking ahead, it has been estimated that by 2025 approximately 60 percent of the world's population will be urban, as compared to only 37 percent in 1990 (Stevens 1992). Urban growth in the United States has been dramatic, progressing from 5 percent of the population living in cities in 1790, to 14 percent in 1850, to 50 percent in 1920, to approximately 75 percent in the 1990s. The percentage of people living in cities in the industrialized world is leveling off, and the most dramatic rates of urbanization in recent years are found in the **less developed countries (LDCs).** Rural peoples in Asia, Africa, and Latin America have been flocking to cities in such numbers that these three continents now contain 13 of the 15 largest cities in the world (see Table 16-1). This rapid urban growth in LDCs is problematic because, unlike the more gradual urbanization in North America and Europe, which was stimulated by a strong industrial base, urbanization in Asia, Africa, and Latin America often lacks the industrial base to support the large numbers of rural people looking for employment.

THE SOCIOCULTURAL NATURE OF CITIES

The numbers dealing with urban growth, however, tell only part of the story. To report that São Paulo, Brazil, has 16.5 million people tells us nothing about whether people in that city think and behave differently from people in rural Brazil. Since the mid-nineteenth century, sociologists, anthropologists, and social theorists have recognized fundamental structural differences between cities and rural societies. Most of the basic theoretical distinctions made in the last century addressed rural–urban differences. German sociologist Ferdinand Tonnies spoke of the *Gemeinschaft,* or intimate community (characterized by personal ties and family connections) versus the *Gesellschaft,* or impersonal association (characterized by self-interest and short-term relationships). French sociologist Emile Durkheim focused on two different types of social cohesion. Rural, small-scale societies were held together by *mechanical solidarity* (little division of labor, shared values, and a mutuality of interest), whereas urban, complex societies were held together by *organic solidarity* (considerable division of labor and mutual interdependence). In the United States, Lewis Henry Morgan made a similar distinction between *societas,* small-scale (rural) societies based on personal ties, and *civitas,* more complex (urban) systems characterized by property relations. In the first half of the twentieth century, other theorists made similar distinc-

= *In recent decades the most spectacular growth of cities has occurred in the developing world—as shown here in Mexico City—not in western Europe or North America.*

TABLE 16-1

The World's 15 Largest Cities

RANK	CITY	COUNTRY	POPULATION (1994) (MILLIONS)	POPULATION (2015) (MILLIONS)
1	Tokyo	Japan	26.9	28.9
2	Mexico City	Mexico	16.6	19.2
3	São Paulo	Brazil	16.5	20.3
4	New York	USA	16.3	17.6
5	Mumbai (Bombay)	India	15.1	26.2
6	Shanghai	China	13.6	17.9
7	Los Angeles	USA	12.4	14.2
8	Calcutta	India	11.9	17.3
9	Buenos Aires	Argentina	11.8	13.8
10	Seoul	Korea	11.6	12.9
11	Beijing	China	11.3	15.6
12	Osaka	Japan	10.6	10.6
13	Lagos	Nigeria	10.3	24.6
14	Rio de Janeiro	Brazil	10.1	11.8
15	Delhi	India	9.9	16.8

SOURCE: Robert Famighetti, ed., *The World Almanac and Book of Facts, 1999.* Mahwah, NJ: World Almanac Books, 1998.

tions between rural and urban societies, including Pitirim Sorokin (familistic versus contractual), Charles Cooley (primary versus secondary groups), Howard Becker (sacred versus secular), Aidan Southall (role breadth versus role narrowness), and Robert Redfield (folk versus urban).

In one way or another, these early theorists were suggesting that cities, compared with noncities, were more heterogeneous, competitive, secular, progressive, role specialized, economically interdependent, and stratified. Urbanites, compared with country dwellers, were more impersonal, time conscious, and blasé and less interested in meeting kinship obligations. Moreover, the process of urbanization, according to this view, led inevitably to alienation, the breakdown in primary group relationships, and a number of social ills such as higher rates of crime, divorce, drug use, and homelessness. A corollary was that as people moved from rural to urban areas they experienced major adjustment problems. At the very least, it was understood that as people moved from rural to urban areas, they experienced significant changes in values, behavior, and culture.

In recent decades, however, urban anthropologists have produced a spate of studies that suggest that such a dichotomous rural–urban model is at best overly simplistic (see the Kenya Kinship Study described in Chapter 5). This rural–urban dichotomy is misleading because it assumes a unidirectional flow of migration from rural to urban areas, in much the same way that it occurred in Western countries. Since the 1850s, agriculturally based peoples in the United States have sold the family farm, moved to the cities without ever intending to return, and eventually, perhaps several generations later, moved to the suburbs. Urban anthropologists (unlike their sociologist colleagues, who tend to study urbanization in the developed world) have found that many migrants from LDCs leave their rural communities *temporarily,* fully intending to return in the future. Some migrate for the purpose of meeting particular objectives, such as obtaining a specific sum of money. Others may intend to make the city their permanent home but because of family obligations or the inability to find or keep a job are forced to return to the rural homeland. Thus, in much of the developing world, where urbanization is occurring at such a rapid rate, we have seen a common phenomenon known as the **circulation of labor** between rural and urban areas rather than a single, permanent rural-to-urban migration.

Rather than viewing rural and urban communities as encapsulated social systems, urban anthropologists over the last 25 years have demonstrated how economic and social developments are creating more unified systems in which the village and the city are intimately interrelated. Thus, we should not think of the migrant as the sole object of change, being transformed from country bumpkin to city slicker. Rural and urban areas should instead be viewed as complex fields of social relationships comprising criss-crossing peoples, ideas, and resources. In this view, changes occur not only in the migrants themselves

= *In many large African cities, such as Lagos, Nigeria, people retain their connections to their rural homelands by periodic visiting.*

but also in the rural communities of origin and the urban host communities.

One early study by Joyce Moock (1978–79) looked at rural–urban ties between a group of Abaluyia migrants to Nairobi, Kenya, and their rural kinsmen in Maragoli Location, about 250 miles away. Moock goes well beyond the claim that urban migrants retain ties with their rural homelands and actually suggests that rural and urban residents are part of the same ongoing social system. For example, Moock studied farm-head migrants who engaged in what she called **occupational duality:** the simultaneous management of a cash-cropping farm at home and some type of wage employment in the city. Strong ties are essential if this management of home affairs from afar is to be a viable economic option. As Moock points out, there are

ties or dependencies in both directions. The farm-head migrants depend on their rural kinsmen for land purchase and adjudication of disputes, management of everyday farming routines, and general household management. Rural family members, on the other hand, depend on the urban wage earner for economic assistance, help in finding jobs in the city, and temporary living accommodations when they come to the city. These mutual dependencies result in a periodic movement of both family members and financial resources between town and country. These ties are so strong that in an earlier study of Abaluyia migrants to Nairobi, Thomas Weisner (1972) described the nature of rural–urban networks as involving "one family with two households." Moock's study was one of the earliest, but a number of more recent studies have recognized the two-way nature of urban migration. For example, Robert Rhoades (1996) examines the effects of circular migration on economic development in the rural homelands in southern Spain, Caroline Brettell (1996) provides a look into the lives of Portuguese women migrants and their desire to return to their homeland, and George Gmelch (1996) has studied West Indian migrants to Britain who plan to stay abroad just long enough to satisfy their monetary and educational goals.

Perhaps one of the clearest examples of the interrelationship between rural and urban, and indeed the coexistence of traditional and modern, is the suburban region around the city of Ulaan Baatar, the capital of Mongolia. On the expansive grassland surrounding the city are found hundreds of *gers*—circular, domelike tents used traditionally as residences by nomadic Mongols. The interior of the *ger* is arranged in traditional fashion, with space for males to the left of the door and space for females to the right. The rear of the enclosure is reserved for guests whereas the space near the entrance is for everyday objects for cooking and cleaning. And, it is likely that beside the door of the *ger* will hang a stuffed hedgehog for the purpose of keeping evil from entering the home. Yet, these traditional nomadic dwellings on the edge of the capitol city have taken on a number of urban traits. It is likely that a car will be parked in front of the *ger* and that a vegetable garden (hardly a traditional Mongol source of food) can be found beside it. At night, the *ger* will probably be lit with electric lights, children will be playing video games, and an adult may be surfing the Internet. And, unlike their rural relatives, the inhabitants of these tent cities are not full-time animal herders but may be engineers, doctors, or accountants. Thus, although nomadism and urbanism are thought to be very different, and mutually exclusive, ways of life, the *ger*-dwellers of Ulaan Baatar have managed to integrate many traditional cultural features of nomadism with those of the modern urban world. (Hay-Eadie 1995)

ADAPTATION TO CITY LIFE

Urban anthropologists are interested in exploring how migrants meet their economic, social, and emotional needs once they come to town. How do these strangers to the big city find a job, a place to live, and a network of friends and acquaintances to play out their social lives? One common strategy is to rely on connections, usually kin-based, from the rural homeland. Migrants often contact relatives or people from back home who have already established a residential and occupational foothold in town. We see this phenomenon operating with both rural-to-urban migration and international immigration. It is this beachhead theory of migration that accounts for the many long-standing ethnic neighborhoods in cities in North America. For example, when many Indians were expelled from Uganda in the 1970s, some migrated to Ontario. Once these early immigrants had established a beachhead, many of their kin, friends, and associates who were looking for a new homeland chose Ontario rather than some other part of the world because there were people there they could rely on for help in finding a job and a place to live. This same adaptive strategy is played out in many parts of the world for the simple reason that it works.

But in addition to relying on existing kin-based networks (which are likely to be much smaller than in rural areas), migrants also use as adaptive mechanisms social groups based on voluntary membership. Migrants in both industrialized societies and LDCs use **voluntary associations** in order to get their needs met and to help in the transition from living in rural, traditional societies to large, industrialized ones. The voluntary associations serve a variety of purposes. They are mutual aid societies, lending money to members, giving assistance in finding jobs, providing scholarships to students, facilitating marriage arrangements, and even handling funeral arrangements. They also serve the recreational, social, and friendship needs of their members.

The voluntary associations found in West African cities, described by Kenneth Little (1957) and Elliott Skinner (1974), illustrate how some voluntary associations play an important social function. For example, the *gumbe* association found in Ouagadougou (Burkina Faso) provided members with both organized social activities and a well-enforced set of behavioral codes. To illustrate, the *gumbe* sponsored dances for its members, but also a controlled set of behavioral standards that guided the interactions between males and females attending the dances. Single females were chaperoned at the dances and escorted home safely afterward; young men were allowed to interact with unmarried girls in very circumscribed ways; and in many ways the social structure established at the dances took the place of the rural kin group that traditionally controlled the interaction of unmarried youth.

Voluntary associations, particularly those in LDCs where the contrast between rural and urban is stark, provide individuals with a sense of belonging. This is often

= *Voluntary associations such as the Guardian Angels in New York City help members adjust to urban life by providing professional and recreational networks beyond the family.*

accomplished through the use of many offices and titles within the organization. Although most of these titles carry little authority or responsibility, they do serve to integrate even the least influential members into the group. For example, voluntary associations in Sierra Leone (Little 1967) grant to their members such titles as Reporter, Bailiff, Inspector, Cashier, Clerk, Sultan, Solicitor, Sister, Nurse, and Lawyer. Clearly, these associations are giving their members, particularly those who are marginal to city life, a strong sense of belonging to a group.

•■ CHANGE AND DEVELOPMENT ■•

TODAY'S WORLD is roughly divided into two broad categories of countries, the haves and the have-nots. This dichotomy is sometimes characterized as the industrialized versus the nonindustrialized world or the developed versus the undeveloped. There is considerable disagreement as to the reasons for these differences, but no one can deny the vast differences in material wealth between the richest nations (such as Canada, Switzerland, the United States, and Japan) and the poorest nations (such as Chad, Mozambique, Ethiopia, and Bangladesh). In terms of comparative income, Canada's per capita income is 170 times higher than it is in Mozambique; the average U.S. citizen earns approximately 178 times as much money as the average Ethiopian. Enormous disparities can also be seen in noneconomic measures. To illustrate, the life expectancy in Norway is 77 years but is 47 years in Burkina Faso. The infant mortality rate in Mali is 168 per 1,000 live births, whereas in Finland it is only 6.

How did the modern world become so stratified in terms of economic development? A number of social scientists have offered differing interpretations, but they usually boil down to one of two competing theories. One broad theory explains these vast differences in economic development in terms of the inherent sociocultural differences found between the rich and the poor, the developed and the undeveloped. Often called the **modernization theory,** this model is based on a dichotomy of traditional versus modern that serves not only as an attempted description of reality but also as a planning strategy for bringing about economic development in undeveloped nations. The modern nations are associated with high levels of technology, industrialization, urbanization, formal education, efficient bureaucratic governments, strong market economies, precise reckoning of time, upward mobility based on merit, rapid change, planning for the future, and a decline in the extended family. Traditional nations, on the other hand, have fewer of these characteristics. This modernization theory assumes that in order for undeveloped nations to become developed, they must engage in activities that would make them more like the developed nations. In short, they need to become more modern. The process of economic development would occur through the mechanism of foreign aid from the wealthy nations to the undeveloped nations.

The modernization theory includes many of the same assumptions as the **culture of poverty** notion set forth by Oscar Lewis (1966). Some groups, Lewis argues, remain poor because they are crippled by certain cultural features, passed from generation to generation, that perpetuate poverty. The only way to break the cycle of poverty is to change their culture (that is, their ideas, values, material possessions, and behaviors). In other words, it blames poverty on the poor by suggesting that their countries are undeveloped because of their cultural characteristics, which they pass on to their children. With the help of some foreign aid, designed to change the culture, the poor nations can become more like the wealthy.

The other grand theory of accounting for the disparities between rich and poor nations is what has been called the **world systems theory.** The rich and poor nations of the world are not fundamentally different because of innate cultural features but rather are really part of the same world system. The wealthy countries of the world achieved high levels of development by exploiting other regions, plundering their natural resources, using their people as cheap sources of labor, and dominating their markets. In 1884 at the Conference of Berlin, European powers carved up the entire continent of Africa. The French took large parts of West Africa; the British controlled Nigeria, the Gold Coast, Kenya, Uganda, and the Rhodesias; the Portuguese got Angola and Mozambique; and the tiny country of Belgium took control of the mineral-rich Congo, which was 76 times larger than itself. These nineteenth-century industrializing nations of Europe used these colonies for their plantations and mining operations, used cheap African labor, exported some of their own excess populations to the colonies, and then sold many of their finished products back to the Africans they claimed to be helping. Whereas Europeans actually took political control over the colonies, the United States chose to establish commercial influence through its corporations, mostly in Central and South America. Whether we are talking about corporate imperialism or outright colonialism, the consequences were the same. The exploitation of people and resources by the dominant powers had the effect of retarding economic

▬ *The U.S. family on the left has a per capita income that is roughly 178 times higher than that of the Ethiopian family on the right.*

growth of the subordinate nations. Thus, according to this explanatory theory, economic development is not the result of an enlightened or progressive population but rather the result of one group purposefully increasing its own wealth at the expense of others.

As we begin the twenty-first century, the period of colonialism has all but ended. Spain and Portugal relinquished control over their South American colonies in the nineteenth century. The 1960s witnessed large numbers of African colonies winning their independence. However, turning over the reins of government to local people has not necessarily resulted in complete autonomy. By a process known as **neocolonialism,** the wealthy (former colonial) nations continue to exercise considerable political, economic, financial, and military power over the less developed nations. By virtue of their economic dominance, the industrialized nations control the international markets of the commodities they buy from the LDCs. That is, the industrialized world determines the price on world markets of Ghanaian cocoa, Bolivian tin, or Kenyan coffee. The wealthier nations also lend capital to the less developed nations, which has the effect of turning them into perpetual debtors. Debt can be a major form of control, with the creditors calling many of the shots. Moreover,

CROSS-CULTURAL MISCUE

SOMETIMES WELL-INTENTIONED but short-sighted environmental sanitation programs can go awry when the planners are not sufficiently aware of local cultural realities. Through various types of foreign aid programs, U.S. technicians have made major efforts to introduce sanitary latrines into many developing countries. Although most North Americans do not regard latrines, or outhouses, as the height of sanitation, they do represent a significant advance over some traditional ways of disposing of human waste. Latrines built by U.S. technicians are fashioned after outhouses found in some rural areas of the United States; they are inexpensive wooden structures with a raised seat perforated by several holes. However, this latrine design is not particularly well received in other parts of the world. George Foster relates an incident from El Salvador:

> *Several years ago a coffee planter, interested in the welfare of his employees, built a latrine for each house according to the standard American model. He was upset when his employees refused to use them. Finally an old man offered a suggestion. "Patron, don't you realize that here we are squatters?" . . . Latrines with raised seats seem to cause constipation among people who customarily defecate in a squatting position. (1973:103)*

with the debtor nations obliged to pay considerable interest payments, they never seem to have the surplus capital to invest in their own economic infrastructure.

The maintenance of the wide gap between the rich and the poor nations is also caused by the increasing power and influence in recent years of **multinational corporations.** In some cases multinational corporations directly exploit LDCs, as with the Firestone Rubber Company in Liberia or the United Fruit Company in Central America. More often, however, multinational corporations tend to exploit LDCs simply by doing business as usual. These multinational corporations have assets and power that far exceed those of most of the governments of the developing world. To illustrate, the General Electric Corporation has more assets than over a hundred different independent countries in the world today. Any single multinational corporation may engage in a wide variety of commercial activities, including transportation, manufacturing, and advertising. However they make their profits, one thing is certain: Most of the corporate profits go back to the home country rather than staying in the developing nation.

The modernization approach to economic development suffers from several ethnocentric assumptions. First, modernization theorists take as a given the fact that all peoples in the world would gladly embrace all of the economic, cultural, and social changes inherent in "becoming modern." Second, the theory clearly overestimates the extent to which some non-Western peoples resist modernization, in large part because they ignore the many creative adapta-

tions these peoples have made for centuries. Third, and perhaps most important, modernization theorists assume that traditional people will be better off if they become modern. Because becoming modern is progressive, it is thought, it must be good. They assume that the advantages of becoming modern—such as increased income, better health, and a higher standard of living—are universally beneficial. Even though becoming modern also involves giving up one's traditional culture, modernization theorists see it as a small price to pay for the obvious benefits. We now consider this last point in greater detail.

The present debate in development anthropology revolves around the question of whether raising income levels and standards of living always has a positive effect for all parties concerned. Modernization theorists would answer this question affirmatively, but a number of studies over the past several decades have strongly suggested that economic growth and development do not always lead to an improvement in peoples' lives. Some have even suggested that economic progress (as defined by rising wages, increased GNP, and so on) actually has lowered the quality of life for many non-Western peoples. Despite the best intentions of international development agencies, multimillion-dollar foreign aid projects have often resulted in greater poverty, longer working hours, overpopulation, poorer health, more social pathology, and environmental degradation.

Contrary to conventional thinking, many of the benefits of economic development have been either illusory or

= *Many multinational corporations have more assets than the countries in which they operate, which gives them enormous control over these governments and their economies. This is the case with Hitachi and Xerox operating in Ho Chi Minh City, Vietnam.*

downright detrimental. Attempts to engage non-Western people in programs of planned economic development often result in an increase in diseases in several significant ways. First, many of the new, more modern lifestyles that people assume result in a marked increase in diseases associated with the industrialized world. For example, Charles Hughes and John Hunter (1972) and Ian Prior (1971) found that such diseases as diabetes, heart disease, obesity, hypertension, gout, and high blood pressure increased dramatically after rapid cultural change occurred in areas where they were previously unknown. Second, certain bacterial or parasitic diseases increase precipitously in areas experiencing rapid cultural change. To illustrate, the construction of dams and irrigation systems in the Sudan as part of the Azande development scheme created ideal breeding conditions for the snail larva that causes schistosomiasis, one of Africa's most deadly diseases. And third, health problems in the developing world are further aggravated by the rapid urbanization that often accompanies economic development. People crowding into cities looking for employment are more exposed to contagious diseases, which are made even worse by poor nutrition and unsanitary conditions.

Programs of economic development often lead to people making changes in their dietary habits. In some cases, these dietary changes are voluntary to the extent that some new foods, associated with powerful outsiders, are status symbols. But more often than not, dietary changes occur because of circumstances associated with the objectives of the economic development that are beyond the control of the local people. For example, in an attempt to develop more cash crops (which help to raise wages and bring in foreign exchange capital), non-Western peoples often divert time and energy from growing their normal subsistence crops. The result is that they find themselves spending much of their hard-earned cash on foods that are both costly and nutritionally inferior in order to feed their families. This was the case among Brazilian farmers who had changed from growing food crops to growing sisal, a cash crop used in making rope (Gross and Underwood 1971). Although they were spending most of their income on purchasing food, they were unable to provide adequate nutrition for their families. The study showed that the children of sisal workers were particularly at risk because most of the food went to the adults in order to maintain their strength needed for the strenuous work.

Not only do people who are caught up in economic development often eat less food; they also eat food that is worse for them than their traditional diets. Often these foods, purchased rather than homegrown, are lacking in minerals, vitamins, and protein. Moreover, they are usually processed foods, high in starch and carbohydrates, and contain high levels of refined sugar. The lack of vitamins and minerals leads to increases in nutritionally related diseases and the lack of protein causes kwashiorkor (protein malnutrition), the leading cause of death in Africa and other parts of the developing world. The marked increase in sugar consumption by non-Western peoples has led to a rapid and dramatic deterioration of dental health (see Bodley 1997).

It is possible to show how economic development programs have had deleterious effects on sizeable segments of

A large-scale sisal plantation in Tanzania. Are such agricultural development projects always beneficial to the local people?

the target populations. Not only is people's health negatively affected, but all too often other unfortunate (and usually unanticipated) consequences occur. The natural environment is often destroyed, families break down, social problems increase, and support systems disintegrate. To be certain, there are segments of non-Western populations that benefit from these programs of economic development, but all too often large numbers or even the majority wind up worse off than if the development efforts were never initiated. To point out these negative consequences, however, is not to suggest that we should abandon foreign assistance programs and attempts to raise people's access to material resources. These negative results occur most often when development programs are introduced without the full participation and understanding of the peoples they are designed to help. The target populations need to control their own resources and define their relationship to the changing economy. But in addition to including the local people in the planning and administration of the programs, it is absolutely imperative for program planners to fully understand the dimensions of the local cultures. If we take seriously the notion of the systemic nature of culture, then we must assume that a change in one part of the system is likely to bring about changes in other parts of the system. It is only when development planners understand the nature of those parts, and how they are interrelated, that they can anticipate what some of the negative consequences may be and thus avoid them.

•■ GLOBALIZATION AND ■• WORLD CULTURES

LIKE OTHER SCIENCES, cultural anthropology tries to bring a sense of order and understanding from enormous diversity. Faced with more than 5,000 separate cultures in the world, the science of anthropology has focused on showing the similarities and differences among these many cultures. In doing so, however, the very act of classifying the cultures of the world assumes that each culture is discrete, distinct, and independent of all others. But, as we have attempted to point out in this chapter, all cultures are constantly experiencing changes through innovations (internal) and diffusion (external). Through the process of diffusion, cultures borrow things, ideas, and behavior patterns from other cultures. The amount of cultural diffusion varies with the amount of contact among cultures. That is, the more contact among cultures, the more likely that things, ideas, and behavior patterns will be diffused. This has never been truer than it has since the early 1990s

as the world experiences a new era of rapid societal change known as globalization.

What do we mean by the term *globalization?* It has become one of the most overused and poorly understood words in the English language. To be certain, there have been interconnections between countries and cultures for centuries that have had far-reaching implications for culture change through diffusion. But when the Berlin Wall came down in 1989, the world began to change in some dramatic ways. Forces were unleashed that are having, and will continue to have, profound effects on all cultures of the world. Cultural anthropologists, whether they are studying large industrialized societies or small-scale foragers, cannot afford to ignore both the magnitude and the speed of this world process called globalization.

According to Thomas Friedman (1999), globalization is not just a passing trend but rather is a worldwide phenomenon that has replaced the Cold War system. From 1945 until the late 1980s, the nations and cultures of the world were compartmentalized into two major camps: the communist bloc and the free world. However, with the demise of world communism, so powerfully symbolized by the physical dismantling of the Berlin Wall, the world is experiencing (at a very rapid pace) a new type of integration of markets, technology, and information that is oblivious to both national and cultural borders. This post–Cold War globalization is driven by free-market capitalism and the idea that the more a country opens up its markets to free trade, the healthier its economy will become. The economics of globalization involve lowering tariff barriers while at the same time privatizing and deregulating national economies. The North American Free Trade Agreement (NAFTA) and the European Economic Union are two examples of the recent globalization of markets. The result of the globalization of markets is that goods and services from all over the world will make their way into other cultures. In actual fact, the way globalization has worked so far is that largely American products have been exported to other cultures on a global scale.

At the same time that world trade barriers are falling, there is a concomitant revolution going on in the world of information technology. In the mid-1980s only a handful of people in the world could operate a computer. Today computers are nearly as common in the home as the radio was in the 1940s. Moreover, the development of digitization, fiber optics, satellite communication, and the Internet now enables people to communicate with one another instantaneously. During the Cold War days, grandparents in Pennsylvania would have had to wait several weeks to see a photograph of a new grandchild born in Istanbul. Today, however, a photo of the new baby can be taken in Istanbul with a digital camera, loaded into a laptop computer, and sent via email to the grandparents on the other side of the globe in a matter of minutes. In short, these revolutionary developments in information processing are greatly facilitating the exchange of ideas across national and cultural boundaries.

New York Times correspondent Thomas Freidman discusses the various dimensions of globalization in a recent book entitled *The Lexus and the Olive Tree* (1999). Here he provides an insightful glimpse into our very rapidly changing world—a world dominated by global business and the rapid exchange of information. Friedman makes a number of interesting contrasts between the Cold War and post–Cold War eras:

- ▶ The defining symbol of the Cold War era was the Wall, an immovable presence that functioned to separate people and ideas; the hallmark of globalization, on the other hand, is the Internet that functions to integrate people by facilitating communication.
- ▶ The concept of weight has been replaced by speed. During the Cold War, the operative question was, How big is your missile? whereas the mantra for the new millennium is, How fast is your modem?
- ▶ Whereas the mentality during the Cold War was "us" versus "them," the emerging globalized world sees all people as competitors.
- ▶ And finally, to use a sports analogy, the Cold War era was like two sumo wrestlers trying to knock each other out of the ring, whereas the era of globalization is like sprinters continually racing to be the first to get their share of global markets.

Clearly, the end of the Cold War helped to facilitate this new era of globalization, but it did not, in and of itself, cause it to happen. Other monumental changes since the late 1980s have defined globalization. First, the world has experienced a revolution in computer technology, which has made communication faster and cheaper for a rapidly growing segment of the world's population. To illustrate, the speed of computers during the 1990s has doubled every 18 months while the space on disks has increased 60 percent every year. Moreover, voice, music, videos, and photos can be digitized and sent cheaply and quickly over fiber-optic cable.

Second, there have been fundamental changes in the way we invest our money. Whereas during the Cold War era investing was done by the large banks, insurance companies, and investment firms, today it is, to a much larger degree, in the hands of individuals. At least in the industrialized world, individuals, not multibillion-dollar firms, are managing their own investments through mutual funds and 401K pension accounts. The ability to move one's personal investment funds around has been made even easier by e-trading on the Internet, which eliminates the need for a broker.

And third, there has been a fundamental change in the flow of information all over the world. As pointed out in Chapter 12, the walls and barriers so prominent during the Cold War era allowed governments to control their populations through systematic control of information. As recently as the mid-1980s, copy machines in Russia and China were unavailable to anyone other than government officials because they threatened the government's control of the flow of information. Today, however, the availability of the Internet permits the spread of ideas (and ideologies) across national boundaries without governmental interference. Consequently, the likelihood of cultural diffusion is greatly increased.

Anthropologist John Yellen (1990) has shown how a total culture (the Kalahari !Kung) can change when exposed to foreign goods and ideas. The Kalahari !Kung of southwest Africa have served for much of the twentieth century as one of the best examples of a foraging society (see Chapter 7). Nevertheless, since the 1970s, the !Kung have experienced dramatic cultural changes. As recently as 1968 when Yellen first conducted fieldwork, the !Kung were general foragers, with men hunting with bows and poisoned arrows and the women gathering edible plants. The band, the basic unit of social organization, was fluid in its membership to the extent that families could readily join other bands that were having greater success at procuring food. With the major group values of sharing and reciprocity, security for the !Kung was ensured by giving rather than hoarding, because during hard times a person could cash in on their accumulated obligations.

By the mid-1970s, however, the !Kung that Yellen had studied were experiencing some major cultural transitions by adopting many of the lifeways of the neighboring Bantu peoples. Many families had begun to plant fields and keep goats, a means of livelihood unheard of just a decade earlier. Traditional grass huts were beginning to be replaced by more substantial (and permanent) mud structures. !Kung began to substitute manufactured clothing for their traditional skin garments, and even though bows and arrows were still made, they were primarily for selling to the tourist market rather than for use as hunting tools. And, there was a major infusion of cash and consumer goods into !Kung society.

CROSS-CULTURAL MISCUE

MANY MULTINATIONAL CORPORATIONS assume that they can conduct business abroad in much the same way they do at home. A case in point is Federal Express when it initiated its European operations. Wanting to standardize its procedures, FedEx established 5:00 P.M. as its deadline for package pickup in Spain without realizing that many Spaniards work in their offices until 8:00 P.M. or even later. This failure to understand differences in work culture between Spain and the United States resulted in their initially losing a good deal of business in the global economy (Pearl 1991).

Along with these changes in material culture, the !Kung began to place less emphasis on personal intimacy, sharing, and interdependence. The spatial layout of the !Kung camps changed from a circular arrangement with the doors facing one another to a linear layout that gave families greater privacy; the distance between huts increased; and the hearth, which had been traditionally a focal point of socializing, became located inside each hut rather than outside. Yellen also found increasing hoarding of material goods purchased with the newfound cash. As the !Kung accumulated more and more possessions, they became less mobile and less willing to continue their seminomadic foraging lifestyle. These changes indicated that the !Kung were retreating from their traditional behavior of sharing and interdependence. The major impetus for the relatively sudden changes in culture, according to Yellen, was not a disenchantment with the foraging lifestyle but rather the introduction of money and commodities into !Kung culture. With the globalization of world markets and the free flow of information via the Internet, the likelihood of far-reaching cultural changes occurring among similar small-scale societies is greatly increased.

The long-term effects of globalization on the 5,000-plus cultures of the world has yet to be fully realized. Some suggest that globalization will eventually lead to a general homogenization of cultures into a single global culture (Jameson 1990). They argue that the rapid flow of money, commodities, and information to every corner of the world, if allowed to continue unchecked, will tend to eradicate cultural differences. An unfettered free enterprise system, open markets, advertising, and the free flow of information, it is suggested, will force local peoples to abandon their traditional values, ideologies, and preferences. For those who hold this homogenization interpretation, the case of the Kalahari !Kung, discussed above, is an excellent example of how the introduction of new commodities and ideas can transform a culture into something entirely different.

In recent years, however, an alternative view has emerged that suggests that globalization, rather than totally changing cultures, can stimulate local cultures to redefine themselves in the face of these external forces. In other words, local cultures, although eventually changing some features, will reaffirm many others by entering into a dialogue with global forces, thereby creating various hybrid cultures. In one such case, Rosalva Aida Hernandez Castillo and Ronald Nigh (1998) have examined the effects of globalization on a local group of Mam (Mayan-speaking) coffee growers in Chiapas, Mexico. Of all Latin American countries, Mexico, as a full participant in NAFTA, is up to its eyeballs in globalization. In terms of agriculture, the Mexican government has brought about a number of reforms designed to (1) discourage collective agriculture while encouraging individual agricultural entrepreneurs, (2) encourage cash crops over basic food crops, and (3) increase overall agricultural productivity for world trade purposes.

Despite the national efforts to transform more traditional types of communal agriculture, in 1988 the Mam started their own organic coffee growers cooperative that was an interesting blend of modern technologies and a deliberate reaffirmation of traditional values. With more than 1,200 members and annual export revenues of over $7 million, the Mam cooperative sells its gourmet organically grown coffee all over the world, has acquired a coffee processing plant, and is planning to build an instant coffee production facility. By any standards one might choose, the Mam cooperative is a highly successful global player. Yet, they have not earned their success at the expense of their traditional values, which are participatory democracy, equity, environmental protection, and the use of traditional organic farming methods rather than reliance on chemical fertilizers. The Mam have used the same communication

The 5th Wave
By Rich Tennant

"Before the Internet, we were only bustin' chops locally. But now, with our Web site, we're bustin' chops all over the world."

technology that has exposed people to Big Macs and iMacs for the purpose of strengthening, not weakening, their traditional cultural values. They have used promotional trips to international trade fairs, the telephone, e-mail, and the Internet to link up with indigenous peoples and ecologically conscious consumers in other parts of the world. In fact, their corporate marketing image, a curious blend of old and new, emphasizes that their coffee is organically grown by socially responsible descendants of the Mayans. Clearly, such an image combines their traditional identity with a brand of coffee that appeals to a specific market of gourmet coffee drinkers from Tokyo to New York. These contacts and experiences have enabled the Mam organic coffee growers

to reinforce many traditional values, accept some new ones from the rest of the world, and essentially reinvent or redefine their traditional culture without forsaking it.

Our discussion of globalization in this section has focused on how the intensification of the flow of money and information throughout the world may be affecting the process of culture change. Globalization has been presented as a new planetary reality, which was unleashed with the fall of the Berlin Wall. The era of globalization links (for good and for bad) Wall Street with the streets of the poorest sections of Jakarta, Nairobi, and Mexico City. Even though some observers see globalization as the savior of humankind, others see it as a boom to the rich and a curse for the poor. Although the revolutions in technology, open markets, and information flow have stimulated production, consumerism, and rapid communication, these same forces have been blamed for joblessness, economic collapse in Southeast Asia, political corruption, environmental destruction, public services reduction, and a growing gap between the rich and the poor. The private sectors of world economies stand to benefit most from this unregulated (or minimally regulated) free-trade situation. Businesses have demonstrated little concern about the human and environmental costs of globalization. However, 1999 witnessed a number of high-visibility protests by organized labor movements, environmentalist groups, and other organizations dealing with human justice. Open protests at the annual World Economic Forum in Davos, Switzerland, and the violent protests at the World Trade Organization meeting in Seattle are but two examples of growing popular resistance to unrestrained free trade throughout the world. It will be interesting to see whether world leaders will continue to view profits and the law of the market as the major parameters or whether they will develop a conscience and begin addressing these pressing human issues for all of the world's population.

SUMMARY

1. Although the rate of change varies from culture to culture, no cultures remain unchanged. The two principal ways that cultures change are internally through the processes of invention and innovation and externally through the process of diffusion.

2. Inventions can be either deliberate or unintentional. Although intentional inventors usually receive the

most recognition, over the long run, unintentional inventors have probably had the greatest impact on cultural change. Because they are not bound by conventional standards, many inventors and innovators tend to be marginal people living on the fringes of society.

3. It is generally recognized that the majority of cultural features (things, ideas, and behavior patterns) found in any society got there by diffusion rather

than invention. The following generalizations can be made about the process of diffusion: Cultural diffusion is selective in nature, it is a two-way process, it is likely to involve changes in form or function, some cultural items are more likely candidates for diffusion than are others, and it is affected by a number of important variables.

4. Acculturation is a specialized form of cultural diffusion that involves forced borrowing under conditions of external pressure. Some anthropologists have described situations of acculturation in which the nondominant culture has voluntarily chosen the changes, whereas others claim that acculturation always involves some measure of coercion and force.

5. Because the parts of a culture are to some degree interrelated, a change in one part is likely to bring about changes in other parts. This insight from cultural anthropology should be of paramount importance to applied anthropologists, who are often involved directly or indirectly with planned programs of cultural change.

6. Among the barriers to cultural change are the following: Some societies can maintain their cultural boundaries through the exclusive use of language, food, and clothing; some societies can resist change in their culture because the proposed change is not compatible with their existing value systems; and some societies resist change because they are unwilling to disrupt existing social and economic relationships.

7. In many parts of the world, urbanization does not occur as a simple flow of migrants from rural areas to urban areas but rather as a circulation of people between these areas. In order to understand the sociocultural aspects of urbanization today, it is important to view the rural area, the urban areas, and the people who move between them as parts of a complex system of change.

8. Planned programs of change have been introduced into developing countries for decades under the assumption that they benefit the local people. But a number of studies have shown that although some segments of the local population may benefit, many more do not.

9. The forces of globalization (intensification of the flow of money, goods, and information) that have occurred since the late 1980s have made the study of culture change more complex. In some cases, globalization may be responsible for an accelerated pace of change in world cultures. In other situations, the forces of globalization may stimulate traditional cultures to redefine themselves.

KEY TERMS

acculturation	modernization theory
circulation of labor	multinational corporations
culture of poverty	neocolonialism
invention	occupational duality
less developed countries (LDCs)	urbanization
linked changes	voluntary associations
marginal people	world systems theory

SUGGESTED READINGS

Bernard, H. R., and P. J. Pelto, eds. *Technology and Social Change.* 2d ed. Prospect Heights, IL: Waveland Press, 1987. A collection of 13 essays discussing the effects of modern technology on non-Western cultures.

Bodley, John H. *Victims of Progress.* 3d ed. Mountain View, CA: Mayfield, 1990. An important book that examines the sometimes disastrous effects of Westernization and industrialization on tribal societies. Bodley discusses the high price small-scale societies pay for "progress" and the role that Western institutions play in this cultural devastation.

Clifford, James. *Routes: Travel and Translation in the late Twentieth Century.* Cambridge, MA: Harvard University Press, 1997. Whereas in the past anthropologists traveled to remote areas to study relatively isolated cultures, today Clifford finds cultures colliding with one another. Clifford examines diasporic peoples, unexplored Western influences on indigenous peoples, and the effects of globalization on those cultures traditionally studied by anthropologists.

Friedman, Thomas. *The Lexus and the Olive Tree: Understanding Globalization.* New York: Farrar, Straus, and Giroux, 1999. A readable primer on the process of globalization, which in the 1990s replaced the Cold War system. Globalization involves the integration of markets, technology, and information across national borders, and it is having important consequences on all societies, particularly on the types of societies normally studied by anthropologists.

Kottak, Conrad P. *Assault on Paradise: Social Change in a Brazilian Village.* New York: McGraw-Hill, 1998. A readable and highly personal account of changes occurring in Arembepe, a fishing village in Brazil. The book chronicles the culture changes that have occurred since he first conducted fieldwork in 1962 up until the present.

Pelto, P. J. *The Snowmobile Revolution: Technology and Social Change in the Arctic.* Menlo Park, CA: Benjamin/Cummings, 1973. A study of sociocultural change documenting how a single technological device, the snowmobile, brought about vast economic and social changes among the reindeer-herding Skolt Lapps of Finland.

Rogers, Everett M. *Diffusion of Innovations.* 3d ed. New York: Free Press, 1983. A quantitative, up-to-date, and richly documented study of the mechanism of cultural diffusion that discusses the history of diffusion research, how innovations are generated, rates of adoption of innovations, diffusion networks, and change agents.

Spindler, Louise S. *Culture Change and Modernization: Mini-Models and Case Studies.* Prospect Heights, IL: Waveland Press, 1984. A discussion of the process of cultural change for introductory students, drawing examples from many ethnographic studies.

Tonkinson, Robert. *The Jigalong Mob: Aboriginal Victors of the Desert Crusade.* Menlo Park, CA: Benjamin/Cummings, 1974. In this study of sociocultural change among a group of Australian aborigines, the author provides a wealth of data on how one group was able to maintain its ethnic pride and traditional values in the face of Western colonialism.

On the Net

Many industrialized countries have foreign assistance programs that provide economic development funds for poorer, less developed nations. For example, the United States administers foreign assistance programs through the United States Agency for International Development (USAID); in Canada the same function is performed by the Canadian International Development Agency (CIDA). Students in the United States should contact the USAID home page:

http://www.info.usaid.gov/

Canadian students should contact the CIDA home page:

http://www.acdi-cida.gc.ca/

After selecting the appropriate agency, browse the site and make a list of the various accomplishments of the agency over the years. Make a list of the types of economic assistance programs USAID and CIDA have sponsored around the world over the past several decades.

1. Both USAID and CIDA have devoted a substantial amount of money in the last five years to the NIS countries. What are the NIS countries? What has been the justification for this large amount of assistance? What types of specific projects have USAID and CIDA sponsored in the NIS countries since 1990?
2. Conduct a subject search for the organization known as Cultural Survival. Once on that home page, write a one-page paper answering the following questions:
   a. What is the purpose of the organization?
   b. What types of projects does the organization sponsor?
   c. After consulting the section dealing with the organization's published journal *Cultural Survival Quarterly,* what are some themes for upcoming issues of the journal?

Chapter Seventeen

THE FUTURE OF ANTHROPOLOGY

WHAT WE WILL LEARN:

▼

What are indigenous cultures and
how are they endangered?

▼

How have cultural anthropologists
contributed to our understanding of
complex, industrialized societies?

▼

What must anthropologists do
to ensure that their findings will
be used by policymakers?

▼

*Kayapo chief from Brazil with
anthropologist Daryll Posey.*

O ne need not be a scholar of cultural change to notice that the pace at which cultures are changing is accelerating with every decade. By comparison, the everyday

lives of our grandparents seem simple and slow moving. Today many people are becoming overwhelmed by how quickly their cultures are changing. In fact, in 1971 Alvin Toffler coined the term *future shock,* which he defined as the psychological disorientation resulting from living in a cultural environment that is changing so rapidly that people feel they are constantly living in the future. With the start of the new millennium, Toffler's notion of future shock is more true than ever before.

Cultural change is occurring at such an accelerated pace today that it is often difficult to keep up with all of the changes. Moreover, because of the recent revolution in transportation and electronic communications, the world is getting smaller. Today it is possible to travel to the other side of the earth on an SST (supersonic transport) in about the same time it took our great-grandparents to travel 30 miles in a horse and carriage. Via satellite we can see instant transmissions of live newscasts from anywhere in the world. And, as was discussed in the previous chapter, the globalization of commodities and information flow is indeed bringing all of the world's population closer to the notion of living in a global village. Because of this rapid and dramatic increase in our capacity to communicate with and travel to other parts of the world, the likelihood of cultures diffusing has increased dramatically in recent decades.

If the cultural world is shrinking, it has led some people to wonder whether the discipline of cultural anthropology is losing its subject matter. Such people argue that it will be just a matter of years before all of the cultures of the world are homogenized into a single culture, leaving the discipline of anthropology without a field of study. If one takes a very traditional view of anthropology—the aim of which

is to document the cultural and biological features of isolated indigenous peoples—then the future of the discipline doesn't hold much promise. It is certainly true that exotic cultures (untouched by the modern world) are few and far between today.

In the twenty-first century, however, only a handful of cultural anthropologists are studying the quickly diminishing number of pristine cultures that were studied at the beginning of the last century. The research interests and activities of the discipline have adapted to the realities of the changing world. The fact that former food-collecting societies are now involved in market economies and consumerism should not lead us to conclude that all cultural differences are disappearing. Even though some of the obvious differences among cultures may be decreasing, there is little evidence to suggest that the world is becoming a cultural melting pot. Thus, despite rapid cultural change, there will certainly be enough cultural diversity to keep anthropologists occupied well into the future.

If cultural anthropologists are no longer seeking out and describing the "uncontaminated" cultures of the world, what is in store for the future of the discipline? Without making any wild prognostications, we can predict that the discipline of cultural anthropology will probably continue to move in the direction it has set for itself in the past several decades. Among the recent trends that are likely to continue well into the future are a concern for the cultural survival of indigenous peoples, a greater emphasis on the study of complex societies such as our own, and greater interest in developing strategies for using anthropological data to solve societal problems. Although we discuss these concerns separately, all three are closely interrelated and, no doubt, affect one another.

•■ CULTURAL SURVIVAL ■• OF INDIGENOUS PEOPLES

IN RECENT YEARS, cultural anthropologists have become increasingly concerned about the rapid disappearance of indigenous populations of the world. According to the World Council on Indigenous Peoples (quoted in Bodley 1982), an indigenous population is any "people living in countries which have populations composed of different ethnic or racial groups who are descendants of the earliest populations which survive in the area, and who do not, as a group, control the national government of the countries within which they live" (166–167). Classic examples of indigenous peoples are the small-scale cultures in Asia, Africa, and the Americas that came under the influence of the colonial powers during the past several centuries.

Many anthropologists are concerned about the survival of these indigenous peoples not because they form the subject matter of much anthropological research, but because their disappearance raises some basic human rights issues. A growing number of cultural anthropologists feel strongly that indigenous populations over the past several centuries have been negatively affected by the onslaught of civilization. Cultural patterns—and in some cases the people themselves—have been eradicated as a direct result of civilization's pursuit of "progress" and economic development.

The industrial revolution in nineteenth-century Europe was "revolutionary" to the extent that it led to explosions in both population and consumerism, which in turn had drastically negative effects on indigenous peoples. The technological efficiency of the industrial revolution resulted in a quantum leap in population growth. To illustrate, before the industrial revolution it took 250 years for the world's population to double, whereas by the 1970s it took only 33 years (Bodley 1982). At the same time that populations were exploding in the industrializing world, there was a corresponding growth in consumerism. If economies were to grow and prosper, production had to be kept high, which could be accomplished only if people purchased and consumed the products of industry. In order to meet the needs of a growing population with ever-increasing desires to consume, people needed to control and exploit natural resources wherever they might be found.

A major motivation for the colonization of the non-Western world was economic in that the natural resources found in Asia and Africa were needed to fuel European factories. The so-called scramble for Africa, which was initiated when the leaders of Europe set national boundaries in Africa at the Conference of Berlin in 1884, was a very "civilized" and "gentlemanly" way of dividing up the continent's natural resources for the industrializing nations of Europe. Unfortunately, the rights of indigenous populations were not protected. In many cases, land and resources needed by the indigenous peoples were simply appropriated for use by the colonial powers. Landless populations were forced to become laborers, dependent on whatever wages the colonial governments and businesses wished to pay. Native resistance to this systematic exploitation was usually met with force. In some cases, large segments of the population were killed or died from European diseases. In other less severe situations, indigenous peoples were economically exploited, systematically kept at the lowest echelons of the society, and forced to give up their traditional identities.

Specific examples of the demise of indigenous populations are all too common in the literature (see, for example, Bodley 1982 and Burger 1987). The tragic annihilation of the population of Tasmania in the nineteenth century is one of the more dramatic examples. Through the use of military force and heavy-handed missionary efforts, not only was the aboriginal culture of Tasmania eliminated, but the people themselves were literally exterminated, many by deliberate killings, because the White settlers wanted the land for sheepherding. Around the turn of the nineteenth century the Germans administered their protectorate in southwest Africa (currently Namibia) on the principle that native populations should give up their land for European use. When the indigenous Herero people refused, the Germans made good on their threats to wage a war of extermination, justifying their military actions on the basis of social Darwinism and White supremacy. But we need not go to the far corners of the earth to find tragic examples of the exploitation of native peoples. The litany of atrocities committed against Native Americans in the name of progress and manifest destiny date back to the earliest European settlements. The massacre of the Pequot in Connecticut in 1637 and the massacre of the Sioux at Wounded Knee in 1890 are just two examples from our own history.

Anthropologists believe that the Brazilian Amazon shelters the largest segment of the world's still isolated populations. In recent years, the most dramatic examples of the degradation of indigenous peoples has come from the Brazilian Amazon, where Indians are being swept away by the relentless frontier of colonialism and economic development. To illustrate, during the 1960s, an Indian village in

Brazil was attacked by a gang of gunslingers allegedly hired by a large Brazilian corporation that wanted the Indians off the land. Shelton Davis (1977) describes the Massacre at Parallel Eleven in which the hired hit men attempted to wipe out the village and its inhabitants by throwing dynamite from a low-flying airplane. During the 1970s, the threats to indigenous peoples, though not quite so blatantly genocide, were no less devastating. By building roads through the Amazonian frontier, the Brazilian government introduced such diseases as influenza and measles to the indigenous peoples of the region. By the beginning of the 1990s, tens of thousands of gold prospectors had invaded the territory of the Yanomamo, extracting millions of dollars worth of gold from the land and leaving the Yanomamo ravaged by disease. In a feeble attempt to protect the indigenous Yanomamo, the Brazilian government ordered the destruction of 110 airstrips built by the gold miners on Yanomamo land. But the miners circumvented the government efforts to destroy their airstrips by using helicopters, which do not require landing strips—an indication of just how difficult it is to protect indigenous peoples from the onslaught of the industrial world (Brooke 1990).

In the early 1990s, however, under the leadership of Sudney Possuelo, the director of Brazil's Indian Protection Agency, the remaining 23,000 Yanomamo Indians have been protected (at least temporarily) on the world's largest reservation (over 20 million square acres). Possuelo has argued that the indigenous peoples of Brazil deserve governmental protection every bit as much as other endangered species such as jaguars and sea turtles. They need safe havens where they can protect their cultures and build up their dwindling numbers. Nevertheless, it is an uphill battle to preserve the fragile indigenous cultures of Brazil, and cultures elsewhere, because there are many interest groups that do not want to protect them. The monied interests who want to mine or develop the Amazon region contend that establishing reservations to protect the local cultures will prevent the all-important exploitation of the country's vast natural resources; missionaries from a number of different Christian denominations are eager to save their souls; the state petroleum company wants entrée into the rain forest so as to explore for oil reserves; linguists are interested in studying more indigenous languages; and pharmaceutical companies are interested in gaining rights to local knowledge of medicines (Schemo 1999).

Cultural anthropologists have not only been documenting the demise of indigenous peoples, but many have also been using their specialized knowledge to help these endangered cultures survive. In one of the most urgent forms of applied anthropology, a number of cultural anthropologists in recent years have contributed to the efforts of Cultural Survival, Inc., a nonprofit organization based in Cambridge, Massachusetts, that supports projects on five continents designed to help indigenous peoples survive the changes brought about by contact with industrial societies. Founded in 1972, Cultural Survival works to guarantee the land and resource rights of tribal peoples while supporting economic development projects run by the people themselves. As part of their work with Cultural Survival, cultural anthropologists have conducted research on vital cultural issues, served as cultural brokers between the indigenous people and government officials, and published literature informing the public about the urgency of these survival issues. To help support its work, Cultural Survival holds semi-annual bazaars in Cambridge selling high-quality arts and crafts made by the very indigenous peoples they are trying to protect. For those who cannot attend the bazaars in person, Cultural Survival now offers e-Bazaar, an online crafts market. Given the ever-increasing number of indigenous populations that are facing cultural extinction—including the San of southern Africa, the Sherpas of Nepal, and the Kurds in the Middle East—it is likely that cultural anthropologists will continue to apply their expertise to help these people avoid cultural genocide.

•■ THE STUDY ■• OF COMPLEX SOCIETIES

WHEN MOST PEOPLE think of cultural anthropology, they envision an anthropologist, notebook in hand, interviewing a scantily clad native inside a mud hut. Although cultural anthropologists from the United States have traditionally tended to concentrate their research efforts on small-scale, non-Western societies, an increasing number in recent years have turned their attention to studying their own complex societies. A number of factors converged to set this trend in motion. First, a handful of anthropologists after World War II conducted some of the first urban anthropological studies in such places as Timbuktu, Mexico City, and Kampala because the so-called tribal peoples were migrating to cities in increasing numbers during the postwar period. Second, the trend toward the study of complex urban societies by anthropologists was stimulated, at least in the United States, by the growing interest in applied anthropology. After the affluent decade of the 1950s, the 1960s witnessed the rediscovery of ethnicity and poverty, both of which were defined as urban problems. Consequently, U.S. policymakers have been more willing in recent decades to use the findings of cultural anthropologists to help solve some of these pressing social problems at home. Third, anthropologists have turned to the study of various aspects of our own complex society because research opportunities in more traditional societies have diminished. Since gaining independence, many developing countries have been increasingly reluctant to grant research permission to Western anthropologists. Moreover, shortages in research funding have prevented many Western scholars from conducting anthropological studies abroad.

When anthropologists study their own complex societies, however, they encounter some unique problems. One such problem is that cultural anthropologists run the risk of prejudice or distortion because they lack the outsider perspective. Another difficulty—and one that has not been adequately resolved—concerns just how well anthropologists studying complex societies are able to live up to their own tradition of holism. A holistic approach—examining a culture within its total context—is much more manageable when studying a small-scale society comprising several thousand people than it is when studying a social system comprising millions of people, such as New York City. Rather than writing holistic ethnographies of cities, anthropologists operating in urban or complex societies have adopted a more limited focus by studying small ethnic neighborhoods, specialized occupational groups, or other subcultural groups that operate within the more complex whole. Nevertheless, as a field of study, cultural anthropology has a good deal to offer the study of complex societies. For example, cultural anthropologists bring to the study of cities and complex societies a sensitivity to ethnic diversity; a tradition of framing their research problems in broad, holistic terms; and the research method of participant-observation, which provides an important supplement to the more quantitative methods of urban sociologists.

The anthropological study of U.S. society has explored a wide variety of topics. To illustrate, cultural anthropologists in recent years have studied hippie communes, street gangs, the aging, adaptive strategies of urban tramps, Gypsies, and Black urban families. Within a more institutional framework, retirement communities, hospitals, classrooms, factories, and volunteer fire departments have all been subjects of anthropological analysis. People in certain occupations—such as construction workers, railroad engineers, and prostitutes—have been treated as occupational subcultures by some anthropologists. And even certain aspects of popular culture in the United States—football, films, soap operas, Disney World, and food—have all been studied by cultural anthropologists as symbols of our cultural values. Because cultural anthropology involves the comparative study of culture in whatever form it may take—and because the United States provides many interesting cultural variations—this trend toward greater anthropological analysis of our own culture is likely to continue into the future.

·■ THE GREATER USE OF ■· ANTHROPOLOGICAL KNOWLEDGE

THIS INTRODUCTORY textbook in cultural anthropology has been written with an applied perspective. Because introductory students will follow a variety of career patterns, this book has been designed to demonstrate how the insights from anthropology can be used by people from a number of professions. The book has illustrated how anthropological knowledge can be used to solve problems by architects, government officials, businesspeople, medical personnel, educators, foreign aid personnel, court officials, family planners, and others. Although this applied perspective has demonstrated how anthropology has contributed to the solution of societal problems, much still needs to be done to increase the extent to which anthropological knowledge can actually be used by policymakers and decision makers. It is one thing to point out the potential uses of anthropological information, but it is quite another to actually use that information to make a difference in the quality of our lives.

As applied anthropology continues to become more prominent in the twenty-first century, more and more anthropologists with an eye toward practical concerns are seeking new strategies to ensure that anthropological insights will have an impact on the policy process. It is no longer enough for applied anthropologists to simply conduct their research and report their findings. According to Barbara Rylko-Bauer, John Van Willigen, and Ann McElroy (1989), applied anthropologists also need to develop a comprehensive strategy that will maximize the likelihood that their findings will be used by policymakers and decision makers. Such a strategy, they suggest, should include the following elements:

1. Collaboration in the research process between applied anthropologists and potential users will

increase the chances that findings will be used because it demystifies the research, provides opportunities for valuable feedback, and increases the commitment to the research.

2. Applied anthropologists must become familiar with the organizations sponsoring their research. They need to clarify the organization's goals and philosophy, identify the relevant people in the decision-making chain of command, and specify the normal decision-making process.

3. Applied anthropologists must be knowledgeable enough about the community under study to be able to identify possible sources of resistance to using the findings.

4. Because policymakers often need cultural information quickly, applied anthropologists need to develop more time-efficient methods if their findings are to be used.

Thus, applied anthropologists are becoming more astute in structuring their research with an eye toward practical application—a trend that will, no doubt, continue into the future.

In addition to developing strategies for the use of applied research findings, there is an enormous potential for the use of existing anthropological data. As we continue to experience a revolution in communication and transportation, all peoples of the world are being thrown together with increasing frequency. Businesspeople, diplomats, educators, technical assistance personnel, missionaries, scholars, and citizen-tourists are traveling throughout the world in greater numbers than ever before. Unhappily, advances in our understanding of other cultures have not kept pace with the advances in communications and transportation technology. Thus, a growing number of people are expected to perform their professional activities in an unfamiliar cultural environment, but this need not be the case.

For years cultural anthropologists have collected enormous quantities of data on the various cultures of the world. Although information exists on most peoples of the world, it is not always accessible or understandable by nonanthropologists. The great bulk of cultural data is hidden away in obscure anthropological journals and written in language that would require a Ph.D. in anthropology to comprehend. Perhaps one of the greatest challenges facing anthropology as it begins the twenty-first century is to become involved in a process that will make existing anthropological data available and usable to nonanthropologists. In short, anthropologists must themselves become (or train others to become) cultural brokers who translate anthropological findings into terms that nonanthropologists can use to cope more effectively with the cultural environments in which they find themselves.

I realize that asking professional anthropologists to devote more time to writing for nonacademic audiences flies in the face of the traditional academic rewards system. Scholars are given little recognition for writing to general audiences because, many believe, it involves dumbing down. That is, those who write for the general public are seen as doing little other than simplifying—or perhaps oversimplifying—the complicated, intricate, and sophisticated theories and issues of their discipline. Such an enterprise, it is argued, involves no creative thought and contributes no new knowledge.

Now it is true that our academic disciplines have always placed primary emphasis on research that leads to new knowledge—and that is exactly as it should be. This type of scholarly research is absolutely essential for the very survival of our academic disciplines. Nevertheless, in the case of cultural anthropology, there is *also* a need for cultural brokering—or translating the enormous quantities of cultural data into language and concepts that can be *understood* and *used* by people with little or no anthropological experience. Moreover, writing for general audiences should not be viewed as a shabby form of scholarship—a mindless or unchallenging intellectual endeavor. The task of the cultural broker—if it is to be done effectively—is every bit as demanding as other scholarly endeavors, for it involves working with large quantities of data, assessing the quality of those data, synthesizing the data, identifying the relationships between the data and certain practical areas of people's professions, and presenting the findings in a challenging and engaging format.

GLOSSARY

acculturation A specific form of cultural diffusion in which a subordinate culture adopts many of the cultural traits of a more powerful culture.

acephalous societies Societies without a political head such as a president, chief, or king.

achieved status The status an individual acquires during the course of her or his lifetime.

adaptive nature of culture The implication that culture is the major way human populations adapt or relate to their specific habitat in order to survive and reproduce.

affinal relatives Kinship ties formed through marriage (that is, in-laws).

age grade Permanent age categories in a society through which people pass during the course of a lifetime.

age organization A type of social organization, found in East Africa and among certain Native American groups, where people of roughly the same age pass through different levels of society together. Each ascending level, based on age, carries with it increased social status and rigidly defined roles.

age set A group of people roughly the same age who pass through various age grades together.

agriculture A form of food production that requires intensive working of the land with plows and draft animals and the use of techniques of soil and water control.

allocation of resources Rules adopted by all societies that govern the regulation and control of such resources as land, water, and their by-products.

ambilineal descent A form of descent that affiliates a person to a kin group through either the male or the female line.

ambilocal (bilocal) residence The practice of a newly married couple taking up residence with either the husband's or the wife's parents.

American historicism Headed by Franz Boas, a school of anthropology prominent in the first part of the twentieth century that insisted upon the collection of ethnographic data (through direct fieldwork) prior to making cross-cultural generalizations.

analyzing data One of five stages of fieldwork in which the cultural anthropologist determines the meaning of data collected in the field.

ancestor worship The worshiping of deceased relatives. These souls are considered supernatural beings and fully functioning members of a descent group.

anthropological linguistics The scientific study of human communication within its sociocultural context.

applied anthropology The application of anthropological knowledge, theory, and methods to the solution of specific societal problems.

arbitrary nature of language The meanings attached to words in any language are not based on a logical or rational system but rather are arbitrary.

archaeology The subfield of anthropology that focuses on the study of prehistoric and historic cultures through the excavation of material remains.

arranged marriage Any marriage in which the selection of the spouse is outside the control of the bride and groom.

artifacts A type of material remain (found by archaeologists) that has been made or modified by humans, such as tools, arrowheads, and so on.

ascribed status The status a person has by virtue of birth.

assimilation The process of absorbing a racial or ethnic group into the wider society.

attitudinal data Information collected in a fieldwork situation that describes what a person thinks, believes, or feels.

authority Legitimate power exercised with the consent of the members of a society.

avunculocal residence The practice of a newly married couple taking up residence with or near the husband's mother's brother.

balanced reciprocity The practice of giving with the expectation that a similar gift will be given in the opposite direction either immediately or after a limited period of time.

band societies Bands are the basic social unit found in many hunting-and-gathering societies; these societies are characterized by being kinship based and having no permanent political structure.

barbarism The middle of three basic stages of a nineteenth-century theory developed by Lewis Henry Morgan that all cultures evolve from simple to complex systems: savagery, barbarism, and civilization.

barter The direct exchange of commodities between people that does not involve a standardized currency.

behavioral data Information collected in a fieldwork situation that describes what a person does.

bicultural perspective The capacity to think and perceive in the categories of one's own culture as well as in the categories of a second culture.

big men/big women Self-made leaders, found widely in Melanesia and New Guinea, who gain prominence by convincing their followers to contribute excess food to provide lavish feasts for the followers of other big men or big women.

bilateral descent A type of kinship system whereby individuals emphasize both their mother's kin and their father's kin relatively equally.

binary oppositions A mode of thinking found in all cultures, according to Claude Lévi-Strauss, based on opposites, such as old–young, hot–cold, and left–right.

bound morphemes A combination of two or more phonemes.

bourgeoisie A Marxian term referring to the middle class.

breadwinner A traditional gender role found in the United States that views males as being responsible for the economic support and protection of the family.

bride service Work or service performed for the bride's family by the groom for a specified period of time either before or after the marriage.

bridewealth (bride price) The transfer of goods from the groom's lineage to the bride's lineage to legitimize marriage.

capital goods Goods or wealth used to purchase or produce other goods.

cargo cults Revitalization movements in Melanesia intended to bring new life and purpose into a society.

carrying capacity The maximum number of people a given society can support given the available resources.

caste A rigid form of social stratification in which membership is determined by birth and social mobility is nonexistent.

census taking The collection of demographic data about the culture being studied.

chiefdoms An intermediate form of political organization in which integration is achieved through the office of chiefs.

circulation of labor As compared to the unidirectional flow of people from rural to urban areas, the circulation of labor involves the continuous movement of people from rural to urban and back again.

civilization A term used by anthropologists to describe any society that has cities.

clans Unilineal descent groups comprised usually of more than 10 generations consisting of members who claim a common ancestry even though they cannot trace step-by-step their exact connection to a common ancestor.

class A ranked group within a stratified society characterized by achieved status and considerable social mobility.

closed systems of communication Communication systems that cannot create new sounds or words by combining two or more existing sounds or words.

code switching The practice of using different languages or forms of a language depending on the social situation.

coercive theory of state formation Argument that the state came into existence as a direct result of warfare.

cognatic descent A form of descent traced through both females and males.

collaterality Refers to kin related through a linking relative.

collecting data Stage of fieldwork involving selection of data-gathering techniques and the gathering of information pertinent to the hypothesis being studied.

communal cults Societies where groups of ordinary people conduct religious ceremonies for the well-being of the total community.

conflict theory A theory of social stratification that argues that society is always changing and in conflict because individuals in the upper stratum use their wealth, power, and prestige to exploit those below them.

consanguineal relatives One's biological or blood relatives.

corporate lineages Kinship groups whose members engage in daily activities together.

council of elders A formal control mechanism composed of a group of elders who settle disputes among individuals within a community.

crime Harm to a person or property that is considered illegitimate by a society.

cross cousins Children of one's mother's brother or father's sister.

Crow system A kinship system, associated with matrilineal descent, in which similar terms are used for (1) one's father and father's brother, (2) one's mother and mother's sister, and (3) one's siblings and parallel cousins.

cultural anthropology The scientific study of cultural similarities and differences wherever and in whatever form they may be found.

cultural boundary maintenance The practice of cultural groups keeping themselves separate from other cultural groups.

cultural diffusion The spreading of a cultural trait (that is, material object, idea, or behavior pattern) from one society to another.

cultural ecology An approach to the study of anthropology that assumes that people who reside in similar environments are likely to develop similar technologies, social structures, and political institutions.

cultural emphasis of a language The idea that the vocabulary in any language tends to emphasize words that are adaptively important in that culture.

cultural materialism A contemporary orientation in anthropology that holds that cultural systems are most influenced by such material things as natural resources and technology.

cultural relativism The idea that cultural traits are best understood when viewed within the cultural context of which they are a part.

cultural universals Those general cultural traits found in all societies of the world.

culture of poverty An interpretation of poverty that suggests that poor people pass certain cultural features on to their children that tend to reinforce and perpetuate poverty.

culture shock A psychological disorientation experienced when attempting to operate in a radically different cultural environment.

dance Intentional rhythmic nonverbal body movements that are culturally patterned and have aesthetic value.

degradation ceremonies Deliberate and formal societal mechanisms designed to publicly humiliate someone who has broken a social norm.

dependent variable A variable that is affected by the independent variable.

descent Tracing one's kinship connections back through a number of generations.

descriptive linguistics The branch of anthropological linguistics that studies how languages are structured.

deviance The violation of a social norm.

diachronic analysis The analysis of sociocultural data through time, rather than at a single point in time.

diffusionism *See* cultural diffusion.

diglossia The situation in which two forms of the same language are spoken by people in the same language community depending on the social situation.

displacement The ability that humans have to talk about things that are remote in time and space.

distributive justice *See* universalism.

division of labor The set of rules found in all societies dictating how the day-to-day tasks are assigned to the various members of a society.

document analysis Examination of data such as personal diaries, newspapers, colonial records, and so on to supplement information collected through interviewing and participant-observation.

double descent A system of descent in which individuals receive some rights and obligations from the father's side of the family and others from the mother's side.

double workload Where employed married women, particularly those with children, are both wage employed and primarily responsible for housework and child care.

dowry The transfer of goods or money from the bride's family to the groom or groom's family in order to legalize or legitimize a marriage.

dysfunction The notion that some cultural traits can cause stress or imbalance within a cultural system.

ecclesiastical cults Highly complex religious systems consisting of full-time priests.

ecofacts Physical remains found by archaeologists that were used by humans but not made or reworked by them (for example, seeds and bones).

economic anthropology A branch of the discipline of anthropology that looks at systems of production, distribution, and consumption most often in the nonindustrialized world.

economics The academic discipline that studies systems of production, distribution, and consumption, most typically in the industrialized world.

egalitarian societies Societies that recognize few differences in status, wealth, or power.

EGO The person in kinship diagrams from whose point of view we are tracing the relationship.

emic view A perspective in ethnography that uses the concepts and categories that are relevant and meaningful to the culture under analysis.

enculturation The process by which human infants learn their culture.

endogamy A rule requiring marriage within a specified social or kinship group.

epidemiology The study of the occurrence, distribution, and control of disease in populations.

Eskimo system The kinship system most commonly found in the United States; it is associated with bilateral descent. Usually, a mother, father, brother, and sister are found in a nuclear family.

ethnic group A group of people sharing many of the same cultural features.

ethnocentrism The practice of viewing the customs of other societies in terms of one's own; the opposite of cultural relativism.

ethnographic mapping A data-gathering tool that locates where the people being studied live, where they keep their livestock, where public buildings are located, and so on in order to determine how that culture interacts with its environment.

ethnography The anthropological description of a particular contemporary culture by means of direct fieldwork.

ethnolinguistics The study of the relationship between language and culture.

ethnology The comparative study of cultural differences and similarities.

ethnomusicology The study of the relationship between music and other aspects of culture.

ethnoscience A theoretical school popular in the 1950s and 1960s that tries to understand a culture from the point of view of the people being studied.

etic view A perspective in ethnography that uses the concepts and categories of the anthropologist's culture to describe another culture.

event analysis Photographic documentation of events such as weddings, funerals, and festivals in the culture under investigation.

evolutionism The nineteenth-century school of cultural anthropology, represented by Tylor and Morgan, that attempted to explain variations in world cultures by the single deductive theory that they all pass through a series of evolutionary stages.

exogamy A rule requiring marriage outside of one's own social or kinship group.

extended family A family form that includes two or more related nuclear families.

extramarital activity Sexual activity outside marriage.

features Archaeological remains made or modified by people that cannot easily be carried away, such as house foundations, fireplaces, and post holes.

female genital mutilation A traditional practice, found in Africa and the Middle East, of performing dramatic and traumatic operations on the genitalia of girls and young women.

female infanticide The killing of female children.

femininity The social definition of femaleness, which varies from culture to culture.

feminization of poverty Refers to the high proportion of female-headed families below the poverty line, which may result from the high proportion of women found in occupations with low prestige and income.

fictive kinship Relationships among individuals who recognize kinship obligations although the relationships are not based on either consanguineal or affinal ties.

fieldwork The practice in which an anthropologist is immersed in the daily life of a culture in order to collect data and test cultural hypotheses.

folklore Unwritten verbal arts that can take a variety of forms such as myths, legends, and folktales.

folktales Stories from the past that are instructive, entertaining, and largely secular in nature.

food collecting A form of subsistence that relies on the procurement of animal and plant resources found in the natural environment.

forensic anthropology A form of applied anthropology that uses certain insights from physical anthropology to help identify victims of crimes and disasters.

formalists Those economic anthropologists who suggest that the ideas of Western economics can be applied to any economic situation.

free morphemes Morphemes that appear in a language without being attached to other morphemes.

French structuralism A theoretical orientation that holds that cultures are the product of unconscious processes of the human mind.

function The contribution that a particular cultural trait makes to the longevity of the total culture.

functionalism/functional theory A theory of social stratification holding that social stratification exists because it contributes to the overall well-being of a society.

functional unity A principle of functionalism that states that a culture is an integrated whole consisting of a number of interrelated parts.

gender The way members of the two sexes are perceived, evaluated, and expected to behave.

gender ideology A system of thoughts and values that legitimizes sex roles, statuses, and customary behavior.

genderlects Linguistic gender differences.

gender roles Expected ways of behaving based on a society's definition of masculinity and femininity

gender stratification A division in society where all members are hierarchically ranked according to gender.

genealogizing A technique of collecting data in which the anthropologist writes down all the kin relationships of informants in order to study the kinship system.

generalized reciprocity The practice of giving a gift with an expected return.

genetics The study of inherited physical traits.

genocide The systematic attempt to eliminate entire cultures or racial groups.

ghost invocation The practice of a living person (typically an elder) calling forth the wrath of ancestor gods against an alleged sinner.

ghostly vengeance The belief that ancestor gods (ghosts) will punish sinners.

globalization The worldwide process, dating back to the fall of the Berlin Wall, which involves a revolution in information technology, a dramatic opening of markets, and the privatization of social services.

glottochronology The historical linguistic technique of determining the approximate date that two languages diverged by analyzing similarities and differences in their vocabularies.

grammar The systematic ways that sounds are combined in any given language to send and receive meaningful utterances.

graphic arts Forms of art that include painting and drawing on various surfaces.

Hawaiian system Associated with ambilineal descent, this kinship system uses a single term for all relatives of the same sex and generation.

heterosexual Sexual desire toward members of the opposite sex.

hija An archaic rhetorical art form found in some Arabic cultures involving boastful self-praise and abusive insults.

historical linguistics The study of how languages change over time.

holism A perspective in anthropology that attempts to study a culture by looking at all parts of the system and how those parts are interrelated.

homosexual Sexual desire toward members of one's own sex.

honor killings A euphemism referring to a practice found in various Middle Eastern cultures whereby women are put to death at the hands of their own family members because they are thought to have dishonored the family.

horizontal function of kinship The ways in which all kinship systems, by requiring people to marry outside their own small kinship group, function to integrate the total society through marriage bonds between otherwise unrelated kin groups.

horticulture A form of small-scale crop cultivation characterized by the use of simple technology and the absence of irrigation.

housewife A traditional gender role found in the United States that views females as responsible for child rearing and domestic activities.

human paleontology *See* paleoanthropology, paleontology.

Human Relations Area Files (HRAF) The world's largest anthropological data retrieval system used to test cross-cultural hypotheses.

human sexuality The sexual practices of humans, usually varying from culture to culture.

hunting and gathering A food-getting strategy involving the collection of naturally occurring plants and animals.

hydraulic theory of state formation The notion that early state systems of government arose because small-scale farmers were willing to surrender a portion of their autonomy to a large government entity in exchange for the benefits of large-scale irrigation systems.

hypothesis An educated hunch as to the relationship among certain variables that guides a research project.

incest taboo The prohibition of sexual intimacy between people defined as close relatives.

independent variable The variable that can cause change in other variables.

individualistic cults The least complex form of religious organization in which each person is his or her own religious specialist.

industrialization A process resulting in the economic change from home production of goods to large-scale mechanized factory production.

infant mortality Infant death rate.

informant A person who provides information about his or her culture to the ethnographic fieldworker.

innovations Changes brought about by the recombination of already existing items within a culture.

intermediaries Mediators of disputes among individuals or families within a society.

interpreting data The stage of fieldwork, often the most difficult, in which the anthropologist searches for meaning in the data collected while in the field.

interpretive anthropology A contemporary theoretical orientation that holds that the critical aspects of cultural systems are such subjective factors as values, ideas, and worldviews.

invention New combinations of existing cultural features.

Iroquois system A system associated with unilineal descent in which the father and father's brother are called by the same term, as are the mother and mother's sister.

jati Local subcastes found in Hindu India.

kibbutz A communal farm or settlement in Israel.

kindred All of the relatives a person recognizes in a bilateral kinship system.

kinship system Those relationships found in all societies that are based on blood or marriage.

kula ring A form of reciprocal trading found among the Trobriand Islanders involving the use of white shell armbands and red shell bracelets.

labor specialization *See* division of labor.

language family A grouping of related languages.

law Cultural rules that regulate human behavior and maintain order.

legends *See* folktales.

Leopard-skin Chief An example of an intermediary found among the Nuer of the African Sudan.

less developed countries (LDCs) Countries that have a relatively low gross national product (GNP) and low annual family income.

levirate The practice of a man marrying the widow of a deceased brother.

liberation theater A type of theatrical production using high levels of audience participation and aimed at bringing about social change.

liberation theology A form of Catholicism found widely through South and Central America in which priests and nuns became actively involved in programs for social justice for the poor.

lineages Unilineal descent groups whose members can trace their line of descent to a common ancestor.

lineality Kin related in a single line such as son, father, and grandfather.

linked changes Changes in one part of a culture brought about by changes in other parts of the culture.

magic A system of supernatural beliefs that involves the manipulation of supernatural forces for the purpose of intervening in a wide range of human activities and natural events.

Mahdist movements A term used to describe revitalization movements in the Muslim world.

male gender bias A preference found in some societies for sons rather than daughters.

marginal people Nonmainstream people who are at the fringes of their own culture.

market exchange A form of distribution where goods and services are bought and sold and their value determined by the principle of supply and demand.

masculinity The social definition of maleness, which varies from society to society.

matriarchy The rule of domination of women over men.

matrilineal descent A form of descent whereby people trace their primary kin connections through their mothers.

matrilocal residence The practice of a newly married couple living with the wife's family.

mechanical solidarity A type of social integration based on mutuality of interests found in societies with little division of labor.

millenarian movements Social movements by a repressed group of people, which foresees better times at a specific time in the future.

modernization theory The theory that explains economic development in terms of the inherent sociocultural differences between the rich and the poor.

moieties Complementary descent groups that result from the division of a society into two halves.

monogamy The marital practice of having only one wife at a time.

moots Informal hearings of disputes for the purpose of resolving conflicts, usually found in small-scale societies.

morphemes The minimal linguistic forms (usually words) that convey meaning.

morphology The study of the rules governing how morphemes are turned into words.

multilinear evolution Mid-twentieth-century anthropological theory of Julian Steward who suggested that specific cultures can evolve independently of all others even if they follow the same evolutionary process.

multinational corporations Large corporations that have economic operations in a number of different countries throughout the world.

myths Stories that transmit culturally meaningful messages about the universe, the natural and supernatural worlds, and a person's place within them.

nation A group of people who share a common identity, history, and culture.

nativistic movements A religious force for social change found among Native Americans.

negative reciprocity A form of economic exchange between individuals who try to take advantage of each other.

negative sanctions Punishment for violating the norms of a society.

neocolonialism The economic, political, and military influence that developed nations continue to exert over less developed countries, even though the official period of colonization ended in the 1960s.

neoevolutionism A twentieth-century school of cultural anthropology, represented by White and Steward, that attempted to refine the earlier evolutionary theories of Tylor and Morgan.

neolithic revolution A stage in human cultural evolution (around 10,000 years ago) characterized by the transition from hunting and gathering to the domestication of plants and animals.

neolocal residence The practice of a newly wedded couple taking up their residence in a place independent from both the husband's and the wife's family.

nomadism A lifestyle involving the periodic movement of human populations in search of food or pasture for livestock.

nonverbal communication The various means by which humans send and receive messages without using words (for example, gestures, facial expressions, and touching).

nouveau riche People with newly acquired wealth.

nuclear family The most basic family unit composed of wife, husband, and children.

nutritional deprivation A form of child abuse involving withholding food; can retard learning, physical development, or social adjustment.

oath The practice of having God bear witness to the truth of what a person says.

occupational duality A practice found in many traditionally agricultural parts of the world in which an individual will spend part of the year working on the farm and another segment of the year working as a wage earner, most likely in an urban area.

occupational segregation The predominance of one gender in certain occupations.

Omaha system A kinship system that emphasizes patrilineal descent. In this system the mother's patrilineal descent is distinct only by sex and not by one's generation.

on-farm research A type of applied agricultural research based on anthropological field methods.

open systems of communication Systems of communication that can create new sounds or words by combining two or more exisitng sounds or words.

optimal foraging theory A theory that foragers look for those species of plants and animals that will maximize their caloric intake for the time spent hunting and gathering foods.

ordeal A painful and possibly life-threatening test inflicted on someone suspected of wrongdoing.

organic analogy Early functionalist idea that holds that cultural systems are integrated into a whole cultural unit in much the same way that the various parts of a biological organism (such as a respiratory system, circulatory system) function to maintain the health of the organism.

organic solidarity A type of social integration based on mutual interdependence; found in societies with a relatively elaborate division of labor.

paleoanthropology The study of human evolution through fossil remains.

paleontology The specialized branch of physical anthropology that analyzes the emergence and subsequent evolution of human physiology.

paleopathology The study of disease in prehistoric populations.

pan-tribal mechanisms Mechanisms such as clans, age grades, and secret societies found in tribal societies that cut across kinship lines and serve to integrate all of the local segments of the tribe into a larger whole.

parallel cousins Children of one's mother's sister or father's brother.

participant-observation A fieldwork method in which the cultural anthropologist lives with the people under study and observes their everyday activities.

particularism The propensity to deal with other people based on one's particular relationship to them rather than according to a universally applied set of standards.

pastoralism A food-getting strategy based on animal husbandry found in regions of the world that are generally unsuited for agriculture.

patrilineal descent A form of descent whereby people trace their primary kin relationships through their fathers.

patrilocal residence The practice of a newly married couple living with the husband's family.

peasantry Rural peoples, usually on the lowest rung of society's ladder, who provide urban inhabitants with farm products but have little access to wealth or political power.

phonemes The smallest sound contrasts in a language that distinguish meaning.

phonology The study of a language's sound system.

photography The use of a 35mm camera or videocamera to document the ecology, material culture, and even social interaction of people when conducting ethnographic fieldwork.

phratries A unilineal descent group composed of a number of related clans.

physical anthropology (biological anthropology) The subfield of anthropology that studies both human biological evolution and contemporary racial variations among peoples of the world.

plastic arts Forms of artistic expression that involve molding certain forms, such as sculpture.

pluralistic societies Societies composed of a number of different cultural or subcultural groups.

political coerciveness The capacity of a political system to enforce its will on the general population.

political integration The process that brings disparate people under the control of a single political system.

polyandry The marriage of a woman to two or more men at the same time.

polygyny The marriage of a man to two or more women at the same time.

population biology The study of the interrelationship between population characteristics and environments.

population transfer The practice of physically relocating a minority group from one area to another.

positive sanctions A mechanism of social control for enforcing a society's norms through rewards.

postmodernism A school of anthropology that advocates the switch from cultural generalization and laws to description, interpretation, and the search for meaning.

postpartum sexual abstinence taboo A husband and wife abstaining from any sexual activity for a length of time after the birth of a child.

potlatch A form of competitive giveaway found among the Northwest Coast American Indians that serves as a mechanism for both achieving social status and distributing goods.

power The capacity to produce intended effects on oneself, other people, social situations, or the environment.

preferential cousin marriage A preferred form of marriage between either parallel or cross cousins.

prestige Social honor or respect within a society.

primatology The study of nonhuman primates in their natural environments for the purpose of gaining insights into the human evolutionary process.

problem-oriented research A type of anthropological research designed to solve a particular societal problem rather than to test a theoretical proposition.

production A process whereby goods are obtained from the natural environment and altered to become consumable goods for society.

project Camelot An aborted U.S. Army research project designed to study the cause of civil unrest and violence in developing countries; created a controversy among anthropologists as to whether the U.S. government was using them as spies.

proletariat The term used in conflict theories of social stratification to describe the working class who exchange their labor for wages.

property rights Western concept of individual ownership, an idea unknown to some non-Western cultures where a large kinship group, instead of the individual, determines limited rights to property.

proxemic analysis The study of how people in different cultures use space.

psychic unity A concept popular among some nineteenth-century anthropologists who assumed that all people when operating under similar circumstances will think and behave in similar ways.

psychological anthropology The subdiscipline of anthropology that looks at the relationships between cultures and such psychological phenomena as personality, cognition, and emotions.

public opinion What the general public thinks about some issue. When public opinion is brought to bear on an individual, it can influence his or her behavior.

purdah Rules involving domestic seclusion and veiling for women in small towns in Iraq, Iran, and Syria.

race A subgroup of the human population whose members share a greater number of physical traits with one another than they do with those of other subgroups.

rank societies Societies in which people have unequal access to prestige and status but not unequal access to wealth and power.

rape A type of sexual violence usually targeted at women; forced sexual activity without one's consent.

rebellion An attempt within a society to disrupt the status quo and redistribute the power and resources.

reciprocal exchange The equal exchange of gifts between the families of both the bride and groom to legitimize marriage.

reciprocity A mode of distribution characterized by the exchange of goods and services that have approximately equal value between parties.

redistribution A form of economic exchange in which goods (and services) are given by members of a group to a central authority (such as a chief) and then distributed back to the donors, usually in the form of a feast.

religious nationalism A phenomenon that is occurring in many parts of the world today in which traditional religious principles are merged with the workings of government.

research clearance Permission of the host country in which fieldwork is to be conducted.

research design Overall strategy for conducting research.

research proposal A written proposal required for funding of anthropological research that spells out in detail a research project's purpose, hypotheses, methodology, and significance.

revitalization movements Religious movements designed to bring about a new way of life within a society.

revolution An attempt to overthrow the existing form of political organization, the principles of economic production and distribution, and the allocation of social status.

rites of passage Any ceremony celebrating the transition of a person from one social status to another.

rites of solidarity Any ceremony performed for the sake of enhancing the level of social integration among a group of people.

role ambiguity Confusion as to how one is expected to behave.

sanctions Any means used to enforce compliance with the rules and norms of a society.

Sapir–Whorf hypothesis The notion that a person's language shapes her or his perceptions and view of the world.

Satanists Individuals belonging to a group of people who worship Satan.

savagery The first of three basic stages of cultural evolution in the theory of Lewis Henry Morgan; based on hunting and gathering.

segmentation The process that takes place within a lineage whereby small subdivisions of a lineage will oppose one another in some social situations but will coalesce and become allies in other social situations.

separatist Christian churches Small-scale churches that break away from the dominant church to gain greater political, economic, social, and religious autonomy.

serial monogamy The practice of having a succession of marriage partners but only one at a time.

sex drive Desire for sexual activity.

sex roles *See* gender roles.

sexual asymmetry The universal tendency of women to be in a subordinate position in their social relationships with men.

sexual dimorphism Refers to the physiological differences between men and women.

shaman A part-time religious specialist who is thought to have supernatural powers by virtue of birth, training, or inspiration.

shamanistic cults Forms of religion in which part-time religious specialists called shamans intervene with the deities on behalf of the clients.

shifting cultivation (swidden, slash and burn) A form of plant cultivation in which seeds are planted in the fertile soil prepared by cutting and burning the natural growth; relatively short periods of cultivation are followed by longer periods of fallow.

silent trade A form of trading found in some small-scale societies in which the trading partners avoid face-to-face contact.

small-scale society A term used to refer to those societies that have relatively small populations, minimal technology, and little division of labor.

social control Mechanisms found in all societies that function to encourage people not to violate the social norms.

social functions of cattle The use of livestock by pastoralists not only for food and its by-products but also for purposes such as marriage, religion, and social relationships.

socialization Teaching the young the norms in a society.

social mobility The ability of people to change their social position within the society.

social norms Expected forms of behavior.

social stratification The ranking of subgroups in a society according to wealth, power, and prestige.

sociolinguistics A branch of anthropological linguistics that studies how language and culture are related and how language is used in different social contexts.

sociometric tracking A data-gathering method that social scientists use to measure different types of interaction among people.

sondeo A research strategy of on-farm research involving the use of informal interviews and participant-observation by teams of agricultural and social scientists.

song duel A means of settling disputes over wife stealing among the Inuit involving the use of song and lyrics to determine one's guilt or innocence.

sorcery The performance of certain magical rites for the purpose of harming other people.

sororate The practice of a woman marrying the husband of her deceased sister.

specialized political roles When large numbers of people are required to carry out very specific tasks such as law enforcement, tax collection, dispute settlement, recruitment of labor, and protection from outside invasion.

spouse abuse A form of violence usually targeted at women.

standardized currency A medium of exchange that has well-defined and understood value.

state A particular type of political structure that is hierarchical, bureaucratic, and centralized and has a monopoly on the legitimate use of force to implement its policies.

state system of government A bureaucratic, hierarchical form of government composed of various echelons of political specialists.

stratified societies Societies characterized by considerable inequality in all forms of social rewards—that is, power, wealth, and prestige.

structural functionalism A school of cultural anthopology, associated most closely with Radcliffe-Brown, that examines how parts of a culture function for the well-being of the society.

structured interview An ethnographic data-gathering technique in which large numbers of respondents are asked a set of specific questions.

subcultures A subdivision of a national culture that both shares some features with the larger society and also differs in some important respects.

Sudanese system An extremely particularistic and descriptive kinship system found in North Africa that is associated with patrilineal descent.

supernatural belief systems A set of beliefs found in all societies that transcend the natural, observable world.

synchronic analysis The analysis of cultural data at a single point in time, rather than through time.

syntax The linguistic rules, found in all languages, that determine how phrases and sentences are constructed.

theory A general statement about how two or more facts are related to one another.

transformational The quality of an artistic process that converts an image into a work of art.

transhumance Movement pattern of pastoralists in which some of the men move livestock seasonally while the other members of their group, including women and children, stay in permanent settlements.

tribal societies Small-scale societies composed of a number of autonomous political units sharing common linguistic and cultural features.

tribute The giving of goods (usually food) to a chief as a visible symbol of the people's allegiance.

unilineal descent Tracing descent through a single line (such as matrilineal or patrilineal) as compared to both sides (bilateral descent).

unilinear evolution A theory held by anthropologists such as Tylor and Morgan attempting to place particular cultures into specific evolutionary phases.

universal evolution White's approach to cultural evolution, which developed laws that apply to culture as a whole and argued that all human societies pass through similar stages of development.

universal functions A functionalist idea that holds that every part of a culture has a particular function.

universalism The notion of rewarding people on the basis of some universally applied set of standards.

universal male dominance The notion that men are dominant over women in all societies.

unstructured interview An ethnographic data-gathering technique—usually used in early stages of one's fieldwork—in which interviewees are asked to respond to broad, open-ended questions.

urbanization The process by which an increasing number of people live in cities.

varnas Caste groups in Hindu India that are associated with certain occupations.

vertical function of kinship The way in which all kinship systems tend to provide social continuity by binding together different generations.

vision quest A ritual found among a number of Plains Indian cultures where through visions people establish special relationships with spirits who provide them with knowledge, power, and protection.

voluntaristic theory of state formation The theory that suggests that stable systems of state government arose because people voluntarily surrendered some of their autonomy to the state in exchange for certain benefits.

voluntary association A political, occupational, religious, or recreational group, usually found in an urban area, that people join freely and that often helps in the adjustment to urban life.

warfare Armed conflict between nation-states or other politically distinct groups.

wealth The accumulation of material objects that have value within a society.

wicca A modern-day movement of witches and pagans.

witchcraft An inborn, involuntary, and often unconscious capacity to cause harm to other people.

woman exchange A form of marriage whereby two men exchange sisters or daughters as wives for themselves.

world systems theory An attempt to explain levels of economic development in terms of the exploitation of the poor by the rich nations of the world, rather than in terms of innate socioeconomic characteristics of each.

BIBLIOGRAPHY

Adams, Bert, and Edward Mburugu. 1994. "Kikuyu Bride-wealth and Polygyny Today." *Journal of Comparative Family Studies* 25(2):159–66.

Agosin, Marjorie. 1987. *Scraps of Life: Chilean Arpilleras.* Toronto: William Wallace Press.

Amadiume, Ifi. 1987. *Male Daughters, Female Husbands.* London: Zed Books.

Amory, Cleveland. 1969. *Introduction: The 1902 Edition of the Sears, Roebuck Catalogue.* New York: Bounty Books.

Anderson, Richard L. 1990. *Calliope's Sisters: A Comparative Study of Philosophies of Art.* Englewood Cliffs, N.J.: Prentice-Hall.

Appell, G. N. 1978. *Ethical Dilemmas in Anthropological Inquiry: A Case Book.* Waltham, Mass.: Crossroads Press.

Ardrey, Robert. 1968. *The Territorial Imperative.* New York: Atheneum.

Baba, Marietta. 1986. "Business and Industrial Anthropology: An Overview." *NAPA Bulletin* 2, National Association for the Practice of Anthropology (a unit of the American Anthropological Association).

Bagash, Henry H. 1981. *Confessions of a Former Cultural Relativist.* Santa Barbara, Calif.: Santa Barbara City College Publications.

Bamberger, Joan. 1974. "The Myth of Matriarchy: Why Men Rule in Primitive Society." In *Women, Culture and Society.* Michelle Zimbalist Rosaldo and Louise Lamphere, eds. Pp. 263–80. Stanford, Calif.: Stanford University Press.

Barfield, Thomas. 1993. *The Nomadic Alternative.* Englewood Cliffs, N.J.: Prentice-Hall.

Barnes, Sandra T. 1990. "Women, Property, and Power." In *Beyond the Second Sex: New Directions in the Anthropology of Gender.* Peggy Reeves Sanday and Ruth G. Goodenough, eds. Pp. 253–80. Philadelphia: University of Pennsylvania Press.

Barrett, Richard A. 1991. *Culture and Conduct: An Excursion in Anthropology.* Belmont, Calif.: Wadsworth.

Beals, Alan. 1962. *Gopalpur: A South Indian Village.* New York: Holt, Rinehart and Winston.

Beals, Ralph L., Harry Hoijer, and Alan R. Beals. 1977. *An Introduction to Anthropology.* 5th edition. New York: Macmillan.

Beattie, John. 1960. *Bunyoro: An African Kingdom.* New York: Holt, Rinehart and Winston.

———. 1964. *Other Cultures: Aims, Methods, and Achievements in Social Anthropology.* New York: Free Press.

Behar, Ruth. 1993. *Translated Woman: Crossing the Border with Esperanza's Story.* Boston: Beacon Press.

Benedict, Ruth. 1946. *The Chrysanthemum and the Sword.* Boston: Houghton Mifflin.

Benet, Sula. 1976. *How to Live to Be a Hundred: The Lifestyle of the People of the Caucasus.* New York: Dial Press.

Bensman, Joseph, and Arthur Vidich. 1987. *American Society: The Welfare State and Beyond.* Rev. edition. South Hadley, Mass.: Bergin and Garvey.

Bernard, H. Russell. 1988. *Research Methods in Cultural Anthropology.* Newbury Park, Calif.: Sage Publications.

Betzig, Laura. 1988. "Redistribution: Equity or Exploitation?" In *Human Reproductive Behavior: A Darwinian Perspective.* Laura Betzig, M. B. Mulder, and Paul Turke, eds. Pp. 49–63. Cambridge: Cambridge University Press.

Birket-Smith, K. 1959. *The Eskimos.* 2nd edition. London: Methuen.

Blacker, J. G. C., and P. R. Forsyth-Thompson et al. 1979. *Report on the 1976 Swaziland Population Census.* Volume 1. Unpublished manuscript.

Blunt, Peter. 1980. "Bureaucracy and Ethnicity in Kenya: Some Conjectures for the Eighties." *Journal of Applied Behavioral Science* 16(3):336–53.

Boal, Augusto. 1979. *Theater of the Oppressed.* London: Pluto Press.

Boas, Franz. 1911. *Handbook of American Indian Languages.* Bureau of American Ethnology. Bulletin 40.

———. 1911. *The Mind of Primitive Man.* New York: Macmillan.

———. 1919. "Correspondence: Scientists as Spies." *The Nation.* December 20, p. 797.

Boddy, Janice. 1989. *Wombs and Alien Spirits: Women, Men and Zar Cult in Northern Sudan.* Madison: University of Wisconsin Press.

Bodley, John. 1982. *Victims of Progress.* 2nd edition. Palo Alto, Calif.: Mayfield.

———. 1997. "The Price of Progress." In *Applying Anthropology: An Introductory Reader.* 4th edition. Aaron Podolefsky and Peter Brown, eds. Pp. 373–81. Mountain View, Calif.: Mayfield.

Bohannan, Paul, and Philip Curtin. 1988. *Africa and Africans.* Prospect Heights, Ill.: Waveland Press.

Bowen, Elenore Smith. 1964. *Return to Laughter.* Garden City, N.Y.: Doubleday.

Brettell, Caroline. 1996. "Women Are Migrants Too." In *Urban Life: Readings in Urban Anthropology.* 3rd edition.

George Gmelch and Walter Zenner, eds. Pp.245–58. Prospect Heights, Ill.: Waveland Press.

Brooke, James. 1990. "Brazil Blows Up Miners' Airstrip, Pressing Its Drive to Save Indians." *New York Times,* May 23.

Brooks, Geraldine. 1990. *Wall Street Journal,* October 10, p. A16.

Brown, Donald E. 1991. *Human Universals.* New York: McGraw-Hill.

Brown, Judith. 1970. "A Note on the Division of Labor by Sex." *American Anthropologist* 72:1073–78.

Brown, Karen McCarthy. 1991. *Mama Lola: A Vodou Priestess in Brooklyn.* Berkeley: University of California Press.

Buckley, T. 1993. "Menstruation and the Power of Yurok Women." In *Gender in Cross Cultural Perspective.* Caroline B. Brettell and Carolyn F. Sargent, eds. Pp. 133–48. Englewood Cliffs, N.J.: Prentice-Hall.

Burger, Julian. 1987. *Report from the Frontier: The State of the World's Indigenous Peoples.* London: Zed Books/Cultural Survival Report 28.

Burton, M. L., L. A. Brudner, and D. R. White. 1977. "A Model of the Sexual Division of Labor." *American Ethnologist,* 4:227–51.

Campbell, Bernard G. 1979. *Mankind Emerging.* 2nd edition. Boston: Little, Brown.

Campbell, Lyle. 1999. *Historical Linguistics: An Introduction.* Cambridge, Mass.: MIT Press.

Carneiro, Robert. 1970. "A Theory of the Origin of the State." *Science,* August 21, p. 733–38.

Carpenter, Edmund. 1973. *Eskimo Realities.* New York: Holt, Rinehart and Winston.

Carvajal, Doreen. 1998. "Better Living Through Sorcery." *New York Times,* October 26, p. E1.

Casagrande, Joseph B. 1960. "The Southwest Project in Comparative Psycholinguistics: A Preliminary Report." In *Men and Cultures: Selected Papers of the Fifth International Congress of Anthropological and Ethnological Sciences.* Anthony F. C. Wallace, ed. Pp. 777–82. Philadelphia: University of Pennsylvania Press.

Cassel, John. 1972. "A South African Health Program." In *Make Men of Them.* Charles C. Hughes, ed. Chicago: Rand McNally.

Chagnon, Napoleon A. 1983. *Yanomamo: The Fierce People.* 3rd edition. New York: Holt, Rinehart and Winston.

———. 1992. *Yanomamo: The Last Days of Eden.* 5th edition. San Diego: Harcourt Brace Jovanovich.

Chambers, John, ed. 1983. *Black English: Educational Equity and the Law.* Ann Arbor, Mich.: Karoma Publishers.

Chambers, Veronica, et al. 1999. "Latino America: Hispanics Are Hip, Hot, and Making History." *Newsweek,* July 12, p. 48.

Chance, Norman A. 1990. *The Inupiat and Arctic Alaska: An Ethnography of Development.* Fort Worth: Holt, Rinehart and Winston.

Charle, Suzanne. 1999. "A Far Island of Cultural Survival." *New York Times,* July 25, section 2, pp. 1, 28.

Childe, V. Gordon. 1936. *Man Makes Himself.* London: Watts.

Chomsky, Noam. 1957. *Syntactic Structures.* The Hague: Mouton.

———. 1972. *Language and Mind.* New York: Harcourt Brace Jovanovich.

Cipollone, Nick, Steven Hartman Keiser, and Shravan Vasishth, eds. 1998. *Language Files: Materials for an Introduction to Language and Linguistics.* 7th edition. Columbus: Ohio State University Press.

Cohen, Eugene N., and Edwin Eames. 1982. *Cultural Anthropology.* Boston: Little, Brown.

Cohen, M. N., and G. J. Armelagos, eds. 1984. *Paleopathology at the Origins of Agriculture.* New York: Academic Press.

Coleman, Richard P., and Lee Rainwater. 1978. *Social Standing in America.* New York: Basic Books.

Collier, Jane F., and J. Yanagisako, eds. 1987. *Gender and Kinship: Essays Toward a Unified Analysis.* Stanford, Calif.: Stanford University Press.

Collins, Chuck, Betsy Leondar-Wright, and Holly Sklar. 1999. *Shifting Fortunes: The Perils of the Growing American Wealth Gap.* Boston: United for a Fair Economy.

Collins, John J. 1975. *Anthropology: Culture, Society and Evolution.* Englewood Cliffs, N.J.: Prentice-Hall.

Condon, John. 1984. *With Respect to the Japanese: A Guide for Americans.* Yarmouth, Mass.: Intercultural Press.

Condon, John, and Fathi Yousef. 1975. *An Introduction to Intercultural Communication.* Indianapolis: Bobbs-Merrill.

Coote, Jeremy, and Anthony Shelton, eds. 1992. *Anthropology, Art, and Aesthetics.* Oxford: Clarendon Press.

Council of the American Anthropological Association. 1971. *Statement on Ethics: Principles of Professional Responsibility.* May (as amended through November 1976).

Counts, David. 1995. "Too Many Bananas, Not Enough Pineapples, and No Watermelon at All: Three Object Lessons in Living with Reciprocity." In *Annual Editions: Anthropology, 1995–1996.* Elvio Angeloni, ed. Pp. 95–98. Guilford, Conn.: Dushkin.

Counts, G. S. 1925. "The Social Status of Occupations: A Problem in Vocational Guidance." *School Review* 33 (January): 16–27.

Cowan, Betty, and Jasbir Dhanoa. 1983. "The Prevention of Toddler Malnutrition by Home-Based Nutrition Education." In *Nutrition in the Community: A Critical Look at Nutrition Policy, Planning, and Programmes.* D. S. McLaren, ed. Pp. 339–56. New York: Wiley.

Cowan, J. Milton. 1979. "Linguistics at War." In *The Uses of Anthropology.* Walter Goldschmidt, ed. Pp. 158–68. Washington, D.C.: American Anthropological Association.

Cronk, Lee. 1989. "Strings Attached." *The Sciences* (May–June): 2–4.

D'Antoni, Tom, and Alex Heard. 1998. "Subway Spirits." *New York Times Magazine,* October 25, p. 23.

Dahlberg, Frances. 1981. "Introduction." In *Woman the Gatherer.* New Haven, Conn.: Yale University Press.

Davis, Kingsley, and Wilbert Moore. 1945. "Some Principles of Stratification." *American Sociological Review* 10 (April): 242–49.

———. 1988. "Wives and Work: A Theory of the Sex-Role Revolution and Its Consequences." In *Feminism, Children, and the New Families.* Sanford Dornbusch and Myra Strober, eds. Pp. 67–86. New York: Guilford Press.

Davis, Shelton H. 1977. *Victims of the Miracle: Development and the Indians of Brazil.* Cambridge: Cambridge University Press.

Deardorff, Merle. 1951. "The Religion of Handsome Lake." In *Symposium on Local Diversity in Iroquois Culture.* W. N. Fenton, ed. Washington D.C.: Bureau of American Ethnology, Bulletin 149.

Dembo, Richard, Patrick Hughes, Lisa Jackson, and Thomas Mieczkowski. 1993. "Crack Cocaine Dealing by Adolescents in Two Public Housing Projects: A Pilot Study." *Human Organization* 52(1):89–96.

Deutsch, Claudia H. 1991. "Anthropologists Probe Company Cultures." *Charlotte Observer,* February 24, p. C11.

De Vita, Philip R., ed. 1992. *The Naked Anthropologist: Tales from Around the World.* Belmont, Calif.: Wadsworth.

De Vita, Philip R., and James D. Armstrong. 1993. *Distant Mirrors: America as a Foreign Culture.* Belmont, Calif.: Wadsworth.

Diamond, Jared. 1987. "The Worst Mistake in the History of the Human Race." *Discover,* May, pp. 64–66.

Diamond, Jared. 1993. "Speaking with a Single Tongue." *Discover,* February.

Diamond, Stanley. 1960. "Introduction: The Uses of the Primitive." In *Primitive Views of the World.* Stanley Diamond, ed. Pp. v–xxix. New York: Columbia University Press.

Domhoff, William G. 1990. *The Power Elite and the State: How Policy Is Made in America.* New York: DeGruyter.

Dorjahn, Vernon. 1959. "The Factor of Polygyny in African Demography." In *Continuity and Change in African Cultures.* William R. Bascom and M. J. Herskovits, eds. Chicago: University of Chicago Press.

Downs, James F. 1971. *Cultures in Crisis.* Beverly Hills: Glencoe Press.

Dresser, Norine. 1996. *Multicultural Manners: New Rules of Etiquette for a Changing Society.* New York: Wiley.

Dundes, Alan. 1965. "What Is Folklore?" In *The Study of Folklore.* Alan Dundes, ed. Englewood Cliffs, N.J.: Prentice-Hall.

Durkheim, Emile. 1933. *Division of Labor in Society* (G. Simpson, trans.). New York: Macmillan.

Dyson-Hudson, Rada, and Neville Dyson-Hudson. 1980. "Nomadic Pastoralism." *Annual Review of Anthropology* 9:15–61.

Dyson-Hudson, Rada, and Eric A. Smith. 1978. "Human Territoriality: An Ecological Reassessment." *American Anthropologist* 80:21–41.

Eastman, Carol. 1983. *Language Planning: An Introduction.* San Francisco: Chandler and Sharp.

Errington, Frederick, and Deborah Gewertz. 1987. *Cultural Alternatives and a Feminist Anthropology: An Analysis of Culturally Constructed Gender Interests in Papua New Guinea.* Cambridge: Cambridge University Press.

Ervin-Tripp, Susan. 1964. "An Analysis of the Interaction of Language, Topic, and Listener." *American Anthropologist* (special publication) 66:86–102.

Esber, George S. 1977. *The Study of Space in Advocacy Planning with the Tonto Apaches in Payson, Arizona.* Doctoral dissertation, University of Arizona.

———. 1987. "Designing Apache Homes with Apaches." In *Anthropological Praxis: Translating Knowledge into Action.* Robert M. Wulff and Shirley J. Fiske. Pp. 187–96. Boulder, Colo.: Westview Press.

Evans-Pritchard, E. E. 1940. *The Nuer.* Oxford: Oxford University Press.

Faludi, Susan. 1991. *Backlash: The Undeclared War Against American Women.* New York: Crown.

Farb, Peter. 1968. "How Do I Know You Mean What You Mean?" *Horizon* 10(4):52–57.

Faris, James C. 1972. *Nuba Personal Art.* Toronto: University of Toronto Press.

Ferguson, B. 1984. "Re-examination of the Causes of Northwest Coast Warfare." In *Warfare, Culture, and Environment.* R Ferguson, ed. Pp. 267–328. New York: Academic Press.

Ferguson, Brian R. 1995. *Yanomami Warfare: A Political History.* Sante Fe: School of American Research Press.

Ferguson, Charles A. 1964. "Diglossia." In *Language in Culture and Society: A Reader in Linguistics and Anthropology.* Dell Hymes, ed. Pp. 429–39. New York: Harper & Row.

Ferraro, Gary. 1980. *Swazi Marital Patterns and Conjugal Roles: An Analysis and Policy Implications.* Unpublished report submitted to USAID, Mbabane, Swaziland. May.

———. 1983. "The Persistence of Bridewealth in Swaziland." *International Journal of Sociology of the Family* (Spring): 1–16.

———. 1998. *The Cultural Dimension of International Business.* Englewood Cliffs, N.J.: Prentice-Hall.

Fetterman, David M. 1987. "A National Ethnographic Evaluation of the Career Intern Program." In *Anthropological Praxis: Translating Knowledge into Action.* Robert M. Wulff and Shirley J. Fiske, eds. Pp. 243–52. Boulder, Colo.: Westview Press.

Fetterman, David M. 1988. "A National Ethnographic Evaluation: An Executive Summary of the Ethnographic Component of the Career Intern Program Study." In *Qualitative Approaches to Evaluation in Education: The Silent Scientific Revolution.* David Fetterman, ed. Pp. 262–73. New York: Praeger.

———. 1989. *Ethnography: Step by Step.* Newbury Park, Calif.: Sage Publications.

Finke, Roger, and Roger Stark. 1992. *The Churching of America, 1976–1990: Winners and Losers in Our Religious Economy.* New Brunswick, N.J.: Rutgers University Press.

Forde, Daryll. 1967. "Double Descent Among the Yako." In *African Systems of Kinship and Marriage.* A. R. Radcliffe-Brown and Daryll Forde, eds. Pp. 285–332. London: Oxford University Press (orig. 1950).

Fortes, M., and E. E. Evans-Pritchard. 1940. *African Political Systems.* London: Oxford University Press.

Foster, George M. 1967. *Tzintzuntzan: Mexican Peasants in a Changing World.* Boston: Little, Brown.

———. 1973. *Traditional Societies and Technological Change.* 2nd edition. New York: Harper & Row.

Fox, Robin. 1967. *Kinship and Marriage.* Baltimore: Penguin Books.

Freilich, Morris, Douglas Raybeck, and Joel Savishinsky, eds. 1990. *Deviance: Anthropological Perspectives.* South Hadley, Mass.: Bergin and Garvey.

Fried, Morton H. 1967. *The Evolution of Political Society: An Essay in Political Anthropology.* New York: Random House.

Friedl, John, and John E. Pfeiffer. 1977. *Anthropology: The Study of People.* New York: Harper & Row.

Friedman, Thomas L. 1999. *The Lexus and the Olive Tree.* New York: Farrar, Straus, and Giroux.

Fuller, Graham. 1999. "Islam Is the Answer to Indonesia's Crisis." *New Perspectives Quarterly* (Summer): 32–33.

Galanti, Geri-Ann. 1991. *Caring for Patients from Different Cultures: Case Studies from American Hospitals.* Philadelphia: University of Philadelphia Press.

Gardner, R. Allen, and Beatrice T. Gardner. 1969. "Teaching Sign Language to a Chimpanzee." *Science,* August 15, pp. 664–72.

Garfinkle, H. 1956. "Conditions of a Successful Degradation Ceremony." *American Journal of Sociology* 61:420–24.

Geertz, Clifford. 1973. "Deep Play: Notes on Balinese Cockfights." In *The Interpretation of Cultures.* Clifford Geertz, ed. Pp. 412–53. New York: Basic Books.

———. 1973. *The Interpretation of Cultures.* New York: Basic Books.

———. 1983. *Local Knowledge: Further Essays in Interpretive Anthropology.* New York: Basic Books.

———. 1984. "Distinguished Lecture: Anti Anti-Relativism." *American Anthropologist* 86 (June): 263–78.

Gibbs, James L. 1963. "The Kpelle Moot." *Africa* 33(1).

Girdner, Linda. 1989. "Custody Mediation: Taking the Knowledge Act on the Policy Road." In *Making Our Research Useful: Case Studies in the Utilization of Anthropological Knowledge.* John Van Willigen, Barbara Rylko-Bauer, and Ann McElroy, eds. Pp. 55–70. Boulder, Colo.: Westview Press.

Glossow, Michael. 1978. "The Concept of Carrying Capacity in the Study of Cultural Process." In *Advances in Archaeological Theory.* Michael Schiffler, ed. Pp. 32–48. New York: Academic Press.

Gmelch, George. 1994a. "Lessons from the Field." In *Conformity and Conflict.* 8th edition. James P. Spradley and David McCurdy, eds. Pp. 45–55. New York: HarperCollins.

———. 1994b. "Ritual and Magic in American Baseball." In *Conformity and Conflict.* 8th edition. James P. Spradley and David McCurdy, eds. Pp. 351–61. New York: HarperCollins.

———. 1996. "A West Indian Life in Britain." In *Urban Life: Readings in Urban Anthropology.* 3rd edition. George Gmelch and Walter Zenner, eds. Prospect Heights, Ill.: Waveland Press.

Goldschmidt, Walter. 1979. "Introduction: On the Interdependence Between Utility and Theory." In *The Uses of Anthropology.* Walter Goldschmidt, ed. Washington, D.C.: American Anthropological Association.

Goldstein, Melvyn C. 1987. "When Brothers Share a Wife." *Natural History* 96(3):39–48.

Goode, William J. 1963. *World Revolution and Family Patterns.* New York: Free Press of Glencoe.

Goodenough, Ward H. 1956. "Componential Analysis and the Study of Meaning." *Language* 32:195–216.

Gorer, G., and J. Rickman. 1949. *The People of Great Russia.* London: Cresset.

Gottlieb, Alma. 1990. "Rethinking Female Pollution: The Beng Case (Cote d'Ivoire)." In *Beyond the Second Sex: New Directions in the Anthropology of Gender.* Peggy Reeves Sanday and Ruth G. Goodenough, eds. Pp. 113–38. Philadelphia: University of Pennsylvania Press.

Gough, Kathleen. 1959. "The Nayars and the Definition of Marriage." *Journal of the Royal Anthropological Institute* 89:23–34.

Gouldner, Alvin. 1960. "The Norm of Reciprocity: A Preliminary Statement." *American Sociological Review* 25:161–78.

Gray, Robert F. 1960. "Sonjo Brideprice and the Question of African 'Wife Purchase.'" *American Anthropologist* 62:34–57.

Grindal, Bruce. 1972. *Growing Up in Two Worlds: Education and Transition Among the Sisla of Northern Ghana.* New York: Holt, Rinehart and Winston.

Gross, Daniel, and Barbara A. Underwood. 1971. "Technological Change and Caloric Costs: Sisal Agriculture." *American Anthropologist* 73(3):725–40.

Hafner, Katie. 1999. "Coming of Age in Palo Alto: Anthropologists Find a Niche Studying Consumers for Companies in Silicon Valley." *New York Times,* June 10, p. D1.

Hagen, E. 1962. *On the Theory of Social Change.* Homewood, Ill.: Dorsey Press.

Hall, Edward T. 1969. *The Hidden Dimension.* Garden City, N.Y.: Doubleday.

Hanna, Judith Lynne. 1979. *To Dance Is Human: A Theory of Nonverbal Communication.* Austin: University of Texas Press.

Harner, Michael J. 1973. "The Sound of Rushing Water." In *Hallucinogens and Shamanism.* Michael J. Harner, ed. Pp. 15–27. New York: Oxford University Press.

Harris, Grace. 1972. "Taita Bridewealth and Affinal Relations." In *Marriage in Tribal Society.* Meyer Fortes, ed. Pp. 55–87. Cambridge: Cambridge University Press.

Harris, Marvin. 1968. *The Rise of Anthropological Theory.* New York: Thomas Y. Crowell.

———. 1977. *Cannibals and Kings: The Origins of Culture.* New York: Random House.

———. 1979. "Comments on Simoons' Questions in the Sacred Cow Controversy." *Current Anthropology* 20:479–82.

———. 1979. *Cultural Materialism: The Struggle for a Science of Culture.* New York: Random House.

———. 1979. "The Yanomamo and the Cause of War in Band and Village Societies." In *Brazil: Anthropological Perspectives: Essays in Honor of Charles Wagley.* M. Margolis and W. Carter, eds. Pp. 121–32. New York Columbia University Press.

———. 1984. "A Cultural Materialist Theory of Band and Village Warfare: The Yanomamo Test." In *Warfare, Culture, and Environment.* R. B. Ferguson, ed. Pp. 111–40. Orlando: Academic Press.

———. 1990. "Potlatch." In *Annual Edition: Anthropology, 1990–91.* Elvio Angeloni, ed. Pp. 88–93. Guilford, Conn.: Dushkin.

———. 1991. *Cultural Anthropology.* 3rd edition. New York: HarperCollins.

Hart, C. W. M., and Arnold R. Pilling. 1960. *The Tiwi of North Australia.* New York: Holt, Rinehart and Winston.

Hart, C. W. M., Arnold Pilling, and Jane Goodale. 1988. *The Tiwi of North Australia.* 3rd edition. New York: Holt, Rinehart and Winston.

Hatch, Elvin. 1985. "Culture." In *The Social Science Encyclopedia.* Adam Kuper and Jessica Kuper, eds. P. 178. London: Routledge and Kegan Paul.

Hawkes, K., and J. O'Connell. 1981. "Affluent Hunters? Some Comments in Light of the Alyawara Case." *American Anthropologist* 83:622–26.

Hay-Eadie, Terence. 1995. "Tents in the City." *New Internationalist,* April, p. 30.

Hecht, David. 1998. "Standing Up to Ancient Custom." *Christian Science Monitor,* June 3, p. 1.

Hecht, Michael L., Mary Jane Collier, and Sidney Ribeau. 1993. *African American Communication: Ethnic Identity and Cultural Interpretation.* Thousand Oaks, Calif.: Sage Publications.

Hecht, Robert M. 1986. "Salvage Anthropology: The Redesign of a Rural Development Project in Guinea." In *Anthropology and Rural Development in West Africa.* Michael M. Horowitz and Thomas M. Painter, eds. Pp. 13–26. Boulder, Colo.: Westview Press.

Heider, Karl. 1979. *Grand Valley Dani: Peaceful Warriors.* New York: Holt, Rinehart and Winston.

Heller, Scott. 1988. "From Selling Rambo to Supermarket Studies, Anthropologists Are Finding More Non-Academic Jobs." *Chronicle of Higher Education,* June 1, A24.

Hellinger, Daniel, and Dennis Judd. 1991. *The Demographic Facade.* Pacific Grove, Calif.: Brooks/Cole.

Henschen, Beth, and Edward Sidlow. 1999. *America at Odds: The Essentials.* Belmont, Calif.: Wadsworth.

Hern, Warren M. 1992. "Family Planning, Amazon Style." *Natural History* 101(12):30–37.

Hernandez Castillo, Rosalva Aida, and Ronald Nigh. 1998. "Global Processes and Local Identity Among Mayan Coffee Growers in Chiapas, Mexico." *American Anthropologist* 100(1):136–47.

Herskovits, Melville. 1967. *Dahomey: An Ancient West African Kingdom.* Volume 1. Evanston, Ill.: Northwestern University Press (orig. 1938).

———. 1972. *Cultural Relativism: Perspectives in Cultural Pluralism.* New York: Vintage Books.

Hickerson, Nancy P. 1980. *Linguistic Anthropology.* New York: Holt, Rinehart and Winston.

Hildebrand, P. 1981. "Combining Disciplines in Rapid Appraisal: The Sondeo Approach." *Agricultural Administration* 8:423–32.

Hill, Carole, and Roy S. Dickens. 1978. *Cultural Resources: Planning and Management.* Boulder, Colo.: Westview Press.

Hill, K., H. Kaplan, K. Hawkes, and M. Hurtado. 1985. "Men's Time Allocation to Subsistence Work Among the Ache of Eastern Paraguay." *Human Ecology* 13:29–47.

Hill, Kim, Hillard Kaplan, Kristen Hawkes, and Magdalena Hurtado. 1987. "Foraging Decisions Among Ache Hunter-Gatherers: New Data and Implications for Optimal Foraging Models." *Ethology and Sociobiology* 8.

Hockett, C. F. 1973. *Man's Place in Nature.* New York: McGraw-Hill.

Hodge, Robert W., Paul M. Siegel, and Peter H. Rossi. 1964. "Occupational Prestige in the United States, 1925–1963." *American Journal of Sociology* 70 (November): 286–302.

Hodgson, Marshall. 1974. "Our Place on Earth." In *Learning About Peoples and Cultures.* Seymour Fersh, ed. Pp. 19–23. Evanston, Ill.: McDougal, Littell.

Hoebel, E. A. 1960. *The Cheyennes: Indians of the Great Plains.* New York: Holt, Rinehart and Winston.

———. 1972. *Anthropology: The Study of Man.* 4th edition. New York: McGraw-Hill.

Hostetler, John, and Gertrude Huntington. 1971. *Children in Amish Society: Socialization and Community Education.* New York: Holt, Reinhart and Winston.

Howard, Beth. 1991. "Ape Apothecary: Self-prescribing Chimps Lead Researchers to Nature's Medicine Cabinet." *Omni* 13, p. 30.

Howell, N. 1986. "Feedbacks and Buffers in Relation to Scarcity and Abundance: Studies of Hunter-Gatherer Populations." In *The State of Population Theory.* D. Coleman and R. Schofield, eds. Pp. 156–87. Oxford: Basil Blackwell.

Hughes, Charles C., and John M. Hunter. 1972. "The Role of Technological Development in Promoting Disease in Africa." In *The Careless Technology: Ecology and International Development.* M. T. Farvar and John P. Milton, eds. Pp. 69–101. Garden City, N.Y.: Natural History Press.

Hunt, Linda M., Jacqueline Pugh, and Miguel Valenzuela. 1995. *What They Do Outside the Doctor's Office: Understanding and Responding to Diabetes Patients' Strategic Adaptations of Self-Care Behavior.* Paper given at the meetings of the Society for Applied Anthropology, Albuquerque, N.M., April.

Husain, Tariq. 1976. "Use of Anthropologists in Project Appraisal by the World Bank." In *Development from Below: Anthropologists and Development Situations.* David C. Pitt, ed. Pp. 71–81. The Hague: Mouton.

Hymes, Dell. 1977. "Discovering Oral Performance and Measured Verse in American Indian Narrative." *New Literary History* 8(3):431–57.

Information Please Almanac. 1991. 44th edition. Boston: Houghton Mifflin.

Isaac, B. 1990. "Economy, Ecology, and Analogy: The !Kung San and the Generalized Foraging Model." In *Early Paleoindian Economies of Eastern North America.* B. Isaac and K. Tankersley, eds. Pp. 323–35. Greenwich, Conn.: JAI Press.

James, Preston E. 1966. *A Geography of Man.* 3rd edition. Waltham, Mass.: Blaisdell.

Jameson, Frederic. 1990. *Postmodernism, or the Cultural Logic of Late Capitalism.* Durham, N.C.: Duke University Press.

Janson, H. W. 1986. *History of Art* (revised by Anthony F. Janson). New York and Englewood Cliffs, N.J.: Harry Abrams and Prentice-Hall.

Janzen, Jorg. 1994. "Resettlement Schemes for Nomads: The Case of Somalia." In *Atlas of World Development.* Tim Unwin, ed. Pp. 268–70. Chichester: Wiley.

Jeffers, Robert, and Ilse Lehiste. 1979. *Principle and Methods for Historical Linguistics.* Cambridge, Mass.: MIT Press.

Jehl, Douglas. 1999. "Arab Honor's Price: A Woman's Blood." *New York Times,* June 20, p.1.

Joans, Barbara. 1984. "Problems in Pocatello: A Study in Linguistic Understanding." *Practicing Anthropology* 6(3/4).

Jordan, Cathie, Roland Tharp, and Lynn Baird-Vogt. 1992. "Just Open the Door: Cultural Compatibility and Classroom Rapport." In *Cross Cultural Literacy: Ethnographies of Communication in Multiethnic Classrooms.* Marietta Saravia-Shore and Steven F. Arvizu, eds. Pp. 3–18. New York: Garland.

Jorgensen, Danny L. 1989. *Participant Observation: A Methodology for Human Studies.* Thousand Oaks, Calif.: Sage Publications.

Kaplan, David, and Robert Manners. 1986. *Culture Theory.* Englewood Cliffs, N.J.: Prentice-Hall.

Kasarda, John D. 1971. "Economic Structure and Fertility: A Comparative Analysis." *Demography* 8(3):307–18.

Kaslow, Amy. 1995. "Helping Women Seen as Boosting World Prosperity." *Christian Science Monitor,* August 24, p.1.

Katzner, Kenneth. 1975. *The Languages of the World.* New York: Funk & Wagnalls.

Keefe, Susan E. 1988. "The Myth of the Declining Family: Extended Family Ties Among Urban Mexican-Americans and Anglo-Americans." In *Urban Life: Readings in Urban Anthropology.* 2nd edition. George Gmelch and Walter Zenner, eds. Pp. 229–39. Prospect Heights, Ill.: Waveland Press.

Keenan, Elinor. 1974. "Norm-makers, Norm-breakers: Uses of Speech by Men and Women in a Malagasy Community." In *Explorations in the Ethnography of Speaking.* Richard Bauman and Joel Sherzer, eds. Pp. 125–43. London: Cambridge University Press.

Kelly, Robert L. 1995. *The Foraging Spectrum: Diversity in Hunter Gatherer Lifeways.* Washington, D.C.: Smithsonian Institution Press.

Khazanov, Anatoly M. 1994. *Nomads and the Outside World.* 2nd edition. Madison: University of Wisconsin Press.

Kilbride, Philip. 1997. "African Polygyny: Family Values and Contemporary Changes." In *Applying Anthropology: An Introductory Reader.* Aaron Podolefsky and Peter Brown, eds. Mountain View, Calif.: Mayfield.

Kilpatrick, D. G., C. N. Edwards, and A. K. Seymour. 1992. *Rape in America: A Report to the Nation.* Arlington, Va.: The National Victim Center.

Kirsch, A. T. 1985. "Text and Context: Buddhist Sex Roles/Culture of Gender Revisited." *American Ethnologist* 12:302–20.

Kluckhohn, Clyde. 1949. *Mirror for Man: Anthropology and Modern Life.* New York: Wittlesey House (McGraw-Hill).

Knauft, B. 1987. "Reconsidering Violence in Simple Human Societies: Homicide Among Gebusi of New Guinea." *Current Anthropology* 28:457–500.

Kohls, L. Robert. 1984. *Survival Kit for Overseas Living.* Yarmouth, Maine: Intercultural Press.

Kosmin, Barry A., and Seymour Lachman. 1993. *One Nation Under God: Religion in Contemporary American Society.* New York: Crown.

Kottak, Conrad P. 1987. *Anthropology: The Exploration of Human Diversity.* 4th edition. New York: Random House.

Kramer, Cheris. 1974. "Folk Linguistics: Wishy-Washy Mommy Talk." *Psychology Today* 8(1):82–85.

Kroeber, A. L. 1917. "The Superorganic." *American Anthropologist* 19(2):163–213.

Kroeber, A. L., and C. Kluckhohn. 1952. *Culture: A Critical Review of Concepts and Definitions.* Papers of the Peabody Museum of American Archaeology and Ethnology 47(1).

Kuczynski, Alex. 1999. "Running Cupid's Wall Street Office." *New York Times,* February 14, section 3, p. 11.

Kuper, Hilda. 1986. *The Swazi: A South African Kingdom.* 2nd edition. New York: Holt, Rinehart and Winston.

Kuznar, Lawrence. 1996. *Reclaiming a Scientific Anthropology.* Thousand Oaks, Calif.: Sage Publications.

La Fontaine, Jean. 1963. "Witchcraft in Bagisu." In *Witchcraft and Sorcery in East Africa.* J. Middleton and E. Winter, eds. Pp. 187–220. New York: Praeger.

Labov, William. 1972. *Sociolinguistic Patterns.* Philadelphia: University of Pennsylvania Press.

Lamont-Brown, Raymond. 1999. "Japan's New Spirituality." *Contemporary Review,* August, pp. 70–73.

Lane, Belden C. 1989. "The Power of Myth: Lessons from Joseph Campbell." *The Christian Century* 106 (July 5): 652–54.

Lanier, Alison. 1979. "Selecting and Preparing Personnel for Overseas Transfers." *Personnel Journal* (March): 160–63.

Lee, Dorothy. 1993. "Religious Perspectives in Anthropology." In *Magic, Witchcraft, and Religion: An Anthropological Study of the Supernatural.* 3rd edition. Arthur C. Lehmann and James E. Myers, eds. Pp. 10–17. Mountain View, Calif.: Mayfield.

Lee, Richard B. 1968. "What Hunters Do for a Living, or How to Make Out on Scarce Resources." In *Man the Hunter.* Richard B. Lee and Irven DeVore, eds. Pp. 30–48. Chicago: Aldine-Atherton.

Lehmann, Arthur C., and James E. Myers, eds. 1985. *Magic, Witchcraft, and Religion: An Anthropological Study of the Supernatural.* Palo Alto, Calif.: Mayfield.

———. 1993. *Magic, Witchcraft, and Religion.* 3rd edition. Palo Alto, Calif.: Mayfield.

Leighton, Dorothea, and Clyde Kluckhohn. 1948. *Children of the People.* Cambridge: Cambridge University Press.

Lepowsky, Maria. 1990. "Big Men, Big Women, and Cultural Autonomy." *Ethnology* 29(1):35–50.

Levine, John R., Carol Baroudi, and Margaret Levine Young. 1999. *The Internet for Dummies.* 6th edition. San Mateo, Calif., IDG Books Worldwide.

Lévi-Strauss, Claude. 1969. *The Elementary Structures of Kinship.* Boston: Beacon Press.

Lewis, I. M. 1965. "The Northern Pastoral Somali of the Horn." In *Peoples of Africa.* James Gibbs, ed. Pp. 319–60. New York: Holt, Rinehart and Winston.

Lewis, Oscar. 1952. "Urbanization Without Breakdown." *Scientific Monthly* 75 (July): 31–41.

———. 1955. "Peasant Culture in India and Mexico: A Comparative Analysis." In *Village India: Studies in the Little Community.* McKim Marriott, ed. Pp. 145–70. Chicago: University of Chicago Press.

———. 1966. "The Culture of Poverty." *Scientific American,* October, pp. 19–25.

Lewis-Williams, J. D., and T. A. Dowson. 1988. "The Signs of All Times: Entoptic Phenomena in Upper Palaeolithic Art." *Current Anthropology* 29(2):201–45.

Lightfoot-Klein. 1989. *Prisoners of Ritual: An Odyssey into Female Genital Circumcision in Africa.* Binghamton, N.Y.: Haworth.

Linton, Ralph. 1936. *The Study of Man.* New York: Appleton-Century-Crofts.

Little, Kenneth. 1957. "The Role of Voluntary Associations in West African Urbanization." *American Anthropologist* 59(4):579–96.

———. 1967. "Voluntary Associations in Urban Life: A Case Study of Differential Adaptation." In *Social Organization: Essays Presented to Raymond Firth.* Maurice Freedman, ed. Chicago: Aldine.

Llewellyn, K., and E. Adamson Hoebel. 1941. *The Cheyenne Way: Conflict and Case Law in Primitive Jurisprudence.* Norman: University of Oklahoma Press.

Lloyd, Marion. 1999. "Affirmative Action Dispute Leads to Violence at a Top Medical School in India." *Chronicle of Higher Education,* April 23, p. A58.

Lomax, Alan, et al. 1968. *Folk Song Style and Culture.* Washington, D.C.: American Association for the Advancement of Science.

Low, Setha M. 1981. *Anthropology as a New Technology in Landscape Planning.* Unpublished paper presented at the meetings of the American Society of Landscape Architects.

Lowie, Robert. 1963. "Religion in Human Life." *American Anthropologist* 65:532–42.

Lutz, William D. 1995. "Language, Appearance, and Reality: Doublespeak in 1984." In *Anthropology: Annual Editions 95/96.* Elvio Angeloni, ed. Guilford, Conn.: Dushkin.

MacFarquhar, Emily. 1994. "The War Against Women." *U.S. News and World Report,* March 28, pp. 42–48.

Malinowski, Bronislaw. 1922. Argonauts of the Western Pacific. New York: Dutton.

———. 1927. *Sex and Repression in Savage Society.* London: Kegan Paul.

Mandelbaum, David G. 1970. *Society in India.* Volume 1. Berkeley: University of California Press.

Marksbury, Richard A., ed. 1993. *The Business of Marriage: Transformations in Oceanic Matrimony.* Pittsburgh: University of Pittsburgh Press.

Marshall, Donald S. 1971. "Sexual Behavior on Mangaia." In *Sexual Behavior: Variations in the Ethnographic Spectrum.* Donald S. Marshall and Robert Suggs, eds. Pp. 103–62. New York: Basic Books.

Marshall, Lorna. 1965. "The !Kung Bushmen of the Kalahari Desert." In *Peoples of Africa.* James Gibbs, ed. Pp. 243–78. New York: Holt, Rinehart and Winston.

Marx, Karl. 1909. *Capital* (E. Unterman, trans.). Chicago: C. H. Kerr (orig. 1867).

Matloff, Judith. 1998. "Russian Hard Times a Boon to Native Peoples." *Christian Science Monitor,* November 20, p. 7.

Mauss, M. 1954. *The Gift* (I. Cunnison, trans.). New York: Free Press.

Maybury-Lewis, David. 1992. *Millennium; Tribal Wisdom and the Modern World.* New York: Viking Press.

McClelland, D. C. 1960. *The Achieving Society.* New York: Van Nostrand.

McGee, R. J. 1990. *Life, Ritual and Religion Among the Lacandon Maya.* Belmont, Calif.: Wadsworth.

McGlynn, Frank, and Arthur Tuden, eds. 1991. *Anthropological Approaches to Political Behavior.* Pittsburgh: University of Pittsburgh Press.

McKenzie, Joan L., and Noel J. Chrisman. 1977. "Healing Herbs, Gods, and Magic: Folk Health Beliefs Among Filipino-Americans." *American Journal of Nursing* 77(5):326–29.

Mead, Margaret. 1928. *Coming of Age in Samoa.* New York: Morrow.

———. 1950. *Sex and Temperament in Three Primitive Societies.* New York: Mentor (orig. 1935).

———. 1956. *New Lives for Old.* New York: Morrow.

Meek, Charles K. 1972. "Ibo Law." In *Readings in Anthropology.* J. D. Jennings and E. A. Hoebel, eds. New York: McGraw-Hill.

Mehrabian, Albert. 1981. *Silent Messages.* 2nd edition. Belmont, Calif.: Wadsworth.

Mendonsa, Eugene. 1985. "Characteristics of Sisala Diviners." In *Magic, Witchcraft, and Religion: An Anthropological Study of the Supernatural.* Arthur C. Lehmann and James E. Myers, eds. Pp. 214–24. Palo Alto, Calif.: Mayfield.

Merton, Robert K. 1957. *Social Theory and Social Structure.* Glencoe, Ill.: Free Press.

Michrina, Barry P., and Cherylanne Richards. 1996. *Person to Person: Fieldwork, Dialogue, and the Hermeneutic Method.* Albany: State University of New York Press.

Middleton, John. 1965. *The Lugbara of Uganda.* New York: Holt, Rinehart and Winston.

Middleton, John, and Greet Kershaw. 1965. *The Kikuyu and Kamba of Kenya.* London: International African Institute.

Middleton, John, and David Tait, eds. 1958. *Tribes Without Rulers: Studies in African Segmentary Systems.* London: Routledge and Kegan Paul.

Miller, Annetta, Bruce Shenitz, and Lourdes Rosado. 1990. "You Are What You Buy." *Newsweek,* June 4, pp. 59–60.

Miller, Barbara D. 1993. "Female Infanticide and Child Neglect in Rural North India." In *Gender in Cross Cultural Perspective.* Caroline Brettell and Carolyn Sargent, eds. Pp. 423–35. Englewood Cliffs, N.J.: Prentice-Hall.

Miller, Lisa. 1999. "The Age of Divine Disunity," *Wall Street Journal,* February 10, p. B1.

Mills, C. Wright. 1956. *The Power Elite.* New York: Oxford University Press.

Mills, George. 1957. "Art: An Introduction to Qualitative Anthropology." *Journal of Aesthetics and Art Criticism* 16(1):1–17.

Mincer, Jillian. 1994. "How Schools Shortchange Girls." *New York Times,* January 9 (Education Life), p. 27.

Miner, Horace. 1953. *The Primitive City of Timbuctoo.* Philadelphia: American Philosophical Society.

Moller, V., and G. J. Welch. 1990. "Polygamy, Economic Security, and Well-Being of Retired Zulu Migrant Workers." *Journal of Cross Cultural Gerontology* 5:205–16.

Montagu, Ashley. 1972. *Touching: The Human Significance of the Skin.* New York: Harper & Row.

Montana, Cate. 1999. "Tribe That Killed a Whale: Allies Say Traditions Not Wrong, Just Different." *Indian Country Today,* May 24.

Moody, Edward J. 1993. "Urban Witches." In *Magic, Witchcraft, and Religion: An Anthropological Study of the Supernatural.* 3rd edition. Arthur C. Lehmann and James E. Myers, eds. Pp. 231–37. Mountain View, Calif.: Mayfield.

Morgan, L. H. 1871. *Systems of Consanguinity and Affinity of the Human Family.* Washington, D.C.: Smithsonian Institution.

———. 1963. *Ancient Society.* New York: World (orig. 1877).

Morin, Richard, and Megan Rosenfeld. 1998. "With More Equity, More Sweat." *Washington Post,* March 22, p. A1.

Morris, Desmond, Peter Collett, Peter Marsh, and Marie O'Shaughnessy. 1979. *Gestures: Their Origins and Distribution.* New York: Stein and Day.

Mulder, Monique B. 1988. "Kipsigis Bridewealth Payments." In *Human Reproductive Behavior: A Darwinian Perspective.* Laura Betzig, M. B. Mulder, and Paul Turke, eds. Pp. 65–82. Cambridge: Cambridge University Press.

Murdock, George. 1945. "The Common Denominator of Cultures." In *The Science of Man in the World Crisis.* Ralph Linton, ed. P. 123. New York: Columbia University Press.

———. 1949. *Social Structure.* New York: Macmillan.

———. 1967. "Ethnographic Atlas: A Summary." *Ethnology* 6(2):109–236.

———. 1968. "The Current Status of the World's Hunting and Gathering Peoples." In *Man the Hunter*. Richard B. Lee and Irven DeVore, eds. Pp. 13–20. Chicago: Aldine-Atherton.

Murphy, R. F., and L. Kasdan. 1959. "The Structure of Parallel Cousin Marriage." *American Anthropologist* 61:17–29.

Murray, Gerald F. 1984. "The Wood Tree as a Peasant Cash-Crop: An Anthropological Strategy for the Domestication of Energy." In *Haiti—Today and Tomorrow: An Interdisciplinary Study*. Charles R. Foster and Albert Valdman, eds. Pp. 141–60. Latham, N.Y.: University Press of America.

———. 1986. "Seeing the Forest While Planting the Trees: An Anthropological Approach to Agroforestry in Rural Haiti." In *Politics, Projects, and People: Institutional Development in Haiti*. Derick W. Brinkerhoff and J. Garcia-Zamor, eds. Pp. 193–226. New York: Praeger.

———. 1987. "The Domestication of Wood in Haiti: A Case Study in Applied Evolution." In *Anthropological Praxis*. Robert Wulff and Shirley Fiske, eds. Pp. 223–40. Boulder, Colo.: Westview Press.

Mwamwenda, T. S., and L. A. Monyooe. 1997. "Status of Bridewealth in an African Culture." *Journal of Social Psychology* 137(2):269–71.

Nader, Laura, and H. F. Todd, Jr. 1978. *The Disputing Process: Law in Ten Societies*. New York: Columbia University Press.

Nakao, Keiko, and Judith Treas. 1990. *Occupational Prestige in the United States Revisited: Twenty-Five Years of Stability and Change*. Paper presented at the annual meetings of the American Sociological Association.

Nanda, Serena. 1990. *Neither Man nor Woman: The Hijras of India*. Belmont, Calif.: Wadsworth.

———. 1992. "Arranging a Marriage in India." In *The Naked Anthropologist*. Philip De Vita, ed. Pp. 137–43. Belmont, Calif.: Wadsworth.

Nash, Jesse W. 1988. "Confucius and the VCR." *Natural History*, May, pp. 28–31.

National Center for Victims of Crime & National Crime Victims Research and Treatment Center. 1992. *Rape in America: A Report to the Nation*. Arlington, Va.: National Center for Victims of Crime.

National Opinion Research Center. 1947. "Jobs and Occupations: A Popular Evaluation." *Opinion News* 9 (September): 3–13.

Nelson, Richard. 1993. "Understanding Eskimo Science." *Audubon*, September/October, pp. 102–9.

Nettl, Bruno. 1980. "Ethnomusicology: Definitions, Directions, and Problems." In *Music of Many Cultures*. Elizabeth May, ed. Pp. 1–9. Berkeley: University of California Press.

Nettl, Bruno, and Philip V. Bohlman, eds. 1991. *Comparative Musicology and Anthropology of Music*. Chicago: University of Chicago Press.

Newman, Katherine S. 1988. *Falling from Grace: The Experience of Downward Mobility in the American Middle Class*. New York: Free Press.

Oberg, Kalervo. 1960. "Culture Shock: Adjustments to New Cultural Environments." *Practical Anthropology* (July/August): 177–82.

Oliver, Douglas. 1955. *A Solomon Island Society*. Cambridge, Mass.: Harvard University Press.

O'Meara, Tim. 1990. *Samoan Planters: Tradition and Economic Development in Polynesia*. Fort Worth: Holt, Rinehart and Winston.

Pachon, Harry P. 1998. "Buenos Dias California." *Unesco Currier*, November, p. 31–32.

Paige, K. E., and J. M. Paige. 1981. *The Politics of Reproductive Ritual*. Berkeley/Los Angeles: University of California Press.

Paredes, J. Anthony. 1992. "'Practical History' and the Poarch Creeks: A Meeting Ground for Anthropologist and Tribal Leaders." In *Anthropological Research: Process and Application*. John Poggie, Billie R. DeWalt, and William W. Dressler, eds. Pp. 209–26. Albany: State University of New York Press.

Parker, Arthur C. 1913. *The Code of Handsome Lake, the Seneca Prophet*. Albany: New York State Museum Bulletin, No. 163.

Parker, Patricia L., and Thomas F. King. 1987. "Intercultural Mediation at Truk International Airport." In *Anthropological Praxis*. Robert Wulff and Shirley Fiske, eds. Pp. 160–73. Boulder, Colo.: Westview Press.

Parsons, Talcott. 1951. *The Social System*. New York: Free Press.

Parsons, Talcott, and E. Shils. 1952. *Toward a General Theory of Action*. Cambridge, Mass.: Harvard University Press.

Pasternak, Burton, Carol Ember, and Melvin Ember. 1976. "On the Conditions Favoring Extended Family Households." *Journal of Anthropological Research* 32(2):109–23.

Peacock, James L. 1986. *The Anthropological Lens*. Cambridge: Cambridge University Press.

Pearl, Daniel. 1991. "Federal Express Finds Its Pioneering Formula Falls Flat Overseas." *Wall Street Journal*, April 15, p. A8.

Pelto, Pertti J. 1973. *The Snowmobile Revolution: Technology and Social Change in the Arctic*. Menlo Park, Calif.: Benjamin/Cummings.

Pennar, Karen. 1991. "Women Are Still Paid the Wages of Discrimination." *Business Week*, October 18.

Philips, Kevin. 1991. *The Politics of Rich and Poor*. New York: HarperCollins.

Plotkin, Mark. 1995. "Through the Emerald Door." In *Annual Editions: Anthropology 1995–96*. Elvio Angeloni, ed. Guilford, Conn.: Dushkin.

Polanyi, Karl. 1957. "The Economy as Instituted Process." In *Trade and Market in the Early Empires*. Karl Polanyi, Conrad Arensberg, and Harry Pearson, eds. Pp. 243–70. New York: Free Press.

Porterfield, Elaine. 1999. "How to Throw a Good Potlatch: Just Add Whale." *Christian Science Monitor*, May 25, p. 2.

Price, T. Douglas, and James A. Brown. 1985. *Prehistoric Hunter Gatherers: The Emergence of Cultural Complexity*. Orlando: Academic Press.

Prior, Ian. 1971. "The Price of Civilization." *Nutrition Today* 6(4):2–11.

Pryor, F. L. 1986. "The Adoption of Agriculture." *American Anthropologist* 88:879–97.

Radcliffe-Brown, A. R. 1950. "Introduction." In *African Systems of Kinship and Marriage*. A. R. Radcliffe-Brown and D. Forde, eds. Pp. 1–85. London: Oxford University Press.

Ramanamma, A., and U. Bambawale. 1980. "The Mania for Sons: An Analysis of Social Values in South Asia." *Social Science and Medicine* 14:107–10.

Raphael, D., and F. Davis. 1985. *Only Mothers Know: Patterns of Infant Feeding in Traditional Cultures*. Westport, Conn.: Greenwood Press.

Rasmussen, Knud. 1927. *Across Arctic America*. New York: G. P. Putnam's Sons.

Read, Margaret. 1960. *Children of Their Fathers: Growing Up Among the Ngoni of Nyasaland*. New Haven, Conn.: Yale University Press.

Renaud, Michelle L. 1993. "We're All in It Together: AIDS Prevention in Urban Senegal." *Practicing Anthropology* 15(4):25–29.

———. 1997. "Applied Anthropology at the Crossroads: AIDS Prevention Research in Senegal and Beyond." *Practicing Anthropology* 19(1):23–27.

Renzetti, Claire M., and Daniel J. Curran. 1992. *Women, Men, and Society*. Boston: Allyn & Bacon.

Reynolds, Simon. 1998. *Generation Ecstasy*. Boston: Little Brown.

Rhoades, Robert. 1996. "European Cyclical Migration and Economic Development: The Case of Southern Spain." In *Urban Life: Readings in Urban Anthropology*. 3rd edition. George Gmelch and Walter Zenner, eds. Pp. 279–92. Prospect Heights, Ill.: Waveland Press.

Richards, Audrey I. 1960. "The Bemba—Their Country and Diet." In *Cultures and Societies of Africa*. Simon and Phoebe Ottenburg, eds. Pp. 96–109. New York: Random House.

Rickford, John R. 1999. "Suite for Ebony and Phonics." In *Applying Anthropology: An Introductory Reader*. 5th edition. Aaron Podolefsky and Peter J. Brown, eds. Pp. 176–80. Mountain View, Calif.: Mayfield.

Roberts, John M. 1967. "Oaths, Autonomic Ordeals, and Power." In *Cross Cultural Approaches: Readings in Comparative Research*. Clellan S. Ford, ed. New Haven, Conn.: HRAF Press.

Robinson, Linda. 1998. "Hispanics Don't Exist." *U.S. News and World Report*, May 11, p. 26.

Robinson, Richard. 1984. *Internationalization of Business: An Introduction*. New York: Dryden Press.

Rogers, Everett M. 1973. *Communication Strategies for Family Planning*. New York: Free Press.

———. 1983. *Diffusion of Innovations*. 3rd edition. New York: Free Press.

Rohner, Ronald P., and Evelyn C. Rohner. 1970. *The Kwakiutl: Indians of British Columbia*. New York: Holt, Rinehart and Winston.

Rooney, James F. 1961. "Group Processes Among Skid Row Winos." *Quarterly Journal of Studies of Alcohol* 22:444–60.

Rosen, Lawrence. *The Anthropologist as Expert Witness*. Mimeographed paper on file with the Applied Anthropology Documentation Project at the University of Kentucky.

Rosenfeld, Jerry. 1971. *Shut Those Thick Lips: A Study of Slum School Failure*. New York: Holt, Rinehart and Winston.

Ross, M. H. 1986. "Female Political Participation." *American Anthropologist* 88:843–58.

Rylko-Bauer, Barbara, John Van Willigen, and Ann McElroy. 1989. "Strategies for Increasing the Use of Anthropological Research in the Policy Process: A Cross-Disciplinary Analysis." In *Making Our Research Useful*. John Van Willigen, Barbara Rylko-Bauer, and Ann McElroy, eds. Boulder, Colo.: Westview Press.

Sahlins, Marshall. 1968. "Notes on the Original Affluent Society." In *Man the Hunter*. R. B. Lee and I. DeVore, eds. Pp. 85–89. Chicago: Aldine.

———. 1972. *Stone Age Economics*. Chicago: Aldine-Atherton.

Salisbury, Richard F. 1976. "The Anthropologist as Societal Ombudsman." In *Development from Below: Anthropologists and Development Situations*. David C. Pitt, ed. Pp. 255–65. The Hague: Mouton.

Samovar, Larry A., and Richard E. Porter. 1991. *Communication Between Cultures*. Belmont, Calif.: Wadsworth.

———. 1994. *Intercultural Communication: A Reader*. Belmont, Calif.: Wadsworth.

Samuelson, Paul, and William Nordhaus. 1989. *Economics*. 13th edition. New York: McGraw-Hill.

Sapir, Edward. 1929. "The Status of Linguistics as a Science." *Language* 5:207–14.

Scaglion, Richard. 1987. "Customary Law Development in Papua New Guinea." In *Anthropological Praxis*. Robert Wulff and Shirley Fiske, eds. Pp. 98–107. Boulder, Colo.: Westview Press.

Schemo, Diana Jean. 1999. "The Last Tribal Battle." *New York Times Magazine*, October 31, pp. 70–77.

Scheper-Hughes, Nancy. 1989. "Death Without Weeping." *Natural History*, October.

Schlegel, Alice. 1990. "Gender Meanings: General and Specific." In *Beyond the Second Sex: New Directions in the Anthropology of Gender.* Peggy R. Sanday and R. G. Goodenough, eds. Pp. 21–41. Philadelphia: University of Pennsylvania Press.

Scrimshaw, Susan C. M. 1976. *Women's Modesty: One Barrier to the Use of Family Planning Clinics in Ecuador.* Monographs of the Carolina Population Center. Pp. 167–83.

Selzer, Richard. 1979. *Confessions of a Knife.* New York: Simon & Schuster.

Service, Elman R. 1966. *The Hunters.* Englewood Cliffs, N.J.: Prentice-Hall.

———. 1975. *Origins of the State and Civilization.* New York: Norton.

———. 1978. *Profiles in Ethnology.* 3rd edition. New York: Harper & Row.

Sharff, Jagna W. 1981. "Free Enterprise and the Ghetto Family." *Psychology Today,* March.

Sheets, Payson D. 1993. "Dawn of a New Stone Age in Eye Surgery." In *Archaeology: Discovering Our Past.* 2nd edition. Robert J. Sharer and Wendy Ashmore, eds. Pp. 470–72. Mountain View, Calif.: Mayfield.

Sheflen, Albert E. 1972. *Body Language and the Social Order.* Englewood Cliffs, N.J.: Prentice-Hall.

Shimonishi, R. 1977. *Influence of Culture and Foreign Language Learning: A Contrastive Analysis in Terms of English and Japanese Passive Based on Japanese Culture.* Unpublished master's thesis, University of Kansas, Lawrence.

Shostak, Marjorie. 1983. *Nisa: The Life and Words of a !Kung Woman.* New York: Vintage Books (Random House).

Sieber, Roy. 1962. "Masks as Agents of Social Control." *African Studies Bulletin* 5(11):8–13.

Simpson, George E., and J. Milton Yinger. 1985. *Racial and Cultural Minorities: An Analysis of Prejudice and Discrimination.* 5th edition. New York: Plenum.

Singer, Barry, and Victor Benassi. 1981. "Occult Beliefs." *American Scientist* 69(1):49–55.

Singer, Merrill. 1985. "Family Comes First: An Examination of the Social Networks of Skid Row Men." *Human Organization* 44(2):137–42.

Skinner, Elliott P. 1974. *African Urban Life: The Transformation of Ouagadougou.* Princeton, N.J.: Princeton University Press.

Slobin, Mark, and Jeff T. Titon. 1984. "The Music Culture as a World of Music." In *Worlds of Music: An Introduction to the Music of the World's Peoples.* Jeff T. Titon et al., eds. Pp. 1–11. London: Collier Macmillan Publishers.

Smith, Anthony D. 1976. *Social Change: Social Theory and Historical Processes.* London: Longman.

Smith, E. A. 1983. "Anthropological Applications of Optimal Foraging Theory: A Critical Review." *Current Anthropology* 24:625–51.

Smith, Susanna. 1995. "Women and Households in the Third World." In *Families in Multicultural Perspective.* Bron Ingoldsby and Susanna Smith, eds. Pp. 235–67. New York: Guilford Press.

Spain, Daphne, and Suzanne M. Bianchi. 1996. *Balancing Act: Motherhood, Marriage, and Employment Among American Women.* New York: Russell Sage Foundation.

Spindler, Louise S. 1984. *Culture Change and Modernization.* Prospect Heights, Ill.: Waveland Press.

Spradley, James. 1970. *You Owe Yourself a Drunk.* Boston: Little, Brown.

Spring, Anita. 1986. "Women Farmers and Food in Africa: Some Considerations and Suggested Solutions." In *Food in Sub-Saharan Africa.* Art Hansen and Della E. McMillan, eds. Boulder, Colo.: Lynne Rienner Publishers.

Stack, Carol. 1975. *All Our Kin: Strategies for Survival in a Black Community.* New York: Harper & Row.

Steiner, Christopher B. 1990. "Body Personal and Body Politic: Adornment and Leadership in Cross-Cultural Perspective." *Anthropos* 85:431–45.

Stenning, Derrick J. 1965. "The Pastoral Fulani of Northern Nigeria." In *Peoples of Africa.* James Gibbs, ed. Pp. 363–401. New York: Holt, Rinehart and Winston.

Stephens, William N. 1963. *The Family in Cross Cultural Perspective.* New York: Holt, Rinehart and Winston.

Stevens, W. K. 1992. "Humanity Confronts Its Handiwork: An Altered Planet." *New York Times,* May 5, pp. B5–B7.

Stewart, T. D. 1979. "Forensic Anthropology." In *The Uses of Anthropology.* Walter Goldschmidt, ed. Pp. 169–83. Washington, D.C.: American Anthropological Association.

Stoller, Paul. 1989. *Fusion of the Worlds: An Ethnography of Possession Among the Songhay of Niger.* Chicago: University of Chicago Press.

Strathern, Marilyn. 1984. "Domesticity and the Denigration of Women." In *Rethinking Women's Roles: Perspectives from the Pacific.* Denise O'Brien and Sharon Tiffany, eds. Pp. 13–31. Berkeley: University of California Press.

Sturtevant, William. 1964. "Studies in Ethnoscience." *American Anthropologist* 66(3) Part 2:99–131.

Sullivan, Thomas J., and Kenrick Thompson. 1990. *Sociology: Concepts, Issues, and Applications.* New York: Macmillan.

Sundkler, Bengt. 1961. *Bantu Prophets of South Africa.* 2nd edition. London: Oxford University Press.

Sutherland, Anne. 1994. "Gypsies and Health Care." In *Conformity and Conflict: Readings in Cultural Anthropology.* 8th edition. James P. Spradley and David McCurdy, eds. Pp. 407–18. New York: HarperCollins.

Takahashi, Dean. 1998. "Doing Fieldwork in the High-Tech Jungle." *Wall Street Journal,* October 27, p. B1.

Talmon, Yohina. 1964. "Mate Selection in Collective Settlements." *American Sociological Review* 29:491–508.

Tannen, Deborah. 1990. *You Just Don't Understand: Women and Men in Conversation.* New York: Morrow.

Tarde, Gabriel. 1903. *The Laws of Imitation* (Elsie Clews Parsons, trans.). New York: Holt.

Taylor, Brian K. 1962. *The Western Lacustrine Bantu.* London: International African Institute.

Tedlock, Barbara. 1991. "From Participant Observation to the Observation of Participation: The Emergence of Narrative Ethnography." *Journal of Anthropological Research* 47(1):69–94.

Thomson, David S. 1994. "Worlds Shaped by Words." In *Conformity and Conflict.* 8th edition. James P. Spradley and David McCurdy, eds. Pp. 73–86. New York: Harper-Collins.

Tiger, Lionel, and Robin Fox. 1971. *The Imperial Animal.* New York: Holt, Rinehart and Winston.

Tischler, Henry L. 1990. *Introduction to Sociology.* 3rd edition. Forth Worth: Holt, Rinehart and Winston.

Toffler, Alvin. 1971. *Future Shock.* New York: Bantam Books.

Treiman, Donald J. 1977. *Occupational Prestige in Comparative Perspective.* New York: Academic Press.

Tripp, Robert. 1985. "Anthropology and On-Farm Research." *Human Organization* 44(2):114–24.

Truzzi, Marcello. 1993. "The Occult Revival as Popular Culture: Some Observations on the Old and the Nouveau Witch." In *Magic, Witchcraft, and Religion: An Anthropological Study of the Supernatural.* 3rd edition. Arthur C. Lehmann and James E. Myers, eds. Pp. 397–405. Mountain View, Calif.: Mayfield.

Turnbull, Colin. 1965. "The Mbuti Pygmies of the Congo." In *Peoples of Africa.* James Gibbs, ed. Pp. 281–317. New York: Holt, Rinehart and Winston.

———. 1981. "Mbuti Womanhood." In *Woman the Gatherer.* Frances Dahlberg, ed. Pp. 205–19. New Haven, Conn.: Yale University Press.

———. 1982. "The Ritualization of Potential Conflict Between the Sexes Among the Mbuti." In *Politics and History in Band Societies.* Eleanor Leacock and Richard Lee, eds. Cambridge: Cambridge University Press.

Tylor, Edward B. 1871. *Origins of Culture.* New York: Harper & Row.

———. 1889. "On a Method of Investigating the Development of Institutions: Applied to Laws of Marriage and Descent." *Journal of Royal Anthropological Institute* 18:245–69.

United Nations. 1995. *The World's Women 1995: Trends and Statistics.*

U.S. Bureau of Labor. 1990. *Employment and Earnings* 37, January 1.

U.S. Bureau of the Census. 1993. *Statistical Abstract of the United States, 1993.* 113th edition. Washington, D.C.: U.S. Government Printing Office.

U.S. Department of Justice. 1990. *Uniform Crime Reports.* Washington, D.C.: U.S. Department of Justice.

U.S. National Commission on the Causes and Prevention of Violence. 1969. *Justice: To Establish Justice, To Ensure Domestic Tranquility.* Washington, D.C.: U.S. Government Printing Office.

Van Erven, Eugene. 1992. *The Playful Revolution: Theatre and Liberation in Asia.* Bloomington: Indiana University Press.

Van Gennep, Arnold. 1960. *The Rites of Passage.* Chicago: University of Chicago Press (orig. 1908).

Vanneman, Reeve, and L. W. Cannon. 1987. *The American Perception of Class.* Philadelphia: Temple University Press.

Van Willigen, John. 1993. *Applied Anthropology: An Introduction.* Rev. edition. Westport, Conn.: Bergin and Garvey.

Van Willigen, John, Barbara Rylko-Bauer, and Ann McElroy. 1989. *Making Our Research Useful.* Boulder, Colo.: Westview Press.

Vilakazi, Absolon L. 1979. *A Study of Population and Development.* Mbabane: Ministry of Agriculture and Cooperatives.

Vincent, Joan. 1990. *Anthropology and Politics: Vision, Traditions, and Trends.* Tucson: University of Arizona Press.

Wagner, Gunter. 1949. *The Bantu of North Kavirondo.* London: Published for the International African Institute by Oxford University Press.

Wallace, Anthony F. C. 1966. *Religion: An Anthropological View.* New York: Random House.

Ward, Martha C. 1971. *Them Children: A Study in Language Learning.* New York: Holt, Rinehart and Winston.

Weber, Max. 1946. *From Max Weber: Essays in Sociology.* (Hans Girth and C. Wright Mills, trans. and eds.). New York: Oxford University Press.

———. 1947. *The Theory of Social and Economic Organizations* (Talcott Parsons, trans.). New York: Oxford University Press.

Weiner, E. 1994. "Muslim Radicals and Police Hunt Feminist Bangladeshi Writer." *Christian Science Monitor,* July 26, p. 6.

Weismantel, Mary. 1995. "Making Kin: Kinship Theory and Zumbagua Adoptions." *American Ethnologist* 22(4): 685–709.

Weisner, Thomas S. 1972. *One Family: Two Households: Rural-Urban Ties in Kenya.* Doctoral dissertation, Harvard University.

Whelehan, Patricia. 1985. "Review of *Incest: A Biosocial View* by Joseph Shepher (New York: Academic Press, 1983)." *American Anthropologist* 87:677.

White, Benjamin. 1973. "Demand for Labor and Population Growth in Colonial Java." *Human Ecology* 1(3):217–36.

White, D. R., M. L. Burton, and M. M. Dow. 1981. "Sexual Division of Labor in African Agriculture." *American Anthropologist* 83:824–49.

White, Leslie. 1959. *The Evolution of Culture.* New York: McGraw-Hill.

Whiting, John W., and Irvin L. Child. 1953. *Child Training and Personality: A Cross Cultural Study.* New Haven, Conn.: Yale University Press.

Whiting, Robert. 1979. "You've Gotta Have 'Wa.'" *Sports Illustrated,* September 24, pp. 60–71.

Whitman, William. 1963. "The San Ildefonso of New Mexico." In *Acculturation in Seven American Indian Tribes.* Ralph Linton, ed. Gloucester, Mass.: Peter Smith (orig. 1940).

Whyte, M. K. 1978. *The Status of Women in Preindustrial Societies.* Princeton, N.J.: Princeton University Press.

Williams, Florence. 1998. "In Utah, Polygamy Goes Suburban." *Charlotte Observer,* February 28, p. G3.

Williams, Thomas R. 1967. "Field Methods in the Study of Culture." New York: Holt, Rinehart and Winston.

———. 1969. *A Borneo Childhood: Enculturation in Dusun Society.* New York: Holt, Rinehart and Winston.

Wilson, Monica. 1960. "Nyakyusa Age Villages." In *Cultures and Societies of Africa.* Simon and Phoebe Ottenberg, eds. Pp. 227–36. New York: Random House.

Winkelman, M. J. 1987. "Magico-Religious Practitioner Types and Socioeconomic Conditions." *Behavioral Science Research* 22.

Winter, Edward H. 1956. *Bwamba: A Structural Functional Analysis of a Patrilineal Society.* Cambridge: Published for the East African Institute of Social Research by W. Heffer.

Witherspoon, Gary. 1977. *Language and Art in the Navajo Universe.* Ann Arbor: University of Michigan Press.

Wittfogel, Karl. 1957. *Oriental Despotism: A Comparative Study of Total Power.* New Haven, Conn.: Yale University Press.

Wolf, Arthur. 1968. "Adopt a Daughter-in-Law, Marry a Sister: A Chinese Solution to the Incest Taboo." *American Anthropologist* 70:864–74.

Wolf, E. 1964. *Anthropology.* Englewood Cliffs, N.J.: Prentice-Hall.

Womack, Mari, and Judith Marti. 1993. *The Other Fifty Percent: Multicultural Perspectives on Gender Relations.* Prospect Heights, Ill.: Waveland Press.

"Women Still Lack Representation—Interparliamentary Union Report." *Women's International Network News,* Winter 2000, 26(1), p. 80.

Wood, Julia T. 1994. "Gender, Communication, and Culture." In *Intercultural Communication: A Reader.* 7th edition. Larry Samovar and Richard Porter, eds. Pp. 155–65. Belmont, Calif.: Wadsworth.

World Almanac and Book of Facts, 1996. 1995. New York: World Almanac.

Ya'ari, Ehud, and Ina Friedman. 1991. "Curses in Verses." *Atlantic* 267(2):22–26.

Yellen, John. 1990. "The Transformation of the Kalahari !Kung." *Scientific American,* April, pp. 96–104.

CREDITS

Chapter One
1 © Karan Kapoor/Corbis; 4 © Glynn Isaac/AnthroPhoto; 5 Courtesy of Gary Ferraro 6 © Gianni Tortoli/Photo Researchers, Inc.; 9 © A. Ramey/Woodfin Camp & Associates; 14 © R. Lord/The Image Works; 15 © Bill Gillette/Stock, Boston

Chapter Two
21 © Penny Tweedie/Panos Pictures; 24 (right) © Dasho/AnthroPhoto, file #396; 24 (left) © Vittoriano Rastelli/Corbis; 28 AP/Wide World Photos; 29 © Christopher Bissell/Tony Stone Images; 31 Andrea Booher/Tony Stone Images; 32 (right) Courtesy of Gary Ferraro, photo by Ginger Wagner; 32 (left) © Jeffrey L. Rotman/Corbis; 35 © Tim Davis/Photo Researchers, Inc.

Chapter Three
41 © Carl Purcell/Photo Researchers, Inc. 42; © Courtesy, Dr. Karen Ramey Burns; 43 © Robert Brenner/Photo Edit; 44 © Billy E. Barnes/Photo Edit; 45 Corbis; 49 © Daemmrich/The Image Works; 51 Courtesy of Elizabeth Briody; 54 © David Austen/Stock, Boston

Chapter Four
59 © Adrian Arbib/AnthroPhoto, file #3690; 61 Brown Brothers; 65 Bettmann/Corbis; 67 © Stephanie Maze/Corbis; 68 © Mary Kate Denny/Photo Edit; 69 © Ken Heyman/Woodfin Camp & Associates; 70 © Mark C. Burnett/Stock, Boston; 76 Courtesy of Ruth Behar

Chapter Five
80 © Peggy/Yoram Kahana/Peter Arnold, Inc.; 82 (left) © Momatiuk/Eastcott/Woodfin Camp & Associates; 82 (right) © Amanda Merullo/Stock, Boston; 85 © Irven DeVore/AnthroPhoto; 87 © K. Cannon-Bonventre/AnthroPhoto, file #46; 90 © Dorothy Little/Stock, Boston; 94 © Crawford/AnthroPhoto, file #6037; 95 © Edward Tronick/AnthroPhoto, file #7172; 101 Courtesy of Gary Ferraro

Chapter Six
104 © Terrace/AnthroPhoto, file #101; 109 © Terrace/AnthroPhoto, file #0177; 118 Courtesy of Gary Ferraro; 119 © Gary A. Conner/Photo Edit; 122 © Camerique/H. Armstrong Roberts; 125 Courtesy of Gary Ferraro; 128 Loren Santo/Tony Stone Images

Chapter Seven
131 © Nathan Benn/Woodfin Camp & Associates; 133 (left) R. Krubner/H. Armstrong Roberts; 133 (right) © Morgan/AnthroPhoto, file #0466; 136 © Lee/AnthroPhoto, file #1194; 143 © Mike Yamashita/Woodfin Camp & Associates; 146 © Mike Yamashita/Woodfin Camp & Associates; 148 (top) © Jane Tyska/Stock, Boston; 148 (bottom) © David Austen/Stock, Boston

Chapter Eight
155 Travelpix/FPG International; 157 © Tobias Everke/Liaison Agency; 163 © DPA/The Image Works; 166 © Bonnie Kamin/Photo Edit; 168 © Washburn/AnthroPhoto, file #386; 170 © DeVore/AnthroPhoto, file #7214; 171 © David Young-Wolff/Photo Edit; 172 © DeVore/AnthroPhoto, file #6221

Chapter Nine
179 © Alan Oddie/Photo Edit; 182 © Bob Daemmrich/Stock, Boston; 185 ZEFA/H. Armstrong Roberts; 187 DTP/The Image Works; 190 © Paola Koch/Photo Researchers, Inc.; 194 © Robert Caputo/Stock, Boston; 201 © Momatiuk/Eastman/The Image Works; 202 D. Degnan/H. Armstrong Roberts

Chapter Ten
205 © South American Pictures/Tony Morrison; 207 © Keren Su/Stock, Boston; 210 © R. Rouchon/Explorer-Robert Harding Picture Library; 213 Courtesy of Gary Ferraro

Chapter Eleven
228 Suzanne Murphy/Tony Stone Images; 230 Tom Mendoza/Los Angeles Daily News/CORBIS-Sygma; 233 © Bio (A. Compost)/Peter Arnold, Inc.; 235 © Cary Wolinsky/Stock, Boston; 236 © David Austen/Stock, Boston; 240 © David Young-Wolff/Photo Edit; 242 © Dominic Harcourt-Webster/Robert Harding Picture Library; 243 © John Elk/Stock, Boston; 244 © Michael Newman/Photo Edit

Chapter Twelve
250 H. Armstrong Roberts; 253 © Kal Muller/Woodfin Camp & Associates; 257 © Kul Bhatia/Photo Researchers, Inc.; 258 © Louise Gubb/The Image Works; 262 Reuters/CORBIS-Bettmann; 265 James Nelson/Tony Stone Images; 272 © Photo Edit

Chapter Thirteen
277 © Daniel Laine-Hoa-Qui/Viesti Associates; 279 Reuters/Jeff Christiansen/Archive Photos; 281 © M. Konner/AnthroPhoto, file #2557; 284 (left) © Andrew Lichtenstein/The Image Works; 284 (right) © Alon Reininger/Contact Press; 285 © Joseph Sohm/Stock, Boston; 288 © Alan Sussman/The Image Works; 290 © Bob Daemmrich/Sygma; 292 © Robert Brenner/Photo Edit; 296 © Josef Polleross/The Image Works

Chapter Fourteen
301 © David Austen/Stock, Boston; 304 © D. D. Morrison/The Picture Cube/Index Stock; 306 AP/Wide World Photos; 309 Gary Brettnacher/Tony Stone Images; 314 © Kal Muller/Woodfin Camp & Associates; 316 © Tobias Schneebaum; 322 © Shandiz/CORBIS-Sygma

Chapter Fifteen
325 M. Koene/H. Armstrong Roberts; 327 © Peter Moszyaki/Panos Pictures; 328 © Camerique; 329 © Emil Meunch/Photo Researchers, Inc.; 331 © Adam Woolfit/Woodfin Camp & Associates; 332 Courtesy of Gary Ferraro; 333 © Steve Benbow/Stock, Boston; 335 © Marion Patterson/Photo Researchers, Inc.; 339 © Kal Muller/Woodfin Camp & Associates; 341 © Michael Newman/Photo Edit; 344 © Laski/Sipa Press

Chapter Sixteen
348 © Paul Chesley/Tony Stone Images; 351 © R. Ford/H. Armstrong Roberts; 356 © J. Boisberranger-Hoa-Qui/Viesti Associates; 358 © A. Ramey/Woodfin Camp & Associates; 360 © Betty Press/Woodfin Camp & Associates; 361 © K. Tanaka/Woodfin Camp & Associates; 363 (left) © Jim Pickerall/Stock, Boston; 363 (right) © Betty Press/Woodfin Camp & Associates; 364 © Steve Benbow/Stock, Boston; 365 © Lynn McLaren/The Picture Cube/Index Stock; 369 © 5th Wave, www.the5thwave.com

Chapter Seventeen
372 © Lionel Delevingne/Stock, Boston

INDEX

Note: A *t* following a page number indicates tabular material, an *f* following a page number indicates a figure, and a *b* following a page number indicates a boxed feature.

AAA. *See* American Anthropological Association
Abaluyia culture, 360
Abkhasian culture, 165–166
Abortion, sex-selective, gender exploitation and, 243
Abundance, within food-collecting societies, 135–136
Abuse, gender-based, 242–244
Acculturation, 352–353
Acephalous societies, 258–259, 263
  social control in, 263–267
Ache culture, 134
Achieved status, 282
Acquired immunodeficiency syndrome, anthropology and, 88–89*b*
Action anthropology, 42. *See also* Applied anthropology
Adaptive nature of culture, 34
Administrator/manager, applied anthropologist as, 52
Adolescence, Mead's study of, 68
Adolescent drug dealers, ethnographic study of, 45–48
Advocacy anthropology, 42. *See also* Applied anthropology
Advocate, applied anthropologist as, 42, 51
Affinal relatives, 206, 210
Affluence of food-collecting societies, 135–136
Africa. *See* East Africa; South Africa; West Africa
African Americans
  ebonics and, 116–117*b*
  extended family ties among, 202
Age
  division of labor by, 165–166
  gender stratification by, 234
  kinship classification by, 210
Age grades, 266–267
Age organizations, 266–267, 267*f*
Age set, 266–267
Agricultural research
  anthropology and, 96–97*b*
  definition of, 132
Agriculture, 132, 139, 146–148
  changes associated with, 139–140
  land ownership/resource allocation and, 159–162
Agroforestry Outreach Project (AOP), 62–63*b*
Agta culture, 233
AIDS, anthropology and, 88–89*b*
Alaska. *See also* Eskimo culture; Inuit culture
  Inupiaq culture, 152
Allocation of resources, 157–162
Amazon, Brazilian, cultural survival of indigenous peoples and, 374–375
Ambilineal descent, 218
Ambilocal (bilocal) residence, 197

American Anthropological Association (AAA)
  code of ethics of, 54, 56–57
  web site of, 20
American Anthropologist (journal), 3
American English. *See also* English language
  cross-cultural miscues related to, 121*b*
American historicism, 64–65, 77*t*
American Indians. *See* Native Americans
Amish society
  anthropology and, 310–311*b*
  education of children and, 24–25, 310–311*b*
  as subculture, 23–25
Analysis of data, 85
Ancestor worship/ancestral cults, 265–266, 316–317
  social control and, 265–266, 308
Ancient Society (Morgan), 61
Androgyny, 230–231
Animals (herd). *See also* Cattle
  keeping of (pastoralism), 132, 142–146
Anthropological linguistics, 3*t*, 7, 104–130. *See also* Language
Anthropological theory, 59–79, 77*t*
  American historicism, 64–65, 77*t*
  applied anthropology and, 62–63*b*
  cultural materialism, 74–75, 77*t*
  diffusionism, 62–64, 77*t*
  ethnoscience, 71–74, 77*t*
  evolutionism, 60–62, 77*t*
  French structuralism, 70–71, 77*t*
  functionalism, 65–67, 77*t*
  neoevolutionism, 69–70, 77*t*
  postmodernism, 75–76, 77*t*
  psychological anthropology and, 67–69, 77*t*
Anthropology, 1–20
  applications of, 14–16, 41–58. *See also* Applied anthropology
    future of anthropology and, 376–377
  archaeology and, 3*t*, 5–7
  branches of, 3–4, 3*t*
  building skills for twenty-first century and, 16–17
  contributions of, 13–17
  cultural, 3*t*, 7–10. *See also* Cultural anthropology
  definition of, 2–3
  economic, 10
    science of economics and, 156–157. *See also* Economics/economic systems
  educational, 9–10, 198–199*b*
  forensic, 42
  future of, 372–377
  linguistics and, 3*t*, 7, 104–130. *See also* Language
  medical, 8–9
    application of, 52–53*b*
    tribal pharmacology and, 150–151*b*

physical, 3*t*, 4–5
principles of, 11–13
psychological, 10, 67–69, 77*t*
understanding enhanced by, 13–14
urban, 8, 13, 358–362
AOP. *See* Agroforestry Outreach Project
Apache culture, 26–27*b*
Apartheid system, 296
Applied anthropologists. *See also* Applied anthropology
  areas of responsibility of, 56–57
  as employees outside academic settings, 45
  future of anthropology and, 376–377
  involvement of in given project, 50
  specialized roles of, 51–53
Applied anthropology, 14–16, 41–58, 376–377. *See also* Applied anthropologists
  agricultural development in West Africa and, 216–217*b*
  agricultural research and, 96–97*b*
  AIDS and, 88–89*b*
  Amish society and, 310–311*b*
  anthropological theory and, 62–63*b*
  architecture and, 26–27*b*, 286–287*b*
  art and, 336–337*b*, 342–343*b*
  business culture and, 72–73*b*
  class stratification and, 286–287*b*
  court-ordered child custody and, 224–225*b*
  definition of, 42
  ebonics and, 116–117*b*
  educational programs and, 36–37*b*
  environmental impact studies and, 354–355*b*
  ethics of, 54–57
  examples of, 45–50
  family planning and, 238–239*b*
  family ties of skid row men and, 183*b*
  future of anthropology and, 376–377
  Hawaiian children and, 198–199*b*
  hija rhetoric and, 342–343*b*
  language and, 126–127*b*
  legal systems and, 270–271*b*
  market research and, 174–175*b*
  mediation and, 46–47*b*, 52–53
  nepotism and, 160–161*b*
  pastoralism and, 144–145*b*
  political organization and, 254–255*b*
  pure anthropology compared with, 43–44
  reforestation in Haiti and, 62–63*b*
  religion and, 310–311*b*
  sexuality and, 238–239*b*
  special features of, 50–53
  tribal pharmacology and, 150–151*b*
  in twentieth century, 44–50, 45*t*
Arabic states. *See* Middle East